New Testament Theology

New Testament Theology

Exploring Diversity and Unity

Frank J. Matera

Westminster John Knox Press
LOUISVILLE • LONDON

Scripture quotations from the New Revised Standard Version of the Bible are copyright © 1989 by the Division of Christian Education of the National Council of the Churches of Christ in the U.S.A. and are used by permission.

The author gratefully acknowledges the permission he has received to use material previously published in *The Catholic Biblical Quarterly*, *Theological Studies*, and *The Gift of the Church* (Liturgical Press).

"New Testament Theology: History, Method, and Identity." *CBQ* (2005): 1–21.

"Christ in the Theologies of Paul and John: A Study in the Diverse Unity of New Testament Theology." *TS* 67 (2006): 237–56.

"Theologies of the Church in the New Testament." *The Gift of the Church: A Textbook on Ecclesiology in Honor of Patrick Granfield O. S. B.* Ed. Peter C. Phan. (Collegeville: Liturgical Press, 2000), 1–21.

Book design by Sharon Adams
Cover design by Lisa Buckley

First edition
Published by Westminster John Knox Press
Louisville, Kentucky

This book is printed on acid-free paper that meets the American National Standards Institute Z39.48 standard. ♾

PRINTED IN THE UNITED STATES OF AMERICA

07 08 09 10 11 12 13 14 15 16 — 10 9 8 7 6 5 4 3 2 1

Libary of Congress Cataloging-in-Publication Data

Matera, Frank J.
  New Testament theology : exploring diversity and unity / Frank J. Matera.
    p. cm.
  Includes bibliographical references (p.   ).
  ISBN 978-0-664-23044-9 (alk. paper)
  1. Bible. N.T.—Theology. 2. Bible. N.T.—Criticism, interpretation, etc. I. Title.
  BS2397.M38 2007
  230'.0415—dc22

                                                                              2007003350

Contents

A Complete Table of Contents

Preface

The most important New Testament theology of the twentieth century was Rudolf Bultmann's classic work, *Theologie des Neuen Testaments*. Published between 1948 and 1953, it dominated the discussion of New Testament theology in the second half of the twentieth century. Other scholars wrote New Testament theologies, but their works remained in the shadow of Bultmann's creative synthesis, which presented the theology of the New Testament in a powerful and convincing manner. But as nearly all scholars recognize, this great work was flawed. Bultmann focused almost exclusively on the theologies of Paul and John, both of which were especially amenable to his existential analysis of the New Testament. In doing so, he neglected other writings of the New Testament, relegating them to a second-class status because they did not present the kerygma as an urgent call to existential decision in the way that Paul and John did.

New Testament scholarship has made many advances since Bultmann published his great synthesis. Scholars have found and employed new methods such as social science analysis, feminist hermeneutics, and narrative criticism to interpret the text. Moreover, contemporary scholarship has a greater appreciation for the theological richness of the material that Bultmann neglected. Consequently, the theologies of the Synoptic Gospels and the theologies of the deuteropauline writings play a greater role in New Testament theology today than they did in Bultmann's synthesis.

In recent years there has been a revival of New Testament theology, especially in Germany. The discipline has moved out of Bultmann's shadow and approached its task with renewed confidence. Moreover, there is a trend to identify the theological unity of the New Testament theology as well as its diversity.

The present work makes no pretension at being a new and original synthesis that replaces what has preceded it. I am keenly aware of my limitations and indebtedness to those who have gone before me. My purpose has been to provide students and colleagues, especially systematic theologians, with a synthesis of the theologies in the New Testament that will enable them to see the diverse unity of New Testament theology. The expression "diverse unity" refers to two aspects of New Testament theology. On the one hand, there is an undeniable theological diversity in the writings of the New Testament that we cannot and should not dismiss. On the other, for those who read the New Testament as a witness to God's self-revelation in Christ, there is an inner unity that binds these writings together. It is this inner unity, which resides in the diversity of the New Testament, that I have sought to uncover.

This work builds upon two earlier books: *New Testament Ethics: The Legacies of Jesus and Paul* (1996), and *New Testament Christology* (1999). In those works I dealt with particular aspects of New Testament theology, ethics and Christology. In this work I have sought to describe the theological logic of each New Testament writing with a view to explaining how the diverse theologies in the New Testament are ultimately related to one another.

Although this book is my own work, I am indebted to several research assistants at the Catholic University of America who read, corrected, and offered constructive criticism: Geoffrey Miller, Eric Johnson, and Sherri Brown. I am especially grateful to my colleague and friend Ronald Witherup, who graciously read the entire manuscript and offered helpful and encouraging advice. Finally, I express my thanks to Jon Berquist and Westminster John Knox Press for their support of this project.

Frank J. Matera
Andrews-Kelly-Ryan Professor of New Testament
The Catholic University of America
Washington, DC

Abbreviations

AB	Anchor Bible
AnBib	Analecta biblica
AUSS	*Andrews University Seminary Studies*
BBR	*Bulletin for Biblical Research*
BDAG	Walter Bauer, *A Greek-English Lexicon of the New Testament and Other Early Christian Literature*. Rev. and ed. Frederick William Danker. 3rd ed. Chicago: University of Chicago Press, 2000
BETL	Bibliotheca ephemeridum theologicarum lovaniensium
Bib	*Biblica*
CBQ	*Catholic Biblical Quarterly*
DLNT	*Dictionary of the Later New Testament and Its Developments*. Ed. R. P. Martin and P. H. Davids. Downers Grove, IL: InterVarsity Press, 1997
DrewG	*Drew Gateway*
EDNT	*Exegetical Dictionary of the New Testament*. Ed. H. Balz and G. Schneider. 3 vols. ET Grand Rapids: Eerdmans, 1990–1993
ET	English translation
ExpTim	*Expository Times*
GBS	Guides to Biblical Scholarship
GNS	*Good News Studies*
HBT	*Horizons in Biblical Theology*
HNTC	Harper's New Testament Commentaries
HTKNT	Herders theologischer Kommentar zum Neuen Testament
HUT	Hermeneutische Untersuchungen zur Theologie
ICC	International Critical Commentary
JBL	*Journal of Biblical Literature*
JR	*Journal of Religion*
JSNT	*Journal for the Study of the New Testament*

JSNTSup	Journal for the Study of the New Testament: Supplement Series
JTC	*Journal for Theology and the Church*
JTS	*Journal of Theological Studies*
KD	*Kerygma und Dogma*
KJV	King James Version
LXX	Septuagint
MdB	*Le Monde de la Bible*
MTZ	*Münchener theologische Zeitschrift*
NAB	New American Bible
NASB	New American Standard Bible
NEB	New English Bible
NIGTC	New International Greek Testament Commentary
NIV	New International Version
NovT	*Novum Testamentum*
NovTSup	Novum Testamentum Supplements
NRSV	New Revised Standard Version
NTL	New Testament Library
NTM	New Testament Message
NTS	*New Testament Studies*
NTT	New Testament Theology
PTMS	Princeton Theological Monograph Series
RSPT	*Revue des sciences philosophiques et théologiques*
RSV	Revised Standard Version
SB	Sources bibliques
SBLDS	Society of Biblical Literature Dissertation Series
SBS	Stuttgarter Bibelstudien
SBT	Studies in Biblical Theology
SJT	*Scottish Journal of Theology*
SNTSMS	Society for New Testament Studies Monograph Series
SP	Sacra pagina
StABH	Studies in American Biblical Hermeneutics
SubBi	Subsidia biblica
Sup	Supplement
TJT	*Toronto Journal of Theology*
TS	*Theological Studies*
USQR	*Union Seminary Quarterly Review*
WBC	Word Biblical Commentary

Introduction

New Testament Theology

New Testament theology is the culmination and goal of exegesis, a discipline by which biblical scholars mediate the fruit of their research in a comprehensive manner to a wider audience. From its inception New Testament theology has been a Protestant project intended to assist and renew dogmatic theology, though, in recent years, Catholics have contributed to the discipline as well.[1] The purpose of this book is to provide its readers with an overview of the diverse unity of the theology in the New Testament. Before we proceed to this task, however, it will be helpful to summarize how others have conceived of the work of New Testament theology.

HISTORY AND METHOD
OF NEW TESTAMENT THEOLOGY

Although others were already engaged in the work of biblical theology, Johann Philipp Gabler's inaugural lecture to the faculty of Altdorf in 1787 is usually

---

1. For a history of the growth and development of biblical and New Testament theology, see D. A. Carson, "New Testament Theology," *DLNT* 796–814; Wilfrid J. Harrington, *The Path of Biblical Theology* (Dublin: Gill and Macmillan, 1973); Gerhard Hasel, *New Testament Theology: Basic Issues in the Current Debate* (Grand Rapids: Eerdmans, 1978); Hans-Joachim Kraus, *Die biblische Theologie: Ihre Geschichte und Problematik* (Neukirchen-Vluyn: Neukirchener Verlag, 1970); Heikki Räisänen, *Beyond New Testament Theology: A Story and a Program* (2nd ed.; London: SCM, 2000). For recent trends in New Testament theology, see Gerhard Barth, "Über Probleme und Trends bei neutestamentlichen Theologien," *KD* 48 (2002): 261–75; John R. Donahue, S.J., "The Changing Shape of New Testament Theology," *TS* 50 (1989): 314–35; idem, "The Literary Turn and New Testament Theology: Detour or New Direction?" *JR* 76 (1996): 250–75; Robert Morgan, "New Testament Theology," in *Biblical Theology: Problems and Perspectives* (ed. Steven J. Kraftchick, Charles D. Myers Jr., and Ben C. Ollenburger; Nashville: Abingdon, 1995), 104–30; Mogens Müller, "Neutestamentliche Theologie als biblische Theologie: Einige grundsätzliche Überlegungen," *NTS* 43 (1997): 475–90; C. Kavin Rowe, "New Testament Theology: The Revival of

regarded as the programmatic statement for modern biblical theology.[2] Convinced that the Scriptures (especially the New Testament) were "the one clear source from which all true knowledge of the Christian religion is drawn" (p. 134), Gabler called for a biblical theology, "pure and unmixed with foreign elements" (p. 142), that would provide dogmatic theology with the universal and unchanging truths of Scripture. He distinguished between biblical theology, which is historical in origin, and dogmatic theology, which is didactic in nature, "teaching what each theologian philosophises rationally about divine things, according to the measure of his ability or of the times, age, place, sect, school, and other similar factors" (p. 137). Biblical theology, as befits its historical approach, is "always in accord with itself," even though it may be elaborated in different ways, whereas dogmatic theology is subject to change. The first task of a true biblical theology then is to provide an accurate, historical description of the ideas found in the sacred writings. The second is to compare these ideas with one another in order to determine which are universal and enduring. In this way, biblical theology can provide dogmatic theology with the enduring and universal truths of Scripture.[3]

Scholars quickly embraced the first part of Gabler's project, a historical presentation of the theology in the Scriptures. Georg Lorenz Bauer produced a four-volume work that marked the beginning of New Testament theology as an independent discipline.[4] Ferdinand Christian Baur provided a controversial interpretation of early Christian history and doctrine in terms of a struggle between Gentile and Jewish Christianity,[5] and Bernhard Weiss and Heinrich Julius Holtzmann wrote comprehensive handbooks of New Testament theology that meticulously examined the doctrinal systems (*Lehrbegriffe*)

---

a Discipline: A Review of Recent Contributions to the Field," *JBL* 125 (2006): 393–419; Dan O. Via, *What Is New Testament Theology?* (GBS; Minneapolis: Fortress, 2002).

2. Johann Philipp Gabler, *Oratio de iusto discrimine theologiae biblicae et dogmaticae regundisque recte utriusque finibus* ("On the proper distinction between biblical and dogmatic theology and the specific objectives of each"). Page numbers refer to the English translation provided by John Sandys-Wunsch and Laurence Eldredge, "J. P. Gabler and the Distinction between Biblical and Dogmatic Theology: Translation, Commentary, and Discussion of His Originality," *SJT* 33 (1980): 133–58.

3. Gabler later distinguished between biblical theology in a broader and narrower sense. The first, "true Biblical Theology," had the task of developing a historical and systematic exposition of biblical religion; the second, "pure Biblical Theology" would then present the unchanging teaching of the Bible. See Hendrikus Boers, *What Is New Testament Theology? The Rise of Criticism and the Problem of a Theology of the New Testament* (GBS; Philadelphia: Fortress, 1979), 33–35.

4. Georg Lorenz Bauer, *Biblische Theologie des Neuen Testaments*, 4 vols. (Leipzig: Weygand, 1800–1802). For a summary of its contents, see William Baird, *History of New Testament Research*, vol. 1: *From Deism to Tübingen* (Minneapolis: Fortress, 1992), 188–94.

5. Ferdinand Christian Baur, *Vorlesungen über neutestamentliche Theologie* (ed. F. F. Baur; Leipzig: Fues, 1864). For a summary of Baur's interpretation of early Christianity, see Baird, *History of New Testament Research*, 1:262–69.

of the various New Testament writers.[6] But the second part of Gabler's project (providing dogmatic theology with the universal truths of Scripture) was abandoned. Instead of becoming a servant of dogmatic theology, biblical theology soon became its rival.

Disappointed with the direction of New Testament theology taken in the handbooks of Weiss and Holtzmann, William Wrede wrote an essay in 1897 entitled "The Task and Methods of 'New Testament Theology,'" which called for a purely historical approach.[7] In his view, New Testament theology should be "totally indifferent to all dogma and systematic theology" (p. 69), no longer confined by the limits of the canon or the doctrine of inspiration. Whereas Holtzmann's New Testament theology sought to set forth "in a scientific way the religious and ethical content of the canonical writings of the New Testament," Wrede advocated "the history of early Christian religion and theology" (p. 84). New Testament theology should explain *"what was believed, thought, taught, hoped, required and striven for* in the earliest period of Christianity; not what certain writings say about faith, doctrine, hope, etc." (pp. 84–85). Wrede concluded that the name of the discipline, "New Testament theology," was wrong in both of its terms. New Testament theology should be more concerned with religion than with theology, and it should not restrict itself to the canonical writings of the New Testament. The appropriate name for the subject matter is "early Christian history of religion, or rather: the history of early Christian religion and theology" (p. 116).

Wrede's project was never brought to completion.[8] The rise of dialectical theology after the First World War resulted in a renewed interest in the theological dimension of New Testament theology that found its greatest achievement in Rudolf Bultmann's *Theology of the New Testament*.[9] A fascinating marriage of existential philosophy and a history-of-religions approach, Bultmann's work

6. Bernard Weiss, *Biblical Theology of the New Testament*, 2 vols. (Edinburgh: T. & T. Clark, 1882; German original, 3rd ed. 1880, 1st ed. 1868); Heinrich Julius Holtzmann, *Lehrbuch der neutestamentlichen Theologie*, 2 vols. (2nd ed.; Tübingen: Mohr [Siebeck], 1911; 1st ed. 1896–97). Although it was not as characterized by the doctrinal systems approach, one should also note the work of Willibald Beyschlag, *New Testament Theology or Historical Account of the Teaching of Jesus and of Primitive Christianity according to the New Testament Sources*, 2 vols. (Edinburgh: T. & T. Clark, 1895; German original, 1891–92).

7. Page references are to "The Task and Methods of 'New Testament Theology,'" in *The Nature of New Testament Theology* (ed. Robert Morgan; SBT, 2/25; Naperville: Allenson, 1973; German original, 1897), 69–116. The German title (*Über Aufgabe und Methode der sogenannten neutestamentlichen Theologie*) is more revealing of Wrede's viewpoint than is the English title.

8. Heikki Räisänen (*Beyond New Testament Theology*, 31) notes that the work that came the closest to fulfilling Wrede's project was the unfinished work of Johannes Weiss, *Earliest Christianity: A History of the Period A.D. 30–150*, 2 vols. (ed. Frederick C. Grant; New York: Harper, 1959; German original, 1914).

9. Rudolf Bultmann, *Theology of the New Testament*, 2 vols. (New York: Scribner, 1951–55; German original, 1948–53).

went beyond the canon as Wrede proposed, but it was also a profound work of kerygmatic theology. Although other New Testament theologies followed, none presented a more compelling reading of the New Testament, even though Bultmann's work was essentially a theology of Paul and John.[10]

Distinguished by a number of methodological proposals and the appearance of several New Testament theologies, the 1990s began a new period in New Testament theology. For example, the monograph of Heikki Räisänen, *Beyond New Testament Theology*, advocates a return to Wrede's proposal but in a modified form.[11] Räisänen acknowledges that New Testament theology "may be a legitimate part of self-consciously ecclesial theology." But those "who work in a broader academic context might want to abandon such an enterprise" (p. 8). New Testament theology should be replaced with two different projects: "the history of early Christian thought" and "critical, philosophical, ethical and/or theological 'reflection on the New Testament', as well as on its influence on our history and its significance for contemporary life" (p. 8). The audience for this project should be broader than the church so that biblical studies can serve society as a whole. Such a global perspective requires that this discipline be conceived in terms of critical information rather than proclamation, making the Christian tradition comprehensible to others and relating it to other traditions (p. 158). The recent work of Gerd Theissen, *The Religion of the Earliest Churches*,[12] which Räisänen deems worthy to replace Bultmann's classic synthesis (p. 146), is an example of what Räisänen means by going "beyond" New Testament theology.[13]

---

10. Among German scholars there were works by Hans Conzelmann, *An Outline of the Theology of the New Testament* (New York: Harper & Row, 1969; German original, 1968); Oscar Cullmann, *Salvation in History* (NTL; London: SCM, 1967; German original, 1965); Leonhard Goppelt, *Theology of the New Testament*, 2 vols. (Grand Rapids: Eerdmans, 1981–82; German original, 1975–76); Joachim Jeremias, *New Testament Theology: The Proclamation of Jesus* (New York: Scribner, 1971; German original, 1971); Werner Georg Kümmel, *The Theology of the New Testament according to Its Major Witnesses: Jesus—Paul—John* (Nashville: Abingdon, 1973; German original, 1969); Karl Hermann Schelkle, *Theology of the New Testament*, 4 vols. (Collegeville, MN: Liturgical Press, 1971; German original, 1968–76). In the English-speaking world there were works by Donald Guthrie, *New Testament Theology* (Downers Grove, IL: InterVarsity Press, 1981); George Eldon Ladd, *A Theology of the New Testament* (Grand Rapids: Eerdmans, 1974); Leon Morris, *New Testament Theology* (Grand Rapids: Zondervan, 1986); Alan Richardson, *An Introduction to the Theology of the New Testament* (New York: Harper & Brothers, 1958).

11. Räisänen's work was originally published in 1990. All references are to the 2nd edition, in which Räisänen has added considerable material and refined this thesis.

12. Gerd Theissen, *The Religion of the Earliest Churches: Creating a Symbolic World* (Minneapolis: Fortress, 1999; German original, 1999). Theissen describes his program as "an attempt to give a scholarly description and analysis of primitive Christian religion. It seeks to describe the content of that religion in such a way that it is accessible to men and women whether or not they are religious" (p. xiii). Whereas a theology of the New Testament is written from an "internal perspective" to describe its theology for Christians, Theissen writes at a certain distance (though he is a committed believer) to describe Christian faith for those who are not necessarily believers.

13. Räisänen, however, does not agree with Theissen's positive estimation of the growth and development of the New Testament canon. See *Beyond New Testament Theology*, 142–46.

Reacting against the approaches of Räisänen and Wrede, Peter Balla has defended the discipline of New Testament theology.[14] He argues the following points: (1) that historical study does not exclude the study of theology, if the definition of theology is understood broadly enough; (2) that there are important arguments, rooted in history, for limiting New Testament theology to the writings of the canon; (3) that the formation of the canon was not an arbitrary ecclesiastical decision; and (4) that there is a unifying theology in the New Testament rooted in early creedal formulas. Accordingly, New Testament theology is a descriptive, historical enterprise that deals with the canonical writings of the New Testament. It is not a normative discipline, nor should it try to prove the claims of the New Testament. One need not be a believer to practice it.

Challenging the modern project of New Testament theology that Gabler inaugurated, A. K. M. Adam criticizes New Testament theology for its modernity.[15] By "modernity" he means (1) a commitment to novelty and progress and opposition to tradition; (2) a concern with questions of chronology; (3) a commitment to a rationalized scholarly practice; and (4) a stance that is intellectually elitist and antipopulist (p. 47). Instead of engaging in historical reconstruction, a postmodern New Testament theology would formulate "an interpretation that begins with the sense one makes of the New Testament" and then restate it in a different way (p. 180). Thus "the New Testament theologian's interpretation would continue the discourse of the canonized text in keeping with the theologian's (and the audience's) sense of the New Testament" (p. 180). Such a project would focus on the canonical writings and be explicitly theological in nature, as implied by the name of the discipline. The task, then, is neither the history of early Christianity (Wrede, Räisänen) nor a historical description of the theology in the New Testament (Balla) but a theological interpretation that makes sense of the New Testament.

Finally, Philip Esler has recently put forward his proposal for New Testament theology in which he offers a model "that encompasses the psychological, social, intercultural, and theological dimensions of communion." His overall aim is "to propose that such interpretation involves communion between modern Christians and the people who wrote these texts in various parts of the Mediterranean world ca. 50–150 CE."[16] Esler maintains that when the people "from whom we would so learn are closest to God's irruption into the world in the life, death, and resurrection of his Son," they represent the "primordial pattern of the new life this made possible."[17]

---

14. Peter Balla, *Challenges to New Testament Theology: An Attempt to Justify the Enterprise* (Peabody, MA: Hendrickson, 1997).

15. A. K. M. Adam, *Making Sense of New Testament Theology: "Modern" Problems and Prospects* (StABH 11; Macon, GA: Mercer University Press, 1995).

16. Philip F. Esler, *New Testament Theology: Communion and Community* (Minneapolis: Fortress, 2005), 65.

17. Ibid., 254.

SOME RECENT NEW TESTAMENT THEOLOGIES

Several New Testament theologies have appeared since the 1990s.[18] Viewed from A. K. M. Adam's perspective these works remain "modern" in their orientation. Most organize their material either diachronically or thematically, with one author (Hahn) employing both approaches.

Diachronic approaches investigate the theology of individual writings or blocks of material in a chronological order. The recent works of Georg Strecker and Joachim Gnilka offer two examples. Although Strecker adopts the customary title, *Theology of the New Testament*, he makes no claim to delineate "the" theology of the New Testament, "since the theological unity of the New Testament documents suggested by this term cannot be presupposed" (p. 2). Instead, he investigates and presents the New Testament writings "according to their own structures of thought, in relation to their own historical and literary contexts" (p. 3). His purpose is not to write a history of early Christian religion or theology but "to investigate the theological conceptions advocated by the New Testament authors on the basis of the theological (church) traditions they had received" (p. 3). Strecker's approach, then, is redactional in nature, seeking the theology of the New Testament writers in light of their editorial activity.

Gnilka is also interested in the traditions the New Testament writers employed. Accordingly, he begins each part of his work with a brief description of the traditions (*Vorgaben*) that underlie the material under discussion.[19] Gnilka, however, is more sensitive to the narrative and rhetorical elements of the writings. He makes some connections between blocks of material such as John and the Synoptics, Paul and the deuteropaulines, and in a final chapter

---

18. The following works have appeared since 1990: G. B. Caird, *New Testament Theology* (completed and edited by L. D. Hurst; Oxford: Clarendon, 1994); Brevard S. Childs, *Biblical Theology of the Old and New Testaments: Theological Reflection on the Christian Bible* (Minneapolis: Fortress, 1992); Joachim Gnilka, *Theologie des Neuen Testaments* (HTKNT Sup 5; Freiburg: Herder, 1994); Ferdinand Hahn, *Theologie des Neuen Testaments*, 2 vols. (Tübingen: Mohr Siebeck, 2002); Hans Hübber, *Biblische Theologie des Neuen Testaments*, 3 vols. (Göttingen: Vandenhoeck & Ruprecht, 1990, 1993, 1995); Walter Schmithals, *The Theology of the First Christians* (Louisville: Westminster John Knox Press, 1997; German original, 1994); Georg Strecker, *Theology of the New Testament* (Louisville: Westminster John Knox Press, 2000; German original, 1996); Peter Stuhlmacher, *Biblische Theologie des Neuen Testaments*, 2 vols. (Göttingen: Vandenhoeck & Ruprecht, 1992, 1999); François Vouga, *Une théologie du Nouveau Testament* (MdB 43; Geneva: Labor et Fides, 2001); Ulrich Wilckens, *Theologie des Neuen Testaments*, vol. 1, parts 1–4 (Neukirchen-Vluyn: Neukirchener Verlag, 2002, 2003, 2005); Alfons Weiser, *Theologie des Neuen Testaments*, vol. 2: *Die Theologie des Evangelien* (Kohlhammer Studienbücher 8; Stuttgart: Kohlhammer, 1993).

19. The overall structure of Gnilka's book is similar to Strecker's: (a) the theology of Paul, (b) the theology of the Synoptic evangelists, (c) the theology of the Johannine writings (but not Revelation), (d) the theology of the writings after Paul (Colossians and Ephesians, the Pastorals, Hebrews, Revelation, 1 Peter, Jude, 2 Peter). He discusses 2 Thessalonians and James in separate excursuses.

he summarizes the various ways in which the New Testament writings present Christ, the human condition, redemption, eschatology, the church and its relation to Israel, sacraments, and faith, thereby suggesting how a thematic study might be organized. In his view, however, the richness of the New Testament manifests a variety that cannot always be reconciled, for example, the tensions between present and future eschatology, justification by faith according to Paul and according to James, and models of the church that are charismatic and those that are based upon office. This variety arises from the different faith experiences of the New Testament writers (p. 464). If there is a unifying principle of New Testament theology, it is to be sought in the kerygma of Jesus' death and resurrection (pp. 462–63).[20]

The works of G. B. Caird and François Vouga are good examples of thematic approaches. Caird views New Testament theology as a historical discipline whose purpose is descriptive rather than dogmatic and apologetic (p. 1). New Testament theology is "involved with the reconstruction of the past, a past accessible to us not by direct scrutiny but only through the interrogation of witnesses" (p. 3). Caird proposes a conference-table approach and views himself as presiding over a conference of "faith and order" at which there will be at least twelve participants: the four evangelists; Paul; the Pastor; the authors of Hebrews, James, 1 Peter, 2 Peter, and Jude; John the seer; and still others if Paul cannot speak for 2 Thessalonians, Colossians, and Ephesians. The participants should speak for themselves, but as "the chair" of the conference, Caird will determine the agenda, the order in which the questions will be posed, and from time to time he will take the sense of the meeting (p. 19).

Whereas Caird views New Testament theology as a historical and descriptive discipline, François Vouga offers a theological and hermeneutical interpretation that focuses on the human subject in light of God's revelation in Christ. He argues that the writings of the New Testament are concerned with a new understanding of human existence and demand to be read and understood as if written *for us* (p. 19). Two consequences follow from this. First, a New Testament theology is not an introduction to the New Testament or a history of its literature. Second, the discipline should investigate the relevance of the New Testament writings for the Christian faith (p. 20).

Vouga insists that the theological diversity of the New Testament is a constitutive element of the unity of Christianity in the apostolic period. Therefore, rather than examine each writing individually, he purposely juxtaposes diverse writings and blocks of material in order to highlight the diverse unity

---

20. This appears to be the reason that Gnilka prefaces his presentation of a given writing or block of material with a discussion of *Vorgaben*, the materials or traditions with which a particular writer worked.

of New Testament theology. In doing so, Vouga effects the kind of dialogue among the writings of the New Testament that Caird promises but does not fully achieve.

The projects of Peter Stuhlmacher and Ferdinand Hahn are more difficult to categorize. Stuhlmacher's work is diachronic in approach, as is the first volume of Hahn's New Testament theology, but Stuhlmacher explicitly identifies his project as a work of biblical theology, by which he means a theology of the New Testament rooted in the theology of the Bible.[21] Although Hahn does not identify his work in this way, it belongs to the same category inasmuch as it interprets the theology of the New Testament in light of the entire Bible. Both authors insist that the message and work of the earthly or pre-Easter Jesus play a central role in New Testament theology,[22] and they explicitly call upon New Testament theology to deal with the unity as well as with the diversity of the New Testament.[23]

The recent New Testament theologies of I. Howard Marshall and Frank Thielman provide careful analyses of the theology in the individual writings of the New Testament, but neither tries to arrange its material chronologically. Thielman purposely follows the canonical order of the writings, whereas Marshall highlights the role that the theme of "mission" plays in the theology of the New Testament.[24] The distinctive aspect of both works is the manner in which each consistently relates the theologies of the diverse writings to one another in order to disclose the inner unity of New Testament theology.

THE TASK OF NEW TESTAMENT THEOLOGY

The task of New Testament theology has been described and carried out in a variety of ways: (1) as a history of early Christian religion or thought; (2) as

---

21. In a small volume entitled *How to Do Biblical Theology* (PTMS 38; Allison Park, PA: Pickwick, 1995), 11–12, Stuhlmacher writes that a biblical theology of the New Testament must elucidate four things: "First, it must be shown that the New Testament message of faith comes thoroughly from the Old Testament and that the Old Testament testimonies pointed forward to the events of fulfillment in the New Testament. Second, it must set forth that God, through the mission, passion, resurrection of Jesus, provided salvation for Jews and Gentiles at a time when both were still godless and unbelieving sinners (Rom 5:6, 8). Third, the historical development and diversity of the post-Easter testimony to Christ and to the faith must be traced and explained. Fourth and finally, it must be shown how the Old and New Testaments came together to form the two-part Christian canon, where the theological center of the canon lies, and what hermeneutical demands it places upon theological exegesis."

22. Stuhlmacher, *Theologie* (1:40–50), and Hahn, *theologie* (1:30–32), prefer the term "earthly Jesus" to "historical Jesus."

23. Stuhlmacker, *Theologie*, 2:287; Hahn, *Theologie*, 1:770.

24. I. Howard Marshall, *New Testament Theology* (Downers Grove, IL: InterVarsity Press, 2004); Frank Thielman, *Theology of the New Testament: A Canonical and Synthetic Approach* (Grand Rapids: Zondervan, 2005).

a descriptive presentation of the diverse theologies in the New Testament; (3) as a thematic statement of the theology of the New Testament; (4) as a theological interpretation of the New Testament intended to engage the contemporary believer. The various ways in which scholars have constructed their works suggest that one can ascribe a variety of tasks to New Testament theology ranging from historical reconstruction to kerygmatic proclamation. But if New Testament theology is to be clear about its identity, it needs to clarify its task further. Two points need to be made here.

First, although Wrede and Räisänen assigned the discipline traditionally called New Testament theology the task of writing a history of early Christian religion or thought, for the sake of clarity it would be better to identify the discipline that carries out that task as the history of early Christian religion or thought and to acknowledge that the discipline called New Testament theology has a specifically theological task. The history of early Christian religion or thought is of immense value to New Testament theology, but it is not New Testament theology. Inasmuch as the New Testament communicates its theology through specific narrative and epistolary forms, a theology of the New Testament ought to be a literary and theological analysis of the New Testament writings rather than a history of early Christian thought.

Second, although many New Testament theologies provide reliable descriptions of the theologies in the writings of the New Testament, these works are primarily expositions of the diverse theologies in the New Testament. As many of their authors readily acknowledge, their works are not concerned with the unity of New Testament theology, nor do they offer a theology of the New Testament.

For those who ascribe scriptural status to the writings of the New Testament, the task of New Testament theology should be bolder. For inasmuch as they identify these writings as Scripture, which bears witness to God's self-revelation, they suppose that these writings possess an inner coherence that is ultimately rooted in God's self-revelation. New Testament theology, then, should seek to provide a theological interpretation of the New Testament that integrates and relates the diverse theologies of the New Testament into a unified whole without harmonizing them, as elusive as that task may be.

One way to achieve this goal would be to take into account the implied narrative that underlies what the New Testament writings claim about Israel, Jesus, and the church. Such an approach would allow New Testament theology to communicate what the New Testament writings say about God through the narratives they tell or presuppose. This task would be historical and literary, descriptive and interpretive, and ultimately theological. It would be *historical* because it must respect the historical dimension of the writings; *literary* because it would focus on the narrative and rhetorical dimensions of the writings; *descriptive* because it would seek to provide a faithful account of the implicit and explicit theological claims of the writings;[25] *interpretive* because the act of careful description is a hermeneutical task; *theological* because it would be an expression of faith seeking to understand what it already believes about the God who is revealed in the story of Israel, Jesus, and the church.

THE METHOD AND APPROACH OF THIS WORK

This work begins with two assumptions: (1) there is a rich diversity in the way the New Testament writers express the experience of salvation the first believers enjoyed because of God's salvific work in Christ; (2) there is an underlying unity in the diverse theologies of the New Testament.

The diverse ways in which the New Testament writers express the experience of salvation is evident from the variety of genres they employ to communicate their message: narratives about Jesus and the early church; letters addressed to communities of believers to encourage and sustain them in their new life; and a book of prophecy (apocalyptic in nature) that warns and comforts its readers about what is soon to happen. Moreover, there are also differences within these literary genres. For example, the approach of the Johannine Gospel differs from that of the Synoptic Gospels, and the Johannine Letters are different in tone than the Pauline Letters. There are also distinctive emphases within the individual Pauline letters, just as there are distinctive emphases within each of the Synoptic Gospels.

It is not surprising that these writings express their understanding of what God has accomplished in a variety of ways since different circumstances occasioned the twenty-seven writings that make up the New Testament. In writing their Gospels, letters, and prophecy, the authors of the New Testament were responding to specific problems and issues within the emerging church. They were not writing essays commissioned for a volume that would someday be called "The New Testament." The diverse theologies in the New Testament are the result of the diverse circumstances and situations that occasioned its writings.

My first task in this book, then, is to describe the distinctive ways in which these writings express the experience of salvation God has effected in Christ. In doing so, I frequently refer to a particular author's theology or theological vision. This is not to suggest that the New Testament writers were theologians engaged in an explicitly theological task. They were not. But they were concerned about God's relationship to humanity, and humanity's new relationship

---

25. Strecker (*Theology of the New Testament*, 2) correctly notes, "Since all expressions of religious experience imply structures of believing comprehension, even if the authors of the New Testament documents were not necessarily aware of this in particular cases, such cognitive structures were also fundamental to the New Testament's witness of the act of God in Jesus Christ."

to God in Christ. Profoundly convinced that God had been active in Christ in a new and distinctive manner, they were communicating an experience of salvation. The theology of their writings, then, may not be a systematic theology, but it is akin to a pastoral theology that tries to make sense of what God has done, is doing, and is about to complete.

My second task in this book is to identify the underlying unity of the diverse theologies in the New Testament. Although it is in the conclusion of this work that I deal most explicitly with the question of the unity of New Testament theology, I address the issue throughout this work as I try to explain why the various writings of the New Testament describe, in such different ways, the experience of salvation that God has wrought in Christ.

The four parts of this book deal with the theology in the writings of the New Testament under the following headings: The Synoptic Tradition; The Pauline Tradition; The Johannine Tradition; Other Voices. By arranging the material in this manner, I suggest that there are three great theological traditions within the New Testament, as well as other voices. Each of the three great traditions has a distinctive starting point that influences the way in which the writings in these traditions present their theology.

The starting point of the Synoptic tradition is Jesus' proclamation of the kingdom of God. For the Gospel of Mark the gospel of the kingdom is God's own good news, which Jesus proclaims.[26] In the Gospel of Matthew Jesus requires his disciples to practice the kind of righteousness that is appropriate to the kingdom. In Luke–Acts the emphasis shifts to the salvation that the kingdom brings. The Acts of the Apostles provides a fitting transition to the Pauline tradition inasmuch as it witnesses to the way in which the one who proclaimed the kingdom was taken up into the church's proclamation about the kingdom.

The starting point of the Pauline tradition is the gospel about Jesus Christ: the good news of what God has accomplished in the death and resurrection of his Son. Thus, even though many of the Pauline letters were composed before the writings of the Synoptic tradition, in this work I treat the Pauline tradition after the Synoptic tradition in order to highlight the movement from the gospel about the kingdom to the gospel about the bringer of the kingdom. Rather than present a synthesis of Paul's theology and deal with the deuteropauline letters separately, in part two I investigate the entire Pauline corpus. I distinguish between the nondisputed and the disputed letters but argue that all of the letters are part of a Pauline tradition that has its origin in the great apostle. In this part I highlight significant theological themes such as election, the cross, justification by faith, the preexistent and cosmic Christ, the church as the body of

---

26. "Gospel" is capitalized when it refers to one of the four Gospels. When it refers to the proclamation of the message it is lowercased.

Christ, the epiphany of Christ, and the importance of handing on and preserving the Pauline tradition.

The starting point for the Johannine tradition is the incarnation: the Gospel's affirmation that the word became flesh and the insistence of the Johannine Epistles that Jesus, in all of his humanity, is the Christ, the Son of God. This starting point determines the particular shape of Johannine theology. The decision to treat the Fourth Gospel apart from the Synoptics is not intended to denigrate this Gospel's witness to Jesus but to highlight its distinctive theology. Although there is a long tradition of associating the book of Revelation with the Johannine tradition, the starting point of Revelation's theology—God's victory in the slaughtered lamb—argues for treating it separately.

In part four I treat the "other voices" in the New Testament. Although they do not belong to any one of the three great traditions, they make significant contributions to the theology of the New Testament. The Letter to the Hebrews begins with Christ's high priesthood and develops one of the most sophisticated christologies in the New Testament. The Letter of James focuses on the wisdom that comes from above and then makes an important contribution to the ethical teaching of the New Testament. First Peter focuses on the sufferings of Christ and provides a rich teaching about the Christian life, while 2 Peter and Jude concern themselves with the threat of false teaching and contribute to the church's understanding of the danger that error poses to its life.

I conclude this book with a substantial reflection on the diverse unity of New Testament theology. I make use of five categories to summarize the master story of the New Testament: (1) humanity in need of salvation, (2) the bringer of salvation, (3) the community of the sanctified, (4) the life of the sanctified, and (5) the hope of the sanctified. These themes correspond to the theological categories of (1) Christian anthropology and soteriology, (2) Christology, (3) ecclesiology, (4) ethics, and (5) eschatology, but they are not intended as a theological straightjacket to control the "unruly theology" of the New Testament. They are the outline of a master story that underlies the writings of the New Testament. This master story and the experience of salvation to which it witnesses provide the foundation for the unity of New Testament theology. The diverse starting points of the story (the kingdom of God, the gospel about Christ's death and resurrection, and the incarnation) help to explain why the writings of the New Testament present the master story differently.

There are many reasons not to write a New Testament theology: the subject is too vast; there is too much diversity in the New Testament; the discipline stifles the life force of the New Testament; theology does not respect history; the project is too subjective. But there are some good reasons to engage in the task: a New Testament theology can provide readers with an overview of the New Testament; it makes important connections among the writings of the New Testament that one might otherwise overlook; it wrestles with the unity of

God's revelation in Christ; its results can be of assistance to systematic theology. In this New Testament theology I do not pretend to accomplish everything, nor is it the only way to write a New Testament theology. But I hope to present readers with a way to see the whole picture so that they may stand in awe and wonder before the multifaceted mystery that is God in Christ.

PART ONE

The Synoptic Tradition

The Synoptic tradition comprises the Gospels of Matthew, Mark, and Luke and, for the purposes of this work, the Acts of the Apostles. Although the precise literary relationship among these Gospels is disputed, most scholars work with some form of the two-source hypothesis. That is, they assume that Mark is the earliest of the three Gospels and that Matthew and Luke, writing independently of each other, employed the Markan Gospel as their primary source as well as a collection of Jesus' teachings commonly designated as "Q." In addition to these two sources, Matthew and Luke had access to additional material, unique to their Gospels, commonly designated "M" and "L."[1] Since Mark is the earliest of the three Gospels, written about A.D. 70, perhaps at Rome, it is advantageous to begin with a description of its theology before proceeding to a discussion of the theology in the Gospels of Matthew and Luke, even though the canon places the Gospel according to Matthew at the beginning of the New Testament. This procedure allows one to see the growth and development in the traditions about Jesus from Mark to Matthew and Luke. Moreover, since Luke composed another work (the Acts of the Apostles), which is so closely related to his Gospel that scholars often speak of the whole work as "Luke–Acts," it is advisable to follow the order Mark, Matthew, Luke–Acts in order to observe how Luke envisions the transition from the preaching of Jesus about the kingdom of God to the proclamation of the early church about its risen Lord.

---

1. Whereas the Q material seems to have come from a written source, which may have gone through several redactions, the history of the material designated "M" and "L" is more obscure. In this work, "M" designates material peculiar to the Gospel of Matthew (for example, the infancy narrative, the parable of the Sheep and the Goats), and "L" material peculiar to the Gospel of Luke (for example, the infancy narrative, the parables of the Good Samaritan and the Prodigal Son).

The theological analysis that follows has a twofold goal: (1) to present the message of Jesus as mediated through the Synoptic writers, and (2) to summarize the theological contribution of each evangelist. The first goal acknowledges that the Synoptic Gospels are more than historical reports of what Jesus said and did. They are proclamations of the gospel that summon people to faith and repentance in light of what God accomplished through the life, death, and resurrection of his Son. Jesus' message, then, is mediated through the prism of each Gospel. This message is rooted in historical events, but it is not merely a historical report. It is the message of the earthly Jesus, but it is not a neutral report of what he said.[2] Rather, presenting Jesus' message from the perspective of resurrection faith, the Gospels call people to faith. Although this presents problems for the historian who seeks to establish what Jesus actually said and did, this is the way in which the Gospels present "the gospel" about the one whom they proclaim, and it is the way in which they ought to be read.

The second goal—to summarize the theological stance of each evangelist—is necessary because each evangelist recounts the story of Jesus from a particular vantage point. For example, the Gospel of Mark presents the gospel in light of the inbreaking kingdom of God, the Gospel of Matthew describes the righteousness the kingdom requires, and the Gospel of Luke highlights the age of salvation and the reversal of fortunes that the kingdom effects. This is not to say the theology of the evangelists has hidden or overshadowed the message of Jesus. Indeed, one suspects that the evangelists would be embarrassed to learn that contemporary scholars place such emphasis on their particular message, as if the theology of the evangelists is more important than Jesus' proclamation. The Gospel writers were not proclaiming their own message but the gospel of, and the gospel about, Jesus. They communicated this message, however, from a distinctive perspective in response to their own experience of the gospel and the needs of those for whom they wrote.

The three chapters that follow deal with the message of the Synoptic writers: Mark, Matthew, and Luke. In the chapter on the Gospel of Mark I summarize the essential elements of the gospel of the kingdom of God that Jesus proclaimed and the gospel that the church proclaimed about him in light of his death and resurrection. In the chapter on the Gospel of Matthew I highlight the ethical, ecclesial, and eschatological dimensions of Jesus' proclamation of the kingdom and the church's proclamation about him, again in light of his death and resurrection. Finally, in the chapter on Luke–Acts I show how

---

2. The traditions about Jesus in the Gospels have now received a literary setting that determines their meaning within the Gospel. Form critics speculate about the original *Sitz im Leben* of the material and redaction critics try to determine how the evangelists employed the traditions they received. This work, which is more literary in nature, tends to focus on the text in its present literary setting.

the one who proclaimed the message of the kingdom of God became the content of the message that the first Christians proclaimed.

Although the Gospel of John also provides an account of Jesus' ministry, it is treated after the Pauline writings because of its distinctive starting point: the incarnation of the eternal Word of God. With this new starting point, the Fourth Gospel tells its story of Jesus in light of the sending of the Son into the world to reveal the Father to the world rather than in light of Jesus' proclamation of the kingdom of God. This starting point also distinguishes the Johannine tradition from the Pauline tradition, whose starting point is God's redemptive work in Christ's death and resurrection. Consequently, there is a theological logic in moving from the Synoptic tradition to the Pauline tradition to the Johannine tradition. The Synoptic tradition recounts Jesus' proclamation of the kingdom into which Jesus enters by his saving death and resurrection, and the Pauline tradition proclaims God's redemptive work in Christ's death and resurrection, whereas the Johannine tradition views God's work in Christ from the perspective of the incarnation.

1

A Theology of the Kingdom of God

The Gospel of Mark

The Gospel of Mark begins with the appearance of John the Baptist and then narrates the events of Jesus' ministry in Galilee and Jerusalem that lead to his crucifixion, death, and resurrection. In terms of genre, the "Gospel" is akin to a Greco-Roman life of an eminent person, but it differs in its purpose and goal inasmuch as it proclaims God's saving work in Jesus and summons its audience to repent and believe in the gospel it proclaims.[1] This Gospel, then, can be described as a "kerygmatic narrative" since it preaches the gospel through the story it tells.

The story the Gospel narrates is the medium through which the evangelist communicates his theological understanding of what God accomplished through Jesus of Nazareth, whom the Gospel identifies as the Messiah, the Son of God. Consequently, it is somewhat misleading to speak about "the theology of Mark" as if the evangelist were trying to develop an explicit Christology, soteriology, ecclesiology, or eschatology. The Markan evangelist surely had his own understanding of the Christ and his significance for humanity, but he chose to communicate this understanding through a narrative rather than a systematic analysis of Jesus' person and work. After reading or listening to the entire Gospel, the audience should have an understanding of God's work in Christ and its implication for the life of faith. In the case of the Markan Gospel, the audience will discover important implications for its understanding of God's rule in creation, God's Messiah, and the life of discipleship.

The story by which Mark communicates his understanding of the gospel is deceptively simple. Apart from its introduction (1:1–13) and conclusion (16:1–8), it consists of three parts:

---

1. On the genre of the Gospels, see Richard A. Burridge, *What Are the Gospels? A Comparison with Graeco-Roman Biography* (SNTSMS 70; Cambridge: Cambridge University Press, 1992).

1:14–8:30	Jesus' initial proclamation of the kingdom of God
8:31–10:52	Jesus' revelation of the mystery of the Son of Man
11:1–15:47	Jesus' messianic work in Jerusalem

In the introduction (1:1–13) the Markan narrator provides the audience with privileged information about Jesus' identity and his relationship to God to which the characters in the narrative, who will appear later, are not privy.[2] In this way Mark lays the groundwork for the dramatic irony that will characterize his narrative. This privileged information presents Jesus as "the one who is more powerful" (*ho ischyroteros*), the Spirit-anointed Son of God who overcomes Satan in the wilderness.

In the first part of the narrative (1:14–8:30), Jesus proclaims God's own good news that the time is fulfilled and the kingdom of God is at hand. Jesus' exorcisms and mighty deeds show that God's rule has made its appearance in his ministry, and his teaching and parables reveal the mystery of the kingdom. He chooses twelve disciples to be with him, and eventually he sends them on mission. Despite his mighty deeds and authoritative teaching, Jesus encounters opposition from Israel's religious leaders. Moreover, even though Peter confesses that Jesus is the Messiah, the disciples do not comprehend the mystery of the kingdom he reveals to them or the mystery of his messianic destiny.

In the second part of the narrative (8:31–10:52), after Peter confesses that Jesus is the Messiah, Jesus reveals that his messianic destiny is that of the Son of Man who must be rejected by the religious leaders, handed over to the Gentiles, crucified, put to death, rise from the dead, and return as the glorious Son of Man. But just as the disciples are unable to comprehend the mystery of the kingdom of God, so are they unable to grasp the mystery of the Son of Man and thus the true nature of discipleship.

In the third part of the narrative (11:1–15:47), the question of Jesus' authority and his temple ministry in Jerusalem become the occasion for the religious leaders to hand him over to Pilate. Condemned as a messianic pretender who has threatened to destroy the temple, Jesus is put to death by the Romans as "the King of the Jews." After Jesus dies, however, a Roman centurion confesses that Jesus truly was God's Son—the first time within the narrative that a human character recognizes that Jesus is the Son of God.

The Gospel concludes with the account of the women at the empty tomb and the command of the young man to tell Peter and the other disciples that the risen One has gone before them to Galilee as he promised.[3]

2. The "Markan narrator" is the voice that tells the story. This omniscient narrator guides readers through the story, providing them with narrative comments (unknown to the characters of the story) crucial for understanding what is happening. For example, the readers of Mark's narrative know that Jesus is the Messiah, the Son of God, but the human characters within the Gospel story do not.

3. The Gospel of Mark has four endings: (1) the ending at 16:8, attested by the best manuscripts; (2) a shorter ending after 16:8 that recounts how the women reported the young man's

The Markan Gospel is propelled by a plot of conflict: conflict between Satan and the kingdom of God; conflict between Jesus and the religious leaders; conflict between Jesus and his disciples.[4] Aware that the inbreaking of the kingdom means the end of his rule, Satan and his minions try to reveal Jesus' identity prematurely in order to obstruct God's rule. Concerned about their authority, the religious leaders refuse to accept Jesus' God-given authority, thereby unwittingly opposing God's rule. Eager to secure positions of honor in the coming kingdom, Jesus' disciples fail to grasp the mystery of the kingdom, which requires a suffering Messiah whose disciples must follow him in the way to the cross.

Although the Markan evangelist communicates his theology through the story he tells, one writing a theology of the New Testament seeks to organize and, to some extent, systematize the implicit theology of the narrative. This can be done by using traditional theological categories such as Christology, soteriology, ecclesiology, and eschatology, or it can be accomplished by employing the theological categories that the Gospel itself uses. In the case of the Markan Gospel, the central concept that undergirds all others is "the gospel," that is, the good news Jesus proclaimed and the good news that the church now proclaims about him. Reflection on this concept leads to a consideration of the kingdom of God and the herald of that kingdom. Since the gospel of the kingdom requires faith and conversion, it implies the gathering of a people who live as a community of disciples in light of God's inbreaking rule and in anticipation of the return of the Son of Man. The theological structure of the Gospel narrative, therefore, suggests that its theology can be organized in the following way: (1) the proclamation of the gospel; (2) the gospel of God as the inbreaking of God's rule; (3) the gospel about Jesus Christ, the herald of the kingdom of God; (4) the community of disciples and the kingdom of God; (5) the return of the Son of Man and the kingdom of God.

THE PROCLAMATION OF THE GOSPEL

The word "gospel" can be construed in two ways: (1) as referring to a genre of literature, for example, one of the four canonical Gospels; or (2) as the announcement of good news proclaimed by a messenger (*angelos*). Although the Gospel of Mark is now viewed as a "Gospel," a genre of literature, the evangelist employs the word in the second sense, the announcement or proclamation of good news. Used as a purely secular term, "gospel" (*euangelion*)

---

message to Peter and his companions; (3) a longer ending comprising 16:9–20; and (4) a version of the longer ending that contains the Freer logion, which occurs after 16:14.

4. On the plot of Mark's Gospel, see Jack Dean Kingsbury, *Conflict in Mark: Jesus, Authorities, Disciples* (Minneapolis: Fortress, 1989).

refers to the good news of events such as the birth of a child or a military victory. Used as a religious term within the New Testament, it refers to the good news of God's victory in and through Christ, which brings salvation to humanity. The term occurs most frequently in the Pauline writings, but it also plays a central role in the Markan Gospel, where it appears eight times.[5] Although the noun never occurs in the Septuagint, the Greek version of the Old Testament, the verb "to announce good news" (*euangelizein*) does, especially in the book of Isaiah. This usage is especially helpful for understanding the noun in the Markan Gospel since Isa. 52:7 relates this good news to God's rule, what Jesus calls the kingdom of God: "As springtime upon the mountains, as the feet of one preaching good news (*euangelizomenou*) of peace, as one preaching good news (*euangelizomenos*): I will make known your salvation, saying, O Zion, your God shall reign" (LXX Isa. 52:7; my translation).

The manner in which the Markan Gospel begins indicates the centrality of the gospel: "The beginning of the gospel of Jesus Christ, the Son of God" (1:1). The precise meaning of this verse, however, is not clear. Understood as a subjective genitive, "the gospel of Jesus Christ" would be the good news that Jesus proclaimed about the kingdom of God. Understood as an objective genitive, the sense would be the good news about Jesus that the rest of the Gospel will narrate. Since Jesus' proclamation does not begin until 1:15, however, it is best to interpret the phrase in the second sense: the beginning of the gospel about Jesus Christ, the Son of God. This meaning does not exclude the first since the gospel message about Jesus inevitably relates the message he preached. In this verse, then, the evangelist provides his audience with a surplus of meaning that helps to resolve a central theological problem: the relationship between the message Jesus proclaimed and the church's proclamation about him. The Markan answer can be stated in this way: in proclaiming a message about Jesus, the church relates Jesus' own message of the kingdom since the church's proclamation *about* Jesus includes the preaching *of* Jesus.

According to the Markan Gospel, the gospel about Jesus Christ begins with the appearance of John the Baptist, whose prophetic ministry the prophet Isaiah announced (1:2; the scriptural citation is actually a mixed quotation from Isa. 40:3 and Exod. 23:20). This gospel includes Jesus' ministry of preaching, teaching, and healing, as well as the account of his death and resurrection, and it anticipates the parousia when the kingdom of God will come in power. The Markan understanding of the gospel, then, is broader in scope than the Pauline notion, which focuses on the event of Christ's death and resurrection but has little to say of Jesus' ministry. For Mark the gospel includes the story of Jesus' ministry as well as the event of his saving death and resurrection. To proclaim

---

5. Mark 1:1, 14, 15; 8:35; 10:29; 13:10; 14:9. It is also found in 16:15.

the gospel is to tell the story of Jesus, a story that includes the gospel of the kingdom that Jesus proclaimed.

Mark begins the first part of his Gospel (1:14–8:30) with Jesus' preaching, which is described as "the gospel of God" (1:14). Like "the gospel of Jesus Christ," the phrase "the gospel of God" can be understood in two ways. If the phrase is construed as a subjective genitive, God is the subject of the phrase, and it refers to God's own good news: "The time is fulfilled, and the kingdom of God has come near" (1:15). If the phrase is construed as an objective genitive, God is the object of the phrase, and it refers to the good news about God. In this case the sense would be the good news about God that Jesus brings: the time of waiting and preparation has been fulfilled and God's kingdom is about to make its appearance. As with "the gospel of Jesus Christ" there is a surplus of meaning: the gospel that Jesus preaches is about God, but it is also God's own good news that Jesus brings as the herald of the gospel. God is the origin of Jesus' gospel.

The next verse (1:15) clearly articulates the content of this gospel and the moral demands it makes on those who hear it. In terms of content, God's good news proclaims that the time of preparation and waiting has ended. Corresponding to the fulfillment of this time is the arrival of the kingdom: the kingdom of God "has come near" (*ēngiken*). Once more the meaning of the Greek is ambiguous, since the verb could refer to the presence of or to the imminent arrival of the kingdom. The rest of the gospel narrative, however, will show that even though the kingdom has not arrived in power, it is already present in a hidden way in Jesus' ministry. For in proclaiming the kingdom, in exorcising demons, and in doing mighty works, Jesus makes God's rule present.

The appropriate response to the gospel is to repent and believe in the gospel, that is, to believe in God's good news that the time is fulfilled and the kingdom is at hand (1:15). The Gospel narrative that follows presents numerous examples of people who exhibit such faith, as well as of people who do not. But in every instance the demand of the gospel is clear: one must believe that Jesus is the one through whom God is effecting his final or eschatological rule. One must believe Jesus' proclamation that there has been a decisive change of time. The time of servitude to Satan has ended, for the time of God's rule has begun.

These two concepts ("the gospel of Jesus Christ" and "the gospel of God") are the foundation for Mark's theology, functioning as a kind of shorthand for what the Markan evangelist proclaims through his Gospel. The good news about Jesus Christ is the good news that Jesus Christ proclaimed when he announced God's good news of the inbreaking kingdom of God. The gospel about Jesus and the gospel that Jesus proclaims are subsumed under God's gospel that the kingdom of God has come near. To entrust oneself to this gospel is to entrust oneself to the gospel Jesus proclaimed before his death and to the gospel the church proclaims after his resurrection.

The intimate relationship between Jesus and the gospel he preaches is stated in two other sayings about the gospel. When describing the demands of discipleship, Jesus says, "For those who want to save their life will lose it, and those who lose their life *for my sake, and for the sake of the gospel,* will save it" (8:35). And in responding to Peter's statement that the disciples have left everything to follow him, Jesus replies, "Truly, I tell you, there is no one who has left house or brothers or sisters or mother or father or children or fields, *for my sake and for the sake of the gospel,* who will not receive a hundredfold now in this age—houses, brothers and sisters, mothers and children, and fields, with persecutions—and in the age to come eternal life" (10:29–30). In both sayings Jesus equates himself with the gospel he preaches so that those who follow him and lose their lives for him do so for the sake of the gospel—God's own good news that the kingdom is at hand. Conversely, those who lose their lives for the sake of the gospel or embark upon the path of discipleship to proclaim the gospel are doing this for the sake of Jesus. Since the person of Jesus and the proclamation of the gospel are so intimately related, discipleship is no longer limited to the time of Jesus' earthly ministry but has become a possibility for people of every age. What people do for the sake of the gospel, they do for the sake of Christ; what they do for the sake of Christ, they do for the sake of the gospel.

In two other statements about the gospel, the Markan evangelist shows that the gospel must be preached in the time after Jesus' death. The first occurs in Jesus' final discourse in which he discusses the events that must take place before he returns as the glorious Son of Man to gather the elect (13:9–11). He warns his disciples that before this happens they will be handed over to councils, beaten in synagogues, and brought before governors and kings to give testimony on his behalf. But they should not worry beforehand what they will say because the Holy Spirit will speak through them. During this instruction, in a parenthetical remark, Jesus notes, "And the gospel must first be proclaimed to all nations" (13:10). The saying indicates that the persecution of the disciples, no matter how intense, does not mean that the end is at hand. The gospel must first be preached to all the nations before the end of the ages and the return of the Son of Man. Since Jesus supposes that his disciples will preach the gospel in the period before his return, the content of the gospel they proclaim will be the gospel about him as well as the gospel of God's inbreaking kingdom that Jesus proclaimed. Moreover, since the disciples preach in the period after Jesus' resurrection, they preach about a kingdom that has entered a new stage because Jesus has already entered into the fullness of the kingdom by his saving death and resurrection.

The second statement about the kingdom occurs at the beginning of the passion narrative, when some object to the actions of a woman who anoints Jesus rather than sell the ointment and give the proceeds to the poor (14:3–9). Jesus responds, "Truly I tell you, wherever the gospel is proclaimed in the whole world, what she has done will be told in remembrance of her" (14:9). Here the gospel is the gospel about Jesus Christ that includes the gospel of God, which Jesus proclaimed. Like the previous passage it looks to the period after Jesus' death and resurrection when the story of Jesus and his preaching will be told again and again. Each time it is told, Jesus' prophecy will be fulfilled.

The best manuscript tradition concludes the Gospel of Mark at 16:8, but there are a number of other endings. In the longer ending of 16:9–20 the risen Lord instructs his disciples, "Go into all the world and proclaim the gospel to the whole creation" (16:15). Although the longer ending is a later conclusion to the Gospel, Jesus' commission to preach the gospel to the whole world coheres with what he says in the final discourse: the gospel must be preached to all of the nations before the end occurs. This gospel is the gospel about Jesus Christ, which the Markan Gospel narrates. It includes the story of Jesus' ministry as well as the saving events of his death and resurrection. In relating the gospel about Jesus Christ, disciples proclaim the gospel of God that Jesus Christ proclaimed—the inbreaking kingdom of God—since the gospel that Jesus preached has become the gospel the church proclaims about him. To preach this gospel and surrender one's life for it is to embrace the kingdom of God and follow Jesus in the way of discipleship.

THE GOSPEL OF GOD AS THE INBREAKING OF GOD'S RULE

If the gospel is the central concept that organizes Mark's theology, the content of the gospel is twofold: God's good news about the kingdom and the church's proclamation of what God has accomplished in his Son, Jesus Christ. This section deals with the first aspect of the gospel: the gospel that Jesus preached about the inbreaking kingdom of God. The next will consider the gospel about Jesus Christ.

Jesus' proclamation of the kingdom appears abruptly and without preparation, in part because the Markan evangelist presupposes that his audience already knows that the kingdom of God was the central message Jesus proclaimed. After John's arrest, Jesus appears announcing the gospel, "The time is fulfilled, and the kingdom of God (*hē basileia tou theou*) has come near; repent, and believe in the gospel" (1:15). The evangelist never explains the origin of this message or why it is central to Jesus' teaching. He simply presents Jesus' initial preaching in terms of the kingdom of God. Thus the listener may assume that God, who identified Jesus as his beloved Son and anointed him with the Spirit, has also entrusted him with the gospel of the kingdom and the authority to inaugurate God's rule.

Although 1:14–15 is the only time that the Markan evangelist explicitly recounts Jesus' proclamation of the kingdom, Jesus' initial preaching serves as a thematic statement that determines what follows. The audience is meant to understand that Jesus regularly preached and taught about the kingdom of God, even when there are no explicit references to the kingdom in his preaching. For example, on several occasions the evangelist notes that Jesus was teaching but does not describe the content of his teaching (1:21, 22; 2:13; 6:2, 6, 34), and on another occasion he relates that Jesus was speaking "the word" but does not explain the content of this word (2:2). In light of Jesus' initial proclamation, however, it is evident that the content of his "teaching" and the "word" he speaks are always related to the kingdom. The same is true for the numerous exorcisms and mighty deeds that Jesus performs, especially in the first part of the Gospel (1:16–8:30). Exorcisms are concrete proofs that God's rule is invading and overcoming Satan's realm through Jesus' ministry. Likewise, when Jesus heals the sick or overcomes the chaos of nature, his mighty deeds indicate that God is establishing his rule by means of Jesus' ministry. The whole of Jesus' ministry, then, both word and deed, proclaims the kingdom of God.

Everything that Jesus says or does is in some way related to the proclamation of the kingdom. For example, he teaches with authority, acts as Lord of the Sabbath, and makes unconditional demands on those whom he calls to discipleship because he knows that the kingdom of God is making its appearance in his ministry. Conversely, the religious leaders oppose Jesus and dispute his right to act with such authority, especially in relation to the Sabbath and their human traditions, because they refuse to believe that God is manifesting his rule over creation and history through Jesus' ministry. They see, but they do not perceive. They hear, but they do not understand that the kingdom of God has made its appearance in Jesus' ministry. As for Pilate, he hands Jesus over to be crucified as a messianic pretender because he has been told that Jesus' preaching about the kingdom is an attempt to restore the kingdom of David at Rome's expense. Even Jesus' death is related to his preaching of the kingdom of God since it has been divinely appointed that the fate of the Messiah is the destiny of the Son of Man who must suffer, die, and rise from the dead before returning with his Father's angels to gather the elect into the kingdom of God. When the Son of Man returns, the kingdom of God will be revealed in power, and no one will be able to deny its presence.

The kingdom of God is a metaphor for God's rule over creation and history. When Jesus proclaims the time is fulfilled and the kingdom of God has come near, he asserts two things. First, the long period during which humanity has waited for God to act in a final and definitive manner has ended. Second, God is now manifesting his rule over creation and history in a new and unparalleled way. This, of course, does not mean that God had ceased to rule over history and creation. God is always the Lord of creation and history. The proclamation of the kingdom, however, does reveal that something is awry in creation and history. The numerous healings and exorcisms that Jesus performs suggest that humanity has failed to submit to God's rule and that its history has gone astray. Humanity has fallen under the power of Satan. Consequently, the religious leaders misunderstand the nature of Jesus' exorcisms when they accuse him of being possessed and casting out demons by Beelzebul, the prince of demons (3:22). Despite their accusations, Jesus' exorcisms show that Satan's rule is coming to an end. Jesus has entered the house of the strong man (Satan), bound him, and plundered his property (3:27). The appearance of the kingdom of God, then, discloses that humanity has been entrapped in a predicament from which it cannot extricate itself unless God manifests his rule in a new and decisive manner. This is precisely what God does through Jesus' ministry, death, and resurrection.

Although powerful, the initial manifestation of the kingdom of God is hidden and can be perceived only by those to whom the mystery of the kingdom is disclosed (4:10–12). Jesus reveals this mystery to his disciples through a series of parables in chapter 4. His explanation (4:13–20) of the parable of the seed (4:2–9) is the key to understanding his ministry. The seed that the sower (Jesus) sows is the word (*logos*), that is, the message of the kingdom. The word receives a variety of responses. Some of the seed (Jesus' preaching about the kingdom) never bears fruit, but the seed that falls on fertile soil produces a harvest that surpasses every expectation. Even though God's rule is hidden now, it will be revealed at harvest time. Other sayings and parables in this chapter make a similar point. Just as one does not hide a lamp but puts it on a lampstand for all to see, so the proclamation of the kingdom is meant to bring light to all (4:21–22). At the present time, one cannot know how or when the kingdom will appear in power since it is like seed a farmer sows only to discover one day that the harvest is at hand (4:26–29). The beginnings of the kingdom, then, are small and insignificant, like a mustard seed, and its growth is imperceptible. But when the kingdom appears in power it provides a resting place where all can dwell (4:30–32). The manner in which the Markan Gospel portrays the kingdom of God in chapter 4 indicates that it is a mystery that can be perceived only by those who believe that Jesus is the herald of God's rule. This mystery proclaims that God's reign is already present in a hidden way and will be revealed in power at the end of the ages. At the present time this rule can be perceived and understood only by those to whom the mystery is revealed. All others stand outside, seeing but not perceiving, hearing but not understanding (4:11–12).

Although the kingdom has not yet come in power, Jesus promises that "there are some standing here who will not taste death until they see that the kingdom of God has come with power" (9:1). This promise comes immediately after a saying about the parousia (8:38) and immediately before the account of Jesus' transfiguration (9:2–8). Thus it could refer either to the parousia or to the transfiguration. The difficulty with the first solution is that the parousia did not occur in the lifetime of Jesus' contemporaries, whereas the difficulty with the second is that the transfiguration occurs only six days later. An alternate solution is to relate Jesus' promise to the resurrection, after which his disciples experienced the coming of the kingdom in power when the risen Son of Man appeared to them as the one who had already entered into the realm of God's transcendent kingdom. Jesus' command to Peter, James, and John not to tell anyone about what they had seen at the transfiguration "until after the Son of Man had risen from the dead" (9:9) suggests that this is the best solution. Only then will others understand their report about the transfiguration since they will have experienced the power of the kingdom in the risen Son of Man—the one who has already entered into the realm of God's rule.

Although the kingdom of God is a dynamic reality that refers to God's rule rather than to a space or location, Jesus portrays the kingdom as something into which one must strive to enter. He warns his disciples that it is better for them "to enter the kingdom of God with one eye than to have two eyes and be thrown into hell" (9:47). He laments how hard it is for the rich to enter the kingdom of God (10:23–25). Each of these sayings is connected to a series of other sayings that speak about entering into life or inheriting eternal life, thereby suggesting that entering into the kingdom means entering into life or inheriting eternal life. For example, 9:43–48 consists of three admonitions not to fall into temptation. In the first two (9:43–46), Jesus warns that it is better to enter life maimed or lame than to have two hands, or two feet, and be thrown into hell. In the third (9:47), however, he no longer speaks of entering into life but of entering into the kingdom of God, suggesting that the kingdom is a metaphor for the fullness of life. To enter the kingdom of God is to enter into the realm of life, as the Johannine Gospel will show.

In 10:17 a rich man asks what he must do *to inherit eternal life*. But when he leaves, unwilling to sell his possessions and follow Jesus (10:21–22), Jesus tells his disciples how hard it is for the rich *to enter into the kingdom of God* (10:23–25), thereby equating the kingdom of God with the fullness of life. The kingdom of God, then, is a realm into which disciples enter when they submit themselves to the rule of God. When they enter into this realm of life, they inherit eternal life. Once more, however, there is a tension between the present and future dimensions of the kingdom. When disciples submit to God's rule they already experience life, but they will not inherit the fullness of life until they enter into God's rule in the way that Jesus already has through his death and resurrection.

Jesus expresses the relationship between death and the kingdom of God in a statement he makes at the Last Supper: "Truly I tell you, I will never again drink of the fruit of the vine until that day when I drink it new in the kingdom of God" (14:25). Taken as a vow of abstinence, Jesus means that he will not share in this final Passover with his disciples because his death is at hand. That death, however, will not prevent him from experiencing the kingdom of God he has preached throughout his ministry. To the contrary, he affirms that even though he will die he will celebrate the Passover anew, and when he does it will be in the kingdom of God. Rather than frustrate the appearance of the kingdom, Jesus' death becomes the paradoxical way by which he enters into the kingdom. For by surrendering his life, he receives it anew through the resurrection of the dead.

The kingdom of God is the focus of Jesus' ministry, the purpose for which God sent him into the world. It is the reason why others oppose him and he must die. A dynamic reality that is already present in a hidden fashion during Jesus' ministry, it will be revealed in power at his resurrection and at the parousia of the Son of Man. It must be proclaimed to all the nations, however, before Jesus returns. In the meantime, those who submit to God's rule are already entering into the realm of life.

THE GOSPEL ABOUT JESUS CHRIST, THE HERALD OF THE KINGDOM OF GOD

Jesus proclaimed the inbreaking kingdom of God. But in the time after his death and resurrection the church proclaims Jesus Christ as the herald of the kingdom of God. In doing so the church does not neglect the gospel about the kingdom that Jesus preached, but the gospel that the church now preaches includes the good news about Jesus, whose ministry inaugurated the kingdom and whose death and resurrection enables the kingdom to come in power. In the case of the Markan Gospel, the gospel of Jesus Christ includes the account of his ministry as well as the good news of his saving death and resurrection, the events by which Jesus entered the transcendent realm of the kingdom of God. The person of Jesus, his identity, and saving work are irrevocably linked to the message he preaches about the kingdom of God. To know who Jesus is and what he has done is to understand the nature of the kingdom whose coming he heralds. To comprehend the mystery of the kingdom is to recognize his identity and his saving work. Therefore, just as the Markan Gospel presents the kingdom as a mystery that can be understood only by those to whom the mystery is given, so there is a mystery about Jesus' identity that is revealed only to those who believe that the crucified One is the messianic Son of God, whose destiny is the destiny of the Son of Man, who must suffer, die, and rise from the dead before returning in his Father's glory.

Because the Markan Gospel is a narrative, its Christology of Jesus is in the form of a narrative Christology.[6] Instead of employing explicit christological statements that tell the audience who Jesus is, the evangelist shows the significance of Jesus' person through the story he tells. The narrative effect of the story can be summarized in this way: Jesus Christ is the crucified Messiah, the Son of God, who can be recognized only by those who understand his destiny in light of the suffering Son of Man, who gives his life as "a ransom for many" (10:45). This Christology can be presented by examining the meaning and relationship of the three major terms the evangelist applies to Jesus.

Jesus the Messiah

The Markan Gospel begins by identifying its central figure as "Jesus Christ, the Son of God" (1:1). This verse indicates that the predicate *Christos* has become so intimately associated with the name "Jesus" that it functions as part of Jesus' name. But the Markan evangelist is aware of the titular use of *Christos*, so that even if he presents "Christ" as part of Jesus' name, he never forgets its messianic sense. For Mark, Jesus has become so associated with Israel's messianic hopes that he can now be identified as Jesus Christ.

The nature of Jesus' messiahship plays a central role in the Markan Gospel. At the close of the first part of the Gospel, Peter confesses that Jesus is the Messiah (8:29). At the climactic moment of Jesus' trial before the Sanhedrin, the high priest asks him if he is the Messiah, the Son of the Blessed One (14:61), and Jesus responds affirmatively (14:62). The Sanhedrin then hands Jesus over to Pilate, who hands him over to be crucified as "the King of the Jews" (15:26), an indication that Jesus was crucified as a messianic pretender. At the crucifixion, the chief priests and the scribes deride Jesus as the Messiah, the King of Israel (15:32). The Markan Gospel, then, presents Jesus as the Messiah. In doing so it recasts messianic expectations in light of Jesus the crucified and risen Messiah. Rather than identify Jesus in light of traditional messianic expectations such as those found in Psalms of Solomon 17 and 18, the evangelist defines messianic expectations in light of what God has done in Jesus.[7]

6. On the Christology of Mark's Gospel, see Jack Dean Kingsbury, *The Christology of Mark's Gospel* (Philadelphia: Fortress, 1983); Frank J. Matera, *New Testament Christology* (Louisville: Westminster John Knox Press, 1999), 5–26; Rudolf Schnackenburg, *Jesus in the Gospels* (Louisville: Westminster John Knox Press, 1995), 17–73.

7. Although there were many ways of envisioning the Messiah and the messianic age in the intertestamental period, these two psalms, which do not belong to the canonical writings, provide an excellent description of a royal Davidic messiah who would free Israel from the oppression of its enemies and then rule Jerusalem in righteousness. On the differences in messianic hope, see Jacob Neusner, William S. Green, and Ernest Frerichs, eds., *Judaisms and Their Messiahs at the Turn of the Christian Era* (Cambridge: Cambridge University Press, 1987).

After Peter confesses that Jesus is the Messiah (8:29), Jesus sternly orders the disciples "not to tell anyone about him" (8:30). He then teaches them about the Son of Man, who "must undergo great suffering, and be rejected by the elders, the chief priests, and the scribes, and be killed, and after three days rise again" (8:31). The juxtaposition of these sayings, especially the command to silence, has led some to suggest that Jesus rejects Peter's confession, as if he were saying, "Enough of this talk!" But this can hardly be correct, since the Markan evangelist presents Peter's confession in juxtaposition to a series of blatantly false opinions about Jesus. Thus, when Jesus asks his disciples who do people say he is, the disciples reply, "John the Baptist; and others, Elijah; and still others one of the prophets" (8:28, which echoes 6:14–16). Jesus then asks the disciples who they think he is, and Peter correctly confesses that he is the Messiah. Jesus does not allow his disciples to reveal this (8:29–30) because, even though this messianic confession is formally correct, it has not taken into account the mystery of Jesus' messiahship. Peter and the disciples do not yet understand what Jesus will teach them about the mystery of the Son of Man (8:31; 9:31; 10:33–34).

Jesus calls into question the traditional Davidic understanding of messiahship in another episode. He asks, "How can the scribes say that the Messiah is the son of David?" (12:35). Quoting Ps. 110:1, he notes that in this psalm, which he attributes to David, David addresses the Messiah as his Lord. But if the Messiah is David's Lord, how can he be David's son, since no father addresses his son as his Lord? With this startling exegesis Jesus calls into question the scribal teaching that the Messiah is the son of David, suggesting that the Messiah is more than the son of David (12:35–37). To be sure, earlier in the narrative, as Jesus approached Jerusalem, Bartimaeus addressed him as "Son of David" (10:47, 48), expressing his faith that Jesus could heal him. And when Jesus entered Jerusalem, those who followed him interpreted his entrance as a sign of the imminent arrival of David's kingdom (11:9–10). But Jesus' question about the Messiah in 12:35–37 indicates that Davidic messiahship cannot adequately account for his identity because it does not take into account that he must suffer, die, and rise from the dead.

The Destiny of the Son of Man

The mystery of Jesus' messiahship is irrevocably linked to the destiny of the Son of Man. This term has a complicated and disputed history. Some argue that Israel's messianic expectations included the hope for an apocalyptic figure called the Son of Man who would suddenly appear to deliver Israel. According to this scenario, even Jesus waited for the coming of the Son of Man, and it was only after Jesus' resurrection that the church identified him

with the Son of Man.[8] Others maintain that there was no such hope. Jesus'
sayings about the Son of Man are indebted to the account of Daniel 7, which
uses the image of "one like a son of man" to describe the one to whom God
grants dominion, glory, and kingship after a long period of persecution and
affliction. This one like a son of man is identified with the "holy ones of the
Most High" in Dan. 7:27, most likely the martyrs of the Maccabean revolt.[9]
According to this scenario, Jesus would have appropriated the fate of these
martyrs for himself, confident that just as God vindicated these holy ones by
granting them dominion, glory, and kingship, so God would vindicate him
after his death by granting him power and kingship as the glorious Son of
Man. But before this can happen, Jesus must undergo the fate of the Son of
Man, a destiny of rejection, suffering, and death, which entails divine necessity (dei, Mark 8:31). This second scenario is the most helpful for understanding Mark's narrative Christology.

Only Jesus refers to himself as the Son of Man.[10] In doing so, he points
to his divinely appointed destiny, as well as the power (exousia) he already
enjoys from God during the period of his earthly ministry. First, the Son of
Man must be handed over, suffer, die, and rise again (8:31; 9:12, 31; 10:33;
14:21, 41). Second, after he has been exalted at the right hand of God, he
will return with his Father's angels to gather the elect (8:38; 13:26–27;
14:62). During the period of his earthly ministry, the Son of Man already
enjoys God's power to forgive sins and heal on the Sabbath (2:10, 28); however, he does not come to be served but to serve and to give his life as a ransom for many (10:45). The mystery of the Son of Man is the mystery of Jesus'
messiahship that can no longer be defined by the traditional categories of
Davidic messiahship, which knows nothing of a suffering messiah who will
rise from the dead and return at the end of the ages. Jesus' messiahship
embraces service as well as power. It entails a death that will ransom many
and leads to resurrection. During his earthly ministry, he inaugurates the
kingdom by his humble service. By his resurrection he enters into the kingdom. At his parousia he will manifest the kingdom into which he has already
entered. But whose death has such salvific power and to whom does God
grant such authority?

8. Rudolf Bultmann (Theology of the New Testament [2 vols.; New York; Scribner, 1951–55],
1:28–30) maintains that it was the church that identified Jesus with the coming Son of Man, and
that Jesus himself anticipated the coming of this figure.

9. While some scholars understand the "holy ones of the Most High" as the martyrs of the
Maccabean revolt, others argue that this phrase refers to the angels of God's council. For a fuller
discussion, see Joseph A. Fitzmyer, The One Who Is to Come (Grand Rapids: Eerdmans, 2007),
57–59.

10. While this statement is true inasmuch as no character within the narrative identifies Jesus
as the Son of Man, it should be noted that the Markan narrator refers to Jesus as the Son of Man
in 8:31.

The Messiah, the Son of God

The Gospel of Mark identifies Jesus as God's Son on several occasions. Twice God calls Jesus his beloved Son: at Jesus' baptism and at his transfiguration. In the first instance, Jesus sees the heavens torn apart and the Spirit descending upon him, and a voice proclaims, "You are my Son, the Beloved; with you I am well pleased" (1:11). In the second a cloud overshadows the transfigured Jesus, and a voice echoes the baptismal declaration in a slightly different way, "This is my Son, the Beloved; listen to him" (9:7). Jesus also echoes this declaration in the parable of the vineyard when he says, "He had still one other, a beloved son. Finally he sent him to them, saying, 'They will respect my son'" (12:6). The manner in which Jesus addresses God in the Garden of Gethsemane indicates that he enjoys a unique relationship with God: "Abba, Father, for you all things are possible; remove this cup from me; yet, not what I want, but what you want" (14:36). Jesus' consciousness of his relationship to God is revealed in two other statements, a saying about the Son of Man and a statement about the time of the parousia. In the first he warns, "Those who are ashamed of me and of my words in this adulterous and sinful generation, of them the Son of Man will also be ashamed when he comes in the glory of his Father with the holy angels" (8:38). In the second he discloses his relation to God, "But about that day or hour no one knows, neither the angels in heaven, nor the Son, but only the Father" (13:32). But it is not only Jesus who is aware of this relationship to the Father. During his Galilean ministry, Jesus silences the unclean spirits, who, whenever they see him, fall before him and shout, "You are the Son of God" (3:11). At Jesus' trial, then, the high priest asks him if he is "the Messiah, the Son of the Blessed One" (14:61), equating messiahship and divine sonship. It is only after Jesus has died, however, that a human character within the narrative, a Roman centurion, exclaims, "Truly this man was God's Son!" (15:39).

Jesus' identity as the Son of God plays a central role in the Markan Gospel, and it is not surprising that the Gospel opens with the statement, "The beginning of the good news of Jesus Christ, the Son of God."[11] The designation of Jesus as the "Son" or the "Son of God" can be related to different backgrounds. In the Old Testament, the title was applied to the people of Israel (Exod. 4:22; Jer. 31:9; Hos. 11:1), to the Israelite king (2 Sam. 7:14; Pss. 2:7; 89:26–27), to the just person (Wis. 2:18; 5:5), and to the angels of God (Gen. 6:2, 4; Deut. 32:8; Job 1:6–12), whereas in the Hellenistic world it could be applied to emperors, miracle workers, and philosophers.[12] The manner in which the

---

11. Although the "Son of God" title in 1:1 is supported by a number of important manuscripts, it is also absent from several significant manuscripts. Its presence in Mark 1:1, however, coheres with the evangelist's overall Christology, which understands Jesus as the Son of God.

12. On the background to the title "Son of God," see James D. G. Dunn, *Christology in the Making: A New Testament Inquiry into the Origins of the Doctrine of the Incarnation* (2nd ed.; Grand Rapids: Eerdmans, 1996), 12–64.

Markan Gospel understands these terms, however, is not confined to or exhausted by these categories but must be determined by its narrative, which presents Jesus as the one who surrenders his life as a ransom for many (Mark 10:45; see also 14:24) and as the one whom God raises from the dead (16:6).

The Markan Gospel never defines what it means by "Son of God," but it provides a number of clues. The predicate "beloved" and Jesus' intimate form of address "Abba" indicate that he enjoys a unique relationship to God. The descent of the Spirit upon Jesus at his baptism shows that whereas the Israelite king was anointed with oil on the day of his enthronement, Jesus is the Spirit-anointed Son of God whom God has designated as his Messiah. The power of Jesus to perform mighty deeds, to cast out demons, to forgive sins, to heal on the Sabbath, and to cleanse the temple show that he exercises a God-given authority. His total submission to the will of the Father reveals that he is utterly obedient and dependent on the Father. Not only does Jesus teach others to save their life by surrendering their life (8:35), he provides the perfect example of this teaching by refusing to come down from the cross to save himself (15:27–32).

The second evangelist does not address the question of Jesus' virginal conception as do Matthew and Luke, nor does he develop a teaching on Jesus' preexistence as do John, Paul, and Hebrews. He prefers to express Jesus' sonship in terms of obedience, the radical obedience of the Son who does the will of the Father. For Mark, Jesus' sonship—his unique relationship to God—is part of the mystery of the kingdom of God. The identity of the one who reveals the mystery is hidden until he dies. Only after he dies is his true identity revealed. Only when disciples are willing to identify the crucified Messiah as the Son of God can they confess that Jesus is God's Son. Such a functional Christology does not exhaust the profound mystery of Jesus' person, but neither does it exclude further development in terms of a Christology that includes the virginal conception of Jesus and his preexistence. It does, however, offer a fruitful way to reflect upon Jesus' sonship.

The herald of the kingdom is the Messiah, the Son of God, whose destiny is the way of the Son of Man. His person defines what it means to be Messiah and Son of God.

THE COMMUNITY OF DISCIPLES AND THE KINGDOM OF GOD

The ecclesiology of the Markan Gospel is implicit at best. Unlike the Gospel of Matthew or the Acts of the Apostles, this Gospel makes no explicit reference to the church (*ekklēsia*). Rather it focuses its attention on the community of disciples that Jesus gathers during the period of his earthly ministry, and it envisions a time between his resurrection and parousia when this community will proclaim the kingdom of God (13:9–13), thereby assuming that the community of Jesus' disciples will endure until the parousia. Consequently, a discussion of Markan ecclesiology must examine how the Gospel presents Jesus' disciples and discipleship.[13]

The Markan Gospel presents discipleship within the context of the inbreaking kingdom of God. Thus immediately after Jesus' initial proclamation of the kingdom he calls his first disciples (1:16–20). Their positive response to his call indicates that they have believed in his proclamation of the kingdom, and their willingness to leave their livelihood is a concrete manifestation of their repentance. From the many disciples who follow him, Jesus chooses twelve "to be with him" (3:13–19). The Twelve form an inner circle within a larger circle of those who follow Jesus, the number "twelve" suggesting that Jesus has chosen them to be the nucleus of a renewed Israel. As the Gospel progresses, Jesus defines his "family" in terms of those who do the will of God (3:34) rather than in terms of blood relationship. Moreover, he reveals the mystery of the kingdom to such people and the Twelve, thereby drawing a distinction between those who know the mystery of the kingdom of God and those who do not (4:10–12). Eventually, Jesus gives the Twelve authority over unclean spirits and sends them on a mission to proclaim repentance because the kingdom of God is making its appearance in his ministry (6:7–13). Thus the Markan Gospel presents the disciples as the community of those who embrace the inbreaking kingdom of God and join Jesus in calling others to repentance.

Although Jesus entrusts the mystery of the kingdom to his disciples, they fail to comprehend the full significance of what is occurring in his ministry. They become fearful when caught in a storm at sea, and Jesus must reprimand them: "Why are you afraid? Have you still no faith?" (4:40). They fail to understand the significance of the feeding of the five thousand, and so the Markan narrator comments: "For they did not understand about the loaves, but their hearts were hardened" (6:52). They misunderstand his warning about the leaven of the Pharisees, and Jesus laments: "Do you still not perceive or understand? Are your hearts hardened? Do you have eyes, and fail to see? Do you have ears, and fail to hear?" (8:17–18). Although the disciples receive privileged information about the kingdom of God, they are unable to comprehend its full significance.

The tension between Jesus and his disciples becomes more pronounced when he reveals his destiny to suffer, die, and rise from the dead before returning as the glorious Son of Man to gather the elect into God's kingdom. When Jesus speaks of his messianic destiny (8:31; 9:31; 10:32–34), his disciples do not understand why he must suffer (8:32; 9:32; 10:35–41). Because they do not

---

13. On the disciples and the church in Mark's Gospel, see Ernest Best, *Following Jesus: Discipleship in the Gospel of Mark* (JSNTSup 4; Sheffield: Sheffield University Press, 1981).

comprehend why he must suffer and die, they do not understand what it means to follow him. Accordingly, Jesus instructs them to deny themselves, take up their cross (8:34–38), and embrace a life of discipleship that makes them servants to one another (9:33–37; 10:41–45). As he makes his way to Jerusalem to embrace his destiny as the suffering Son of Man, he provides the disciples with a series of teachings that should guide their life of discipleship now and in the period after his death. The Markan Gospel gathers these instructions into something akin to a "catechism for disciples" that deals with the danger of scandal, the indissolubility of marriage, the dignity of children, and the danger of riches, in light of Jesus' teaching on the kingdom of God (9:42–10:31). Accordingly, disciples must take the most severe precautions to avoid scandal lest they be excluded from the kingdom of God (9:42–47). They must become like children, since the kingdom belongs to those who trust in God just as children trust in their parents (10:14–15). They must be willing to leave everything for the kingdom, since "it is easier for a camel to go through the eye of a needle than for someone who is rich to enter the kingdom of God" (10:25).

In his final discourse about the fate of the temple and his return at the end of the ages (chap. 13), Jesus teaches the disciples that the time between his resurrection and parousia will be a period of affliction for his disciples (13:9–13). Their families will betray them, and they will be brought to trial because of their allegiance to him. During this period, they must preach the gospel (which now includes the story of Jesus as well as the gospel about the kingdom) to all the nations. Those who endure during this period of affliction will be saved (13:13) and numbered among the elect whom the Son of Man will gather at his parousia (13:27). During the period of Jesus' own affliction—the passion—Judas betrays him, Peter denies him, and the community of disciples scatters (14:27, 50). But the risen Lord, the shepherd of the sheep, promises that he will gather his scattered flock in Galilee after his resurrection (14:28; 16:7).

The manner in which the Markan Gospel portrays discipleship suggests that it understands the church as a community of disciples who have embraced Jesus' message of the inbreaking kingdom of God. Because of his death and resurrection, the community now understands the mystery of the kingdom, the nature of discipleship, and the true identity of Jesus as the crucified Messiah. But it is keenly aware that it is only a step away from apostasy if it fails to embrace a discipleship that entails suffering, the cross, and service to others. For the Markan Gospel the church is an eschatological community, that is, a community of disciples who know they are living in the last days before the appearance of the Son of Man. Therefore they must proclaim the gospel of Jesus and the gospel about Jesus to all the nations before the Son of Man returns. If they are faithful to this, they will encounter affliction and persecution. But disciples can be confident that if they endure to the end, they will be numbered among the elect.

The Markan Gospel says little about church structure, though it implies that the Twelve have a central role, provided they become the servants of all and exercise their authority in imitation of the Son of Man, who did not come to be served but to serve (10:41–45). The Markan Gospel never employs the word *ekklēsia*, but it is aware that the community of Jesus' disciples must endure until the parousia so that the gospel will be preached to all the nations. The ecclesiology of Mark's Gospel is implicit and ultimately inadequate, but its main lines are indispensable for any understanding of New Testament ecclesiology.

THE RETURN OF THE SON OF MAN AND THE KINGDOM OF GOD

The mystery of the kingdom of God that Jesus reveals to his disciples is intimately related to the coming of the kingdom. It can be summarized in this way: Although the ministry of Jesus inaugurates the kingdom of God, the kingdom is present in a hidden way that only faith can perceive. At the end of the ages, however, the kingdom will be manifested in such a way that no one will be able to deny its presence. Thus the community of Jesus' disciples lives with an eschatological reservation: on the one hand faith enables it to see and experience God's rule in Jesus' ministry, death, and resurrection; on the other the community's present afflictions are a painful reminder that the final phase of the kingdom has not yet come. This relationship between what has "already" happened and what has "not yet" occurred is a central issue in the Markan Gospel that raises the question of eschatology. Understood as a theological category, eschatology refers to the last or final things that will occur in God's plan of salvation. When these events happen, God's victory will be complete, and the elect will be saved. According to the Markan Gospel these events will occur at the parousia of the Son of Man when the final stage of the kingdom of God will be ushered in.

Although his ministry effects an initial experience of God's rule, Jesus anticipates another stage when the kingdom will come in power. For example, he tells a parable of a farmer who sows seed. The earth produces the stalk, the head, then the grain in the head, and when the grain is ripe the sickle harvests the grain (4:26–29). The parable indicates that the seed for the kingdom has already been sown. At the present time the kingdom is growing, unknown to the world, and it will soon appear in power. Then God's eschatological harvest will occur. But how and when will this occur?

Although the Markan Gospel never explicitly explains how the kingdom of God will come in power, it contains a number of sayings about the coming of the Son of Man that suggest that Jesus' parousia is the eschatological event that effects God's final judgment or salvation. For example, the coming of the Son of Man will be a moment of judgment for those who have been ashamed of Jesus and his words (8:38), a moment when he will be vindicated as the Son of Man who sits at God's right hand (14:62). It will be the moment when the Son of Man will send out the angels to gather the elect (13:26–27), presumably into the kingdom of God. Thus, although the Markan Gospel never explicitly relates the parousia of the Son of Man to the final coming of the kingdom, the Gospel narrative suggests that the parousia of the Son of Man will be the decisive moment of God's eschatological harvest, the moment when people will experience the fullness of salvation inaugurated by Jesus' ministry.

The Markan Gospel, however, is elusive about when the parousia will occur and when the kingdom will come in power. On the one hand, some statements could be interpreted as referring to the appearance of the kingdom in power and the parousia of the Son of Man as something that will occur in the lifetime of Jesus' disciples: "Truly I tell you, there are some standing here who will not taste death until they see that the kingdom of God has come with power" (9:1); "Truly I tell you, this generation will not pass away until all these things have taken place" (13:30). On the other hand, Mark records a statement in which Jesus cautions disciples that neither the angels nor the Son, but only the Father, knows the day or hour when the Son of Man will return (13:32). Therefore disciples must be vigilant, for they do not know when the Son of Man will return (13:33–37).

On face value, it would appear that the Markan evangelist believed that the parousia and the final manifestation of the kingdom would occur in the lifetime of the generation for which he wrote, much as Paul appears to have thought that the parousia would occur in his lifetime (1 Thess. 4:17). If so, both Mark and Paul were mistaken. But they were not wrong in their judgment that the appearance of the kingdom and the Messiah's death and resurrection have inaugurated the penultimate period in God's salvific plan. If the kingdom has appeared, then it will surely be consummated. If the Messiah has been raised from the dead, then he will surely return in glory as the Son of Man.

But it is also possible that Mark understands the sayings of 9:1 and 13:30 in another way, namely, that the kingdom has already come in power (9:1) in the resurrection of the Son of Man, and all the things (13:30) of which Jesus spoke in his eschatological discourse—up to but not including the parousia of the Son of Man—have taken place.[14] If this is so, the Markan Gospel has established an

---

14. In 13:29 Jesus says that when the disciples see "these things taking place" they will know that the appearance of the Son of Man is at hand. "These things" refers to everything leading up to the parousia. In 13:30 Jesus says that this generation will not pass away "until all these things have taken place." If "all these things" includes the parousia, then Jesus expects the parousia to occur in the lifetime of the disciples. But if "these things" refers to the events leading up to the parousia, he is not necessarily saying that the parousia will occur in their lifetime.

eschatological tension that remains intact to this day. All of the preliminary signs leading to the parousia, including the destruction of the temple, have occurred (see 13:4–23). Consequently, the appearance of the Son of Man can occur at any moment. Since not even the Son knows when the parousia will occur (13:32), disciples of every generation must be vigilant and watch (13:33–37).

Mark's eschatology can be summarized in this way. The kingdom made its initial appearance in a hidden way, accessible only through faith, in Jesus' ministry to Israel. It was then revealed in power at the resurrection of the Son of Man. All of the preliminary signs of the parousia, including the destruction of the temple, have occurred. Consequently, the Son of Man can return at any moment. The similarity between Markan and Pauline eschatology can be stated in this way: just as Paul believes that the parousia can occur at any moment because the general resurrection of the dead has begun with the resurrection of the Messiah, so Mark believes that the parousia can occur at any moment because the Son of Man has risen from the dead and the signs preliminary to his coming have occurred.

CONCLUSION

Markan theology begins with the gospel: the gospel that Jesus preached (the inbreaking kingdom of God) and the gospel about Jesus (his ministry, death, resurrection, and the hope of his imminent return). At the heart of this theology is a profound understanding of Jesus as the crucified Messiah, the Son of God, which cannot be understood apart from his destiny as the Son of Man to suffer, die, rise, and come again. The community of disciples that he gathers around him (the church) understands itself as standing between the appearance of the kingdom and its final manifestation. As it awaits its Lord's return, it preaches the gospel to the nations and patterns its life after the model of the one who came to serve and give his life as a ransom for many. When compared with Matthew and Luke–Acts, Mark is lacking in a number of areas. Nonetheless it provides a powerful exposition of the gospel Jesus proclaimed and the gospel the church now preaches about him—the starting point for the Gospels of Matthew and Luke. It provides a profound understanding of God as the one who manifests power in the weakness and folly of the cross.

2

A Theology of the Righteousness of the Kingdom

The Gospel of Matthew

Although the Gospel of Matthew makes use of the Markan Gospel as its primary source, for at least two reasons it narrates the story of Jesus in a different way. First, Matthew employs new traditions about Jesus: a collection of Jesus' sayings commonly designated "Q," and special material (peculiar to Matthew), such as is found in the infancy narrative, commonly designated "M." Second, Matthew's understanding of Jesus' role in Israel's history expresses itself in a distinctive theological vision that goes beyond what the Markan Gospel proclaims about Jesus, his teaching, his disciples, his significance for Israel, and the future coming of the Son of Man.

Because Matthew has access to other sources in addition to Mark's Gospel, and because he so carefully edits his sources, he presents a more complete account of Jesus' life and ministry. For example, the Gospel begins with a genealogy and infancy narrative (1:1–2:23) and gives a more detailed account of John the Baptist's preaching (3:7–12) and Jesus' testing in the wilderness (4:1–11). It presents Jesus' teaching in a series of discourses: the Sermon on the Mount (5:1–7:27), a missionary discourse (10:1–42), a discourse of parables (13:1–52), a discourse on church discipline (18:1–35), a discourse in which Jesus condemns the Pharisees and the scribes (23:1–39), and a farewell discourse about the imminent destruction of the temple and the parousia of the Son of Man (24:1–25:46). The Gospel then concludes with a fuller account of the events that occurred after Jesus' death and burial: the posting of a guard at the tomb (27:62–66), the appearance of the risen Lord to the women (28:9–10), the bribing of the guards (28:11–15), and the appearance of the risen Lord to the eleven disciples in Galilee whom he commissions to make disciples of all the nations (28:16–20). In addition to this material, the Matthean Gospel contains other distinctive traditions such as the account of Peter walking on the sea (14:28–33), Jesus' promise that Peter will be the rock foundation of the church (16:17–19), the curious episode about the temple tax (17:24–27), the suicide of Judas (27:3–10), the dream of Pilate's wife on the eve of Jesus' death (27:19), the frightful cry of the Jewish crowd at Jesus' trial (27:25), and the earthquake that occurs after Jesus' death (27:51–53).

Although this material allows Matthew to develop his Gospel in ways that Mark does not, it is Matthew's theological vision that shapes his story of Jesus in a new and distinctive way. This theological vision presupposes the theology of the Markan Gospel. Consequently, Matthew is essentially faithful to his predecessor's understanding of Jesus as the Messiah, the Son of God, whose destiny is that of the Son of Man who must suffer, die, and rise from the dead before returning as the glorious Son of Man. The kingdom of God, which Matthew normally refers to as "the kingdom of heaven" (a Semitic circumlocution for the kingdom of God, which was probably current in the community for which Matthew wrote) remains the central message of Jesus' proclamation. Likewise Jesus' disciples continue to be the nucleus of a restored Israel that must preach the gospel of the kingdom to the nations before their Lord returns. In retelling the story of Jesus, however, Matthew develops old themes and introduces new ones. For example, whereas the Markan Gospel has little interest in Jesus' Davidic messiahship, Matthew explicitly presents Jesus as the Davidic Messiah, conceived by the power of God's Spirit, the culmination of Israel's history. The most distinctive aspects of Matthew's Gospel, however, are Jesus' interpretation of the Law and the Prophets, his teaching on the righteousness the kingdom requires of disciples, the role of Israel in salvation history, the new gathering of Israel that Jesus explicitly identifies as his church (*ekklēsia*) and that he establishes on the rock foundation of Peter, and the final judgment that the parousia of the Son of Man will inaugurate. Since the Matthean Gospel has a more explicit interest in the righteousness that the kingdom requires, Jesus' relationship to Israel's history, the community that Jesus establishes, and the final judgment, its theology will be presented under the following headings: (1) the gospel of the kingdom and its righteousness; (2) Jesus Messiah, the climax of Israel's history; (3) Israel and the church; (4) parousia and judgment.

THE GOSPEL OF THE KINGDOM AND ITS RIGHTEOUSNESS

The heart of Jesus' proclamation is the inbreaking kingdom of God that Matthew normally calls "the kingdom of heaven" (32 times) rather than "the kingdom of God" (5 times). The two expressions, however, refer to the same reality—the reign of God that is making its appearance in Jesus' ministry (4:17)—and they can be used interchangeably as in 19:23–24. But inasmuch as "kingdom of heaven" points to the realm where God's reign is already acknowledged, it possesses a more explicitly ethical dimension suggesting that people must submit to God's sovereignty on earth as in heaven.[1] So the third petition of the Lord's Prayer reads, "Your will be done, on earth as it is in heaven" (6:10). In this respect the concept of the kingdom of heaven is especially suited for Matthew's Gospel, which emphasizes doing God's will and practicing a greater righteousness.

The Kingdom

Matthew's presentation of the kingdom is more extensive than Mark's. Whereas Mark has fourteen references to the kingdom, Matthew has fifty, thirty-two of which are peculiar to his Gospel.[2] The first announcement of the kingdom comes from John the Baptist, who proclaims the same message that Jesus does at the start of his own ministry, "Repent, for the kingdom of heaven has come near" (3:2; 4:17). This verbal identification heightens the similarity in the mission of John and of Jesus. Later, when Jesus sends his twelve disciples on mission, they are to preach the same message as John and Jesus: "The kingdom of heaven has come near" (10:7). As in Mark 1:15, the nearness of the kingdom is expressed by the elusive verb *ēngiken*, which has the sense of something having drawn so close that one can say it is here even though it has not yet finally arrived. Jesus can tell the Pharisees, "But if it is by the Spirit of God that I cast out demons, then the kingdom of God has come to you (*ephthasen eph' hymas*)" (Matt. 12:28). But other sayings point to the kingdom as a future reality for which believers pray (6:10), at which they will eat with Abraham, Isaac, and Jacob (8:11), and from which some will be excluded because of their lack of faith (8:12). It is a kingdom Jesus still anticipates on the eve of his death (26:29), a kingdom he will bring when he returns as the vindicated Son of Man (16:28).

The kingdom of God belongs to the poor in spirit and to those who are persecuted because of their righteous behavior (5:3, 10). One's status in the kingdom will be determined by careful observance of even the least important commandment, and unless the righteous behavior of Jesus' disciples surpasses that of the scribes and Pharisees, they will not enter the kingdom of heaven (5:19, 20). Therefore disciples must seek the kingdom and its righteousness (6:33); for actions, not words, will determine who enters God's kingdom (7:21–23).

At the beginning of his discourse on behavior in the new community of the church, Jesus teaches his disciples that the greatest in the kingdom will be those who humble themselves as if they were little children (18:1–4; see also

---

1. Ulrich Luz, *Matthew 1–7* (Continental Commentary; Minneapolis: Augsburg, 1989), 167.
2. C. C. Caragounis, "Kingdom of God/Heaven," *Dictionary of Jesus and the Gospels* (ed. Joel B. Green, Scot McKnight, and I. Howard Marshall; Downers Grove, IL: InterVarsity Press, 1992), 417–30, here 426.

19:14). The kingdom is of such surpassing worth that some have voluntarily surrendered marriage for its sake (19:12). Riches can impede entrance into the kingdom (19:23–24). And because entrance into the kingdom requires a new way of acting, the kingdom brings about an unexpected reversal of fortunes for many. Repentant tax collectors and prostitutes who follow the way of righteousness taught by John the Baptist are entering the kingdom ahead of Israel's religious leaders (21:31). Therefore the kingdom will be taken away from a nation that does not produce its fruits (righteousness) and given to one that will (21:43).

The message of the kingdom is the content of Jesus' gospel, and Matthew summarizes this message as "the gospel of the kingdom" (4:23; 9:35; 24:14). The gospel, then, is the good news about the kingdom of heaven that Jesus' ministry inaugurates. Those who repent and believe in this good news—that the kingdom has drawn near in the life and ministry of Jesus—will be saved. They will enter into the kingdom that God has prepared for them from the foundation of the world (25:34). Those who do not will be cast into the outer darkness, where there will be weeping and gnashing of teeth.

Because it is difficult to grasp the elusive nature of the kingdom of heaven, the Matthean Jesus presents a series of parables comparing the kingdom to everyday realities to explain what it is like. The centerpiece of Jesus' exposition of the kingdom is the parable discourse of chapter 13. Although similar in content to the parable discourse of Mark 4, Matthew 13 introduces new material and reveals new facets of the kingdom, especially as regards righteousness, Israel, the church, and the end of the ages. These parables require understanding and can be grasped only by those to whom the mysteries of the kingdom have been revealed.

Jesus reveals the mysteries of the kingdom of heaven to his disciples (13:11), and their ability to bear fruit appropriate to the kingdom is closely related to their understanding of his teaching. When people do not understand, then the evil one snatches the seed that was sown in their hearts (13:19), whereas those who hear the word of the gospel and understand it bear fruit in abundance (13:23). What distinguishes the disciples from the crowds that follow Jesus, then, is their understanding; for although the crowds see and hear they do not understand. Because they do not understand, they fulfill Isaiah's prophecy of a people whose heart has grown dull (Isa. 6:9–10; Matt. 13:13–15). In stark contrast to the crowds, the disciples respond "yes" when Jesus asks, "Have you understood all this?" (13:51).

From the parables the disciples learn that the kingdom is like a field in which someone sows good seed but another comes and sows weeds (13:24–30). Jesus' explanation (13:36–44) teaches them that at the present time the children of the kingdom are living alongside the children of the evil one, but at the end of the ages the Son of Man will send his angels to separate the two, and the righteous will live in the kingdom of their Father. The kingdom is like a net that gathers all sorts of fish, bad as well as good, but at the end of the ages the evil ones will be separated from the righteous (13:47–50). The disciples also learn that the kingdom is like a mustard seed; it is small in appearance but great in its final manifestation (13:31–32). It is like treasure hidden in a field, or like a pearl of great price (13:44–46); it is something for which it is worth sacrificing everything. Many of these parables point to the final appearance of the kingdom when the harvest will occur (13:8, 23). When the kingdom comes, good and evil will be separated (13:30, 41–42, 49–50), and all will find a home within it (13:32). But these parables are also related to the present, since the decision disciples make about Jesus' proclamation now will have final, that is, eschatological, consequences for the future.

Other parables disclose different aspects of the kingdom. The kingdom is like the case of a landowner who hired day laborers at different hours and then paid all of them the same wage—the kingdom is a manifestation of God's grace and generosity (20:1–16). The kingdom is like the case of a king who invited guests to his son's wedding but they did not come, and so he invited everyone he could find—the kingdom will be filled even if the invited guests refuse to come (22:1–14). The kingdom is like the situation of bridesmaids waiting for the bridegroom—only those prepared for its unexpected arrival will enter (25:1–13). Matthew is aware that the kingdom of heaven refers to God's reign, but his Gospel also describes the kingdom as a future reality into which people will enter and eat at God's eschatological banquet. Jesus' proclamation of this kingdom undergirds his interpretation of righteousness and the law, his mission to Israel, the gathering of a renewed Israel (the church), and the coming judgment at which he will preside when he returns as the vindicated Son of Man.

Righteousness

Jesus' proclamation of the gospel of the kingdom has important implications for the moral life of believers, which find their fullest expression in the Sermon on the Mount.[3] By placing the sermon at the beginning of Jesus' ministry, shortly after his initial proclamation of the kingdom (4:17), Matthew shows that there is an intimate connection between the indicative of salvation (the gospel of the kingdom of heaven) and the moral imperative it requires (a righteousness that surpasses that of the scribes and Pharisees). The sermon begins with nine beatitudes and two metaphors (5:3–16) that serve as a preamble to what follows. Next, Jesus makes an important statement about the

---

3. The literature on the Sermon on the Mount is immense, but reliable commentary on it can be found in Dale C. Allison, *The Sermon on the Mount: Inspiring the Moral Imagination* (New York: Crossroad, 1999); Luz, *Matthew 1–7*; and Robert A. Guelich, *The Sermon on the Mount: A Foundation for Understanding* (Waco: Word, 1982).

enduring validity of the law and the prophets and the need for disciples to practice a superior righteousness (5:17–20). He then gives an extended teaching on
righteousness (5:21–7:11) that concludes with a summary of the law and the
prophets (7:12). The sermon ends with a series of harsh warnings about the
importance of putting this teaching into practice (7:13–27). The sermon may
be outlined in this way:

Introduction (5:3–16)
    Enduring validity of the law and the prophets (5:17–20)
    Three teachings on righteousness (5:21–7:11)
        Six contrasting statements (5:21–48)
        Three works of righteousness (6:1–18)
        Seeking the righteousness of the kingdom (6:19–7:11)
    Summary of the law and the prophets (7:12)
Conclusion (7:13–27)

Whereas Paul uses "righteousness" (*dikaiosynē*) in a theological sense to
depict the gift God grants to the justified, Matthew employs it in an ethical
sense to describe the conduct required of those who belong to the kingdom.
Jesus is a model of such righteous behavior. When John the Baptist hesitates
to baptize him, Jesus responds, "Let it be so now; for it is proper for us in this
way to fulfill all righteousness" (3:15). The righteousness to which Jesus refers
is moral conduct appropriate to the kingdom of God, which John has already
announced: "Repent, for the kingdom of heaven has come near" (3:2). Jesus is
also speaking of the ethical nature of this righteousness when he criticizes
Israel's leaders for not believing John, who came to them "in the way of righteousness" (21:32). Therefore, repentant tax collectors and prostitutes are
entering the kingdom of God before them. At the outset of the Gospel, then,
Matthew portrays Jesus as the Son of God who practices the righteousness he
teaches, and at the end of the Gospel even Judas (27:4), Pilate's wife (27:19),
and Pilate himself (27:24) must acknowledge that Jesus is a righteous man.
    In the Sermon on the Mount, Jesus explains the nature of this righteous-
ness in light of the gospel of the kingdom he has been proclaiming throughout Galilee (4:23). In the beatitudes that begin the sermon, he announces that
the kingdom belongs to "the poor in spirit" (5:3) and to "those who are persecuted for righteousness' sake" (5:10). The poor in spirit are those who are
utterly dependent on God. They are the meek, those who mourn because of
the present afflictions of God's people, and they hunger and thirst for righteousness; that is, they seek to live righteous lives. "Those persecuted for righteousness' sake" refers to those who are persecuted for conducting their lives
according to the demands of the inbreaking kingdom of God. They are the
merciful, the pure of heart, the peacemakers. These righteous are persecuted

because they live according to the righteousness for which they hunger and thirst. So the kingdom of heaven belongs to them.

In the body of the sermon Jesus explains the nature and demands of this righteousness in relation to the law and the prophets. In a programmatic statement that clarifies his relationship to the law and the prophets (5:17–20), he tells his disciples that he has not come to abolish the law or the prophets but to fulfill them (5:17). The law will endure until everything is accomplished (5:18). Therefore, it is incumbent upon the disciples to observe and teach all the commandments, even the least important (5:19); for if their righteousness does not surpass that of the scribes and Pharisees, they will not enter the kingdom of God (5:20). The manner in which Matthew employs the verb "to fulfill" in his fulfillment quotations suggests that Jesus is bringing Israel's Scriptures, the law and the prophets, to prophetic fulfillment by his life, ministry, and teaching. On the one hand, he is the embodiment of his people, the perfectly obedient Son of God who practices the righteousness of the kingdom he proclaims. On the other, his prophetic teaching enables people to do the will of God so that they can become perfect as their heavenly Father is perfect (5:48). Therefore, the law will endure until all is accomplished. If Matthew views Jesus' death and resurrection as the moment when all things are accomplished, then the death of the Messiah marks the end of the law and the prophets. But if Matthew views the parousia as the moment when all things will be accomplished, then the law and the prophets *as interpreted by Jesus Messiah* continue to have an abiding validity until that moment. Matthew's view of the law, then, can be summarized in this way. In his teaching and conduct, the Son of God brings the Mosaic law to its prophetic fulfillment. The law and the prophets *as interpreted by Jesus Messiah* will endure until the parousia, when all things are fulfilled. Therefore, his disciples must do even the least commandment of the law *as interpreted by Jesus Messiah*. When they observe the law *as interpreted by Jesus Messiah*, they practice a righteousness superior to that of the scribes and Pharisees because their behavior corresponds to God's will as revealed by the Son of God.

Having assured his disciples that he has not come to abolish the law or the prophets, Jesus presents his teaching on righteousness. The teaching begins with six contrasting statements in which he juxtaposes what the disciples have heard ("You have heard that it was said") with what he says ("But I say to you"). The first half of the contrast recalls a moral injunction from the Scriptures, whereas the second offers Jesus' prophetic interpretation of the law. For example, the ancestors were told, "You shall not murder," a commandment of the Decalogue (Exod. 20:13; Deut. 5:17). They were also warned, "Whoever murders shall be liable to judgment" (Exod. 21:12; Lev. 24:17). In contrast, Jesus tells his disciples that if they are angry they will be liable to judgment; if they insult they will be liable to the council; if they call each other "fool" they will be liable to hell fire (Matt. 5:22). Before they bring their gifts to the altar then they should be reconciled with those with whom they are estranged. Otherwise they will be handed over to judgment. In effect, Jesus' teaching intensifies the law by identifying the root cause of murder: anger, insult, the derogatory remark. Far from abolishing the law, he calls upon disciples to build a fence around the law that protects them from those things that lead to murder. The same pattern holds, in different ways, for the other contrast statements. The law forbids adultery, but Jesus requires his disciples to avoid the lustful glance that leads to adultery (5:27–30). The law allows divorce, commanding a man to notify his wife in writing that he is divorcing her, but Jesus forbids divorce except in the case of *porneia*.[4] The law forbids false oaths, but Jesus forbids oaths because his disciples should be people of utter integrity whose words do not need to invoke God as a witness (5:33–37). The law allows limited retribution, but Jesus forbids vengeance (5:38–42). The law requires its adherents to love their neighbor and hate their enemy, but Jesus requires his disciples to love their enemies as well as their neighbors (5:43–47). Although the text of Leviticus does not speak of hating one's enemies ("You shall not take vengeance or bear a grudge against any of your people, but you shall love your neighbor as yourself; I am the LORD," Lev. 19:18), Jesus formulates this contrast in a way that reflects how the love commandment was often practiced: love for the neighbor was extended to those within the community of Israel, whereas those outside the community were treated as enemies.

Jesus' contrasting statements bring the law and the prophets to their prophetic fulfillment by revealing the original intention of God's law, a meaning the religious leaders have obscured by their human traditions (Matt. 15:3). Jesus requires his disciples to be perfect (*teleios*) as their heavenly Father is perfect (5:48; also see 19:21). This means to be whole and undivided in their allegiance to God, to be perfect in their observance of the law *as taught by Jesus Messiah*, teaching and observing even the least important commandment (5:19). To be sure these contrasting statements are not, nor are they intended to be, a complete commentary on the law. Nor do they form a new law that is sufficient to itself. But when disciples grasp the inner dynamic of Jesus' teaching, then they have understood the hermeneutical principle that he has applied to the law in order to recover God's original will.

After revealing the prophetic meaning of the law, the Messiah warns his disciples not to practice their righteousness (NRSV "piety") for others to see (6:1–18). The works of righteousness or piety that Jesus has in view are almsgiving, prayer, and fasting. Those who practice their works of righteousness

---

4. The precise meaning of this word in Matthew's divorce clause is disputed. While some construe it as referring to sexual immorality, others argue that it refers to marriages between people who are too closely related to each other by blood. Thus, whereas the NRSV translates the text as "except on the ground of unchastity," the NAB translates it as "unless the marriage is unlawful."

for others to see already have their reward—human praise—whereas those who practice them in secret will be rewarded by their heavenly Father, who sees all that they do in secret. People who practice almsgiving, prayer, and fasting for others to see are divided in loyalty since they want to please God and human beings. Jesus calls them hypocrites because they are like actors whose true identity is hidden behind a mask. They appear to be righteous before God but in reality are seeking human praise. In contrast to them, those who practice almsgiving, prayer, and fasting in secret are whole and entire in their devotion to God; they are perfect (5:48). In his woes against the Pharisees and the scribes, Jesus calls them "hypocrites" (23:27) because they appear to be righteous but are in fact full of hypocrisy and lawlessness (23:28). In the sermon, however, he warns his disciples that if their loyalty is divided when they practice righteousness, they will no longer be perfect but numbered among the hypocrites.

The third part of Jesus' teaching on righteousness (6:19–7:11) is not as clearly structured as the first two. Nonetheless, righteousness remains the central theme: "But strive first for the kingdom of God and its righteousness, and all these things will be given to you as well" (6:33). The material can be outlined as follows.

6:19–21	One's treasure is where the heart is
6:22–23	The healthy eye enlightens the whole person
6:24	No one can serve two masters
6:25–33	*Seek the kingdom and its righteousness*
7:1–5	Do not judge
7:6	Do not give what is holy to dogs
7:7–11	Ask and you will receive

The central unit (6:25–33) is Jesus' admonition not to be anxious but to seek the kingdom of God and its righteousness, then everything good will follow. To seek the kingdom and its righteousness, however, one must be single-hearted in devotion to God. One's heart must be with God (6:19–21); one's eye must be sound so that one is single-minded (6:22–23); and one must serve only God (6:24). Those who seek the kingdom and its righteousness do not judge others (7:1–5) or give the mysteries of the kingdom to those who are not prepared to receive them (7:6). They approach God knowing that if they ask, they will receive (7:7–11). Viewed in this way, the central theme of the third teaching on righteousness echoes the injunction of 5:48, "Be perfect, therefore, as your heavenly Father is perfect."

Before concluding his teaching on righteousness, Jesus returns to the theme of the law and the prophets in order to summarize his teaching on righteousness: "In everything do to others as you would have them do to you; for this is the law and the prophets" (7:12). This golden rule is similar to the remark Jesus makes after teaching that the most important commandment is to love God, and the second is to love one's neighbor as oneself: "On these two commandments hang (*krematai*) all the law and the prophets" (22:40). This love commandment is the hermeneutical principle Jesus employs to interpret the meaning of the law and the prophets. The superior righteousness he requires of his disciples is an expression of love for God and neighbor.

The conclusion of the sermon (7:13–27) emphasizes the importance of doing Jesus' teaching on righteousness. His disciples can discern the false prophets in their midst by the "fruit" they produce. Good trees bear good fruit—righteousness—whereas rotten trees bear rotten fruit, which in the Matthean moral world is lawlessness (7:15–20). On the day of judgment many who called Jesus "Lord" will be exposed as workers of lawlessness (*hoi ergazomenoi tēn anomian*) because they did not do the will of his Father (7:21–23). Everything then is a matter of "doing" Jesus' words. Whereas foolish disciples hear but do not do, wise disciples hear and do what Jesus requires (7:24–27).

The themes and metaphors that Jesus introduces in the sermon appear throughout the Gospel. John warns the Pharisees and the Sadducees that if they do not bear good fruit they will suffer the fate of rotten trees that are cut down and cast into the fire (3:7–10). Using the same metaphor, he issues a similar warning to the Pharisees (12:33–37). Entrance into the kingdom of heaven requires them to bear the fruit of righteousness and do God's will (21:31). This is why the Lord's Prayer, with its petition, "Your will be done, on earth as it is in heaven" (6:10), occurs at the center of the sermon. It is also the reason that Jesus prays in the Garden of Gethsemane, "My Father, if this cannot pass unless I drink it, your will be done" (26:42). Not only does Jesus the Son of God teach a way of righteousness; he is the perfect model of the righteousness he demands.

The moral world of the Matthean Gospel can be summarized in this way. The righteous are those who do God's will by following the law as interpreted by Jesus Messiah. They are like healthy trees that bear good fruit. Their lives are characterized by keeping the commandments, loving God and their neighbor. Because they are perfect in their devotion to God, they are sons and daughters of the kingdom of the Son of Man, and they enter the kingdom of heaven. In contrast to them the lawless are those who do not do God's will because they do not put Jesus' words into practice. They are like unhealthy trees that bear rotten fruit. Their lives are characterized as lawless and hypocritical. They are sons and daughters of the evil one and will not enter the kingdom of heaven.

Does such morality do away with God's grace? Is there an irreconcilable difference between Paul and Matthew, the former the representative of justification by grace, the latter of justification by works? Paul calls Christ the end of the law (Rom. 10:4); Matthew insists that Jesus did not come to abolish the law and the prophets (5:17). Matthew presents righteousness in terms of conduct; Paul insists upon the righteousness that comes from God. Paul is keenly aware of the power of sin that frustrates a person's ability to do God's will; Matthew appears more sanguine about the ability of humans to do God's will. Despite these differences, the Matthean Gospel insists upon God's initiative in the work of salvation since the kingdom of heaven comes from God. If people live a righteous life, it is because the kingdom of heaven has made its appearance in Jesus' life and ministry. If they do God's will, it is because the Son of God has revealed God's will to them and made them sons and daughters of the kingdom. Matthew's analysis of the human predicament is not as profound as Paul's, and he has not reflected as much as Paul has on the role of God's Spirit in the moral life of the believer, but his metaphor of good and bad trees suggests that the moral life is the fruit of the kingdom of heaven. This is why Jesus tells his disciples, "Every plant that my heavenly Father has not planted will be uprooted" (15:13). Those who produce the good fruit of righteousness have been planted by Jesus' heavenly Father.

JESUS MESSIAH, THE CLIMAX
OF ISRAEL'S HISTORY

The manner in which Matthew begins his Gospel indicates what he wants to say about Jesus: Jesus is the Messiah, the one who embodies and relives the history of his people and so brings Israel's history to its climax. Matthew makes this point by beginning his account with a genealogy "of Jesus the Messiah, the son of David, the son of Abraham" (1:1), and by identifying the events of Jesus' birth as the fulfillment of Israel's prophetic promises. In this way Matthew highlights the salvation-historical significance of Jesus.

The New Israel

The genealogy partitions Israel's history into three periods, each consisting of fourteen generations (1:17): from the time of Abraham to David, from the time of David to the Babylonian exile, and from the time of the exile to the appearance of the Messiah. The appearance of four women (Tamar, Ruth, the wife of Uriah, Mary) in a genealogy, which is otherwise populated by men, is surprising. The presence of these women, however, highlights the unexpected ways in which God has guided Israel's history to ensure the birth of the Messiah. Judah's offspring, Perez and Zerah, are the result of an incestuous union with his daughter-in-law Tamar (see Genesis 38). Boaz's son, Obed, is the result of a union with a Moabite woman, Ruth (see the book of Ruth). David's son Solomon is the result of a union with Bathsheba, who had been the wife of Uriah, and with whom David had previously committed adultery (see 2 Samuel 11). The greatest irregularity in this genealogy, however, is the birth of the Messiah, who is born of a virgin, through the power of the Holy Spirit rather than through the agency of a human father. By these irregular births, the genealogy shows how God has guided Israel's history to ensure the birth of the Messiah.

But the Messiah is more than the son of David, the son of Abraham. He represents God's people and relives their history. For example, just as Moses escaped Pharaoh's attempt to kill the male children of Israel, so Jesus escapes Herod's slaughter of the male children of Bethlehem (Matt. 2:16–18). Just as Israel migrated to Egypt to escape famine, so the Messiah and his family flee to Egypt to escape Herod (2:13–15). Just as God called his son, Israel, out of Egypt, so God calls his son, the Messiah, out of Egypt (2:15). In the period of Jesus' testing in the wilderness (4:1–11) there is a similar correlation between what happens to Jesus and what happened to Israel of old. Both find themselves in the wilderness: Israel for forty years, Jesus for forty days. Both are hungry and without food when tested. But whereas Israel was disobedient and rebelled against God, Jesus repels the devil by quoting Deut. 8:3, "One does not live by bread alone, but by every word that comes from the mouth of God" (Matt. 4:4). And whereas Israel fell into idolatry during the period of its wilderness wandering, Jesus wards off Satan by quoting Deut. 6:13, "Worship the Lord your God, and serve only him" (Matt. 4:10). Thus Matthew establishes a contrast between God's son Israel and Jesus the Son of God. Whereas Israel was disobedient during the period of its wilderness testing, Jesus is the obedient Son of God who trusts in the power of God to save him. It is significant, then, that Satan tests Jesus precisely in his capacity as God's Son by challenging him, "If you are the Son of God . . ." (4:3, 6). The same test occurs at Jesus' passion when the passersby mock him, "If you are the Son of God, come down from the cross" (27:40). In a similar fashion, the chief priests, scribes, and elders mock and test him, "He trusts in God; let God deliver him now, if he wants to; for he said, 'I am God's Son'" (27:43).

At the beginning of his Gospel, Matthew frequently quotes from Israel's Scriptures to show that the birth and ministry of Jesus are the fulfillment of God's promises. For example, the irregularity of Jesus' birth is the fulfillment of Isa. 7:14, "The virgin shall conceive and bear a son" (Matt. 1:23). The birth of Jesus in Bethlehem accords with the promise of Mic. 5:2 that the ruler and shepherd of God's people will be born in Bethlehem (Matt. 2:6). The slaughter of the innocent children is foretold by Jer. 31:15 (Matt. 2:18). When God calls Jesus out of Egypt, the words of Hos. 11:1 are fulfilled, "Out of Egypt I called my son" (Matt. 2:15). The decision to settle Jesus' family in Nazareth—even though the family of the Messiah comes from Bethlehem—is the fulfillment of what is written in the prophets, "He will be called a Nazorean" (2:23).[5] Finally, when Jesus begins his ministry in Galilee, Matthew views this as the fulfillment of Isa. 9:1–2 since the Messiah's ministry will bring the light of the gospel to "Galilee of the Gentiles" (Matt. 4:15–17). These quotations show that Jesus the Messiah is the fulfillment of the prophetic promises God made to his people and that Israel's history of salvation finds its climax in the ministry of Jesus the Messiah.

After the opening of the Gospel, Matthew continues to develop Jesus' identity in relationship to Israel. Jesus' great Sermon on the Mount (chaps. 5–7) reveals that he is the authoritative teacher and interpreter of God's law. Consequently, "the crowds were astonished at his teaching, for he taught them as one having authority, and not as their scribes" (7:28–29). The series of mighty deeds that Jesus performs in chapters 8–9 indicate that he is as powerful in deed as he is authoritative in word. When he heals a mute possessed by a demon, therefore, they exclaim, "Never has anything like this been seen in Israel" (9:33). Because he is Israel's Messiah, Jesus summons twelve disciples—who are destined to judge the twelve tribes of Israel (19:28)—to go "to the lost sheep of the house of Israel" and proclaim, "The kingdom of heaven has come near" (10:5–7).

In an important discussion about the salvation-historical significance of John the Baptist (11:7–15), Jesus explains that John was more than a prophet; he was the messenger whom Scripture said would prepare the way for the Messiah (Mal. 3:1; Isa. 40:3). John does not belong to the time of Old Testament prophecy, since the prophets and the law prophesied until his coming (Matt. 11:13). He is Elijah returned to life, the one sent to restore all things before the Messiah appears (11:14; 17:10–12). In the Matthean Gospel John even proclaims "the kingdom of heaven" (3:2). Nevertheless, since he stands only at the dawn of the kingdom, "the least in the kingdom of heaven is greater than he" (11:11). By contrast, Jesus is the one who inaugurates the kingdom for which John has been sent to prepare Israel.

The Matthean Jesus is deeply aware of the salvation-historical significance of his role in Israel's history. Defending his disciples' behavior on the Sabbath, he tells the Pharisees that "something greater than the temple is here" (12:6). In another controversy, he informs the scribes and Pharisees, "Something greater than Jonah is here . . . something greater than Solomon is here" (12:41, 42). When revealing the mysteries of the kingdom of heaven to his disciples, he explains how blessed they are; "many prophets and righteous people longed to see what you see, but did not see it, and to hear what you hear, but did not hear it" (13:17). When the temple tax collectors ask Peter if Jesus pays the temple tax (an annual tax levied upon every adult Jewish male over twenty to sup-

---

5. The source of the quotation is unknown. It may be Isa. 11:1, where the future Davidic king is referred to as a *nēṣer* ("branch"); or Judg. 13:5, 7, where the savior Samson is referred to as a *nāzîr* ("nazirite").

port the temple sacrificial system),[6] Jesus asks Peter if kings take tribute from their children (*hyioi*) or from others. When Peter responds "from others," Jesus concludes that the children are free from such tribute (17:26). The implication of Jesus' statement is that he need not pay the temple tax because, as the Son of God, he is the messianic Lord of the Temple.

The remaining fulfillment quotations support Jesus' unique role in God's salvation-historical plan. For example, when Jesus heals the possessed and cures the sick, Matthew quotes from Isa. 53:4, "This was to fulfill what had been spoken through the prophet Isaiah, 'He took our infirmities and bore our diseases'" (Matt. 8:17). To explain why Jesus withdraws from the Pharisees, Matthew presents an extensive quotation from Isa. 42:1–4 that portrays Jesus as the gentle servant of the Lord who brings justice and in whom the Gentiles will hope (Matt. 12:18–21). Jesus' parable discourse is interpreted by a quotation from Ps. 78:2 that presents the parables as the revelation of "what has been hidden from the foundation of the world" (Matt. 13:35). When Jesus enters Jerusalem as its meek and humble king (21:5–7), Matthew interprets this in light of a quotation from Zech. 9:9. Through these fulfillment quotations, it is evident that the major events of Jesus' life are the fulfillment of Israel's messianic promises. Just as Paul portrays Jesus as the new Adam who is obedient, whereas the old Adam was not, so Matthew portrays Jesus as the new Israel who is obedient, whereas Israel of old was not.

The Messianic Son of God

To appreciate Matthew's theological understanding of Jesus it is necessary to say something about his presentation of Jesus as the Messiah and the Son of God. As in the Gospel of Mark, "Messiah" and "Son of God" are the principal confessional titles Matthew employs to identify Jesus. Several texts verify this: God's revelation of Jesus as his beloved Son at the baptism (Matt. 3:17) and transfiguration (17:5); Peter's confession of Jesus as "the Messiah, the Son of the living God," at Caesarea Philippi (16:16); and the statement of the centurion and those with him at Jesus' death, "Truly this man was God's Son!" (27:54). But Matthew also goes beyond his Markan source and presents a more exalted portrait of Jesus as the Messiah, the Son of the living God. For example, Matthew begins with a genealogy that identifies Jesus as the Messiah (1:1, 16, 17), David's royal descendant. He then narrates the circumstances surrounding "the birth of Jesus the Messiah" (1:18) and shows that he was born in Bethlehem of Judea, "where the Messiah was to be born" (2:4). Matthew refers to Jesus' activity as "the works of the Messiah" (*ta erga tou Christou*, 11:2,

---

6. W. D. Davies and Dale C. Allison, Jr. *The Gospel according to Matthew*, vol. 3 (ICC; Edinburgh: T. & T. Clark, 1991), 743.

NAB), and Jesus reminds his disciples that they have only one teacher, the Messiah (23:10), namely, Jesus.

Other texts indicate that Jesus' messianic identity plays a central role in this Gospel: Jesus' warnings about false messiahs who will appear at the time of the great tribulation (24:5, 23–24), the mockery of him as a messianic pretender (26:68), and Pilate's sarcastic remarks about Jesus the Messiah (27:17, 22). Like the Gospel of Mark, however, the Matthean Gospel interprets the title "Messiah" in light of Jesus rather than Jesus in light of traditional messianic concepts. Therefore, the genealogy that establishes Jesus' Davidic origin also subverts it when it says, "And Jacob the father of Joseph the husband of Mary, *of whom Jesus was born*" (1:16). This curious change in the pattern of the genealogy, which otherwise emphasizes the paternity of each descendant, is resolved only when the angel informs Joseph that Mary has conceived her child through the power of God's Spirit (1:20). Jesus is a royal descendant of David because Joseph, a descendant of David, adopts him into David's line. Consequently, Matthew can identify Jesus as the Son of David and still relate the Markan controversy story that calls into question the traditional notion of the Davidic Messiah (22:41–45; see Mark 12:35–37). Jesus is a royal descendant of David because Joseph, son of David, has adopted him into the royal line. But God, not David, is the Messiah's true father. When Matthew employs the title "son of David," therefore, he does not intend a powerful warrior-king but the meek and humble Messiah who heals the infirmities of his people. This is why "son of David" is so frequently found in the speech of people of little account. Marginalized individuals such as the blind (Matt. 9:27; 20:30, 31), the Canaanite woman (15:22), and children (21:15) recognize Jesus as the messianic son of David, but Israel's religious leaders do not.[7]

Matthew cannot embrace the "son of David" title without qualification, because, like Mark, he knows that Jesus' true identity is rooted in his divine sonship. Jesus is the Messiah because he is God's Son. Matthew, however, presents Jesus' sonship in new ways. First, he points to the agency of God's Spirit in the conception of Jesus (1:18, 20), thereby forestalling any suggestion that Jesus is merely an adopted son of God, as were Israel's kings of old (Ps. 2:7). Second, he no longer enforces the secret of Jesus' sonship, which, in Mark's Gospel, is disclosed only after Jesus' death. When Jesus rescues the disciples from a storm at sea, they worship him, "Truly you are the Son of God" (Matt. 14:33). At Caesarea Philippi, Peter confesses that Jesus is the Messiah, the Son of the living God (16:16). At Jesus' crucifixion, the religious leaders deride him, "If you are the Son of God, come down from the cross. . . . He trusts in God; let God deliver him now, if he wants to; for he said, 'I am God's Son'"

---

7. This point is made by Jack Dean Kingsbury, *Matthew: Structure, Christology, Kingdom* (Philadelphia: Fortress, 1975), 99–103.

(27:40, 43). These references to Jesus as the Son of God during Jesus' lifetime do not mean that those who confess him as God's Son understand the full implications of what they are saying, but they do emphasize that Jesus was always God's Son and during his lifetime his disciples understood something of his unique relationship to God, though there was more to learn from his death and resurrection.

It is not surprising then that within the Matthean Gospel Jesus frequently and openly says "my Father" when referring to God (7:21; 10:32, 33; 11:27; 12:50; 15:13; 16:17; 18:10, 19, 35; 20:23; 25:34; 26:29, 39, 42, 53) and that he often refers to God as "your Father" or "your heavenly Father" when speaking to his disciples (5:16, 45, 48; 6:1, 4, 6, 8, 14, 15, 18, 26, 32; 7:11; 10:20, 29; 18:14). He talks in this way because he enjoys a unique relationship to the Father. Confidently addressing God as "Father" in 11:25–26, he exclaims, "All things have been handed over to me by my Father; and no one knows the Son except the Father, and no one knows the Father except the Son and anyone to whom the Son chooses to reveal him" (11:27). This remarkable statement, so Johannine in tone, reveals the intimate relationship between the Father and the Son that allows Jesus to call God "my Father" and to encourage his disciples to see God as their "heavenly Father," since the Son of God makes them children of the kingdom and so children of their heavenly Father.

Jesus' intimate relationship with God finds its fullest expression in the appearance of the risen Christ to the eleven disciples on the mountain in Galilee. Here Matthew presents Jesus as the exalted and risen one to whom the Father has given all authority in heaven and on earth. The disciples, whose mission was once limited to the lost sheep of Israel (10:5–6), must now make disciples of all the nations, baptizing them in the name of the Father, the Son, and the Holy Spirit (28:18–19). This Trinitarian formula relates Jesus to the Father and the Spirit in an unparalleled way, leaving no doubt about the exalted status and divine nature of the one whom the Gospel presents as the Messiah, the Son of the living God. Just as the greetings of the Pauline letters place Christ on a level with God ("Grace to you and peace from God our Father and the Lord Jesus Christ," 1 Cor. 1:3), so the ending of Matthew's Gospel puts the risen Lord on a level with the Father and the Spirit.[8]

The Son receives all authority in heaven and on earth because, rather than try to save himself from the cross, he obediently surrenders his life to the Father and trusts that God will raise him from the dead. Jesus dies as the faithful and obedient Son of God because he understands that his destiny is that of the Son of Man who must suffer, die, and rise from the dead (Matt. 16:21; 17:22–23;

8. For yet another Trinitarian formula, see 2 Cor. 13:13. To be sure, the New Testament writers did not yet understand the full Trinitarian implications of these formulas as they would be developed in the third and fourth centuries, but they did plant the "seeds" for the church's later Trinitarian theology.

20:17–19). In the infancy narrative, the angel already indicated the salvation-historical significance of the child by instructing Joseph to name him "Jesus" because he will save his people from their sins (1:21). It is not surprising, then, that the adult Messiah interprets his death as a ransom for many (20:28) and the shedding of his blood as bringing about the forgiveness of sins (26:28). When a great earthquake occurs after the Messiah's death that leads to the resurrection of the holy ones (27:50–53), it is an unmistakable sign that the new age has begun in which the exalted Son rules with the fullness of God's authority.

Although Jesus' exalted status as the risen One to whom the Father has given all authority is not revealed until the end of the Gospel, his status already shines forth in Matthew's presentation of the earthly Jesus. This is why the disciples recognize him as the Son of God even during his earthly ministry, and why they and others address him as "Lord" (*kyrios;* for example, 8:2, 6, 21, 25; 14:28, 30; 15:22, 25, 27; 17:4, 15). To be sure, *kyrios* can be a simple form of address meaning nothing more than "sir." But in the Matthean Gospel, it also points to the one who is the exalted and risen Lord. It is not surprising then that those who approach Jesus seeking his favor often do so in a posture of worship (*proskynein;* 8:2; 9:18; 15:25; 20:20), just as the magi worshiped the newborn king of the Jews (2:11), and the women and disciples worshiped the risen Lord (28:9, 17).

To summarize, Matthean Christology is firmly grounded in its Markan source, but it moves beyond Mark's Christology. It presents Jesus as (1) the embodiment and culmination of his people's history and promises, (2) the royal Davidic Messiah, (3) the one whose sonship is revealed throughout his ministry, and (4) the exalted and risen Lord to whom the Father has entrusted all authority in heaven and on earth.

ISRAEL AND THE CHURCH

Because Jesus is Israel's promised Messiah, he directs his mission to the lost sheep of the house of Israel. He tells a Gentile woman who seeks a cure for her daughter, "I was sent only to *the lost sheep of the house of Israel*" (15:24). When he sends his twelve disciples on mission he explicitly instructs them, "Go nowhere among the Gentiles, and enter no town of the Samaritans, but go rather to *the lost sheep of the house of Israel*" (10:5–6). Matthew reinforces this picture of Jesus who confines his preaching to the house of Israel through a number of summary statements that describe Jesus as going throughout Galilee and teaching in synagogues (or cities), proclaiming the good news of the kingdom, and curing the sick (4:23; 9:35; 11:1). Jesus' exclusive mission to Israel is not surprising. The Matthean genealogy has presented him as the culmination of Israel's history. The angel has instructed Joseph to name the child

"Jesus, for he will save his people from their sins" (1:21). In the words of the prophet Micah (Mic. 5:3), the Messiah is the one "who is to shepherd my people Israel" (2:6). By the end of the Gospel, however, a major change takes place. The risen Lord commissions his eleven disciples to "make disciples of *all nations*, baptizing them in the name of the Father and of the Son and of the Holy Spirit, and teaching them to obey everything that I have commanded you" (28:19–20). This movement from an exclusive mission to Israel to a universal mission that includes the nations raises the question of Israel and the church. How did Jesus' exclusive mission to Israel become a universal mission to all the nations? What is the relationship between Israel and the church?

Israel

Because Israel is God's people, Matthew tends to employ the noun *laos* when speaking of Israel and *ethnē* when referring to the Gentiles. But within the narrative, Israel is most prominently represented by the crowds that follow Jesus and the religious leaders who oppose him. The religious leaders (Pharisees, scribes, Sadducees, high priests) form a united front in their opposition to Jesus, and it quickly becomes apparent that they do not accept his gospel about the kingdom. The Pharisees assert that Jesus casts out demons by the ruler of the demons (9:34). They accuse his disciples of violating the Sabbath (12:1–8), and they seek to entrap him as well. When their plan fails, they plot to destroy him (12:9–14). They and the scribes criticize Jesus' disciples for breaking the traditions of the elders (15:1–2). Jesus, in turn, accuses them of violating God's law for the sake of their traditions (15:3–20). When the Pharisees and Sadducees ask for a sign, Jesus calls them an evil and adulterous generation (16:1–4), and he cautions his disciples to beware of their teaching (16:5–12). The Pharisees continue to test Jesus (19:3), and, with the Herodians, they plot to entrap him by what he says (22:15). In a series of harsh woes (23:1–36), Jesus eventually condemns the scribes and Pharisees as hypocrites for not practicing what they preach (23:3) and for excluding people from the kingdom of heaven (23:13). In a final apostrophe to Jerusalem, Jesus prophesies that its house will be left desolate, a prediction of the destruction of the city and its temple that occurred in A.D. 70 (23:37–39).

Matthew's portrayal of the people begins more favorably but ends with a harsh judgment. At the outset of Jesus' ministry, large crowds follow him (4:25). They are utterly astounded by his great sermon because he teaches with authority (7:28–29). When he heals a possessed man they exclaim, "Never has anything like this been seen in Israel" (9:33), whereas the Pharisees respond, "By the ruler of the demons he casts out demons" (9:34). But all is not well with the people. Astonished by the faith of a Gentile centurion, Jesus warns that the heirs (*hoi huioi*) of the kingdom will be cast into the outer darkness

(8:10–12). Shortly after the crowds have expressed their amazement at his teaching and mighty deeds, Jesus upbraids "this generation" as a fickle lot that is satisfied neither with him nor with John (11:16–19). He then condemns the Galilean towns in which he performed most of his mighty deeds because they did not repent (11:20–24). He speaks to the crowds in parables (chap. 13) because they do not perceive or understand (13:13). Midway through the discourse, he withdraws from the crowds and explains everything to his disciples (13:36), who will be the nucleus of a renewed and repentant Israel, the community of the church.

Jesus' most damaging indictment against Israel comes in a series of parables that prepare for his mandate to make disciples of all nations. The first, that of the workers in the vineyard, a parable (20:1–16) peculiar to Matthew, provides an allegorical interpretation of God's dealings with Israel and the nations. Although Gentile believers are the last to be called into the vineyard, they receive the same wage as Israel, which has been working since the beginning. The remaining three parables (the two sons, the tenant farmers, and the wedding feast; 21:28–22:14) occur together, with the central parable making the most explicit statement about the future of Israel and the nations: "The kingdom of God will be taken away from you and given to a people that produces the fruits of the kingdom" (21:43). This harsh indictment, found only in Matthew's Gospel, indicates that Israel will lose its exclusive status among the nations because it has not produced the fruit of righteousness that the kingdom requires. Israel has become like the son who says he will work in his father's vineyard but does not (21:28–32) and like the wedding guests who were invited but did not come (22:1–14). Therefore, the gospel of the kingdom is now offered to a people (*ethnei*, literally, "a nation") that will produce the fruits of righteousness. This people will be the church, a repentant and restored Israel composed of Gentiles as well as Jews. But lest the church become overconfident, Jesus warns that those who have been invited to take the place of the original guests will be expelled if they do not have the proper wedding garment, which, in Matthew's parlance, refers to deeds of righteousness (22:12–14).

The decisive turning point in Israel's history comes with the tragic cry of the people, "His blood be on us and on our children!" (27:25), a text found only in Matthew's Gospel. In this terrifying cry, the people employ a cultic formula (see 2 Sam. 1:16; 1 Kgs. 2:32–33) whereby they accept responsibility for what is about to occur. For Matthew, who is responsible for the text, the people's cry signifies a turning point in Israel's salvation history: the gospel of the kingdom will no longer be preached exclusively to the lost sheep of the house of Israel but to all the nations, and the church that results will be a new and repentant Israel—what Paul calls the Israel of God (Gal. 6:16). If Matthew introduced this cry in light of the fall of Jerusalem, he probably interpreted the city's destruction as God's punishment on the people of Jesus' generation and their children who witnessed the fall of Jerusalem. But any attempt to make the Jewish people of every age responsible for the death of the Messiah, or to employ this text to justify anti-Semitism, betrays its meaning.

The Church

If the crowds and the religious leaders are the characters through whom Matthew portrays Israel's response to Jesus, Jesus' disciples are those through whom Matthew presents his understanding of the church. To be sure, the church did not exist during the time of Jesus' earthly ministry, nor is it Matthew's intention to present an explicit ecclesiology. But the manner in which he portrays the nature of discipleship, and Jesus' promise to build his church on the rock foundation of Peter, provide fruitful ways to investigate Matthew's understanding of the church.

Jesus' choice of twelve disciples (Matt. 10:1–4), whom he intends to be the eschatological regents of Israel (19:28), indicates that the Twelve will be the nucleus of a renewed Israel. To prepare the disciples for their role of restoring Israel, Jesus teaches them to practice a righteousness that exceeds that of the scribes and Pharisees (5:20), and he reveals the mysteries of the kingdom of heaven to them (13:11) so that they will be scribes trained for the kingdom of heaven (13:52). Unlike Israel, which did not understand the parables of the kingdom (13:13), the disciples have understood (13:51). They even worship Jesus as the Son of God (14:33), thereby anticipating the day when they will worship him as the risen Lord (28:17). Peter's confession at Caesarea Philippi, however, is the moment when Jesus reveals his intention to establish the community of disciples as his congregation, the church (*ekklēsia*). The sequence of events is illuminating. First, Jesus asks who people say the Son of Man is, and the disciples respond: John the Baptist, Elijah, Jeremiah, or one of the prophets. Next he asks who do they say he is, and Peter answers, "You are the Messiah, the Son of the living God" (16:16). In response, Jesus pronounces a beatitude upon Peter that makes the following points: (1) Jesus' heavenly Father is the one who has revealed Jesus' identity to Peter; (2) therefore Jesus will build *his* church on Peter (*Petros*) the rock (*petra*), and the powers of death will not prevail over it; (3) Jesus will entrust Peter with "the keys of the kingdom of heaven" so that what he binds on earth will be bound in heaven, and what he looses on earth will be loosed in heaven.

The intimate connection between Peter's divinely inspired confession and Jesus' promise indicates that the faith of the church is the faith Peter has confessed: Jesus is the Messiah, the Son of the living God. Because Peter is the historical connection between Jesus and the faith of the church, he serves as the "rock" foundation on which Jesus will build the church. Jesus explicitly identifies this *ekklēsia* as *his* church, thereby indicating that he has the universal church in view.[9] Employing a metaphor from Isa. 22:22 (the key of the house of David), Jesus grants Peter "the keys of the kingdom of heaven," but instead of continuing the imagery of opening and shutting, he employs the rabbinic metaphor of loosening and binding. Given Jesus' warning, immediately preceding this episode, that his disciples should beware of the teaching of the Pharisees and Sadducees (Matt. 16:5–12), and given his indictment of the scribes and Pharisees as those who "lock people out of the kingdom of heaven" (23:13), the keys of the kingdom must refer to Peter's role in opening the kingdom of heaven to others, and the power of binding and loosening must be something similar to the process of making legal decisions. But in this case the halakic decisions concern teaching related to the kingdom of heaven: teaching in which Jesus has already instructed his disciples in order to make them scribes of the kingdom of God.[10]

In 18:18 all of the disciples are given a similar power so that what Peter receives, they receive, but there are significant differences between the two texts. First, there is no reference to the power of the keys in 18:18. Second, whereas Jesus is clearly referring to the universal church ("my church") in 16:18, the reference to the "church" in 18:17 is to a local congregation so that the binding and loosening in 18:18 refers to the power of the local congregation to expel recalcitrant members. If this is so, the Matthean text ascribes a unique role to Peter as the foundation stone of Jesus' church, the one entrusted with rabbinic-like authority to bind and loose in matters of teaching related to the kingdom of heaven.

Although Peter enjoys a central role in Matthew's vision of Jesus' church, the church is essentially a community of disciples in which the greatest are those who humble themselves as if they were little children (18:1–4). Therefore, disciples should view themselves as "little ones" who believe in Jesus. They should take every precaution not to scandalize other disciples (18:6–7) and to avoid anything that will cause them to falter in their own faith (18:8–9). Should a fellow disciple ("one of these little ones") go astray, the others should search for the lost one with the diligence of a shepherd who leaves his flock in search of a single stray sheep (18:10–14). The Matthean Jesus even establishes a process of correction for disciples who have erred. It begins with a private admonition; next it involves two or three other disciples; finally the entire church is involved before excluding the unrepentant disciple (18:15–20). Within this community, there is no limit to forgiveness (18:21–22), because their heavenly Father has forgiven a debt that disciples could never hope to repay (18:23–35).

9. The expression "the universal church" belongs to the theological vocabulary of a later period. It is used here to make the point that Matthew is not simply thinking of a local congregation but of the congregation that embraces all who believe in Jesus.

10. On this point see the exegesis of John P. Meier, *Matthew* (NTM 3; Wilmington, DE: Glazier, 1980), 175–83.

The church is not the kingdom of heaven, but the disciples are children (*huious*) of the kingdom (13:38) because they practice a superior righteousness and have been entrusted with the mysteries of the kingdom of God. To the extent that disciples are children of the kingdom who seek the kingdom and its righteousness (6:33), there is a congruence between kingdom and church. But since the kingdom is an eschatological reality that will only appear in its fullness at the end of the ages, the church cannot identify itself as the kingdom of heaven. Jesus' explanation of the parable of the weeds (13:36–43) suggests that at the present time the church is a community in which evildoers are present as well as the righteous. This intolerable situation will be resolved when the Son of Man returns and sends his angels to remove such evildoers from the midst of his kingdom. To the extent that Matthew envisions the situation of the church in this parable, there is an overlap between the kingdom of the Son of Man and the church, though the two cannot simply be equated with each other.

The relationship between Israel and the church can be summarized in this way. Israel was the heir of the kingdom, but the kingdom has now been given to the church because Israel did not produce the righteousness of the kingdom. The church consists of Gentile as well as Jewish believers, and it now preaches the gospel of the kingdom to all the world (24:14) in order to make disciples of all nations. Israel is not excluded from this mission, but it has lost its exclusive status. In Matthew's view this church of Gentile and Jewish believers is the restored Israel, the Israel of God.

PAROUSIA AND JUDGMENT

The knowledge that there will be a final (and so eschatological) judgment plays a central role in Matthew's understanding of the gospel of the kingdom and of the righteousness it requires. Matthew employs a rich vocabulary and numerous images to describe this eschatological or end-time reality. For example, his Gospel refers frequently to Gehenna (5:22, 29, 30; 10:28; 18:9; 23:33), a place where the wicked will be punished by fire, and it often employs the imagery of fire to describe the coming judgment (3:10, 12; 7:19; 13:40, 42, 50). In two instances it speaks of eternal fire (18:8; 25:41). The word "judgment" (*krisis*) occurs regularly (5:21–22; 10:15; 11:22, 24; 12:41, 42), and there is a reference to the day of judgment (12:36) as well as to the judgment of Gehenna (23:33). In speaking of the fate of the condemned, Matthew describes them as being cast into the outer darkness (8:12; 22:13; 25:30), where there will be weeping and gnashing of teeth (8:12; 13:42, 50; 22:13; 24:51; 25:30). A number of parables found only in his Gospel (M material) also deal with the theme of judgment or the parousia: the parable of the weeds (13:24–30), which Jesus decodes for his disciples (13:36–43); the parable of the net cast into the sea (13:47–50); the parable of the unmerciful servant (18:23–35); the parable of the wise and the foolish virgins (25:1–13); and the parable of the sheep and the goats (25:31–46). In addition to these distinctively Matthean parables, there are others that Matthew shares with Luke (Q material) that also deal with the themes of judgment or parousia: the parable of the wise and foolish builders (7:24–27); the parable of the two ways (7:13–14); the parable of the wedding banquet (22:1–14); the parable of the thief who comes unexpectedly at night (24:42–44); the parable of the faithful and unfaithful servants (24:45–51); and the parable of the talents (25:14–30). Of the parables that Matthew shares with Mark, the parable of the wicked tenants is the most explicit in its reference to judgment (21:33–46).

The theme of judgment is intimately related to the gospel of the kingdom of heaven and the righteousness it demands. At the outset of the Gospel, John the Baptist calls for repentance because the kingdom of heaven has come near, and he warns the Pharisees and Sadducees to bear fruit worthy of repentance; otherwise they will be thrown into the fire of God's coming wrath (3:7–10). At the end of his sermon, Jesus warns his disciples about false prophets in their midst who are like rotten trees because they do not bear the fruit of righteousness; they will be cut down and thrown into the fire (7:15–20). Therefore disciples must do the will of Jesus' heavenly Father if they hope to enter the kingdom of God (7:21–23). Otherwise they will suffer an incalculable loss when the floodwaters of God's judgment burst forth (7:24–27). The parable of the sheep and the goats indicates that this judgment will affect everyone. The criterion for judgment will be good and evil deeds: what people have done to the least members of Jesus' new family (25:40, 45), they will have done to him. Since "the least of Jesus' family members" are the missionaries Jesus and the church have sent to proclaim the gospel of the kingdom, Matthew's understanding of judgment is intimately related to the proclamation of the gospel of the kingdom.[11] Those who receive Jesus' disciples receive him (10:40), and those who give his disciples even a cup of cold water will not lose their rewards (10:42). Those who refuse to repent and fail to produce fruit worthy of the kingdom will be condemned, whereas those who repent and bear the fruit of righteousness will escape the coming wrath by entering the kingdom of heaven.

In addition to the motifs outlined above, Matthew makes use of images such as the coming wrath of God, the fire of Gehenna, the day of judgment, and the outer darkness where there will be weeping and gnashing of teeth. Moreover, he employs the motif of the parousia of the Son of Man in a way that goes beyond his Markan source. For Mark the parousia is the moment when the vin-

---

11. Note that Jesus uses similar language in 10:42; 18:6, 10, where he likens his disciples to children.

dicated Son of Man comes in power and glory to send the angels to gather his elect (Mark 13:26–27), but there is no description of the Son of Man exercising a role of judgment in the Markan Gospel. The situation is different in Matthew. At the end of the ages, the Son of Man will send his angels to separate evildoers from the righteous and to cast them into the fiery furnace where there will be weeping and gnashing of teeth (Matt. 13:41–42). The Son of Man will come with his angels and "repay everyone for what has been done" (16:27). The Son of Man will be seated on his throne, and his disciples will judge the twelve tribes of Israel (19:28). All of the tribes of the earth will mourn when they see the sign of the Son of Man (24:30), presumably because they know their judgment is near. The Son of Man will come in his glory with the angels and sit on his glorious throne to judge the nations (25:31–32). In Matthew's Gospel, then, the parousia of the Son of Man has a twofold purpose. On the one hand, it will be the moment when the vindicated Son of Man will come with his angels to gather the elect into the kingdom of heaven, on the other it will be the moment when the Son of Man will judge the righteous and the wicked.

Because the parousia of the Son of Man is of ultimate significance to the church, Matthew introduces a series of parables to exhort the church to be vigilant and ready for the coming of its Lord. Disciples are not to mistake the period between Jesus' resurrection and parousia as a time that will continue indefinitely (24:48; 25:5, 19) but as an opportunity to produce fruit appropriate to the kingdom—righteousness. They are to be like faithful servants who watch over their Lord's household (24:45–51), like wedding attendants whose lamps are filled with oil (the fruit of righteousness) as they wait for the bridegroom (25:1–13), and like industrious servants who multiply the wealth (righteousness) their Lord has entrusted to them (25:14–30). Those who are not vigilant will be cast into the outer darkness where there will be weeping and gnashing of teeth (24:51; 25:30); they will be excluded from the messianic banquet (25:10–12).

Matthew, like Mark, understands that there is a relationship between the destruction of Jerusalem and the parousia of the Son of Man. The desecration of the temple (24:15), the flight from the city (24:16–22), and the appearance of messianic pretenders (24:23–26) are the signs that portend the parousia of the Son of Man (24:30), but only the Father knows the exact moment of the parousia (24:36). Therefore, lest the church be swept away like the contemporaries of Noah who were not prepared for the flood, it must be vigilant because the Son of Man will come at an unexpected hour (24:44).

Jesus' words in 24:34 ("Truly I tell you, this generation will not pass away until all these things have taken place") suggest that Matthew expects the parousia to occur within the lifetime of the disciples, unless the phrase "all these things" refers to the events prior to, but not including, the parousia. The text of 10:23 in Jesus' missionary discourse also seems to anticipate that the parousia will occur in the lifetime of the disciples ("For truly I tell you, you will not have gone through all the towns of Israel before the Son of Man comes"). As was the case with the Gospel of Mark, there is an unresolved tension in the Matthean text. The evangelist is aware that the parousia is imminent, but he acknowledges that neither the Son nor the angels know when it will occur (24:36), suggesting that vigilance is more important than calculating times and seasons.

Parousia and judgment are inextricably linked in Matthew's Gospel because each concept is ultimately related to the gospel of the kingdom of heaven. Since entrance into the kingdom of heaven requires a superior righteousness, disciples will be judged on the basis of what they have done rather than on the basis of what they have said. And because the gospel of the kingdom is being preached to the whole world, even the nations will be judged by the Son of Man. Since the parousia of the Son of Man ushers in the final phase of the kingdom of heaven, the parousia will be the moment when this eschatological judgment occurs. When it does, the vindicated Son of Man will play the decisive role in judging the nations.

Matthew's emphasis on judgment has led some to view him as a proponent of righteousness by doing good works whereas Paul proposes a righteousness based on faith. Although it is true that Matthew emphasizes doing righteousness in a way that Paul does not, Paul is keenly aware that all must stand before the judgment seat of Christ/God (2 Cor. 5:10; Rom. 14:10). Judgment plays a central role in Paul's theology because he knows that even though believers are justified by what God has done, they will be judged by what they have done. Matthew does not develop a theology of justification, but he understands that the gracious offer of the kingdom requires an appropriate response. Therefore, although believers will be judged on the basis of their behavior, the grace of God has already been bestowed upon them by the inbreaking kingdom of God and by the death and resurrection of their Lord. The Matthean Gospel, like the Letter of James, reminds disciples that they must be "doers of the word, and not merely hearers who deceive themselves" (Jas. 1:22).

3

A Theology of the Salvation
the Kingdom Brings

Luke–Acts

Like Matthew, Luke drew upon the Gospel of Mark and the collection of Jesus' sayings commonly designated "Q" to compose his Gospel. In addition to these sources, he had access to an extensive amount of material peculiar to his Gospel, which is commonly designated "L." The addition of this special material and the distinctive manner in which Luke employs his sources results in a new story that fulfills his promise "to write an orderly account" (1:3). This orderly account begins with parallel stories of the announcement, birth, and circumcision of John and Jesus (1:5–2:40). The episode of the twelve-year-old Jesus in the temple who is already conscious of his unique relationship to God (2:41–52) then serves as a transition to the appearance of John the Baptist in the wilderness and to the baptism and testing of Jesus (3:1–4:13). After his baptism and testing in the wilderness, Jesus carries out his Spirit-filled ministry in Galilee (4:14–9:50). When the time draws near for him "to be taken up" (9:51), he determines to go to Jerusalem, where he must suffer and die. In 9:51–19:44 Luke describes this fateful journey as a period when Jesus teaches his disciples, calls the crowds to repentance, and finds himself in conflict with Israel's religious leaders.[1] Once in Jerusalem, Jesus teaches in the temple in his capacity as Israel's Messiah (19:45–21:38). Israel, however, does not recognize the Messiah in its midst, and Jesus is put to death as a messianic pretender (22:1–23:56). The suffering and death of Jesus, however, are part of God's plan for the Messiah to enter into his

---

1. Luke's description of Jesus' journey to Jerusalem is one of the most distinctive aspects of his Gospel. It contains a great deal of material from Luke's special source, "L," as well as Q material, which Matthew has chosen to put in the Sermon on the Mount. Scholars, however, are not in agreement about the theological purpose or organizing principle of the section. For an important study on this section, see David P. Moessner, *Lord of the Banquet: The Literary and Theological Significance of the Lukan Travel Narrative* (Minneapolis: Fortress, 1989). See also Frank J. Matera, "Jesus' Journey to Jerusalem (9:51–19:46): A Conflict with Israel," *JSNT* 51 (1993): 57–77.

glory. So after the Messiah suffers, he is raised from the dead and "carried up into heaven" (24:1–53). Luke's orderly account follows this outline:

1:1–4	A Prologue
1:5–2:52	The infancy narratives of John and Jesus
3:1–4:13	The appearance of John and Jesus
4:14–9:50	Jesus' ministry in Galilee
9:51–19:44	Jesus' journey to Jerusalem
19:45–21:38	Jesus' ministry in the temple of Jerusalem
22:1–24:53	Jesus' passion, death, resurrection, and ascension

The account of Jesus' earthly ministry, however, is not the whole story that Luke tells. In the Acts of the Apostles, he continues the narrative begun in the Gospel and shows how the salvation inaugurated by the Messiah was extended to Israel and the Gentiles despite the Messiah's death; for, even though human beings rejected and killed God's Messiah, God raised him from the dead.[2] This resurrected Messiah, the promised heir of David's dynasty, is now enthroned at God's right hand, and from his heavenly throne he dispenses the Spirit, the gift of the Father, and guides the progress of the church, the repentant and reestablished Israel.

Luke tells a single story of salvation that has its origins in the promises God made to Israel. The climax of this story is the appearance of Jesus of Nazareth, Israel's Messiah, a prophet like Moses, the Son of God. This story continues in the story of the church, the portion of Israel that embraces Jesus as the Messiah. This reestablished Israel consists of Jewish and Gentile believers. Because Luke tells a single story, his two writings, which contemporary scholars call "Luke–Acts," can and should be studied together.

THE UNITY OF LUKE–ACTS

Luke–Acts is a unified work. The Acts of the Apostles develops theological themes introduced in the Gospel, and the narrative of Acts presupposes what has already occurred in the Gospel. The reason for this symbiotic relationship is not difficult to explain. Luke recounts the story of God's plan of salvation, which is rooted in the story of Israel. From Luke's perspective, then, the

---

2. Acts makes use of a number of "contrast formulas" to show that whereas human beings put Jesus to death, God vindicated him by raising him from the dead (Acts 1:23–24; 3:13–15; 4:10; 5:30–31; 10:39–40; 13:28–30). Many of these formulas focus on what the people of Israel or their leaders did during the passion, thereby raising the question of responsibility for the death of Jesus. See Frank J. Matera, "Responsibility for the Death of Jesus according to the Acts of the Apostles," *JSNT* 39 (1990): 77–93.

Gospel is not merely the story of Jesus any more than Acts is merely the story of the church. Luke–Acts narrates a single story of redemptive history rooted in Israel's story and God's plan of salvation.

The canonical order of the New Testament, however, separates Acts from the Gospel of Luke by placing the Fourth Gospel between them. From a canonical perspective this makes eminent sense since the canonical order allows Acts to function as a bridge between the story of Jesus as narrated in the four Gospels and the story of the church as told in Acts. Moreover, Acts now provides a canonical framework for reading the apostolic letters of Paul, James, Peter, John, and Jude, which follow Acts. But there are several indications that Luke intended his two works to be read as a unified narrative.[3] A New Testament theologian who hopes to retrieve Luke's theological vision should study the Gospel of Luke and Acts as two volumes of a single work: Luke–Acts.

Indications of Literary Unity

The prefaces of the Gospel (1:1–4) and of Acts (1:1–2) point to the literary unity of Luke's project. In the Gospel preface, Luke states his intention to write an orderly account "of the events that have been fulfilled among us" (1:1). Since Luke writes as a Christian of the second or third generation, these "events" include the salvific events he will narrate in Acts as well as the events of Jesus' ministry.[4] In the preface of Acts (1:1–2), Luke summarizes the essential content of his Gospel as "all that Jesus did and taught from the beginning until the day when he was taken up to heaven, after giving instructions through the Holy Spirit to the apostles whom he had chosen." Thus just as the Gospel preface envisions the events Luke will narrate in Acts, so the preface of Acts recapitulates the story he has already told in the Gospel.

Like the prefaces of Luke–Acts, the manner in which the Gospel ends and Acts begins highlights the literary unity of Luke's project. At the end of the Gospel, the risen Lord shows his apostles that he is truly risen (24:36–43). He then opens their minds to understand from the Scriptures that the Messiah had to suffer and rise from the dead (24:45–46), "and that repentance and forgiveness of sins is to be proclaimed in his name to all nations, beginning from Jerusalem" (24:47). Since the apostles are his witnesses, they must stay in Jerusalem until they "have been clothed with power from on high" (24:49). Jesus is then "carried up into heaven" (24:51), and the apostles return to Jerusalem, where they continually bless God in the temple (24:52–53). With this account

---

3. For an important essay on the unity of the Gospel and Acts, see I. Howard Marshall, "Acts and the 'Former Treatise,'" in *The Book of Acts in Its Ancient Literary Setting* (ed. Bruce W. Winter and Andrew D. Clark; The Book of Acts in Its First Century Setting 1; Grand Rapids: Eerdmans, 1993), 163–82.

4. Ibid., 177.

of the ascension, Luke completes the theme of the ascension announced at the beginning of Jesus' journey to Jerusalem ("When the days drew near for him to be taken up," 9:51), and he ends his Gospel where it began, in the temple of Jerusalem.

Acts opens with a second account of Jesus' ascension. This account, however, occurs forty days after the resurrection, giving the risen Lord ample time to provide his apostles with convincing proofs of his resurrection so that they can witness to it, and further instructing them about the kingdom of God. The risen Lord tells the apostles that they will be baptized with the Holy Spirit (1:5) and be his witnesses "in Jerusalem, in all Judea and Samaria, and to the ends of the earth" (1:8). When Jesus is taken from the apostles, two men in white robes remind the apostles that the Lord will return, as he departed, at the parousia (1:10–11), thereby indicating that this is not the time for the apostles to concern themselves with questions about when the parousia will occur but to witness to the resurrection. So the apostles return to Jerusalem to await the gift of the Spirit.

Like the prefaces, the manner in which the Gospel ends and Acts begins indicates that Luke is telling a unified narrative. The ending of the Gospel leads into the beginning of Acts, and the beginning of Acts recalls the ending of the Gospel inasmuch as both deal with similar material: proof of the Lord's resurrection (Luke 24:36–43; Acts 1:3); the commissioning of the apostles to be his witnesses of the resurrection (Luke 24:48; Acts 1:8); instructions to wait in Jerusalem for the gift of the Spirit (Luke 24:48; Acts 1:4–5); and accounts of the Lord's ascension (Luke 24:50–53; Acts 1:9).[5] Moreover, whereas the beginning of Acts recalls the major theme of Jesus' preaching (the kingdom of God; Acts 1:3), the ending of the Gospel foreshadows the major theme of the apostles' preaching, repentance for the forgiveness of sins (Luke 24:47). This interlocking pattern reminds readers that even though Acts begins a new phase of the story, the story it tells is the resumption of a story already begun.

The central role of Jerusalem and its temple in Luke–Acts provides Luke with yet another way to relate his two volumes to each other. The Gospel begins in the temple of Jerusalem with an angelic announcement to Zechariah (1:5–25), and it concludes with the apostles returning to Jerusalem, where they continually bless God in the temple as they await the gift of the Spirit (24:52–53). Acts also begins with the apostles returning to Jerusalem after the ascension to wait

5. The two different accounts of the ascension are puzzling. According to the Gospel, the ascension occurs on the day of Jesus' resurrection, whereas according to Acts it takes place forty days after Easter. If the accounts are taken as historical, there is no way to reconcile them. Viewed from a literary perspective, however, the accounts function in this way. In the Gospel the ascension brings closure to the Gospel story, whereas in the Acts of the Apostles it opens the story of Acts. Since the apostles will be witnesses to Jesus' resurrection, the risen Lord spends forty days with his apostles before being taken up into heaven, in order to show them that he is risen and alive and provide them with further instruction about the kingdom of God (Acts 1:3).

for the gift of the Spirit (1:12). Once empowered by the Spirit, they become the eschatological rulers of that portion of Israel that repents and believes that Jesus is the Messiah, preaching to the people of Israel in the temple area as Jesus did (see Acts 1–5). From Jerusalem their witness to the Lord's resurrection spreads to Judea, to Samaria, and to the ends of the earth. Jerusalem then becomes the center of a reestablished and repentant Israel, so that even Paul, the great missionary to the Gentiles, repeatedly visits the city,[6] and James boasts to him, "You see, brother, how many thousands of believers there are among the Jews, and they are all zealous for the law" (Acts 21:20). Jerusalem, however, becomes a place of intense opposition to the apostles, just as it was for Jesus during his ministry.[7] Moreover, just as Jesus once made a fateful journey to Jerusalem (Luke 9:51), where he was put to death, so Paul determines to visit Jerusalem (Acts 19:21), where he is arrested and undergoes his own "passion" as a prisoner for the Lord. The story of the Spirit-filled Messiah then continues in the story of his Spirit-filled witnesses: the apostles, Stephen, and Paul. Just as Jesus came with a message of salvation and was rejected, so his followers come with a message of salvation and are rejected.

The infancy narrative (Luke 1:5–2:52) and Jesus' inaugural sermon in the synagogue of Nazareth (4:16–30) highlight the literary unity of Luke–Acts by announcing themes that Luke will develop throughout his two-volume work. The infancy narrative begins with great expectations that the promises made to Abraham and David are about to be fulfilled. For example, the angel Gabriel tells Mary that God will give her son the throne of David, and he will rule over the house of Jacob forever (1:32–33; an allusion to the promises made to David in 2 Sam. 7:12–16). Mary proclaims that God has remembered his mercy in accordance with the promises made to Abraham and his descendants (Luke 1:54–55). Zechariah says that God has raised up a mighty savior in the house of David (1:69) and has been mindful of the covenant he made to Abraham (1:72–73). When Simeon takes the child into his arms he says that he has seen God's salvation for Israel and the Gentiles (2:29–32). The prophet Anna speaks of the child to all in the temple who await the redemption of Israel (2:38). By the end of the Gospel, however, the messianic expectations of the infancy narrative have not materialized, and the two disciples on the road to Emmaus lament that Jesus has not fulfilled their expectations (24:21). How God fulfills these messianic promises is revealed only in Acts. There Peter teaches the

---

6. Paul visits Jerusalem after his call/conversion (Acts 9:23–30). He and Barnabas bring famine relief to the church of Jerusalem (11:30), and they represent the church of Antioch at the Jerusalem conference (15:1–29). Paul then returns to the city after his second missionary journey (18:22) and after his third missionary journey (21:17), at which time he is arrested and held prisoner in Jerusalem before being sent to Caesarea and then Rome.

7. During the first part of Acts, the religious leaders oppose the preaching of the apostles, arresting Peter and John (Acts 4:1–3), forbidding them to teach in the name of Jesus (4:18), and eventually arresting all of the apostles (5:17–18).

people of Jerusalem that God has enthroned Jesus as his Messiah by raising him from the dead (Acts 2:30–32), and Paul proclaims that God has fulfilled his promises to Israel by Jesus' resurrection (Acts 13:32–33). The resurrection of the Messiah is thus the fulfillment of the promises God made to Israel; it is the hope of Israel (Acts 26:6–8).

Jesus' inaugural sermon (Luke 4:16–30) is the story within the story that reveals the plot of Luke–Acts: Jesus comes with a gracious offer of salvation because his ministry is the fulfillment of Isaiah's prophecy; it is the "today" of salvation (4:16–21). Confronted by this gracious offer of salvation from their native son, the synagogue worshipers are taken aback that such an offer should come from the prophet they know as "Joseph's son" (4:22). Because of their skepticism, Jesus intimates that God's gift will be offered to others, as happened in the days of Elijah and Elisha (4:23–27). Incensed by this, his compatriots seek to kill him (4:28–30). This pattern of a gracious offer of salvation, that is refused and then offered to others is repeated in the lives of the Spirit-filled figures that dominate Acts: Peter, John, Stephen, and Paul. At the beginning of Acts, the apostles come with a renewed offer of salvation and a second chance for Israel to repent, but the religious leadership rejects them. Stephen also comes with a gracious offer of salvation only to be rejected. His speech shows that this pattern has occurred repeatedly in Israel's history (Acts 7:1–53). Prophetic figures such as Joseph and Moses and most recently Jesus have come to Israel with a gracious offer of salvation, only to be rejected. The same pattern occurs in the ministry of Paul, who goes from synagogue to synagogue preaching the gospel, only to be rejected. Consequently, he threatens to go to the Gentiles (13:46; 18:6; 28:28).[8] The story of Luke–Acts, then, is a story of a gracious offer of salvation that is rejected and then offered to others. Those who accept this offer—Jew and Gentile alike—are the reestablished Israel. Those who refuse it separate themselves from this reestablished Israel.

Theological Unity

The literary unity of Luke–Acts is an indication of the religious message Luke seeks to impart through his narrative: because Jesus was the Messiah, his ministry was the climax of Israel's redemptive history that continues in the life of a reestablished and repentant Israel, the church. This theological claim can be verified from Luke's understanding of God's purpose in history.

In Luke's view the definite plan or purpose of God underlies the "events" he narrates. This plan is evident from vocabulary such as "the plan" or "purpose

8. Luke appears to employ a literary technique here to make the case that Israel received repeated warnings that it did not heed. Thus, even though Paul twice threatens to go to the Gentiles (Acts 13:46–47; 18:6), he continues to preach to Jews in the synagogues until he reaches Rome. His final warning at Rome, however, is his last and most decisive (28:25–28).

of God" (*hē boulē tou theou*), the divine necessity that certain things "must" (*dei*) happen, the manner in which God "appoints" or "determines" (*horizō*) what happens or must be "fulfilled" (*plēroō*). David served this plan (Acts 13:36), and the Messiah was crucified "according to the definite plan and foreknowledge of God" (Acts 2:23; see also 4:28). At Miletus Paul reminds the elders of Ephesus that he never failed to tell them "the whole purpose of God" (20:27). By refusing John's baptism, the Pharisees and lawyers rejected this plan (Luke 7:30), and even after the resurrection of the Messiah they still oppose it (Acts 5:38–39).

Because God's plan or purpose underlies all that happens in Israel's history, certain things "must" (*dei*) occur. The twelve-year-old child already knows that he *must* be in his Father's house (Luke 2:49). Jesus *must* proclaim the good news of the kingdom of God (4:43). There is a divine necessity underlying his journey to Jerusalem (13:33) because the Son of Man *must* suffer, die, and rise from the dead (17:25; 24:7), and the Messiah "*must* suffer in order to enter into his glory" (24:26). In short, everything written in the Scriptures about Jesus *must* be fulfilled (22:37; 24:44).

This theme of divine necessity continues in Acts. The Scriptures about Judas *must* be fulfilled (Acts 1:16, 20). Paul's life falls under a divine necessity. He is told what he *must* do (9:6) and how much he *must* suffer for the sake of the name he once persecuted (9:16). In Thessalonica the former persecutor proves "that it was *necessary* for the Messiah to suffer and to rise from the dead" (17:3). The risen Lord instructs Paul that as he has testified in Jerusalem, "so you *must* bear witness also in Rome" (23:11), and an angel tells him that he *must* stand before the emperor (27:24). Nothing happens by chance. Everything has a purpose—God's purpose. Because God's plan underlies all that happens, certain events occur by divine necessity.

God has ordained or determined (*horizō*) that certain things happen. For example, the fate of the Son of Man has been *determined* (Luke 22:22), presumably by God, so that Peter can say that Jesus was handed over according to a plan *determined* by God (Acts 2:23). Because God determined the events of Jesus' life, the apostles testify that Jesus is "the one *ordained* by God as judge of the living and the dead" (Acts 10:42), and Paul affirms that God has "*fixed* a day on which he will have the world judged in righteousness by a man whom he has appointed" (17:31). In a word, all of the redemptive events that Luke narrates had to happen because they were part of a plan that God determined. This is why Jesus tells his apostles that everything written about him in the "law of Moses, the prophets, and the psalms must be fulfilled (*plērōthēnai*)" (Luke 24:44). Having learned this from the risen Lord, Peter preaches that God *fulfilled* what had been foretold through all the prophets "that his Messiah would suffer" (Acts 3:18), and Paul notes that the residents of Jerusalem and their leaders unwittingly *fulfilled* the words of the prophets they read every Sabbath by condemning Jesus (13:27).

Luke reveals the scope of this redemptive plan in Stephen's speech and in Paul's inaugural sermon at the synagogue of Antioch in Pisidia. In these speeches first Stephen and then Paul present selective summaries of Israel's history to show how that history came to its climax in the ministry of Jesus of Nazareth.

Stephen's speech (Acts 7:2–53) is the most complete, albeit selective, account of Israel's history in Acts. It begins with the call and migration of Abraham, with whom God made a covenant of circumcision. It narrates the jealousy of the patriarchs who sold Joseph into slavery. It tells the story of Moses and Israel in Egypt and the wilderness, and it alludes to how Joshua brought the people into the promised land where Solomon eventually built the temple. From Stephen's perspective, however, this history has been a continual rejection of the savior figures whom God sent to Israel (Joseph, Moses, the prophets). This rebellious history comes to its climax in the rejection of the Righteous One (7:52). As in the case of Jesus' inaugural sermon, Stephen's speech is the story of Luke–Acts in miniature.

Like Jesus, Paul delivers his inaugural sermon in a synagogue after the law and the prophets have been read (13:16–41). Like Stephen, he provides a selective account of Israel's history. God chose their ancestors, making them great in Egypt, and then rescued them from Egypt. He put up with them for forty years in the wilderness, and he led them into the promised land. He set up judges until the time of Samuel when Israel asked for a king, and so God gave them Saul and then David. At this point Paul affirms, "Of this man's [David] posterity God has brought to Israel a Savior, Jesus, as he promised" (13:23). Addressing his audience as "you descendants of Abraham's family, and others who fear God" (13:26), he reminds them that this message of salvation is intended for them. He explains that the residents of Jerusalem and their leaders did not recognize who Jesus was (the Messiah), nor did they understand the prophetic words they read each Sabbath. Thus they ironically fulfilled what they did not understand by condemning Jesus, but God raised him from the dead. Employing Psalms 2 and 16, Paul establishes that Jesus' resurrection was the fulfillment of David's prophetic word. For Paul the whole history of Israel points to Jesus as the Davidic Messiah whom God installed as Messiah at the resurrection.

Although both of these histories are selective, they indicate how firmly Luke roots his narrative in the story of Israel's redemptive history. Luke cannot conceive of the story of Jesus and the church apart from the story of Israel. Israel's redemptive history finds its climax in the Messiah, since the law of Moses, all of the prophets, and the Psalms speak of the Messiah.

Some contemporary readers may object to Luke's scheme of redemptive history as artificial, and to his understanding of God's plan as rigid. Another "selective" reading of history, they will contend, could find another climax in

Israel's history. Moreover, if God has so determined the fate of the Son of Man, how can one speak of human freedom and responsibility? But Luke is viewing the matter from another vantage point: the faithfulness of God. By highlighting Israel's redemptive history and God's divine plan, he affirms that God has been faithful to Israel. The appearance of Jesus of Nazareth was not an aberration or interruption of God's redemptive plan but its climax. For Luke, any other understanding of the events that happened "among us" would call into question God's faithfulness to Israel.

For Luke God's plan of salvation is a seamless garment woven by the prophecies of Moses and the prophets that the Messiah would suffer, die, and be raised from the dead. Faith in Jesus as the Messiah then is not an aberration from, or denial of, the law or the prophets; it is its fulfillment. Any sober reading of Israel's Scriptures, Luke would contend, will show that Jesus is the promised Messiah, since there is one underlying story that informs Israel's sacred writings and "the events that have been fulfilled among us" (Luke 1:1), namely, "that God who brought salvation to his people in the Old Testament continues to do this, especially through Jesus Christ."[9] That "sober reading," however, must be done in light of the resurrection, since even Luke acknowledges that people cannot understand what the law and the prophets say about the Messiah unless the Messiah opens their minds to understand the Scriptures (Luke 24:45).

The literary unity of Luke–Acts and the story it tells is a theological statement about Israel's redemptive history and God's faithfulness to Israel. The God of Israel has been and remains faithful to his people, for in Jesus the promised Messiah has come to Israel with a gracious offer of salvation. For Luke the story of Jesus and the church is rooted in the story of Israel, and the story of Israel finds its culmination in the story of Jesus and the church.

A SAVIOR WHO IS MESSIAH AND LORD

Luke's Christology follows the pattern established by his Markan source: Jesus is the Messiah, the Son of God, whose destiny is the destiny of the Son of Man who must suffer, die, and rise before returning at the end of the ages. But Luke also diverges from his Markan source in some significant ways. First, he gives greater prominence to Jesus as the promised Davidic Messiah than does Mark so that "Messiah" becomes his preferred christological title. Second, in addition to telling the story *of* Jesus, he recounts the proclamation of the early church *about* Jesus and narrates how the risen Lord guided the church's mission. The

9. Robert F. O'Toole, *The Unity of Luke's Theology: An Analysis of Luke–Acts* (GNS 9; Wilmington, DE: Glazier, 1984), 17.

result is a Christology that places Jesus within the full sweep of Israel's history as well as the life of the early church.[10] This section deals with (1) the beginning of Luke's Christology as presented in the Gospel, which portrays Jesus as the messianic Son of God who follows the destiny of the Son of Man, and (2) the completion of that Christology in the Acts of the Apostles, which presents Jesus as the God's exalted Messiah and Lord.

The Gospel: The Beginning of Luke's Christology

The infancy narrative begins with great expectations that God is about to fulfill his promises to Israel. At the annunciation, the angel Gabriel tells Mary that her child will be called "Son of God" (1:35) and that God will give him the throne of his ancestor David. Mary's son will reign over the house of Jacob forever, and his kingdom will endure forever (1:32–33), thereby fulfilling the promises made to David through the prophet Nathan (2 Sam. 7:13–16). At Jesus' birth, angels announce to shepherds that a savior has been born who is "the Messiah, the Lord" (Luke 2:11).[11] When the aged Simeon sees "the Lord's Messiah" (2:26), he proclaims, "My eyes have seen your salvation, which you have prepared in the presence of all peoples, a light for revelation to the Gentiles and for glory to your people Israel" (2:30–32); and in the temple the prophet Anna speaks of the child "to all who were looking for the redemption of Jerusalem" (2:38). From the outset of the narrative then there is no mistaking Jesus' identity. He is the Son of the Most High, the promised Davidic Messiah, a savior for Gentiles and Jews, the one who will redeem Israel. Elizabeth already recognizes the child as her "Lord" when she asks Mary, "And why has this happened to me, that the mother of *my Lord* comes to me?" (1:43),[12] and the twelve-year-old Jesus already understands that the temple is his Father's house (2:49). In sum, the Lukan infancy narrative shows the faithfulness of God to his covenant promises by presenting Jesus as the promised Davidic Messiah. Anyone who does not know the story that follows will suppose that Jesus is about to restore the Davidic monarchy.

When John the Baptist begins his ministry, the people of Israel wonder if he might be the Messiah (3:15). But readers who have been privy to the infancy narrative already know that even though John is the prophet of the Most High

---

10. Although the Gospels of Mark and Matthew also reflect the preaching of the early church, only Acts recounts the preaching of the early church about Jesus.

11. Luke purposely employs the title "savior" to undermine the claims of Caesar, who was acclaimed as the savior of his people. For Luke the true benefactor and savior of the people is the one who is Messiah and Lord.

12. In narrative comments throughout the Gospel, the Lukan narrator refers to Jesus as "the Lord," thereby indicating the perspective from which he tells the story (see 10:1; 11:39; 13:15; 17:5).

(1:76), it is Jesus whom God has raised up from the house of Israel as its mighty savior (1:69). Aware of his important but limited role in God's plan for Israel's salvation, John assures the people that after him a more powerful one is coming who will baptize them with "the Holy Spirit and fire" (3:16). When Jesus appears the Holy Spirit descends upon him, and God identifies Jesus as his Son when the heavenly voice declares: "You are my Son, the Beloved; with you I am well pleased" (3:22). After this heavenly declaration, Luke introduces Jesus' genealogy (3:23–38). But since the infancy narrative has already intimated that Jesus was born of a virgin because the power of the Most High overshadowed Mary (1:34–35), Luke forestalls any notion that Jesus is the physical descendant of Joseph by noting, "Jesus was about thirty years old when he began his work. He was the son (*as was thought*) of Joseph" (3:23). The genealogy traces Jesus' lineage from Joseph through David and Abraham to Adam, and finally to God. Like Matthew, Luke affirms that Jesus belongs to the royal lineage of David through Joseph, and that he is a true son of Israel, a descendant of Abraham. But he also goes further than Matthew. As a son of Adam, the Jewish Messiah is the representative of, and he belongs to, the whole human race. Most importantly, he is the Son of God.

In the scenes that follow, Luke portrays Jesus as the Spirit-filled Son of God whom the Spirit leads into the wilderness (4:1), where Satan tests him to see if he is truly God's Son (4:3, 9). Filled with the power of the Spirit (4:14), the Spirit-anointed Son of God returns to Galilee, where he begins his ministry with an inaugural sermon in the synagogue of Nazareth (4:16–30). There, after reading from Isaiah, where the prophet declares, "The Spirit of the Lord is upon me, because he has anointed me to bring good news to the poor . . ." (4:18; cf. Isa. 61:1–2; 58:6), Jesus proclaims, "Today this Scripture has been fulfilled in your hearing" (Luke 4:21), thereby disclosing that he is the Spirit-filled Messiah who brings release to captives, sight to the blind, freedom to the oppressed, and a year of favor to Israel (4:18–19).

Jesus' Galilean ministry (4:14–9:50) effects the salvation he announced in the synagogue of Nazareth. The power of the Lord is with him to heal (5:17; 6:19; 8:46), and he calls sinners to repentance (5:32). The people of Israel recognize that a great prophet has appeared in their midst (7:16), though Simon the Pharisee has his doubts (7:39). When John sends messengers to ask Jesus if he is the one who is to come (that is, the Messiah), Jesus responds by telling them to report what they have seen and heard: "The blind receive their sight, the lame walk, the lepers are cleansed, the deaf hear, the dead are raised, the poor have good news brought to them" (7:22). The Messiah of Israel is the Spirit-anointed Son of God, who brings good news to the poor just as he proclaimed in his inaugural sermon.

Whereas Peter's confession comes suddenly and somewhat unexpectedly in Mark's Gospel, given the incomprehension of Jesus' disciples, Luke provides a clearer connection between Peter's confession and Jesus' ministry.[13] Peter now confesses that Jesus is "the Messiah of God" (9:20) immediately after Jesus feeds the five thousand in the wilderness, and his confession echoes Simeon's words in the infancy narrative that he would not die before seeing "the Lord's Messiah" (2:26). For Luke, Jesus is preeminently Israel's Messiah, and within his Gospel "Messiah" and "Son of God" are interchangeable titles. Thus when the demons shout, "You are the *Son of God!*" Jesus silences them, "because they knew that he was the *Messiah*" (4:41). Luke's account of Jesus' Galilean ministry presents him as the Messiah who is the Spirit-anointed Son of God. This Messiah brings salvation to Israel "today" by preaching to the poor, healing the sick, and raising the dead. Through Jesus' prophetic and messianic ministry, God visits his people.

Luke understands that Jesus' messiahship cannot be fully expressed in traditional messianic categories, since the fate of the Son of Man will be the destiny of the Messiah. Therefore, after Peter's confession, Jesus orders his disciples not to tell anyone that he is the Messiah, saying, "The Son of Man must undergo great suffering, and be rejected by the elders, chief priests, and scribes, and be killed, and on the third day be raised" (9:22). Similar predictions occur in 9:44 and 18:31–33, but after each of them Luke notes that the disciples did not understand because "its meaning was concealed" (9:45) or "hidden from them" so that they could not "grasp what was said" (18:34). Jesus, however, is keenly aware that he must suffer and die, and at his transfiguration (9:31) even Moses and Elijah discuss his impending "departure" (*exodos*).

When Jesus realizes that the time has drawn near for him "to be taken up," he resolutely sets his face toward Jerusalem (9:51) because he knows that he must suffer and die before he can be taken up. The reference to being taken up (*analēmpseōs*) refers to Jesus' ascension, which can occur only after he has suffered and died. Aware that he must suffer before entering into his glory (see 24:26), he determines to complete his messianic destiny as outlined in his sayings about the suffering of the Son of Man.

In the journey that follows (9:51–19:44), Jesus calls Israel to repentance (13:5, 6–9) because the kingdom of God has made its appearance (10:9, 11), but he encounters opposition, especially from Israel's leaders (11:37–54). When Jesus draws near to the city, he weeps because he knows that it does not recognize God's visitation in his messianic ministry (19:41–44). Nevertheless, he spends the final days of his life teaching the people of Israel in his Father's house, the temple (19:47–48; 21:37–38). Although the religious leaders do not accept Jesus as the Messiah, they understand the messianic claims of his temple ministry. Therefore, when he stands before their council, they ask if he is

---

13. Luke accomplishes this by omitting the material of Mark 6:45–8:26, what is usually referred to as Luke's "great omission."

the Messiah (22:67). When Jesus replies that he is about to be enthroned at God's right hand (22:69), they ask, "Are you, then, *the Son of God?*" (22:70). The use of "Messiah" and "Son of God" again shows how the two titles are interchangeable (see 4:41): the enthroned Son of God is the Messiah. Convinced that Jesus has presented himself as the Messiah, Israel's leaders deliver him to Pilate, accusing him of claiming to be "the Messiah, a king," and perverting the nation (23:2), a reference to Jesus' temple ministry. Tested and mocked as a Messiah who cannot save himself (23:35, 39), Jesus dies as the innocent (23:4, 14, 22, 41) and righteous (23:47) Messiah who entrusts himself to his Father (23:46).

After the resurrection, the veil of incomprehension that has prevented the disciples from understanding Jesus' predictions of his suffering and death is lifted. At the empty tomb angels remind the women of what Jesus told them when in Galilee, "that the Son of Man must be handed over to sinners, and be crucified, and on the third day rise again" (24:7). Next the risen Lord teaches two disciples on the road to Emmaus that it was necessary for the Messiah to suffer in order to enter into his glory, interpreting all of the passages in the law of Moses and the prophets written about him (24:25–27). Finally, he instructs the eleven apostles that everything written about him in the law of Moses, the prophets, and the Psalms had to be fulfilled (24:44), and he opens their minds to understand the Scriptures (24:45). The death of Israel's Messiah cannot be reduced to a miscarriage of justice since it was the fulfillment of what is written in Israel's Scriptures (24:46). That plan, however, is evident only *after* the Lord's resurrection so that one can understand what Moses, the prophets, and the Psalms wrote about the Messiah only in light of the Messiah's resurrection. This is why the risen Lord must open the minds of his apostles to understand the Scriptures (24:45). This is why Israel will be given a second chance to repent of what it did in ignorance (Acts 3:17).

Acts: The Completion of Luke's Christology

Left to itself, the Christology of Luke's Gospel is incomplete since it does not explain how the great expectations of the infancy narrative are fulfilled. When does Jesus ascend the throne of David (Luke 1:32)? How does he rule over the house of Jacob forever? In what sense does his kingdom endure forever (1:33)? Luke answers these questions by recounting the preaching of the early church about Jesus as reported in the speeches of Peter and Paul.[14] In addition to these speeches, the risen Lord plays an active role in Acts as he guides the mission of the church.

---

14. For a careful analysis of these speeches, see Marion L. Soards, *The Speeches in Acts: Their Content, Context, and Concerns* (Louisville: Westminster John Knox Press, 1994).

Acts begins by summarizing the forty-day period between Jesus' resurrection and ascension as a time when the risen Lord appeared to his apostles, showing them by many convincing proofs that he was alive,[15] speaking to them about the kingdom of God, instructing them to remain in Jerusalem where they will be baptized with the Holy Spirit, and commissioning them to be his witnesses in Jerusalem, Judea, and Samaria. Only after this period of proof and instruction is Jesus taken from their midst (Acts 1:3–9). The resurrection appearances of these forty days are crucial for understanding the Christology Luke develops, since they qualify the apostles to be trustworthy witnesses to the resurrection and the kingdom of God. During this period, which climaxes in the ascension, the apostles begin to understand how God has enthroned Jesus as Messiah by raising him from the dead. It is not surprising then that they ask, "Lord, is this the time when you will restore the kingdom to Israel?" (1:6). Although Jesus responds that it is not for them to know the times and periods God has set, their question is not ill-advised.[16] For if Jesus is risen and alive, then he is the Messiah. And if he is the Messiah, then the kingdom will be restored. But as the speeches of Acts will show, Jesus is the Messiah who has been enthroned at God's right hand, and the kingdom will be more inclusive than a restored Davidic monarchy; it will bring about the universal restoration that only God's enthroned Messiah can effect (see Peter's remarks about this universal restoration in 3:21).

Peter's sermon at Pentecost (2:14–36) clearly indicates that the risen Lord has made his apostles insightful interpreters of Scripture. Quoting from Psalm 16, Peter now understands and explains that when David wrote, "For you will not abandon my soul to Hades, or let your Holy One experience corruption" (Acts 2:27), he was not speaking of himself, since he died and was buried. Rather, David was a prophet, and he knew that God had promised to put one of his descendants on his throne. Therefore, he was speaking of the resurrection of the Messiah when he said, "He was not abandoned to Hades, nor did his flesh experience corruption" (2:31). Furthermore, since David did not ascend into heaven, Peter concludes that David was speaking of the Messiah's exaltation or enthronement at God's right hand when he said in Psalm 110, "The Lord said to my Lord, 'Sit at my right hand, until I make your enemies your footstool'" (Acts 2:34–35). Through this messianic exegesis of Psalms 110 and 16, Peter resolves the issues raised by the infancy narrative of how Jesus ascends to the throne of David and rules over the house of Israel forever (Luke 1:32–33): God enthroned Jesus as Lord and Messiah at the resurrection (Acts 2:36).

Peter delivers his next speech (Acts 3:12–26) in the temple area after healing a man who had been lame from birth. He refers to Jesus as God's "servant"

---

15. According to Luke 24:42–43 and Acts 10:41, Jesus ate and drank with them after his resurrection.

16. The point is made by Robert C. Tannehill, *The Narrative Unity of Luke–Acts: A Literary Interpretation*, vol. 2: *The Acts of the Apostles* (Minneapolis: Fortress, 1990), 15.

(3:13), "the Holy and Righteous One" (3:14), and "the Author of life" (3:15). He contrasts the action of the people who rejected and handed Jesus over to Pilate with that of God who raised him from the dead (3:13–15). Nevertheless, Peter is now aware that the people and their leaders acted in ignorance and unwittingly fulfilled what all the prophets foretold: that God's Messiah would suffer (3:18), precisely what Jesus taught the apostles after his resurrection (Luke 24:46). Therefore, Peter exhorts the people to repent so that their sins will be wiped away and God may send the Messiah appointed for them, that is, Jesus, "who must remain in heaven until the time of universal restoration that God announced long ago through his holy prophets" (Acts 3:19–21). Next, Peter identifies Jesus as the prophet whom Moses foretold when he said, "The Lord your God will raise up for you from your own people a prophet like me. You must listen to whatever he tells you. And it will be that everyone who does not listen to that prophet will be utterly rooted out of the people" (3:22–23, quoting from Deut. 18:18). He reminds them that all of the prophets since Samuel predicted these days and that they are the descendants of the prophets and of the covenant God made with Abraham (Acts 3:24–25). God's purpose in raising his servant Jesus from the dead, then, was to bless them and turn them from their wicked ways (3:26). In this brief speech, Peter places Jesus within the full sweep of God's redemptive plan that begins with the prophetic promises God made to Abraham, Moses, and the prophets. That plan finds its climax in the resurrection and will not be complete until the enthroned Messiah returns to restore all things.

When Peter must defend his actions before the religious leaders who are annoyed that he teaches the people and proclaims the resurrection of the dead (4:2), he delivers a speech (4:8–12) in which he explains that the lame man has been healed by the name of Jesus Christ of Nazareth whom they crucified but God raised from the dead (4:10). Displaying his new understanding of Israel's Scriptures, he employs Psalm 118 to identify Jesus as the stone rejected by them that has become the cornerstone (Acts 4:11). Peter is now aware that there is salvation in no other name under heaven save the name of Jesus Christ of Nazareth (4:12). At the heart of his christological defense is the resurrection, the act by which God enthroned Jesus as his Messiah.

In a further speech to the religious leaders (5:29–32), Peter and the apostles affirm that they must obey God rather than human beings because God raised up Jesus whom they killed by hanging him on a tree. Alluding to the enthronement of Jesus as the Messiah, Peter notes that God exalted him at his right hand "as Leader and Savior that he might give repentance to Israel and forgiveness of sins" (5:31). Because they are witnesses to the resurrection, as is the Holy Spirit whom God grants to those who obey him (5:32), Peter and the apostles know that Jesus is the enthroned Messiah who rules over the house of Jacob forever.

Peter's sermon to the household of Cornelius (10:34–43) provides a summary of Jesus' ministry to Israel. Having recently learned that God shows no partiality (10:28, 34), Peter begins by identifying Jesus as "Lord of all" (10:36), of the Gentiles as well as of the Jews. He then reviews the course of Jesus' ministry, which began in Galilee after the baptism that John announced until the day Jesus was put to death. Once more, Peter draws a contrast between what human beings did ("They put him to death by hanging him on a tree," 10:39) and God's response ("but God raised him on the third day," 10:40). Peter and the rest of the apostles can witness to the resurrection since they ate and drank with him after he rose from the dead (10:41), and they now testify that "he is the one ordained by God as judge of the living and the dead" (10:42). The sermon concludes with Peter's testimony that all of the prophets testify that those who believe in Jesus will have their sins forgiven. This sermon (the first addressed to a non-Jewish audience) points to the significance of Jesus for Gentiles even as it continues to ground the story of Jesus in the story of Israel.

Paul's inaugural sermon at Pisidian Antioch (13:16–41) has already been discussed in relation to its significance for the unity of Luke–Acts. But the sermon is also important for understanding Luke's Christology since Paul employs Psalm 16 as did Peter in his sermon at Pentecost. Paul's sermon, however, emphasizes Jesus' Davidic ancestry, insisting that God brought a savior to Israel from David's posterity (13:22–23). As did Peter, Paul reminds his audience that they are the descendants of Abraham and that this message of salvation has been sent to them (13:26). He notes that by condemning Jesus the religious leaders of Jerusalem unknowingly fulfilled the words of the prophets, which they read every Sabbath. But God raised Jesus from the dead, and he appeared to the apostles who are now his witnesses. Paul then employs Psalms 2 and 16 to show "that what God promised to our ancestors he has fulfilled for us, their children, by raising Jesus; as also it is written in the second psalm" (Acts 13:32–33). What God promised the ancestors is that he would bring forth a savior from David's descendants, namely, the Messiah (13:23). Once more the resurrection is the key to unlocking Luke's Christology. Through the resurrection, God enthroned Jesus as the promised Messiah, and now that he has been enthroned as Messiah there is forgiveness of sins in his name. The Lukan Paul, however, expresses this in a distinctively Pauline way, "By this Jesus everyone who believes is set free from all those sins from which you could not be freed by the law of Moses" (13:39).

These speeches and sermons provide a rich Christology that completes the Christology begun in the Gospel, explaining how God installed Jesus as his Messiah when he raised him from the dead. In doing this, they introduce a number of new titles to explain the significance of Jesus and his work: God's servant (3:13), the Holy and Righteous One (3:14), the Author of life (3:15), the prophet like Moses (3:22), and the Lord of all (10:36). But all of these titles remain subordinate to Luke's major christological category for understanding Jesus: Messiah. Because Jesus is the enthroned Messiah who sits at God's right hand until he comes again, he is rightly called "Lord." This designation, which can also refer to God,[17] confirms Jesus' exaltation as the enthroned Messiah. It is not surprising then that "Lord" and "Lord Jesus" are the ways Luke most frequently refers to Jesus in Acts now that Jesus has been enthroned as God's Messiah.[18]

"Son of God" and "Son of Man," which play central roles in the Gospel, occur once in Acts. When Stephen is about to die, he exclaims, "I see the heavens opened and the Son of Man standing at the right hand of God!" (7:56). This Son of Man, who stands at God's right hand, is none other than the one whom God vindicated and enthroned as his Messiah. But now that Jesus has been exalted as God's Messiah, Jesus' designation for himself, "Son of Man," no longer plays a prominent role in Acts. In 9:20 Luke reports that the newly converted Saul proclaimed Jesus as the "Son of God" in the synagogues of Damascus and then notes how Saul confounded the Jews in Damascus by proving that Jesus is "the Messiah" (9:22). As he did in Luke 4:41, Luke again equates "Son of God" and "Messiah." But whereas "Son of God" continued to play a prominent role in the Gospel, it all but disappears from Acts since God has vindicated Jesus by raising him from the dead and enthroning him as Lord and Messiah. Within Acts, then, "Lord" and "Messiah" are the ways in which Luke prefers to identify Jesus, and all other titles are best understood in relationship to them. The Son of God is the enthroned Messiah and so the exalted Lord; the Son of Man will return as the Messiah who is presently in heaven until "the time of universal restoration" (Acts 3:21). It is significant, then, that Acts concludes with Paul proclaiming the kingdom of God and teaching about the Lord Jesus Christ (28:31). The kingdom of God was the central message of the earthly Jesus and the content of his teaching at the beginning of Acts (1:3), and the identification of him as "the Lord Jesus Christ" brings together Luke's central christological affirmations about Jesus: he is the exalted Lord, the enthroned Messiah.

Although Luke presents Jesus as the enthroned Messiah "who must remain in heaven until the time of universal restoration" (3:21), this Messiah is not absent or unconcerned about the needs of the church. He appears to Saul and Ananias when it is time to make Saul his chosen instrument to bring his name before Gentiles, kings, and the people of Israel (9:1–19). In recounting his call to the inhabitants of Jerusalem, Paul relates how the risen Lord commissioned

17. It is usually apparent in Acts when "Lord" refers to God and when it refers to Jesus, but in several instances it is not. Although this leaves the reader of Acts uncertain about Luke's intention, it suggests that the relationship between God and Jesus is so close that Luke can use "Lord" in this ambiguous way.

18. The designation of Jesus as "Lord" (*kyrios*) or "Lord Jesus" points to his exalted status, which derives from his enthronement as God's Messiah.

him to go to the Gentiles (22:17–21). After Paul's trials in Jerusalem, the Lord "stood near him" and said, "Keep up your courage! For just as you have testified for me in Jerusalem, so you must bear witness also in Rome" (23:11). Moreover, "the Spirit of Jesus" guides Paul's mission (16:7–10). In a word, although the Messiah is presently enthroned in heaven, he is not absent from the church.

Luke's Christology presents Jesus within the full sweep of God's redemptive plan. Jesus is the promised Messiah of whom Moses and all the prophets spoke. Because God has raised him from the dead, he is the enthroned Messiah who will bring about a universal restoration. In the time between the resurrection and this final restoration, the Messiah sits at God's right hand guiding the church.

SALVATION FOR ISRAEL AND FOR THE NATIONS

Those who believed in Jesus during the days of his earthly ministry experienced salvation in the mighty deeds he performed on their behalf, in the forgiveness of their sins, and in the reversal of fortunes the kingdom of God effected for them. After Jesus' resurrection from the dead and the outpouring of the Holy Spirit, this salvation was offered to Israel and the Gentiles through the preaching of the early church. Luke's understanding of the salvation Jesus offered, which the resurrection makes available to all who believe in the name of Jesus, is at the heart of Luke's theology. Consequently, any study of who Jesus is (Christology) remains incomplete until it takes into consideration the "benefits" Christ brings (soteriology).[19] Put simply, Luke–Acts offers a more complete presentation of the salvation the gospel brings than do the Gospels of Mark and Matthew.[20]

A New Era of Salvation

The Lukan infancy narrative proclaims that the birth of the Messiah inaugurates a new era of salvation for Israel and the nations. Mary's canticle celebrates the reversal of fortunes that the Savior God, the Mighty One of Israel, is already effecting in her life and in the lives of the poor and downtrodden (Luke 1:46–55). Zechariah praises God for raising up a mighty savior (literally, "a horn of salvation") from the lineage of David (1:69) so that Israel will experience salvation from its enemies (1:71). At Jesus' birth, an angel of the Lord

19. This point is made throughout the important work of Arland J. Hultgren, *Christ and His Benefits: Christology and Redemption in the New Testament* (Philadelphia: Fortress, 1987).

20. See the essay by Augustin George, "Le vocabulaire de salut," *Études sur l'oeuvre de Luc* (SB; Paris: Gabalda, 1978), 307–20.

tells shepherds that a savior has been born who is the Messiah, the Lord (2:11). The aged Simeon praises God because in the child Jesus he has seen the salvation God has prepared for all peoples, "a light for revelation to the Gentiles" and glory for the people of Israel (2:32). In the temple the prophet Anna speaks of the child "to all who were looking for the redemption of Jerusalem" (2:38). In a word, Israel will experience a new age of salvation because the covenant promises God made to Abraham are about to be fulfilled (1:55, 72–73) through the house of David (1:69). Sins will be forgiven. Fortunes will be reversed. Israel will worship God in holiness and righteousness. Jerusalem will be delivered. Even the Gentiles will share in this salvation.

This age of salvation takes form when John the Baptist appears in the wilderness "proclaiming a baptism of repentance for the forgiveness of sins" (3:3), just as his father Zechariah prophesied (1:76–77). Like Mark, Luke interprets the appearance of John in light of Isaiah's prophecy as "the voice of one crying out in the wilderness: 'Prepare the way of the Lord, make his paths straight'" (3:4). More importantly, he extends the quotation to read, "Every valley shall be filled, and every mountain and hill shall be made low, and the crooked shall be made straight, and the rough ways made smooth; *and all flesh shall see the salvation of God*" (3:5–6, quoting Isa. 40:3–5 according to the LXX), thereby highlighting the universal dimension of the salvation that is about to appear in Jesus' ministry.

A Ministry of Salvation

In Luke's Gospel the formal inauguration of Jesus' ministry begins with his sermon in the synagogue of Nazareth, where he proclaims that his ministry is the fulfillment of Isaiah's prophecy.[21]

> The Spirit of the Lord is upon me,
> because he has anointed me
> to bring good news (*euangelisasthai*) to the poor.
> He has sent me to proclaim release to the captives
> and recovery of sight to the blind,
> to let the oppressed go free,
> to proclaim the year of the Lord's favor.
> (4:18–19, a composite of Isa. 61:1–2 and 58:6)

This proclamation of "good news" is the purpose of Jesus' ministry (Luke 4:43), and it defines the salvation God offers through him. The verb Luke employs to describe this activity (*euangelizein*, "to proclaim good news") occurs

---

21. Although this sermon is often designated as Jesus' inaugural sermon at Nazareth, it is clear from 4:14–15 that Jesus' ministry is already well under way. From a literary point of view, however, this is an inaugural sermon since it is the first time within the narrative that Jesus proclaims the gospel he preaches.

frequently in Luke–Acts.[22] In the Gospel the content of this good news is the kingdom of God (4:43; 8:1; 16:16), which is bringing about a reversal of fortunes in favor of the poor and dispossessed (see Jesus' beatitudes and woes, 6:20–26). In those instances when Luke simply reports that Jesus was preaching good news (7:22; 9:6; 20:1), one can assume the kingdom of God is the content of his good news.

Jesus' ministry confirms what he proclaims in his inaugural sermon and shows how the kingdom brings about salvation. His healings and exorcisms release those whom Satan oppresses and holds captive (4:31–37; 13:10–17). His table fellowship with sinners (5:29–30; 15:1–2) and his authoritative declaration that their sins have been forgiven (7:48) indicate that in his ministry God is offering Israel a year of divine favor, a jubilee that remits sin, the most serious of all debts. So when John the Baptist sends messengers to ask Jesus if he is the one who is to come, Jesus points to the mighty works he has been doing on behalf of Israel: "The blind receive their sight, the lame walk, the lepers are cleansed, the deaf hear, the dead are raised, the poor have good news brought to them" (7:22). As in the Gospel of Mark, Jesus' healings and exorcisms are concrete indications of the inbreaking kingdom of God that is already present in Jesus' ministry. They are examples of how salvation affects people here and now by freeing them from sin and sickness, the oppression of evil spirits, and restoring them to the human community.

The salvation Jesus brings can be understood only in light of the inbreaking kingdom of God that he preaches. Through his ministry the kingdom has drawn near (*ēngiken*, 10:9, 11). It has come upon people (*ephthasen*, 11:20). It is even among them (*entos hymōn estin*, 17:21). To the extent that the kingdom is already here, people experience salvation through Jesus' ministry. But since the kingdom has not yet arrived in its final manifestation (19:11), no one has experienced the fullness of salvation, nor will they until they enter the kingdom. Therefore, when someone asks Jesus if only a few will be saved, he warns, "Strive to enter through the narrow door; for many, I tell you, will try to enter and will not be able" (13:24). In one of his favorite metaphors, Jesus describes the kingdom as a great banquet at which the patriarchs, the prophets, and people from every corner of the earth will be present. But the kingdom will also effect a great and final reversal, and many who think they will eat bread in the kingdom of God will be excluded because they did not recognize God's offer of salvation in Jesus' ministry (13:28–30; 14:15–24).

Jesus comes to call people to repentance (5:32; 13:1–9; 19:10). He forgives sins (5:23; 7:48), and he proclaims the gracious forgiveness that God offers

---

22. The verb occurs only once in Matthew (11:5, a Q saying) and not at all in Mark. In Luke it occurs in 1:19; 2:10; 3:18; 4:18, 23; 7:22; 8:1; 9:6; 16:16; 20:1. In Acts it occurs in 5:42; 8:4, 12, 25, 35, 40; 10:36; 11:20; 13:32; 14:7, 15, 21; 15:35; 16:10; 17:18.

(15:1–32) so that people will be able to enter the kingdom. His association with sinners and his table fellowship with them is a cause for controversy and scandal to many, but it is also an initial experience of the salvation that will be fulfilled in the kingdom of God. At the end of the Gospel the risen Lord ensures that this offer of salvation will continue when he teaches his apostles that "repentance and forgiveness of sins is to be proclaimed in his name to all nations, beginning from Jerusalem" (24:47).

To summarize, the salvation Jesus proclaims during his earthly ministry is a present reality that already affects people "today" (4:21; 19:9; 23:43). It restores them to health and releases them from Satan's bondage; it offers forgiveness and effects a reversal of fortunes. It is also a future reality that will not be fully experienced until the final manifestation of God's kingdom. The most prominent aspect of this salvation is the forgiveness of sins, which enables people to enter the kingdom. In Acts the church will offer this forgiveness as well as the gift of the Spirit, in Jesus' name.

Salvation in Jesus' Name

Salvation remains a central theme in Acts as the church continues to proclaim the forgiveness of sins (2:38; 5:31; 10:43; 13:38; 26:18) and the kingdom of God (8:12; 14:22; 19:8; 28:23, 31). But now that Jesus has been raised from the dead and entered into the kingdom, where he is enthroned as Messiah, it is apparent that the kingdom he preached has entered a new phase. Jesus is enthroned as Messiah at God's right hand, and the gift of the Spirit has been given to the church. Accordingly, the church proclaims salvation in Jesus' name. For Israel, this salvation means the fulfillment of God's covenant promises and the restoration of God's people as was intimated in the infancy narrative. For the Gentiles, this salvation is an opportunity to become part of the renewed and reestablished people of God. For all, it means forgiveness of sins, the gift of the Spirit, entrance into the kingdom, and resurrection from the dead.

The outpouring of God's Spirit at Pentecost indicates that a period of renewal has begun and that "the last days" have arrived (Acts 2:17–21). Accordingly, at Pentecost Peter exhorts his fellow Israelites to repent of their role in the death of the Messiah whom God has raised up, and to be baptized in the name of Jesus Christ so that their sins may be forgiven and they may receive the Holy Spirit (2:38). After healing a lame man in the temple, Peter again urges his listeners to repent so that their sins will be wiped away and the times of renewal or refreshment (*kairoi anapsyxeōs*) that accompany the messianic age will come upon them (3:20). When Israel's leaders ask Peter and John by what power or name they do these things, Peter responds that the lame man was healed "by the name of Jesus Christ of Nazareth" whom they crucified but God raised (4:10). He then proclaims, "There is salvation in no one else, for there is no other name under heaven among mortals by which we must be saved" (4:12).

Luke communicates the essential content of his soteriology through Peter's sermons and speeches: in raising Jesus from the dead, God has made him the source of salvation for all who believe in his name. Those who rejected Jesus must repent and be baptized in his name if they wish to be saved. Those who repent and are baptized will have their sins forgiven, receive the gift of the Holy Spirit, and become part of a restored Israel that will enjoy the benefits of the messianic age; for God has exalted Jesus "at his right hand as Leader and Savior that he might give repentance to Israel and forgiveness of sins" (5:31).

Paul's sermon in the synagogue of Pisidian Antioch is another expression of Lukan soteriology. The Lukan Paul reminds his Jewish audience that this message of salvation was sent to them (13:26) and that what God promised their ancestors he has fulfilled in raising Jesus from the dead (13:32–33). For this reason, forgiveness is being proclaimed through the one whom God raised up (13:37–38). And "by this Jesus everyone who believes is set free from all those sins from which you could not be freed by the law of Moses" (13:39). On the next Sabbath, when Paul meets with a negative response, he and Barnabas reply, "It was necessary that the word of God should be spoken first to you. Since you reject it and judge yourselves to be unworthy of eternal life, we are now turning to the Gentiles. For so the Lord has commanded us, saying, 'I have set you to be a light for the Gentiles, so that you may bring salvation to the ends of the earth'" (13:46–47). Although Paul and Barnabas continue to preach to the Jews, Paul repeats these words at Corinth (18:6) and Rome (28:28), warning that if they do not accept this renewed offer of salvation, it will be given to the Gentiles.

The offer of salvation to the Gentiles, however, is not merely the result of Israel's refusal, as the conversion of Cornelius and his household shows (10:1–48); it is God's plan of salvation for Israel and the nations. Accordingly, when some of the circumcised object to what Peter has done (11:2), he explains the whole affair and concludes, "If then God gave them the same gift that he gave us when we believed in the Lord Jesus Christ, who was I that I could hinder God?" (11:17). The church at Jerusalem replies, "Then God has given even to the Gentiles the repentance that leads to life" (11:18). Later, when certain members of the church insist that unless Gentile converts are circumcised they cannot be saved (15:1–2), Peter responds that since God has given the Gentiles the Holy Spirit just as he gave it to Jewish believers, cleansing their hearts by faith, then God makes no distinction between Gentile and Jew (15:9). "On the contrary," Peter asserts, "we believe that we will be saved through the grace of the Lord Jesus, just as they will" (15:11). Although the Pauline teaching of justification by faith does not play a major role in Acts, Paul's statement at Antioch of Pisidia (13:39) and Peter's declaration at the Jerusalem conference (15:11) indicate that

Luke understands its meaning: Gentiles and Jews are saved by faith in Jesus Christ because there is no other name under heaven by which they can be saved.

While Luke shows that those who believe in Jesus already experience salvation through the gift of the Spirit and the forgiveness of their sins, he is also aware that their salvation is not complete. The day of "universal restoration" will not occur until the enthroned Messiah returns (3:21), and believers must pass through many persecutions before they can enter the kingdom of God (14:22). Because God has raised Jesus from the dead, however, Luke is confident that God will bring about this moment of universal restoration and that believers will finally enter the kingdom of God. Thus an essential aspect of Luke's soteriology is his understanding of the resurrection of the dead, which plays such a prominent role in Paul's defense speeches in the latter part of Acts.

When defending himself before the Sanhedrin, Paul exclaims, "Brothers, I am a Pharisee, a son of Pharisees. I am on trial concerning the hope of the resurrection of the dead" (23:6). When he defends himself before the Roman governor Felix, he says, "I have a hope in God—a hope that they themselves also accept—that there will be a resurrection of both the righteous and the unrighteous. . . . It is about the resurrection of the dead that I am on trial before you today" (24:15, 21). And when he defends himself before King Agrippa, he again affirms that he is on trial on account of his hope in the promises made by God to Israel's ancestors, namely, the resurrection of the dead (26:6–8). So he concludes his defense, "To this day I have had help from God, and so I stand here, testifying to both small and great, saying nothing but what the prophets and Moses said would take place: that the Messiah must suffer, *and that, by being the first to rise from the dead, he would proclaim light both to our people and to the Gentiles*" (26:22–23).

Paul's final words indicate that Luke understands the intimate connection between the resurrection of Christ and the general resurrection of all believers, as does Paul in 1 Corinthians 15. Because God has raised Jesus from the dead, those who believe in him can be assured that they will also share in the general resurrection of the dead, a process that has already begun with the resurrection of the Messiah.

The Dimensions of Salvation

Luke's understanding of salvation can be summarized under four headings: (1) the agents of salvation, (2) the beneficiaries of salvation, (3) the time of salvation, and (4) the gifts of salvation.[23]

The primary agent of salvation is the savior God of Israel (Luke 1:47), the God who is faithful to his covenant promises. It is this God who raised up a

---

23. This point is made by George, "Vocabulaire de salut," 307–8.

savior for Israel (Luke 2:11; Acts 5:31; 13:23) and who comes to Israel with a gracious offer of salvation. Although human beings reject Jesus and his offer of salvation, God raises him from the dead. As the vindicated and exalted agent of God's salvation, the Messiah sends other Spirit-endowed figures (his apostles, Stephen, Philip, Paul) with a renewed offer of salvation just as he sent agents of salvation to his people Israel (Acts 7:2–53).

The immediate beneficiaries of God's salvation are those who accept the salvation offered by Jesus and those who come in his name. Stories of individuals who accept this offer abound in Luke–Acts. But the salvation God offers through Jesus and proclaimed by those who come in the name of the risen Lord is ultimately directed to a people. Because Jesus is *Israel's* Messiah, Israel is the first to hear the good news of the kingdom. After Jesus' resurrection, the church continues to preach to Israel because "the message of this salvation" (Acts 13:26) was sent to the people of Israel and their descendants. But since God's salvation is universal in scope (Luke 3:6), the Messiah is also "a light for revelation to the Gentiles." Luke is concerned with how both individuals and peoples embrace or reject this offer of salvation, for just as individuals reject or embrace salvation so do larger groups of people such as Israel and the Gentiles.

The salvation God offers Israel and the Gentiles through Jesus Christ is a reality that people can already experience. It occurs in history because it is part of history. For Luke salvation occurs "today." *Today* a savior is born (Luke 2:11). *Today* the prophecy of Isaiah is fulfilled in Jesus (4:21). *Today* salvation comes to the house of Zacchaeus (19:9). *Today* the repentant criminal will be with Jesus in paradise (23:43). The present dimension of salvation that people experience "today" is the assurance of God's faithfulness to his covenant promises. But salvation is also an eschatological reality that will not be complete until the parousia, the final coming of the kingdom, the general resurrection of the dead, and the restoration of all things.

At the present time, the gift of salvation is experienced in a multiplicity of ways: the restoration of health, the recovery of sight, freedom from demons and magical powers, the forgiveness of sins, the gift of the Spirit, a common life of sharing in a community of believers. Other dimensions of salvation, such as the restoration of Israel, are still in the process of being realized. Still others will not be complete until the end of the ages when the kingdom of God will appear and the dead will be raised. Therefore, although believers can already experience the reality of salvation, there are dimensions of salvation for which they still long and desire.

Luke is a balanced writer who understands the tension between salvation that is already experienced but not yet finally realized. When he is compared with Matthew and Mark, however, it is apparent that Luke gives greater emphasis to the present dimension of salvation than they do. His double work chronicles the story of Jesus and the ongoing progress of the Word and its impact on the lives of those who embrace it. If salvation is merely future and there is no experience of it in the present, then there is little motivation to embrace it. To Luke's credit, he shows how the gift of salvation affects believers here and now.

ISRAEL AND THE CHURCH

Just as Luke's soteriology is linked to his Christology, so his ecclesiology is related to his Christology and soteriology. For Luke, the church is a community of "the last days," an eschatological community inaugurated by the outpouring of the Spirit at Pentecost upon those who first believed in Jesus as the Messiah. To enter into this "community of disciples" is to embark upon a "way" of salvation. In Luke's view this community is the heir of the promises made to historical Israel, not because it has replaced Israel but because it is that portion of Israel that has repented and believed in Jesus as the Messiah. From Luke's perspective there has been a "division" within Israel.[24] On the one hand, a significant portion of Israel repented and believed in Jesus as the Messiah. This restored Israel is the church. On the other, a large portion of Israel has not repented, and Luke tends to describe this part of Israel, especially in the latter part of Acts, as "the Jews."[25] They belong to historical Israel, but by refusing to accept Jesus as the Messiah they have forfeited the covenant promises. Luke's view of "the Jews," of course, is problematic for contemporary Christians given the anti-Jewish sentiments it can encourage.[26] But before commenting on his view of "the Jews," it is necessary to investigate Luke's understanding of Israel and the church.

The People of God

Luke is a theologian of redemptive history inasmuch as he traces the history of salvation that began with God's covenant promises to Israel and found its climax in the appearance of the Messiah. This concern for Israel and the relationship of Israel's history to Jesus is evident throughout Luke–Acts. In the canticles of the infancy narrative and in the speeches of Acts, Luke frequently refers to the promises God made to Israel through the covenants and prophets. Luke's most

24. The point is made by Jacob Jervell, *Luke and the People of God: A New Look at Luke–Acts* (Minneapolis: Augsburg, 1972), especially 41–74, "The Divided People of God: The Restoration of Israel and Salvation for the Gentiles"; and idem, *The Theology of the Acts of the Apostles* (NTT; Cambridge: Cambridge University Press, 1996), 35–43.

25. The concordance shows that Luke uses the terms "Israel" and "Israelite" primarily in the first part of Acts, whereas "the Jews" appears more frequently in the second part of Acts.

26. For a penetrating and controversial study of Luke's attitude toward the Jews, see Jack T. Sanders, *The Jews in Luke–Acts* (Philadelphia: Fortress, 1987).

detailed accounts of Israel's history, however, occur in Stephen's speech and in Paul's sermon at Antioch of Pisidia. Through Stephen's speech, Luke shows that God has persistently sent Israel a series of savior figures, culminating in the appearance of "the righteous one" (7:52) whom Israel rejected. Through Paul's speech at Antioch in Pisidia, he recounts Israel's history from a vantage point that shows how the promises made to Israel point to the one whom the inhabitants of Jerusalem and their leaders failed to recognize and so condemned (13:27). After Paul recounts this history, some follow him and Barnabas (13:43), but others contradict him (13:45). Through these speeches, Luke shows how Israel has rejected those whom God has sent with a gracious offer of salvation, thereby showing that present division in Israel over the Messiah is a pattern in Israel's history. Yet, as Augustin George notes, Luke consistently portrays Israel as the object of God's favor. Luke is the only evangelist to speak of the election of the patriarchs (Acts 13:17), of God's covenant with them (Luke 1:72; Acts 3:25; 7:8), and especially of his promises to Abraham (Luke 1:73; Acts 3:25; 7:5, 17), to David (Acts 2:30; 13:23, 34), and to the patriarchs (Acts 13:32; 26:6). For Luke, Israel is the people of the promise more than the people of the law.[27]

Israel at the Threshold of the Messiah's Ministry

Through the infancy narrative and the preaching of John the Baptist, Luke presents a hopeful picture of Israel at the threshold of the messianic age. The major characters of the infancy narrative (Zechariah and Elizabeth, Mary and Joseph, Simeon and Anna) are pious Israelites who observe all the prescriptions of the law. Mary's canticle portrays God as mercifully coming to the assistance of his "servant Israel" in accordance with the promises made to Abraham (Luke 1:54–55). Zechariah's canticle blesses the God of Israel for visiting and bringing redemption to his people (1:68) by raising up a savior from the dynasty of David, just as the prophets had foretold (1:69–70), thereby showing God's faithfulness to the covenant made with Abraham (1:72–73). Simeon identifies the child as the glory of Israel (2:32), and in the temple Anna speaks of him to all who are awaiting the redemption of Israel (2:38). At the outset of John's ministry, great crowds flock to him asking what they must do (3:10–14). Filled with expectation as they stand at the threshold of a new age, the people of Israel wonder if John might be the Messiah (3:15).

Within this favorable presentation of Israel, however, Luke signals that not all of Israel will receive Jesus as the Messiah. Simeon predicts that the child will be the fall and rise of many in Israel and a sign of contradiction (2:34). John the Baptist calls the crowds that have come for his baptism a brood of vipers, and he warns that if Israel does not repent God will raise up new off-

---

27. George, "Israël," *Études sur l'oeuvre de Luc*, 87–125, here 89.

spring for Abraham. In a word, Luke already hints that there will be a division in God's people when the Messiah appears.

Israel during the Ministry of the Messiah

Jesus' ministry evokes a variety of responses from Israel. During the period of his Galilean ministry (4:14–9:50), Jesus teaches in synagogues (4:15)[28] and preaches the good news of the kingdom to Israel (4:43). At the outset, his ministry receives a favorable response from the crowds. People are astonished by his ministry and glorify God (5:26). They proclaim that a great prophet has arisen among them and that God has visited his people (7:16). But there are indications that not all is well. Jesus' compatriots at Nazareth drive him out of the synagogue when he comes with a gracious offer of salvation (4:28–29). His ministry enrages the scribes and Pharisees (6:11), and Jesus complains that "this generation" is fickle (7:31–35), faithless, and perverse (9:41). Nevertheless, there are disciples who leave everything to follow him (5:11), and from these disciples he chooses twelve apostles (6:13) whom he sends to proclaim the good news of the kingdom to Israel (9:1–6). These apostles are destined to be the eschatological rulers of a restored Israel (22:28–30).[29] Therefore, Jesus reveals the mysteries of the kingdom of God to them and his disciples (8:10). Although many people respond positively to Jesus during the period of his Galilean ministry, not all of Israel will receive him.

Great crowds follow Jesus as he journeys to Jerusalem (12:1; 14:25), but it soon becomes apparent that Israel has not repented. In Jesus' view, the present generation is an evil generation (11:29), and he calls the people of this generation "hypocrites" (12:56) for not repenting at his preaching (13:1–9). He warns those in the crowds that follow him that there will be a great reversal and they are in danger of being excluded from the messianic banquet (13:22–30). Therefore as he journeys to Jerusalem, he cautions his disciples about the hypocrisy of the Pharisees (12:1), and he tells them that he will be a cause of division. Households will be divided because of him (12:49–53). In a word, Jesus' journey to Jerusalem is a period of conflict with Israel, a time when it becomes apparent that even though great crowds follow him, not all of the people in these crowds have repented at his preaching.

During the period of Jesus' journey to Jerusalem (9:51–19:44), Israel's leaders intensify their opposition to him. He denounces the Pharisees and scholars of the law for their hypocrisy (11:37–52), and in turn they act with hostility toward him and plot against him (11:53–54). As he journeys to Jerusalem,

28. Note, however, that in 4:44 Luke says that Jesus preached in the synagogues of Judea.
29. See Jervell, "The Twelve on Israel's Thrones: Luke's Understanding of the Apostolate," *Luke and the People of God*, 75–112.

therefore, Jesus pronounces a lament over the city, predicting that its house will be abandoned (13:34–35). As he approaches the city, he weeps because it has not recognized the time of its visitation (19:41–44).

Luke portrays the period of Jesus' ministry in Jerusalem (19:45–21:38) as a time when the Messiah takes possession of his Father's house (see 2:49), the temple, in order to teach God's people. At the beginning (19:47–48) and at the end (21:37–38) of Jesus' temple ministry, Luke notes that Jesus taught the people every day in the temple, much to the displeasure of Israel's leaders. Alarmed by Jesus' teaching ministry, the religious leaders ask him by what authority he does these things (20:2).[30] Although he refuses to answer their question (since they will not answer his question about John the Baptist), he tells them the parable of the tenant farmers (20:9–19), which implicitly identifies them as those who have rejected the one whom God has chosen to be the "cornerstone." He also warns, "Everyone who falls on that stone will be broken to pieces; and it will crush anyone on whom it falls" (20:18). Although the people are "spellbound" (19:48) by Jesus' teaching and gather early each morning to listen to him (21:38), the city does not recognize that his temple ministry is a time of divine visitation (19:44). For this reason the city and its temple will be destroyed (21:5–6, 20–24).

As a result of Jesus' temple ministry, the religious leaders look for a way to put him to death; for they understand all too well that his temple ministry is an implicit claim to messiahship. When he stands before Israel's leadership, therefore, the central issue is whether he is the Messiah (22:66–67). When the religious leaders bring him to Pilate, their main accusation is that he has perverted the nation by forbidding the people to pay taxes and claiming that he is the Messiah (23:2).[31] For Luke, then, the central issue is Jesus' teaching, which began in Galilee, continued during the period of his great journey to Jerusalem, and came to a climax in Jerusalem.[32] By that teaching he has claimed messianic authority, thereby threatening the authority of Israel's religious leaders. Though he is convinced of Jesus' innocence, Pilate hands him over to the chief priests, the leaders, and the people (23:13–25), and Jesus is put to death. Despite this negative portrayal of the people and their leaders, after Jesus dies Luke notes that the crowds who had gathered to watch the spectacle returned home "beating their breasts" (23:48), thereby suggesting that a portion of Israel has begun to repent.

Luke's understanding of Israel within the Gospel can be summarized in this way. Although Israel is God's elect people, the appearance of the Messiah has brought about a division within this people. On the one hand, Jesus' disciples

---

30. Their question does not refer simply to the cleansing of the temple, which Luke recounts in an abbreviated form in 19:45, but to Jesus' teaching ministry, since Luke notes that they ask the question when he is teaching in the temple area (20:1).

31. Luke presents this as one charge, perverting the nation, which is then specified in two ways: preventing the people from paying taxes and claiming that he is the Messiah.

32. This teaching, of course, is his good news about the kingdom.

believe that he is the Messiah, and they now form the nucleus of a restored Israel that will emerge as the church after his resurrection, even though they failed to remain faithful at the critical moment. On the other hand, the vast majority of people have finally been swayed by their leaders to reject Jesus,[33] though many of them will repent and join the community of believers when the apostles witness to the resurrection in Acts.

Israel during the Time of the Church

The Acts of the Apostles begins with the risen Lord commissioning his disciples to be his witnesses "in Jerusalem, in all Judea and Samaria, and to the ends of the earth" (1:8). This commission structures the narrative that follows so that the church's witness begins in Jerusalem (2:1–5:42), moves beyond the city to the regions of Judea and Samaria (6:1–9:43), and then goes to the ends of the earth (10:1–28:31).[34]

The witness of the church in Jerusalem provides Israel with a renewed offer of salvation to which thousands of the city's inhabitants respond by repenting and accepting baptism in Jesus' name (2:37, 41, 47; 4:4; 5:14). As a result of these mass conversions, James will boast to Paul, "You see, brother, how many thousands of believers there are among the Jews, and they are all zealous for the law" (21:20). The purpose of these conversions in the opening chapters of Acts (2–5) is to show that the community of believers—the church—is that portion of Israel that has repented of its role in the Messiah's death.[35] Consequently, it has become a reestablished Israel, with the apostles as its rulers. This community of believers, which continues to frequent the temple and to observe the law, is not a separate or different entity from historical Israel, even though it leads a distinctive communal life (2:42–47; 4:32–37). It is the messianic community of the last days, God's eschatological community, a reestablished Israel, God's *ekklēsia*.

Although the church experiences initial success among the Jewish inhabitants of Jerusalem, Israel's religious leaders oppose the apostles just as they opposed Jesus during the period of his temple ministry.[36] They refuse to accept the apostles' witness that Jesus has been raised. They are fearful that just as

---

33. This is a literary statement of how Luke perceives the matter. It is not necessarily an accurate historical statement of what happened.

34. See the more detailed outline of Acts in Gerhard Krodel, *Acts* (Proclamation Commentaries; Philadelphia: Fortress, 1981), 8–9.

35. A constant element of the speeches of Acts is to accuse the people and/or their leaders for their role in the Messiah's death. One must be careful in interpreting this "theological" theme, which can give the mistaken impression that all the inhabitants consented to Jesus' death.

36. Just as Jesus carried out a ministry within Jerusalem's temple calling Israel to repentance at the end of the Gospel, so the apostles carry out a ministry within Jerusalem's temple calling Israel to repentance toward the beginning of Acts.

Jesus' temple ministry captivated the people and led them astray, so the preaching of the apostles in the temple area will do the same. In effect, the opposition of the religious leaders becomes a struggle over the leadership of Israel, and there is a division within the people. Those who accept the witness of the apostles are incorporated into a restored Israel that is the church, whereas those who align themselves with the religious leaders remain part of what Peter calls "this corrupt generation" (2:40).

A decisive turn of events occurs with the martyrdom of Stephen (chap. 7). The "Jerusalem springtime" described in Acts 2–5 comes to an end, and the church faces a severe persecution in the Holy City. This persecution, however, paradoxically contributes to the spread of the Word in Judea and Samaria, where those who had been scattered by the persecution begin to preach the Word (8:1), thereby fulfilling the risen Lord's commission to be his witnesses to Judea and Samaria (see 1:8).

The conversion of Cornelius (10:1–48) and the descent of the Holy Spirit upon him and his household is the Pentecost of the Gentiles (see 10:44–48), and it inaugurates the witness to the ends of the earth. From this point on the church begins its witness to the Gentiles,[37] especially through the preaching of Paul. This is not to say that Paul preaches only to Gentiles. In most instances he begins his preaching in the synagogues of the Diaspora, where he can be assured of an audience composed of Jews as well as of God-fearing Gentiles. Thus Jews will continue to hear the Word (13:16; 14:1; 17:1, 10; 18:4; 19:8) and many will believe, but the days of the mass conversions, as described in Acts 2–5, have ended. Now there is regular Jewish opposition to Paul's preaching, and on three occasions (at Antioch of Pisidia, 13:46–47; at Corinth, 18:6; and at Rome, 28:28) he warns the Jews who oppose him that he will go to the Gentiles. Despite these warnings, Paul continues to preach in synagogue after synagogue. The division of Israel that resulted from the witness of the apostles in Jerusalem is repeated in the Diaspora (14:4). Although some Jews continue to respond positively (17:11–12), others do not (17:4–9). The witness of the church that Jesus has been raised from the dead and enthroned as God's Messiah has divided Israel.

The Church and Israel

Luke employs a variety of terms for the community of those who accept Jesus as the enthroned Messiah. Those who are converted and believe are called "those who believe" (2:44; 4:4, 32; 5:14; 11:17; 15:5, 11; 21:20; 22:19). They

---

37. In most instances the gospel is preached to Gentiles who have attached themselves to the synagogue, most likely as "God-fearers." Such Gentiles were sympathetic toward Judaism but had not yet become converts to it. Cornelius is the prime example of such a God-fearer.

form a new family and so are called *adelphoi* (1:15, 16; 6:3; 9:30; 11:1, 29; 12:17; 15:7, 13, 22, 23; 21:17, 20). They are disciples (6:1, 2, 7; 9:1, 26). They belong to a "way" of salvation (9:2; 22:4; 24:14, 22). They are the "saints" or the "holy ones" who have been set aside and consecrated for service (9:13; 26:10). And of course, they belong to a community that Luke calls the "church" (*ekklēsia*, 5:11; 8:1, 3; 9:31; 11:22; 12:1, 5; 15:4, 22; 18:22).[38] Although Luke identifies the community in these different ways, he does not present the church as a new people who supplant the people of Israel. Brought into existence by the creative power of God's Spirit at Pentecost, the community of the church has its origin in the people of Israel. This is why it attaches itself to the temple and continues to practice circumcision and the law, though it will eventually dispense its Gentile members from the Mosaic law (15:1–29). The community of believers, the church, is and remains Israel, albeit repentant and restored. Those Jews who refuse to believe Jesus is the Messiah remain part of historical Israel, but in Luke's view they are part of a corrupt generation that was complicit in the death of the Messiah (2:40). They have become stubborn and recalcitrant (28:25–27). They have not heeded the prophet of whom Moses spoke (Deut. 18:15), "The Lord your God will raise up for you from your own people a prophet like me. You must listen to whatever he tells you. And it will be that everyone who does not listen to that prophet will be utterly rooted out of the people" (Acts 3:22–23; see also 7:37). They have become a "stiff-necked people, uncircumcised in heart and ears . . . forever opposing the Holy Spirit," as did their ancestors (7:51).

Given the long history of anti-Jewish sentiment among many Christians, Luke's judgment on Israel is a frightful indictment. Luke–Acts places a heavy burden of responsibility on the inhabitants of Jerusalem and their leaders for the death of Jesus (2:23; 3:13–14; 4:10; 5:30; 7:52; 10:39; 13:27–29) that goes beyond the historical evidence. Although certain Jews were complicit in the death of Jesus, it is historically implausible that *all* the inhabitants of Jerusalem or *all* of their leaders were. In this regard, one needs to say quite clearly that Luke claims too much. A purely Lukan perspective makes it difficult for Christians to appreciate the faithfulness and piety of generations of Jewish people in the period after the New Testament. A more fruitful approach to Lukan theology would be to reappropriate his understanding of the church as a restored and repentant Israel. Viewed in this way, the church is not a "new Israel" that replaces Israel. It is and remains Israel understood as God's covenant people. As for that portion of Israel that continues to exist today without believing in Jesus as the Messiah, the Lukan view needs to be balanced by what Paul writes in Romans 9–11. God has not rejected his people (Rom. 11:1), "for the gifts and the calling of God are irrevocable" (11:29).

---

38. George, "Israël," 110–11.

THE MORAL LIFE WITHIN
THE MESSIANIC COMMUNITY

Entrance into the church, the community of believers who proclaim that Jesus is Messiah and Lord, requires repentance and conversion.[39] Those who repent and believe are baptized in the name of Jesus and live within a community that waits for the consummation of all things. As members of a restored Israel, their lives are to be characterized by an ethic rooted in the law and the prophets and brought to perfection in the life and teaching of the Messiah. Luke presents this moral teaching in two ways: through the ministry and teaching of Jesus, and through the life and preaching of the early church. In both cases this teaching begins with a call to repentance. Those who repent become part of a new community in which they experience the forgiveness of sins.

Luke does not offer the profound and insightful analysis of the human condition that characterizes the theology of Paul and John. He does not portray sin as a power that makes it impossible for human beings to do the law as does Paul, nor does he view the human condition in the dualistic terms of light and darkness, truth and falsehood, life and death, in the way that the Fourth Evangelist does.[40] Without offering a profound analysis of the human condition, Luke assumes the need for forgiveness. This need for forgiveness is apparent at the dawn of the messianic age, during Jesus' ministry, as well as after his death and resurrection.

The Need to Repent

As the messianic era dawns, John the Baptist preaches "a baptism of repentance for the forgiveness of sins" (Luke 3:3) in order to prepare Israel for the Messiah's advent. John assumes that the crowds that come to be baptized are in profound need of repentance, calling them a "brood of vipers" (3:7).[41] When the people ask what they should do to repent (3:10, 12, 14), John gives concrete instructions that, in one way or another, have to do with the proper use of possessions and money.

---

39. See the important study by George, "La conversion," *Études sur l'oeuvre de Luc,* 351–68. On the moral life in Luke–Acts, see Rudolf Schnackenburg, *Die sittliche Botschaft des Neuen Testaments* (2 vols., HTKNT Sup 1–2; Freiburg: Herder, 1986–88), 2:134–47; Wolfgang Schrage, *The Ethics of the New Testament* (Philadelphia: Fortress, 1988), 152–61; Siegfried Schulz, *Neutestamentliche Ethik* (Zurich: Theologischer Verlag), 466–84.

40. Although there are some contrasts between light and darkness in Luke–Acts, this is not a persistent theme. Two examples are the canticle of Zechariah, "to give light to those who sit in darkness and in the shadow of death" (Luke 1:79), and Paul's words in Acts 26:18, "to open their eyes so that they may turn from darkness to light and from the power of Satan to God, so that they may receive forgiveness of sins and a place among those who are sanctified by faith in me."

41. Note that the parallel text of Matthew (3:7) calls the Pharisees and Sadducees a brood of vipers.

In the Lukan Gospel, Jesus' ministry begins with the proclamation of a year of jubilee, "the year of the Lord's favor" (4:19), rather than with a call to repent, as is the case in the Gospels of Matthew (4:17) and Mark (1:15). This is not to say that repentance plays a secondary role in the Lukan Gospel. Immediately after his inaugural sermon, Jesus insists that he must proclaim the good news of the kingdom to other towns (Luke 4:43). But by beginning with Jesus' inaugural sermon, Luke emphasizes that Jesus' proclamation of the kingdom and his call to repentance are a gracious offer of salvation. During this "year of favor" Jesus forgives, dines with, and welcomes sinners (5:20, 27–32; 7:36–50). When the religious leaders question his behavior, he replies, "I have come to call not the righteous but sinners to repentance" (5:32). Through Jesus' gracious presence, people become aware of their sinfulness (5:8).

After his ministry in Galilee, as he journeys to Jerusalem, Jesus reproaches the Galilean cities that did not repent (10:13–16), and he sternly warns the crowds that follow him that if they do not repent they will perish (13:1–5, 6–9). During this journey he presents some of his most important teaching on forgiveness (the parables of the lost sheep, the lost coin, the lost son; 15:3–32) because the Pharisees and scribes complain that he "welcomes sinners and eats with them" (15:2). When some are convinced that they are righteous and despise others (18:9), Jesus tells the parable of the Pharisee and the tax collector (18:10–14). Then, to the dismay of many, he stays in the house of Zacchaeus, whom the crowds identify as a sinner (19:7). But Jesus responds, "Today salvation has come to this house, because he too is a son of Abraham. For the Son of Man came to seek out and to save the lost" (19:9–10). Thus, even as Jesus warns people of the impending doom they face if they do not repent, he continues to associate with those who are sinners in order to show that in his ministry God's year of favor has arrived.

After his resurrection Jesus commissions his apostles to proclaim repentance and forgiveness of sins in his name to all the nations, beginning in Jerusalem (24:46–47). At Pentecost, when the inhabitants of Jerusalem ask what they must do (Acts 2:37), Peter answers, "Repent, and be baptized every one of you in the name of Jesus Christ so that your sins may be forgiven; and you will receive the gift of the Holy Spirit" (2:38). Peter's response outlines the basic structure of the moral life for the new community. Those who wish to enter this community must first repent. In the case of the inhabitants of Jerusalem, they must believe in the one whom they rejected as the Messiah and be baptized into his name, an action that will result in the forgiveness of their sins and the gift of the Spirit. Peter makes a similar demand in the temple precincts, but this time he notes that the gift of their repentance will lead to "the time of universal restoration that God announced long ago through his holy prophets" (3:21). He warns that if the people do not repent they will be rejecting the prophet that Moses foretold and "be utterly rooted out of the people" (Acts 3:23; see Deut. 18:15–20).

When the gospel is preached beyond Jerusalem, even Gentiles repent, believe, accept baptism, and receive the Spirit. See the accounts of the Ethiopian eunuch (Acts 8:26–40), the household of Cornelius (10:1–48), the jailer at Philippi (16:30–34), and Paul's preaching at Athens (17:22–34). For Gentiles repentance means turning to "the living God" (14:15) because God "has fixed a day on which he will have the world judged in righteousness by a man whom he has appointed" (17:31). As for Diaspora Jews and God-fearers who already believe in this living God, they must turn to Jesus as the Messiah.[42] As Paul looks back on his missionary career, he reminds the elders of Ephesus, "I did not shrink from doing anything helpful, proclaiming the message to you and teaching you publicly and from house to house, as I testified to both Jews and Greeks about repentance toward God and faith toward our Lord Jesus" (20:20–21). In his defense before Agrippa, he says that he "declared first to those in Damascus, then in Jerusalem and throughout the countryside of Judea, and also to the Gentiles, that they should repent and turn to God and do deeds consistent with repentance" (26:20); for the one who called him commissioned him "to open their eyes so that they may turn from darkness to light and from the power of Satan to God, so that they may receive forgiveness of sins and a place among those who are sanctified by faith in me" (26:18).

To summarize, in Luke–Acts the moral life begins with repentance that leads to faith, baptism, and a new life defined by the gift of the Spirit.

A Community of Disciples

As Jesus calls Israel to repentance because the kingdom of God is at hand, he gathers disciples who leave everything to follow him (Luke 5:1–11, 27). The conditions he imposes upon his disciples are extreme since there is nothing more urgent than preaching the kingdom of God, not even one's family (9:59–62). He warns the crowds that follow him that if they wish to be his disciples they must calculate the cost of following him. Unless they are willing to renounce all of their possessions, they cannot be his disciples (14:25–33).

This community of disciples, at the center of which are the twelve apostles (6:12–16), forms the nucleus of a repentant and restored Israel that will emerge as the church in Acts, though its members will still be called disciples. The teaching with which Jesus provides his disciples is the foundation for the moral life they will live in this community of like-minded disciples.

The core of Jesus' moral teaching is the Sermon on the Plain (6:20–49), the Lukan counterpart to the Matthean Sermon on the Mount. But whereas the

---

42. Luke does not hold Jews in the Diaspora responsible for the death of Jesus. Those who are responsible, in his view, are the inhabitants of Jerusalem and their leaders.

Sermon on the Mount presents Jesus' teaching as the fulfillment of the law and the prophets and instructs disciples how to practice the righteousness of the kingdom, the Sermon on the Plain makes no reference to the law and the prophets, or to the righteousness of the kingdom. Its central theme is the need for Jesus' disciples to love their enemies (6:27–36). In developing this teaching, Jesus disavows the principle of reciprocity; that is, his disciples should not love others because others will love them in return, since even those who are evil act in this way. Disciples must love others without expecting anything in return. At the heart of Jesus' ethic, then, is a love that extends to one's enemy and refuses to retaliate when injured.

But if Jesus revokes the principle of reciprocity in his teaching on love, he explicitly invokes it in his warning not to judge others. He teaches his disciples that if they do not judge they will not be judged, if they do not condemn they will not be condemned, and if they forgive they will be forgiven (6:37–38). It is imperative then that they pay attention to their own faults before correcting the faults of others (6:39–42).

As in the Sermon on the Mount, Jesus admonishes his disciples to produce good fruit and to act upon his words; otherwise they will be swept away by God's judgment (6:43–49). As in the Matthean Gospel, the moral life is a matter of doing good. The key to understanding the Lukan sermon, however, is found in the initial woes and beatitudes that preface it (6:20–26). Once more, the difference between Matthew and Luke is significant. Whereas the Matthean beatitudes are capable of being read as ethical imperatives inasmuch as they present a behavior or attitude that can be emulated ("blessed are the meek"), the Lukan beatitudes describe a condition in which people already find themselves ("Blessed are you who are poor"). They are a salvation-historical expression of the grace that the kingdom of God is already effecting, namely, a reversal of fortunes in favor of the poor, the hungry, the weeping, and those despised on account of the Son of Man. God has come to the assistance of such people and is effecting a reversal of fortunes on their behalf, not because of anything they have done but because they are in need of salvation. Because of this imminent reversal of fortunes, disciples must practice a love that does not expect anything in return. In this way they will be merciful, as is their heavenly Father (6:36).

In addition to the Sermon on the Plain, Luke provides an extensive body of teaching on the life of discipleship in the section of his Gospel devoted to Jesus' journey to Jerusalem (9:51–19:44). Throughout the journey, Jesus frequently converses with his disciples, the crowds, and the religious leaders so that it is necessary for Luke to remind his readers that Jesus is actually on a journey to Jerusalem (9:51; 10:38; 13:22; 18:31; 19:11, 28). Within this section, Luke incorporates much of his special material ("L"), as well as material from "Q" that Matthew places in the Sermon on the Mount. The result is a kind of "catechism" or "handbook" for disciples on topics such as prayer (11:1–13), the danger of hypocrisy (11:37–54), discipleship (14:25–33; 17:1–10), conversion (13:1–9), the need for humility in light of the coming reversal of fortunes (14:7–14, 15–24), vigilance (12:35–48), forgiveness (15:3–32), and the parousia (17:22–37; 19:11–27). Jesus' most distinctive teaching, however, deals with the proper use of possessions.

He warns the crowds of the danger of greed (12:13–15, 16–21) and instructs his disciples to trust in God rather than wealth (12:22–34). If they have possessions, they are to use them wisely in order to enter the kingdom (16:1–13). They are not to be like the Pharisees, whom Luke characterizes as lovers of money (16:14), nor like the rich man who neglected the needs of the poor (16:19–31). Warning his disciples of the dangers of riches, he says that it is easier for a camel to pass through the eye of a needle than for a rich person to enter into the kingdom of God (18:18–30). In effect, Luke makes the correct use of possessions a measure of discipleship. Disciples must use their possessions to relieve the needs of others, otherwise they will be swept away in the great reversal that the inbreaking kingdom is effecting. Because of the demands of the kingdom, disciples must leave everything to follow Jesus (14:33), something Peter and his fellow apostles have already done (18:28).

In the period after the resurrection, the correct use of possessions continues to play a central role in the life of disciples, who now live within the community of the church. In his descriptions of the Jerusalem community (Acts 2:42–47; 4:32–35) Luke notes, "All who believed were together and had all things in common; they would sell their possessions and goods and distribute the proceeds to all, as any had need" (2:44). Later he writes, "Now the whole group of those who believed were of one heart and soul, and no one claimed private ownership of any possessions, but everything they owned was held in common" (4:32). Luke presents Barnabas as an example of someone who sold his property and laid the proceeds at the feet of the apostles (4:36–37), whereas Ananias and Sapphira fail as disciples because they secretly withhold from the apostles some of the proceeds of their sale (5:1–11).

Although there are numerous speeches in Acts, they say little about the moral life apart from the need to repent, believe, and be baptized. Luke supposes that disciples will live in community according to Jesus' teaching. Moreover, even though the Spirit plays a major role in guiding the church, Luke does not develop the relationship between the Spirit and the moral life in the way Paul does, namely, that it is impossible to live the moral life apart from life in the Spirit. Luke may have believed that the Spirit, who guides and directs the church, is also of assistance to the moral life of the believers, but he never develops this teaching. Luke never considers the anthropological and soteriological issues that Paul and John do.

The Law in Luke–Acts

Luke's understanding of the law stands somewhere between Matthew's insistence that Jesus has come to fulfill the law and the prophets (5:17) and Paul's assertion that Christ is the end of the law (Rom. 10:4). Luke does not present Jesus' teaching in terms of a greater righteousness as does Matthew, nor does he argue against justification by works as does Paul. The law continues to function as a moral guide within the church, but its observance is not the distinguishing mark of the moral life.

The only point at which Luke presents the law in a somewhat negative light is in Peter's comment at the Jerusalem conference, "Now therefore why are you putting God to the test by placing on the neck of the disciples a yoke that neither our ancestors nor we have been able to bear?" (Acts 15:10). In all other instances, Luke portrays the law in a positive manner. The infancy narrative, for example, presents Zechariah and Elizabeth as righteous Israelites who observe all the commandments of the law (Luke 1:6), as do Jesus' parents (2:22, 27, 41). Simeon is righteous and devout (2:25), and the Messiah is circumcised (2:21).[43]

Although Jesus' behavior on the Sabbath is a source of controversy, he never criticizes the Sabbath or the law. He regularly attends the synagogue service (4:16), and when a lawyer inquires what he must do to inherit eternal life, Jesus asks what is written in the law. When the lawyer summarizes the law as love of God and love of neighbor, Jesus replies, "You have given the right answer; do this, and you will live" (10:28). Later, a ruler asks him the same question (18:18), and Jesus answers, "You know the commandments: 'You shall not commit adultery; You shall not murder; You shall not steal; You shall not bear false witness; Honor your father and mother'" (18:20). In telling the ruler that he is still deficient in one area, Jesus is not criticizing the law but summoning the ruler to follow him as his disciple.[44]

Luke makes a salvation-historical distinction between the time of the law and the prophets and the preaching of the kingdom of God, which is marked by the preaching of John the Baptist. John was the last and greatest of the prophets who prepared for the coming of the Messiah, but the least in the kingdom of God is greater than John (7:28; 16:16). The good news of the kingdom, however, does not mean the end of the law, as Jesus notes when he says, "But it is easier for heaven and earth to pass away, than for one stroke of a letter in the

43. See the article by Jacob Jervell, "The Circumcised Messiah," *The Unknown Paul: Essays on Luke–Acts and Early Christian History* (Minneapolis: Augsburg, 1984), 138–45.

44. Note that Luke omits the controversy between Jesus and the Pharisees found in Mark 7:1–23, in which the Markan narrator notes that Jesus declared all foods clean (Mark 7:19), thereby abolishing the food laws for Jew as well as Gentile. It is not until Acts that the question of the food laws is addressed, first in the conversion of the household of Cornelius (10:15) and then at the Jerusalem conference (15:23–29).

law to be dropped" (16:17). The preaching of the kingdom inaugurates a new period in which the commandments of the law remain in force, and in which Jesus presents Israel with a moral teaching on love that requires disciples to do even more than the law commands.

In Acts Luke portrays the Jerusalem church as law-observant (21:20). Its members gather in the temple area, and they enjoy the esteem of the people (5:13). In Luke's view, the accusations that Stephen and Paul speak against the law and the temple are false, and Paul's defense speeches in the final part of Acts show that even though he believes that Jesus is the Messiah, Paul remains a loyal Jew who embraces everything found in the law and the prophets. The only discernible difference between Paul and the Pharisees is that whereas they hope for the general resurrection of the dead, he believes that this resurrection has already begun in the resurrection of Israel's Messiah.

The law is not problematic for Luke in the way that it is for Paul; Luke is aware of the Pauline teaching of justification by faith, though he does not express it as sharply as does Paul. In the synagogue of Antioch of Pisidia the Lukan Paul says, "Let it be known to you therefore, my brothers, that through this man forgiveness of sins is proclaimed to you; by this Jesus everyone who believes is set free from all those sins from which you could not be freed by the law of Moses" (13:38–39). At the Jerusalem conference Peter says, "We believe that we will be saved through the grace of the Lord Jesus, just as they will" (15:11).[45] These are the only two references to Paul's teaching on justification in Acts, and they hardly have the theological force and depth of Paul's extended teaching in Romans and Galatians. But they do attest to Luke's understanding that there is no salvation apart from Christ, something that Luke clearly affirms through Peter's words, "There is salvation in no one else, for there is no other name under heaven given among mortals by which we must be saved" (4:12). For Luke the moral prescriptions of the law are in force for Gentile as well as Jewish believers, though Gentiles are not obligated by the ritual prescriptions of the law. The ability of people to do the law is not the problem for Luke that it is for Paul because Luke does not analyze the human predicament in the way Paul does. But he is as aware as they are that there is no salvation apart from Christ.

The moral life for Luke can be summarized in this way. The appearance of the Messiah and his resurrection require people to repent, to be baptized, to believe in Jesus as the Messiah, and to live in a community of like-minded believers. Believers will follow the moral prescriptions of the law they have inherited from Israel and live a life of discipleship distinguished by the proper use of possessions and a love that extends even to their enemies.

---

45. Note that in v. 9 Peter even speaks of God cleansing the hearts of the Gentiles by faith.

HOPE WITHIN THE COMMUNITY OF DISCIPLES

Believers live in hope and expectation that the salvation they already experience will be brought to completion.[46] Luke–Acts expresses this hope for ultimate redemption in several ways: the final manifestation of the kingdom of
God, the coming of the Son of Man; the resurrection of the dead; the last judgment; and the restoration of all things. Jesus' teaching about the kingdom, the
coming of the Son of Man, and the final judgment are the principal ways
through which Luke develops this eschatological hope in the Gospel, whereas
in Acts he shifts the focus to the return of the Messiah, the general resurrection of the dead, and the restoration of all things. This shift is not surprising
since the resurrection of the Messiah is the beginning of the general resurrection of the dead, even if there is an extended period of time between these two
events. Although Luke never explicitly connects all the elements noted above
into an all-embracing eschatological scenario, a "composite view" of his eschatology could be expressed in this way. Jesus, the Son of Man, will return as the
enthroned Messiah. His coming will signal the resurrection of the dead, the
appearance of the kingdom of God in power, final judgment, and the restoration of all things. Those judged worthy of eternal life will enter into the kingdom, whereas those judged unworthy will be punished. In addition to this
scenario of final redemption, Luke–Acts describes the salvation and punishment of individuals immediately after death, without trying to harmonize the
latter scenario with the former.

The Final Appearance of God's Rule

Like the other Synoptic evangelists, Luke understands that the kingdom of
God is making its appearance in Jesus' ministry and that Jesus' followers
already experience the kingdom and the salvation it brings. For example, when
Luke describes Jesus as "proclaiming the good news" (*euangelizō*, 4:18; 7:22;
20:1), and when Luke links the proclamation of this good news with the kingdom (4:43; 8:1; 16:16), he suggests that the good news of the kingdom is an
initial, albeit incomplete, experience of salvation. For Luke, the salvation-
historical period of the law and the prophets continues up to and includes the
preaching of John the Baptist, whereas the salvation-historical period of the
kingdom of God begins with Jesus' preaching of the kingdom and extends into
the period of the church (16:16; see also 7:28).[47] When Jesus sends the seventy
on mission, they are to proclaim that "the kingdom of God has come near

46. On the eschatology of Luke, see the important study of George, "L'eschatologie," *Études
sur l'oeuvre de Luc*, 321–47, to which this section is indebted.
47. There is no need for a third period of salvation history, the time of the church, such as proposed by Hans Conzelmann, *The Theology of St. Luke* (New York: Harper & Row, 1961).

(*ēngiken*)" (10:9; see also 10:11). He then tells the crowds that his exorcisms are signs that the kingdom of God has come upon them (*ephthasen*, 11:20). When the Pharisees ask when the kingdom of God will come, he responds, "The kingdom of God is not coming with things that can be observed; nor will they say, 'Look, here it is!' or 'There it is!' For, in fact, the kingdom of God is among you (*entos hymōn estin*)" (17:20–21). In a word, the kingdom of God is already present, albeit in a hidden way, in Jesus' ministry, as the parables of the yeast and the mustard seed attest (13:18–21).

This hidden presence of the kingdom is an essential building block of Luke's eschatology. For if the kingdom of God has made its appearance in Jesus' ministry, then God will surely bring it to fulfillment. At one point Jesus describes the final manifestation of the kingdom as a great banquet at which people from every corner of the earth will gather to eat with the patriarchs and prophets but from which many who expect to be included will be excluded because God's rule is effecting a reversal of fortunes (13:22–30; 14:15–24). On the eve of his death, Jesus anticipates his participation in this banquet (22:16–18).

Although some thought that the kingdom would appear suddenly during his Jerusalem ministry (19:11), Jesus' parable of the coins (19:12–27) cautions that the kingdom will not appear immediately. For, just as the nobleman of the parable returns only *after* he has obtained kingship (19:12–15), so the kingdom will not be inaugurated until Jesus returns after being enthroned as Messiah. It is not surprising, then, that after his resurrection Jesus continues to teach his apostles about the kingdom of God (Acts 1:3) and that they ask if now is the time when he will restore the kingdom to Israel (Acts 1:6). The kingdom of God, however, will not appear in its final form until "the Son of Man" returns (Luke 21:31). In the Gospel Jesus promises that some of his contemporaries will see the kingdom before they die (Luke 9:27), but after his resurrection he also cautions his apostles that it is not for them to know "the times or periods that the Father has set by his own authority" (Acts 1:7). So the church continues to wait for and to preach the coming of the kingdom throughout Acts (8:12; 14:22; 19:8; 28:23). In the final scene of Acts, Paul is still "proclaiming the kingdom of God and teaching about the Lord Jesus Christ" (28:31). The question of when the kingdom of God will come is ultimately related to the question of the coming of the Son of Man.

The Day of the Son of Man

As in the other Synoptic Gospels, the return of Jesus as the Son of Man plays an important role in Luke's eschatology. The Son of Man will be ashamed of those who are ashamed of him and of his words "when he comes in his glory and the glory of the Father and of the holy angels" (Luke 9:26; see Matt. 16:27; Mark 8:38). Conversely, those who acknowledge Jesus before others, "the Son of Man also will acknowledge before the angels of God" (Luke 12:8). At the end of the ages, after a series of unmistakable cosmic signs, "People will faint from fear and foreboding of what is coming upon the world, for the powers of the heavens will be shaken. Then they will see 'the Son of Man coming in a cloud' with power and great glory" (21:26–27). Although Jesus speaks in the third person about the Son of Man, as though the Son of Man were an eschatological figure for whom he waits, Jesus is referring to himself as the one who must suffer and die before returning at the end of the ages.

Although the total Gospel narrative indicates that the coming of the Son of Man and the final appearance of the kingdom of God are related to each other, the evangelists rarely explain that relation. On two occasions, however, Luke brings the two concepts together. In the first, immediately after Jesus warns that the Son of Man will be ashamed of those who are ashamed of him *when he comes in his glory* (9:26), he notes, "But truly I tell you, there are some standing here who will not taste death before they see *the kingdom of God*" (9:27), thereby suggesting that the coming of the Son of Man and the appearance of the kingdom are interrelated. The second occasion is more explicit. After describing the coming of the Son of Man "with power and great glory" (21:27), Jesus says, "When you see these things taking place, you know that the kingdom of God is near" (21:31).[48] The appearance of the Son of Man, then, will result in the final manifestation of the kingdom of God. But when will the Son of Man come?

Like the other Synoptic evangelists, Luke reports Jesus' final discourse, which is occasioned by his prediction that the temple will be destroyed (21:5–6). When asked when this will happen, Jesus explains what will occur before the city's destruction (the appearance of false messiahs, wars, insurrections, famines, plagues, and the persecution of his disciples; 21:8–19). Then he describes the destruction of Jerusalem (21:20–24), which "will be trampled on by the Gentiles, until the times of the Gentiles are fulfilled" (21:24). Finally, he predicts the coming of the Son of Man (21:25–28). But whereas Mark explains that the Son of Man will appear "after that suffering" (13:24; *meta tēn thlipsin ekeinēn*), thereby drawing a relationship between the destruction of Jerusalem and the coming of the Son of Man, Luke does not. Writing fifteen to twenty years after the city's demise, he no longer views its destruction by the Romans as the immediate prelude to the coming of the Son of Man. The time between Jerusalem's destruction and the coming of the Son of Man is "the times of the Gentiles" (Luke 21:24), that period when the church must bring its witness of the resurrection to the ends of the earth. When this period is completed, the Son of Man will return.

---

48. George ("L'eschatologie," 324) notes that Luke is the only evangelist to mention the kingdom of God in his apocalyptic discourse.

By breaking the connection between the destruction of Jerusalem and the coming of the Son of Man, and by introducing the time of the Gentiles, Luke makes sense of the apparent "delay of the parousia" by insisting upon a period during which the church must preach to the Gentiles before the Son of Man comes. The introduction of this period, however, does not mean that Luke no longer has a lively hope for the Lord's return, for he continues to report Jesus' words, "Truly I tell you, this generation will not pass away until all things have taken place" (21:32). Taken literally, this means that the events described in chapter 21 will occur before the last of Jesus' contemporaries dies.

For Luke, however, it is more important to be vigilant than to inquire when these things will take place since the day of the Son of Man will come suddenly and unexpectedly. Disciples must be like faithful and vigilant servants because the Son of Man will come at an hour they do not expect (12:35–40). Disciples who think that the coming of their master has been delayed will be punished since he will come unexpectedly (12:41–48). In what is sometimes called Luke's "small apocalypse" (17:22–37), Jesus does not announce any signs for discerning the coming of the Son of Man, but he does warn his disciples that the day of the Son of Man will be revealed suddenly and unexpectedly. Immediately following this discourse about the day of the Son of Man, Luke recounts the parable of the persistent widow (18:1–8), at the end of which Jesus remarks, "And will not God grant justice to his chosen ones who cry to him day and night? Will he delay long in helping them? I tell you, he will quickly grant justice to them. And yet, when the Son of Man comes, will he find faith on earth?" (18:7–8). Although Luke believes that the time between the Lord's resurrection and parousia will be longer than originally expected, he maintains a lively hope in the coming of the Son of Man, which will occur suddenly and unexpectedly.

The Eschatological Hope of the Early Church

The only reference to the Son of Man in Acts is Stephen's cry at the moment of his martyrdom, "I see the heavens opened and the Son of Man standing at the right hand of God!" (7:56). This text is significant for two reasons. First, it does not speak of the coming of the Son of Man. Rather, Stephen sees the Son of Man *standing* at God's right hand and welcoming him into heaven.[49] Second, it implies that Stephen will be with the Son of Man immediately after his death; he will not have to wait for the parousia. What, then, has happened to the eschatological hope of the Gospel, which is linked with the coming of the Son of Man?

Although Acts does not have the same eschatological urgency as the Gospel, eschatological hope continues to play a vital role in Acts. The community of

---

49. In his comment to the Sanhedrin, Jesus speaks of the enthronement of the Son of Man at the right hand of the power of God (Luke 22:69).

believers is aware that it is living in the "last days" foretold by the prophet Joel since God has poured his Spirit upon them (2:16–21) through the agency of the enthroned Messiah (2:32–33). It understands that Jesus is the enthroned Messiah, "who must remain in heaven until the time of universal restoration that God announced long ago through his holy prophets" (3:21). So Peter tells the household of Cornelius that Jesus "is the one ordained by God as judge of the living and the dead" (10:42). When Paul speaks at Athens he proclaims that God "has fixed a day on which he will have the world judged in righteousness by a man whom he has appointed, and of this he has given assurance to all by raising him from the dead" (17:31). Moreover, at the very outset of Acts, after Jesus is taken up into heaven, the angelic figures reprimand the apostles, "Men of Galilee, why do you stand looking up toward heaven? This Jesus, who has been taken up from you into heaven, will come in the same way as you saw him go into heaven" (Acts 1:11). Hope for the Lord's return remains an important element in the eschatology of Acts, but since Jesus has been enthroned in heaven, and since the time of the Gentiles must be fulfilled, the church's primary task is to witness to the resurrection until the enthroned Messiah returns.

Paul's speeches toward the end of Acts show how this witness to the resurrection becomes an expression of eschatological hope. Affirming that he is a Pharisee, Paul insists that he is on trial "concerning the hope of the resurrection of the dead" (23:6; see also 24:21; 26:6). He believes "that there will be a resurrection of both the righteous and the unrighteous" (24:15). For this reason, just as he warned the Athenians there will be a day of judgment at which the risen Christ will preside (17:31), he discusses "justice, self-control, and the coming judgment" (24:25) with the Roman governor Felix. The foundation for Paul's eschatological teaching on the general resurrection of the dead and the judgment that will attend it is the resurrection of the Messiah; for by being the first to rise from the dead, the Messiah now proclaims light to both Jews and Gentiles (26:23) through those who preach in his name.

The eschatology of Acts can be summarized in this way. The resurrection of the Messiah portends the general resurrection of the dead when all will be judged. The Messiah is presently enthroned in heaven, but when he returns he will effect a long-awaited universal restoration.

The Fate of the Individual after Death

On a few occasions Luke narrates episodes that deal with the fate of the individual after death. For example, Jesus replies to the repentant criminal, "Truly I tell you, today you will be with me in Paradise" (Luke 23:43), and Stephen sees the Son of Man standing at the right hand of God welcoming him into paradise. When teaching his disciples to be courageous in the face of persecution, Jesus says, "Do not fear those who kill the body, and after that can do nothing more. But I will warn you whom to fear: fear him who, after he has killed, has authority to cast into hell. Yes, I tell you, fear him!" (12:4–5). In the parable of the rich fool God says to the rich man, "You fool! This very night your life is being demanded of you. And the things you have prepared, whose will they be?" (12:20). To be sure, both of these texts are hortatory in nature, and it is not their purpose to develop a systematic eschatology, but they do suggest that just as the reward of Stephen and the repentant thief came immediately after death, so punishment will be swift and immediate. The parable of the rich man and Lazarus makes the same point in a more developed manner (16:19–31). The rich man dies and finds himself in Hades, whereas poor Lazarus is already with Abraham (16:23).

All of the texts mentioned above focus on the fate of individuals immediately after death without any consideration of the eschatological scenario developed in conjunction with the kingdom of God, the coming of the Son of Man, and the general resurrection of the dead. In this regard Luke is similar to Paul, who can also envision an immedate union with the Lord after death (2 Cor. 5:1–10; Phil. 1:23), even though his eschatology tends to focus on the parousia and the general resurrection of the dead. Luke's purpose is not to develop an alternate eschatological scenario but to affirm that reward and punishment affect individuals immediately after death as well as at the end of the ages. These two scenarios cannot and need not be harmonized, for each intends to make its own point, namely, (1) that the community of believers will experience final salvation at the coming of the Son of Man, when the kingdom of God will appear and the dead will be raised; and (2) that the individual will experience salvation or punishment immediately after death, even if the final consummation is yet to come.

To summarize, Luke's eschatology is multifaceted and makes use of a variety of images to communicate its message: the kingdom of God, the coming of the Son of Man, and the general resurrection of the dead. But none of this would be possible apart from Luke's overriding conviction that God has raised Jesus from the dead. For, when all is said, Luke's eschatological vision rests on the church's witness to the resurrection.

THE THEOLOGICAL SIGNIFICANCE OF LUKE–ACTS

Although Luke's two-volume work does not manifest the penetrating theological analysis of the Pauline or Johannine writings, it is a remarkable theological achievement for at least two reasons. First, it inscribes the story of Jesus into the story of Israel, thereby providing the New Testament with its most complete account of God's redemptive history. It is Luke–Acts more than any other New Testament writing that narrates the ongoing story of Israel in the life of

Jesus and the church and, from a Christian perspective, brings closure to Israel's redemptive story as narrated in its sacred writings. Second, Luke–Acts functions as a kind of "bridge" within the New Testament. On the one hand, it is a bridge from Jesus to the early church that shows how Jesus became the object of the church's proclamation even as the church continued to proclaim the kingdom of God. Put in contemporary jargon, Luke–Acts explains the movement from the "historical Jesus" to the "Christ of faith." On the other hand, Luke–Acts is a bridge to the epistolary literature of the New Testament, especially the Pauline writings, establishing a narrative and theological framework for the Pauline letters and the writings attributed to Peter, John, and James, whom Paul calls the "pillar apostles" (Gal. 2:9).[50]

Luke's Account of Redemptive History

Luke's account of redemptive history has often been denigrated as an example of "early Catholicism" because it supposedly shifts the emphasis from Christology to ecclesiology and from an eschatology that anticipates an imminent parousia to one that seeks to resolve the problem of the delayed parousia. In this view Luke effectively replaces eschatology with salvation history.

There is, of course, some truth to the charge. Luke's two-volume work is not as theologically charged as the writings of Paul and John in which the new age already penetrates the old. Luke does not (and probably cannot) provide the insightful analysis of the human condition and of the Christ event that John and Paul do. He approaches his task as a religious historian who wants to know how the events of his day are related to Israel's history. To this end, he inscribes the story of Jesus and the church into the story of Israel.

This story of redemptive history is necessarily selective. Luke is the one who has chosen which events to include or exclude, and he is the one who "plots" the story in terms of Israel's repeated rejection of the savior figures sent to it, culminating in the Messiah's death. Other New Testament writers have also inscribed the story of Jesus into the story of Israel. For example, through his genealogy and fulfillment quotations Matthew presents Jesus as the climax of Israel's history, whereas Paul views Christ as Abraham's singular descendant (Gal. 3:16) and as the goal or end of the law (see Rom. 10:4). But no writer of the New Testament presents a more complete account of redemptive history than Luke. This history focuses on Israel's messianic expectations and culminates in the appearance of the Messiah. It continues in the story of the church and will be concluded only when the enthroned Messiah returns to restore all things. It is Luke who reminds New Testament theology that every reading of

---

50. This James is not James the apostle, one of the Twelve, but James the brother of the Lord of whom Paul speaks in Galatians 1–2.

the story of Jesus and the church must be inscribed into the story of Israel. In this regard, his two-volume work is a biblical theology of Jesus and the church.

A Bridge from Jesus to the Church

The Gospels of Matthew and Mark are already proclamations of the church. In recounting the good news that Jesus proclaimed about the kingdom of God, they tell the good news about Jesus, who announced the kingdom of God. Luke–Acts, however, goes further by explicitly reporting the preaching of the early church in the Acts of the Apostles, particularly in the speeches of Peter, Stephen, and Paul. In these speeches the church explicitly witnesses to the resurrection of Jesus and proclaims forgiveness of sins in his name. While the church must continue to preach about the kingdom of God (Acts 28:31), it now makes the resurrection of Jesus the explicit content of its message, affirming that there is salvation in no other name.

The historical question of how Jesus became the Christ of the church's faith is an enduring question for New Testament scholarship. Luke–Acts does not provide a historical answer to this question, but it does offer a theological response rooted in its theology of Christ's resurrection. Jesus became the Christ of faith because God raised him from the dead. The one who proclaimed the good news of the kingdom became the object of the church's good news about the kingdom because God raised him and enthroned him as Lord and Messiah (Acts 2:36). As the enthroned Messiah, Jesus has entered into the kingdom he preached. For this reason when the church proclaims the risen Lord it continues to preach about the kingdom in which Jesus now reigns as the enthroned Messiah.

The death of Jesus plays a prominent role in Acts as well as in the Gospel, but Luke does not focus on its redemptive value to the extent that Paul or Mark does.[51] For Luke the resurrection of Jesus is the decisive event that effects salvation. The resurrection is the "bridge" that explains how Jesus became the Christ of faith and why the church made Jesus the content of its proclamation without abandoning his message of the kingdom of God.

A Bridge to Paul and the Pillar Apostles

The placement of Acts between the Four Gospels and the remaining writings of the New Testament is significant from a canonical perspective. In addition to erecting a bridge from Jesus to the church, this arrangement provides a bridge from the story of the church to the apostolic writings of the New Tes-

---

51. This point should not be exaggerated, however, since Luke does record statements that point to the redemptive value of Christ's death. See Luke 22:20; Acts 20:28.

tament by offering readers of the New Testament a narrative context for reading the letters of Paul, Peter, James, and John.

There are, to be sure, numerous differences between the way in which Luke depicts Paul in his story and how Paul presents himself in his letters. Moreover, many of the letters attributed to Paul in the New Testament may have been written by others in his name (2 Thessalonians, Colossians, Ephesians, and the Pastoral Letters). Nevertheless, Acts does allow those who read Paul's letters (and those attributed to him) to place the great apostle within a narrative that tells the story of the emerging church. To be sure, the story is not always historically accurate, and there are times when the reader will garner more accurate information from Paul's writings. From a canonical and literary perspective, however, it is the story of Acts that enables readers to inscribe Paul into a larger theological narrative that has its origins in Israel's history.

What is true for Paul is true for the writings of the "pillar apostles." For even if the letters attributed to James, Peter, and John were written by others in their names, Acts provides a narrative and canonical context for understanding their writings. Although this story may not be the hermeneutical key for interpreting these writings, it provides readers of the New Testament with a narrative framework for understanding the great figures of the early church, thereby contributing to the narrative unity of the New Testament.

To summarize, the significance of Luke's work is its narrative theology that inscribes the story of Jesus and the church into the story of Israel, and the writings of Paul, Peter, James, and John into the story of the church.[52]

---

52. Whereas Protestantism tends to understand "the story" of the New Testament in terms of Paul, Catholicism is more apt to view the New Testament story through the purview of Luke–Acts.

PART TWO

The Pauline Tradition

The Pauline tradition stands as the second great tradition in the New Testament. Like the Synoptic tradition, it anticipates the coming of God's kingdom and proclaims the gospel of God: God's own good news about Jesus Christ. But whereas the Synoptic tradition proclaims the gospel through a narrative that includes Jesus' proclamation of the kingdom of God, the Pauline tradition communicates the gospel through a series of letters that focus on God's redemptive work in Christ's death and resurrection. Consequently, apart from a few references to Jesus' early life, the Pauline tradition focuses like a laser beam on Christ's death and resurrection as the decisive moment of God's salvific work. This is not to imply that Christ's death and resurrection are of less importance to the Synoptic writers—to the contrary. But whereas the Synoptic writers view Christ's proclamation of the kingdom as an essential part of the gospel they proclaim, the Pauline tradition has made the preacher of the kingdom the content of the gospel it proclaims. Jesus, who has already entered into the transcendent realm of God's kingdom by his death and resurrection, has become the subject of the gospel. The starting point of the Pauline tradition, then, is God's redemptive work in Christ's death and resurrection. It is this starting point that explains the similarities and differences between the Synoptic and Pauline traditions. For whereas the Synoptic writers present their theologies in light of the inbreaking kingdom of God, the Pauline tradition presents its theologies in light of the one who has already entered the kingdom.

The Pauline tradition consists of thirteen letters, which occur in the following order in the canon of the New Testament: Romans, 1 and 2 Corinthians, Galatians, Ephesians, Philippians, Colossians, 1 and 2 Thessalonians, 1 and 2 Timothy, Titus, and Philemon. This canonical order is determined by two principles. First, the letters that are addressed to churches precede those addressed to individuals. Second, the longer letters in each category tend to precede the shorter ones. The position of the Letter to the Romans, at the beginning of this canonical order, gives that letter pride of place within the Pauline corpus, and it invites "the canonical reader" to read the rest of Paul's letters in its light. Although many would dispute this principle for reading the Pauline Letters, most would agree that Romans represents the most complete expression of Paul's theology.

The canonical ordering of the letters, however, does not correspond to the chronological order in which they were written. Although there is no unanimity about the sequence in which the letters were composed, most would agree that Paul wrote 1 Thessalonians before the Corinthian correspondence, that he composed Galatians before Romans, and that the Corinthian correspondence precedes the Letter to the Romans. The placement of Galatians, Philippians, and Philemon, not to mention the deuteropauline letters (see below), is more difficult to determine.[1]

Although the New Testament attributes thirteen letters to Paul, many contemporary scholars question the Pauline authorship of Ephesians, Colossians, 2 Thessalonians, 1 and 2 Timothy, and Titus, designating them as deuteropauline, and the remaining seven letters (Romans, 1 and 2 Corinthians, Galatians, Philippians, 1 Thessalonians, and Philemon) as the nondisputed Pauline correspondence. If this critical judgment is correct, several letters of the Pauline corpus were written in Paul's name but not by Paul.[2]

This distinction between the nondisputed and the deuteropauline letters presents New Testament theologians with a methodological problem. Should one make a sharp distinction between the nondisputed and the disputed letters (deuteropauline letters) in a presentation of Pauline theology, or should one focus on the canonical corpus of the Pauline writings? A canonical approach to New Testament theology could take one of two directions. It could consider the letters individually, in the order in which they occur within the canon, or it could present a synthesis of the entire Pauline corpus.[3] Although both

1. Raymond E. Brown (*An Introduction to the New Testament* [New York: Doubleday, 1997]) proposes the following dates for the Pauline Letters: 1 Thessalonians, 50 or 51; 2 Thessalonians, 51–52 if by Paul, no way of knowing if pseudonymous; Galatians, 54–55; Philippians, 56, 58–60, or 61–63, depending on its place of origin; Philemon 55, 58–60, or 61–63, depending on its place of origin; 1 Corinthians, 56–57; 2 Corinthians, 57; Romans, 57–58; Colossians, 54–56 or 61–63, or the 80s if it is pseudonymous; Ephesians, the 60s if by Paul, the 90s if it is pseudonymous; Titus, 65 if by Paul, toward the end of the first century if it is pseudonymous; 1 Timothy, 65 if by Paul, toward the end of the first century if it is pseudonymous; 2 Timothy, 64, if by Paul, late 60s or toward the end of the first century if it is pseudonymous.

2. Although 2 Thessalonians, Colossians, Ephesians, and the Pastorals are usually identified as deuteropauline letters, several scholars argue for the Pauline authorship of 2 Thessalonians, Colossians, and 2 Timothy, and some support the Pauline authorship of all thirteen letters.

3. Thomas R. Schreiner's monograph, *Paul, Apostle of God's Glory in Christ: A Pauline Theology* (Downers Grove, IL: InterVarsity Press, 2001), is a recent attempt to present a synthesis of Paul's theology making use of all thirteen letters. He writes, "The Pauline theology offered here is distinctive in that all thirteen letters ascribed to Paul are mined to decipher his theology" (p. 10).

approaches respect the canonical shape of the material, each presents particular problems. A canonical synthesis of all thirteen letters runs the risk of minimizing and overlooking the theological differences within the Pauline corpus, whereas a study of the letters in their canonical order will find it difficult to take into account the development of Pauline theology since such a presentation would begin with Romans, Paul's most mature and developed letter. Therefore, although a canonical approach has the merits of protecting the Pauline writings from the changing currents of historical research that at one moment may judge 2 Thessalonians or Colossians to be deuteropauline and at another as written by Paul, this approach tends to blend and conceal rather than reveal the distinctive voices within the Pauline corpus.

Most New Testament theologians, therefore, distinguish between the nondisputed and the disputed (that is, deuteropauline) letters. They begin with a systematic presentation of Paul's theology as found in the nondisputed letters, and then they treat the disputed letters in what they perceive to be the chronological order in which they were composed, for example, Colossians, Ephesians, the Pastorals (1–2 Timothy and Titus), and 2 Thessalonians.[4] There are several advantages to this approach. First, it allows one to distinguish between Paul's theology and the theology of those who wrote in his name. Second, it provides a systematic presentation of Paul's thought. Third, by distinguishing between the nondisputed and the disputed correspondence, it highlights the theological development in Pauline theology. But there are also problems. First, there is often an unspoken assumption that the deuteropauline tradition represents a decline—if not a betrayal—of Paul's theology. Second, if this approach draws too sharp a distinction between the nondisputed and the disputed Pauline letters, it fails to see the many ways in which the disputed letters develop and even enhance the teaching of the nondisputed Pauline letters.

How then should New Testament theologians construct a theology of the letters attributed to Paul? To answer this question, we must be clear about what we are trying to accomplish. If the goal is to present a historical account of Paul's own theology, then we surely need to distinguish clearly between what Paul wrote and what others wrote in his name. In doing this, we must be ready to acknowledge that what we say about "Paul's theology" will inevitably be incomplete since we know only what is available in the nondisputed correspondence.[5] On the other hand, if New Testament theologians understand their work as a literary and theological endeavor, then our primary task is to

---

4. This is how the New Testament theologies of Rudolf Bultmann, Joachim Gnilka, Ferdinand Hahn, Peter Stuhlmacher, and most others approach the task. Hans Hübner's New Testament theology is different inasmuch as it treats each letter individually.

5. To write a complete account of Paul's theology, a scholar would need access to everything Paul wrote. But this is no longer possible since it is evident from 1 Cor. 5:9 that Paul wrote at least one letter that has long since been lost.

construct a theology of the writings themselves. In this case, it is more appropriate to investigate the theological content of each letter before proceeding to a synthesis of the Pauline letters. Such an approach must take into account the historical background of the letters since the Pauline writings are "occasional" in nature; that is, each was written in response to a specific occasion.[6] The focus, then, will be on the writings themselves, and the goal will be to uncover the theological and religious dimension of each letter.[7]

In this New Testament theology I proceed in the following way. First, I begin with a description of the implicit or explicit theology in each letter in order to allow each writing to speak for itself. To be sure, the Pauline Letters were not composed as theological tracts. The word "theology," then, is employed in a rather broad manner to signify how a particular letter construes God's salvific activity in relationship to humanity. To put it another way, in this work I seek to determine how the writing understands the human condition in light of what God has done in Christ. Consequently, in this descriptive theology I investigate the theological logic of each letter. I ask what the letter says or implies about the human condition in relationship to God, to Christ, and to the Spirit. I inquire about the claims the letter makes about salvation and what it says about the future of those who believe in Christ. When appropriate, I ask how the letter inscribes its implied story of God, Christ, and the Spirit into the story of Israel. To be sure, not every letter answers these questions. But these are the kinds of questions a New Testament theologian should put to the Pauline writings if one hopes to uncover their theology, inchoate though it may be.

Second, taking into consideration the authorship of the Pauline Letters and their relative chronological development, in this study of Pauline theology I organize the letters attributed to Paul into five groups, each with its own focus:[8] (1) the Thessalonian correspondence in light of its election theology; (2) the Corinthian correspondence in light of its theology of the cross and the resurrection of the dead; (3) Galatians and Romans in light of their theology of justification by faith apart from doing the works of the Mosaic law; (4) Philippians, Philemon, Colossians, and Ephesians in light of the imprisoned apostle's the-

6. To say that the Pauline Letters are "occasional" is to acknowledge that they are real correspondence because they respond to questions and problems raised in the Pauline churches. This is even true for Ephesians, which is often viewed as a general letter sent to Pauline churches in Asia Minor, since it addresses the needs of these Pauline congregations.

7. While New Testament theologians are concerned with the historical reconstruction of a particular author's thought, they must also concern themselves with the theology of the writing that the author has produced. Consequently, in addition to speaking of Paul's own theology (which requires historical reconstruction), it is possible to speak of the theology of the Pauline writings (the letters in their present canonical form). These two approaches should be viewed as complementary, the second building upon and learning from the first.

8. Except for 2 Thessalonians, I treat all of the deuteropauline letters after the nondisputed Pauline letters. Letters that are generally acknowledged to have been written earlier (1 Thessalonians and the Corinthian correspondence) I treat first.

ology; and (5) the Pastoral Epistles (1 and 2 Timothy and Titus) in light of their theology of handing on the Pauline tradition to a new generation.[9]

These five groups are not airtight compartments, as if Paul's election theology is found only in his Thessalonian correspondence, or as if his theology of the cross and the resurrection is present only in the Corinthian correspondence. There is a strong strain of election theology in all of the Pauline correspondence, and Christ's death and resurrection play a central role in all of the letters. But certain themes characterize particular letters inasmuch as the Pauline correspondence is occasional in nature. For example, justification plays an important role in Galatians and Romans because Paul must defend and explain the law-free gospel he preaches to Gentiles, whereas the cosmic dimension of Christ and the church play a central role in Colossians and Ephesians because these letters must interpret Christ and the church for a new time and a new situation. The purpose of this grouping, then, is to highlight what is distinctive about the letters gathered in each group.

---

9. The fourth category is the most problematic, since it includes two letters that are usually viewed as deuteropauline (Ephesians and Colossians) and since there is no single theme that binds all four writings together, apart from the fact that they were, or claim to have been, written while Paul was in prison. Earlier commentators referred to these letters as the Captivity Epistles, and it is this older terminology that inspires this grouping.

4

A Theology of Election

The Thessalonian Correspondence

Scholars have disputed the relationship between 1 and 2 Thessalonians for more than a century.[1] Whereas some argue that Paul is addressing a new problem in 2 Thessalonians occasioned by a heightened expectation that the parousia is at hand, others maintain that 2 Thessalonians is a pseudonymous letter composed toward the end of the first century. Although this debate is important for reconstructing the history of Christian origins and Paul's theological thought, these letters can and should be treated together since they share a common theology of election as well as a vibrant hope for the Lord's parousia.

The occasion for 1 Thessalonians can be summarized as follows. After leaving Thessalonica, Paul tried to return several times, but Satan thwarted his plans (2:18). Therefore, he sent Timothy to strengthen and encourage the community during its time of affliction and to learn about the progress of its faith (3:1–5). Timothy has recently returned from Thessalonica with an encouraging report that the community has remained steadfast in its faith despite a severe affliction (3:6–8). Overjoyed by this report, Paul writes a paraenetic letter to encourage the Thessalonians in their faith and to remind them of what he has already taught them.[2] This paraenesis is necessary because the faith that the Thessalonians have embraced has alienated them from their compatriots, leaving them with a sense of social dislocation.[3] To counter this

---

1. For a history of this debate, see Raymond F. Collins, *Letters That Paul Did Not Write: The Epistle to the Hebrews and the Pauline Pseudepigrapha* (GNS 28; Wilmington, DE: Glazier, 1988).

2. Paraenesis is moral exhortation with which the audience is already familiar. It reminds the audience of what it already knows or should know. First Thessalonians is a paraenetic letter inasmuch as Paul reminds the Thessalonians of what he has already taught them, and it exhorts them to adopt a pattern of behavior with which they should be familiar from his earlier teaching.

3. This social dislocation derives from the fact that they no longer participate in the religious practices of their compatriots. From the point of view of their compatriots, the new faith the Thessalonians have embraced is a deviant religious practice that threatens the good order of society.

sense of alienation and dislocation, Paul reminds the Thessalonians of the gospel he preached to them. Their acceptance of that gospel has made them members of a new family, the eschatological community of God's chosen and elect people, the church. To strengthen them in their faith, Paul points to their new status as God's chosen and elect people and of the hope they have in the Lord's parousia (1:9–10; 2:19; 3:12–13; 4:13–18; 5:1–3, 23–24).

If 2 Thessalonians was written by Paul, as many contend, it is responding to a new crisis at Thessalonica: some members of the community are urging that the day of the Lord is at hand, or that it has already come (2:2).[4] Accordingly, Paul writes to correct this misunderstanding and remind the Thessalonians that certain events must occur before the Lord returns. If 2 Thessalonians is pseudonymous, as others maintain, it is difficult to identify the letter's occasion apart from saying that someone, writing in Paul's name, seeks to enlist the apostle's authority in resolving a serious misunderstanding about the parousia. As in 1 Thessalonians, election theology plays a central role in 2 Thessalonians.

ELECTED AND CHOSEN BY GOD

The theological logic of 1 Thessalonians can be summarized as follows. Through Paul's preaching of the gospel, God has called and chosen the Thessalonians to be members of the sanctified community that is the church. God's will for them, then, is their sanctification. As members of a sanctified community that has received the gift of the Spirit, they must live their lives in holiness so that they can stand blameless before the Lord on the day of his parousia.

The Gospel

The gospel (*euangelion*) Paul proclaims is God's own good news about his Son, Jesus Christ, whom Paul identifies as the Lord.[5] Although Paul speaks of the gospel as "our message of the gospel" (1 Thess. 1:5) as if it were his own message, he is profoundly aware that what he proclaims is "the gospel of God," God's own good news, which God entrusted to Paul and his coworkers (2:2, 4, 8, 9). Since the content of God's gospel is Christ, Paul can also speak of "the gospel of Christ" (3:2), by which he means the gospel about Jesus Christ, the

---

4. The Greek of 2 Thess. 2:2 (*hōs hoti enestēken hē hēmera tou kyriou*) can be rendered "that the day of the Lord is at hand" (NAB), or "that the day of the Lord is already here" (NRSV). In the first instance, the parousia is perceived as imminent, in the second it is perceived as having arrived.

5. This is the way in which Paul most frequently refers to Jesus in 1 Thessalonians: the Lord, the Lord Jesus, our Lord Jesus Christ. See 1:1, 3, 6, 8; 2:15, 19; 3:8, 11, 12, 13; 4:1, 2, 6, 15, 16, 17; 5:19, 23, 28. *Kyrios* refers to Jesus' exalted status at God's right hand because God has raised him from the dead.

good news whose content is Christ. Paul has already instructed the Thessalonians in this gospel, and he presupposes that they are acquainted with its essential content. Accordingly, this letter is paraenetic in nature, and its primary concern is to encourage the Thessalonians and remind them of what they should already know about the gospel.[6]

The letter contains several clues about the gospel Paul preached at Thessalonica, the most important of which is a summary of his original message: "For the people of those regions report about us what kind of welcome we had among you, and how you turned to God from idols, to serve a living and true God, and to wait for his Son from heaven, whom he raised from the dead—Jesus, who rescues us from the wrath that is coming" (1:9–10). This synopsis of Paul's gospel suggests that when he first preached to the Thessalonians, he summoned them to turn from idols to serve the living and true God—the God of Israel—because God is about to deal with human sinfulness in a final and decisive manner. The indisputable sign that this end-time judgment is at hand is the resurrection of God's Son, Jesus, whom God raised from the dead. Having been raised from the dead, the Son will return from heaven to deliver, from the coming wrath of God, those who turn from idols to the living and true God.[7]

In another text Paul reminds the Thessalonians that God has destined them not for "wrath" but for salvation "through our Lord Jesus Christ, who died for us, so that whether we are awake or asleep we may live with him" (5:9–10). Christ's salvific death on their behalf ("for us," *hyper hēmōn*) leads to life with Christ, even for those who have died. Like Christ's death, the resurrection is the believer's assurance of future life with Christ. Writing about the effects of Christ's resurrection, Paul says: "For since we believe that Jesus died and rose again, even so, through Jesus, God will bring with him those who have died" (4:14). The content of God's gospel about Christ, then, can be summarized as follows: Christ has died "for us" and his resurrection is the assurance of future life with him. Those who believe in him and turn to the living and true God—the God of Israel—will be rescued from the coming wrath that will occur at the parousia of God's Son.

Although the gospel is proclaimed in human words, it is not a human word: it is the very word of God (2:13). It comes "in power and in the Holy Spirit and with full conviction" (1:5). A word about the Lord Jesus Christ, the gospel sounds forth as if it were a mighty trumpet (1:8). This word brings affliction as well as the joy that comes from the Holy Spirit (1:6): affliction because others will oppose the gospel; joy because the Spirit of God dwells in those who accept the gospel.

---

6. The frequent use of the phrase "as you know" in 1 Thessalonians indicates that the material is not entirely new to the audience. This point is made by Abraham Malherbe, *Paul and the Thessalonians: The Philosophic Tradition of Pastoral Care* (Philadelphia: Fortress, 1987), 50–51.

7. Note the similarity of this theology with that in Acts 3:19–21; 14:15–17; 17:30–31.

Paul preaches the gospel by the example of his life as well as by his words. Therefore, he presents himself to his converts as a model to be imitated. By imitating him, his converts imitate the Lord whom they cannot see.[8] Because the Thessalonians have imitated Paul (1:6), they have become an "example" (*typon*) for believers in Macedonia and Achaia (1:7) so that the "word of the Lord," the gospel message about Christ, has sounded forth from them like a mighty trumpet (1:8). In 2:1–12, then, Paul describes the integrity of his ministry among the Thessalonians to provide them with a model of behavior they can emulate.

Election

The proclamation of the gospel is an offer of salvation rooted in God's election. Because the Thessalonians have believed in the gospel of God, Paul reminds them that God has chosen and elected them. At the outset of the letter (1:4), Paul recalls their election (*tēn eklogēn hymōn*), and he addresses them as "beloved by God" (*ēgapēmenoi hypo tou theou*). This election theology inscribes the Thessalonians into the story of Israel, God's beloved and elect people. Just as God called Israel to be his chosen people, so he calls those who believe the gospel into the sanctified community of the *ekklēsia* that dwells in God the Father and Jesus Christ the Lord (1:1).

In another explicit statement about their election, Paul urges the Thessalonians to conduct themselves in a way worthy of the God who calls (*kalountos*) them into his kingdom and glory (2:12). The *ekklēsia* is the elect and chosen community of those who are being called into God's kingdom. Employing the language of election in the context of moral exhortation, Paul reminds the Thessalonians that God called (*ekalesen*) them not "to impurity" but "in holiness" (4:7). Because the Thessalonians are God's chosen and elect people, God's will for them is their "sanctification" (*hagiasmos*, 4:3). Paul is once more inscribing the Thessalonians into the story of Israel, thereby suggesting that just as God called Israel to be holy as God is holy (Lev. 19:2), so God now calls the *ekklēsia* of the Thessalonians to be holy as God is holy. Reminding them that they must be blameless at the day of the Lord's parousia, Paul assures them that the God who calls (*kalōn*) them is faithful and will accomplish this (1 Thess. 5:24).

Election, however, does not preserve one from tribulation and persecution in the present life. This is why Paul sent Timothy to strengthen and encourage the Thessalonians in their faith during the time of their affliction. They should not

---

8. Paul speaks of imitation rather than following Christ in the way of discipleship. For whereas Jesus' disciples could see and follow him, Paul's converts could not. Consequently, they had to imitate someone who could present them with a model of what it means to be a believer. By imitating Paul, they imitate Christ since Paul has perfectly conformed himself to Christ's death and resurrection.

be disturbed by persecution, because Paul has already told them that they are destined for this (*eis touto keimetha*, 3:3). He employs the same language when he reminds the Thessalonians, "For God has destined us not for wrath (*ouk etheto hēmas ho theos eis orgēn*) but for obtaining salvation through our Lord Jesus Christ" (5:9). God's election, then, results in both persecution and salvation.

The election of the Thessalonians is grounded in their experience of the Spirit. The gospel came to them in power and in the Holy Spirit (1:5). They have experienced the joy of the Spirit (1:6), and God has given them his Holy Spirit (4:8) to guide them in the moral life. Consequently, Paul can affirm that they have been taught by God (*theodidaktoi*) to love one another (4:9). Because the Spirit dwells in their midst, they must be careful not to extinguish the Spirit or to despise prophecy (5:19–20). The presence of the Spirit within their community indicates that they, like Israel of old, have been chosen and elected by God. Should the Spirit disappear from their midst, their election would surely be in doubt.

The Moral Life of the Elect

Moral exhortation plays an important role in 1 Thessalonians since the proclamation of the gospel summons those who have been called and chosen to live within the sanctified community of the *ekklēsia* until the Lord returns to rescue them from the coming wrath. As members of this sanctified community, the elect must live holy lives so that they can be blameless at the Lord's parousia (3:13; 5:23). In Paul's view the Thessalonians are already distinguished by their work of faith, their labor of love, and the steadfastness of their hope (1:3), what later theology would identify as the theological virtues because they are empowered by God's Spirit. References to these "virtues" abound in this letter: faith (1:3, 8; 3:2, 5, 6, 7, 10; 5:8), love (1:3; 3:6, 12; 4:9; 5:8, 13), and hope (1:3; 4:13; 5:8). The manner in which Paul describes them in 1:3 indicates that they require a continuous effort on the part of the Thessalonians: their "work" is their ongoing faith in the gospel; their "labor" is their ongoing love for one another; and their "steadfastness" in face of persecution and affliction is the expression of their hope in the parousia.

Because the moral life of those chosen and elected by the gospel is a labor and a work that requires steadfastness, Paul exhorts the Thessalonians to live as members of a sanctified community that has been consecrated and set apart so that they will be blameless on the day of the parousia. Since God's will is their holiness, they must refrain from all *porneia* (4:3; "fornication," NRSV; "immorality," NAB). *Porneia* characterizes the life of those who do not know the living God. God, however, called the Thessalonians not to impurity but to holiness (4:7). Their sanctified community, which has been called to be holy, should be distinguished by the love its members extend to one another. As members of a new family,[9] which is the sanctified community of the church, the Thessalonians practice the ancient virtue of *philadelphia* ("brotherly love," "mutual love") in an entirely new way. Whereas this virtue formerly had in view the love of blood brothers for each other, it now includes all the brothers and sisters who make up the family of the church.

This moral life, however, is not merely the result of human effort. The sanctified community lives a life of holiness through the power of the Holy Spirit that God has bestowed upon it (4:8), and its members live as a new family in which they love each other because they have been taught by God (4:9). By reminding the Thessalonians that God has given them the Spirit, and in saying that they have been taught by God (*theodidaktoi*), Paul alludes to Ezekiel's promise of the Spirit (Ezek. 36:27; 37:14), a promise that plays a prominent role in Paul's new covenant theology in 2 Corinthians 3.[10] By referring to the role of the Spirit in the moral life of the Thessalonians, then, Paul inscribes them into the story of Israel and intimates that they participate in this new covenant.

The sanctified community lives the moral life in anticipation of the parousia so that as God's elect they may stand blameless before the Lord (1 Thess. 3:13; 5:23). Since that day will come suddenly and without warning, believers must be vigilant and alert. They no longer belong to the darkness or to the night, for they are children (*huioi*) of the light and of the day. Viewing the moral life as comparable to a military struggle, Paul likens their faith and love to a breastplate and their hope for salvation to a helmet (5:8). Protected by this armor, they will be able to prevail in the moral life until the day of the Lord's parousia.

The Hope of the Elect

Hope for the parousia plays a prominent role in 1 Thessalonians. At the end of chapter 1, Paul recalls how the Thessalonians turned from idols to serve the living God and await the coming of his Son whom he raised from the dead, Jesus, who rescues them from the coming wrath (1:9–10). At the end of chapter 2, he writes that the Thessalonians will be his crown in whom he will boast at the parousia (2:19). At the end of chapter 3, he prays that they will be blameless in holiness before God at the parousia of the Lord (3:13). At the end of chapter 5, he makes a similar prayer-wish (5:23). But it is at the end of chapter 4 (4:13–18) and at the beginning of chapter 5 (5:1–11) that he makes his most complete statement about the parousia.

---

9. Paul's frequent use of "brothers and sisters" is one way in which he reinforces, for his converts, that they belong to a new family, the community of the church. Although they may have lost their old families because of their new faith, they have become members of a new and larger household.

10. On Paul's new covenant theology, see T. J. Deidun, *New Covenant Morality in Paul* (AnBib 89; Rome: Biblical Institute Press, 1981).

In 4:13–18 Paul addresses a specific question: what will happen to those who have already died? Will they be excluded from the salvation that Christ will bring at his parousia? In response to this query, Paul draws a relationship between the resurrection of Christ and the resurrection of the believer, a relationship he will develop further in 1 Corinthians 15. Here, however, the essential point is that death cannot separate believers from Christ since those who have died as Christians will be raised from the dead. Those who believe that Jesus died and rose can be confident, then, that even if they die before the parousia, God will gather them at Jesus' return (1 Thess. 4:14). Speaking on the authority of "a word of the Lord" (*en logō kyriou*, 4:15),[11] in 4:16–17 Paul briefly outlines a scenario for the parousia. First, the Lord will descend from heaven at the appropriate time ("with a cry of command, with the archangel's call and with the sound of God's trumpet") and the dead in Christ will rise first. Then those who are still alive will be "caught up" (*harpagēsometha*) with them in the clouds to meet the Lord in the air. Finally Paul concludes, "And so we will be with the Lord forever" (4:17).

This description of the parousia is sparse and raises as many questions as it answers. What will be the fate of those who are left behind? Will believers go out to meet the Lord in order to escort him to earth or to be brought to heaven by him? The text does not address these questions since Paul's primary concern is to assure the Thessalonians that those who have died as believers will not be excluded from the salvation Christ will bring at his parousia.

Although Paul appears to think that the parousia is imminent and even reckons with the possibility that he may be alive when it occurs ("Then we who are alive," 4:17), he discourages speculation about its appearance (5:1–11). The parousia will occur suddenly, at a moment people least expect. There is no need to speculate about its arrival (5:1). It is sufficient to know that the parousia will come "like a thief in the night" (5:2). For this reason believers must live as children of the day and children of the light.

AFFLICTION AND THE KINGDOM OF GOD

Although many argue that 2 Thessalonians is pseudonymous, the remarkable similarity between the theology of 1 and 2 Thessalonians justifies treating the two together. As in 1 Thessalonians, Paul (or the one who writes in his name) employs an election theology to assure the Thessalonians that God will vindicate them on the day of the Lord's parousia. Therefore, they must remain steadfast despite persecution and affliction so that they will be deemed worthy

---

11. Here Paul appears to refer to a prophetic oracle that he, or a prophet within the community, spoke.

of the kingdom of God for which they are suffering. Those who are leading idle or disorderly lives, because they mistakenly think that the parousia has come or is at hand, must imitate Paul by working for their living.

The Meaning of Persecution and Affliction

In 1 Thessalonians Paul reminded the Thessalonians that they were destined for affliction, something he told them when he first preached the gospel to them (3:3–4). Although he assured them that they would be rescued from the wrath of God that is coming upon those who refuse to turn to the living and true God (1:10; 5:9), his description of the parousia in 4:13–18 did not deal with questions of judgment and retribution since his concern was to assure his converts that those who died believing in Christ would be raised to new life at the parousia. Second Thessalonians, however, addresses a different situation. The question is no longer, "What will happen to believers who die before the parousia?" but "Do the intense persecutions and afflictions of the present mean that the day of the Lord has arrived?" Accordingly, even though he has already taught the Thessalonians that they are destined for affliction because of their faith in the gospel, Paul now explains the meaning of the persecutions and afflictions they are enduring by relating them to the kingdom of God and the Lord's parousia.

At the outset of the letter, Paul assures the Thessalonians that God will repay with affliction those who are presently afflicting them (2 Thess. 1:5–6). Paul now describes the parousia as a moment when Jesus will suddenly appear with his mighty angels in blazing fire to punish those who do not acknowledge God or obey the gospel he (Paul) has proclaimed about Jesus. Such people will suffer the penalty of eternal destruction and be separated from the Lord (1:9). Thus, whereas the description of the parousia in 1 Thess. 4:13–18 focused on the salvation Christ will bring to those who have believed in him, 2 Thess. 1:5–10 is primarily concerned with the fate of those who are afflicting the elect and refusing to obey the gospel. The purpose of the afflictions the elect are presently enduring is to make them worthy of the kingdom of God, for which they are suffering (1:5). Paul concludes this section with a prayer that recalls his election theology: "To this end we always pray for you, asking that our God will make you worthy of *his call* and will fulfill by his power every good resolve and work of faith, so that the name of our Lord Jesus may be glorified in you, and you in him, according to the grace of our God and the Lord Jesus Christ" (1:11–12).

The Mystery of Iniquity

The severe affliction that has come upon the Thessalonians, however, has led some to conclude "that the day of the Lord is already here" (2:2). Although Paul warned the Thessalonians that there is no way to calculate when the parousia will occur, since it will come "like a thief in the night" (1 Thess. 5:2), he explains that the parousia will not happen until certain events take place: the apostasy (*apostasia*) and the revelation of a lawless figure (*ho anthrōpos tēs anomias*, 2 Thess. 2:3). Paul is convinced that the mystery of lawlessness is already at work (2:7), but something (2:6) or someone (2:7) is still restraining this lawless figure, who will arrogate to himself prerogatives that belong to God. Consequently, the parousia is not as imminent as some believe, nor has it already taken place, since the apostasy has not yet occurred and the lawless one has not yet appeared. When the lawless one is revealed, however, the Lord will destroy him "with the breath of his mouth, annihilating him by the manifestation of his coming" (2:8).[12] The present afflictions of the Thessalonians, then, do not mean that the day of the Lord has come or that it is at hand.

After this third description of the events surrounding the parousia (the first two being 1 Thess. 4:13–18 and 2 Thess. 1:5–10), Paul again draws upon his election theology to strengthen the Thessalonians in their new identity in Christ. They are loved by the Lord (Jesus) because God has chosen them "as the first fruits for salvation through sanctification by the Spirit and through belief in the truth" (2:13). They have been called through the gospel so that they can obtain the glory of the Lord Jesus Christ (2:14). This is why they should stand firm and hold to the traditions they have received rather than be deceived into believing that the day of the Lord is here (2:15). The meaning of their afflictions is not that the day of the Lord is at hand, or that it has already occurred, but that they have been chosen by God.

Living an Orderly Life

If the problem of the *ataktoi* ("the idle," NRSV; "the disorderly," NAB) is related to the mistaken notion that the day of the Lord is at hand or is already here, then some people are "living in idleness" (3:6), and not according to the tradition they received from Paul, because they think that the day of the Lord is at hand or has already arrived. Consequently, they no longer work for their living. To combat this misunderstanding, Paul reminds the Thessalonians of what he has already taught them in 1 Thess. 4:11 ("to aspire to live quietly, to mind your own affairs, and to work with your hands"). The Thessalonians are to imitate Paul, who was not idle when he was among them. Rather than eat someone else's food, he toiled night and day so that he would not be a burden to the Thessalonians (2 Thess. 3:7–8). Those who are living in idleness, therefore, must work quietly and earn their own living (3:12). Although the day of the Lord will come

---

12. The identity of the lawless figure is no longer known. Paul supposes that his audience is aware of whom and of what he is speaking. The lawless one appears to be the antitype of Christ, one who opposes all that Christ stands for.

suddenly, hope for the Lord's parousia does not excuse believers from living and working in the world in a responsible way. It is with this understanding of the parousia that Paul presents himself to the Thessalonians as a model to be imitated. For even though he is firmly convinced that the Lord will return soon, he works to support himself as he preaches the gospel.

CONCLUSION

The theological structure of the Thessalonian correspondence revolves around three concepts: (1) the proclamation of the gospel of God; (2) the election of the Thessalonians to be a sanctified community; and (3) the parousia of the Lord. Its major theological themes can be summarized as follows. Through the proclamation of the gospel, God calls and elects people to the sanctified community of the church. God's will for the elect is their sanctification. Therefore, those who live within the sphere of the sanctified community must refrain from what is immoral and unclean so that they can stand blameless before God on the day of the Lord's parousia, when Christ will gather the elect (even if they have died before his appearance) and punish those who are afflicting God's chosen ones. Because the elect enjoy the gift of the Spirit, they are taught by God and love one another as brothers and sisters who are members of a new family, the church. Those who have been chosen and elected to be members of this sanctified community, however, are also destined for persecution and affliction for the sake of the kingdom of God. By enduring such affliction, they show that they are worthy of the kingdom of God for which they are suffering.

5

A Theology of the Cross and
of the Resurrection from the Dead

The Corinthian Correspondence

Paul's Corinthian correspondence echoes a number of theological themes found in his Thessalonian correspondence: an election theology rooted in the gracious call of the gospel, an ecclesiology that views the church as a sanctified community in which the Spirit plays an active role, and an eschatology that looks to the Lord's parousia as the moment of God's final and definitive victory. In addition to these themes, 1 and 2 Corinthians introduce a number of new theological motifs: the wisdom and power of God manifested in the weakness and folly of the cross; the paradoxical nature of apostolic ministry; the relationship between the resurrection of Christ and the general resurrection of the dead; and Christian freedom and responsibility within the believing community, to mention a few. The introduction of these new themes is not unexpected given the length of the Corinthian correspondence and the variety of issues that Paul encountered at Corinth. What is surprising is that the apostle was able to apply the gospel to new issues in so many creative ways. The gospel of what God has done in Christ remains the theological center of Paul's thought so that the diverse ways in which he expresses his theology arise from the changing circumstances to which he applied the gospel rather than from a fundamental change in his theology.

The new circumstances that Paul encountered at Corinth can be summarized as follows. At some point after leaving Corinth and settling in Ephesus, Paul wrote a letter to the Corinthians that is no longer preserved. He alludes to this letter in 1 Cor. 5:9, "I wrote to you in my letter not to associate with sexually immoral persons." In response to that letter, the Corinthians wrote their own letter to Paul raising a number of issues and questions. Paul refers to this letter in 1 Cor. 7:1, "Now concerning the matters about which you wrote." About the same time, Paul received an oral report from a group of people associated with a woman named Chloe about divisions within the community ("For it has been reported to me by Chloe's people that there are quarrels among you, my brothers and sisters," 1:11). Paul probably heard a similar report from a delegation headed by one of his converts, Stephanas, to whom he alludes in 1:16 and 16:17. It was in response to these oral reports about divisions within the church and to the Corinthians' own letter to Paul that Paul wrote the letter now identified as 1 Corinthians.[1]

Although Paul hoped that his response to the Corinthians would resolve their problems, it did not. About the time that he wrote 1 Corinthians, Paul also sent Timothy to Corinth to remind the congregation of Paul's "ways in Jesus Christ" (1 Cor. 4:17). On his return Timothy appears to have reported that there were continuing problems at Corinth. Consequently, Paul visited the community, only to be rebuffed by one of its members, a painful episode to which Paul alludes in 2 Cor. 2:5–11. Grieved and disappointed that the community did not come to his defense, Paul returned to Ephesus and wrote a harsh letter to the Corinthians, to which he refers in 2 Cor. 2:1–4, 9, and 7:12. Like the letter alluded to in 1 Cor. 5:9, this letter is no longer extant. Delivered by Titus, it called the community to repentance. When Paul finally met Titus in Macedonia and learned that the community had repented, he was overjoyed (2 Cor. 7:5–16). It is at this point that Paul sent the Corinthians the letter now identified as 2 Corinthians. In this letter he reviews the recent events that have transpired between him and the community (1:12–2:13; 7:5–16); he provides the community with an extended reflection on the nature of apostolic ministry (2:14–7:4); he encourages the Corinthians to complete the collection for the church of Jerusalem, which they had undertaken a year earlier (8:1–9:15); and he deals with the issue of intruding missionaries (sarcastically dubbed "superapostles"), who had come to Corinth and called into question Paul's apostolic ministry (10:1–13:13).[2]

The content of Paul's Corinthian correspondence is occasioned by the specific circumstances of the Corinthian congregation. Consequently, when he writes about baptism, the Eucharist, the gift of the Spirit, the resurrection of the dead, or the nature of his apostolic ministry, he does so within the context of problems and questions occasioned by the particular circumstances of the Corinthian church. In doing so, Paul develops a theology of these issues by applying the gospel of what God has done in Christ's saving death and life-giving resurrection to the particular circumstances of the Corinthian commu-

---

1. The Corinthians appear to have raised the following issues in their letter to Paul: the advisability of sexual abstinence in marriage; whether the unmarried should marry; the freedom of believers to eat food previously sacrificed to idols; the relative importance of spiritual gifts, especially speaking in tongues and prophecy.

2. The relationship between Paul and the Corinthian community is complicated and disputed, especially the circumstances behind the writing of 2 Corinthians and the question of the letter's literary integrity. For a fuller discussion, see Frank J. Matera, *II Corinthians: A Commentary* (NTL; Louisville: Westminster John Knox Press, 2003), 15–32.

nity. For example, when he writes about marriage and virginity in 1 Corinthians 7, Paul must first respond to an ascetical group that abstains from marital relations and is trying to dissuade other believers from marrying. When he discusses the resurrection of the dead, he is responding to those who have called into question the nature and necessity of a bodily resurrection. In his response to these issues, Paul is not so much trying to develop a theology of marriage and virginity or a theology of the resurrection of the dead as he is endeavoring to resolve a series of practical issues in light of the gospel he preaches.

This does not mean that Paul's Corinthian correspondence is theologically irrelevant, or that these letters are less theological than Romans and Galatians, where he wrestles with the question of justification by faith. Paul's Corinthian correspondence is filled with theological reflection, and at the heart of that reflection is a profound theology of the cross, which might never have come to light if Paul did not have to deal with the issues he encountered at Corinth. In other words, it was the new circumstances Paul faced at Corinth that led him to reflect on the implications of the gospel for a community of believers who were profoundly convinced of the power of the Spirit within their lives but did not fully comprehend the relationship between this experience of the Spirit and the proclamation of a crucified Messiah.

Consequently, Paul finds himself in a strange and unsettling situation. It is not that the Corinthians have abandoned the truth of the gospel, such as he feared was happening in the churches at Galatia, or that the Corinthians had lost enthusiasm for the gospel. If anything, the Corinthians were filled with enthusiasm and had begun to shape the gospel according to their own powerful experience of the Spirit. Filled with the Spirit, they experienced the freedom of the gospel in ways that were sometimes disturbing to Paul, as is apparent from his criticism of their slogans about freedom and knowledge in 1 Cor. 6:12–13; 8:1–3. The Corinthians had an intense experience of salvation. They valued baptism and those who baptized them, and they ate the spiritual food, that is, the Eucharist. In a word, the Corinthians had taken the gospel to new heights. But in doing so, they did not make any place for the weakness and folly of the cross. They did not understand that in the weakness and folly of the crucified Christ the hidden wisdom of God is revealed. Paul's quarrel with his Corinthian converts, then, was that they had not yet fully appropriated the gospel.

Because they did not comprehend how the wisdom and power of God could be revealed in the cross, they were mistaking the powerful manifestation of the Spirit in their midst for the fullness of salvation: they were already reigning with Christ; they were filled with all knowledge; they thought of themselves as beyond the dangers of the flesh. It is in order to address this situation of "spiritual enthusiasm" that Paul develops his theology of the cross in the Corinthian correspondence. Although this theology is most powerfully developed in the opening chapters of 1 Corinthians, it underlies all that Paul writes in 1 and 2 Corinthians. The major theological themes of Paul's Corinthian correspondence, then, will be reviewed in light of this theology of the cross under the following headings: (1) the wisdom of God and the word of the cross; (2) the sanctified community and the worshiping assembly; (3) apostolic ministry in light of the cross; and (4) the resurrection of Christ and the general resurrection of the dead.

THE WISDOM OF GOD AND THE WORD OF THE CROSS

The Corinthians appear to have understood the gospel as a spiritual wisdom imparted to them at the time of their baptism. If this was all that the Corinthians affirmed, Paul would not have disagreed; for he also acknowledged that the gospel imparted wisdom. Moreover, even though he insists that Christ sent him not to baptize but to proclaim the gospel (1 Cor. 1:17), baptism plays a central role in his theology as the sacrament by which believers are baptized "into one body," which is Christ, and "made to drink of one Spirit" (12:13).[3] But the Corinthians had gone further. They were aligning themselves with the particular apostle or representative of that apostle who had baptized them, arguing that the one who baptized them also equipped them with a particular wisdom or knowledge. Consequently, the community was in danger of falling into factions.[4] Claiming that they possessed a superior wisdom and knowledge or superior spiritual gifts such as the ability to speak in tongues, certain members of the community were setting themselves in opposition to other members of the community who did not possess these spiritual gifts or the same knowledge and wisdom. Mistaking their powerful experience of the Spirit for an indication that they were already reigning with Christ (4:8), these spiritual enthusiasts did not see any need to associate themselves with the sufferings of the crucified Christ. Therefore, even though Paul had handed on the gospel to the Corinthians when he first preached to them (15:1–5), they did not understand the relationship between the wisdom and knowledge they claimed, the Spirit they experienced, and the message about the cross. Left to themselves, they would have developed a gospel in which an esoteric wisdom and knowledge played a central role without any reference to the cross of Christ. In a word, they were on their way to a kind of Gnosticism that valued the wis-

---

3. Paul acknowledges that he baptized Crispus, Gaius, and the household of Stephanas at Corinth (1 Cor. 1:14–16), but he purposely downplays his baptismal ministry at Corinth because the Corinthians have exaggerated the importance of the one who baptized them.

4. Paul also speaks of those who align themselves with Christ. Christ, of course, did not baptize any of them, but there may have been one faction that sought to outdo the others by claiming a special relationship to Christ rather than to a particular apostle.

dom and knowledge of the gospel at the expense of the cross.[5] Although Paul affirmed the central roles of wisdom, knowledge, and the Spirit in the gospel, he understood the relationship of the wisdom of God, the power of the Spirit, and the message about the cross in a very different way.

It is within this context that Paul develops his theology of the cross in 1:18–2:5, where he relates "the message about the cross" (*ho logos . . . ho tou staurou*, 1:18) to the power and wisdom of God. This "message about the cross" is another way of referring to "the gospel," as is the expression "the mystery of God" (*to mystērion tou theou*), which Paul employs in 2:1. But in coining the phrase "the message about the cross," which occurs only here, Paul clearly intends to emphasize an aspect of the gospel that the Corinthians neglected.[6] By this expression, he shows that the cross is an indispensable element of the gospel he preaches. This message about the cross is the paradoxical proclamation of a crucified Messiah, a "stumbling block" (*skandalon*) to Jews and "foolishness" (*mōria*) to Gentiles. This "proclamation" (*kērygma*) scandalized Paul's Jewish contemporaries because it contradicted the law, which says that "anyone hung on a tree is under God's curse" (Deut. 21:23). Since Jesus was "hung on a tree" (the cross) the inevitable conclusion is that he was under God's curse, an accusation Paul employs to his benefit in Gal. 3:13: "Christ redeemed us from the curse of the law by becoming a curse for us—for it is written, 'Cursed is everyone who hangs on a tree.'"[7] To put it boldly, a "crucified messiah" is an oxymoron, a contradiction in terms, for a crucified messiah is a messiah under God's curse. But if the proclamation of a crucified messiah was a scandal for Jews, it was utter foolishness to Gentiles, who lived in a world where crucifixion was reserved for slaves, violent criminals, and political insurgents. The very notion of a savior who could not save himself but suffered a death reserved for slaves, criminals, and rebels was utter folly.[8] From the perspective of human wisdom, then, the message of the cross is foolishness.

But it is precisely the metaphor of the cross, in all of its offensiveness, upon which Paul insists; for in and through the death of the crucified Jesus, God paradoxically reveals himself to a world that did not know God through its own wisdom. This message about the cross also reveals the true condition of the

5. Some have argued that there was already an early form of Gnosticism at Corinth. Others maintain that what Paul encountered at Corinth was an incipient form of Gnosticism, a way of viewing Christ that would eventually lead to Gnosticism.

6. Paul refers to the cross more times than any other New Testament writer, but the word does not occur as frequently in the Pauline writings (10 times), or in the New Testament (27 times), as one might expect. When Paul employs the word, he tends to focus on the scandal of the cross, as he does here. See Gal. 5:11; 6:12, 14; Phil. 2:8; 3:18. The deuteropauline correspondence employs the word to speak of the salvific dimension of Christ's death on the cross (Eph. 2:16; Col. 1:20; 2:14). These letters do not speak of the scandal of the cross in the way that 1 Corinthians does.

7. Luke employs the expression "to hang on a tree" in Acts to refer to Jesus' death by crucifixion (Acts 5:30; 10:39).

8. For the historical background to crucifixion in the ancient world, see Martin Hengel, *Crucifixion in the Ancient World and the Folly of the Message of the Cross* (Philadelphia: Fortress, 1977).

world by disclosing that what the world esteems as wisdom, God counts as folly, and what the world counts as power, God esteems as weakness. The message of the cross, then, reveals a God whom the world did not and could not know on the basis of its own wisdom. It exposes the true condition of a world living according to standards that it evaluates as power and wisdom but which God views as weakness and foolishness.

Paul's theology of the cross is a theology about God and the way in which God has chosen to save humanity.[9] Although one would have expected God to save humanity through a powerful display of wisdom and power that the world would have immediately recognized, God chose to save humanity through the folly and weakness of the cross. But Paul insists that the weakness of God is stronger than human strength, and the foolishness of God is wiser than human wisdom. For this reason, the word of the cross stands in contradiction to every human attempt to determine how God should act. The message about the cross is the beginning of a dialectical theology that affirms that every theology which does not take into account the cross of Christ is inadequate.

This does not mean that it is impossible to know God. For although humanity failed to know God on the basis of its own wisdom, it can know God through the message of the cross on the basis of faith. Consequently, those who believe are on the way to salvation, whereas those who view the message of the cross as foolishness are perishing. The contrast and paradox that Paul establishes in 1 Cor. 1:18–25 can be diagrammed as follows:

The message of the cross	foolishness	to those perishing
	but	
	the power of God	to those being saved
	for	

Jews demand signs
Greeks desire wisdom
but
Paul proclaims Christ crucified
a stumbling block to Jews
foolishness to Gentiles
but

to those who are called	Jews and Greeks alike
the power of God	
the wisdom of God	
for	

| God's foolishness | is wiser than human wisdom |
| God's weakness | is stronger than human strength |

---

9. This point is made by Victor Furnish, *The Theology of the First Letter to the Corinthians* (NTT; Cambridge: Cambridge University Press, 1999), 40–46.

The contrasts that Paul establishes between (1) those who are being saved and those who are perishing, (2) those who believe and those who do not, (3) power and weakness, and (4) wisdom and foolishness, are mediated by the message about the cross. Those who believe and are being saved understand that the cross is the power and wisdom of God, whereas those who refuse to believe are perishing because they see the cross as utter weakness and folly.

Paul verifies this theology of the cross in two ways, by the circumstances that attended the call of the Corinthians (1:26–31) and by the manner in which he initially proclaimed the gospel to them (2:1–5). Reminding the Corinthians of their call, he notes that the majority of them were not among the powerful or well-bred when God called them. But it was precisely because of their lowly and despised circumstances that God chose them: to shame the wise and the strong, "to reduce to nothing the things that are" (1:28). God's purpose in electing them was to forestall all human boasting. Therefore, the wisdom, righteousness, sanctification, and redemption they now enjoy come from God through the crucified Messiah. The very election of the Corinthians, then, is a verification of the message about the cross. For just as God manifested power and wisdom in the weakness and folly of the cross, so God manifested power and wisdom by choosing the weak and the foolish to confound the powerful and the wise. This theology of the cross, which forestalls any boasting in one's election, gives a new and added dimension to the election theology of the Thessalonian correspondence.[10]

Paul's own proclamation of the gospel at Corinth provided him with a second way to substantiate his message about the cross. Referring to the message about the cross as "the mystery of God," he insists that he did not proclaim this mystery in "lofty words or wisdom" (2:1). Rather, he preached the gospel of a crucified Christ lest "the cross of Christ" be emptied of its power (1:17). When he proclaimed this offensive message about the cross, the power of God was revealed so that the faith of the Corinthians now rests on the power of God rather than on human wisdom (2:5).

Having said that he did not proclaim the mystery of God in lofty words or wisdom, Paul insists that the gospel he preaches does impart wisdom to those who are mature in faith (2:6). However, whereas the Corinthians grounded their wisdom in the person of the one who had baptized them—confusing the wisdom of God with human wisdom—Paul maintains that the wisdom he imparts is not his own but the secret and hidden wisdom of God revealed by the Spirit. This is why Paul calls the gospel "the mystery of God" (2:1), for the wisdom it discloses is the hidden purpose of God, decreed long ago and now

---

10. Jürgen Becker (*Paul: Apostle to the Gentiles* [Louisville: Westminster John Knox Press, 1993], 197–216) notes that Paul enriches the election theology of 1 Thessalonians with a theology of the cross in the Corinthian correspondence.

revealed in Christ. This mystery of God is not a wisdom the world could have attained on the basis of its own wisdom; otherwise its rulers would not have crucified "the Lord of glory" (2:8).[11] It is a wisdom taught by the Spirit, not by human beings (2:13).

To explain what he means by being taught by the Spirit, Paul distinguishes between those who belong to the realm of what is merely natural and those who belong to the realm of the Spirit. Since the mystery of God can be revealed by the Spirit only to those who live in the realm of the Spirit, those who are merely natural cannot discern the wisdom God reveals in the crucified Christ. Because the Spirit does not dwell in them to instruct them, they look at the cross as foolishness and weakness. In contrast to the natural person (*psychikos*), the spiritual person (*pneumatikos*) is the one instructed in the mysteries of God through the Spirit (2:14–15). It is this Spirit who communicates spiritual things to those who are spiritual.

But if the Corinthians have already received the Spirit, why is the mystery of God about the cross hidden from them? Although Paul acknowledges that all who have been baptized into Christ live in the realm of the Spirit, he is aware that not all are mature (*teleios*) in Christ. Factions and divisions among believers indicate that they are still living in a merely human way even though they have been baptized into Christ. Such people are *sarkikoi* because they are living in a manner that characterizes those who live in the realm of the flesh (3:3). They are immature believers; they are "as infants in Christ" (*hōs nēpiois en Christō*, 3:1). By making this distinction between those in Christ who are mature and those who are not, Paul shows that he is a realist. He does not view the Spirit as a force that magically transforms people with or without their cooperation. This is why he can even call those who have been baptized into Christ *sarkikoi* when they live in a way that does not correspond to the message about the cross.

The relationship of the message of the cross, the Spirit, and the wisdom of God can be summarized as follows. The wisdom the Spirit reveals is the hidden mystery of God revealed in the message about the cross. When this message is appropriated by faith, the wisdom and power of God are revealed in the weakness and folly of the cross. Without the Spirit, the cross is emptied of its power because there would be no resurrection. Without the cross, the wisdom and power of God remain hidden, for God has chosen to act through the foolishness and weakness of the cross. Only when the cross and the Spirit are related to each other are the power and wisdom of God revealed. Because the Corinthi-

---

11. "The Lord of glory" is a rather unusual expression, and this is the only place it occurs, suggesting to some that it may have been a way in which the Corinthians referred to Christ. But even if the expression came from the Corinthian church, it is not foreign to Paul's theology, which insists that Jesus is the image of God, the one on whose face God's own glory is reflected (2 Cor. 3:18; 4:4–6).

ans emphasized the life of the Spirit apart from the folly and scandal of the cross, they fell short of the mystery of God revealed in the crucified Christ.

THE SANCTIFIED COMMUNITY
AND THE WORSHIPING ASSEMBLY

That the church plays a central role in Paul's Corinthian correspondence is evident from the numerous times he employs the term *ekklēsia* in these two letters. Of the many uses of *ekklēsia* in the New Testament, more than one-fourth occur in 1 and 2 Corinthians.[12] That the church should play a central role in Paul's letters is not surprising since, apart from his letters to individuals, Paul normally addresses specific communities of believers.[13] Nonetheless, the frequency with which he speaks about the *ekklēsia* in his Corinthian correspondence is striking, and it is best explained by the circumstances that occasioned these letters: the oral reports Paul received about the congregation and the letter that the congregation sent to him, which together raised a number of issues pertinent to the moral life of the Corinthians and their worshiping assembly. Because of these circumstances, it was necessary for Paul to remind the Corinthians of their new status as a sanctified community that worshiped God and acclaimed Jesus as its Lord in the power of the Spirit. Paul, then, is not writing an ecclesiology any more than he set out to write a theology of the cross. Once more he is applying the gospel to the situation he encountered at Corinth. In the case of 1 and 2 Corinthians, this application of the gospel explains what it means for the church to be a sanctified community in light of God's call, manifested in and through the cross of Christ.

The Church and the Church of God

The Greek word *ekklēsia* derives from two words, the preposition *ek* ("from," "out of") and the verb *kalein* ("to call"), giving the meaning "called out." From an etymological point of view, then, *ekklēsia* is well suited to Paul's election theology inasmuch as he views the *ekklēsia* as the congregation of those whom God has called forth through the death and resurrection of his Son. In secular use, the word referred to an assembly of free men who were entitled to

---

12. Of the 114 occurrences of *ekklēsia* in the New Testament, 38 appear in the nondisputed Pauline letters (Romans, 5 times; 1 Corinthians, 21 times; 2 Corinthians, 9 times; Galatians, 3 times; Philippians, 2 times; 1 Thessalonians, 2 times; Philemon, 1 time) and 18 in the disputed Pauline letters (Ephesians, 9 times; Colossians, 4 times, 2 Thessalonians, 2 times; 1 Timothy, 3 times).

13. Although the letter to Philemon is addressed to an individual, it greets the church in Philemon's house. Romans is something of an anomaly since its greeting does not identify the recipients as the church at Rome. But it is clear that Paul views the believers at Rome as forming a church inasmuch as he refers to a number of house churches in Romans 16.

vote.[14] This is how Luke employs it in Acts 19:39. For Paul and other New Testament writers, however, *ekklēsia* now refers to the Christian assembly or congregation that consists of those who call on the name of the Lord Jesus Christ. The fuller expression, *ekklēsia tou theou* ("the church of God"), identifies this assembly as belonging to God because the God and Father of Jesus Christ is the one who called it into being through the death and resurrection of his Son. Jürgen Roloff suggests that "this formulation might have come into existence as the translation of *qᵉhal 'ēl* ['congregation of God'], which is attested in apocalyptic Judaism as a term for the eschatological company of God."[15] Whatever the precise origins of the term, the New Testament writers gave *ekklēsia* a religious dimension that cannot be understood apart from God's call in Jesus Christ.

In his Corinthian correspondence, Paul tends to employ *ekklēsia* in one of three ways. First, it can refer to the local congregation that makes up the Corinthian church. A good example is found in 1 Cor. 11:18, "For, to begin with, when you come together as a church (*en ekklēsia*), I hear that there are divisions among you; and to some extent I believe it." From this verse, it is evident that the church comes into being when it assembles as a body of believers. (*Ekklēsia* also refers to the local congregation in 1 Cor. 6:4; 14:4, 5, 12, 19, 23, 28, 34.) Second, just as Paul refers to the Corinthian assembly of believers as an *ekklēsia*, so he calls other assemblies "churches" as well. For example, he speaks of the churches of Galatia (1 Cor. 16:1), Asia (1 Cor. 16:19), and Macedonia (2 Cor. 8:1). Or he refers to "every church" (1 Cor. 4:17), "other churches" (2 Cor. 11:8), "all the churches of the saints" (1 Cor. 14:33), or simply "the churches" (2 Cor. 8:23; 11:28). Thus there are numerous churches or congregations. Third, Paul speaks of "the church of God." For example, in 1 Cor. 1:2 and 2 Cor. 1:1, he greets "the church of God that is in Corinth." In 1 Cor. 10:32 he says that he gives no offense "to Jews or to Greeks or to the church of God," and in 11:22 he rebukes the Corinthians for showing "contempt for the church of God." In 15:9 he acknowledges that he once persecuted "the church of God." Paul can also use this expression in the plural, as he does in 11:16, "We have no such custom, nor do the churches of God." Thus "each local community was in essence *the* church of God."[16]

Paul's use of *ekklēsia tou theou* in 1 Cor. 15:9 and Gal. 1:13, where he writes that he persecuted "the church of God," suggests that he may have had in mind something more than the local congregation. For Paul, the church of God, which originated in the Jerusalem community, is embodied in all of the congregations that call upon the name of the Lord, Gentile as well as Jewish. Con-

---

14. *EDNT* 1:411.
15. Ibid.
16. Donald Guthrie, *New Testament Theology* (Downers Grove, IL: InterVarsity Press, 1981), 743.

sequently, although he does not explicitly distinguish between the local assembly and what later theology would call the universal church—a concept Colossians and Ephesians broach when they present the church as the body of Christ and Christ as its head—Paul intimates that the church is more than the sum of its congregations.[17]

The Sanctified Community

Paul's concept of the church is intimately related to his presentation of it as a sanctified community, which in turn is related to his theology of election and his theology of the cross. This is apparent in Paul's greeting to the Corinthians: "To the church of God that is in Corinth, to those who are sanctified in Christ Jesus, called to be saints, together with all those who in every place call on the name of our Lord Jesus Christ, both their Lord and ours: Grace to you and peace from God our Father and the Lord Jesus Christ" (1 Cor. 1:2–3). Here Paul identifies the church of God that is in Corinth in three ways. First, it is a community of the sanctified in Christ Jesus (*hēgiasmenois en Christō Iēsou*). Second, it is a community of people called to be holy (*klētois hagiois*). Third, it is a community associated with other congregations throughout the world who call on the name of the Lord Jesus Christ.

The church is a sanctified community not because of anything it has done but because those who call upon the name of the Lord have been washed, sanctified (*hēgiasthēte*), and justified "in the name of the Lord Jesus Christ and in the Spirit of our God" (1 Cor. 6:11). Consequently, their sanctification is not their own but comes from Jesus Christ, "who became for us wisdom from God, and righteousness and sanctification (*hagiasmos*) and redemption" (1:30). This sanctification, then, derives from God in Christ, who has consecrated them and set them apart for service to God, just as Israel of old was set apart and consecrated for service to God (Exod. 19:6).

Because the church consists of those who have been sanctified, consecrated, and set apart, its members are "called to be saints" (*klētois hagiois*, 1 Cor. 1:2). Although the translation of the NRSV is technically correct, it can be misleading if it is primarily interpreted in terms of attaining moral holiness. This meaning, to be sure, is included in the concept of holiness, but it is not its primary sense. When Paul writes that the Corinthians have been "called to be saints," he means that they are the object of God's elective love in Jesus Christ, whose death and resurrection have consecrated and set them aside for service to God. Thus the text might be better rendered, "called to sanctification" or

---

17. Although Paul never develops a specific teaching about the universal nature of the church, his understanding of the church as the body of Christ (discussed below under "The Worshiping Community") implies the universal nature of the church inasmuch as there cannot be more than one body of Christ.

even "called to be set apart." This sanctification, which refers to the holiness God has already communicated to believers in Christ, implies a corresponding moral holiness. But the emphasis remains on the sanctification believers have already received through Christ. It is this sanctification or holiness from God that enables and summons them to live a moral life.

The church of God in Corinth calls upon the name of Jesus Christ as their Lord with other churches throughout the world. This association of the church of God at Corinth with other sanctified communities points to an intimate union in Christ, which churches everywhere have with one another as a result of their election and faith in Jesus their Lord. It also intimates, though it does not explicitly say so, that the many congregations that call upon the name of the Lord belong to the one church of God. The opening greeting of 1 Corinthians, then, summarizes the essential nature of the church: it is an elect community that has been sanctified in Christ. Therefore, it is to live as a community of the sanctified, that is, of those who have been consecrated and set aside for service to God.

In the opening chapters of 1 Corinthians (1:10–4:21), Paul's task is to persuade the sanctified community at Corinth that it cannot be faithful to its vocation as a sanctified community if it falls into rivalries and factions based on allegiance to particular apostles. Consequently, he calls the community to "be united in the same mind and the same purpose" (1:10). To make his point, Paul insists that the Corinthians owe their existence as a church to Christ, who was crucified for them and into whose name they were baptized (1:13). God chose and called them as a church from among the weak and foolish to confound the wisdom and power of the world (1:26–31). Thus the election of the church is intimately related to the message about the cross.

Although many had baptized and preached at Corinth, a fact that accounts for the rivalries within the community, the growth of the church comes from God rather than from those who minister to it. Apostolic ministers are merely "God's servants" (3:9), "servants of Christ and stewards of God's mysteries" (4:1). Since these ministers belong to God and Christ, and since it is God who gives the church its growth, the church is "God's field, God's building" (3:9), and its foundation is Jesus Christ (3:11). Therefore, it is rightly called God's temple because God's Spirit dwells within it (3:16–17).

The point of Paul's argument in 1:10–4:21, then, is that there is no place for rivalry and factions within the church of God because the church does not belong to those who preach the gospel but to God who called it into being through the message about the cross. Because the church of God belongs to God, it must "be united in the same mind and the same purpose" (1:10), for it has been called to be a sanctified community, the temple and dwelling place of God.

Threats to the Sanctity of the Community

Although the Corinthians undoubtedly thought of themselves as God's sanctified community, since they had experienced such a powerful outpouring of the Spirit, they do not appear to have understood the full implications of their election to this sanctified community.[18] Consequently, in 5:1–11:1 Paul addresses a number of issues that, if left untended, would have threatened the life of the sanctified community: the case of a man living in an immoral relationship with his father's wife (5:1–13); the anomaly of believers asking nonbelievers to adjudicate lawsuits between believers (6:1–8); the situation of those who continue to engage in prostitution (6:9–20); a movement that encouraged sexual abstinence within marriage and appears to have discouraged marriage (7:1–40); and participation in idolatry (8:1–11:1). From Paul's perspective each of these issues, in one way or another, threatens to compromise the God-given holiness and sanctity of the community. Consequently, Paul must remind the Corinthians that there are certain boundaries beyond which they may not trespass if they are to remain the sanctified community of the church.

For example, in the case of the man living in an immoral relationship with his father's wife, Paul reminds the community that they are like a new batch of unleavened bread because Christ, their paschal lamb, has been sacrificed for them. Therefore, they must cast out the immoral man from their midst if they are to remain a sanctified community (5:7). To those who bring lawsuits against fellow believers to nonbelievers, Paul asks, "Do you not know that the saints will judge the world?" (6:2). In this way he reminds the community that it is the community of the last days destined to judge angels (6:3). Consequently, if it cannot judge its own disputes, it betrays its deepest identity. To those who continue to frequent prostitutes, Paul reminds them that they were washed, sanctified, and justified at the time of their baptism into Christ (6:11). Consequently, their bodies now belong to Christ (6:15); they are temples of the Holy Spirit (6:19). For this reason, they must shun *porneia* ("immorality," NAB; 6:18). To those who encourage sexual abstinence within marriage and discourage the unmarried from marrying, Paul reminds them of the danger of immorality (7:2). He himself is a practicing celibate, and he would like others to follow his example (7:7). But he is keenly aware that this is a gift, and not all have such self-control (7:7). He is willing to allow the married to abstain from sexual relations for a time in order to devote themselves to prayer, but

18. Becker (*Paul: Apostle to the Gentiles*, 199–201) suggests that the problems between Paul and the Corinthians may have been caused by a clash of cultures. He argues that what the Corinthians thought was perfectly acceptable behavior, given their Hellenistic culture, Paul perceived as immoral and unacceptable, given his Jewish background.

they eventually must come together lest Satan tempt them and the sanctity of the community be violated by immorality.[19] Likewise, he would like the unmarried to remain as they are, if they can, since "the appointed time," the parousia, is close at hand (7:29). But again, Paul is a realist. Those who cannot exercise self-control should marry lest they fall into immorality and compromise the sanctity of the community.

Finally, Paul admonishes those who mistakenly believe that they are immune from immorality because they have been baptized and participate in the Eucharist. He reminds them that Israel of old was baptized into Moses, ate and drank the same spiritual food (the manna in the wilderness) and the same spiritual drink (the water from the rock), and yet this sanctified community, which had its own sacraments, fell into idolatry (10:1–5). Paul insists that the sanctified community of the church should learn from the story of the sanctified community of Israel. The members of the church must not become idolaters or indulge in sexual immorality. Baptism and the Eucharist are not magical rites that preserve believers from immorality and idolatry. Consequently, believers must flee all idolatrous worship (10:14), remembering that their *koinōnia* ("participation") in the Eucharist is a *koinōnia* in Christ. They cannot be *koinōnous* ("partners") of demons by participating in idolatrous worship and be partners of Christ (10:20–21). As members of the sanctified community, they belong to Christ and no other.

To summarize, in 5:1–11:1 Paul deals with a number of issues that threaten the sanctity of the community. His application of the gospel to these issues focuses the attention of the Corinthians on the nature of the community to which they belong. As the church of God, they have been called into being as a community of the washed, the sanctified, the justified (6:11), a community bought at a price (6:20), namely, the death of Christ. Although Paul does not expect believers to flee the world—as if believers could live without associating with the immoral of the world (5:9–10)—he does urge them to expel those believers who practice immorality lest the sanctity of the community be compromised. Paul sees the church as a community of the sanctified that lives in the world and yet remains apart from the immorality and idolatry of the world. Believers will associate with nonbelievers, many of whom are immoral. But they must not tolerate immorality or idolatry in their community because God has called them, in Christ, to holiness. This is precisely what Paul already reminded the Thessalonians when he wrote, "For this is the will of God, your sanctification (*hagiasmos*): that you abstain from fornication (*porneias*). . . . For God did not call us to impurity (*akatharsia*) but in holiness (*en hagiasmō*)" (1 Thess. 4:3, 7).

---

19. When Paul writes, "This I say by way of concession, not of command" (1 Cor. 7:6), the concession refers to their desire to abstain from conjugal relations. He is not saying that he allows marriage by way of concession.

The Worshiping Community

In 1 Cor. 11:2–14:40 Paul deals with a number of problems that threaten to disrupt the internal life of the church at worship: the conduct of women who prophesy within the worshiping assembly (11:2–16); the conduct of the Corinthians at the fellowship meals that accompany their celebration of the Lord's Supper (11:17–34); rivalries and disputes within the community about the gifts of the Spirit (12:1–14:33a; 14:37–40); and the problem of women speaking publicly when the community gathers as a church (14:33b–36). Although the issues with which Paul deals in these chapters are foreign and strange to contemporary believers, the manner in which he responds to them reveals a great deal about his understanding of the church, its worship, and its sacraments.

A Eucharistic Assembly

Paul refers to the Eucharist in 1 Corinthians on two occasions. In the first (10:14–22), he warns those who think that their "knowledge" allows them to participate in idolatrous worship and still share in the Eucharist. In order to dissuade them, he reminds them that when they celebrate the Lord's Supper, the cup of blessing they bless is a communion or participation (*koinōnia*) in the blood of Christ, and the bread they break is a communion or participation in the body of Christ. The celebration of the Eucharist, then, is not a mere memorial service but an intimate union with a living Lord, which is incongruous with idolatrous worship. Consequently, those who participate in the Eucharist cannot share in both the cup of demons (idolatrous worship) and the cup of the Lord (the Eucharist) since participation in one excludes participation in the other. The Eucharist identifies the church as a community that belongs to a particular Lord whose lordship cannot be compromised, and the celebration of the Eucharist provides the church with a profound reminder of its unity in Christ. For although the community is made up of many members, it forms one body because all partake of the one bread (10:17).

In 11:17–34 Paul reminds the community of the significance of the Eucharist once more. But whereas the occasion for his first discussion (10:14–22) was the danger of idolatry, the occasion for this discussion (11:17–34) is the manner in which the community gathers for the fellowship meal that precedes the Eucharist. A fellowship meal that should have embraced all the members of the community has become a discriminatory meal during which some eat to excess while the poorer members of the community go hungry (11:17–22). Confronted with this anomaly that undermines the unity of the church, Paul reminds the Corinthians of the eucharistic tradition he has handed on to them, concluding that "as often as you eat this bread and drink the cup, you proclaim the Lord's death until he comes" (11:26). He then exhorts the Corinthians to examine themselves before they participate in the Eucharist lest they eat and drink "without discerning the body" (11:29). He concludes by advising the community that when it gathers to eat, it should wait for everyone, so that all can participate in the meal. Those who are too hungry to wait should eat at home (11:33–34).

The manner in which Paul reminds the community of what it already knows indicates that the Eucharist plays a central role in its life. This is true even if the community does not completely understand the full significance of its action, namely, that the sacrament is an intimate participation in the life of Christ and a proclamation of his death until he comes again. The celebration of the Lord's Supper, then, is meant to identify the church as a community that belongs to the one Lord and proclaims his death until he returns at the parousia, when there will be no further need to celebrate the Eucharist. In the period before the Lord's return, the Eucharist is the sacramental way in which the church proclaims the death of its Lord. This sacramental proclamation of his death does not do away with the need to preach the message of the cross, nor does the proclamation of the cross make the celebration of the Eucharist irrelevant. But whereas the preaching of Christ crucified is the way in which the church evangelizes the world, the celebration of the Eucharist is the manner in which it proclaims the message about the cross in worship until the Lord returns. In doing so, it submits itself in obedience to its Lord by its participation in the one bread and the one cup, a sharing that excludes allegiance to any other lord.

One Body

Paul is aware that there are a variety of gifts, services, and activities within the church that derive from the same Spirit, the same Lord, the same God (12:4–6). Therefore, he compares the church to a body, arguing that just as the body has many members, all of which are intended for the common good of the body, so the church has many members whose diverse gifts are for the common good. The analogy that Paul draws between the body and the church expands upon a well-known metaphor comparing society to a body.[20] The remarkable aspect of Paul's analogy, however, is the manner in which he relates the image of the body to Christ.

He begins with an opening statement that disrupts the expected analogy. Instead of saying that just as the body is one and has many members, so it is with the church, he writes, "For just as the body is one and has many members, and all the members of the body, though many, are one, so it is with Christ (*houtōs kai ho Christos*)" (12:12). Thus he implies that the church is the body of Christ, even though he does not make this explicit until 12:27. To support the relationship he draws between the body and Christ, he alludes to what may

20. On this point see the discussion in Raymond F. Collins, *First Corinthians* (SP 7; Collegeville, MN: Liturgical Press, 1999), 458–59.

have been a creedal or baptismal formula reminiscent of that found in Gal. 3:28, noting that all were baptized "into one body" (*eis hen sōma*) by the one Spirit, and "were all made to drink of one Spirit" (12:13). Since those who are baptized are baptized into Christ, the one body into which all were baptized is the body of Christ. At the moment of their baptism, then, believers entered into the body of Christ. It was at that moment that they were made to drink of the one Spirit that provides the church with a variety of gifts.[21] Baptism into the body of Christ, then, is the way in which believers enter into the Spirit-filled community of the church.

Having drawn a relationship between the body and Christ—rather than between the body and the church—Paul explains that the body is composed of many parts, each of which is necessary for the body to function properly (12:14–26). After this detailed image, he concludes, "Now you are the body of Christ (*hymeis de este sōma Christou*) and individually members of it" (12:27). With this statement, Paul makes two points. First, what was implicitly stated earlier ("For just as the body is one . . . , so it is with Christ") is now made explicit. In a way that Paul does not fully explain, the community of believers—the church—can be called "the body of Christ." Second, just as each believer has been baptized into Christ, so each is a member of Christ's body. Thus the baptized belong to the body of Christ corporately as a community of believers and individually as members of Christ's body. Belonging to Christ, then, can be viewed from two vantage points: (1) from the perspective of the community of believers that is one body in Christ, and (2) from the vantage point of the individual members of the church, each of whom is a member of Christ's body with a particular role to play.

Although Paul explicitly says, "You are the body of Christ," the precise meaning of the phrase is unclear. Is the genitive (*sōma Christou*) to be taken as indicating possession, giving the meaning that the church *belongs* to Christ? Or is it to be construed as pointing to identity: the church *is* the body of Christ present in the world today? Neither interpretation is completely satisfactory. Whereas the first seems to claim too little, given Paul's statement that believers have been baptized into one body (12:13), the second is in danger of claiming too much, as if the church is the Lord's alter ego. Paul's statement in Rom. 12:4–5 is more nuanced: "For as in one body we have many members, and not all the members have the same function, so we, who are many, are one body in Christ (*hen sōma esmen en Christō*), and individually we are members of one another." Rather than say, "You are the body of Christ," Paul writes, "We are

---

21. Although the imagery of "drinking" might suggest that Paul is referring to the Eucharist, the context indicates that he has baptism in view. In one Spirit all were baptized into the one body, and entering into that body the baptized received ("were made to drink") the one Spirit. See C. K. Barrett, *A Commentary on the First Epistle to the Corinthians* (HNTC; New York: Harper & Row, 1968), 289.

one body in Christ." The formulation of Romans suggests that what Paul writes in 1 Corinthians stands somewhere between the two interpretations noted above (possession and identity). The image of the church as the body of Christ is not merely a metaphor for possession nor can it be taken in the full sense of identity. The church is truly the body of Christ, but it does not take the place of Christ its Lord. Ephesians and Colossians provide a helpful way forward when they portray the church as the body of Christ and Christ as the head of the church (Eph. 4:15–16; Col. 1:18), thereby showing that while the church is truly the body of Christ, Christ remains its Lord.[22]

A Variety of Gifts

Because believers were made to drink of the one Spirit at their baptism, the church possesses a variety of spiritual gifts. In 1 Cor. 12:8–10 Paul lists the utterance of wisdom, the utterance of knowledge, faith, gifts of healing, the working of miracles, prophecy, the discernment of spirits, various kinds of tongues, and the interpretation of tongues among these gifts, emphasizing that they come from the same Spirit. In 12:27–28 he speaks of different roles or offices within the body of Christ as gifts of the Spirit: apostles, prophets, teachers, deeds of power, gifts of healing, forms of assistance, forms of leadership, various kinds of tongues. In order to remind the Corinthians that various members of the body play different roles within it, he asks, "Are all apostles? Are all prophets? Are all teachers? Do all work miracles? Do all possess gifts of healing? Do all speak in tongues? Do all interpret?" (12:29–30).

In chapter 14 Paul takes up the immediate issue that occasions his discussion of the gifts of the Spirit (12:1–11): the significance and role of "tongues" within the worshiping assembly. Because of its esoteric nature, this gift was especially prized by the Corinthians and occasioned rivalries between those who possessed the gift and those who did not. The manner in which Paul responds to this problem provides further insight into his understanding of the church as a local assembly gifted by the Spirit.

Although Paul possesses the gift of tongues and would like others to share in the same gift (14:5, 18), he places greater value on the gift of prophecy. For whereas those who speak in tongues "build up" or edify themselves, those who prophesy "build up the church" by their ability to interpret the speech of those who speak in tongues (14:4). Those who speak in tongues speak not to others but to God, and nobody understands them because they are speaking "mysteries in the Spirit" (14:2–4).[23] Of itself, the gift of tongues does not build up

---

22. However, whereas in Romans and 1 Corinthians Paul is speaking of the church as the local congregation, Ephesians and Colossians are speaking of the universal church.

23. These mysteries of the Spirit appear to be divine mysteries known only to God. The one who speaks in tongues utters them but is not able to reveal or explain them; thus the need for prophecy.

the church. If the church is to be built up, there is need for someone to interpret the "mysteries of the Spirit" uttered by those who speak in tongues. The relative importance of the gifts of the Spirit to the church, then, does not derive from the esoteric or spectacular nature of the gift but from the gift's ability to build up the church. When Paul lists the different gifts that function as roles or offices within the church, therefore, apostles, prophets, and teachers stand at the head of the list because they play the most significant roles in building up the church (12:28–29). When the church comes together as a worshiping assembly, then, everything should be done to ensure that it will be built up. If there is no one who can interpret tongues, those who possess the gift of tongues should remain silent within the worshiping assembly (14:28) since the purpose of their gift is not to edify themselves but to build up the church.

An Orderly Assembly

Paul's discussion of spiritual gifts in 12:1–14:40 reveals that the Corinthian community was especially gifted. To employ contemporary jargon, it was a charismatic community. Nevertheless, Paul insists that the worshiping assembly should also be an orderly assembly that respects the custom of the other churches of God. Consequently, when women prophets prayed and prophesied in the worshiping assembly with their heads unveiled, Paul's final argument is: "We have no such custom, nor do the churches of God" (11:16)—referring to women prophesying while unveiled, not to their prophesying. When he learns that women are publicly speaking when the congregation gathers as a church, he argues, "As in all the churches of the saints, women should be silent in the churches. . . . For it is shameful for a woman to speak in church" (14:33a–34, 35b), perhaps referring to a public gathering or meeting of the church rather than to its worship.[24]

Each of these texts presents difficulties for contemporary readers. On the one hand, they appear to contradict each other since Paul assumes that women can prophesy and pray in the worshiping assembly, but he excludes them from speaking in the assembly. Likewise, they appear to contradict the spirit of equality that Paul manifests in Gal. 3:28, "there is no longer male or female; for all of you are one in Christ." Given the continuing debate about the precise situation that occasioned these texts, and the repeated suggestion that 1 Cor. 14:33b–36 is a later interpolation, the meaning of the texts is contested. From the point of view of Paul's ecclesiology, however, both texts argue for order within the worshiping assembly, as do Paul's instruction about the order of worship in 14:26–33a, where he concludes, "For God is a God not of disorder but of peace." Contemporary readers need not adopt Paul's views about

---

24. Here the "church" refers to the coming together of the community as a church, God's congregation, rather than to a building.

how women should be attired or the need for them to be silent in a gathering of the assembly, but the underlying point he makes in these texts remains important: the church ought to be an ordered assembly that witnesses to the God of peace rather than to a god of disorder. Therefore, although contemporary believers will order their own congregational life differently than did the churches of the New Testament period, the goal of structuring the church in an orderly way, without extinguishing the power of the Spirit within the church (see 1 Thess. 5:19), must be respected.

Conclusion

This discussion of the church in 1 Corinthians can be summarized as follows. The church is a sanctified community because its members, who have responded in faith to the message about the cross, have been elected and sanctified by God in Jesus Christ. This sanctified community is God's own assembly, the church of God, God's field, God's building, the temple of God. Because it has been consecrated and set aside for service to God, the church must flee from all immorality and idolatry. Like Israel of old, it must be holy because God is holy. The local assembly of the church is the body of Christ, constituted by its baptism into the one body of Christ. Each time it celebrates the Eucharist, it participates in the life of its Lord and proclaims his death until he comes again, thereby witnessing to the message about the cross. As a worshiping assembly, it is gifted with a variety of gifts that come from the same Spirit, all of which are intended to build up the church. This worshiping community, under the powerful guidance of the Spirit, is nonetheless an ordered assembly because it belongs to the God of peace rather than to a god of disorder.

APOSTOLIC MINISTRY IN LIGHT OF THE CROSS

Paul's understanding of his apostleship is intimately related to his theology of the cross, as well as to his theology of the church as a called and sanctified community. More importantly, the manner in which he exercises his apostleship is a concrete manifestation of the gospel he preaches. On the one hand, as the minister of a new covenant he exercises a ministry of the Spirit that reveals the glory of God shining on the face of Christ, who is the image of God. On the other, the afflictions and sufferings he endures for the gospel are the ways in which he carries in his body the death or the dying of Jesus (2 Cor. 4:10).[25]

---

25. According to BDAG, the term that Paul employs here, *nekrōsis*, can refer to death as a process, "death," "putting to death," or to the cessation of a state or activity, "deadness," "mortification." The first interpretation fits the context best. Paul is in the process of dying because of the dangers and afflictions he endures for the sake of Jesus. Thus he is carrying "the dying of Jesus" within his body.

To be faced with Paul's apostolic ministry is to be confronted with the gospel he preaches.

Because he exercises this ministry for the sake of the church, there is an intimate bond between Paul and the communities he establishes. He is their father in Christ, and members of the congregation are his dear children in Christ (1 Cor. 4:14–15). The community is his letter of recommendation, a letter written on his own heart for all to see and read (2 Cor. 3:1–3).[26] The community is a chaste virgin that he has promised in marriage to Christ, and which it is his duty to present to Christ on the day of the Lord's parousia (2 Cor. 11:2). It is imperative for Paul, then, that the community live out its vocation as a sanctified congregation if it is to be Christ's bride. It is also imperative for Paul, as the founding apostle of the community, to do everything in his power to preserve the church from defilement.

There is an intimate connection, then, between Paul's theology of the cross, his understanding of apostolic ministry, and his ecclesiology. The gospel of Christ's death and resurrection is the pattern for Paul's ministry, and this pattern determines the way in which he cultivates and forms the churches entrusted to his care.

But just as Paul developed his theology of the cross and his understanding of the church in light of the situation that occasioned his Corinthian correspondence, so he develops his understanding of apostolic ministry in light of the problems and crises he faced at Corinth. In 1 Corinthians 1–4 he reflects on the nature of apostolic ministry in order to dissuade the Corinthians from attaching themselves to particular apostles and falling into rival factions. In 1 Corinthians 9 he uses the example of his ministry to persuade the stronger members of the community to refrain from insisting upon their rights, just as he has sacrificed many of his legitimate rights as an apostle for the sake of the gospel. But it is in 2 Corinthians that Paul presents his most extended exposition of apostolic ministry.

The immediate occasion for this discussion of apostolic ministry in 2 Corinthians was a crisis in Paul's relationship with the church that has several dimensions: (1) the continuing problem of immorality at Corinth; (2) Paul's painful visit to Corinth after writing 1 Corinthians; (3) the harsh letter he sent to the community in response to this visit; (4) Paul's refusal to accept financial support from Corinth; and (5) the presence of intruding apostles whose powerful ministry and willingness to accept the financial patronage of the Corinthians called into question Paul's ministry among certain factions at Corinth. If 1 Corinthians is about the Corinthian community, 2 Corinthians is about Paul.

26. Paul is referring to his apostolic work of establishing the church at Corinth. The work that he has already done at Corinth is something that all can read, even though it is written on his heart, because it is visible in the community he has established.

Second Corinthians is perhaps the most personal of Paul's letters. It is a letter in which he opens his heart to the Corinthians and asks them to do the same (2 Cor. 6:11–13; 7:2–4). The personal character of the letter, however, does not mean that it is any less theological. As Paul reflects upon his ministry, he develops a profound theology of the new covenant, of suffering and affliction, of reconciliation, and of power in weakness. In doing so, he relates his theology of the cross to the ministry he exercises and the community he founded at Corinth.

The underlying structure of Paul's theology of apostolic ministry can be summarized under four headings: (1) a ministry of a new covenant; (2) a ministry confirmed by suffering and affliction; (3) a ministry of reconciliation; and (4) a ministry of power in weakness.

A Ministry of a New Covenant

In 2 Cor. 3:6 Paul identifies himself as the minister of "a new covenant."[27] This statement occurs within the wider context of 2:14–4:6, a section in which Paul draws a bold contrast between his own ministry and the ministry of Moses, arguing that whereas the ministry of Moses veiled the glory of God, his ministry reveals the glory of God because it is a ministry of a new covenant.

Paul is conscious that the claims he makes for his ministry are extravagant. But he is also aware that he has been called to be an apostle "of Christ Jesus by the will of God" (1 Cor. 1:1; 2 Cor. 1:1). His apostleship is not something of his own choosing but a call grounded in his encounter with the risen Lord, who commissioned him to be an apostle. So he writes, "Am I not an apostle? Have I not seen Jesus our Lord?" (1 Cor. 9:1; see also 15:8–10). Because he was *chosen* to be an apostle, an obligation has been imposed upon him to preach the gospel (9:16). Consequently, Paul views himself as God's prisoner led in a triumphal procession (2 Cor. 2:14–16). As God's "prisoner," he spreads the fragrance of the knowledge of God by the gospel he preaches. To those who are perishing because they refuse to accept the gospel, this fragrance is the stench of death, but to those who are being saved by the gospel, it is the fragrance of life.

Aware that no one is competent for such a ministry, Paul asks, "Who is sufficient for these things?" (2 Cor. 2:16). The answer, of course, is no one. But since Paul has been called by the risen Lord, he replies, "our competence is from God, who has made us competent to be ministers of a new covenant, not of letter but of spirit; for the letter kills, but the Spirit gives life" (3:5b–6). It is his apostolic call, then, that allows Paul to make the bold comparison he does between his ministry and the ministry of the greatest figure in Israel's history, Moses, the mediator of the Sinai covenant.

---

27. Paul's only other reference to the new covenant occurs in the eucharistic tradition of 1 Cor. 11:23–26, where he writes, "This cup is the new covenant in my blood" (11:25).

It is not Paul's purpose to denigrate Moses or the Sinai covenant. He understands the profound role that Moses and Sinai played in Israel's history. But the salvific event of Christ's death and resurrection and the outpouring of God's Spirit have convinced Paul that the new covenant foretold by Jeremiah (Jer. 31:31–33) and the outpouring of the Spirit promised by Ezekiel (Ezek. 36:26) have arrived. Therefore the ministry that Paul exercises as an apostle of Christ assures him that he has been called to be the minister of a new covenant.[28]

To explain what he means by his new covenant ministry, Paul draws a comparison between his own ministry and the ministry of Moses (2 Cor. 3:7–18). He calls the ministry of Moses one of death and condemnation, whereas his ministry is one of life and righteousness. He calls Moses' ministry one of death and condemnation because, even though it was revealed in glory on Mount Sinai, it did not provide Israel with the Spirit that gives life. It was a ministry of the letter because it was mediated by the written code of the law rather than by the Spirit.[29] By way of contrast, Paul's ministry is a ministry of the Spirit and of life, the fulfillment of the promises made through Jeremiah and Ezekiel.

In 2 Cor. 3:12–18 Paul makes his boldest statements. Recalling the episode from the book of Exodus, which recounts how Moses veiled his face after speaking with God on Mount Sinai lest the Israelites see the reflected glory of God on his face and die (Exod. 34:29–35), Paul asserts that he acts more boldly than Moses did. For whereas Moses put on a veil to prevent the Israelites from gazing on the glory of God reflected on his face, Paul's ministry reveals the glory of God so that believers now see God's glory "with unveiled faces" (2 Cor. 3:18). Paul, of course, is speaking metaphorically, and he is reinterpreting the story of Moses in light of his new understanding of Christ. Paul seems to suppose that Moses knew that the glory of God, reflected on his face, was coming to an end. Therefore he purposely put a veil over his face to keep the Israelites from gazing upon this glory, which he knew would end.[30] The hearts and minds of the Israelites, however, were hardened, and they insisted upon looking at the glory on the face of Moses, even though it was a glory destined to end. Applying this episode to the situation of his contemporaries, Paul says that when they hear the reading of the old covenant, that veil is still present,

28. Paul is not the only minister of this new covenant. Throughout 2 Corinthians he often employs the plural ("we") when speaking of this ministry. Although some of these plurals are literary plurals, which refer to Paul alone, others refer to all the ministers of this new covenant.

29. Paul does not take up the issue of the law in his Corinthian correspondence in the way he does in Romans and Galatians. He does not oppose doing the works of the law and faith in Christ, because the question of justification by faith rather than by doing the works of the law was not an issue at Corinth. Here Paul is indicating that the old covenant, of which Moses was a minister, was not empowered by the Spirit in the way that his new covenant ministry is.

30. Thus Moses is not trying to deceive the people. Rather, aware that the glory of his ministry was destined to pass away, he tries to prevent the Israelites from gazing upon this glory that will be set aside. This, of course, is Paul's Christian interpretation of the text rather than a literal reading of it.

for it can only be removed by Christ. But when one turns to the Lord, the veil is removed, so that those who believe in Christ look "with unveiled faces" and see the glory of the Lord. As they view that glory reflected on the face of Christ, the image of God (4:4, 6), they are transformed from glory to glory.

When Paul calls his ministry the ministry of a new covenant, then, he identifies himself as the minister of the covenant prophesied by Jeremiah, a covenant empowered by the Spirit as promised by Ezekiel. Paul does not claim to be greater than Moses, but he is fully convinced that he has been called to administer a covenant that is more glorious because it is empowered by the Spirit in a way that the Sinai covenant was not. When Paul preaches the gospel of the crucified Christ, then, those who "hear" the gospel "see" the glory of God on the face of the Christ, who is the image of God (4:4). For Paul this extraordinary ministry results from a new act of creation whereby the God who commanded light to shine in darkness enlightened Paul's heart so that he might know the glory of God, which shines on the face of Jesus Christ (4:6). Having learned that Christ is the image of God, on whose face shines the glory of God, Paul, the minister of a new covenant, preaches the message about the cross so that those who *hear* may *see* the glory of God.

A Ministry Confirmed by Suffering and Affliction

As the minister of a new covenant, Paul is aware that the power of his ministry belongs to God and not to himself. Employing the metaphor of a fragile earthen jar that can be broken and destroyed at any moment, he writes, "But we have this treasure in clay jars, so that it may be made clear that this extraordinary power belongs to God and does not come from us" (4:7). In this metaphor, the clay jar is Paul's mortal body that is wasting away day by day as he suffers affliction for the sake of the gospel, whereas "the extraordinary power" (*hē hyperbolē tēs dynameōs*) is the power of the gospel that is paradoxically manifested through his ministerial sufferings and afflictions for it.[31]

Just as Paul affirms that God paradoxically manifests his power and wisdom in the weakness and folly of the cross, so he insists that the life-giving power of the gospel is revealed through the suffering and afflictions that the ministers of the new covenant endure for the sake of the gospel. Describing himself as "afflicted in every way" (4:8), he says that he carries "the death of Jesus" (*tēn nekrōsin tou Iēsou*, 4:10) in his body. This striking expression, which occurs nowhere else in Paul's writings and which might better be rendered "the dying

31. Just as Paul began his discussion of the ministry of a new covenant in 2 Cor. 2:14–4:6 with the metaphor of prisoners being led in triumphal procession, so he begins his discussion of apostolic suffering in 4:7–5:10 with the metaphor of the clay jar. In both instances, the metaphors point to Paul's fragility and weakness as an apostle.

of Jesus," highlights Paul's union with Christ's suffering and death. The affliction he suffers in his body for the sake of the gospel manifests the death or
dying of Jesus, and this dying paradoxically reveals the life of Jesus. Paul's purpose, then, in carrying the *nekrōsis* of Jesus in his mortal body is to make the
life of Jesus visible in his mortal body (4:10). Thus he concludes, "we are always
being given up to death for Jesus' sake, so that the life of Jesus may be made
visible in our mortal flesh. So death is at work in us, but life in you" (4:11–12).

Paul is not substituting his sufferings for Christ's sufferings. Nor is he claiming that his sufferings are redemptive in the way that Christ's sufferings are
redemptive. But he is firmly convinced that those who preach the gospel about
the cross must manifest the message about the cross in their lives. More than an
annoyance, the sufferings of Paul's new covenant ministry embody and illustrate
the gospel he preaches. Consequently, when the church looks at the sufferings
and affliction of its apostolic ministers, it sees the death or dying (*nekrōsis*) of
Jesus. As it contemplates the afflictions of Paul, whose inner nature is being
renewed day by day (4:16), it sees the life of Jesus already present in the suffering apostle. Suffering and affliction for the sake of the gospel, then, become a
way for the ministers of the new covenant to preach the gospel about the cross.

Paul's understanding of his apostolic sufferings was born of personal experience. At the beginning of 2 Corinthians, he alludes to a particularly harsh
affliction he experienced in Asia, when he "despaired of life itself" (1:8).[32] That
experience, which seemed like a death sentence, taught him to rely on "God
who raises the dead" (1:9) rather than on himself. Although Paul undoubtedly
experienced affliction and hardship prior to this, what he endured in Asia gave
him a more profound understanding of the purpose of his sufferings and afflictions and their significance for his ministry. In the benediction of 2 Corinthians (1:3–7), for example, he identifies God as "the God of all consolation" who
comforts him (Paul) in his afflictions so that he can console those in affliction
with the same consolation he has received from God. He now understands that
his afflictions are for the consolation and salvation of others. By enduring
affliction for the sake of the gospel, he provides his converts with a living example of someone whose afflictions have resulted in consolation because the God
of all consolation—the God who raises the dead—is at work in the midst of
affliction. Affliction endured for the sake of the cross, then, mirrors the suffering of Christ. And just as Christ was raised from the dead, so those who are
afflicted will be consoled because the God of all consolation is the God who
raises the dead.

---

32. Although the precise nature of this affliction is unknown, it seems to have played a major
role in the development of Paul's ministry. On this point see A. E. Harvey, *Renewal through Suffering: A Study of 2 Corinthians* (Studies of the New Testament and Its World; Edinburgh: T. & T.
Clark, 1996).

This is not to say that Paul deliberately pursues suffering and affliction. The afflictions and sufferings he endures are the inevitable outcome of a ministry that preaches a crucified Messiah. They come from those who reject a gospel that contradicts the wisdom of this world. From Paul's perspective, authentic apostolic ministry will always involve affliction for the sake of the gospel, whereas a ministry devoid of such suffering is suspect.

Suffering and affliction for the gospel are a badge of honor for Paul, and on several occasions he lists his apostolic sufferings in order to show the relationship between his ministry and the message about the cross. To correct the boasting of those who think they are already reigning with Christ, Paul provides an extended hardship list in which he contrasts the high esteem in which the Corinthians hold themselves with the sufferings he and other apostolic ministers endure for the sake of the gospel (1 Cor. 4:9–13). At the end of the list he concludes, "We have become like the rubbish of the world, the dregs of all things, to this very day."[33] And after describing himself as the minister of a glorious new covenant, in 2 Cor. 4:7–12 he provides a list of his sufferings in order to show that he carries the death/dying of Jesus in his mortal body for the sake of the community. Then, after presenting himself as Christ's ambassador, who calls people to reconciliation, he provides a list of the afflictions he has suffered for the sake of the gospel (6:3–10). Paul's most extended hardship list, however, occurs in 11:22–12:10, where he provides a catalogue of his apostolic sufferings in order to boast in his weakness as an apostle, concluding that when he is weak, then he is strong (12:10). In every instance the purpose of Paul's apostolic suffering is to preach the paradoxical message about the cross: that God manifests power and wisdom through the weakness and folly of the cross.

A Ministry of Reconciliation

The message about the cross is a message of reconciliation. Therefore, in 2 Cor. 5:11–21 Paul describes himself as an ambassador for Christ through whom God appeals to humanity to be reconciled to God. This message of reconciliation is grounded in the death of Christ. Firmly convinced that Christ's death has a salvific value for all humanity, in 5:14–15 Paul draws a comparison between the death of Christ who died for all, on the one hand, and humanity, on the other.

---

33. In 1 Cor. 4:13 Paul writes, "We have become like the rubbish (*perikatharmata*) of the world, the dregs (*peripsēma*) of all things, to this very day." According to BDAG the first term refers to "that which is removed as a result of a thorough cleansing" and the second "to that which is removed by the process of cleansing." Paul may be making the ironic point that he and his fellow apostolic ministers, inasmuch as they are the world's scapegoats, ironically cleanse the very world that despises them, as if they were so much rubbish. See Barrett, *First Corinthians*, 112–13.

One has died *for all*;
> therefore *all have died.*

And he died *for all,*
> so that those who live
> might live no longer for themselves,
> but for him

who died and was raised *for them.*

The phrase "one died for all" (*heis hyper pantōn*) establishes the fundamental contrast and points to the redemptive nature of Christ's death. But what does it mean to say that one man died for all? Paul suggests an answer in the discussion that follows. First he writes, "if any one is in Christ, he is a new creation" (5:17, RSV). Second, he notes, "For our sake he made him to be sin who knew no sin, so that in him we might become the righteousness of God" (5:21). In the first text, Paul presents Christ as a representative figure, the one in whom God's new creation has already begun.[34] Consequently, those who have been incorporated into Christ participate in this new creation, already effective in the one whom God has raised from the dead. In the second (5:21), Paul employs the same preposition he does in 5:14–15, *hyper* ("for"), to emphasize that it was "for" the sake of humanity that God made Christ "sin" so that humanity might become "the righteousness of God." This striking formula does not mean that Christ became a sinner, for Paul says that Christ did not know sin. Rather, it points to a kind of divine interchange similar to that in Gal. 3:13, where Paul notes that Christ redeemed humanity from the curse of the law by becoming a curse. As in Galatians, Paul employs the language of interchange in 2 Corinthians to show that at God's initiative Christ stood in the human condition (which Paul describes in Rom. 7:14 as being under the power of sin) so that humanity could stand in righteousness before God. To affirm that Christ died *for* all, then, means that by his death Christ stood as humanity's representative before God, effecting the reconciliation that humanity could not. Consequently, those who are *in* Christ have died with Christ and are part of a new creation in Christ.[35]

Paul insists that this work of reconciliation is from God, who reconciled humanity to himself through Christ, and has given this ministry of reconciliation to the ministers of the new covenant (2 Cor. 5:18). As a minister of this new covenant, Paul has been entrusted with the message of reconciliation: "in Christ God was reconciling the world to himself" (5:19). Ministers of the new

---

34. Although Paul does not refer to Adam here, he seems to be drawing upon his understanding of Christ as the eschatological Adam, as he does in 1 Corinthians 15 and Romans 5.

35. Morna D. Hooker (*Not Ashamed of the Gospel: New Testament Interpretations of the Death of Christ* [Grand Rapids: Eerdmans, 1994], 20–46, here 36) explains this view of Christ's death. She notes, "*Christ died, not instead of the human race, but as their representative*: in some mysterious sense, the whole of humanity died on Calvary."

covenant then are ambassadors *for* Christ. Just as God once made an appeal through Christ for humanity to be reconciled, so the ministers of the new covenant make a similar appeal, "be reconciled to God" (5:20). In saying this, Paul does not imply that humanity can reconcile itself to God. Rather, he affirms that as the minister of a new covenant he calls upon humanity to embrace the reconciliation God has already extended through the death of the one man, the crucified Christ. In this way the message about the cross is the foundation for Paul's ministry of reconciliation.

A Ministry of Power in Weakness

Paul is Christ's ambassador, the minister of a new covenant, who calls people to be reconciled with God through the gospel he preaches. Entrusted with this ministry, he reflects the paradoxical message about the cross in the way he exercises his ministry. This is especially apparent in 2 Corinthians 10–13, where he relates his ministry to the paradoxical message about the cross by boasting in his weakness so that the power of Christ might be manifested in and through his ministry.

In 2 Corinthians 10–13 Paul must deal with a serious crisis in his ministry. Apostles whom he sarcastically dubs "superapostles" (11:5; 12:11) have come to Corinth, and in Paul's view, they have intruded upon his missionary field (10:13–16). Although they boasted that they were equal to Paul, Paul views them as "false apostles" and "deceitful workers" who have disguised themselves as apostles of Christ (11:13). His harsh language about these intruders reflects the seriousness of the crisis he faced at Corinth. Although the precise nature of the crisis is disputed, its main contours can be summarized as follows. Whereas Paul refused to be supported by the Corinthian community, the intruding apostles did not. Rhetorically gifted preachers, they called into question the nature of Paul's ministry. On the one hand, they (or their supporters) accused him of writing powerful letters but of being weak and contemptible in speech when present in person (10:10). On the other, they criticized his refusal to be supported by the Corinthians as an insult to the community (11:7–11; 12:11–13).[36]

From Paul's perspective, the crisis raised by the presence of these apostles struck at the heart of the gospel. Therefore, he criticizes the Corinthians for being too eager to accept those who proclaim "another Jesus," "a different spirit," "a different gospel." This "different gospel" proclaims Jesus and the Spirit, but it is a gospel that boasts in the power of Jesus and of the Spirit at the expense of the weakness and folly of the cross. It is a gospel that evaluates

---

36. The issue of patronage probably stands behind this accusation. Certain members of the community may have wanted to support Paul in order to become his patrons. But Paul, unlike the intruding apostles, resisted such patronage lest it become a way for others to exercise undue influence and control over him.

the ministers of the gospel in terms of their rhetorical skills, their powerful deeds, and perhaps their ecstatic experiences. It is a gospel that requires the minister of the gospel to be a powerful figure who honors the community by accepting its patronage.

Faced with this different gospel and its view of ministry, Paul defends his ministry by relating it to the paradoxical message of the cross and boasting in his weakness. The theological argument of 2 Corinthians 10–13, then, recalls the theology of the cross Paul developed in 1 Cor. 1:18–2:5. There he explained the paradoxical manner in which God manifested his power and wisdom in the weakness and folly of the cross. Here he shows how apostolic ministers paradoxically reveal the power of God through the weakness of their ministry. Just as affliction and suffering endured for the sake of the gospel proclaim the gospel, so the weakness of the new covenant minister paradoxically reveals the power of the gospel.

Paul's argument finds its theological climax in a section that can be entitled "Foolish Boasting" (2 Cor. 11:1–12:13). At the outset of this section, it is evident that Paul does not want to boast in his ministry since it would violate the principle he quotes in 1 Cor. 1:31 and 2 Cor. 10:17, "Let the one who boasts, boast in the Lord." Moreover, he is aware that God chose the weak to shame the strong "so that no one might boast in the presence of God" (1 Cor. 1:29). But since the intruding apostles are boasting "according to human standards" (2 Cor. 11:18), he decides that he will also boast—but in an entirely unexpected way.

First, since all boasting is foolish, he will dare to boast, provided the Corinthians understand that he is acting foolishly (2 Cor. 11:16; 12:11). Second, he will boast only of those things that show his weakness (11:30; 12:5, 9). When he finally engages in boasting, then, he presents an extended catalogue of his apostolic sufferings and failures (11:22–12:10), and he concludes, "I have been a fool! You forced me to it" (12:11). This foolish boasting, however, is the vehicle by which Paul makes his point about the nature of his ministry and its relationship to the gospel he preaches.

Through his sufferings on behalf of the gospel he has learned that "power is made perfect in weakness" (12:9), so that whenever he is weak, then he is strong (12:10). The key to understanding these paradoxical statements is found in 13:4:

> For he was crucified in weakness,
>> but lives by the power of God.
> For we are weak in him,
>> but in dealing with you we will live with him
>> by the power of God.

Here Paul draws an analogy between the death and the resurrection of Christ on the one hand, and the weakness and life of the apostolic minister on the other, which can be explained as follows. Just as the crucifixion of Christ was a moment of utter weakness that became the occasion for God to manifest power through the resurrection, so the weakness of the new covenant minister is the occasion for the power of God to manifest itself anew. By embracing weakness, apostolic ministers associate themselves with Christ's death in the hope of his life-giving resurrection. Therefore, any ministry that boasts in its own accomplishments rather than in the Lord betrays the message about the cross it proclaims. For Paul, the ministers of the new covenant must be completely identified with the gospel they proclaim, and the gospel they proclaim must inform their lives.

Paul's understanding of his ministry can be summarized as follows. He is the minister of a new covenant that reveals the glory of God shining on the face of the crucified and risen Christ. As the minister of this new covenant, he is an ambassador for Christ who proclaims that God reconciled the world to himself by Christ. In order to proclaim this gospel, Paul carries the death/dying of Christ in his mortal body so that he can reveal the life of Christ to others. He boasts of his weakness in order to associate himself with the weakness of the crucified Christ, whom he preaches through the message about the cross.

THE RESURRECTION OF CHRIST AND THE GENERAL RESURRECTION OF THE DEAD

Paul's theology of the cross must not be separated from his understanding of the resurrection of the dead. For whenever Paul speaks of the cross, he has the power of the resurrection in view, as is apparent in 2 Cor. 13:4, "For he was crucified in weakness, but lives by the power of God." But Paul's most important discussions about the resurrection of Christ and the resurrection of the believer occur in 1 Corinthians 15 and 2 Corinthians 5. In the first text, he must deal with a specific problem within the community: some members of the congregation have called into question the general resurrection of the dead. In the second, he must deal with a problem related to his own ministry: the suffering and the affliction he endures as an apostle appears to call into question the power of the resurrection.

The Resurrection of the Dead

Paul takes up the question of the resurrection of the dead in 1 Corinthians 15 because some are saying, "there is no resurrection of the dead" (15:12). It is difficult to say exactly what lies behind this statement. It could be taken as a denial of the afterlife, as Paul seems to imply when he writes, "If for this life only we have hoped in Christ, we are of all people most to be pitied" (15:19). Or it might be construed as an understanding of the afterlife that did not include the resurrection of the body, as Paul implies when he raises what appears to be a Corinthian objection to the notion of a bodily resurrection, "But someone will ask, 'How are the dead raised? With what kind of body do they come?'" (15:35). Whatever the precise problem was, there is no doubt about Paul's position: there is an intimate union between the resurrection of Christ and the resurrection of those who believe in him because Christ's resurrection was the firstfruits of a larger harvest that will be reaped at the parousia, when the general resurrection of the dead will occur. To believe in the resurrection of Christ is to hope for the general resurrection of the dead. To deny the general resurrection of the dead is to deny the resurrection of Christ.

Because Paul's teaching about the resurrection is central to his gospel, he reminds the Corinthians of the gospel he proclaimed to them by repeating a tradition that was handed on to him and that he in turn handed on to them.[37]

> What I in turn had received:
>> that Christ died for our sins
>>> *in accordance with the scriptures,*
>> and that he was buried,
>> and that he was raised on the third day
>>> *in accordance with the scriptures,*
>> and that he appeared to Cephas,
>> then to the twelve.
>
>> (15:3b–5)

By repeating this tradition Paul summarizes the essential elements of the gospel: (1) Christ truly died; (2) his death was redemptive; (3) God raised him from the dead; (4) Christ's death and resurrection fulfilled Israel's prophetic Scriptures; and (5) the risen Lord was seen by reliable witnesses.

Paul goes on to say that Christ appeared to more than five hundred at one time, to James, and to all of the apostles. Last of all, he appeared to Paul. Consequently, there are numerous witnesses beyond the circle of the Twelve to whom the risen Lord appeared (15:6–8). Before taking up the question of the general resurrection of the dead, then, Paul establishes two points: (1) the resurrection of Christ is foundational for the gospel that he and others preach; (2) Christ was seen by or appeared to (*ōphthē*) a host of reliable witnesses who can testify that he was raised bodily.

Having established the centrality of Christ's death and resurrection for the gospel, Paul argues that there is an intimate connection between Christ's

---

37. It is difficult to determine where the tradition that Paul handed on to the Corinthians ends. Does it continue through v. 7, the appearance to James? Or does it end at v. 5, with the appearance to Cephas and the Twelve? Barrett (*First Corinthians*, 342), following Jeremias, thinks that the primitive tradition concludes after v. 5, the appearance to Peter and the Twelve.

resurrection and the resurrection of those who believe in him. The resurrection of Christ was not an isolated event that affected only Christ; it was the beginning of the general resurrection of the dead that will occur at the parousia, when Christ returns. In the period between Christ's resurrection and the general resurrection of the dead, Christ is presently reigning, in fulfillment of Ps. 110:1, and is subjecting all things to himself (1 Cor. 15:25). When the parousia occurs, the dead will be raised and the last enemy, "death," will be destroyed. Then Christ will hand over the kingdom to his Father, and the Son himself will be subjected to the one (God) who subjected everything to him. And so God will be all in all (15:26–28).

The resurrection of Christ, then, is the "firstfruits" of a larger harvest yet to be reaped. It was necessary if the woeful effects of Adam's sin were to be reversed. For just as death entered the world through a human being (Adam), so the resurrection of the dead must come through a human being (Christ, the eschatological Adam).

But what does it mean to speak about the resurrection of the dead? What does it mean to say that Christ was raised bodily? It is this question about the bodily resurrection that was a point of contention between Paul and some at Corinth. For whereas Paul assumes the bodily continuity between the earthly body and the resurrection body, those who questioned the resurrection of the dead did not understand how or why the dead will be raised bodily.

In the second part of chapter 15, Paul addresses the question of the bodily resurrection by way of analogy. He argues that resurrection means transformation of the body rather than resuscitation. Consequently, there is a continuity and a discontinuity between the earthly body and the risen body analogous to the continuity and discontinuity between the seed that is sown and the plant that grows. On the one hand, there is no immediate likeness between the seed that is planted and the plant that grows, but on the other there is continuity since the plant comes from the seed. So it is with the earthly and risen body. The earthly body is perishable because it is subject to death, dishonorable because it is subject to sin, and weak because it must die. But when it is raised by the power of God's Spirit, the risen body is no longer subject to the powers of sin and death; it is imperishable, glorious, and powerful. The physical body (*sōma psychikon*) dies and is raised as a spiritual body (*sōma pneumatikon*, 15:42–44).

To explain how this is possible, Paul returns to the Adam-Christ comparison he introduced earlier, when he said that just as death came through a human being, so the resurrection of the dead must come through a human being (15:21). Paul now explains what he meant. Adam, the first man, was a "living being" (*psychēn zōsan*) from whom the human race descended; he was "from the earth" (15:45, 47). Christ, the last Adam, became a "life-giving spirit" (*pneuma zōopoioun*) by his resurrection from the dead. Raised from the dead, Christ is the "one from heaven" (15:45, 47). Therefore, just as humanity bears the image of Adam, the earthly body that is destined to die, so humanity will bear the image of the risen Christ, the risen body that is immortal.

Not everyone will die, however—many will be alive when the Lord returns. But even the living must be transformed if they are to enter the realm of God's incorruptible kingdom. Thus at the parousia, "in the twinkling of an eye" (15:52), the living and the dead will be changed and transformed. The perishable and mortal body will put on imperishability and immortality, and death will be destroyed (15:53–55).

Paul's description of the risen body is indebted to his encounter with the risen Lord, whom he identifies as "the image of God," on whose face shines "the glory of God" (2 Cor. 4:4, 6). That revelation of Jesus Christ as the glorious Son of God taught Paul that Jesus is the one who has already been transformed by the power and glory of God at his resurrection from the dead. In describing the resurrection body of the believer, therefore, Paul is describing the body of the risen Lord who appeared to him. For the body that the risen Christ already enjoys is the body that the believer will inherit at the general resurrection of the dead. Christ is the one who has fulfilled humanity's destiny as portrayed in Psalm 8.[38] This is why Christ is called the new, that is, the eschatological, Adam. The bodily resurrection of the dead is central to the gospel because humanity is destined to be what the risen Lord has become. If Christ's body has been raised and transformed by the glory of God, the bodies of those who believe in him will experience the same power of God at the general resurrection of the dead.

A Building from God

Paul returns to the question of the resurrection body in 2 Cor. 5:1–10. However, whereas in 1 Corinthians 15 he spoke about the general resurrection of the dead that will occur at the parousia, in 2 Corinthians 5 he writes in a more personal way of his profound confidence that, even if he dies, he will be clothed with a resurrection body. Since Paul's discussion in 2 Corinthians is so personal, some interpreters have argued that 2 Corinthians 5 represents a change in Paul's understanding of the resurrection of the dead. In their view Paul is introducing an intermediate stage between the death of the individual and the general resurrection of the dead. During this intermediate period, believers will be present to the Lord but not yet in possession of the resurrection body they will inherit at the parousia, when the general resurrection of the dead will occur.

---

38. Paul alludes to this in 1 Cor. 15:27, "For 'God has put all things in subjection under his feet.'" In the psalm it is God's intention to subject all things to humanity; in Christ this has already begun.

Although it is possible that Paul's thought about the resurrection developed, it is unlikely that there was a significant shift in his understanding of the resurrection between the writing of 1 and 2 Corinthians. The new way in which Paul presents the resurrection of the dead in 2 Corinthians is better explained by the circumstances he faced rather than by a change in his theological understanding of the resurrection. These new circumstances can be summarized as follows. Whereas in 1 Corinthians Paul must show his audience that (1) the resurrection of Christ implies the general resurrection of the dead, and (2) the resurrection body is a body that has been transformed by the power of God's Spirit, in 2 Corinthians he must show the Corinthians how the power of the resurrection is already at work in the sufferings and afflictions of the minister of the new covenant. Consequently, whereas 1 Corinthians presents a view of the general resurrection as an eschatological event that will occur at the Lord's parousia, 2 Corinthians focuses on the way in which the power of the resurrection already impinges upon the life of the apostolic minister now. In doing this, Paul has not forgotten that the resurrection of the dead is an eschatological event. He still hopes and waits for his resurrection body. But he is profoundly aware that the power of the resurrection is already at work in his mortal body.

Paul prepares for his discussion of the resurrection body in 2 Cor. 5:1–10 by reflecting on his apostolic sufferings (4:7–18). He views his mortal body as a fragile clay jar that can be destroyed at any moment. He is "afflicted," "perplexed," "persecuted," and "struck down." He carries in his body "the death of Jesus" and is "given up to death." Everything that the world can see about him, namely, his outer nature, is wasting away. From a merely human vantage point, Paul is about to be defeated by death. But despite what the world sees, Paul is confident that his inner nature, which the world cannot see, is "being renewed day by day" by the power of Christ's resurrection that is already at work within him, even though Paul has not yet been raised from the dead. This is why Paul writes, "So death is at work in us, but life in you" (4:12). Paul's experience in Asia has taught him to believe in the God who raises the dead, and in no other (1:10); therefore he is confident that the God who raised the Lord Jesus will raise him from the dead (4:14).

It is in light of this discussion about the power of Christ's resurrection in the midst of his apostolic sufferings (4:7–18) that Paul affirms his confidence that a resurrection body awaits him. This discussion begins with a series of contrasts that recall the contrasts Paul has already established between his inner and outer nature (4:16–18). Earlier he described his mortal body as a fragile clay jar that can be broken at any moment (4:7). Now he compares it to a fragile earthly tent that can be collapsed at any moment, affirming that if this tent should be folded (by his death), he has a "building from God," a "heavenly dwelling," namely, the resurrection body (5:1–2). In 5:3–4 he expresses his profound hope that he will not be found "unclothed" (without a resurrection body) but that he will be clothed (with a resurrection body) so that what is mortal (his earthly body) can be swallowed up by life when he assumes his resurrection body. Next, in 5:5 Paul affirms his confidence that God is the one who will effect this change, the very God who has already given him the Spirit as the guarantee of what is to come, resurrection from the dead. Paul then concludes that so long as he is in this body, he is away from the Lord. He continues to walk by faith, however, confident that one day he will be at home with the Lord, before whose judgment seat he must stand (5:6–10).

If 5:1–10 is read apart from its context, it may seem that Paul's understanding of the general resurrection of the dead, which he developed in 1 Corinthians 15, has given way to a more personal view of death and resurrection in 2 Corinthians 5. But this is not the case. Paul is surely aware of what he has already said about the destiny of humanity. But now he applies it to himself in a personal way in order to proclaim his profound faith in the power of Christ's resurrection, despite the sufferings he presently endures. Instead of the language of transformation, Paul now speaks of a tent being replaced by a permanent building, of being clothed with a heavenly dwelling so that what is mortal may be swallowed up by life.

Although some have argued that Paul is reckoning with an intermediate state between death and resurrection because he is no longer confident he will be alive at the Lord's parousia, this is not the purpose of his discussion in 2 Corinthians 5. His goal is to affirm his confidence in the resurrection in face of his apostolic sufferings. It is likely that Paul thought that those who died in Christ were already with the Lord in some way, even though they had not yet been raised from the dead, but this is not the point of Paul's discussion in 2 Corinthians 5.[39]

To summarize, in his Corinthian correspondence Paul presents the resurrection of the dead from two vantage points: (1) the general resurrection of all who believe in Christ; (2) the power of Christ's resurrection that already empowers believers so that they can be confident that, when their earthly body is destroyed, they will be clothed with resurrection glory.

CONCLUSION

The main contours of Paul's theology in 1 and 2 Corinthians are expressed through his theology of the cross, his presentation of the church as a sanctified community, his understanding of himself as the minister of a new covenant

---

39. Paul's statement in Phil. 1:23 ("I am hard pressed between the two: my desire is to depart and be with Christ, for that is far better") suggests that he believes he will be united with Christ, in some way, even if he dies before the parousia and the general resurrection of the dead.

who calls people to be reconciled to God, and his confidence in the resurrection of the dead. His theology of the cross and his faith in the power of the resurrection inform his apostolic ministry of reconciliation. His paradoxical message about the cross assures the community that it has been elected and chosen by God. His apostolic ministry manifests, in an equally paradoxical way, the wisdom of the cross and the power of the resurrection. Consequently, those who see the apostle see the gospel he preaches in and through his apostolic ministry. The message about the cross and the power of the resurrection form the content of Paul's preaching and the reason for his apostolic ministry. They call the sanctified community into being. The community that lives in accordance with the wisdom of the cross through the power of the resurrection is a sanctified community. The apostolic ministers who embody this message in their lives are ministers of a new covenant who serve this sanctified community.

6

A Theology of Righteousness

Galatians and Romans

Although written to different communities, Romans and Galatians share several common themes, for example, the preeminent role of Abraham in God's plan of salvation history, the inability of human beings to justify themselves before God by doing the works of the law, the need to believe in the promises of God that have come to their fulfillment in the appearance of the Christ, the salvific value of Jesus' death, and the need for those justified on the basis of faith to live a moral life characterized by love and empowered by God's Spirit. In each letter Paul draws a series of sharp contrasts between doing the works of the law and believing in Christ, living according to the flesh and living according to the Spirit. In each Paul also forcefully argues that a person cannot be justified in God's sight by doing the works of the Mosaic law, since righteousness is God's gracious gift that comes through faith. Abraham provides the example par excellence of the kind of faith God requires, a trusting faith in God's promises. Through such faith, one is delivered from the realm of sin and death and transferred to the realm of the Spirit. Thus one is justified in God's sight. It is not too much to say that the theology of Romans and Galatians is at the heart of Paul's understanding of what God has accomplished in Christ, as long as one remembers that the theology of these letters is not the whole of Paul's theology.

This theology of righteousness that binds Romans and Galatians together was forged in response to questions and problems that account for the distinctive character of each letter. Thus, whereas Paul composed Galatians as a polemical response to those who called into question the truth of the law-free gospel he preached among the Gentiles, thereby threatening the ecclesial life of the congregations Paul had established in Galatia, Romans is akin to a letter essay in which the apostle carefully presents the major themes of the gospel he preaches among the Gentiles to a community that has heard of him but has not yet seen or heard him preach this gospel. It is not surprising then that Paul returns to many of the themes of Galatians and presents them in a more complete and nuanced manner in Romans. For example, Romans 7 mollifies Paul's rather harsh presentation of the law in Galatians 3, and his discussion of the human predicament in Romans 1–3 develops his rather brief statement in Galatians about the human situation apart from Christ. The growth and development in Paul's theology as seen in Romans, then, can be accounted for, at least in part, by the new circumstances that occasioned Romans.[1] This point, however, should not be pressed too far, as if Galatians represents an early or immature theology of righteousness and the law, and Romans a more mature theology. These letters, after all, were written toward the end of Paul's missionary work, within a few years of each other.[2] The difference between them is the result of the particular situation that gave rise to each. On the one hand, a serious crisis, which called into question the truth of the gospel Paul proclaimed among the Gentiles, occasioned Galatians. On the other hand, the need for Paul to clarify his gospel for a congregation he had not founded, but hoped to visit, occasioned Romans.

Despite the different situations that led to them, Romans and Galatians are Paul's most important testimonies to his teaching on justification by faith apart from doing the works of the Mosaic law. Of course, other letters speak of justification and righteousness, most notably Philippians, Ephesians, 2 Timothy, and Titus,[3] but justification by faith is not the central and unrelenting theme in them that it is in Galatians and Romans. In this chapter, then, I focus on Paul's theology of justification by faith and its implications for the Christian life as developed first in Galatians, then in Romans.

THE TRUTH OF THE GOSPEL: GALATIANS

The occasion for Galatians can be summarized as follows. Jewish Christian missionaries had come to Galatia and taught Paul's Galatian converts that if they wished to perfect their faith in Israel's Messiah, the Christ, they must be incorporated into the people of Israel by observing the covenant of circumcision God established with Abraham and the Mosaic covenant God established with Israel at Sinai. Consequently, they urged the Galatians to accept circumcision and do

1. There has been a major debate about the "occasion" of Romans. This debate is presented in a collection of articles edited by Karl F. Donfried, *The Romans Debate* (rev. ed.; Peabody, MA: Hendrickson, 1991). A. J. M. Wedderburn (*The Reasons for Romans* [Minneapolis: Fortress, 1991]) also presents a thorough study of the issue.

2. This statement is accurate if one accepts the later dating of Galatians, which is usually associated with the North Galatian Hypothesis. It is not as accurate if one accepts an early dating for Galatians, which is usually associated with the South Galatian Hypothesis.

3. See Phil. 3:7–11; Eph. 2:9–10; 2 Tim. 1:8–9; Titus 3:5.

"the works of the law."[4] It is difficult to know to what extent these Jewish Christian missionaries, whom Paul calls "agitators" and whom scholars name "the teachers" or "Judaizers," introduced the language of justification or righteousness into their argument, but Paul certainly did. In response to this "crisis," which called into question his apostleship and the truth of the gospel he preached to the Galatians, Paul mounts a vigorous argument to persuade his Gentile converts that it is not necessary for them to be circumcised and do the works of the law in order to be justified and declared righteous in God's sight. Paul insists that God's covenant promises to Abraham (that all the nations would be blessed in him) had a singular descendant (*sperma*) in view—the Christ. Consequently, those who have been incorporated into Christ are Abraham's descendants because they have been incorporated into Abraham's singular descendant, the Christ. There is no need for those who are in Christ to be circumcised. Paul argues that the Galatians have already been justified, because of what God accomplished in Christ's saving death and resurrection, pointing out that the empirical proof of their justification is their dynamic experience of the Spirit. They need not do the works of the law in order to be justified because they are already justified. They now live in the realm of the Spirit, and if they allow the Spirit to lead and guide them, they will fulfill the law through the love commandment.

The issue at Galatia concerned the truth of the gospel that Paul preached to the Galatians when he proclaimed a gospel that did not require them to be circumcised and do the works of the law but to entrust themselves to what God had already accomplished for them through Christ's death and resurrection. Although Paul may not have explicitly told the Galatians, "You are justified by faith rather than by doing the works of the law," he now formulates the essence of the gospel—the truth of the gospel he preaches among the Gentiles—in this way. Most simply put, Galatians is a sustained argument in which Paul seeks to persuade the Galatians not to seek their righteousness before God by having themselves circumcised and doing the works of the Mosaic law. At the heart of this argument, and at the center of Paul's theology, is an issue that he identifies as "the truth of the gospel" (2:5, 14). Is God's act in Christ sufficient for justification or must it be supplemented by something else?

Paul's Apostleship and the Truth of the Gospel

The apostle and the gospel he preaches are one. To call into question Paul's apostleship is to call into question the gospel he preaches, and to call into

---

4. This phrase, which has been at the center of controversy in recent Pauline study, is peculiar to Paul, although it has recently been found in a document from Qumran (4Q394–399, MMT, *Miqṣat Ma'aśê ha-Torah* [Some observances of the Torah]). Although most would agree that it refers to the prescriptions or commandments of the Mosaic law, some would limit it, at least in Galatians, to those commandments that specifically identified Jews as such in the Gentile world: circumcision, dietary prescriptions, Sabbath observance.

question the gospel he preaches is to call into question his apostleship. This is why Paul begins Galatians with such a strong affirmation that his apostleship did not have a human origin (*ouk ap' anthrōpōn*), nor was it mediated through human agents (*oude di' anthrōpou*). Rather, it came "through Jesus Christ and God the Father, who raised him from the dead" (1:1). In making this statement, Paul defines his apostleship in light of the call he received when God revealed his Son to him—what is commonly called Paul's conversion or his Damascus road experience. Although the early church gave a preeminent place to the apostleship of "the Twelve" whom Jesus chose to be with him, Paul's understanding of his apostleship is not an arbitrary use of the term "apostle"—at least from his point of view. He is an apostle because of an apocalyptic event, "a revelation of Jesus Christ" (*apokalypseōs Iēsou Christou*, 1:12), through which God revealed his Son to him (1:15–16). On the basis of this experience, Paul knows that he has been sent to preach the gospel to the Gentiles just as Peter had been sent to the circumcised (2:7–8). To be sure, Paul was not acquainted with or a follower of the earthly Jesus, as were the original apostles, but his experience of the risen Lord and the commission he received to preach the gospel was as true as theirs. Just as they did not receive their apostleship and commission to preach the gospel from or through human beings, neither did he.

Since Paul did not receive his apostleship from or through human beings, he did not receive the gospel he preached from human beings, nor was he taught it (1:12). Like his apostleship, it was communicated in that moment when God revealed his Son to him and called him to be an apostle to the Gentiles. To be sure, Paul received traditions from the early church and learned from those who were in Christ before him. But the gospel, the good news that Jesus is God's Son, "who gave himself for our sins to set us free from the present evil age" (1:4), was given to Paul through a revelation from God the Father and Jesus Christ. This is not to say that Paul immediately understood every implication of this gospel or that there was no further growth in his understanding of it. To the contrary! Paul worked out the ramifications of this gospel in his preaching, teaching, and missionary activity. But "the truth of the gospel," its most profound meaning, was apparent to him. He now knew that the one whom he once judged to be a cursed messiah was the very Son of God, the perfect reflection of God's glory. All else followed from this. There is an intimate relationship, then, between Paul's apostleship and the gospel, and this led him to defend his gospel again and again. In the moment God revealed his Son to him, Paul received his call and the gospel he would preach among the Gentiles. To deny his claim to apostleship is to call into question the gospel he preaches; to call into question the gospel he proclaims is to deny his claim of apostleship.

It is not surprising that Paul makes use of extended autobiographical material in Galatians (1:13–2:14) to persuade his converts of the truth of the gospel he preached to them. In this statement, he portrays his past life as the life of one who was more zealous for the law than his contemporaries, to the point of persecuting the church of God (1:13–14). He describes his call to preach the gospel among the Gentiles (1:15–17). He highlights the limited scope of his first visit to Jerusalem and the reaction of the Judean congregations to his conversion (1:18–24). He recounts the decisive meeting in Jerusalem with the pillar apostles who recognized the grace of his apostleship (2:1–10), and he recalls the conflict in Antioch, at which he rebuked Cephas (Peter) for betraying the truth of the gospel (2:11–14).

By this autobiographical statement, Paul makes several points. First, the contrast between his former zeal for the law and the law-free gospel he now preaches highlights a decisive change in his life that, from Paul's perspective, can be explained only by an act of God: the former zealot for the law now preaches Christ instead of the law because God revealed his Son to him. Second, Paul's insistence that he did not immediately go up to Jerusalem after this revelation but went off to Arabia, where he probably began his preaching of the gospel, is a subtle indication that his apostleship came directly from God and Jesus Christ. There was no need for the pillar apostles at Jerusalem to interpret the revelation for him, or to authenticate his call, or to commission him to preach the gospel.[5] Paul immediately understood the content and meaning of the revelation. Third, at the decisive meeting at Jerusalem, at which Paul did not yield for a moment so that he might preserve the truth of the gospel for his Gentile converts, the pillar apostles acknowledged that God was active in Paul's apostolate to the uncircumcised just as God was active in Peter's apostolate to the circumcised. In a word, the pillar apostles did not commission Paul to be an apostle. They recognized the divine origin of his call. Fourth, the crisis at Antioch, at which Paul rebuked Peter, presents Paul as defending the truth of the gospel in face of overwhelming odds. Thus, even though Paul sought and valued communion with the pillar apostles, he understood that his apostleship did not depend on their approval but on a divine call that communicated the gospel to him.

Paul's understanding of his apostleship is unique in the New Testament. No other writer makes such bold claims, nor does the defense of apostleship play such a central role in any of the writings outside the Pauline corpus. The reason for this is the origin of Paul's call and its relationship to the gospel he preaches. Paul's apostleship cannot be reduced to the role of a messenger commissioned or sent from one community to another. His apostleship is a prophetic call, comparable to the call of Jeremiah or the servant in the book of Isaiah. In this call, the gospel is revealed and Paul is commissioned, not by

---

5. In the Acts of the Apostles, Luke develops his portrait of Paul differently. Writing at a later period, perhaps the mid-eighties, Luke presents a more ideal portrait of Paul, which shows Paul to be in a close relationship to the mother church in Jerusalem.

human beings but by God and Jesus Christ. It is impossible to understand the claims of Paul's gospel apart from the claims he makes about his apostleship. Thus, if one is to embrace the Pauline gospel, one must accept the claims Paul makes about his apostleship. Put another way, just as the claims of the early church are rooted in its witness to the resurrection, so the claims of the Pauline gospel are rooted in Paul's call to be an apostle of Jesus Christ to the nations.

The Truth of the Gospel

If Paul's apostleship is the starting point for understanding the theological claims of Galatians, "the gospel" is the concept that underlies all that he says. This gospel is the good news he proclaims, namely, what God has effected through the death and resurrection of Jesus Christ. Although it is difficult to determine the precise content of Paul's original preaching to the Galatians, his rebuke at the beginning of chapter 3 suggests that he proclaimed a crucified Christ to them, just as he did to the Corinthians (see 1 Cor. 1:23): "You foolish Galatians! Who has bewitched you? It was before your eyes that Jesus Christ was publicly exhibited as crucified!" (Gal. 3:1). In this verse, Paul reminds the Galatians that his original proclamation of the gospel presented them with a graphic visual image of the crucified One. The purpose of this graphic presentation, however, was not to indulge a morbid curiosity but to highlight the paradoxical nature of the act whereby God redeemed them and to impress upon them that, through his death, Christ gave himself for their sins to free them from the present evil age (1:4). For Paul, this death was an act of personal and individual love, leading him to proclaim that he now lives "by faith in the Son of God, *who loved me and gave himself for me*" (2:20).[6] Paul, of course, has not forgotten the central role of the resurrection (see 1:1), and it is inconceivable that he would have preached a crucified Christ without announcing the resurrection. Indeed, he could hardly make so many references to the Spirit if he had not first proclaimed the resurrection. Given the nature of the crisis at Galatia, however, Paul focuses on the death of Christ, presupposing that his Gentile converts are fully aware of Christ's resurrection. At Galatia the issue is not the resurrection of the dead, as it was at Corinth, but the significance of Christ's death.

The gospel of a crucified messiah whom God had risen from the dead, a messiah who had died "for our sins," was undoubtedly similar to the gospel that numerous other missionaries preached throughout the Mediterranean basin, some giving greater emphasis to Christ's death, others to his resurrection. But when Jewish Christian missionaries came to Paul's Galatian congregations and insisted that the Galatians be circumcised and do the works of the Mosaic law, Paul denounced their gospel as "a different gospel" (1:6). Paul, of course, is not

---

6. The phrase can also be taken as a subjective genitive, "by the faith of the Son of God."

suggesting that there are two equally valid versions of the gospel. Any gospel that contradicts the law-free gospel he proclaimed is a perversion of the gospel of Christ (1:7), and those who proclaim it are accursed (1:8–9). Paul's strong reaction to this other gospel can be explained only by his understanding of the sufficiency of Christ's saving death and resurrection. If Paul's Gentile converts must be circumcised and do the works of the law *in addition to believing in Christ*, then what God accomplished in Christ's saving death and resurrection was not sufficient for salvation. If the other gospel is correct, Paul's gospel is not.

It is doubtful that Paul's opponents called into question the sufficiency of Christ's death and resurrection so explicitly. As believers deeply committed to Christ *and* the Jewish law, they may have viewed faith in Christ as God's way of enabling people to do the works of the law. But in light of his call and conversion, Paul saw a deeper issue. If righteousness can be attained through the law, then why did Christ die (2:21)? And if the law could truly bring life, righteousness would have come through the law (3:21). For Paul, the sending of God's Son implied that Christ did something that the law could not and was never intended to accomplish: to bring people righteousness and life. For the Pauline gospel, then, Christ replaced the law, and any attempt to impose something in addition to faith in Christ called into question the sufficiency of what God has done in Christ.

It is this understanding of the Christ's death and resurrection that leads Paul to speak of "the truth of the gospel" (2:5, 14), which he summarizes in this way: "We ourselves are Jews by birth and not Gentile sinners; yet we know that a person is justified not by the works of the law but through faith in Jesus Christ. And we have come to believe in Christ Jesus, so that we might be justified by faith in Christ [or, "the faith of Christ"], and not by doing the works of the law, because no one will be justified by the works of the law" (2:15–16). This statement occurs within the context of the crisis at Antioch, where Peter and other Jewish Christians, including Barnabas, withdrew from table fellowship with Gentile believers when a delegation loyal to James came to survey the situation at Antioch. Astonished at this "hypocrisy" (2:13), Paul confronts Peter for not acting in accord with "the truth of the gospel," and he asks, "If you, though a Jew, live like a Gentile and not like a Jew, how can you compel the Gentiles to live like Jews?" (2:14). In other words, if Peter was willing to set aside the dietary prescriptions of the law to eat with Gentiles, how can he compel Gentiles to observe that law because partisans of James have arrived? Peter and the other Jewish Christians acted hypocritically, and in doing so they betrayed the truth of the gospel that a person is not justified on the basis of doing the legal prescriptions of the law but on the basis of faith in what God has accomplished in Christ.

The context of this episode indicates that Paul faces a social as well as a theological problem. On what basis, if any, can Jewish and Gentile believers share table fellowship with each other? Can Jewish believers set aside the dietary prescriptions of the law as Peter and others did prior to the arrival of the partisans of James at Antioch? Or must Gentile believers adopt a Jewish way of life in order to share table fellowship with Jewish believers? Paul's understanding of Christ's death and resurrection provides him with an answer that those loyal to James found difficult to accept: Gentile believers need not adopt a Jewish way of life in order to share table fellowship with Jewish believers because they have already been fully integrated into the community of Israel through faith in Christ. Conversely, Jewish believers are no longer bound by such dietary prescriptions, although they may continue to practice them, provided they do not deny the truth of the gospel that a person is justified on the basis of faith rather than on the basis of doing the works of the law.

The Antioch incident is a salutary reminder that there is a social dimension to Paul's teaching on justification on the basis of faith. Jewish and Gentile believers are related to each other through their common faith in Christ. Consequently, the law must no longer be employed to separate Israel from the nations. The significance of Paul's teaching on justification, however, is also profoundly theological, affecting the believer's relationship to God. Previous to the moment when God revealed his Son to Paul, Paul made a sharp distinction between Jews, who had the benefit of God's law and so knew the divine will, and Gentiles, who did not and so were accounted sinners. But in light of Christ, Paul now understands that no one is justified or acquitted by God on the basis of doing the works of the law. By these works of the law, Paul means *all* the prescriptions or commandments of the Mosaic law, even though he may have circumcision, dietary prescriptions, and Sabbath observance primarily in view, due to the Antioch incident.[7] If works of the law could have effected justification or acquittal, there would have been no need for Christ to give himself for sins to rescue humanity from the present evil age (1:4), or for God to send his Son to redeem those under the law (4:4–5). Christ's death and resurrection convinces Paul that acquittal before God's tribunal is not the outcome of doing the works of the law. How then is justification attained? According to Paul, it is the result of faith, the faith of Christ, which is the basis for faith in Christ.[8]

7. At Antioch the primary issue seems to have been the dietary prescriptions of the law: must Gentile believers observe the dietary prescriptions of the law if they wish to share table fellowship with Jewish believers in Christ? Whereas Paul said no, certain Jewish Christians from Jerusalem argued that Gentile believers must observe these prescriptions if they wished to share table fellowship with Jewish believers.

8. The faith of Christ is Christ's own faithfulness, his obedience to God. In 2:16 the phrases *dia pisteōs Iēsou Christou* and *ek pisteōs Christou* can be taken as either subjective or objective genitives (the faith of Christ or faith in Christ). If they are construed as subjective genitives, as many argue, then Paul is saying that a person is not justified by the works of the law but by Christ's act of faithful obedience to God—the faith of Christ. This interpretation, it must be emphasized, does not do away with the need to believe in Christ, for in the very same verse Paul writes *kai hēmeis eis Christon Iēsoun episteusamen* ("And we have come to believe in Christ Jesus").

This faith in Christ is not a mere intellectual exercise, such as is criticized in Jas. 2:14–26. It is faith that entrusts itself to what God has done, confident that God has justified the sinner. Consequently, the choice is between doing the works of the law or relying on what God has done in Christ. In the first instance, people implicitly rely upon themselves to do the legal prescription of the law in order to be acquitted by God. In the second, they trust in God to acquit them on the basis of what God has done for them in Christ. Fearful that the Galatians are dangerously close to relying on Christ *and the law*, Paul warns that if they want to be justified by the law, they will cut themselves off from Christ; they will fall from grace (Gal. 5:4).

The truth of the gospel that Paul preaches, and that he will not compromise, can be summarized as follows. Through Christ's death and resurrection, God has justified humanity; that is, God has pronounced a gracious judgment of acquittal. This justification or right standing before God is not the result of doing the works of the law, for one can only embrace it as a gracious gift granted on the basis of faith. Consequently, any gospel that requires believers to do the works of the law *in addition* to what God has done in Christ betrays the truth of the gospel. The gospel that God offers, and that Paul preaches, is a gospel of grace that can be appropriated only by faith.

The Law in Light of the Gospel

Paul's acceptance of the gospel resulted in a new understanding of the Mosaic law, which he once fervently embraced. Previous to his call and conversion, he was zealous for the traditions of his ancestors, far beyond his contemporaries, to the point of persecuting the church of God. For, in his view, Jesus' followers disregarded God's law. But when God revealed his Son to him, Paul reevaluated his previous understanding of the law in light of the gospel he preached. This rethinking of the law undoubtedly occurred throughout his ministry, although the conference at Jerusalem, the incident at Antioch, and the crisis at Galatia were key moments in his reassessment of the law's role in God's salvific plan.

Apart from Romans, Paul's most extensive discussion about the law is in Galatians, where he must persuade his Gentile converts not to subject themselves to the Mosaic law by accepting circumcision. Given the crisis he faces, it is not Paul's intention to present a carefully nuanced discussion of the law. Rather, employing a variety of rhetorical strategies, he seeks to persuade his Gentile converts to hold fast to the truth of the gospel he preached to them. What he writes about the law in Galatians, then, needs to be understood within the context of a crisis that threatened the very life of his Gentile congregations. In a less polemical setting, Paul may well have written differently, as he eventually did in Romans.

Paul's presentation of the law was meant to counter, at least in part, what Jewish Christian missionaries were teaching his converts: they had made a good start by believing in Christ, but now they must have themselves circumcised and do the works of the law if they wished to be fully incorporated into the people of Israel as descendants of Abraham. Indeed, the agitators may even have employed many of the texts about the law that Paul uses in this letter, for example, the threatening curse of the law upon those who do not do the works of the law (Deut. 27:26, quoted in Gal. 3:10; see also Deut. 28:58–68) and the promise of life for those who do the works of the law (Lev. 18:5, quoted in Gal. 3:12). Given the crisis at Galatia and his new understanding of the law, Paul draws a distinction between the promises God had spoken to Abraham and the Mosaic law, which was given through the mediation of angels four hundred and thirty years after the promises (3:16–18). Because God had always intended to "justify the Gentiles by faith," God revealed the gospel to Abraham when he promised, "All the nations shall be blessed in you" (3:8, quoting Gen. 12:3). Consequently the promises God made to Abraham, directly and without a mediator, enjoy a salvation-historical priority to the law, not only because God gave them before the law but because they announced the gospel of justification by faith. These promises, according to Paul's reading of Gen. 12:7, had a singular "seed" or "offspring" in view, the Christ (Gal. 3:16; see also Gen. 17:7–10; 22:17–18). All who have been baptized into Abraham's singular offspring, the Christ, are heirs of the promises God made to Abraham, even if they are not circumcised (Gal. 3:29).

What then was the purpose of the law (3:19)? Was the law opposed to God's promises (3:21)? In response to the first question, Paul answers that the law had a temporary role: "It was added for (*charin*) transgressions, until the descendant came to whom the promise had been made" (3:19, NAB). The enigmatic phrase "for (*charin*) transgressions" can be understood in several ways: (1) God added the law to provoke transgressions; (2) God added the law to make people aware of their transgressions; (3) God added the law to control transgressions. Whereas the first two interpretations provide a decidedly negative view of the law, the third is more positive and preferable in light of the phrase that follows, "until the descendant came to whom the promise had been made." In other words, God provided the law as a temporary remedy for sin until Christ should appear. But when Christ appeared and dealt decisively with sin, the law's salvation-historical role ended.

In response to the second question (Is the law opposed to the promise?), Paul answers: "Certainly not! For if a law had been given that could make alive, then righteousness would indeed come through the law" (3:21). The premise here and throughout Galatians is that righteousness does not come through the law. This state of affairs, however, does not mean that the law stands in opposition to God's promises. For whereas the purpose of the promises was that "the blessing of Abraham might come to the Gentiles" (3:14), it was never the purpose of the law to effect life-giving righteousness. Why? Because humanity was under the "power of sin" so that the blessing promised to Abraham's descendant, the Christ, might be given to all who believe on the basis of faith (3:22).

The law, then, had a temporary role in God's salvific plan, something Paul would never have accepted before he came to faith in Christ. In light of Christ and of his own missionary experience, however, he now realizes that the law is subservient to the promises God made to Abraham four hundred and thirty years earlier, though not in opposition to them, since it was never the purpose of the law to effect righteousness. Before Christ came, the law functioned as a disciplinarian (*paidagōgos*), guarding and protecting those under its care until the promised offspring of Abraham, the Christ, appeared. When the offspring appeared, the law's role of watching over and guarding those under its rule was completed (3:23–25).

Although Paul maintains that the law is not opposed to the promises of God, he draws a contrast between law and promise, arguing that whereas the promises of God require faith and bring a blessing to those who believe, the law requires works and puts those who fail to do its works under the threat of a curse. Paul develops this contrast in 3:6–14, one of the most disputed passages in Galatians. He begins by presenting Abraham as the model believer to whom God reckoned righteousness because he believed in God, concluding that those who believe (*hoi ex pisteōs*) are blessed with faithful Abraham (3:6–9). Next, Paul warns that those who rely on the works of the law (*hosoi . . . ex ergōn*) place themselves under the threat of a curse since Deut. 27:26 reads, "Cursed is everyone who does not observe and obey all the things written in the book of the law" (Gal. 3:10). If one does not carry out all that the law prescribes, then one will fall under a curse rather than a blessing. But it was precisely to free those under the threat of this curse that Christ died on the cross, under the curse of the law. Thus Paul writes, "Christ redeemed us from the curse of the law, by becoming a curse for us—for it is written, 'Cursed is everyone who hangs on a tree'" (3:13, quoting Deut. 21:23). The result of Christ's death is that the blessing of Abraham, which Paul identifies as "the promise of the Spirit," has come upon the Gentiles through faith in Christ (Gal. 3:14).

In Paul's view "no one is justified before God by the law" (3:11) since the law operates on the principle of doing the works it prescribes rather than on the basis of faith. To be sure, the law promises life to those who do its works— "Whoever does the works of the law will live by them" (3:12, quoting Lev. 18:5)—but no one does all the works of the law, not even those who are urging the Galatians to be circumcised (Gal. 6:13). Righteousness, which is equivalent to life, comes from a relationship of faith rather than from doing the works of the law—"The one who is righteous will live by faith" (3:11, quoting Hab. 2:4). It is foolish, then, for the Galatians to have themselves circumcised and assume the yoke of obeying the entire law; for, if they seek to be justified by legal observance, Christ will be of no avail to them (Gal. 5:3–4) since he died to redeem them from the threatening curse of the law (3:13).

The main outlines of Paul's thinking about the law in Galatians can be summarized as follows. The law had a temporary role in God's salvific plan. It was not meant to effect justification or to give life but to function as a kind of disciplinarian—protecting those under its care from sin until Christ should appear. As a disciplinarian, it required complete obedience from those who put themselves under its threatening curse. This, of course, was not the way Paul's Jewish contemporaries viewed the law, and to their ears Paul's words must have sounded blasphemous. How could the law be described as temporary and be placed in such a subservient position to the promises God made to Abraham? Paul's understanding of the law, however, is not so much a logical deduction from what is already in Israel's Scriptures as it is a new understanding of the law in light of his call/conversion, and this understanding leads to a fresh exegesis of old texts. Other Jewish Christians did not come to the same conclusions about the law and were undoubtedly puzzled by Paul's exegesis. But they did not undergo the same experience he did. Paul's teaching on the law, then, cannot be understood apart from his apostolic call, the gospel he received, and the crisis he confronted at Galatia.

The Gospel and the Moral Life

One of the most puzzling aspects of Paul's theology is his understanding of the moral life. If those who believe in Christ are no longer under the law and are not required to *do* all of the prescriptions of the law, how can they live a moral life? Paul responds to this question in the final chapters of the letter, where he provides the Galatians with an important moral exhortation (5:1–6:10 or 5:13–6:10).[9] This exhortation, however, should not be construed as an afterthought to his discussion on righteousness and the law, as if the letter's real argument is found in the first four chapters. Paul's moral exhortation is integral to the statement he makes on behalf of the truth of the gospel. For if he cannot persuade his Gentile converts, who are no longer under the law, that they can live a moral life, the Galatians will agree with Paul's opponents that his gospel is defective. Paul develops his argument through a number of opposing concepts: the Spirit and the flesh, freedom and slavery, fulfilling the law and doing the law.

The first pair of opposing concepts—the Spirit and the flesh—is the most important since it underlines the other contrasts Paul will develop. This Spirit

---

9. It is difficult to determine where the exhortation of Galatians begins: at 5:1 or 5:13. In my view 5:1–12 is Paul's final argument on behalf of justification by faith, and 5:13 is the beginning of his moral exhortation. See Frank J. Matera, "The Culmination of Paul's Argument to the Galatians: Gal 5:1–6:17," *JSNT* 32 (1988): 79–91.

to which Paul refers is the power of God that the Galatians received when they entrusted themselves to the gospel he preached (3:2, 5). According to Paul's reading of Israel's Scripture, the gift of the Spirit is the fulfillment of the promises God made to Abraham: "All the nations shall be blessed in you" (Gen. 12:3, as quoted in Gal. 3:8). This is why Paul writes, "Christ redeemed us from the curse of the law . . . in order that in Christ Jesus the blessing of Abraham might come to the Gentiles, *so that we might receive the promise of the Spirit through faith*" (3:14). Put another way, God has given Abraham innumerable descendants from among the Gentiles by granting them the Spirit through faith. It is this Spirit that enables believers to live a moral life, a point Paul also makes in 1 Thessalonians, where he writes that the Thessalonians "have been taught by God to love one another" (1 Thess. 4:9), and which he develops in 2 Corinthians 3, where he describes his ministry as the ministry of a new covenant empowered by the Spirit (2 Cor. 3:6). Since the Galatians have already received this Spirit apart from doing the works of the law (Gal. 3:1–5), Paul calls upon them to live by the Spirit, to be led by the Spirit, and to be guided by the Spirit (5:16, 18, 25). In contrast to the power of God's Spirit stands the flesh, understood as all that is mortal and so corruptible. Understood as a moral force, the flesh (*sarx*) refers to the appearance of things—what people can see and touch, and so what they are tempted to rely and depend upon for their life. Paul comes dangerously close to relating the works of the law to the realm of the flesh, sensing that those who put themselves under the law are tempted to rely upon the works of the law for their justification precisely because such works are so visible and tangible. The concepts of the flesh and the Spirit, then, refer to two different realms, one empowered by God, the other dependent upon all that is mortal and so corruptible.

The moral life is a choice of submitting oneself to the power of God's Spirit or to the power of the flesh. In the first instance, human beings rely on the power of the Spirit; in the second they rely on the power of what is perceptible, tangible, and ultimately corruptible. Thus Paul warns the Galatians that if they sow to their own flesh, they will reap a corruptible harvest; whereas if they sow to the Spirit, they will reap eternal life (6:8). The Spirit and flesh stand in opposition to each other, so that a person cannot please both. Either one carries out the desires of the flesh or one carries out the urging of the Spirit. The true remedy for the moral life, then, is to live by the Spirit (5:16–18). Those who do so will not do "the works of the flesh." Rather, the Spirit will produce its singular fruit in them: "love, joy, peace, patience, kindness, generosity, faithfulness, gentleness, self-control" (5:22–23). This is not to say that the moral life of the believer is without struggle; those who belong to Christ must "crucify the flesh" with its passions and desires (5:24); they must die to their former way of life. The power to do this, however, does not come from themselves but from the Spirit of God.

Paul's second contrast is the opposition between freedom and slavery. According to Paul's anthropology, humanity was in the period of its spiritual minority before Christ appeared. The Gentiles did not know the God of Israel and were enslaved to beings that masqueraded as gods but in fact were "weak and beggarly elemental spirits" (4:9). Paul evaluates the situation of Israel before the coming of Abraham's true heir in a similar way. Abraham's descendants were "under the law" (3:23; 4:5), which functioned as their disciplinarian (3:24). They were like an heir destined to inherit his father's household but still no different from a slave, since heirs are under the care of guardians and trustees until they attain their age of majority. Employing this example (4:1–3), Paul views the time of the law as the period of Israel's spiritual minority, when the Jewish people were "enslaved to the elemental spirits of the world" (4:4), an enigmatic phrase that may refer to the elemental structures of religion, and so to the law. The moral life, then, is a choice between freedom and a yoke of slavery that Paul equates with the law (5:2). Those who have been elected, however, have been called to freedom (5:13). They are no longer under the law (5:18) or subject to its tutelage. They are free to be led and guided by the Spirit. Paul, however, is aware that some may misinterpret freedom from the law as a license to do whatever they want. In this case, what should be an opportunity to live by the guidance of the Spirit becomes an occasion for self-indulgence. Playing on the concept of slavery, Paul urges those who have been set free to "enslave" themselves to one another through loving service (5:13). Freedom from being under the law is not a warrant to do whatever one wants but an opportunity to live by the Spirit.

Paul's third contrast—doing the law and fulfilling the law—is elusive and illuminating. On the one hand it is elusive, since it appears to be a matter of semantics. Whereas those who have themselves circumcised are obligated "to obey the entire law" (*holon ton nomon poiēsai*, 5:3), those who have been freed from being under the law fulfill the law through the love commandment: "For the whole law is summed up (*peplērōtai*) in a single commandment, 'You shall love your neighbor as yourself'" (5:14). This concept of fulfilling what the law requires through the love commandment, rather than doing its many precepts, presupposes an understanding of what Paul means by "the law of Christ" when he writes, "Bear one another's burdens, and in this way you will fulfill the law of Christ (*anaplērōsete ton nomon tou Christou*)" (6:2). If by this expression Paul means a new law, with specific prescriptions given by Jesus that replaced the Mosaic law, there is no indication what these prescriptions are. It is more probable, then, that Paul has in mind the Mosaic law as exemplified in the life of Christ, who by his saving death "gave himself for our sins" (1:3) and "loved me and gave himself for me" (2:20). Paul looks upon the life of Jesus as the fulfillment of the law because Jesus' death for others was the perfect embodiment of the command to love one's neighbor as oneself. Love, then, is the fulfillment of the law. It is difficult to say if Paul is aware of Jesus' summary of the law. If he is, it is puzzling that his own summary differs from Jesus' summary, which includes love of God as well as love of neighbor (Mark 12:28–34).

On the other hand, Paul's concept of fulfilling the law through the love commandment provides an important insight to his understanding of the moral life. Although believers are not under the precepts of the law, they do not disregard its moral demands. Rather, they approach them from another vantage point—not as individual commandments to be observed in order to stand in a right relationship to God but as prescriptions that are fulfilled when one loves as Christ loved. Put another way, those who are under the guidance of the Spirit and love their neighbor as Christ loved cannot but fulfill the law. Although Paul does not explicitly distinguish between the ceremonial and moral prescriptions of the Mosaic law, one suspects that when he speaks of fulfilling the law, it is primarily the moral prescriptions of the law that he has in view. Other laws, such as circumcision, dietary prescriptions, and Sabbath observance are matters of indifference for Gentiles. What matters is the new creation God has effected in Christ, not circumcision or the lack of it (6:15).

To summarize, those who follow the truth of the gospel as Paul preached it at Galatia must live a moral life, but they no longer do this by observing the law's several prescriptions. For just as Christ is the source of their righteousness, so the Spirit is the source of their moral life.

Israel, the Church, and the Truth of the Gospel

At the end of Galatians, Paul notes that the new creation God has established in Christ is more important than circumcision or the lack of it. Paul then pronounces a blessing of peace and mercy upon all who follow this rule of the new creation "and upon the Israel of God" (6:16). Like "the law of Christ," this enigmatic expression has puzzled commentators. Is Paul referring to historical Israel, a portion of Israel within all of Israel, or does he have in view the church composed of those Jewish and Gentile Christians who live according to the rule of the new creation? Given the argument of Galatians, it seems more likely that Paul has in view Jewish and Gentile Christians who understand that circumcision, or the lack of it, is no longer important in the new creation God has effected in Christ. After all, Paul has devoted nearly all of chapter 3 to persuading his Gentile converts that they are Abraham's descendants if they have been incorporated into his singular offspring, who is Christ. The Israel of God, then, provides a good starting point for exploring Paul's understanding of Israel and the church in light of the gospel.

The concept of the church does not play as significant a role in Galatians as it does in the Corinthian correspondence. The only reference to the church at Galatia is in the letter's opening, where Paul greets "the churches of Galatia" (1:2). In the rest of the letter, Paul speaks directly to the Galatians without any reference to the leadership within these communities, apart from a remark about teachers in 6:6, since Paul's primary concern is to assure the Galatians that they need not be circumcised to be counted among Abraham's offspring. Accordingly, Paul has more to say about Abraham's descendants than he does about the church. This discussion of Abraham's descendants presupposes an understanding of salvation history that begins with the promises God made to Abraham, which find their culmination in Christ. In this scheme, the period of the law is a parenthesis within God's plan, but the giving of the law was never intended to change the original stipulations of the covenant God made to Abraham. For Paul, salvation history begins with Abraham and finds its climax in Christ. Nothing is said of the Davidic covenant or of Israel's messianic hope.

This salvation history is further developed in the allegory based on Abraham's two sons (4:21–31). Here Paul argues that the two children and their mothers represent two covenants. The slave woman Hagar and her son Ishmael correspond to the covenant of Sinai "bearing children for slavery," whereas the free woman Sarah and her son Isaac represent a covenant, which Paul does not name, that leads its children to freedom. Although the text is often taken as referring to Judaism and Christianity, Paul is probably speaking about his law-free gospel and the gospel of circumcision advocated by those who have intruded into his missionary territory. If so, he is making a distinction between those who would require Gentile converts to adopt a Jewish way of life and those who do not. The Judaizers may be physically descended from Abraham, but they belong to a line of descent that traces its origins to Hagar and leads its children into slavery. From a historical point of view, this makes little sense since Paul's exegesis is precisely what he says it is, an allegory. The point he wishes to make about Abraham and his descendants, however, is clear: it is possible to be physically descended from Abraham and still be in slavery.

For Paul the church is the Israel of God, or perhaps better expressed, the Israel of God is the church, that is, those Jewish and Gentile believers who rely on faith rather than doing the works of the law for their justification. The church is not a new Israel. It does not replace or displace historical Israel. In Paul's view one finds God's Israel in the church, a community of Gentile and Jewish believers that relies on faith. Paul does not discuss the fate of historical Israel in Galatians, as he does in Romans 9–11, since he is more concerned about the relationship of his Gentile congregations to Jewish Christian communities such as the church at Jerusalem. He would prefer to maintain good relations with the Jerusalem church, in which the pillar apostles play a prominent role, but not at the cost of the truth of the gospel. One can suppose that Paul was quite willing to allow such Jewish congregations to continue in their practice of the law, provided they were willing to acknowledge the right of his Gentile congregations to live apart from the law.

Conclusion

In recent years there have been many competing views of Galatians.[10] The traditional Lutheran perspective argues that Paul, like Luther, opposed every attempt to establish one's righteousness before God on the basis of doing good works. This interpretation is not opposed to good works, but it is deeply convinced that a person cannot be justified before God on the basis of good works. Every attempt to do so is boasting before God. In recent years "the new perspective" on Paul has argued that Luther's concern and Paul's concern were different. Whereas Luther opposed any attempt to gain one's righteousness by doing good works, Paul opposed those who tried to impose a Jewish way of life on his Gentile converts. Put another way, whereas Paul's concern was social in nature, Luther's was personal. Others have argued that Galatians exhibits an apocalyptic theology—a divine invasion intended to free humanity from the demonic powers that threatened it.[11] Each of these approaches has understood something the others have neglected. The "new perspective" on Paul urges that the theology of justification has important social ramifications, and it has shown that, in Galatians, Paul employs this theology to defend the rights of his Gentile converts. Paul's theology of justification, however, is not merely a social teaching; it has important soteriological ramifications for the moral life of the individual, as the traditional Lutheran notion argues. Finally, Paul does indeed speak in apocalyptic language, opposing spirit and flesh, law and faith, this age and the age to come, the old and the new creation. What happened in Christ was a kind of divine invasion that freed humanity from the present evil age. Paul's own initial experience of the gospel was an apocalyptic event, a "revelation of Jesus Christ" (1:12). In this revelation Paul was called to be an apostle and received the gospel he preached, and in light of this revelation he rethought his understanding of Israel and its law. Apart from this revelation it is impossible to make sense of Paul's theology.

THE RIGHTEOUSNESS OF GOD: ROMANS

The importance of Paul's Letter to the Romans is beyond dispute, and it rightly stands at the beginning of the Pauline corpus, not only because it is the longest of the apostle's extant letters but because it is his most cogent statement of the gospel he preached. Whether Paul wrote Romans as a kind of summary of his

10. See Stephen Westerholm, *Perspectives Old and New on Paul: The "Lutheran" Paul and His Critics* (Grand Rapids: Eerdmans, 2004). This work provides an informative account of recent Pauline interpretation in light of the traditional Lutheran understanding of Paul and the "new perspective" developed by James D. G. Dunn and E. P. Sanders.

11. The most prominent exponent of this view is J. Louis Martyn, *Galatians: A New Translation with Introduction and Commentary* (AB 33A; New York: Doubleday, 1997).

theology, especially his understanding of justification by faith, is a matter of continuing scholarly discussion.[12] But even if he did not, generations of believers have viewed this letter as the essence of the apostle's teaching on justification by faith. The theological importance of this letter and the pride of place the canon grants it has led many to evaluate and understand Paul's other writings in light of Romans.[13]

Although all concur that Romans is central to Paul's theology, there is less agreement about the historical situation that occasioned it. Did Paul write to address divisions between Jewish and Gentile believers at Rome, as suggested by 14:1–15:13, where he addresses the problem of the "weak" and the "strong" in the Roman community? Was he writing to present his gospel to believers whom he had long desired to visit (1:13) in order to proclaim the gospel to them (1:15) and correct distortions of his gospel (3:8) in the hope that they would assist him with his mission to Spain (15:28)? Did the apostle write this letter with a view to his impending visit to Jerusalem, where he expected to encounter opposition to the law-free gospel he had been preaching among the Gentiles, even though he was bringing a collection gathered from his Gentile congregations to the poor of the church at Jerusalem (15:30–32)? Or was Romans occasioned by all of these and still other reasons history will never uncover?[14] Whatever the answer, it is clear that Paul is writing toward the end of his missionary career in the eastern Mediterranean basin, that he is on his way to Jerusalem to bring a gracious gift of money from his Gentile congregations to the church of Jerusalem, and that he intends to go to Rome and then undertake a mission to Spain (15:22–33).

Although there are disputes about the structure of individual sections, the overall movement of Romans is clear. After the letter's introduction (1:1–15), there is an extended discussion of the need for, the nature of, and the results of the righteousness that God has effected in Jesus Christ (1:16–8:39). This discussion of the righteousness that God grants on the basis of faith rather than on the basis of doing the works of the law leads to a consideration of the faithfulness of God despite the failure of God's covenant people to submit to this righteousness (9:1–11:36). In light of this discussion of righteousness, which dominates chapters 1–11, Paul takes up the question of how those who have

---

12. The view of Romans as Paul's last will and testament, argued by Günther Bornkamm ("The Letter to the Romans as Paul's Last Will and Testament," in *Romans Debate*, 16–28), is not as popular today as it once was, since scholars insist that Romans, like all of Paul's letters, is an occasional writing.

13. For example, James D. G. Dunn (*The Theology of Paul the Apostle* [Grand Rapids: Eerdmans, 1998]) employs Romans as a template for his Pauline theology.

14. Wedderburn (*Reasons for Romans*, 5–6) writes: "we shall in fact find that no one single reason or cause will adequately explain the writing of Romans; rather the explanation is to be found in a constellation or cluster of different circumstances, each contributing in its own way to the writing of the letter and thus to our understanding of it."

been justified on the basis of faith should live this new life of righteousness (12:1–15:13). In the remaining portion of the letter, Paul discusses his travel plans (15:14–33), commends Phoebe (the bearer of the letter), and extends greetings to numerous believers at Rome (16:1–16), before concluding with a final admonition, blessing, and doxology (16:17–27).[15] Romans, then, consists of three major parts (1:16–8:39; 9:1–11:36; 12:1–15:13), each of which develops some aspect of the letter's central theme, the righteousness of God.

The theology of Romans is indebted to the theology of Galatians. For example, Romans echoes and develops what Galatians says about the promises God made to Abraham and the inability of human beings to attain righteousness on the basis of doing the works of the law. It relates the Spirit to God's work of justification and affirms the Spirit's central role in the moral life. Romans, however, presents these themes in a less polemical way, and it gives greater attention to a number of issues Galatians raises but never develops, for example, the sinfulness of human beings apart from Christ and the place of Israel in God's plan of salvation. The most distinctive characteristic of Romans, however, is the unrelenting manner in which it speaks of God. The entire letter is about the righteousness or uprightness of God, God's faithfulness to his covenant promises, the way in which God deals with humanity, Gentile as well as Jew. This righteousness is God's integrity and God's unexpectedly gracious way of dealing with sinners. In this letter, then, Paul affirms and, to the extent that any human being can, defends the uprightness of God.

The theology of Romans is best approached by beginning with "the gospel of God" (1:1), which is God's power for salvation (1:16). This gospel, in which God's righteousness is revealed (1:17), graciously comes to humanity, which finds itself under God's wrath because of its disobedience. Despite the sinful condition of humanity, or rather precisely because of it, God justifies the ungodly on the basis of faith rather than on the basis of doing the works of the law, thereby reconciling humanity, freeing it from the power of sin, and granting it the gift of the Spirit. Although the greater part of Israel has not responded to this gracious offer in Jesus Christ, Paul insists that God has not been unfaithful to the covenant people, nor has God rejected Israel. Israel will be saved in God's way. In the period before this final act of God's justice, those who have been justified must live in accordance with the righteousness that God has bestowed upon them through the gospel Paul preaches. The major topics to be treated, then, are the following: (1) the gospel of God; (2) the human predicament apart from the gospel; (3) God's gracious gift of salvation; (4) the need for faith; (5) the righteousness of God toward Israel; and (6) the moral life.

15. The doxology, Rom. 16:25–27, has always been problematic since it occurs in several different places in the manuscript tradition, most notably after 14:23 and 16:24.

The Gospel of God

Romans is about "the gospel of God" (1:1). Understood as an objective genitive, the phrase means the gospel about God. Taken as a subjective genitive, the
focus is on God's own gospel, God's good news of what has been accomplished
in Christ. The fact that Paul also speaks about "the gospel of his Son" (1:9) and
the "gospel of Christ" (15:19) suggests that God is the subject and Christ is the
object of the gospel. Thus the gospel is God's own good news of what God has
done in his Son, Jesus Christ. To be sure, the gospel proclaims something about
God whenever it speaks of Christ, and it includes the good news of the kingdom that Jesus once proclaimed. But in Romans the focus is decidedly on God
as the active agent so that "the gospel of God" refers to God's own good news,
and "the gospel of Christ" to the content of that good news.

But if the gospel is God's own good news, how can Paul proclaim it? How
can he dare to say "according to my gospel" (2:16; 16:25)? As in Galatians, Paul's
right to call God's gospel his own is rooted in his apostolic call, when God set
him apart for the gospel of God (1:1). The gospel, then, does not belong to Paul
as if he were its author. He can claim it as his gospel only because God designated him to proclaim it. But inasmuch as he has been set aside and consecrated
to preach this gospel, he can call the gospel of God "my gospel." Paul, however, does not see the need to defend his apostleship in Romans as he did in
Galatians. Instead, he presents his apostolic ministry in the language of worship and cult. Thus he worships (*latreuō*) God with his spirit by preaching the
gospel (1:9). He is "a minister (*leitourgon*) of Christ Jesus to the Gentiles in
the priestly service (*hierourgounta*) of the gospel of God, so that the offering
(*prosphora*) of the Gentiles may be acceptable, sanctified by the Holy Spirit"
(15:16). Paul's apostolic ministry of preaching God's gospel, then, is akin to a
priestly offering, in this case an offering of Gentile believers.

In the opening verses of Romans (1:1–6), Paul carefully outlines the content of the gospel he preaches as well as its relationship to his apostleship. First,
the gospel is not his own message, for he has been called and set apart for the
gospel of God. Second, for all of its newness, the gospel stands in continuity
with the prophetic promises recorded in Israel's Scriptures. Thus Paul argues
that when Israel's Scriptures are correctly understood, they lead to Christ.
Third, the content of these promises is about God's Son, whom Paul describes
from two perspectives. In terms of his human descent (*kata sarka*), the Son
belongs to the line of David, from whom the promised Messiah was to come.
But in terms of his resurrection from the dead, he was appointed Son of God
in power "according to the spirit of holiness" (*kata pneuma hagiōsynēs*). That is,
the resurrection began the Son's messianic enthronement and revealed him to
be God's Son. Fourth, it is this Son, whom Paul calls "Jesus Christ our Lord,"
who gave Paul the grace of apostleship to bring about the obedience of faith

among the Gentiles. The gospel of God, which Paul preaches, then, is the gospel about Christ, the son of David, the Son of God, the one to whom the Scriptures point. Its purpose is to bring all people to the obedience that is faith.

Although the content of the gospel is a crucified Messiah, Paul is not ashamed of the gospel (1:16a). He is confident that God, and so the gospel, will be victorious (see 8:31–39). There are two reasons for Paul's confidence. First, although the gospel is proclaimed by human beings, it is not a human word: "it is the power of God for salvation to everyone who has faith, to the Jew first and also to the Greek" (1:16b). To speak of the gospel as "the power of God for salvation" is to affirm that when the gospel is proclaimed, God is at work rescuing people from their sinful situation. Paul describes this condition in 1:18–3:20 and the new life that God's salvific work brings in 6:1–8:39. As for Paul, he has already experienced the power of the gospel at work in his ministry. In Asia and Greece, Christ was at work in him, bringing about the obedience of the Gentiles (15:18), and it was "by the power of signs and wonders, by the power of the Spirit of God," that he proclaimed the gospel of Christ (15:19). Thus, just as God's power was disclosed in the gospel Jesus proclaimed, so God's power is manifested through the gospel Paul proclaims. This gospel, however, can be appropriated only by faith. For this reason, Paul insists on the need to believe in the gospel rather than rely on doing the works of the law in order to be justified. Moreover, even though he has been set aside to preach this gospel to the Gentiles, he willingly acknowledges that there is a salvation-historical order: to the Jews first, and then to the Gentiles. The failure of the greater part of Israel to accept the gospel causes Paul intense grief and raises the question of God's faithfulness to the covenant people.

The second reason why Paul is not ashamed of the gospel is that "in it the righteousness of God is revealed through faith for faith; as it is written, 'The one who is righteous will live by faith'" (1:17). The righteousness or uprightness of God (*dikaiosynē theou*), like the gospel of God, can be taken as an objective or subjective genitive. Taken as an objective genitive, it refers to the righteousness that God graciously confers upon the ungodly. This is certainly the sense of the expression in 2 Cor. 5:21 and Phil. 3:9, but here and in Rom. 3:5, 21, 22, and 10:3 the righteousness of God is best construed as a subjective genitive that points to God's own uprightness, God's righteousness, God's integrity, God's covenant faithfulness in the face of human infidelity. God manifests this righteousness "toward humanity when through the death and resurrection of Jesus Christ he brings about the vindication and acquittal of sinful human beings."[16] Paul is not ashamed of the gospel, then, and he is confident that it will not disappoint him, for it is the power of God that leads to

---

16. Joseph A. Fitzmyer, *Romans: A New Translation with Introduction and Commentary* (AB 33; New York: Doubleday, 1992), 106.

salvation. When it is proclaimed, it reveals the utter integrity of God, who acquits sinners on the basis of what has been accomplished in his Son, Jesus Christ. The one response the gospel requires is faith, the faith Scripture describes when it testifies to the gospel, "The one who is righteous will live by faith" (1:17, quoting Hab. 2:4).

The Human Predicament apart from the Gospel

A gospel that has the power to bring everyone to salvation implies that humanity is in dire need of salvation. Humanity may be unaware of its predicament, and it may deny that it finds itself in a situation from which it cannot extricate itself. But a gospel that presents itself as the only way to salvation reveals something of the human condition that was not previously known and could not be known apart from this revelation. The gospel of God, then, contains the seeds of a profound anthropology that Paul develops in Romans through his exposition of the wrath of God (1:18–3:20), the disobedience of Adam (5:12–21), and the power that is sin, which results in death, takes advantage of the law, and exercises dominion over humanity (6:1–7:25). In effect, Paul analyzes the human condition from three vantage points: (1) the reality that all have transgressed God's law and are under the wrath of God, (2) the origin of sin, and (3) the power of sin. To be sure, Paul's goal is more rhetorical than analytical since his purpose is to persuade his readers that all have sinned—Jew as well as Gentile. Consequently, all stand in need of the salvation that only the gospel of God can bring. But behind this rhetorical tour de force is an insightful theological understanding of the human condition that later theology would call original sin.

The Wrath of God

The opening verse of 1:18–3:20 functions as the theme for all that will follow: "For the wrath of God is revealed from heaven against all ungodliness and wickedness of those who by their wickedness suppress the truth." This "wrath of God" (*orgē theou*) is the mirror image of the "righteousness of God" (*dikaiosynē theou*), which is revealed in the gospel of God. Those who have been graciously acquitted by the death of Christ now experience the wrath of God as the righteousness of God, whereas those who suppress the truth of God experience the righteousness of God as the wrath of God. Just as the righteousness of God is revealed in the gospel, so the wrath of God is being revealed "from heaven" (1:18). This wrath of God is a cosmic event that humanity can see and experience in the results of its own sinful behavior. But it is not to be construed as an emotion, as if God became "angry" with humanity.[17] Rather,

---

17. On the wrath of God, see Herman Ridderbos, *Paul: An Outline of His Theology* (Grand Rapids: Eerdmans, 1975), 108–14.

it is God's just and impartial response to sin. The wrath of God is the consequence of, and the punishment for, sin.

Paul's initial indictment of humanity is its refusal to acknowledge God, even though "what can be known about God is plain to them, because God has shown it to them" (1:19). Humanity has understood something of God's eternal power and divine nature in and through the created universe, and so it is without excuse because it has suppressed the truth of God. But although it has known something of God from the created world, it has refused to honor God or to give him thanks. Choosing to worship the creature rather than the Creator, humanity exchanged the glory of the immortal God for images of God's mortal creatures. The root sin, then, which is at the origin of all sin, is idolatry; and it is this idolatrous worship of the creature rather than worship of the Creator that characterizes the human situation the gospel addresses.

The wrath of God is already being revealed against such behavior, but not necessarily in the way one might expect. To be sure, there will be a day of wrath when God's righteous judgment will be revealed (2:5, 16), but the wrath of God is already being revealed in humanity's sinful folly. For rather than immediately punishing humanity by an act of cosmic judgment, God has delivered humanity to its own lusts and impurity that leads to bodily degradation (1:24), to degrading passions (1:26), and to a debased understanding of reality (1:28). Because the creature has forsaken the Creator, God has abandoned humanity to its own devices, allowing it to do what it wishes, no matter how degrading or lustful. The consequence of this divine wrath, which is already revealed, is as frightful as the last judgment. For having worshiped the creature rather than the Creator, humanity finds itself in a situation in which it must live with the consequences of its own behavior. Consequently, sin becomes the punishment of sin, and sin leads to the revelation of God's wrath. More frightful still, this sinful situation is a predicament from which humanity cannot extricate itself because, having forsaken the glory of God for the glory of the creature, humanity confuses good with evil and evil with good, for it has exchanged the order of creation for the disorder of sin.

Paul's description of human sinfulness in 1:18–32 is usually taken as a description of the sinful condition of the Gentile world. From Paul's Jewish perspective, this is true. The sinfulness of the Gentile world is the result of its refusal to acknowledge God (see Wis. 13:1–14:31). But as Paul develops his argument in Romans 2, it becomes apparent that the Jewish world shares in the same sinful condition even though it has been granted the gift of the law and can boast in the covenant sign of circumcision. Paul's Jewish compatriots may acknowledge the righteousness of God's judgment upon those who do such things as are described in 1:29–32, but they will not escape the judgment of God if they also do them (2:3); for God is a just judge who repays each person according to his or her works (*kata ta erga autou*, 2:6). The righteousness of God means that "God shows no partiality" (2:11). Those who do good works will be given eternal life, whereas those who do not obey the truth will inherit "wrath and fury" (2:7–8). The wrath of God, then, is not only being revealed in the present sinful condition of humankind; there will also be a "day of wrath" (2:5) when God will judge all—Jew as well as Gentile—justly and impartially on the basis of what they have done.

The Gentiles who have sinned apart from the law will be judged on the basis of what they could have known about God's demands from what is already written in their hearts, whereas those who have sinned with full knowledge of the law will be judged on the basis of the law: "For it is not the hearers of the law who are righteous in God's sight, but the doers of the law who will be justified" (2:13). Paul makes an analogous statement about circumcision. Circumcision is of value if one obeys the law (*ean nomon prassēs*, 2:25), but if one transgresses the law, the physical sign of circumcision will be of no avail on the day of judgment. Conversely, if the uncircumcised keep the law, their uncircumcised state will be reckoned as circumcision. No one will be saved on the day of judgment and wrath because they possess the law and the sign of circumcision. It is only those who obey the law who will be justified in God's sight.

Paul's discussion in chapter 2 is indebted to Israel's Scriptures. For example, the statement of 2:6 that God will repay each one according to his or her deeds derives from Ps. 62:12, Prov. 24:12, and Sir. 16:14. Paul's statement that "real circumcision is a matter of the heart" (Rom. 2:29) is an echo of Deut. 30:6, Jer. 4:4, and 9:25. The real challenge is to understand what Paul is saying, in light of the gospel, when he writes that a person is justified not by doing the works of the law but on the basis of faith. How can Paul affirm that God will repay each one according to his or her deeds (Rom. 2:6), that it is not the hearers of the law who are righteous in God's sight but the doers of the law who will be justified (2:13), and then proceed to develop his teaching on justification by faith? Does Paul conveniently forget what he writes here?

Paul may be difficult to understand, and there are surely moments when he appears to contradict himself, but that is not the case here. He is quite insistent that each one will be judged according to deeds, and he clearly states that it is the doers of the law who will be justified before God. But he is equally insistent that there is no one who fulfills all that the law prescribes. In what is admittedly a rhetorical flourish, he employs a catena of scriptural quotations to show that there is no one who is righteous, not even one (3:10–18). The Jewish observer of the Gentile world, of course, has long since determined that Gentiles have suppressed the truth about God through their idolatrous worship. But Paul now accuses his Jewish compatriots of what the prophets said long ago, that even though Israel possesses the law, it violates the law. There is, of course, an advantage to being a Jew since the Jew knows what God requires (3:1–2), but the Jew is no better off since "all, both Jews and Greeks, are under the power of sin" (3:9). With this statement, Paul introduces something he has not yet mentioned, the power of sin. The Jew may know what the law requires, and something of the moral prescriptions of the law may be written in the heart of the Gentile, but neither the Jew nor the Gentile does all that the law requires because both stand under the power of the force Paul calls sin. This power does not refer to the individual transgressions that Jew and Gentile commit against the law and that contemporary believers refer to as "sins." In Paul's theology, sin is a cosmic power that exercises control over humanity to the extent that humanity stands in solidarity with Adam rather than with Christ, a point Paul will develop in chapter 5.

Paul's insistence that it is the doers of the law who will be justified and his teaching on justification by faith, then, are related to each other in the following way. The law demands obedience, and those who do it will be justified. It also threatens judgment on the day of wrath to all who disobey its prescriptions. The reality, however, is that all, Jew as well as Gentile, have transgressed the law because all are under the cosmic power of sin. Consequently, no one will be justified in God's sight by doing the works of the law because nobody does all that the law prescribes. Because nobody does all that the law requires, everybody without exception is liable to the wrath of God that will be revealed on the day of judgment. Just and impartial judge that God is, God will not overlook those who transgress the law. Gentiles suppress the truth of God, and Jews disregard the law that has been given to them because both are under the power of sin. Instead of leading people to justification, then, the law brings about a deeper knowledge of sin. Those who possess the law know what God requires, but they do not do what the law commands. Thus the law increases their knowledge of sin.

Paul's description of the human condition in 1:18–3:20 needs to be understood as both a rhetorical argument and a theological statement. As a rhetorical argument, it is a tour de force intended to sweep readers off their feet. It takes little account of the fact that there are "good" Gentiles and Jews who try to do what God requires, even if they do not do all that God requires. Consequently, one will always be able to object to what Paul says. For example, what is to be said of those righteous and pious Israelites that Scripture extols? But Paul's rhetorical argument is also a profoundly theological statement that there is something awry with the human condition with which the law cannot deal. Human beings transgress God's law on a massive scale, even when they know the law. They transgress God's law because they suppress the truth about God and find themselves enslaved to the cosmic power of sin. They cannot obey God's law because sin insidiously employs the law to frustrate the law. How did this power enter the world?

The Origin of Sin

Paul has provided a powerful description of the sinful condition of humanity (1:18–3:20), but he has not explained the origin of this condition, although he does allude to it when he notes that all "are under the power of sin" (3:9). In chapter 5, however, he finally explains why humanity finds itself under the power of sin, which he personifies as an actor on the human stage. In a contrast that he establishes between Adam and Christ (5:12–21), Paul argues that sin entered the world through one man, Adam, the type (*typos*) of the one who was to come, Christ. But whereas Adam's act of disobedience led to death and condemnation for all of his descendants, Christ's obedience resulted in life and acquittal for all who are incorporated into him. The contrast, then, involves two human beings: Adam, the progenitor of sinful humanity, and Christ, the progenitor of redeemed humanity. Paul draws a similar contrast between Adam and Christ in 1 Cor. 15:21–22, 44–49, when he argues on behalf of the general resurrection of the dead, maintaining that just as death came through a human being (Adam), so the resurrection of the dead comes through a human being (Christ). The Adam-Christ contrast that Paul establishes in Romans, however, is more elaborate and connects death with sin in a way that 1 Corinthians 15 does not.[18]

Paul develops his Adam-Christ comparison in three stages. In the first (5:12–14), he begins a comparison between Adam and Christ that he does not complete. The beginning of the comparison, however, explains the origin of sin and death. Sin entered the world through one man, and death followed. Death then spread to all human beings because all sinned.[19] Paul's basic premise, then, is that Adam's transgression unleashed the power of sin, and with the entrance of sin into the world came yet another power, which Paul identifies as death. More than the physical destruction of the body, death is eternal separation from God. Death is in the service of sin because sin's ultimate goal is to separate the creature from the Creator. This is why the wage that sin pays to those in its service is death (6:23). Sin and death, then, were already in the world in the time before the appearance of the Mosaic law— from the period of Adam to Moses. During this period, human beings transgressed God's commandments, but they were not fully aware of the enormity of what they were doing since the Mosaic law had not yet been promulgated.

---

18. Whereas 1 Cor. 15:45–49 suggests that death is the result of Adam's mortal nature, Rom. 5:12 says that Adam's transgression introduced sin and death into the world. The difference may derive from the fact that in Romans Paul thinks of death as physical and spiritual (separation from God), whereas the physical aspect of death is primarily in view in 1 Corinthians 15.

19. The Greek expression that Paul employs here (*eph hō*) is enigmatic. Fitzmyer (*Romans*, 413–17) lists and evaluates eleven different interpretations. The translation of the NRSV, "because," suggests that death was the result of continued human sinfulness. This translation, however, should not obscure Paul's major premise that Adam's transgression introduced sin into the world.

Nonetheless, even in this period before the law, all were under the power of sin and death, and so all were alienated from God.

In the second stage of his argument (5:15–17), Paul distinguishes between the gift of Christ and the trespass of Adam in order to show that even though the two can be compared, Christ's act of obedience is superior to Adam's act of disobedience. The comparison that will follow, then, does not mean that Adam and Christ are on an equal footing. Christ is superior in every way. Paul describes the consequences of Adam's trespass in three ways. First, as a result of his trespass, many died (v. 15). Second, the judgment following his trespass brought condemnation to all (v. 16). Third, because of this one trespass, death exercised dominion through one man (v. 17). Adam's singular sin, then, had a universal effect, for it resulted in death and condemnation for all. In contrast to Adam, Christ's gift brought justification and life for all. The actions of Adam and Christ, then, affect humanity in diametrically opposed ways; for whereas Adam's disobedience leads to death and condemnation, Christ's obedience leads to life and justification.

Having made the necessary distinctions between the consequences of Adam's and Christ's action, in 5:18–19 Paul completes the comparison he began in verse 12. Just as Adam's trespass led to condemnation, so Christ's act of righteousness led to justification and life for all. Just as many were made sinners by Adam's disobedience, so many were made righteous by Christ's obedience. Although Paul's primary goal in Romans 5 is to demonstrate the superabundant grace of God in Christ as compared to the baleful effects of Adam's transgression, this discussion provides an important insight to Paul's understanding of the human condition and why humanity can be saved only by the gospel of God.

The human predicament is more than a matter of human sinfulness. If this predicament were merely a matter of sinfulness from which humanity could repent, then there would be no need for the gospel of God. The predicament of the human condition is that humanity finds itself under the power of sin that was unleashed by Adam's transgression. In other words, it is as if sin preexisted and was waiting for the right moment to enter the world. Once unleashed, sin exercises its dominion over humanity by separating humanity from God through death. Human beings may be able to repent from their individual sins and transgressions, but they cannot free themselves from the domination of sin or death. Not even the Mosaic law was able to alter this situation. Indeed, when the law finally arrived, it multiplied trespasses (5:20), not because the law was sinful (7:7) but because humanity was already under the power of sin, thanks to Adam's transgression. In the time from Adam to Christ, then, sin and death already reigned, and humanity was in a predicament from which it could not extricate itself, even when the law arrived. Paul employs a variety of expressions to describe this predicament. The "old self" was enslaved to sin (6:6), and sin exercised dominion over the mortal body (6:12). The members of this mortal body were given over to sin as instruments of wickedness so that those under the power of sin belonged to death (6:13). Consequently, those under the power of sin were slaves of sin (6:16), and the members of their bodies were slaves to impurity (6:19). The result of such enslavement was death: the wages of sin (6:23). The power of sin is such that there is no way for humanity to escape this situation.

The Power of Sin

The power of sin can even frustrate the goal and purpose of God's law. Paul explores this strange relationship between sin and law in Romans 7. He is firmly convinced (in a way that is not so apparent in Galatians) that "the law is holy, and the commandment is holy and just and good" (7:12). He is insistent that the law is not to be equated with sin (7:7), nor did it bring death (7:13). The real culprit is sin, which, seeing an occasion in the commandment, took advantage of the commandment. Speaking in the voice of every human who does not know God's law, Paul writes, "I was once alive apart from the law, but when the commandment came, sin revived and I died, and the very commandment that promised life proved to be death to me" (7:9–10). This is not to say that apart from the law human beings lived a morally good life. Rather, before they knew the prescriptions of God's law, they lived in the bliss of ignorance, unaware of the extent to which they violated God's law. But when the law, which promised life, arrived (see Lev. 18:5; Deut. 4:1; 6:24), sin seized the opportunity to "deceive" those under the law just as the serpent deceived Eve (Gen. 3:13). For when the commandment said, "You shall not covet," sin aroused the desire to covet (Rom. 7:7–8). The real culprit, then, is sin, which took advantage of the law in order to produce death so that, through the law, the real nature of sin could be unmasked (7:13).

The law is spiritual (*pneumatikos*) because it comes from God, but those who try to observe it belong to the realm of the flesh; they are *sarkinos* ("fleshly," "carnal," 7:14). They are weak and mortal and destined to perish. Moreover, even if they do not know it, they have been enslaved to the power of sin unleashed by Adam's transgression (5:12). It is this belonging to the realm of the flesh, and being sold under the power of sin, that results in the inner conflict Paul describes: "I do not understand my own actions. For I do not do what I want, but I do the very thing I hate" (7:15). This statement and what follows (7:16–25) is not to be taken as an autobiographical account of Paul's psychological state as regards legal observance before he became a Christian.[20] Nor is it to be construed as a description of the Christian's struggle to live a morally good life. The

---

20. See the helpful discussion in Westerholm, *Perspectives Old and New*, 134–45; and Ridderbos, *Paul: His Theology*, 126–30.

"I" who speaks here is the "I" of unredeemed humanity. It is the "I" of everyone who is in Adam rather than in Christ. It is the "I" of every person under the power of sin. This is the predicament of humanity apart from Christ.

To be sure, Paul's description of unredeemed humanity is not necessarily the concrete experience of every individual who does not belong to Christ. For example, the author of Sirach is quite insistent that the law can be kept: "If you choose, you can keep the commandments, and to act faithfully is a matter of your own choice" (Sir. 15:15). Even Paul could write of his former experience in Judaism that "as to righteousness under the law" he was "blameless" (Phil. 3:6). What Paul writes here, then, should not be taken as the anguished experience of every person apart from Christ, as if that experience could be verified empirically. Rather, this rhetorical tour de force represents Paul's understanding of the human predicament in light of the gospel of God. Having been redeemed by Christ and finding himself no longer under the law but in Christ, Paul looks back at the situation of unredeemed humanity and speaks in its voice with the knowledge he now has in Christ. From this perspective he affirms that those under the law agree that it is good (Rom. 7:16), and in their innermost self they delight in it (7:22), but another law is at work "making me captive to the law of sin that dwells in my members" (7:23).

Unredeemed humanity, then, does not know its real situation. But Paul, speaking in the voice of unredeemed humanity—in light of the gospel of God—clarifies humanity's true situation. He explains the struggle of humanity apart from Christ, a struggle of which unredeemed humanity is not fully aware, just as the Johannine Gospel confronts the world with a light that exposes the darkness that the world denies.

Paul's understanding of the human predicament can be summarized as follows. All have sinned, Jew as well as Gentile, because all are under the power of sin unleashed by Adam's transgression. All are under the power of sin, which brought death into the world and takes advantage of the law to deceive those under the law. Although human beings know what the law requires and even delight in it, no one does the works that the law prescribes because all are under the power of sin.

God's Gracious Gift of Salvation

Having established that humanity finds itself in a sinful situation from which it cannot extricate itself, because it is under the power of sin, Paul shows how the gospel reveals God's salvation for all who believe in what God has accomplished in Christ. Paul describes this salvation in four texts. In 3:21–26 he returns to the theme of the righteousness of God that he introduced in 1:17, employing the concepts of justification, redemption, expiation, and possibly forgiveness, to explain how God dealt with sin through the saving event of

Christ's death. In 5:1–11 he argues that if God justified and reconciled humanity when it was at enmity with God, then it is all the more certain that the justified and reconciled will be saved from the wrath of God. In 5:12–7:6, having
explained the doleful effects of Adam's transgression, he shows that the justified and reconciled are no longer under the rule of sin, death, and the law.
Finally, in 8:1–39 he presents the life of the justified and reconciled in relationship to the Spirit of God. The major themes to be considered, then, are
(1) how God has justified humanity, (2) the hope of the justified and reconciled, (3) the freedom of the justified and reconciled, and (4) the new life in the
Spirit that the justified and reconciled enjoy.

How God Has Justified Humanity

Apart from Christ, humanity finds itself under the wrath of God. Humanity
already experiences this wrath in the consequences of its own sinful behavior.
But it is also faced with an eschatological wrath that will be revealed when God
impartially judges humanity on the basis of its deeds (2:5–6). Because everyone is under the power of sin, no one is righteous before God on the basis of
doing the works of the law. All humanity finds itself alienated from God, in a
sinful condition that it cannot rectify. It is because of this hopeless situation
that God intervenes in an utterly gracious way by manifesting his own righteousness in Christ.

This righteousness of God (*dikaiosynē tou theou*) is God's uprightness, the
manifestation of God's integrity and covenant loyalty. At the beginning of
Romans, Paul writes of the gospel he preaches, "For in it [the gospel] the righteousness of God is revealed through faith for faith" (1:17). He then returns to
this concept in 3:21–26, affirming that the righteousness of God has now been
revealed in Christ in order to deal with the sinful human condition described
in 1:18–3:20. In other words, because humanity found itself in a predicament
from which it could not extricate itself by doing the works of the law (since all
were under the power of sin), God revealed his righteousness, his own way of
dealing with sin, in order to free humanity from its sinful condition. This
righteousness is manifested apart from the law because all are under the power
of sin, which frustrates every human attempt to justify oneself before God on
the basis of doing the works of the law. The law and the prophets, however,
testify to the righteousness of God inasmuch as they point to Christ. Since this
righteousness is manifested apart from the law, it can be appropriated only on
the basis of trusting faith in what God has accomplished in Christ. Paul's
understanding of salvation, then, can be summarized as follows: Since all have
sinned, because all are under the power of sin, no one is justified before God
on the basis of legal observance. Therefore, God has freely justified everyone
on the basis of faith. This gracious offer of salvation to all on the basis of faith
is the revelation of God's righteousness.

God manifests this righteousness in the death of Christ. To explain the significance of this death Paul employs three concepts, justification, redemption, and expiation, and possibly a fourth, forgiveness. He maintains that the death of Christ is the act whereby God accomplishes what humanity could not do on the basis of legal observance because it was under the power of sin. By the death of Christ, God justifies humanity so that it now stands in the right relationship to God, not because it has observed the law but because God has freely justified and acquitted humanity on the basis of Christ's death. To explain why God justifies humanity so freely, Paul introduces the concept of redemption (*apolytrōsis*, 3:24), which in the Greco-Roman world referred to the buying back of slaves or prisoners. The application of this concept to the situation of sinful humanity suggests that Christ's death ransomed and rescued humanity from the power of sin that enslaved and held it captive.[21] God freely justifies humanity by the death of Christ, then, because the death of Christ frees humanity from the power of sin.

Paul provides another reason why God has freely justified humanity on the basis of Christ's death. Drawing on the cultic imagery of the Day of Atonement—when the high priest sprinkled the blood of bulls and goats on the mercy seat (*hilastērion*) within the Holy of Holies (Lev. 16:14–15) to make atonement "for the sanctuary, because of the uncleanness of the people of Israel, and because of their transgressions, all their sins" (Lev. 16:16)—Paul writes that God put forward Christ as a *hilastērion* (Rom. 3:25), the new mercy seat sprinkled with Christ's own blood, thereby atoning for the sins of humanity. Fitzmyer explains the significance of this image in this way: "so it would depict Christ as the new 'mercy seat,' presented or displayed by the Father as a means of expiating or wiping away the sins of humanity, indeed, as the presence of God, of his revelation, and of his expiating power."[22]

Whether Paul introduces a fourth image of forgiveness depends upon how one translates *paresin* in 3:25. Whereas the NRSV reads, "because in his divine forbearance he had passed over (*dia tēn paresin*) the sins previously committed," suggesting that in his mercy God had overlooked sins in the past but is now dealing with them, the NAB reads, "because of the forgiveness (*dia tēn paresin*) of sins previously committed," indicating that Christ's death brought about the forgiveness of sins.[23] Although this is the only occurrence of *paresis* in the New Testament, and although the word normally means "passing over, letting go unpunished," it can be used of "remitting debts and other

21. Although Paul reminds the Corinthians that they were purchased at a price, neither in 1 Corinthians nor here does he develop the image further, as if a price were paid to the devil in order to release humanity.

22. Fitzmyer, *Romans*, 350.

23. This is the reading of the Vulgate: "propter remissionen praecedentium delictorum" (Rom. 3:25).

obligations."[24] This concept of "forgiveness," if correct, contributes to Paul's line of thought in 3:21–26: God justified humanity by Christ's death because that death redeemed sinful humanity from sin. It presented Christ as the mercy seat of atonement, and brought about the forgiveness of sins committed in the past.

To summarize, God manifested his uprightness by freely justifying humanity on the basis of Christ's death because that death was redemptive, atoned for sins, and effected the forgiveness of sins.

The Hope of the Justified and Reconciled

In his discussion of the righteousness of God (3:21–26), Paul explains that God justifies sinners by faith in Christ's death because, by that death, God dealt with sin once and for all. In 5:1–11 Paul relates God's work of justifying sinners to their hope for salvation. He begins by describing the present situation of the justified: they are now at peace with God (5:1) because they have received the gift of reconciliation through Jesus Christ (5:10). This reconciliation is the outcome of justification, for, once acquitted by God, the justified are reconciled with God. They are no longer at enmity with God, nor are they counted among the ungodly, because in Christ God has restored the relationship humanity fractured by its transgressions. Where there was enmity, now there is peace, so that in Christ the justified and reconciled have access to God (5:2).

Paul, however, distinguishes this new situation of justification and reconciliation from the eschatological reality of salvation that will be completed at the end of the ages. The new situation of the justified and reconciled provides them with a firm assurance that they will be saved. For if God justified and reconciled them when they were sinners, they can be all the more confident, now that they are justified and reconciled to God, that God will complete the work of salvation begun in them. For if they were reconciled when they were God's enemies, they will surely be saved now that they have been reconciled (5:9–10). Paul's understanding of salvation, then, is best expressed in a formula that takes into account what has "already" happened and what has "not yet" occurred: already justified and reconciled, believers are not yet saved from the eschatological wrath to come. Because they are "already" justified and reconciled, however, they can be confident that they will be saved, in Christ, on the day of salvation.

Having described God's work of justification in relationship to the righteousness of God (3:21–26), Paul relates justification to God's love for humanity (5:1–11). For just as God manifested his righteousness in and through Christ, so he manifests his love in and through Christ who died "for us" when we were still sinners (5:8). The remarkable aspect of this love is that there is no motivation for it apart from God's love "for us." For inasmuch as all have sinned, all are destined for God's wrath. The day of wrath and judgment, how-

---

24. See BDAG 776.

ever, will now be a day of salvation for the justified and reconciled because of God's love. This love is manifested in Christ's love and poured into the hearts of the justified and reconciled through the Holy Spirit (5:5). The justification of sinners, then, results in reconciliation with God. This reconciliation of the ungodly, in and through Christ, is the way in which God proves his love for us. Consequently, the justified and reconciled have every hope that they will be saved and delivered from God's wrath on the day of salvation.

The Freedom of the Justified and Reconciled

In his comparison of Adam and Christ (5:12–21), Paul explains the origin of the human condition described in 1:18–3:20. Humanity finds itself under the power of sin (3:9) because sin entered the world through Adam's transgression, and, with sin, death spread to all because all sinned (5:12). Humanity, then, finds itself under the powers of sin and death, and Paul speaks of sin and death as exercising dominion or rule over humanity (5:14, 17, 21). The appearance of Christ, however, marks the end of this rule. For just as sin once ruled by means of death, so grace now rules through the righteousness that leads to eternal life in Jesus Christ (5:21).

In Romans 6 Paul explains why believers need not, and should not, sin. They are no longer enslaved to sin because they have died with Christ in baptism, and this sacramental death with Christ has freed them from sin. Put another way, they have been transferred from the realm of Adam to the realm of Christ, and because they are no longer in Adam, they are no longer under the power of sin that Adam's transgression unleashed into the world. Moreover, since they have died with Christ in baptism, death no longer has dominion over them, for if they have died with Christ they will live with him (6:8–9). Finally, since God's grace rules over their lives through righteousness (5:21), they are no longer under the law but under grace (6:14). The justified are free from sin and death, then, and they are no longer under the law. The rule of grace has replaced the rule of the law, the rule of righteousness has replaced the rule of sin, and the rule of life has replaced the rule of death. Whereas those who were in Adam formerly presented themselves as obedient servants to sin, which led to death, those who are in Christ have become obedient servants to righteousness, which leads to life.

But why does Paul insist that the justified are no longer under the law? The law, as Paul affirms, is not to be equated with sin (7:7). But the justified are no longer under the law for the same reason that they are no longer under the power of sin: because they have died to the law "through the body of Christ" (7:4). They belong to Christ rather than to the law. Having died with him through baptism, the justified have been discharged from service to the law so that they can serve God in the new life of the Spirit (7:6), a life that Paul describes in chapter 8. Freedom from law is not intended to lead to moral laxity but to a moral life guided by the Spirit of the living God rather than by the code of a written law whose commandments were holy, just, and good (7:12) but did not have the inner power of the Spirit to bring those under its rule to life.

The Life of the Justified in the Spirit

The justified are no longer under the powers of sin, death, and the law because they have been transferred to the realm of Christ, in whom they experience the power of God's Spirit at work in their lives. Therefore, there is no condemnation for them because the Spirit, which derives from life in Christ, has freed them from the power of sin and death (8:1–2).[25] This new status is the work not of the justified but of God; for, since humanity found itself in a situation from which it could not free itself, God sent his own Son "in the likeness of sinful flesh" to do what humanity could not do because it dwelt in the realm of the flesh.

By sending his own Son "in the likeness of sinful flesh," God dealt with and condemned sin in its own realm, the realm of the flesh (8:3–4). This description of Christ coming "in the likeness of sinful flesh" signifies that Christ took on the fullness of the human condition. That is, he assumed the frailty of the human condition, which belongs to the realm of the flesh and finds itself under the rule of sin. But whereas humanity was unable to do God's will, the Son of God, who assumed the human condition, was obedient to God's will. In this way, Christ dealt with sin in its own realm (the realm of the flesh) and reversed the ever-growing power of sin that Adam unleashed into the world. Expressed in yet another way, if Christ did not enter the human condition in all of its frailty, he would not have defeated sin in its own realm. If Christ did not come in the fullness of the human condition, he would not have been able to condemn sin "in the flesh" (8:3). In effect, Paul supposes something akin to the Johannine understanding of the incarnation (John 1:14), although he does not express this as explicitly as the Fourth Evangelist does.

As a result of God's work in Christ, humanity finds itself with a choice it did not have before. Whereas it formerly stood in solidarity with Adam, it is now possible for humanity to stand in solidarity with Christ, in whom the just requirement of the law (righteousness before God) has finally been fulfilled (Rom. 8:4). Those who stand in solidarity with Christ belong to the realm of the Spirit and live accordingly, whereas those who continue to stand in solidarity with Adam belong to the realm of the flesh and live accordingly. This realm of the flesh is all that is mortal and destined to perish, whereas the realm

---

25. The meaning of the expressions "the law of the Spirit of life" and "the law of sin and death" (8:2) is disputed. Whereas Peter Stuhlmacher (*Paul's Letter to the Romans: A Commentary* [Louisville: Westminster John Knox Press, 1994], 118–19) interprets *nomos* in relation to the Mosaic law, Fitzmyer (*Romans*, 482–83) construes *nomos*, in this instance, as "principle."

of the Spirit refers to the power of God that has been released in and through Christ's saving death and resurrection. The realm of the flesh is hostile to God inasmuch as those who live according to what is merely mortal assert themselves against God. Those in the realm of the flesh do not, and cannot, submit to God's law because they lack the power that comes from the Spirit of God, which Paul also identifies as the Spirit of Christ (see 8:9).

Paul is quite emphatic that since the justified have been transferred to the realm of the Spirit, they no longer belong to the realm of the flesh (8:9). He insists that the present reality of the Spirit, which the justified already enjoy, assures them of final salvation. For if the Spirit of God, which raised Jesus from the dead, dwells in them, that same Spirit will surely raise them from the dead at the general resurrection of the dead. Life in the Spirit, then, has a present and a future dimension. As regards the present, the justified already live in the realm of the Spirit. They are at peace with God and can please God. As regards the future, this present life in the Spirit is the promise and assurance of that final salvation that has not yet occurred but that will come at the parousia and the general resurrection of the dead.

It is this Spirit that makes the justified "children of God" (*huioi theou*), enabling them to call God "Father" (*abba*, 8:15–16). Because they have received the Spirit, the justified are heirs of God and joint heirs with Christ (8:17). Therefore, just as the Father glorified Christ by raising him from the dead, so the Father will glorify them by raising them from the dead. The resurrection glory that Christ, the eschatological Adam, already enjoys is the eschatological destiny of all who enjoy the gift of the Spirit. As Christ has been glorified, so humanity will be glorified.

The Spirit is the "first fruits" (*aparchē*) of this glorification, which will be completed when the mortal bodies of the justified are redeemed (8:23) at the general resurrection of the dead. At that moment, the justified will be revealed as God's children since they will have been fully conformed to the image of God's Son (8:29) through the resurrection of the dead. Thus just as the justified once bore the image of the old Adam, so they will bear the image of the eschatological Adam when their mortal bodies are redeemed from death and glorified at the general resurrection of the dead.

Paul views the glorification of the justified as the final stage of a process that he outlines as follows. Those whom God foreknew, God predestined. Those whom God predestined, God called. Those whom God called, God justified. And those whom God justified, God also glorified (8:30). This scheme summarizes God's purpose for the justified (8:28), assuring them that if they are justified, it is because they were called and predestined by God, who always knew and loved them. If they are justified, they will certainly be glorified. The focus, then, is on the justified, to assure them that they are part of a larger divine plan that has their glorification as its goal.

This language of justification and election, however, raises a question about the justified. Does this mean that God has predestined some for salvation and others for damnation? It is possible to think in this way, given Paul's remark in 9:22 about the "objects of wrath that are made for destruction"; and beginning with Augustine and culminating with Calvin, an important exegetical tradition has often spoken of double predestination: some are destined for salvation, whereas others are destined for damnation.[26] But is this the point of Paul's argument in Romans 8? His immediate concern is the justified, and his purpose is to assure them that they will be glorified since they have been called and predestined by God who knew and loved them from all eternity. To the extent that others embrace the gospel, they will participate in this same divine plan; for, in Christ, God has already justified and reconciled humanity to himself. To the extent that sinful human beings accept this gracious offer of salvation, they will also be glorified since salvation in Christ is available to all on the basis of faith, apart from doing the works of the Mosaic law.

The Need for Faith

Paul's analysis of the human condition shows that a person cannot be justified on the basis of doing the works of the law since the power of sin, unleashed by Adam's transgression, frustrates every attempt to attain righteousness on the basis of legal observance. At the heart of Paul's gospel stands the firm conviction that a person is justified on the basis of faith in what God has accomplished in Christ rather than on the basis of doing the works of the law. Paul affirms that Christ "was handed over to death for our trespasses and was raised for our justification" (4:25).[27] Faith, then, is the response that Paul seeks from his converts, faith that utterly trusts in, and relies on, what God has done in Christ. It is on the basis of this faith that a person is justified before God.

Paul gives thanks for the faith of the Romans, which "is proclaimed throughout the world" (1:8), and he hopes to be encouraged by their faith as well as to encourage them in their faith (1:12). But he is also aware that God has apportioned a different measure of faith to each believer (12:3, 6) so that the faith of some is stronger than the faith of others (14:1). Believers must act in accordance with the measure of faith they possess (14:22–23) rather than judge the behavior of those whose actions proceed from a different measure of faith.

---

26. Augustine discusses predestination in his anti-Pelagian work "On the Predestination of the Saints," Calvin, *Institutes of the Christian Religion* 3.21–24. See the discussion in Westerholm, *Perspectives Old and New*, 3–21, 42–63.

27. Fitzmyer (*Romans*, 389) notes: "This verse is not to be understood as though Paul meant that human trespasses were removed by Christ's death and that human justification was achieved by his resurrection. They are so formulated in a literary parallelism; both effects are to be ascribed to the death *and* resurrection."

Because faith is central to the gospel Paul preaches, the purpose of his ministry is "to bring about the obedience of faith (*hypakoēn pisteōs*) among all the Gentiles" (1:5). This expression can be construed either as the obedience that is faith, in which case the two Greek words stand in apposition to each other, or as the obedience that has its origin in faith, in which case *pisteōs* is taken as a genitive of origin. In either case, it is clear that the faith Paul seeks is not a mere intellectual assent but total obedience to God.[28] Thus Paul is speaking of a very different kind of faith than is the Letter of James, which criticizes those whose faith does not result in doing good works (Jas. 2:14–26).

Paul views his ministry as an urgent mission because he knows that faith comes from hearing. If the gospel is not proclaimed, it will not be heard; and if the gospel is not heard, it will not be believed; and if it is not believed, people will not be justified. Faith comes from what is heard,[29] from the proclamation of the good news of what God has done in Christ (Rom. 10:14–17). Those who respond with trusting faith will be justified in God's presence.

The proclamation of the gospel effects what it proclaims because the gospel "is the power of God for salvation to everyone who has faith" (1:16). When the gospel is proclaimed, "the righteousness of God is revealed through faith for faith" (1:17). This righteousness can be experienced only on the basis of faith. If one hopes to attain the salvation that comes with the resurrection of the dead, one must believe and trust what the gospel proclaims about Christ's saving death and resurrection (10:9). If one wishes to experience the righteousness of God, one must believe and trust in what the gospel proclaims about God's righteousness, which is revealed "through faith for faith" (1:17); that is, it begins and ends with faith. Apart from faith, there is only the revelation of God's wrath (1:18).

Paul argues that even though the law and the prophets testify to God's righteousness, God's righteousness was manifested apart from the law; that is, it did not come about by legal observance since all had sinned. Rather, God manifested his righteousness in and through Jesus Christ (3:25). Since all have sinned and fallen short of God's glory (3:23), God justified and reconciled humanity apart from the law, so that faith is the only way one can appropriate what God has accomplished in Christ. For this reason, Paul insists "that a person is justified by faith apart from works prescribed by the law" (3:28). This is not to say that faith effects justification; otherwise faith would be a work in which humanity could boast. For Paul, faith stands in sharp contrast to works. Whereas those who do the works of the law may be tempted to think that they have a claim to righteousness, those who believe understand that righteousness is a gift upon

---

28. The same phrase occurs in 16:26, thereby forming an inclusion with 1:5. As noted above, however, 16:25–27 has a very complicated textual tradition.

29. The enigmatic text, "and what is heard comes through the word of Christ" (Rom. 10:17), could refer to Christ's own preaching, or more likely preaching about Christ.

which they have no claim since it is the outcome of God's righteousness man-ifested in and through Christ. This is why Paul affirms that Christ's atoning sacrifice is "effective through faith" (3:25) and that God justifies "the one who has faith in Jesus," or, if *ek pisteōs Iēsou* is taken as a subjective genitive, "the one who has the faith of Jesus" (3:26). Since all have fallen under the power of sin, God justifies Gentiles and Jews in the same way, on the basis of faith.[30]

For Paul, the way of faith has become the only access to righteousness since Christ marks the end of the salvation-historical role of the law (10:4). The greater portion of Israel, however, did not understand this. Instead of pursu-ing righteousness on the basis of faith in Christ, Israel pursued its own righ-teousness on the basis of doing the law. Consequently the Gentiles, who were not striving for righteousness, have paradoxically obtained it on the basis of faith in Christ, whereas Israel, which was striving for righteousness on the basis of legal observance, failed to attain it. Israel stumbled on the stumbling stone that is Christ; for instead of believing that God revealed his righteous-ness in Christ, Israel was scandalized by the crucified Messiah (9:30–33). Instead of pursuing God's righteousness, Israel chose to pursue its own righ-teousness, unaware that "Christ is the end of the law so that there may be righ-teousness for everyone who believes" (10:4). Christ marks the end of one period—the time of the law—and the beginning of a new period—the time of faith in Christ. Consequently, righteousness is not a matter of legal observance but of trusting faith in what God has done in Christ. For Paul, this righteous-ness is close at hand. To obtain it, one need only confess Jesus as Lord and believe that God raised him from the dead (10:9). This confession, however, involves a total transformation of one's life since it supposes a dramatic shift of allegiance to a new Lord and a profound faith in the God who raised him from the dead. This is the obedience of faith that is at the heart of Paul's gospel.

The faith of Abraham, described in Romans 4, provides Paul with a con-crete example of what it means to say that a person is justified by faith rather than by doing the works of the law. Paul argues that God credited righteous-ness to Abraham because Abraham believed in God's promise that he would become the father of many nations (4:18). Quoting Gen. 15:6, Paul writes, "Abraham believed God, and it was reckoned to him as righteousness" (Rom. 4:3). This righteousness was not the result of something Abraham did, as if his faith was a work that could merit a recompense for something he had done. Abraham's faith was an act of utter trust that God would accomplish what he promised (that Abraham would be the father of many nations), even though Abraham's body was as good as dead and Sarah's womb was barren (4:19). There was nothing Abraham could do to bring about the accomplishment of

---

30. The slight difference of language in Rom. 3:30 is more rhetorical than substantive, "and he will justify the circumcised on the ground of faith and the uncircumcised through that same faith."

God's promise. He could only trust and hope that God would fulfill what he promised, even though there was no human way for the promise to be fulfilled. Abraham's faith, then, foreshadowed faith in Jesus Christ because he believed in the God "who gives life to the dead and calls into existence the things that do not exist" (4:17). Hoping against hope, Abraham did not weaken in faith but was fully convinced "that God was able to do what he had promised" (4:21). Abraham's faith was credited to him as righteousness not because he did something but because he relied on God.

Paul establishes an important analogy between the faith of Abraham and the faith of those who believe in Christ. For just as Abraham believed that God could bring life from Sarah's barren womb and his aged body, so the Christian believes in the God who raised Jesus from the dead. Christian faith is not merely faith in God. It is faith in the God who raised Jesus from the dead (4:24). It is faith in the God who justifies the ungodly (4:5).

Abraham was among the ungodly when God justified him on the basis of faith. Previous to his call, he was an uncircumcised Gentile. But it was precisely to the uncircumcised and ungodly Abraham that the promises were made. It was the ungodly and uncircumcised Abraham who believed in those promises, even though there was no human way for them to be fulfilled. This historical circumstance (Abraham's uncircumcised state) plays an important role in Paul's theology, and it leads him to conclude that the promises depend not on the law but on faith. Thus God's promises are a matter of sheer grace, and they are available to all who share the faith of Abraham (4:16). For if the promises were not an act of grace, their fulfillment would depend on legal observance, and they would be available only to those under the law. That Abraham was justified on the basis of faith, when he was still uncircumcised (ungodly), suggests to Paul that God's promises and righteousness depend on faith rather than on doing the works of the law. Since the fulfillment of God's promises is a matter of grace, it is those who believe and trust in the promises who are justified.

Faith, then, is a matter of utter trust in God. It is an act of obedience inasmuch as the believer trusts and relies on God. Although it is a human response, it is not a work that merits payment or reward, since it does not accomplish or do anything. The nature of faith is defined by God's promises and the gracious bestowal of righteousness—that blessed state whereby one's sins are forgiven by God (4:7), not because one has been righteous but because one has trusted in the God who is righteous and justifies the ungodly (4:5). Paul's understanding of justification by faith, however, raises an important theological question. Who is the God in whom Paul believes? If a person is justified by God on the basis of faith rather than on the basis of doing the law, has God been unjust toward Israel, which sought its righteousness on the basis of the law but did not achieve it, whereas the Gentiles, who were not seeking righteousness, attained it on the basis of faith (9:30–31)?

The Righteousness of God toward Israel

That the greater part of Israel has not embraced the gospel raises the question of God's covenant faithfulness to his people. Has the plan of God failed? Is God ultimately capricious in the way he extends mercy to some but not to others? Put bluntly, can God be accused of being unjust in dealing with Abraham's descendants? Paul is keenly aware of these questions, and in Romans 9–11 he deals with them in three movements: (1) the word of God has not failed (9:1–29); (2) Israel has failed because it pursued righteousness on the basis of works rather than on the basis of faith (9:30–10:21); (3) the failure of Israel has paradoxically played a role in God's redemptive plan for Israel as well as for the Gentiles (11:1–36).

Deeply distraught that his fellow Israelites have not responded to the gospel, Paul is filled with sorrow and anguish (9:1–5). But he is firmly convinced that the word of God has not failed. Pointing to the manner in which God promised Abraham that his descendants would be counted through Isaac, and recalling the manner in which God chose and loved Isaac rather than Esau before either was born, Paul insists that the word of God has always worked on the basis of promise and election. Consequently, not all of Abraham's physical descendants are his children but only those who belong to the promise God made to Abraham, "It is through Isaac that descendants shall be named for you" (9:7).[31] Moreover, the election of Isaac rather than Esau, before either of them had done or accomplished anything, shows how God's plan is based on grace rather than on human merit.

Paul is aware that God's purpose in electing some rather than others raises another question, and so he asks, "Is there injustice (*adikia*) on God's part?" (9:14). Recalling the way in which God dealt with Pharaoh at the time of the exodus, Paul argues that God's elective purpose cannot be understood apart from God's mercy. Because God is God, God has mercy on whomever he wills, and God hardens the heart of whomever he wills. God's elective purpose does not depend on what human beings will or do but on God's mercy (9:16).

Aware that what he has just said raises further questions, Paul anticipates his audience's objection, "You will say to me then, 'Why then does he still find fault? For who can resist his will?'" (9:19). It is at this point that Paul introduces the image of the potter who makes different objects from the same lump of clay, some for special use, others for ordinary use (9:21). He argues that if a human potter has the discretion to make different kinds of objects from the same material, does not the Creator of the universe have the right—if he should so desire—to make "objects of wrath" that are destined for destruction and "objects of mercy" that have been prepared for glory (9:22–23)? Although

---

31. Paul is not speaking literally, as if physical descent from Isaac makes one a descendant of Abraham. As in Galatians, descent from Isaac means to rely on the promises that God made to Abraham, which find their fulfillment in Christ. It is to belong to the community of faith.

many have argued, on the basis of this text, that Paul is propounding a doctrine of double predestination (God destines some for eternal life and others for eternal damnation), this interpretation reads more into the text than Paul actually says. First, and most importantly, Paul is asking a rhetorical question rather than stating a fact. What if God should decide to act in this way? Does the creature have the right to question the Creator? Second, Paul's purpose is to explain that the reason and purpose for God's elective love, which is rooted in God's mercy, cannot be fully explained. Because God is God, there will always be something in God's elective purpose beyond human comprehension. What the human person can know, however, is that this elective purpose is a manifestation of God's mercy.

To summarize, although the majority of Israel has failed to believe in the gospel, the word of God has not failed, because not all of Abraham's descendants are his physical children. The children of Abraham are those who belong to a line of election rooted in God's inscrutable mercy. The God of Jesus Christ cannot be understood apart from promise, election, and mercy. What appears to be utter capriciousness on God's part is divine election, and what appears to be injustice is divine mercy.

In the second movement of his argument (9:30–10:21), Paul discusses the apparent injustice that Israel has experienced. How is it that the Gentiles, who did not strive for righteousness, have attained it, whereas Israel, which strove "for the righteousness that is based on the law, did not succeed in fulfilling the law" (9:30–31)? The concrete example of Israel's failure raises the question of God from yet another vantage point. For if the godless Gentiles attained righteousness and Israel did not, it would appear that the word of God has failed.

In face of Israel's reversal of fortunes, Paul responds that although Israel strove for the righteousness based on the law, it mistakenly sought this righteousness on the basis of doing the works of the law rather than on the basis of faith. Consequently, instead of submitting to the righteousness of God that God manifested in Christ, Israel sought to establish its own righteousness, unaware that Christ is the salvation-historical terminus of the law (10:4).[32] Israel continued to pursue a righteousness that it thought it could attain by doing the works of the law, when God had already revealed a righteousness in Christ that is available to all through faith. Interpreting a series of texts from Deuteronomy in light of Christ, Paul argues that the righteousness that comes from God is not so far away that it is impossible to retrieve it: it is as close at hand as one's lips and hearts. Therefore, confession on the lips that "Jesus is Lord" leads to salvation, and faith in the heart that "God raised him from the dead" leads to justification.

---

32. The Greek *telos* can be taken as "end" or "goal." It is probably best to take it in both senses: Christ is the end of the law inasmuch as the law finds its prophetic goal in him.

But what if Israel has not heard this gracious gospel? Perhaps Israel is not at fault after all. Since faith comes from hearing the good news, perhaps the gospel has not been preached to Israel. But Paul will have none of this. Quoting from Ps. 19:4, he responds, "Their voice has gone out to all the earth, and their words to the ends of the world" (Rom. 10:18). No, the fundamental problem is not that the gospel has not been preached to Israel but that Israel has been disobedient to the gospel. Consequently, as Isaiah foretold, God has been found by those who did not seek him, and has shown himself to those who did not ask for him, namely, the Gentiles (10:20, quoting Isa. 65:1). Conversely, God has held out his hand all day "to a disobedient and contrary people," namely, Israel (Rom. 10:21, quoting Isa. 65:2). To summarize, then, it is not the word of God that has failed but Israel that has failed. Seeking its own righteousness rather than the righteousness that God revealed in Christ, Israel has been disobedient to God.

In the final movement of his argument (Rom. 11:1–36), Paul addresses the most important question of all, "Has God rejected his people?" (11:1). If the answer is yes, then it is difficult to understand how one can speak of the righteousness of God in any meaningful sense; for if God has rejected Israel, how can those who have been justified in Christ be sure that God will not reject them at some future date? The question of Israel and the question of God, then, should not be separated or addressed separately. To speak of Israel is to speak of God, and to speak of God is to speak of Israel.

Paul immediately answers his question, "God has not rejected his people whom he foreknew" (11:2). Rather, a remnant has been chosen by grace, of whom Paul is an outstanding example, and this elect remnant has attained the destiny God always intended for Israel: a righteousness based on faith in Jesus Christ. As for the rest of Israel, a hardening has come upon it (11:7), and even though it has stumbled on the stumbling stone that is Christ (9:32–33), it has not fallen (11:11). To the contrary, God has paradoxically used their stumbling to bring about the salvation of the Gentiles in order to make Israel jealous. Thus Paul envisions a history in which Israel's rejection brings salvation to the Gentiles, and the salvation of the Gentiles leads Israel to be jealous and embrace the salvation it has rejected. There is no place, then, for Gentile boasting at the expense of Israel. For, if Israel's rejection has led to the reconciliation of the world, its acceptance of the gospel will surely bring about the general resurrection of the dead (11:15).

In the end, Paul views the present condition of that portion of Israel that has not believed as part of the mystery that is God's plan for the salvation of the world. A hardening has come upon Israel until the full number of Gentiles believes in the gospel. In this way, "all Israel will be saved" through the entrance of the full number of the Gentiles (11:26). Paul does not explain how or when this final act of salvation will occur, but he is confident that it will take place because "the gifts and the calling of God are irrevocable" (11:29).

What, then, is the purpose of God's plan, and who is the God in whom Paul believes? God's plan is as paradoxical as the gospel Paul preaches. Once the Gentiles were disobedient, but now they have received God's mercy because of Israel's disobedience. Israel is now disobedient, so that it may receive mercy because of the mercy shown to the Gentiles. In effect, all were disobedient so that God might be merciful to all. God's elective love and mercy is not an exclusive love and mercy; it does not predestine some to salvation and others to damnation. The election of the few paradoxically leads to salvation for the many. The apparent failure of God's plan is, in reality, salvation for the world. God's word has not failed; God is not unjust or capricious; nor has God rejected Israel. God is mysterious, however, and not even Paul fully understands God's ways (11:33–36). But the apostle is firmly convinced that God remains faithful to himself and so to Israel. In the end, God is faithful and merciful, God is mysterious, and his ways are unfathomable. The God of Jesus Christ remains the God of Israel.

The Moral Life

As was the case in Galatians, Paul's gospel of justification by faith may appear to undermine the basis for the moral life. For if a person is not justified on the basis of doing the works of the law (3:20), and if "where sin increased, grace abounded all the more" (5:20), how can one continue to speak of the moral life? Paul alludes to this objection: "But if through my falsehood God's truthfulness abounds to his glory, why am I still being condemned as a sinner? And why not say (as some people slander us by saying that we say), 'Let us do evil so that good may come'?" (3:7–8). Paul's gospel, then, raises two questions. First, what is the basis for the moral life now that Christ has appeared? Second, what is the shape of the moral life of the justified?

The Basis of the Moral Life

To inquire about the basis of the moral life, now that Christ has appeared, is to ask a foundational question: what is the relationship between the indicative of salvation (what God has accomplished in Christ) and the imperative of the moral life (what the believer must do)? This relationship between indicative and imperative is at the core of Paul's moral vision, and yet it is not peculiar to him. It is deeply rooted in the moral praxis of Israel, which saw its observance of the law as a response to God's covenant justice, and it is found in Jesus' call to repentance and righteousness in light of the inbreaking kingdom of God.

For Paul, the moral imperative is rooted in Christ's death and resurrection: because God has manifested his righteousness in Christ's saving death and resurrection, the justified must live a life of total obedience to God, "the obedience of faith" (1:5). Such obedience is not only required; it has been made possible because the justified have been transferred from the realm of the flesh to the realm of the Spirit by being incorporated into Christ, the eschatological Adam. Before and apart from Christ, humanity was in Adam, in solidarity with the one who introduced sin and death into the world. Because it stood in solidarity with Adam, humanity found itself in the realm of the flesh, unable to please God or do the law because it was under the power of sin. But with the appearance of Christ, the eschatological Adam, humanity finds itself in a new situation it did not previously enjoy. No longer condemned to being in solidarity with Adam, it is now possible for humanity to stand in solidarity with the eschatological Adam who was perfectly obedient to God. Incorporated into Christ, humanity finds itself in the realm of the Spirit, empowered to be obedient to God, as was Christ. Paul's moral imperative, then, is rooted in his understanding of the righteousness of God that has been manifested in Christ, the eschatological Adam, who has transferred the justified from the realm of the flesh to the realm of the Spirit. Deeply aware that there is something awry in the human condition, Paul is convinced that one cannot live the moral life apart from God's grace.[33]

For Paul, it is Christ's death and resurrection that make the moral life possible. Inasmuch as the justified have been incorporated into Christ, they have died with him. Through their baptism, that sacramental act whereby the justified are incorporated into Christ, the old self (*ho palaios anthrōpos*) has been crucified with Christ. Consequently, the justified are no longer enslaved to the power of sin (6:6) that Adam unleashed into the world. Their sacramental death in Christ, then, was a death to sin that allows them to live for God (6:11). Whereas formerly sin ruled over their mortal bodies and made them slaves to their passions and agents of wickedness, now they can present their bodies to God as agents of righteousness, for sin no longer rules over them (6:12–14).

Paul contrasts being "under the law" with being "under grace" (6:14) because the law belonged to the period before Christ, when humanity was under the power of sin. Consequently, being "under the law" is not a remedy for sin. The only remedy for sin is freedom from sin, freedom from being in Adam, freedom from the period that Paul characterizes as being "under the law." This is why the concept of "death" plays such a central role in his moral vision. To be free from sin, one must die to sin. To be transferred from being "under the law" to being "under grace," one must die to the law. This is precisely what the justified have done in Christ (7:4). But this dying to the law is not to be equated with a disregard for the moral life, as if Paul were summoning people to an antinomian way of life. To the contrary, his understanding of dying to the law is akin to his understanding of dying to sin; it is a transfer from

---

33. Here Paul stands both in continuity and discontinuity with his Israelite heritage: in continuity inasmuch as Israel understood that it could not do God's will apart from the gift of the law; in discontinuity inasmuch as Paul did not think it possible to fulfill what the law required apart from Christ.

one realm to another, from the rule of the Mosaic law to the realm of God's grace. It is not that the law was sinful (7:7). It simply did not have the power to effect what it commanded. To live the moral life one must be in another realm, the realm of grace, the realm of God's empowering Spirit. This is why Romans 8, with its extensive teaching on the Spirit, plays such a crucial role in Paul's vision of the moral life.

For Paul, there are two ways of life, one characterized by living according to the flesh, the other by living according to the Spirit. The two are mutually exclusive, and there can be no compromise between them. To live according to the flesh is to view reality from a merely human point of view, from the vantage point of sinful Adam, who rebelled against God. To live in such a way is to destine oneself for death, to be hostile to God, to refuse to submit to God's law. To live according to the Spirit is to view reality from the point of view of the Spirit as revealed in Christ, who was perfectly obedient to God. To live in this way is to receive life and be at peace with God. Indeed, living according to the Spirit is the only way to please God, since those who are in the flesh cannot please God (see 8:4–8, 12–17).

Paul's foundational understanding of the moral life, then, can be summarized as follows. Those who are in solidarity with Adam are under the power of sin, in the realm of the flesh, under the law, so that even though they know what the law requires, they cannot accomplish its purposes. Those who are in solidarity with Christ, the eschatological Adam, have died to sin and the law by dying with Christ. They are in solidarity with Christ, in the realm of the Spirit, under grace. It is this new salvation-historical situation that summons and empowers them to live the moral life.

The Shape of the Moral Life

Paul's understanding of the indicative and the imperative in Romans 6–8 might give the impression that there is no need for specific moral instruction since the justified have "died" to sin and now live according to the Spirit. To be sure, Paul insists that the old self was crucified with Christ, so that it is no longer under the power of sin. He is quite emphatic that the justified now live according to the Spirit. The "death" that believers have experienced, and the power of the Spirit they already enjoy, however, does not do away with the need to live a moral life in the concrete circumstances of their life. Nor does it mean that the justified are incapable of sin. To be sure, it is difficult for Paul to believe that they would submit to sin again after they have died with Christ. Since the justified have been empowered by the Spirit, it is difficult for Paul to believe that they would allow themselves to live according to the flesh. But Paul is a realist. He is aware that believers are still living in the period between what God has already done in Christ and God's final act of salvation. It is still possible, though difficult for Paul to believe, that the justified would betray their election.

Since the moral life is a process of growing into an ever deeper union with Christ, Paul regularly provides his converts with moral instruction and exhortation. Romans 12:1–15:13 is the longest of these exhortations, and it provides a good example of how Paul views the concrete shape of the moral life. To be sure, this exhortation is not a systematic presentation of the moral life, as if Paul were writing "an ethic for the justified." But it does reveal some of the principles that underlie his moral reasoning, and it shows that his gospel of justification by faith does not exclude the need for specific moral instruction.

First and most importantly, Paul views the moral life as an act of worship on the part of those whom God has justified. Consequently, he begins by exhorting the justified to present (*parastēsai*) their bodies as "a living sacrifice" (*thysian zōsan*) that will be holy and acceptable to God as their "spiritual worship" (*tēn logikēn latreian*, 12:1). They are not to be conformed to this world but to be transformed by the renewal of their minds so that they can discern God's will (12:2). In these opening verses, Paul echoes themes from his earlier exposition of God's wrath as well as his discussion of how the justified have died to sin in order to live a new life. For example, whereas those under God's wrath degraded their bodies through their lustful passions (1:24), the justified offer their bodies to God as living sacrifices (12:1), as instruments and slaves of righteousness (6:13, 19). Whereas the debased minds of sinful humanity did not acknowledge God (1:28), the minds of the justified are being renewed (*anakainōsei*, 12:2) so that they know God's will and walk in newness (*kainotēti*) of life (6:4), "in the new (*kainotēti*) life of the Spirit" (7:6). The moral life, then, is not merely an ethical project; it is the gift of the renewed self to God; it is an act of spiritual worship that replaces temple sacrifice.

Second, the justified live the moral life within a community of faith. Incorporated into Christ, they are one body in Christ, each a member of the same body (12:3–8). This intimate relationship between the justified has profound consequences for the moral life. It requires believers to think of themselves in relationship to the other members of the community. The moral life, then, is not merely a matter of how individuals conduct themselves before God but of how they conduct themselves before God within a community where it is more important to seek those things that build up the community than it is to insist upon one's own point of view. This is apparent in 14:1–15:13, where Paul seeks to mediate a dispute between the weak and the strong members of the community. Those who form the body of Christ, then, must welcome one another and become servants to one another as Christ welcomed them and became a servant for them (15:7–8). The community of faith, then, is the sphere within which the justified offer themselves to God as living sacrifices.

Third, the community of the justified is not closed in upon itself as if it had no responsibilities to the world at large. Although believers have only one Lord, Jesus Christ, they remain subject to the governing authorities. Paul's discussion about authority and the payment of taxes in 13:1–7 is difficult to apply to every situation since he makes no provision for governing authorities who abuse the authority they have received. But his teaching indicates that the justified should not remove themselves from the political structures of life. The moral life of the believer is lived within the world as well as within the community of faith.

Fourth, Paul does not disregard the moral injunctions of the Decalogue. In 13:8–10 he quotes four of the Ten Commandments and concludes that these, as well as all the other commandments, are "summed up" (*anakephalaioutai*) in the commandment to love one's neighbor as oneself (Lev. 19:18; see also Gal. 5:14). This love must express itself in concrete deeds toward those within the community (see Rom. 12:9–13), but is hardly restricted to the community of faith since Paul exhorts the justified to bless those who persecute them and not to avenge evil (12:14–21). As in Galatians, he views the love commandment as the commandment that fulfills the law. Thus, even though the justified are no longer under the law, they fulfill what it requires when they practice the commandment to love one another as they love themselves.

Finally, the justified must live the moral life with a keen awareness that their salvation is nearer now than it was when they first believed in Christ (13:11–14). This salvation is the resurrection of the dead that will occur at the parousia when the justified will be glorified with Christ and revealed as sons and daughters of God (8:17, 19). The moral life of the believer, then, is lived within a context of hope and anticipation for the final manifestation of God's salvation.

To summarize, Paul's gospel of justification apart from doing the works of the law does not undermine the moral life. Rather, it establishes the moral life on the basis of what God has done in Christ. Sin no longer rules over the lives of the justified, for they now live in the realm of God's grace, where the Spirit empowers them to live a moral life within the community of faith. This life, measured by love, is the sacrifice they offer to God.

CONCLUSION

Romans is one of the most explicitly theological writings of the New Testament. Viewing the human situation in light of the righteousness of God, Romans exposes humanity's profound need for redemption. Apart from Christ, all are under the power of sin, a power that frustrates every human attempt to carry out the righteous decree of God. Consequently, God's righteousness (understood as God's covenant loyalty, faithfulness, and integrity) has been revealed in Christ. Those who entrust themselves to God's righteousness, as manifested in Christ, are freely justified and reconciled to God on the basis of faith. Reconciled and justified, they dwell in the realm of the Spirit, which empowers them to do the just decrees of the law. Living in the realm of the Spirit, believers wait for the fullness of God's salvation: the glorification of their bodies at the general resurrection of the dead. This understanding of the righteousness of God assures Paul that God has not rejected Israel, even though the greater portion of Israel has pursued its own righteousness rather than the righteousness of God revealed in Christ. Therefore, Paul can conclude that in God's way, in God's time, all Israel will be saved. When all is said and done, then, Romans is a letter about God and God's way of effecting salvation for all, Gentiles as well as Jew. The only other writing in the New Testament that focuses so consistently on God is the book of Revelation, a writing that also speaks of God's wrath and final victory. But Romans remains the most subtle and sophisticated writing about God in the New Testament. In light of God's righteousness, it unveils the hidden and unexpected ways in which God effects salvation for all through Christ.

7

A Theology from Prison

Philippians, Philemon, Colossians, and Ephesians

The letters addressed to the Philippians, Philemon, the Colossians, and the Ephesians are often referred to as the "Captivity Epistles" since they portray Paul as writing from prison. None of these letters, however, identifies the place of Paul's imprisonment, and there are serious questions about the Pauline authorship of Colossians and Ephesians. Nevertheless, it is convenient to gather these four writings under the admittedly artificial rubric of a theology from prison.

Although the letters do not share a particular theological theme that distinguishes them from the rest of the Pauline corpus, there are a number of interesting relationships among them. For example, Philippians and Colossians contain christological hymns that play central roles in the theology of each letter. In Philippians the hymn celebrates the abasement and exaltation of the preexistent Christ; in Colossians it proclaims the primacy of the Son in the order of creation and redemption. Philemon and Colossians are linked to each other by a series of names that appear in both letters (Archippus, Onesimus, Epaphras, Mark, Aristarchus, Demas, and Luke), suggesting that even if Colossians is deuteropauline, its author purposely drew a relationship between his letter and Paul's letter to Philemon. Finally, Colossians and Ephesians are similar in their Christology and ecclesiology, each presenting Christ as the head of the church and the church as the body of Christ. In both letters the church has become a cosmic and universal entity because of its relationship to the head, who is the cosmic Christ.

The most common feature of these letters, however, remains the manner in which they portray Paul. Paul is no longer a free man, and in Philippians there is the distinct possibility he may soon be put to death. Despite his imprisonment, the apostle continues to preach the gospel. In Philippians Paul has discovered that there is no chaining the word of God, and that his imprisonment has actually advanced the gospel. In Philemon it is apparent that he has found a way to make converts for Christ even while in prison. In Colossians the apostle views his imprisonment as a way of completing the afflictions of Christ, and, although in prison, he continues to instruct the Colossians from afar. Finally, in Ephesians the great apostle reveals the mystery of God to a new generation of believers who have not seen or heard him in the flesh. Paul's imprisonment, then, is not the end of his apostolic ministry so much as it is a new phase in his relationship with the churches. Instead of ending his ministry, his imprisonment provides him with an opportunity to preach the gospel by letter, by messenger, and most importantly by the example of his sufferings.

In this chapter I will examine the theology of the imprisoned apostle, beginning with Philippians and Philemon and concluding with Colossians and Ephesians, which are usually classified as deuteropauline. In discussing Philippians I will focus on the role that imitation plays in the apostle's theology, whereas in the discussion of Philemon I will highlight the manner in which Christ transforms human relationships. In studying Colossians I will give attention to the mystery of Christ, whereas in Ephesians I will focus on the mystery of the church.

PHILIPPIANS: A THEOLOGY OF IMITATION

Paul's Letter to the Philippians presents a number of problems that continue to plague New Testament scholarship. Among the most important are the literary integrity of the letter, the place of Paul's imprisonment, and the origin and purpose of the passage referred to as "the Christ hymn" (2:6–11).[1] The literary integrity of the letter has been called into question on the basis of internal evidence, leading some to hypothesize that the present canonical form of Philippians is a composite of two or three letters Paul had sent to Philippi.[2] This understanding of Philippians as a composite letter has, in turn, led many to question the traditional view that Paul composed this letter while in prison at Rome.[3] Finally, the origin and purpose of the Christ hymn, which is rightly viewed as the letter's most important theological legacy, have been intensely studied, with

1. For a discussion of these introductory issues, see Udo Schnelle, *The History and Theology of the New Testament Writings* (Minneapolis: Fortress, 1998), 129–43.

2. Becker (*Paul: Apostle to the Gentiles*, 305–31, here 310) argues that Philippians is a composite of two earlier letters: "Philippians B (= 3:2–21; 4:8–9) was inserted into Philippians A (= 1:1–3:1; 4:1–7, 10–23), losing its opening in the process."

3. Many argue that Paul wrote the letter during the period of his imprisonment at Caesarea Maritima (Acts 23:35; 24:26–27), others maintain that he was in prison at Ephesus. Although Acts does not recount such an imprisonment at Ephesus, there are some indications in Paul's letters that he may have been incarcerated there (1 Cor. 15:32 and 2 Cor. 1:8). If Paul wrote from Ephesus, Philippians would have been composed ca. A.D. 55–57; if he wrote from Caesarea, the letter is to be dated ca. 58–60; if it was written from Rome, as traditionally thought, it is to be dated ca. 61–63.

most scholars arguing that Paul is drawing upon and adapting an earlier piece of tradition for his own purposes, perhaps a hymn used in the church's worship.[4]

Scholars continue to debate these introductory issues, but nearly all agree that Philippians merits an important place in any exposition of Pauline theology. Although brief, it develops a number of theological motifs found in the letters that we have investigated thus far. Among these are the imitation of Paul, the difference between the righteousness that comes from God and the righteousness based on legal observance, the parousia and the general resurrection of the dead, the paradoxical message about the cross, and the need to live in a manner worthy of the gospel.

In this letter Paul presents these motifs in a new way because his circumstances have changed. He is now in prison, and he is no longer able to preach the gospel or visit the community. More importantly, he is facing the very real possibility that he will be put to death for the sake of the gospel. As he waits for the outcome of his trial, some are preaching the gospel in a manner they hope will add to his suffering, and the Philippian community, for which Paul has had the deepest affection, is beset by internal dissensions. Moreover, Paul is fearful that the Philippians may soon have to deal with the kind of agitators who caused so many problems for him at Galatia: Judaizing missionaries who preached circumcision and legal observance in addition to faith in Christ.

Given the circumstances of Paul's imprisonment and the troubles his converts were facing at Philippi, one might expect him to be utterly distraught, as he was at the time of the Galatian crisis (Gal. 4:20). But this is not the case. In Philippians, more than in any other letter, the apostle expresses his joy in the midst of adverse and trying circumstances. By sharing in Christ's sufferings, Paul has come to a deeper understanding of the power of Christ's resurrection in his life. Consequently, as he writes this letter, he is filled with a joy that is grounded in his hope for the resurrection, and he explains how the circumstances of his imprisonment have paradoxically resulted in the advancement of the gospel. Having experienced this joy in the midst of suffering, Paul calls upon the Philippians to join others in imitating him (Phil. 3:17); for the Philippians have been given the privilege "not only of believing in Christ, but of suffering for him as well" (1:29).

The narrative line of the letter can be summarized as follows. After greeting the community with its "bishops and deacons" (1:1–2),[5] Paul thanks God

---

4. For a discussion of the issues surrounding this passage, see Ralph P. Martin and Brian J. Dodd, eds., *Where Christology Began: Essays on Philippians 2* (Louisville: Westminster John Knox Press, 1998).

5. This reference to bishops and deacons in the letter opening is atypical of the nondisputed Pauline letters. Paul's greeting to these officeholders, who are usually associated with the Pastoral Letters, raises an interesting question about the structure of the church at Philippi. Perhaps Paul mentioned these officers because they supervised the monetary gift that Epaphras brought him.

because the Philippians have shared in his imprisonment and in his defense and confirmation of the gospel (1:3–11).[6] He then explains how his circumstances have paradoxically advanced the gospel (1:12–26). Next, he exhorts the Philippians to live in a manner worthy of the gospel by being of one mind and behaving in a way that is appropriate for those who belong to Christ, who, although in the form of God, emptied himself to take the form of a slave (1:27–2:30). Having reminded the Philippians of how God exalted the one who humbled himself, Paul warns them not to be misled by those who would require them to be circumcised in order to attain righteousness, presenting himself as a model of someone who has experienced the surpassing righteousness that comes from God (3:1–21). After exhorting two women of the community to end their quarrel, he again calls upon the community to imitate him (4:1–9). Finally, he expresses his gratitude for the monetary gift the Philippians have sent him through Epaphroditus (4:10–20). He then concludes the letter (4:21–23).

The theology of this letter expresses itself in two ways that are intimately related to each other: (1) Paul's invitation to the community to join others in imitating him and (2) his call for the community to appropriate the self-abasing attitude of Christ, who did not insist upon the prerogatives that were rightfully his as one who was equal to God. Accordingly, in this section I will focus on the manner in which Paul presents the pattern of his own life and the pattern of Christ's life as patterns for the Christian life.

The Pattern of Paul's Life

At the beginning (1:12–26), in the middle (3:1–21), and at the end of this letter (4:1–20), Paul invites the Philippians to imitate the pattern of his life. In the opening chapters he recounts his present circumstances in order to show them how his imprisonment has "actually helped to spread the gospel" (1:12). By every human standard, his incarceration and the threat of execution should have discouraged others from preaching the gospel. But contrary to human expectations, his imprisonment has made others more confident "to speak the word with greater boldness and without fear" (1:14). To be sure, some are preaching the gospel "from envy and rivalry" and "out of selfish ambition" in order to add to his sufferings, but others are preaching from "goodwill" because they know that his imprisonment is "for the defense of the gospel" (1:15–17). Despite the evil intentions of the former group, Paul rejoices because Christ is being preached (1:18). Paul's imprisonment, which should

---

6. Paul can say that the Philippians have shared in his imprisonment because they have helped to support him during the time of his incarceration. Consequently, in v. 7 he calls them his *synkoinōnous*, which the NAB aptly translates as "partners" rather than turning it into a verb as does the NRSV, "for all of you share. . . ."

have brought him to the depths of despair, has paradoxically filled him with a joy that can be explained only in light of the gospel he preaches.

Paul does not fear death; indeed, he seems to long for it so that he can be more closely united with Christ. He is more convinced than ever that whether he continues to live or whether he forfeits his life by dying for the gospel, Christ will be exalted in him. Because his entire life is devoted to Christ, he can affirm that "living is Christ"; and because death means final and lasting union with Christ, he can say that "dying is gain" (1:21). If there is any indecision on Paul's part, it is whether to pursue a verdict of acquittal so that he can continue to work for the sake of the gospel or to accept a sentence of death so that he may "depart and be with Christ" (1:23).[7] Paul is torn between the two, but he seems to realize that his converts still need him, and so he hopes to return to them once more (1:21–26).

Paul recounts the circumstances of his imprisonment to the Philippians because they confirm and replicate the paradoxical message about the cross that he preaches. To understand why he endures the sufferings of his imprisonment for the sake of the gospel, then, is to grasp something of why Christ endured the sufferings of the cross for the sake of the kingdom. For just as Jesus' death led to the advancement of the kingdom, so Paul's sufferings are leading to the advancement of the gospel. And just as Christ's death glorified God and meant life for the crucified One, so Paul's death—should it come at this time—will exalt God and mean life for the apostle.

Paul views the Philippians as his partners in the work of the gospel (1:5, 7), and he prays that they will be "pure and blameless" on the day of the Lord's parousia, "having produced the harvest of righteousness (*dikaiosynē*) that comes through Jesus Christ" (1:10–11). But if the Philippians are to reap this harvest, they must suffer for the gospel as Paul is presently doing. Consequently, having shown them how his imprisonment has led to the spread of the gospel, he calls upon them to live "in a manner worthy of the gospel of Christ" (1:27–30). The verb Paul employs here (*politeuomai*) could also be translated "discharge your obligations as citizens,"[8] especially in light of what Paul writes in 3:20, "But our citizenship (*politeuma*) is in heaven." Understood in this way, Paul is encouraging the Philippians to live the gospel by carrying out their duties as a people who are already enrolled as citizens of heaven. To live in a manner worthy of the gospel, the community must be of one mind for "the faith of the gospel" (1:27), thereby forming a united front in face of its opponents. The Philippians must realize that God is giving them the grace that has

---

7. Commentators regularly point to this passage as an indication that Paul is now reckoning with the possibility that he may die before the parousia. This verse suggests that he is thinking of some sort of union with Christ before the general resurrection of the dead.

8. BDAG (s.v. *politeuomai*) notes the meaning "to be a citizen" but lists Phil. 1:27 under the meaning "to conduct one's life."

already been granted to Paul—not only to believe in Christ but to suffer for him. Paul's struggle for the gospel should become their struggle as well.

Paul presents himself to the community as an example of what it means not only to believe in Christ but to suffer for him as well. If the Philippians look at the example of his life, they will know what it is to live in a manner worthy of the gospel of Christ. They will understand that since they are already enrolled as citizens of the heavenly city, they must live as citizens of heaven during the period of their earthly sojourn.

In chapter 3, apprehensive about intruding missionaries who insist upon circumcision and legal observance, Paul again presents his converts with the example of his life in order to dissuade them from pursuing a righteousness based on legal observance. Paul has already experienced that kind of righteousness, and he, more than anyone, can assure them that there is no comparison between a righteousness based on legal observance and the righteousness that comes from God through Jesus Christ. It is imperative, therefore, that the community imitate the pattern of Paul's life in this regard as well.

Paul begins with a brief autobiographical statement of his former way of life. He was circumcised on the eighth day. He is an Israelite, a member of the tribe of Benjamin, and he was born of Hebrew parents. Most importantly, he observed the law as a Pharisee (3:5). He manifested his zeal for the law by persecuting the church, and, in that period when he relied on the law, he could say that he was blameless "as to righteousness under the law" (3:6). Before he knew Christ, he understood himself as someone who had attained a status of righteousness through careful observance of the law. But when he came to know Christ, his self-understanding was dramatically altered. Employing the language of profit and loss, he now reckons as a loss what he formerly counted as gain (righteousness on the basis of legal observance) because it was not a righteousness on the basis of faith in Christ (3:7). It is as if the columns in the accounting book of his life have been reversed.

This dramatic reversal, whereby Paul reckons his former gains as losses, occurred when God revealed his Son to him. In light of that experience, Paul understands the difference between the righteousness he formerly pursued and the righteousness that comes as a free gift from God through Jesus Christ. Paul calls the former "a righteousness of my own that comes from the law," and the latter "the righteousness from God based on faith" (3:9). His former righteousness depended on his zeal for the law, the latter on his faith in Christ.[9] His former righteousness was the result of his effort to observe the law; the righteousness that comes from God is the result of God's grace at work within

---

9. The phrase in 3:9 is read by some commentators as a subjective genitive, "but one that comes through the faith of Christ." This is also the NRSV marginal reading.

him. But before Paul could appropriate this righteousness from God, he had to set aside his former claims to righteousness. Reckoning his former gains as so much "rubbish," he now seeks to know the power of Christ's resurrection and to share in Christ's sufferings so that, like Christ, he can attain to the resurrection of the dead (3:8, 10–11). If the Philippians hope to attain the same goal, they must imitate Paul and seek the righteousness that comes from God rather than that based on legal observance.

Although Paul has relinquished his former righteousness, he knows that he has not yet reached the ultimate goal of his new life in Christ—resurrection from the dead. That goal will be attained only when his body is conformed to Christ's glorified body (*tō sōmati tēs doxēs autou*, 3:21). Therefore, Paul forgets what lies behind him—his former way of life under the law—in order to pursue what lies before him, "the prize of the heavenly call of God in Christ Jesus" (3:14), namely, resurrection from the dead. Those who wish to be "mature" (*teleioi*, 3:15) will follow Paul in the pursuit of this heavenly call to resurrection life.

In 3:17 Paul appeals to the Philippians to imitate him ("join in imitating me, and observe those who live according to the example you have in us") since there are many who are "enemies of the cross of Christ" (3:18). These enemies are best understood as the Judaizing missionaries of whom Paul speaks so harshly at the beginning of this chapter, calling them "dogs," "evil workers," and "those who mutilate the flesh" (3:2). He says that "their god is the belly" because they still insist upon the dietary prescriptions of the law, and that "their glory is in their shame" (3:19) because they require circumcision. In Paul's view such people have confused legal observance with the righteousness that comes from God. Contrasting himself and his converts with these Judaizing missionaries and their adherents, he affirms, "it is we who are the circumcision, who worship in the Spirit of God and boast in Christ Jesus and have no confidence in the flesh" (3:3). In making this claim, Paul affirms that there is no need for his Gentile converts to adopt the physical rite of circumcision, just as he did in Galatians, where he argued that those who belong to Christ are already Abraham's offspring (Gal. 3:29).

Toward the end of this letter, Paul again summons the Philippians to imitate him. He begins by urging two prominent women, Euodia and Syntyche, "to be of the same mind in the Lord" (Phil. 4:2).[10] He then exhorts the community to rejoice and let its gentleness be known to everybody because the Lord is near (4:4–5). Finally, he encourages the Philippians to pursue whatever is honorable, just, pure, pleasing, commendable, and worthy of praise, concluding, "Keep on doing the things that you have learned and received and

---

10. This exhortation, "to be of the same mind," recalls the introduction to the hymn (2:5), which exhorts the Philippians to adopt the "same mind" as Christ Jesus.

heard and seen in me" (4:9). This list of Stoic-like virtues leads to a section in which Paul thanks the community for its monetary support during the period of his imprisonment (4:10–20).[11] In expressing his gratitude to the Philippians, he presents himself as if he were a Stoic philosopher: "I have learned to be content with whatever I have. I know what it is to have little, and I know what it is to have plenty. In any and all circumstances I have learned the secret of being well-fed and of going hungry, of having plenty and of being in need" (4:11–12). But unlike a Stoic, the source of Paul's equanimity is not his self-control but Christ, who strengthens him and through whom he can do all things (4:13).

The theological significance of the pattern of Paul's life for the life of his converts can be summarized in three points. First, the example of the imprisoned Paul shows the community how to suffer for the gospel it believes. Second, the example of Paul, who counts his former gains as losses in order to gain the righteousness that comes from God, shows the community how to counter the threat of Judaizing missionaries. Third, the example of Paul, who is content in whatever circumstances he finds himself, shows the community how to live with the constantly changing circumstances of life through the power of Christ. Since the pattern of Paul's life embodies the gospel he preaches, others can learn how to live the gospel by imitating Paul.

The Pattern of Christ's Life

As important as the pattern of Paul's life is for the community, it is the pattern of Christ's life that plays the central role in Philippians and, more importantly, in the Christian life. This pattern finds its most dramatic expression in the hymnlike passage of 2:6–11, the Christ hymn. Although the origin and structure of the passage are disputed, its function within the letter is evident from the manner in which Paul introduces it. He exhorts the community to make his joy complete by being "of the same mind, having the same love, being in full accord and of one mind" (2:2). Instead of acting out of selfish ambition or looking to their self-interest, the Philippians should regard others as better than themselves and be concerned for the interest of others (2:3–4). To explain what he means, Paul writes: "Let the same mind be in you that was in Christ Jesus" (2:5). The passage that follows, the Christ hymn (2:6–11), provides the Philippians with a dramatic description of the self-effacing pattern of behavior that characterized Christ, a pattern they must adopt in their lives. The hymn consists of two parts, each containing three strophes.

11. Many who argue that Philippians is a composite letter view 4:10–20 as a separate letter of thanksgiving that Paul sent to the community for its monetary gift.

Part One: The Self-Emptying of Christ
   A. The attitude of Christ Jesus
         who, though he was in the form of God,
         did not regard equality with God
         as something to be exploited,
   B. His first act of self-effacement
         but emptied himself,
         taking the form of a slave,
         being born in human likeness.
   C. His second act of self-effacement
         And being found in human form,
         he humbled himself
         and became obedient to the point of death—even death on a cross.

Part Two: The Exaltation of Jesus
   D. The exaltation of Jesus
         Therefore God also highly exalted him
         and gave him the name
         that is above every name,
   E. Universal homage of the exalted One
         so that at the name of Jesus
         every knee should bend,
         in heaven and on earth and under the earth,
   F. Universal confession of the exalted One
         and every tongue should confess
         that Jesus Christ is Lord,
         to the glory of God the Father.

Although the Christology of the hymn plays the central role in most discussions of this passage, it is advisable to begin with a summary of what the passage says about the pattern of Christ's life before investigating the hymn's Christology.[12]

According to the hymn, the pattern of Christ's life was characterized by an attitude of self-effacement that expressed itself in two ways. The first strophe (A) describes this attitude of self-effacement: although he enjoyed equality with God because he was "in the form of God," Christ did not consider his godly status something of which he should take advantage or exploit during the period of his earthly sojourn. As God's Son he could rightly have insisted

---

12. The hymn begins with a pronoun ("who") without identifying its subject. But Paul's introduction in 2:5 shows that the pronoun refers to "Christ Jesus."

on the privileges of his godly status, but he did not consider that status some-thing to be clutched or grasped for his own advantage.[13] In the second stro-phe (B), the hymn points to Christ's first act of self-effacement. The one who was in "the form of God" humbled himself by taking on "the form of a slave." Rather than insisting upon being served because of his godly status, he entered the human condition and served others. The third strophe (C) describes a fur-ther act of self-effacement on Christ's part. Having assumed the human con-dition, the one who was "in the form of God" humbled himself still further by becoming obedient to the point of dying on the cross, a death reserved for slaves. By two acts of self-effacement (B, C), then, wherein he did not insist upon the privileges of his godly status (A), Christ Jesus humbled himself.

The second part of the hymn describes God's response to the self-effacement of the one who humbled himself. In the first strophe (D), the hymn says that God exalted him by giving him the name above every other name. The name, which is not yet mentioned, is *kyrios*, the name that belongs properly to God. Two things follow from God's exaltation of Jesus. First, because Jesus has been exalted as "Lord," he is worthy of homage in heaven and on earth (strophe E). Second, everyone must now confess that "Jesus Christ is Lord" (strophe F).

Although this exaltation follows the self-abasement of Christ, nothing in the act of Jesus' self-abasement required God to exalt the one who humbled himself. That God did exalt the one who humbled himself in such an act of obedience and self-effacement, however, reveals that self-effacement has become the way to exaltation.

What then does Paul mean when he writes, "Let the same mind be in you that *was* in Christ Jesus"? This verse is notoriously difficult to translate since the underlying Greek text lacks a verb. Therefore, others have proposed, as does the NRSV marginal reading, "Let the same mind be in you that *you have* in Christ Jesus." In the first translation, the emphasis is on imitation. The Philippians are to imitate Christ. In the second, the emphasis is on an attitude that the community should have because it dwells in the realm of Christ; it belongs to Christ. The latter translation is preferred by those who argue that believers cannot imitate the self-effacement of the preexistent Son of God, whose death was redemptive. For example, Jürgen Becker writes, "What Christian dies for humanity? What Christian can become poor in such a way that he gives up a heavenly way of life? What Christian can give up equality with God and receive a position of dominion over all reality?"[14] Becker is cor-rect in one respect: Christians cannot imitate Christ in this way. But they can imitate the attitude of their Lord's self-effacement; Jesus did nothing from self-

13. The text does not explicitly refer to "the Son of God," but the title is implied since the text is talking about one who was in the form of God.

14. *Paul: Apostle to the Gentiles*, 318–19.

ish ambition but looked to the interest of others instead. Understood in this way, the hymn provides a pattern for others to imitate.

The Christology of the Christ Hymn

Any discussion of the Christology of the Christ hymn should begin by acknowledging the following. First, the primary purpose of the hymn is to present the Philippians with the pattern of Christ's behavior that should inform their behavior rather than to instruct them in Christology. Second, it is likely that Paul appropriated this passage from the liturgical life of the church and adapted it to his own needs. If he did, it should be evident that he also affirms the implicit Christology of the hymn, even if he supplements it at some points.[15] Third, the hymn focuses on Christ's self-abasement and exaltation without explicitly speaking of the redemptive significance of his death and resurrection. Taken by itself, then, the hymn does not present a complete Christology or soteriology. Nor was it intended to do so, especially if it grew out of the cultic life of the community. Like any good hymn, this hymn seeks to inspire a sense of wonder and awe in the worshiping community, and this it does. Nonetheless, this passage has rightly played a central role in the discussion of Paul's Christology, especially his understanding of the preexistence, the incarnation, and the exaltation of Christ.

The first part of the hymn draws a sharp contrast between two stages in the career of Christ. Although he was "in the form of God," he emptied himself, taking "the form of a slave." It is difficult to translate the noun *morphē* ("form") adequately, and nearly every translation is somewhat misleading. Lucien Cerfaux, however, provides some guidance:

> The word expresses the way in which a thing, being what it is in itself, appears to our senses. If the word is applied to God, his *morphē* will be his deepest being, which cannot be reached by our understanding or sight, precisely because God is *aoratos* [unseen]: in fact the word has meaning here only as referring to the reality of God's being. In the case of the servant, the word means the external appearances which correspond with reality.[16]

The sense of the word, then, is aptly rendered as "nature" or "condition," even though this is not the way in which *morphē* is normally translated. To speak of Christ being in "the form of God" is to say that he enjoyed the very nature or condition of God, and to speak of him taking on "the form of a slave" is to affirm that he truly shared in the nature and condition of what it means to be human. The hymn confirms this understanding of *morphē* in two ways: (1) by equating being "in the form of God" with "equality with God," and (2) by equating

---

15. Many commentators argue that Paul added the phrase "even death on a cross."
16. Lucien Cerfaux, *Christ in the Theology of St. Paul* (New York: Herder & Herder, 1959), 385.

"taking the form of a slave" with "being born in human likeness." Thus the hymn is not saying that Christ appeared to be like God or like a human being but, in fact, was not. Rather, without explaining the inner relationship between God and Christ, it affirms that before taking on the human condition Christ already shared in the nature of God. In affirming this, the hymn makes the most explicit statement about the preexistence of Christ found in the Pauline writings.[17]

This movement from being in the "form of God" to being in the "form of a slave" involved a profound *kenōsis* or self-emptying (*heauton ekenōsen*) on the part of the one who was equal to God. The meaning of this self-emptying is explained by the phrase, "he did not regard equality with God as something to be exploited." The Greek noun that lies behind the phrase "to be exploited" (*harpagmon*) points to something to which one can claim or assert title.[18] Within the context of the hymn, the noun should be understood in light of the equality with God that the preexistent One could rightfully have claimed as his own. Because he was "in the form of God," he could have insisted on the prerogatives of his equality with God during the period of his human sojourn. But instead of insisting upon the privileges of his godly status, he emptied himself. This self-emptying, however, need not and should not be understood as the abandonment of his godly condition, as if Christ ceased being the Son of God by emptying himself of his divine nature, although some forms of kenotic theology have insisted upon this. Rather, it can also mean that the one who could rightfully have insisted on the prerogatives of his godly status divested himself of those privileges in order to live a life of service for others. Thus, as later theology would assert, the incarnate Jesus is true God and true Man.

The second part of the hymn describes the exaltation of the one who humbled himself by dying on the cross, but without any explicit reference to the resurrection. This exaltation occurs through the conferral of the name that is above every other name because it is reserved to God. Accordingly, Jesus is given the name *kyrios* so that every tongue must now confess that "Jesus Christ is Lord." The relationship between the one who was "in the form of God" and the one who was exalted as "Lord" can be summarized as follows. Before the incarnation, Christ enjoyed equality with God because he was "in the form of God." At a particular moment in time, however, the preexistent One set aside the divine prerogatives that were rightfully his to enter into the fullness of the human condition and live a life of service for others. This service for others found its ultimate expression in his death on the cross. In exalting Jesus to the status of "Lord," therefore, God restored the divine prerogatives of the one who emptied himself of them in order to take the form of a slave. This status

17. Paul never explicitly discusses the preexistence of Christ, but he presupposes it, as is apparent in the following texts: Rom. 8:3; 1 Cor. 8:6; 10:4; 2 Cor. 8:9; Gal. 4:4.

18. BDAG (s.v. *harpagmos*) gives the basic meaning as something to which one can claim or assert title by gripping or grasping, thus something claimed.

of lordship includes a dimension that was not present at the beginning. For, whereas the preexistent Christ was "in the form of God," he was not yet acclaimed as Lord. But now, precisely because of his *kenōsis* and exaltation, all must confess that "Jesus Christ is Lord." There is a sense in which the exaltation of Jesus as Lord—made possible through the incarnation—brings a new dimension to the one who was "in the form of God."[19]

The Christ hymn is not the whole of Paul's Christology. Nor should it be read apart from his Christology. But it does complement that Christology by making explicit what is implicit in the Pauline writings: the preexistence and the incarnation of the one now called Christ.

Conclusion

Philippians is an occasional writing rather than a theological tract. It encourages its recipients to suffer for the gospel they believe, exhorts them to communal unity, and warns them of those who are still pursuing righteousness on the basis of legal observance. To achieve these goals, Paul presents the Philippians with the pattern of his own life and the pattern of Christ's life. The pattern of Christ's life is the more important of the two. But if the Philippians want a concrete example of this pattern, they need only look to the example of the suffering and imprisoned Paul, who seeks "to know Christ and the power of his resurrection and the sharing of his sufferings by becoming like him in his death" (3:10). By his suffering for the sake of the gospel, Paul has already conformed himself to the pattern of Christ's self-abasement, which he now exhorts the Philippians to adopt in their lives. If they imitate him, they will understand, as he already does, the joy and equanimity that the gospel brings amid suffering, the righteousness that comes from God, and the power of the resurrection. The theology of this letter is born from an experience of suffering and imprisonment. It is a theology that can be seen in the pattern of Christ's existence, a pattern to which Paul has already conformed his life and to which he now calls the community.[20]

PHILEMON: THE TRANSFORMATION OF RELATIONSHIPS IN CHRIST

Despite its brevity, Paul's letter to Philemon provides an excellent example of how Paul deals with a problem of human relations in light of the gospel he preaches.

---

19. Here there is a similarity with Hebrews, which affirms, "Although he was a Son, he learned obedience through what he suffered" (Heb. 5:8).

20. Michael J. Gorman (*Cruciformity: Paul's Narrative Spirituality of the Cross* [Grand Rapids: Eerdmans, 2004]) has studied this pattern of Christ's life, and its implication for the Christian life, in great detail.

According to this letter, Paul is in prison, although the place of his imprisonment is disputed (Rome, Caesarea, Ephesus). At some time in the past, before the letter was written, Philemon had been converted to Christ by Paul, who now views him as a "brother," a "coworker," and a "partner" on behalf of the gospel. The church meets in Philemon's home, which is most likely in Colossae, since Col. 4:9 describes Philemon's slave Onesimus as "one of you," that is, a Colossian. Although the principal recipient of the letter is Philemon, Paul also includes Apphia and Archippus in the greeting, as well as the church that meets in Philemon's home (Phlm. 2).[21] Thus, more than a piece of personal correspondence, this letter is ecclesial in nature, intended to be read publicly in the gathering of the church. The ecclesial nature of the letter suggests that Paul views the affair of Onesimus, which was surely known to the entire household, as a matter that has important implications for the gospel.

The circumstances that gave rise to the letter are disputed. The traditional view is that the slave Onesimus ran away from Philemon, thereby becoming a fugitive and liable to severe punishment. At some point, by design or by chance, Onesimus meets Paul, who is in prison, and is converted by the apostle to faith in Christ. Having brought Onesimus to Christ, Paul writes to Philemon, asking him to receive his former slave as a brother in Christ. Since the letter never explicitly says that Onesimus ran away from Philemon, however, many commentators argue that Onesimus offended or injured his master in some other way. Knowing his master's profound respect for Paul, Onesimus purposely sought out the apostle to ask him to intervene with Philemon on his behalf. While visiting with Paul, however, Onesimus becomes a Christian. According to this scenario, Philemon is a letter of petition on behalf of Onesimus, who has become a believer, and whom Paul would now like to engage in the service of the gospel.[22]

Paul's appeal that Philemon accept Onesimus no longer as a slave "but more than a slave, a beloved brother" (v. 16), points to the profound change in relationship that has occurred between master and slave as a result of Onesimus's conversion. It is this appeal more than any other that is the climax of the letter. The letter does not so much develop a theology as it presupposes a theology of the new relationship that exists between those who are in Christ. This implied theology of how Christians ought to relate to one another can be seen in the relationships that the letter describes between Paul and Philemon, Paul and Onesimus, and Onesimus and Philemon.

---

21. Apphia, whom Paul describes as "our sister," is most likely Philemon's wife. Paul calls her his sister because of her new relationship to him in Christ; she is a Christian. Archippus, whom Paul calls "our fellow soldier," is most likely Philemon's son. He is mentioned in Col. 4:17. This reference to Archippus at Colossae is another indication that Philemon's household is in Colossae.

22. Joseph A. Fitzmyer (*The Letter to Philemon: A New Translation with Introduction and Commentary* [AB 34C; New York: Doubleday, 2000], 17–22) summarizes and evaluates the different theories for the occasion of Philemon.

Paul and Philemon: Brothers, Coworkers, and Partners in Christ

Paul holds Philemon in the highest esteem. He addresses him as one who is beloved (*agapētō*; NRSV "dear friend") and as a coworker (v. 1). He thanks God for Philemon's love and faith, and he says that the hearts of the saints have been refreshed through him. He also thanks God because other members of the church draw their strength from Philemon's faith, and their sharing in his faith promotes the good they are doing for the sake of Christ. Because of his work on behalf of the gospel, Philemon is the ideal church leader. Not only has he cooperated with Paul in the work of the gospel in the past, his Christian life has become a source of strength for others as well.

Paul appears to have full confidence in Philemon, whom he has brought to the faith. Instead of ordering him what to do, therefore, he urges him out of love to receive Onesimus once more. Paul does not want to do anything without Philemon's consent, in part because he understands the legal relationship that Onesimus has to Philemon as a slave. More importantly, he prefers that whatever good Philemon does be voluntary rather than coerced.

Paul, however, is aware that the relationship between Philemon and Onesimus has been badly damaged, and if there is to be a reconciliation between the two, Paul must provide Philemon with convincing reasons to receive Onesimus in his household once more. To accomplish this Paul builds on the good relationship that he already enjoys with Philemon in Christ to show him that a similar relationship now exists between him and his former slave, Onesimus. Moreover, he suggests that the painful events that have transpired may have been part of God's plan to bring Onesimus to faith so that Philemon might receive him no longer as a slave but as a "beloved brother" (v. 16). Therefore, if Philemon truly considers Paul a "partner" (*koinōnon*, v. 17) in the work of the gospel, he will receive Onesimus as if he were receiving Paul.

In the space of a few verses, then, Paul weaves a subtle web of relationships between himself and Philemon, which he can transfer to Philemon and Onesimus, now that the former slave is "in Christ." Paul and Philemon are brothers, coworkers, and partners in the gospel. Philemon and Onesimus will enjoy a similar relationship, if Philemon receives him as Paul encourages him to do.

Paul and Onesimus: Father and Son in Christ

Paul does not appear to have had any prior relationship with Onesimus, though Onesimus undoubtedly heard and knew of Paul, inasmuch as he was a slave in Philemon's household. If Onesimus was not a fugitive slave, he may have sought out Paul to ask him to intercede with Philemon on his behalf. But in meeting Paul and asking for this favor, he received an unexpected grace.

Onesimus was incorporated into the faith of his master. Paul became Ones-imus's spiritual father, and Onesimus became Paul's dear child in this new faith. Onesimus (the name means "useful"), who had previously been useless to his master for whatever offense he had committed, now became useful to Paul on behalf of the gospel. This relationship between Paul and Onesimus mirrors, in part, the relationship between Paul and Philemon. For just as Paul became the spiritual father of Philemon by bringing him to the faith, so he became the spiritual father of Onesimus, making the two men brothers in Christ and beloved children of Paul. And just as Philemon became Paul's partner in the gospel, so Onesimus has become useful to Paul in the work of the gospel.

The relationship between Paul and Onesimus has been dramatically changed because of their common faith in Christ. For Paul this changed relationship has important implications for the relationship between Philemon and Onesimus, and it will be difficult for Paul to maintain his former relationship with Phile-mon if Philemon does not alter his former relationship with Onesimus.

Philemon and Onesimus: Beloved Children of Paul and Brothers in Christ

The prior relationship of Philemon and Onesimus can be summarized in the words "master" and "slave." As a slave, Onesimus was the property of his mas-ter, a piece of chattel. Although he might have been well educated, he could never have hoped to enjoy a relationship of equality with his master, even though his master might entrust him with great responsibilities. Because Onesimus was Philemon's property, he had no rights of his own. Paul's request to Philemon on Onesimus's behalf, then, is all the more striking and can be understood only in light of the new relationship that Onesimus and Philemon enjoyed in Christ, of which Philemon is not yet aware, and perhaps does not fully comprehend. Paul not only petitions Philemon to welcome Onesimus into his household, he asks him to receive his former slave "no longer as a slave but more than a slave, a beloved brother . . . both in the flesh and in the Lord" (v. 16). With this climactic statement, Paul petitions Philemon to put into practice the mystery of the gospel: "There is no longer Jew or Greek, there is no longer slave or free, there is no longer male and female; for all of you are one in Christ Jesus" (Gal. 3:28). Anyone who is in Christ has become a new creation (2 Cor. 5:17; Gal. 6:15).

Just as the relationships between Paul and Philemon and between Paul and Onesimus were altered by the gospel, so the relationship between Philemon and Onesimus has been altered by the gospel, even if Philemon is not fully aware of it. If Philemon is to retain his former relationship to Paul as a beloved brother, coworker, and partner in Christ, he must find a way to alter his for-mer relationship with Onesimus, even if Onesimus remains his slave.

Slavery and the Gospel

The central theological issue that the Letter to Philemon raises for the contemporary reader is that of slavery. Does the letter permit and condone slavery, even among Christians, or does it plant the seeds for its destruction? The question is not entirely fair since it is not the purpose of the letter to address the issue of slavery or to criticize the social structures of the day. The primary purpose of the letter is more modest: to petition Philemon to welcome and, presumably, to forgive Onesimus for whatever injustice he has committed. The question of the relationship between slavery and the gospel, however, is not inappropriate given Paul's statements about the new creation that God has effected in Christ (2 Cor. 5:17; Gal. 6:15). For if there is a new creation in Christ, how does that new creation affect the old? And if all are one in Christ so that "there is no longer slave or free" (Gal. 3:28; see also Col. 3:11), what is the relationship between slavery and the gospel?

Despite these theological statements of equality in Christ, there is no explicit condemnation of the institution of slavery in the New Testament, nor is there any attempt to challenge the social structures that embraced and depended upon this institution. In 1 Corinthians Paul's basic rule is that believers should continue to lead the life that was assigned to them when they were called (1 Cor. 7:17) because the parousia is at hand. Consequently, slaves should not be concerned about their social status. But, if they can obtain their freedom, they should avail themselves of it (7:21).[23] Moreover, the household codes of Colossians and Ephesians accept the institution of slavery as a given, without protest (Col. 3:22–4:1; Eph. 6:5–9). Although they warn masters not to mistreat their slaves since they have a master in heaven who shows no partiality, they continue to exhort slaves to obey their masters.[24]

This acceptance of the status quo of slavery is, in part, due to the early church's belief that the parousia was at hand, as well as its firm conviction that its citizenship is in heaven. Given its conviction that the world was about to pass away, it is not surprising that the church was not concerned to change the structures of society. For the early Christians, the institution of slavery was a given that they were not yet ready to challenge, and in many instances simply accepted.

Slavery was so pervasive that Paul could use it as a metaphor for the Christian life, given that Christ took on the form of a slave and died the slave's death

---

23. The Greek of 1 Cor. 7:21 (*mallon chrēsai*) is ambiguous so that whereas the NRSV reads "make use of your present condition now more than ever," its marginal reading is "avail yourself of the opportunity."

24. The Pastoral Epistles are even more insistent that slaves be submissive to their masters for the sake of the faith in Christ. See 1 Tim. 6:1–2; Titus 2:9–10. Unlike in Colossians and Ephesians, there are no instructions for masters in the Pastorals.

of crucifixion (Phil. 2:7–8). Thus Paul views himself as a slave of Jesus Christ (Rom. 1:1), and he encourages believers to become slaves to righteousness (Rom. 6:19). In the new creation established in Christ, the one who was a slave, when called by the Lord, is now a free person in regard to the Lord, and the person who was a free person, when called by the Lord, is now a slave of the Lord (1 Cor. 7:22).

At the end of the Letter to Philemon, however, Paul makes an elusive statement that appears to be a petition for Philemon to release Onesimus from his bonds of slavery: "Confident of your obedience, I am writing to you, knowing that you will do even more than I say" (v. 21). Exactly what the "more" is, Paul does not explain. His earlier injunction, however, that Philemon receive Onesimus "no longer as a slave but more than a slave, a beloved brother" (v. 16), may suggest that Paul is petitioning for Philemon's freedom. Such a petition is not a condemnation of slavery, nor is it a petition that Philemon free all of his slaves, but it does indicate that Paul understood the tension between the new reality that exists in Christ and the reality of this old age that still makes a distinction between Jew and Gentile, slave and free, male and female.

The theology that Paul presupposes in his letter to Philemon, then, is the theology of the new creation, which he develops in Galatians and 2 Corinthians. Those who are in Christ are a new creation, and in this new creation the old social distinctions of race, class, and gender no longer prevail. The challenge of the gospel is to bridge the tension between the reality of the world as it is and the reality of this new creation that God has created in Christ. This mystery of this new reality is the central theological theme of Colossians and Ephesians.

COLOSSIANS: THE MYSTERY OF CHRIST

The Pauline authorship of Colossians and Ephesians is disputed.[25] These two letters, whose theology is closely related, are usually classified as deuteropauline. Their literary style is marked by longer and more complex sentences than Paul usually uses, and they often employ a distinctive vocabulary. Their theology tends to focus on (1) the cosmic redemptive work of Christ, who is the head of the church; (2) the cosmic dimension of this church, which is the body of Christ; and (3) the hope and salvation believers already possess in heaven above rather than on the imminence of the parousia. For New Testament theology, however, the central issue is not so much the authorship of these letters as it is their faithfulness, or lack thereof, to the theology found in the nondisputed Pauline correspondence. If the theology of these letters is a legit-

25. For a full discussion of the issues, see Collins, *Letters That Paul Did Not Write*, 132–208.

imate outgrowth of Paul's own theology, then these letters can be viewed as the work of a Pauline school, or of individuals familiar with, and faithful to, the thought of the great apostle. Their disputed authorship, then, is not so much a liability for New Testament theology as it is a vantage point from which to study the growth and development of Paul's thought.

Although in this New Testament theology I view Colossians and Ephesians as deuteropauline letters, I refer to their author as "Paul" since this is the claim that the letters make for themselves. Moreover, since in this New Testament theology I am primarily interested in the theology in the New Testament writings, I must concern myself with the situation of Paul and his readers, as implied in the letters, as well as with a hypothetical reconstruction of the historical circumstances that gave rise to them.

Colossians, more than Ephesians, gives the impression of having been occasioned by a specific situation in Paul's life. According to the letter, Paul is in prison on account of "the mystery of Christ" (Col. 4:3; see also 4:10, 18), although the place of his imprisonment is not disclosed.[26] He is surrounded by a cadre of coworkers, many of whom are named in the letter to Philemon: Tychicus (4:7; see Eph. 6:21); Onesimus (Col. 4:9, see Phlm. 10); Aristarchus, Paul's "fellow prisoner" (Col. 4:10; see Phlm. 24); Mark (Col. 4:10; see Phlm. 24); Jesus/Justus (Col. 4:11); Epaphras (4:12; see Phlm. 23); Luke (Col. 4:14); and Demas (4:14; see Phlm. 24). Although Paul appears to know a great deal about the church at Colossae, he was not its founder, nor is there any indication within the letter that he ever visited there. He has, however, heard of the community's faith and love from its founder, Epaphras, whom Paul identifies as his "beloved fellow servant" and "faithful minister of Christ" on their behalf (Col. 1:7). In addition to laboring among the Colossians, Epaphras has worked on behalf of the gospel in Laodicea and Hieropolis (4:13), cities geographically close to each other in the Lycus Valley. Accordingly, Paul instructs the Colossians to have this letter read in Laodicea after it has been read aloud in Colossae, and he tells them to read the letter he has already sent to the Laodiceans (4:16).

In Colossians, and more so in Ephesians, the person of the apostle begins to loom large, an indication that these letters may have been composed after Paul's death. For example, Paul views his sufferings as "completing what is lacking in Christ's afflictions for the sake of his body, that is, the church" (1:24).[27] As an apostle, he has been commissioned "to make the word of God

26. As is the case with Philemon, commentators have proposed Ephesus, Caesarea, and Rome as possible places for Paul's imprisonment.

27. Paul, of course, does not mean that his personal sufferings are redemptive in the way that Christ's sufferings are. Nor is he implying that there was something lacking in Christ's redemptive work. The expression "Christ's afflictions" (*tōn thlipseōn tou Christou*) refers to the afflictions the church must endure on behalf of Christ, before the completion of all things, rather than to Christ's own afflictions or sufferings. It is these afflictions on behalf of Christ that the apostle endures for the sake of the church, the body of Christ.

fully known, the mystery that has been hidden throughout the ages and generations but has now been revealed to his saints" (1:25–26). This mystery is Christ, who is in them (1:27). At the present time, because of his suffering and imprisonment, Paul is enduring a great struggle for the Colossians and those in Laodicea, as well as for those who have never seen him, so that they may have "the knowledge of God's mystery, that is, Christ himself" (2:2). Consequently, even though Paul may be absent from them in body, he is present to them in spirit (2:5).[28]

While in prison, Paul has learned of a dangerous situation that is threatening, or might threaten, the Colossians: a false teaching, which he identifies as a "philosophy," and which he equates with human traditions and "the elemental spirits of the universe" (2:8). What this "philosophy" is and what Paul means by the "elemental spirits of the universe" (*stoicheia tou kosmou*) are disputed. Moreover, it is not entirely clear if this teaching purports to be Christian.[29] Paul's remarks in 2:8–23, however, suggest the following: (1) The teaching was a merely human invention, which is to be equated with an elementary form of religious teaching according to "the rudiments of the world" (the NRSV marginal reading for *ta stoicheia tou kosmou*). (2) The teaching was syncretistic in nature and included a number of Jewish practices dealing with food, drink, festivals, new moons, and Sabbaths. (3) The teaching promised its devotees a way to worship angels or, perhaps, to view the worship of angels, provided the devotees adopted a series of ascetical practices.[30] (4) Fearful of the cosmic powers, which they believed controlled their fate, the Colossians may have been tempted to adopt this teaching in order to enlist the protection of angels against the cosmic powers.

The central theological issue of Colossians, then, is akin to that of Galatians: the sufficiency of what God has done in Christ. But whereas the agitators at Galatia called into question the sufficiency of Christ by insisting that the Galatians should have themselves circumcised and do the works of the law, the proponents of this philosophy called into question the sufficiency of

---

28. This verse can be read as an indication that Paul has already died. Although he is no longer present to the church in body, he is present to the church in spirit, as this letter shows.

29. A. J. M. Wedderburn ("The Theology of Colossians," in Andrew T. Lincoln and A. J. M. Wedderburn, *The Theology of the Later Pauline Letters* [NTT; Cambridge: Cambridge University Press, 1993], 3–71) discusses the background to Colossians (pp. 3–22). Regarding the *stoicheia*, he notes that it may be misguided "to distinguish too sharply between the two possible senses of *stoicheia* as physical elements and as powers, benign or malign, controlling human life" (p. 8). Regarding the false teaching, he notes, "What remains uncertain is whether the proponents of this teaching against which Colossians is written were Christians, putting forward their views as the true form of Christianity, as was the case in Galatia, or whether they existed outside the Christian community as a seductive alternative to it" (p. 11).

30. The Greek of 2:18 (*thrēskeia tōn angelōn*) can be taken as a subjective or as an objective genitive. Taken as a subjective genitive, it refers to the worship in which angels participate. Taken as an objective genitive, it refers to the worship of angels.

Christ by urging that it is necessary to enlist the assistance of angels in order to be protected from the cosmic powers. As in Galatians, Paul's response is the same: what God has done in Christ is sufficient for salvation: there is no need for angelic protection because the fullness of Deity dwells in Christ (2:19). The theology of Colossians is a response to this teaching, and it can be summarized under the following headings: (1) the mystery of Christ; (2) the mystery of redemption; (3) the mystery of the church; and (4) the mystery of life in Christ.

The Mystery of Christ

Although the figure of Christ plays a central role in all of Paul's correspondence, Colossians is the most explicitly christological letter of the Pauline corpus. This is not to say that it develops a systematic Christology; it does not. But given the nature of the teaching at Colossae that Paul must combat, the figure of Christ necessarily plays a central role in the argument he makes: there is no need to fear the cosmic powers because the fullness of Deity dwells in Christ. Paul lays the foundation for this argument in the hymnlike passage of Col. 1:15–20. As is the case with the Christ hymn of Philippians, the origin and structure of the Colossians hymn are disputed. But there is no disputing the central role of Christ in the hymn and the importance of this passage for Paul's argument.

The hymn can be divided into two (1:15–18a, 18b–20) or three strophes (1:15–16, 17a–18, 18b–20). A division into two strophes, however, each of which begins in the same way (*hos estin*), has the advantage of highlighting the work of Christ in the order of creation (1:15–18a) and in the order of redemption (1:18b–20).

The Order of Creation (1:15–18a)

He is (*hos estin*) the image (*eikōn*) of the invisible God,
the firstborn (*prōtotokos*) of all creation;
for in him all things (*ta panta*) were created
in heaven and on earth,
things visible and invisible,
whether thrones or dominions
or rulers or powers—
all things (*ta panta*) have been created
through him and
for him.

He himself is before all things (*pro pantōn*),
and in him all things (*ta panta*) hold together (*synestēken*).
He is the head (*kephalē*) of the body (*sōmatos*), the church
(*ekklēsia*);

The Order of Redemption (1:18b–20)

he is (*hos estin*) the beginning (*archē*),
the firstborn (*prōtotokos*) from the dead,
      so that he might come to have first place (*prōteuōn*) in everything (*en pasin*).
            For in him all (*pan*) the fullness (*plērōma*) of God was pleased to dwell,
            and through him God was pleased
            to reconcile (*apokatallaxai*) to himself all things (*ta panta*),
               whether on earth or in heaven,
            by making peace through the blood of his cross.

                                   (NRSV slightly revised)

Although the hymn never explicitly identifies its subject, the verses that precede the hymn are explicit: the subject of this hymn is God's beloved Son, in whom there is redemption, the forgiveness of sins (1:13–14). The first strophe (1:15–18a) identifies the Son in two ways: as the image of the invisible God and as the firstborn of all creation. As the image of the invisible God, the Son is not merely a faint and incoherent representation of God, he is the perfect reflection of the God who cannot be seen. As the firstborn of all creation, he is superior to creation in every way because all things were created through and for him. He is the agent and goal of creation, not only of the created order that can be seen but of the created order, in heaven, that cannot be seen. The Son is preeminent in the order of creation, not as a created being, but as the one through whom creation came into existence.[31]

In the final part of the opening strophe (v. 18a), the hymn calls the Son the head of the body, which is identified as the church. At an earlier stage, before the hymn was incorporated into the letter, it is possible that there was no reference to the church, giving the sense that the one through whom and for whom all things were created, in heaven and on earth, is the head of the body, which is the universe. But the present form of the hymn clearly identifies the body as the church, thereby emphasizing that the one who is the head of the church is preeminent in the order of creation.

The second strophe (1:18b–20) begins in the same way as the first, *hos estin* ("he is"), but it moves from the order of creation to the order of redemption. As in the first strophe, the Son is identified in two ways: as the beginning and as the firstborn from the dead. He is the beginning of a new humanity that is being incorporated into his body, the church, because he is the firstborn from the dead. He is the firstborn from the dead because he is the first to have been raised from the dead. Working back from the resurrection to the death of the Son, the hymn coordinates the role of the Son in the order of redemption with

---

31. Here the noun *prōtotokos* ("firstborn") refers to the preeminence of Christ in creation, a dignity accorded to the firstborn, without necessarily suggesting that Christ was the first being to be created by God.

his role in the order of creation. Just as God created all things in heaven and on earth through and for the Son, so God reconciled all things, whether on earth or in heaven, through the Son, by the blood of the cross. Like the Son's role in creation, his role in reconciliation is cosmic in scope.

When it says that "the fullness (*plērōma*) of God" was pleased to dwell in him, the Colossians hymn, like the hymn of Philippians, presupposes the incarnation. But whereas the Philippians hymn refers to the cross to emphasize the self-abasement of the Son, the Colossians hymn refers to the cross to speak of the Son's redemptive work: all things, whether on earth or in heaven, were reconciled to God through the blood of the cross.

The work of creation and the work of redemption, then, find their unity in Christ. On the one hand, everything was created through and for him. On the other, everything was reconciled to Christ through the blood of the cross. Since this work of creation and redemption embraces all things, whether in heaven or on earth, there should be no doubt about the preeminence of Christ. He is the mystery of God because God's plan of creation and redemption is revealed in him. In Christ all the treasures of God's wisdom and knowledge are revealed (2:3). In Christ the fullness of Deity dwells (1:19; 2:9). All other things, whether in heaven or on earth, are mere shadows of reality. The "substance" (*sōma*) belongs to Christ (2:17). As the firstborn from the dead, he has been raised up and is seated at God's right hand until he is revealed in glory (3:1–4). The mystery of Christ then is the revelation of the mystery of God in the order of creation and in the order of redemption.

The Mystery of Redemption

There is an intimate connection in Colossians between Christology and soteriology. For in presenting Christ as the mystery of God, Paul speaks of Christ's redemptive work. Consequently, the mystery of Christ can also be viewed as the mystery of redemption, as is already apparent when Paul explains that the mystery, which he reveals to the Colossians, is "Christ in you, the hope of glory" (1:27).

Previous to the revelation of this mystery, the Colossians belonged to the power of darkness (1:13); they were "estranged and hostile in mind, doing evil deeds" (1:21); they were under "rulers and authorities" (2:15); and they were enslaved to a way of life that Paul identifies with a rudimentary form of religion (2:8, 20). But when the mystery of Christ was revealed, God rescued them from the power of darkness and transferred them into the kingdom of his beloved Son, in whom they have redemption, which is "the forgiveness of sins" (1:13–14).

Colossians does not trace the origin of the human predicament to humanity's refusal to acknowledge God (Rom. 1:18–32), nor does it appeal to the story of Adam to explain how sin and death entered the world by the transgression of one man (Rom. 5:12–21). Rather, it seems to suppose that humanity was once under the sway of cosmic powers and forces who had rebelled against God. Subservient to these "rulers and authorities," humanity was alienated from God and lived according to an elementary form of religious teaching. If this scenario is correct, it may have been this abiding sense of bondage to cosmic powers beyond their control that tempted the Colossians to enter into the worship of angels in order to find protection from these malevolent cosmic forces. But in doing this, the Colossians were merely returning to a rudimentary form of religion, according to Paul.

Just as Galatians affirms that there is no need to submit to circumcision and put oneself under the rule of the Mosaic law in order to be justified, so Colossians argues that there is no need to assuage these cosmic powers. Employing a cosmic imagery that corresponds to the cosmic plight of the Colossians, Paul argues that when they were baptized they underwent a spiritual circumcision whereby their old nature, which was alienated from God, was stripped away. Paul calls this spiritual circumcision "the circumcision of Christ" (Col. 2:11) because it occurred when they entered the sphere of Christ. At their baptism they were buried with him, their old nature died and was stripped away, and they were raised with Christ through their faith in the power of God, who raised him from the dead (2:12). In saying that they were raised up, Paul is not implying that the Colossians have already experienced the resurrection of the dead in the same way that Christ has. But he is affirming that, by their baptism, they have entered a new life that will find its fulfillment when they are revealed in glory with Christ.[32]

Paul employs cosmic imagery to explain how God effected this work of redemption in Christ. Since humanity found itself in a situation of indebtedness to God because it did not carry out the legal requirements of the law, God erased the "bond" or "record" (*cheirographon*) of humanity's indebtedness, with all of its "legal demands" (*dogmasin*), nailing it to the cross (2:14). In this way God disarmed the "rulers and authorities" and, like a victorious general, led them in triumph as his prisoners.

This cosmic imagery is as elusive as it is powerful since it never explains what is meant by the record of humanity's indebtedness or why it was necessary for God to disarm the rulers and authorities and lead them in triumph.

---

32. The parousia does not play a central role in Colossians in the way that it does in the nondisputed Pauline letters, especially 1 Corinthians and 1 Thessalonians. However, Col. 3:4 (*hotan ho Christos phanerōthē hē zōē hymōn*, "When Christ who is your life is revealed") indicates that Colossians is still aware that there will be a future manifestation of Christ, even though it does not speak of the parousia. On this point see Todd Still, "Eschatology in Colossians: How Realized Is It?" *NTS* 50 (2004): 125–38. He notes that although this language is "atypical" (p. 131) of Paul, "It would be both premature and inappropriate, then, to regard Colossians as out of synch with Pauline eschatology based on the facts that the letter lacks eschatological urgency and employs spatial imagery" (p. 132).

The reference to the "legal demands" or "the record" indicates that humanity had violated God's law. Moreover, God's triumph over the "rulers and powers," who are now subject to Christ (2:10), suggests that these cosmic powers had previously rebelled against God. Having rebelled against God, they ruled over humanity, which in turn was disobedient to God, thereby accumulating a bond of indebtedness that the powers and authorities employed to exert their control over humanity. By Christ's death on the cross, however, God freely canceled this debt. Thus, whereas Galatians speaks of Christ becoming a curse in order to free humanity from the threatening curse of the law (Gal. 3:13), Colossians portrays God as nailing the record of humanity's offenses to the cross in order to forgive humanity's trespasses. As different as the imagery is, in both instances these images describe God's gracious forgiveness, which took place on the cross.

This forgiveness of sins required a cosmic act of redemption, for it was not only humanity that needed to be reconciled to God, it was the powers and authorities of the universe as well. Consequently, God reconciled all things to himself, in heaven and on earth, "through the blood of his cross" (Col. 1:20). The death of Christ, as represented by the cross, continues to play a central role in Colossians, but whereas the nondisputed Pauline letters focus on the justification and redemption of sinful humanity, Colossians portrays reconciliation as taking place on a cosmic scale.[33] Since the entire cosmos needed to be reconciled to its Creator, the one through and for whom God created all things reconciled all things to God. This work of reconciliation, therefore, is a new creation.

Because the mystery of Christ is so closely related to the mystery of redemption, there is an intimate relationship between Christ and those who have been reconciled through him. They are "in Christ" (1:2). They live their lives in him (2:6), and they are rooted and built up in him (2:7). In him they have been brought to fulfillment (2:10), and in him they were circumcised (2:11). All of this happened because they were buried with him in baptism, in which they were also raised up with him and were made alive together with him (2:12). With Christ they have died to the *stoicheia tou kosmou* (2:20). Now that they have been raised up with him (3:1), they are to set their minds on the things that are above, where their life is hidden with Christ in God (3:2–3). When Christ is revealed, they will be revealed with him in glory (3:4).

The soteriology and anthropology of Colossians can be summarized as follows. Although all things were created through and for Christ, humanity was alienated from God and subject to cosmic rulers and authorities who rebelled

---

33. Paul, however, does speak of the cosmic dimension of redemption in Rom. 8:18–21, where he notes "that the creation itself will be set free from its bondage to decay and will obtain the freedom of the glory of the children of God."

against God. In a cosmic act of redemption that finds its focal point in the cross, God reconciled the cosmos to himself. As a result of this cosmic drama of redemption, those who are in Christ have experienced the forgiveness of their sins. Through baptism they have died and risen with Christ, and when Christ is revealed in glory, their life with him will be revealed in glory with him. The mystery of redemption is the presence of Christ, in whom the fullness of God dwells, in the life of the believer.

The Mystery of the Church

The mystery of Christ is the mystery of redemption, and this mystery of redemption is presently at work in the church, which Colossians identifies as the body of Christ, whose head is Christ.

In the nondisputed Pauline letters, Paul normally speaks of the *ekklēsia* in relation to the local community. Colossians is still aware of this usage, as is evident from Paul's greeting to Nympha and "the church in her house" (4:15), and in his instruction that this letter be read "in the church of the Laodiceans" (4:16). But Colossians goes beyond the ecclesiology of the nondisputed letters in two ways. First, it presents the church as a cosmic entity. Second, in presenting the church as the body of the cosmic Christ, Colossians no longer employs the metaphor of the body in a functional way, as do Rom. 12:4–8 and 1 Cor. 12:12–27. In Colossians the church is a separate entity, the body of Christ, the place where the mystery of Christ and the mystery of redemption are at work.

The first mention of the church comes at the end of the first strophe of the hymn, where Paul concludes, "He is the head (*kephalē*) of the body (*sōmatos*), the church" (Col. 1:18a). On first reading, this statement appears out of place since the hymn has been speaking of the Son's role in creation (1:15–18a) and has not yet spoken of his work of reconciliation (1:18b–20). The reason for placing the statement at this point, however, is to emphasize that the very one through and for whom God created all things is also the head of the church. In this way the church becomes the place—the body—where God's work of reconciliation, accomplished through the Son, can be seen. The church, then, is a cosmic reality because its head is the one through and for whom all things were created. As the body of Christ, it is the sphere where those who have been reconciled through Christ live and dwell. Inasmuch as the church is the body of Christ, the place where the reconciling work of Christ takes place, it can be identified as "the kingdom of Christ" because it is the sphere where Christ already reigns over every ruler and authority (2:10). Thus Paul prefaces this hymn by saying that God "rescued us from the power of darkness and transferred us into the kingdom of his beloved Son" (1:13).

As the body of Christ, the church suffers afflictions, what Paul identifies as "Christ's afflictions." Therefore, having been commissioned as a "servant" (*diakonos*) of the church, he suffers for the church to complete the afflictions that the church must endure for Christ (1:24–25). The ultimate goal of his ministry is to reveal the hidden mystery of God, which is Christ, so that he can present everyone "mature in Christ" or, as the NEB reads, "to present each one of you as a mature member of Christ's body" (1:28). The church, then, is the sphere where believers continue to suffer on behalf of Christ by enduring "Christ's afflictions" and so come to perfect maturity in him.

In exhorting the Colossians not to allow others to condemn them in matters of food, drink, festivals, new moons, and Sabbath observance, Paul reminds them that these things are only "shadows" but the *sōma* belongs to Christ (2:16–17). Although *sōma* is usually translated "substance" (so NRSV), the context suggests that it can also be rendered as "body" since Paul exhorts the Colossians to hold fast to the "head" from whom "the whole body" is nourished and held together (2:19).[34] Paul's thought can be summarized as follows. These Jewish religious practices were shadows of what was to come; the reality is the body of Christ, which is the church. Rather than pursue these practices and enter into the worship of angels, the Colossians should hold fast to Christ, who is the head of the body, the church; for he is the one who nourishes and holds the church together.

Paul makes another reference to the body in 3:15, "And let the peace of Christ rule in your hearts, to which indeed you were called in the one body." This "peace of Christ" is the reconciliation that God has effected through the blood of Christ, which was shed on the cross (1:20), whereas "the one body" to which the Colossians were called is the church, the body of Christ, the sphere in which this reconciliation is experienced.

The ecclesiology of Colossians can be summarized as follows. The church is the body of Christ because it is the sphere in which God's work of cosmic reconciliation in Christ is seen and experienced. The church, however, does not exist in and for itself. It lives for, and it is nourished by, its head, who is Christ, God's agent of creation and reconciliation. To live in the church is to live in and with Christ.

The Mystery of Life in Christ

In the first two chapters of this letter, Paul explains the mystery of Christ in order to assure the Colossians that they are no longer under the rule of cosmic powers since they have been transferred from the power of darkness into the kingdom of Christ, in whom the fullness of Deity dwells. In the last two

---

34. Margaret Y. MacDonald (*Colossians and Ephesians* [SP 17; Collegeville, MN: Liturgical Press, 2000], 111) makes this point. She translates the phrase, "but the reality is the body of Christ."

chapters, he draws out the practical implications of this mystery in order to show the Colossians how to lead a life "worthy of the Lord" (1:10). Thus Colossians, like Romans and Galatians, affirms that the morally good life is the outcome of the gospel. But whereas Romans and Galatians relate the moral life to Paul's gospel of justification by faith, Colossians relates it to the mystery of Christ through whom all things were created and reconciled to God. This intimate connection between the mystery of Christ and the moral life of the believer is presented at the beginning of Paul's moral exhortation in language indebted to his baptismal theology. "So if you have been raised with Christ, seek the things that are above, where Christ is, seated at the right hand of God. Set your minds on things that are above, not on things that are on earth, for you have died, and your life is hidden with Christ in God. When Christ who is your life is revealed, then you also will be revealed with him in glory" (3:1–4). These verses begin with a statement of the redemptive situation of the Colossians, which they have experienced through their baptism: in baptism they were raised up with Christ, who is seated at God's right hand. This affirmation of their hidden life with Christ leads to a moral imperative: since they are raised up with Christ in baptism, they should set their minds on what is in heaven, where Christ reigns. Finally, Paul provides supporting reasons for this moral indicative: they have already been raised with Christ in baptism, and although their life with him is presently hidden, it will be revealed when Christ appears in glory. The moral life, then, is a process of living out the death and resurrection of Christ that believers already enjoy with Christ through their baptismal union with him.

Paul's understanding of the moral life, then, is rooted in his baptismal theology, which portrays baptism as a spiritual circumcision whereby "the body of the flesh" is put off (2:11). Alluding to this imagery in his moral exhortation, he reminds the Colossians that they have stripped off the old self (*palaion anthrōpon*) and clothed themselves with the new self (*ton neon*), which is being renewed in knowledge according to the image of its creator (3:9–10). Consequently, since their old self was stripped off in the spiritual circumcision, which is baptism, the Colossians should live in accordance with the new self with which they were clothed at baptism. This new self, however, is still in the process of being renewed and will not be completed until Paul presents everyone as "mature in Christ" (1:28). Although this process of renewal is not completed, and although this new life is still hidden in Christ, the social distinctions that separate people from one another no longer apply in Christ. In the renewal that is taking place in Christ, "there is no longer Greek and Jew, circumcised and uncircumcised, barbarian, Scythian, slave and free" (3:11).

Paul explains the implications of this baptismal ethic in two ways. First, in an extended moral exhortation that draws upon this baptism imagery, he calls upon the Colossians to put to death whatever is still of this earth in their life

(3:5–11) and to clothe themselves with those virtues that are appropriate to God's elect (3:12–17). These two imperatives correspond to the two movements of the baptismal theology developed in Colossians. Being buried with Christ in his death requires believers to put to death whatever is of earth, and being raised with Christ requires them to be clothed with a new way of life.

Second, Paul introduces a household code (3:18–4:1) that provides guidance for believers who must continue to live in the old world knowing that their new life is hidden with Christ in God. Paul does not attempt to change or reform the social structures of his day. The community of believers to whom he is writing is too small, and the time before the consummation of all things too brief. He assumes, as does the culture of his day, that wives should be subject to their husbands and that slaves should obey their earthly masters. Yet he plants the seeds for a transformation of these social conventions in a series of subtle phrases that relate the conduct of husbands and wives, parents and children, masters and slaves, to their relationship with the Lord. The old sinful structures of society, such as slavery, continue to exist. But the believer knows that in Christ there is no longer Greek and Jew, slave and free, for Christ is all in all. This knowledge may not immediately change the sinful structures of society, but in time, as the new humanity makes its appearance in the body of Christ, it will become clear that those who live in and with the Lord can no longer tolerate such structures.

To summarize, the moral teaching of Colossians grows out of the mystery of Christ. As humanity enters the body of Christ, which is the church, it grows into full maturity in Christ.

Conclusion

Although Colossians may not have been written by Paul, it is faithful to the theology of the great apostle. Like the nondisputed Pauline letters, it insists upon the sufficiency of Christ for salvation. There is no need to supplement or to add to what God has done in and through Christ. Moreover, like the nondisputed Pauline letters, Colossians points to the intimate connection between the gospel and the moral life. The moral life is not something added to the gospel but the working out of the gospel in daily life. Finally, like the nondisputed Pauline letters, Colossians draws attention to the death of Christ upon the cross as the focal point of God's redemptive act. But there are also new emphases and insights in Colossians, the most important being the cosmic role of Christ and the church in creation and redemption. Colossians no longer argues for justification by faith apart from doing the works of the law. The role of Israel in God's salvific plan is no longer a central issue, in part because Colossians is addressing a new situation, either in the lifetime of the apostle or in a time after his death. Ultimately, however, Colossians is faithful to Paul's theology as it tries to rethink the meaning and significance of Christ for a new time and situation.

EPHESIANS: THE MYSTERY OF THE CHURCH

Scholars have called into question the Pauline authorship of Ephesians for many of the reasons they have questioned the Pauline authorship of Colossians: the language and style of the letter and its theological developments in the areas of Christology, ecclesiology, and eschatology. But in addition to these reasons, the Pauline authorship of Ephesians has long been suspect because there is a relationship between it and Colossians that, in the view of many scholars, is the result of the author of Ephesians employing Colossians as one of its literary sources. Consequently, if Colossians is deuteropauline, the case against the Pauline authorship of Ephesians is all the more compelling.

For New Testament theology the question of the Pauline authorship of Colossians and Ephesians need not be viewed as a liability, as already noted. For if these letters were written in Paul's name by others, they provide a vantage point for investigating how a new generation of Paulinists applied Paul's theological vision to its time and circumstances. In the case of Ephesians, this growth and development can be observed in two ways: the manner in which it expands upon Paul's own theology, and the way in which it uses and develops material from Colossians. But even if Paul were the author of these letters, New Testament theologians would still find themselves in a position of observing and commenting on the growth and development of Paul's thought as found in these two letters. Consequently, whether or not Ephesians was written by Paul, the fundamental task of New Testament theologians in regard to this letter remains essentially the same: to identify and clarify the letter's theology, noting and explaining, when possible, its theological development in comparison to other Pauline writings.

Although Ephesians is similar to Colossians in style and theological thought, there are a number of differences between the two writings. Among the most significant is the way in which they address their implied audiences. Whereas Colossians gives every impression of a writing occasioned by the threat of false teaching, Ephesians is more general in tone. The author does not write in response to a false teaching or a specific problem within the community. Indeed, the letter does not even seem to have been addressed to a particular community of believers, since the words "in Ephesus" are not present in ancient and important manuscripts such as Papyrus 46, Vaticanus, and Sinaiticus. In these manuscripts the letter begins: "Paul, an apostle of Christ Jesus by the will of God, to the saints who are faithful in Christ Jesus" (1:1). In light of this reading, Ephesians is best understood as a circular letter to Gentile Christians in Asia Minor.

Ephesians explicitly identifies Paul as its author, clearly indicating that the apostle is writing from prison (3:1, 13; 4:1; 6:20). There is a formal tone to this letter, however, which gives the impression that the intended audience has never seen or heard Paul in the flesh. Paul appears to be writing to a new generation of Gentile Christians who are the beneficiaries of, but not fully aware of, his earlier struggles to preach the gospel to Gentiles without requiring them to be circumcised and adopt the Mosaic law. If Ephesians is deuteropauline, as many urge, this is precisely the rhetorical voice that the author seeks to establish. He writes as a fervent Paulinist to a new generation of Pauline Christians to remind them of their status in Christ and to urge them to live accordingly. Through the efforts of this Paulinist, the great apostle speaks from the grave to a new generation.

The implied author of Ephesians, to use Andrew Lincoln's phrase, is Paul.[35] The audience is composed of Gentile Christians who have not seen or heard him in the flesh. They are the beneficiaries of his struggles on their behalf, and the challenge they now face is the danger of complacency. In the first three chapters of this letter, therefore, Paul reminds them of God's economy of salvation and his own role in this divine economy. In the final three chapters, Paul presents an extended moral exhortation, rooted in his theological vision of God's economy, in which he calls upon the audience to lead a life worthy of its calling. Since God's economy of salvation plays such a central role in this writing, the theological structure of Ephesians will be examined in light of the following: (1) God's economy of salvation; (2) reconciliation in the economy of salvation; (3) the apostle's role in the economy of salvation; (4) the church in the economy of salvation; and (5) the believer in the economy of salvation.

God's Economy of Salvation

The Greek word *oikonomia* can refer to the responsibility for managing something, for example, the management of a household, or to something that has been arranged or managed, such as a plan. In Eph. 3:2 Paul uses the word in the former sense, when he reminds the recipients of the letter of his "stewardship" (NAB; "commission," NRSV) of God's grace that was given to him on their behalf. But in 1:10 and 3:9 he employs the word in the latter sense and speaks of God's "plan" in relationship to the mystery of his will. This plan of God is

---

35. Andrew T. Lincoln, "The Theology of Ephesians," in Lincoln and Wedderburn, *Theology of the Later Pauline Letters*, 75–166, here 79. Lincoln summarizes the purpose of the work in this way: "It attempts to renew its readers' sense of identity by reminding them of the privileges of the great salvation which they have experienced and of their place in the Church with its highly significant role in God's purpose for the cosmos as a whole. And it attempts this in order to produce the impetus for a renewed resolve to preserve the unity of the Church and to embody the distinctive ethical qualities of the new humanity they have become in Christ" (p. 86).

God's economy of salvation: the manner in which God arranged and determined, before the foundation of the world, how he would reconcile the world
to himself and effect salvation. This concept of a divine economy is akin to the
notion of salvation history, which is more prominent in Luke–Acts and the
nondisputed Pauline writings than it is in Colossians and Ephesians. But whether
one speaks of salvation history or of the divine economy of salvation, the concept refers to God's will, the plan God established in order to effect salvation.

Paul introduces this theme of God's economy in the opening verses of Ephesians (1:3–14), which are akin to a Jewish *berakah*: a thanksgiving blessing that
celebrates the blessings God has bestowed upon his people. In this case the blessing concerns the whole economy of God. The subject of the blessing is God the
Father, who has blessed the recipients of the letter with every spiritual blessing.
This God has made the mystery of his will known in Jesus Christ. Through
Christ the recipients of the letter have heard the word of truth, which is the
gospel of their salvation. Having believed in the gospel, they have been sealed
with the Holy Spirit, who is the pledge (*arrabōn*) of their salvation, an advance
payment for what will be delivered in full when all things are gathered in Christ.

If God is the subject of the blessing, the one from whom every spiritual
blessing comes, Christ is the agent of God's economy, the one in and through
whom God effects this economy of salvation. Paul repeatedly speaks of what
God has done "in" or "through" Christ. First, in Christ God blessed them and
chose them before the foundation of the world to be holy and blameless; and
through Christ, God destined them for adoption as his children (1:3–6). Second, in Christ they have redemption through his blood, the forgiveness of trespasses. In Christ God has made known the mystery of his will, a plan for the
fullness of time, to gather all things in Christ (1:7–10). Third, in Christ believers have obtained an inheritance in accordance with God's purpose, and in
Christ they have heard the gospel and been sealed with the Spirit, the pledge
of their inheritance (1:11–14).

The divine economy, then, begins with God's plan, finds its initial fulfillment in Christ's redemptive death, is presently experienced through the power
of the Spirit[36] (the pledge of their future inheritance), and will be brought to
completion when everything in heaven and on earth is gathered in and finds
its unity in Christ. Like the Colossians hymn, the benediction of Ephesians
outlines the major movements in God's economy of salvation. But whereas the
Colossians hymn is more christologically focused, emphasizing the work of the
Son in creation and redemption, the benediction of Ephesians is more theologically focused, emphasizing God's mystery, the divine economy of salvation
revealed in and through Christ.

---

36. Whereas there is only one reference to the Spirit in Colossians (1:8), there are several in
Ephesians (1:13; 2:18; 3:5, 16; 4:3, 4, 30; 5:18; 6:17, 18).

In a prayer that follows this benediction (1:15–23), Paul asks that the recipients of the letter be enlightened to know the hope to which they have been called and the greatness of God's power (1:18–19). God manifested this power in raising Christ from the dead, seating him at his right hand above every heavenly power, putting all things under his feet, and making him the head of the church, which is his body (1:20–23). This all-encompassing statement of Christ's exaltation recalls what Paul writes in 1 Cor. 15:28. But whereas 1 Corinthians speaks of all things being subjected to Christ in the future, Ephesians goes beyond 1 Corinthians in two ways. First, it says that God has already subjected all things under Christ's feet. Second, it affirms that God has made Christ "the head over all things for the church, which is his body, the fullness of him who fills all in all" (Eph. 1:22–23). In calling Christ "the head over all things," Ephesians goes beyond Colossians, which speaks of Christ as the head of the church but not of the cosmos. For Ephesians, Christ is the head over all things (*kephalē hyper panta*) for the sake of the church. The church, in turn, is his body, the fullness (*to plērōma*) of Christ, who fills all things. On the one hand, then, God has already subjected all things to Christ in fulfillment of Psalm 8 ("and he has put all things under his feet"); on the other, this subjection is still in the process of occurring because the church, the body of Christ, has not yet been brought to its full stature in Christ.

The manner in which Ephesians presents God's economy of salvation can be summarized as follows. In Christ, before the foundation of the world, God chose and elected those who now find themselves in the church. God effected this plan in Christ when he raised him from the dead and exalted him at his right hand, making him the head of all things for the benefit of the church. God's economy of salvation will be completed when all things are finally gathered in Christ, in the church. Ephesians' portrayal of the divine economy then is a subtle interplay of Christology and ecclesiology. On the one hand, the goal of God's economy is to gather all things in Christ; on the other, the church plays a vital role in this consummation since it is the body of Christ, the fullness of the one who is the head of all things. For Ephesians, to be in the church is to be in Christ, and to be in Christ is to be in the church.

Reconciliation in the Economy of Salvation

Discussion of an economy of salvation presupposes humanity's need to be reconciled to God. The benediction of Ephesians already hints at this when it speaks of the redemption that believers have through Christ's blood, but it is not until chapter 2 that Paul explains the former plight of the redeemed. He does this in two ways. First, he explains that once they were dead because of their trespasses and sins. Dead because of their trespasses, they were destined for wrath since they lived according to the passions of their flesh (2:1–3). Second, he reminds them that once they were without Christ, alienated from the commonwealth of Israel, strangers to the covenants with their promises, and so without God and without hope in the world (2:11–12). In a word, those who now find themselves in the church were once alienated from God and Israel.

The new situation of those who have been redeemed is also described in two ways. First, just as God exercised his power by raising Christ and seating him at his right hand, so the redeemed have been made alive with Christ, raised with him, and seated in the heavenly sphere with him.[37] Second, having been incorporated into the body of Christ, the church, they are no longer strangers and aliens but "members of the household of God" (2:19). Paul explains this twofold reconciliation with God and the commonwealth of Israel in two ways. First, believers have been saved by grace through faith. That is, their salvation is a gift from God (2:8). Second, Christ has reconciled Gentile and Jew to each other by breaking down the dividing wall that separated the two, thereby abolishing "the law with its commandments and ordinances" in order to create "one new humanity" (*kainon anthrōpon*), where formerly there was enmity between Gentile and Jew (2:15).

In some ways Ephesians 2 is a synopsis of Paul's theology in Romans. For example, Eph. 2:1–10 summarizes Paul's soteriology as presented in Romans 1–8, and Eph. 2:11–22 provides a synopsis of his theology of Israel developed in Romans 9–11. Ephesians, however, is not so much a summary of Paul's theology as it is a restatement of that theology for a new day. Instead of speaking of justification by faith apart from doing the works of the law, the author of Ephesians says believers are saved by grace through faith. Whereas Paul speaks of believers as already justified and reconciled but not yet saved (Rom. 5:9–10), the author of Ephesians speaks of them as already saved through God's grace (Eph. 2:8). These differences can be explained in light of the way in which the author of Ephesians understands God's divine economy and the new situation to which the letter responds. The author affirms that believers are raised with Christ and seated with him in the heavenly places, because he views the church as the body of Christ, who has been raised and exalted at God's right hand. Consequently, inasmuch as believers belong to the body of Christ, they already share in Christ's resurrection and exaltation, and they are saved, although the author is aware that believers have not yet received their final inheritance. Moreover, since the battles between Paul and his Judaizing opponents belong to the past, Paul's teaching must be updated for a new generation of Pauline Gentiles. What was once a debate about faith in Christ and the works of the Mosaic law is now interpreted in light of God's grace and human striving. A person is not saved by human effort but by the sheer grace of God.

---

37. This marks a development in the theology of Ephesians. For whereas Colossians affirms that believers have been raised up with Christ (Col. 3:1), Ephesians says they are raised up *and seated with Christ* in the heavenly places (2:6).

The teaching of Ephesians about the relationship between Gentiles and Jews is also updated for a new time. Whereas Paul sought to find continuity between historical Israel and his Gentile communities, the author of Ephesians speaks of the church as a new humanity in Christ, in which there is neither Gentile nor Jew. Whereas Paul writes that he upholds the law (Rom. 3:31), the author of Ephesians says that Christ has "abolished the law" with its commandments and ordinances (Eph. 2:15).[38] These new approaches to Israel and the law are the result of a different situation. Addressing a new generation of Gentile Christians, for whom the connection with historical Israel is beginning to fade, the author of Ephesians presents the church as a new entity in which Jew and Gentile are reconciled to God and to each other. Although this new understanding of the church emphasizes the unity of Gentile and Jew in Christ, it has the unfortunate consequence of severing the church's tie with historical Israel in a way that Romans 9–11 does not.

To summarize, reconciliation within God's economy of salvation is effected through the cross, the place where humanity is reconciled to God and where Jew and Gentile are reconciled to each other. Salvation is a matter of grace rather than human effort. The church is the place where this reconciliation is experienced. It is the new humanity that God is effecting in and through Christ.

The Apostle's Role in the Economy of Salvation

Paul's understanding of his apostleship plays a central role in his letters since the gospel he proclaims is rooted in the apostolic call he received when God revealed his Son to him. In Ephesians, however, there is a greater emphasis on the role that the apostle plays in mediating the mystery of God's economy of salvation to the Gentiles. Employing the same word he used in 1:10, when referring to the "plan" or "economy" of God, Paul writes that he has been given *tēn oikonomian tēs charitos tou theou* ("the stewardship of God's grace," 3:2, NAB). This stewardship refers to Paul's apostolic role in mediating the "economy" or "plan" (*oikonomia*) of God to the Gentiles, for whose sake he is suffering in prison.

As the steward of God's economy, Paul enjoys a unique understanding of "the mystery of Christ." In former generations this mystery was hidden, but now the Spirit has revealed it to the "holy apostles and prophets," among whom is Paul (3:5). In 2:20 Paul calls the apostles and prophets the foundation of the church, and in 4:11 apostles and prophets head the list of "gifts" that the exalted Christ gave the church to equip it for ministry. For Ephesians, however, Paul is the great apostle to the Gentiles who provides them with an apostolic link to an earlier generation. As one of the apostles to whom the mystery has been

---

38. Romans does, however, call Christ the *telos* ("goal" or "end") of the law (10:4).

revealed, he enjoys a special insight to God's plan that the recipients of the letter do not. It is his apostolic task to disclose this mystery to a new generation. In the closing of the letter, therefore, he asks the recipients to pray for him so that he can make known "the mystery of the gospel" (6:19), that is, the mystery of God's economy in Christ.

Paul has already spoken of this mystery in the great benediction that opens the letter, where he notes that the mystery of God's will, set forth in Christ, is to gather up all things, whether in heaven or on earth, in Christ (1:3–14). But his most explicit statement of the mystery is found in 3:6: "the Gentiles have become fellow heirs, members of the same body, and sharers in the promise in Christ Jesus through the gospel." Since it is by the proclamation of the gospel that this mystery is revealed, Paul can speak of "the mystery of the gospel" (6:19).

Paul is a servant of this gospel, and although it is his role to reveal the mystery to the saints, he presents himself as "the very least of all the saints" (3:8). Nevertheless, he has been given the grace to preach the riches of Christ to the Gentiles and "to make everyone see what is the plan (*oikonomia*) of the mystery hidden for ages in God who created all things" (3:9). In one of the most striking ecclesiological statements of the New Testament, Paul affirms that the wisdom of God is made known, *through the church*, "to the rulers and authorities in the heavenly places" (3:10). These rulers and authorities are malevolent forces (6:12), whom God has made subservient to Christ (1:21). The wisdom of God has been made known to them by the preaching of the gospel, which reveals God's hidden plan to reconcile Gentile and Jew in the church. Paul's role in God's economy of salvation, then, is cosmic in scope. In addition to revealing God's economy to the saints, his preaching makes the divine plan known, through the church, to the cosmic powers as well.

In Ephesians there is no need for Paul to defend his apostleship or the gospel he preaches. Paul has become the great apostle to the Gentiles, the one who mediates the mystery of Christ to the saints. His apostolic work is to assist others in comprehending God's divine economy in Christ. This focus on Paul's role in the mystery and economy of salvation is not entirely new. In 1 Cor. 2:7–8 Paul writes about the secret and hidden wisdom of God, which none of the rulers of this age understood. In 1 Cor. 4:1 he identifies himself and his fellow apostolic ministers as servants of Christ and stewards (*oikonomous*) of God's mysteries. But whereas in 1 Corinthians the mystery is the revelation of the wisdom of God in the crucified Christ, in Ephesians it is the economy of God's salvation that is manifested in the church, where all things are destined to be gathered in Christ. Although these two concepts of the mystery differ, they are not opposed to each other. In both letters the mystery ultimately concerns Christ. The new circumstances in which Ephesians was composed, however, focus the mystery more explicitly on the church as the place where God's redemptive work in Christ is seen.

The Church in the Economy of Salvation

For Ephesians the church is universal and cosmic in scope because it enjoys an intimate relationship with Christ, who is the head of all things and "fills all in all" (Eph. 1:23). But Christ is also the head of the church, which is his body, the sphere in which God's economy of salvation is presently at work. In Ephesians Paul employs the metaphor of the church as the body of Christ to explain God's economy of salvation in Christ and to exhort the recipients of the letter to live a life worthy of their calling.

Because the church is the body of Christ, it is the place where God's work of reconciliation in Christ is taking place. At one time Gentiles and Jews were at enmity with each other, but now they have been brought together in Christ. To explain how this occurred, Paul employs the imagery of the "dividing wall" that stood in the Jerusalem temple and prevented Gentiles from entering the inner courts of the temple. Identifying that wall with the law, Paul says that Christ broke down that dividing wall by abolishing the law with its commandments in order to create "one new humanity in place of the two" and so "reconcile both groups to God in one body through the cross" (2:15–16). As the body of Christ, the church is the one body in which Jew and Gentile have been reconciled with God, and with each other, through the blood of Christ.

Moving from the metaphor of the body to the metaphor of a building, Paul describes the church as "the household of God," which is built upon the foundation of the apostles and the prophets, to whom the mystery of Christ has been revealed (2:19–20).[39] Built up from this cornerstone, who is Christ, the whole edifice is joined together and growing into "a holy temple in the Lord" (Christ), thereby becoming a dwelling place for God. Understood as the body of Christ, the church is a place of peace and reconciliation for a divided humanity, a building that is being constructed in Christ as a dwelling place for God.

In 5:22–33 Paul employs the metaphor of the church to explain the intimate relationship that ought to characterize Christian marriage. Drawing an analogy between Christ and the church on the one hand, and husband and wife on the other, Paul argues that just as the church is subject to its head, who is Christ, so the wife should be subject to her head, who is her husband. But rather than employ this imagery to secure a dominant role for the husband, Paul reminds his audience of the way in which Christ loved and gave himself for the church in order to present the church to himself as his spotless bride. Consequently, just as Christ, who is the head of the church, loves the church

---

39. Whereas Ephesians speaks of "the household of God" as being built on the foundation of the apostles and prophets, with Christ being the cornerstone (Eph. 2:19–20), in 1 Corinthians Paul says that, "like a skilled master builder" (3:10), he laid a foundation, and "that foundation is Jesus Christ" (3:11). Although there is a tension between the two metaphors, they are not mutually exclusive. In both Christ, not the apostle, is the essential component of the building.

as his own body, so the husband, who is the head of the wife, should love his wife as his own body. At the conclusion of this comparison, Paul recalls the text of Genesis, "For this reason a man will leave his father and mother and be joined to his wife, and the two will become one flesh" (Eph. 5:31, quoting Gen. 2:24). He then concludes, "This is a great mystery, and I am applying it to Christ and the church" (Eph. 5:32). The original mystery is the profound union whereby a man leaves his family to be joined with a woman. Without denying this enduring mystery, Paul applies the text of Genesis to the more profound union of Christ and his church. Just as one can never fully understand the mystery of marriage by which man and woman become one flesh, so one can never fully comprehend the mystery of Christ and the church whereby the church is united to Christ.

To summarize, the church is cosmic and universal in scope because it is one with Christ. It is the place where Gentile and Jew are transformed into a new humanity. Ultimately, however, the church is a mystery within the economy of God's salvation. The primacy of place that Ephesians gives to the church goes beyond the ecclesiology of Paul's nondisputed correspondence, which focuses on the local church. The ecclesiology of Ephesians, however, is not wholly unrelated to that of Paul's nondisputed correspondence. The marriage metaphor of Ephesians 5, for example, can be related to Paul's statement in 2 Cor. 11:2, where he tells the Corinthians, "for I promised you in marriage to one husband, to present you as a chaste virgin to Christ." Paul's references to "the church of God" (1 Cor. 1:2; 10:32; 11:16, 22; 15:9; 2 Cor. 1:1; Gal. 1:13; 1 Thess. 2:14) and "the body of Christ" (1 Corinthians 12 and Romans 12) can be seen as the seedbed for an understanding of the church that includes but goes beyond the local community.

The Believer in the Economy of Salvation

Like Colossians, Ephesians draws an intimate connection between the indicative of salvation and the moral imperative. But whereas the moral indicative of Colossians is rooted in the believer's union with Christ's death and resurrection through baptism, the moral indicative of Ephesians is grounded in the new humanity that the believer has been granted within the sphere of the church.

Paul develops this "ecclesial ethic" at the beginning of his moral exhortation, when he calls upon the recipients of the letter to lead a life worthy of the calling to which they have been called by maintaining "the unity of the Spirit and the bond of peace" (Eph. 4:1–3). The motivation for preserving this unity is sevenfold: there is one body (the church), one Spirit, one hope, one Lord, one faith, one baptism, one God and Father (4:4–6). This list emphasizes the unity in God's economy of salvation, which is presently being worked out within the sphere of the church. Next, Paul explains that the gifts ("that some would be apostles, some prophets, some evangelists, some pastors and teachers"), which Christ bestowed upon the church when he ascended on high, were given to equip the saints for the work of ministry, "for building up the body of Christ" (4:12). As the body is built up, the members of the church come to maturity, "the full stature of Christ" (4:13), who is the head of the body.

Ephesians presents its vision of the moral life in light of its ecclesiology. Since there is only one body, the body of Christ that is the church, the overriding moral imperative is to maintain the unity of the church so that all will be built up into the head of the church, who is Christ. Ephesians supplements this ecclesial exhortation with specific moral exhortations in 4:17–32. Because the recipients of the letter (themselves Gentiles) have become part of the new humanity in the church, they must no longer live as the Gentiles do (4:17). They must put away their old self (*ton palaion anthrōpon*, 4:22) and clothe themselves with the new self (*ton kainon anthrōpon*) "created according to the likeness of God in true righteousness and holiness" (4:24). The language of Ephesians recalls Paul's Adam Christology, but whereas the Adam Christology of 1 Corinthians 15 and Romans 5 is rooted in Christ's death and resurrection, the Adam Christology of Ephesians comes from its understanding of the church as the place where a new humanity is being formed.

For Ephesians, those who are engaged in the moral life must remember who they are so that they can live in a way that accords with their new status in the body of Christ. They must not lie to one another, because they are "members of one another" (4:25). They must not grieve the Holy Spirit, because they were sealed with the Spirit for the day of redemption (4:30). They must imitate God, because they are God's beloved children (5:1). They must live in love, because Christ gave himself for them (5:2). Once they were darkness, but now they are light, therefore they must live as children of the light (5:8). Since they have been taken up into the body of Christ, their moral life is a struggle with cosmic powers and spiritual forces (6:12). It cannot be lived without taking up "the whole armor of God" (6:13).

The moral teaching of Ephesians does not speak of "fulfilling the law" through the love commandment. Nor does Ephesians take up the question of the law in the way that Romans and Galatians do. But the moral teaching that it proposes is similar to that of the nondisputed Pauline correspondence in several ways. It warns people not to engage in immoral behavior. It exhorts them to set aside their old way of life in order to pursue a new life in Christ. It calls upon them to build up and maintain the unity of the church. Most importantly, Ephesians draws an intimate relationship between the moral imperative and the indicative of salvation.

CONCLUSION: COLOSSIANS AND EPHESIANS
IN THE PAULINE TRADITION

Colossians and Ephesians provide a good test case for the diverse unity of the New Testament. On the one hand, they share a number of themes with Paul's theology, as seen in the nondisputed Pauline correspondence. On the other, they introduce new themes that go beyond Paul's theology, thereby establishing a Pauline tradition.

Overall, Colossians and Ephesians agree with the main lines of Paul's theology. For example, they agree upon the centrality of the Christ event in God's economy of salvation, and they draw an intimate connection between the indicative of salvation in Christ and the moral imperative of new life in Christ. They describe the former predicament of the redeemed in terms of sin and alienation from God, and they celebrate redemption as new life with Christ in the community of the church. The cross remains the place where salvation was won, and the resurrection continues to be viewed as the source of new life. The heavenly inheritance may already be in heaven, but it has not yet been fully attained.

Colossians and Ephesians, however, develop Paul's Christology, soteriology, ecclesiology, and eschatology in new ways. In terms of Christology and soteriology, there is a greater emphasis on the exaltation of Christ than there is on the cross of Christ. Christ is now portrayed as a cosmic figure whose redemptive work reconciles all things, in heaven as well as on earth, with God. Most importantly, Colossians and Ephesians portray Christ as the head of the church, which they present as universal and cosmic in scope because it is the body of the cosmic Christ. Consequently, the church plays a more central role in these letters as the place where a new humanity is taking form in Christ. In terms of eschatology, the emphasis is on the hope that believers have "above," in the heavenly places, where they have already been raised up with Christ in baptism, whereas the nondisputed Pauline letters focus on the parousia and the general resurrection of the dead as the consummation of all things. Colossians and Ephesians have not collapsed the future into the present, as if the fullness of salvation has already arrived. They are still aware that the final consummation has not yet taken place but, instead of employing temporal imagery, they have begun to speak of the consummation of all things in terms of what is below and what is above.

These developments of Paul's theology are, in part, the result of the new situation Colossians and Ephesians faced. Whereas Paul found it necessary to defend his law-free gospel against a Judaizing form of Christianity, the authors of Colossians and Ephesians did not. Whereas the question of Israel's destiny and the role of the Mosaic law weighed heavily upon Paul, these were no longer central issues for his disciples. The challenges facing a new generation of Paulinists concerned the role of Christ and the church in a Gentile world, where cosmic powers and forces played a central role in people's lives. In response to this different situation, Paul's followers applied their master's thought to a new day.

8

A Theology of the Pauline Tradition

The Pastoral Epistles

The Pastoral Epistles (1 and 2 Timothy, Titus), which most scholars classify as pseudonymous, form a distinctive group of writings within the Pauline corpus.[1] Addressed to two of Paul's delegates rather than to a particular community of believers, they instruct Timothy and Titus to combat false teaching, to preserve the sound teaching that has been entrusted to them, and to establish order within the church, which is the household of God. It is not surprising then that these letters are often viewed as manuals for pastors charged with the responsibility of maintaining church order and preserving the "deposit of faith."[2]

Frequently measured against the theology of the nondisputed Pauline letters, the Pastoral Epistles have often been seen as a falling away from Paul's apocalyptic theology and as manifestations of early Catholicism. Recent discussion of these letters, however, has been more concerned to understand their theology on its own terms in light of the new situation they address. By studying the theology of these letters on their own terms, scholars have been able to see how one segment of the church preserved the memory of Paul and his theology for a new day.[3]

---

1. Schnelle (*New Testament Writings*, 328–32) presents four reasons why most scholars view the Pastorals as pseudonymous: (1) they presuppose a historical situation that cannot be harmonized with the data of Acts or of the nondisputed Pauline letters; (2) they reflect the problems of a third Christian generation; (3) they manifest distinctive linguistic features; (4) they present a considerably different theology from the nondisputed Pauline letters, lacking important concepts such as the righteousness of God, freedom, the cross, Son of God, the body of Christ. This last point will become more apparent in the development of this chapter.

2. The expression "the deposit of faith" refers to what 1 Tim. 6:20 and 2 Tim. 1:14 call the *parathēkē* (Latin *depositum*). Although the precise content of this deposit is never explained, it appears to be the Pauline gospel as found in the Pastorals, which is presented in terms of an epiphany theology.

3. Authors who have dealt with the Pastorals on their own terms are Lewis R. Donelson, *Pseudepigraphy and Ethical Argument in the Pastoral Epistles* (HUT 22; Tübingen: Mohr [Siebeck], 1986); Philip H. Towner, *The Goal of Our Instruction: The Structure of Theology and Ethics in the Pastoral Epistles* (JSNTSup 34; Sheffield: JSOT Press, 1989); Francis Young, *The Theology of the Pastoral Epistles* (NTT; Cambridge; Cambridge University Press, 1994).

In light of this newer approach, it has become apparent that the Pastorals manifest a coherent theology that addresses an important issue: how can the church faithfully maintain the deposit of faith it has received from the great apostle and his delegates, Timothy and Titus, in the face of false teaching that distorts the gospel? The answer of the Pastorals is that the church must preserve what it has received from Paul and his delegates and entrust it to faithful witnesses who, in turn, will hand on what has been entrusted to them to faithful witnesses who must do the same. Inasmuch as the Pastorals seek to preserve the authentic Pauline tradition by designating faithful witnesses who can be trusted to hand on what has been received from Paul, they establish something akin to a line of succession that can be traced to Paul and his delegates and can assure the church that its faith is rooted in the deposit of faith it has received from Paul and his delegates.

The theological framework of the Pastoral Epistles is determined by their objective, which is to preserve and hand on the Pauline tradition to future generations. Consequently, the persons of Paul, Timothy, and Titus play a central role in these letters. By reminding the church that it has received its faith from Paul and his delegates, the Pastorals assure the church that it is the recipient of sound teaching that leads to salvation and good works. Moreover, the presentation of Paul, Timothy, and Titus within these letters provides church leaders with models of teachers and preachers whom they should emulate. Establishing order in the church, then, plays a central role in the Pastorals, which view the world and the church in an unabashedly hierarchical way. There is one God who wills the salvation of all, and one mediator between God and humanity, Jesus Christ, through whom the savior God has manifested himself. The church is the household of God, and within this household the *episkopos* ("bishop," "overseer") is God's chief steward entrusted with the deposit of faith. There are also *diakonoi* ("deacons," "servants") and *presbyteroi* ("presbyters," "elders") within the household of God who preserve the rich deposit of faith entrusted to the church, just as Timothy and Titus taught and handed on what Paul entrusted to them.

As noted above, most scholars view the Pastorals as pseudonymous, arguing that they were written by a later Paulinist in response to a heterodox teaching, the precise contours of which is debated.[4] In the face of this teaching, which the Pastorals characterize as inordinately concerned with myths,

---

4. Although it is debatable as to whether there is only one author behind the Pastorals, in this chapter I treat the Pastorals as having been written by one author. As regards the false teaching, Schnelle (*New Testament Writings*, 342) characterizes it as an early form of Christian Gnosticism. James A. Aageson ("The Pastoral Epistles, Apostolic Authority, and the Development of the Pauline Scriptures," in *The Pauline Canon* [ed. Stanley E. Porter; Leiden: Brill, 2004], 5–26) argues that the more likely explanation, on the narrative level of the text, is that the false teaching has to do with "the misapplication of the Jewish law" (p. 9).

genealogies, asceticism, and the Jewish law, the author of the Pastorals juxtaposes the sound teaching that the church has received from Paul and his delegates. In doing so, the author establishes a narrative world according to which
Paul writes to Timothy and Titus in order to protect the church from false
teaching. But if Paul was not the author of these letters, it is unlikely that Timothy and Titus were their original recipients. Written in the name of Paul and
addressed to Timothy and Titus, they were intended for church leaders of a
later generation. Thus, even though the great apostle has died, he continues
to instruct the church of a later period, which must deal with a crisis that Paul
foresaw and of which he warned Timothy and Titus long ago, when he told
them what would happen "in the last days."

The pseudonymous nature of these letters, which is often disturbing to
modern readers, need not be viewed as a liability for New Testament theology. For inasmuch as the Pastorals insist that Paul's teaching is foundational
for the church's faith, they initiate a process that will eventually view Paul's letters as Scripture, normative for the life of the church.[5] In handing on Paul's
teaching, however, the Pastorals also interpret it. Consequently, although they
purport to preserve Paul's teaching just as they received it, they are adapting
that teaching in the way that Paul interpreted and adapted his own teaching
to new circumstances.[6]

Although the Pastorals form a distinct unit within the Pauline corpus, they
present their theology in slightly different ways, and they differ in genre from
one another.[7] For example, whereas 1 Timothy and Titus can be viewed as manuals for establishing order in the churches of Ephesus and Crete, respectively,
2 Timothy functions as Paul's final testament to remind Timothy of Paul's past,
exhort him to suffer for the gospel in the present, and warn him of what will
happen in the last days, after Paul has departed. Despite these differences, the
Pastorals assume a theological framework that can be summarized as follows.
The grace and mercy of God, who is Savior, has appeared in the epiphany of
Christ Jesus to save all. Through the mercy of Christ Jesus, Paul has been
entrusted with this gospel of salvation, which he has entrusted to Timothy and
Titus. Timothy and Titus are to hand on what Paul has entrusted to them by
teaching sound doctrine, rebuking false teachers, and designating others to
guide the church, which is the household of God. Sound teaching, which is
rooted in the gospel of salvation, trains and enables those within the household

---

5. This point is made by Aageson, "Pastoral Epistles."

6. For example, in 1 Corinthians Paul weds the election theology of 1 Thessalonians to a theology of the cross because the Corinthians have embraced something akin to a realized eschatology, and in Romans he modifies the harsh critique of the law that he made in Galatians because
he must now deal with objections that his gospel has no place for the law and the election of Israel.

7. For example, the Letter to Titus tends to focus on Jesus as Savior, whereas 2 Timothy
focuses on Jesus as Lord.

of God to do good works. In this chapter I present the theology of the Pastorals under the following headings: (1) the epiphany of God in the epiphany of Christ Jesus; (2) preserving sound teaching: Paul and his delegates; (3) the church as the household of God; and (4) trained for good works.

THE EPIPHANY OF GOD IN THE EPIPHANY OF CHRIST JESUS

Although the primary concern of the Pastorals is to preserve and hand on the deposit of faith within the household of God, this ecclesiological concern is set within a larger theological framework of salvation that can be summarized in the phrase, "the epiphany of God in the epiphany of Christ Jesus."[8] Without this epiphany there would be no salvation, and without salvation there would be no deposit of faith or need for the church. Before we turn to the ecclesial concerns of the Pastorals, therefore, it will be helpful to summarize this theology of salvation in light of the epiphany of God in the epiphany of Christ Jesus.

According to the Pastorals, there are two epiphanies. The first is the appearance of God's grace and mercy in Jesus Christ, which offers salvation to all. This grace trains those who embrace it to renounce their former way of life in order to live lives marked by self-control, uprightness, and godliness (Titus 2:11–12). In this epiphany God manifested his goodness and loving-kindness, and the faithful were saved according to God's mercy, through the waters of baptism and the renewal of the Holy Spirit, not because of any works of righteousness they performed (Titus 3:4–5). God's grace and mercy then were revealed through the epiphany of Christ Jesus, the Savior. This epiphany of God in Jesus Christ, "who abolished death and brought life and immortality to light through the gospel" (2 Tim. 1:10), was not limited to a particular moment in the life of Jesus but was evident in the entire earthly career of Christ Jesus, who came into the world to save sinners (1 Tim. 1:15). This "mystery of our religion" is dramatically summarized in the hymnlike passage of 1 Tim. 3:16:

> He was revealed in flesh,
>   vindicated in spirit,
>   seen by angels,
> proclaimed among Gentiles,
>   believed in throughout the world,
>   taken up in glory.

8. The Greek term *epiphaneia* can be translated as "manifestation" or "appearance." In this chapter, I usually translate it as "epiphany." The noun occurs only six times in the New Testament (2 Thess. 2:8; 1 Tim. 6:14; 2 Tim. 1:10; 4:1, 8; Titus 2:13). In every instance, except 2 Tim. 1:10, it refers to the parousia. The use of *epiphaneia* places greater emphasis on the appearance or manifestation of Christ as a deity.

The passage does not focus on the event of Christ's death and resurrection, although this saving event is surely in view in the phrase "vindicated in spirit." Rather, the emphasis is on the earthly appearance of the one who was revealed in the flesh and then taken up in glory.

The second appearance or manifestation (*epiphaneia*) of Christ will occur at the end of the ages, what Paul normally refers to as the parousia. But whereas Paul coordinates the parousia with the general resurrection of the dead, the Pastorals tend to relate this second epiphany to the last judgment. It is at this epiphany that God will vindicate the elect. Therefore, Timothy must keep the commandment "without spot or blame until the manifestation of our Lord Jesus Christ," which God will bring about "at the right time" (1 Tim. 6:14–15). In view of this coming epiphany, when Jesus Christ will judge the living and the dead, Timothy must proclaim the message he has received from Paul (2 Tim. 4:1–2). Aware that his own death is at hand, Paul looks forward to this epiphany because the Lord will grant him and all who long for the Lord's "appearing" the crown of righteousness (2 Tim. 4:8). This epiphany will be "the manifestation of the glory of our great God and Savior, Jesus Christ" (Titus 2:13).[9]

In addition to these comments about the epiphany of God that has occurred in the epiphany of Christ, the Pastorals make a number of statements about God and Christ that are central to their theological vision. God is described as "the King of the ages, immortal, invisible, the only God" (1 Tim. 1:17), whom "no one has ever seen or can see" (6:16). This living God is the Savior of all people, especially those who believe (4:10). Therefore, God wants everyone "to be saved and to come to the knowledge of the truth" (2:4). But since God cannot be seen, there is need for a mediator. This mediator is Christ Jesus, who once stood before Pontius Pilate (6:13) and "gave himself as a ransom for all" (2:6). Since Christ Jesus abolished death and brought life, those who die with him will live with him, and those who endure with him will reign with him (2 Tim. 2:11–12).[10]

The Pastorals insist that the elect were called according to God's purpose and grace rather than according to their works, in a plan that was given in Christ Jesus "before the ages began" (2 Tim. 1:9). They are aware that Jesus Christ was a descendant of David (2 Tim. 2:8), but they do not focus on his royal mes-

---

9. The text of Titus 2:13 can be construed as referring to Jesus who is God and Savior, or to God, and to Jesus who is Savior. The NAB translates the text in the second way, "as we await the blessed hope, the appearance of the glory of the great God and of our savior Jesus Christ," whereas the NRSV translates the text in the first way, "while we wait for the blessed hope and the manifestation of the glory of our great God and Savior, Jesus Christ." Although it is unusual for the New Testament to call Jesus "God" (but see Rom. 9:5), that seems to be the sense here since the text has only one epiphany in view, the epiphany of Jesus. Because this epiphany is the manifestation of God's power, the epiphany of Jesus is the epiphany of God, allowing Jesus to be called God.

10. This statement is the closest the Pastorals come to speaking of the believer's personal union with Christ.

siahship. The frequent use of "Christ Jesus," however, may be their way of highlighting Jesus' messianic credentials.[11] More important for the Pastorals is the *kyrios* title, which occurs frequently in 1 and 2 Timothy but never in Titus.[12] For Titus the most important title is "Savior," which it applied to both Jesus and God (Titus 1:3, 4; 2:10, 13; 3:4, 6), thereby showing the close and intimate relationship that exists between the savior God and the one who bears the title "Savior." In Titus 2:13 Jesus is called "our great God and Savior" because "the goodness and loving kindness of God our Savior" (3:4) has made its appearance in him. For the Pastorals, the epiphany of Jesus, who is Savior, is the epiphany of the unseen Savior God, the manifestation of God's grace.

The Pastorals are aware of the full sweep of the Christ story: Jesus' Davidic origin, passion, death, resurrection, ascension, and parousia. But they never speak of the saving event of Christ's death and resurrection in quite the same way that Paul does. Nor do they highlight the cross as the place where God paradoxically manifested his wisdom and power and reconciled the world to himself. Building on the Pauline tradition they received, the Pastorals focus their attention on the epiphany of God's salvation that occurred in the appearance of Christ Jesus. This salvation, which occurred in that epiphany, is the fundamental content of the glorious gospel God entrusts to Paul, and that Paul has now entrusted to his delegates. It is this gospel that must be preserved by sound teaching.

PRESERVING SOUND TEACHING: PAUL AND HIS DELEGATES

Because the glorious gospel entrusted to Paul is a gospel of salvation that trains its adherents to live a godly life, it is vital for the church to preserve and hand on the gospel that was entrusted to Paul, and that he entrusted to Timothy and Titus. To achieve this goal, the Pastorals present Paul, Timothy, and Titus as model church leaders from whom later generations can learn. Consequently, just as imitation plays an important role in the nondisputed Pauline correspondence, so it plays a vital role in the Pastorals. But whereas Paul presents himself to his converts as a model of someone who embodies the gospel he preaches, the Pastorals present Paul, Timothy, and Titus as models for those who will function as *episkopoi*, *diakonoi*, and *presbyteroi* in the household of God. By imitating the example of Paul and his delegates, those who follow them will be able to guard and hand on the rich deposit of faith they have received.

11. The name Christ Jesus occurs frequently in 1 and 2 Timothy, only once in Titus (1 Tim. 1:1, 2, 12, 14, 15, 16; 2:5; 3:13; 4:6; 5:21; 6:13; 2 Tim. 1:1, 2, 9, 10, 13; 2:1, 3, 10; 3:12, 15; 4:1; Titus 1:4).

12. For the occurrences of *kyrios*, see 1 Tim. 1:2, 12, 14; 6:3, 14, 15; 2 Tim. 1:2, 8, 16, 18; 2:7, 19, 22, 24; 3:11; 4:8, 14, 17, 18; 4:22.

First Timothy presupposes that Paul, who has left for Macedonia, has asked Timothy to remain in Ephesus in order to instruct certain people not to teach in a different or divisive way (*heterodidaskalein*, 1:3).[13] Paul hopes to return soon, but since he may be delayed, he writes so that Timothy will know how one should behave in the household of God, which is the church (3:14–15). During the period of Paul's absence, Timothy is to occupy himself with the public reading of Scripture, with exhortation, and with teaching (4:13).[14] Most importantly, he is to guard what Paul has entrusted to him (Greek: *tēn parathēkēn*; Latin: *depositum*; 6:20). What Paul has entrusted to Timothy is "the glorious gospel of the blessed God" that was entrusted to him (1:11), and for which he was appointed a herald, an apostle, and a teacher of the Gentiles (2:7).[15] Previous to this, Paul was a blasphemer, a persecutor of the church, a violent man. In his own estimation, he was the foremost of sinners.[16] But Jesus Christ treated him mercifully, making Paul an example of the gospel that he would proclaim: that Jesus Christ came into the world to save sinners (1:13–16). Paul's self-description in 1 Timothy functions in two ways. First, it establishes that the gospel entrusted to Timothy is the same gospel God entrusted to Paul. Second, it presents Paul as the premier example of how Jesus Christ extends grace and mercy to sinners.

Whereas Paul was appointed herald, apostle, and teacher of the Gentiles through his call, Timothy was appointed to his ministry when a council of elders laid hands upon him. This "ordination" was a gift (*charismatos*, 4:14) of the Spirit inasmuch as it was the outcome of prophetic utterances that pointed to Timothy as the one to be ordained (1:18; 4:14).[17] Timothy's office is not given a specific name. He is not called a herald or apostle as Paul is, nor is he identified as a bishop or elder, although it is clear that he ordains others to

---

13. This is an example of how the historical situation presupposed by the Pastoral does not fit what is known from Acts or Paul's own letters since there is no indication in either Paul's own letters or Acts that Paul left Timothy in Ephesus when he went on to Macedonia.

14. Teaching plays an important role in the Pastorals, much more so than it does in Paul's own letters. This is apparent from the extensive vocabulary in the Pastorals dealing with teaching: *didaktikos* ("taught, instructed, imparted"; 1 Tim. 3:2; 2 Tim. 2:24), *didaskalia* ("teaching, instruction"; 1 Tim. 1:10; 4:1, 6, 13, 16; 5:17; 6:1, 3; 2 Tim. 3:10, 16; 4:3; Titus 1:9; 2:1, 7, 10), *didaskalos* ("teacher"; 1 Tim. 2:7; 2 Tim. 4:3), *didaskō* ("to teach, to instruct"; 1 Tim. 2:12; 4:11; 6:2; 2 Tim. 2:2; Titus 1:11), *didachē* ("teaching"; 2 Tim. 4:2; Titus 1:9).

15. Although Paul regularly identifies himself as an apostle in the nondisputed letters, he never calls himself "herald" or "teacher."

16. In Phil. 3:6 Paul writes that he was blameless as to righteousness under the law. Here the pastoral Paul is looking back at his former life in light of his call or conversion.

17. The use of "ordination" here is not exactly accurate since the text of 1 Tim. 4:14 speaks of the laying on of hands. But it was this rite of the laying on of hands that eventually developed into the ordination ceremonies whereby certain members of the community were designated for service to the church. On this topic see Joseph A. Fitzmyer, "The Structured Ministry of the Church in the Pastoral Epistles," *CBQ* 66 (2004): 582–96.

these offices (5:22), and that he is charged with teaching sound doctrine.[18] On the one hand, Timothy is intended to be a model for all bishops, deacons, and elders. On the other, he stands in a unique relationship to Paul because the gospel he has received was directly entrusted to him by the great apostle.

As an immediate successor to Paul, Timothy's first and most important task is to preserve the teaching that Paul entrusted to him. He is to combat false teaching, instruct those within the household of God, and appoint others, who will act as bishops, deacons, and elders within the church. If Timothy does these things, he will be a "good servant" (*kalos diakonos*) of Jesus Christ (4:6).

In 2 Timothy Paul's circumstances have changed dramatically. He is now a prisoner in Rome, where he suffers like a common criminal for the sake of the gospel (2:8–9). Everyone in Asia, except the household of Onesiphorus, has abandoned him (1:15–18) and, at his first defense, no one came to his support (4:16). Paul longs to see Timothy, whose faith he commends (1:4–5). The great apostle is keenly aware that his death is imminent (4:6), and he urges Timothy, who is apparently still in Ephesus, to come to him soon (4:9). Second Timothy functions as Paul's farewell testament. It reminds Timothy of what Paul told him in the past, encourages him to suffer for the gospel, and tells Timothy what will happen in the last days when Paul will no longer be present to the church.

Paul again identifies himself as one appointed to be a herald, apostle, and teacher for the gospel (1:11). He has fought the good fight, finished the race, kept the faith, and now waits for the crown of righteousness, which the Lord will give to him on the day of his appearing (4:7–8), the parousia. Aware that he is about to be put to death, Paul is eager to ensure that what he handed on to Timothy, Timothy will entrust to faithful witnesses (2:1–2). Therefore, he encourages Timothy to rekindle the gift of his ordination, reminding him that he himself laid hands upon him (1:6).[19] He admonishes him not to be ashamed of his testimony to Christ, or of Paul, but to join in suffering for the gospel (1:8), since all who want to live a godly life will be persecuted (3:12). Timothy is to maintain the "sound teaching" he received from Paul and the "good treasure" (*kalēn parathēkēn*) Paul entrusted to him (1:13–14). As Paul's delegate, he must entrust to faithful witnesses what he has heard from Paul so that they will be able to teach others as well (2:2), thereby establishing a tradition of sound teaching that can be traced to Paul himself. Timothy is in a privileged position to do

18. In 1 Tim. 4:6 Timothy is called "a good servant of Jesus Christ," and in 2 Tim. 4:5 "an evangelist."

19. Whereas in 2 Timothy Paul says that he was the one who ordained Timothy, in 1 Tim. 4:14 he writes that the council of elders laid hands upon Timothy. The tension between the two texts can be resolved in light of their genre. In 2 Timothy Paul reminds Timothy of the close bond that exists between them; therefore he says that he was the one who ordained Timothy, perhaps along with the council of elders to whom he refers in 1 Timothy.

this because he has observed Paul's teaching, his conduct, his aim in life, his faith, his patience, his love, his steadfastness, and the persecutions he suffered in Antioch, Iconium, and Lystra (3:10–11).[20] Timothy is a reliable witness and teacher because he knows the one from whom he received the rich deposit of faith (3:14). But Paul warns him that "in the last days" (3:1) people will no longer abide sound doctrine. Therefore, he must do the work of an evangelist and fulfill his ministry (4:3–5).

Whereas Paul presents Timothy with a number of practical guidelines for ordering the life of the church in 1 Timothy, in 2 Timothy he focuses his attention on his personal relationship to Timothy and urges him to join him in suffering for the gospel (1:8). Instead of being ashamed of the gospel, Timothy must join Paul in suffering for it "like a good soldier of Christ Jesus" (2:3). He must rekindle the gift of his ordination, which he received when Paul imposed hands upon him, and he must remember that it was Paul who entrusted him with the deposit of faith. This emphasis on the personal relationship between Paul and Timothy assures the audience of the Pastorals that they have inherited the faith that Paul entrusted to Timothy, and that Timothy entrusted to others. Most importantly, this point reminds the audience, especially the church's officeholders, that they must join Paul and Timothy in suffering for the gospel.

Paul's letter to Titus presupposes a situation similar to the one described in 1 Timothy. Paul, who is still free, has left Titus on the island of Crete in order to put in order what still needs to be done. To accomplish his task, Titus must appoint elders/bishops in every town. As in Ephesus, the church on the island of Crete is threatened by false teaching. Therefore, Titus must "teach what is consistent with sound doctrine" (2:1), and he must be a model of good works so that he can encourage others to be rich in good works, which have been made possible by the grace of God. Once Titus has completed this task, he is to meet Paul at Nicopolis, where the apostle will spend the winter.

While repeating many of the themes found in 1 and 2 Timothy, especially the need to appoint others who will oversee the church and to teach sound doctrine, the Letter to Titus emphasizes the need for Titus to be a model of good works so that he can call others to do the same. This emphasis on good works is related to the letter's overall theme that Jesus Christ has redeemed believers from iniquity in order to prepare "a people of his own who are zealous for good deeds" (2:14). The presbyter-bishop, therefore, of which Titus is a prototype (although there is no reference to his ordination as there is to Tim-

---

20. These sufferings seem to refer to Paul's first missionary journey, as mentioned in Acts, but Barnabas, not Timothy, was Paul's companion on that journey. However, Timothy did accompany Paul on his second missionary journey, when Paul revisited these cities (see Acts 15:36–16:5). But Acts does not record the persecutions mentioned here. This is another example of how difficult it is to coordinate the information in Acts and Paul's own writings with the situation presupposed in the Pastorals.

othy's ordination), must be a model of good works, a man whose words are sound and whose teaching is marked by integrity and gravity (2:7).

By reminding their audiences of the foundational relationship between Paul and his delegates, the Pastorals establish a line of succession that reaches back to the great apostle. This unbroken line assures believers that the teaching they have received is sound since Timothy and Titus have handed on to faithful witnesses what they received from Paul: the deposit of faith that is the glorious gospel of God. To summarize, the narrative world of the Pastorals presupposes a community of faith in which particular individuals have been designated to preserve, teach, and hand on the deposit of faith.

THE CHURCH AS THE HOUSEHOLD OF GOD

The ecclesiology of the Pastorals is both traditional and innovative. On the one hand, the Pastorals continue to make use of rather traditional Pauline terminology in their description of those who belong to the church. The members of the church are still referred to as "the saints" (1 Tim. 5:10) and "the elect" (2 Tim. 2:10; Titus 1:1). They are those who believe (1 Tim. 4:3, 10) and know the truth (1 Tim. 4:3). They are a people for whom Jesus Christ gave himself so that he might redeem them from "all iniquity and purify for himself a people of his own who are zealous for good deeds" (Titus 2:14). On the other hand, the Pastorals begin to view the church as a great household, which they identify as the household of God (1 Tim. 3:5, 15). As the household of God, the church belongs to God. It is "the church of the living God, the pillar and bulwark of the truth" (3:15), which has been entrusted with the mystery of the one revealed in the flesh, vindicated in spirit, seen by angels, proclaimed among the Gentiles, believed in throughout the world, and taken up in glory (3:16). Because the church has been entrusted with this mystery, it is "God's firm foundation," which bears two inscriptions: (1) the Lord knows his own, and (2) those who call upon the name of the Lord must turn away from wickedness (2 Tim. 2:19).[21]

This use of household imagery to describe the church is both traditional and innovative. It is traditional inasmuch as the Pauline churches were house churches, small communities of believers who gathered in the homes of local patrons. It is not surprising, then, that the metaphor of the household should be applied to the church. What is surprising is the thoroughgoing manner in

---

21. The first inscription comes from LXX Num. 16:5 (the story of the rebellion of Korah), whereas the second appears to be a combination of Sir. 17:26 and Isa. 26:13. The first of these two inscriptions draws a comparison between the present rebellion and the rebellion of Korah, reminding the audience of the Pastorals that God knows who belongs to the church. The second is a warning to the members of the church to avoid the evil of this false teaching.

which the Pastorals employ this metaphor. For in addition to calling the church the household of God, they view the order and management of the church as if it were a large household supervised by stewards and serviced by slaves. Moreover, inasmuch as each community is the household of God, all of the communities that constitute the church belong to the great household of God. In this regard, there is an interesting analogy between the Pastorals on the one hand, and Colossians and Ephesians on the other. For just as Colossians and Ephesians applied the Pauline metaphor of the body in a way that referred to the universal church, so the Pastorals have begun to apply the metaphor of the household in a way that has the whole church in view.

The metaphor of the household guides the way in which the Pastorals view the structure and order of the church. For if the church is the household of God, then it must be structured as an orderly household in which all the members know their place and play their role. The Pastorals are especially concerned about good order in the church because the communities they have in view have been infiltrated by false teachers who are disrupting the faith.[22] If the church is to function as the household of God, therefore, it requires stewards and servants who know how to manage the household of God.

In his first letter to Timothy, Paul provides his young delegate with a list of qualifications necessary for those who wish to serve as bishops (3:1–7) and deacons (3:8–13) in the household of God. The bishop must be above reproach, married only once, an apt teacher, a good manager of his own household, and well thought of by those outside the church. Deacons must be serious, hold fast to the mystery of the faith, be married only once, and be good managers of their households. In both lists, the emphasis is on the moral character of the officeholder and the ability to manage one's household well, indicating the central role that administration plays in both offices. That the bishop is referred to in the singular, whereas deacons are referred to in the plural, suggests that the bishop is the one primarily charged with overseeing the affairs of a particular community. Moreover, since the bishop must be an apt teacher, teaching seems to play a more important role in his ministry than in the ministry of the deacon. The reference to women, in the midst of the qualification for deacons (3:11), has often been interpreted as a reference to the wives of deacons. But it may be an indication that women too serve as deacons.[23]

Toward the end of this letter, Paul provides Timothy with guidelines for enrolling older women in what appears to be something akin to an order of widows, which is supported by the church (5:3–16). These women are distin-

---

22. There is no indication that the false teachers are outsiders. The Pastorals give the impression that they are members of the church who have gone astray.

23. If women served as deacons, their teaching role was probably limited to teaching other women (see Titus 2:3–5), since 1 Tim. 2:12 says that Paul does not permit a woman to teach or have authority over a man.

guished for their good works and their pledge not to remarry. Finally, Paul presents Timothy with guidelines for dealing with presbyters or elders (*presbyteroi*, 5:17–20), who apparently oversee the community. Given that Paul does not list any qualification for elders, and that not all of the elders labor at the task of preaching and teaching,[24] Paul may simply be referring to the elder male members of the community, some of whom preach and teach because of the wisdom they have acquired through age.

The picture that emerges from 1 Timothy can be summarized as follows. The local church is supervised by an *episkopos*, who is the chief steward in the household of God. His primary tasks are to administer and teach. He is assisted by deacons, whose tasks are less clearly defined. There are also presbyters or elders, members of a ruling council, some of whom preach and teach. Widows play an important role in the community by the good works they perform. The *episkopos* is not yet the monarchial bishop portrayed in the letters of Ignatius of Antioch, and the threefold office of bishop, presbyter, and deacon has not yet emerged.[25] But 1 Timothy is moving in this direction.

There are no lists of qualifications for officeholders in 2 Timothy, but in his letter to Titus, Paul provides Titus with instructions for appointing "presbyters" or "elders" (*presbyterous*) in every town (1:5–9). These elders are to be blameless and married only once, and there appears to be no difference between them and the bishop since Paul equates the elders mentioned in 1:5 with the bishop mentioned in 1:7. Thus, whereas 1 Timothy speaks of the bishop and elders, Titus seems to have in view elders who function as the bishop or supervisor of a local church. The presbyter-bishop described in Titus is appropriately called "God's steward" (1:7) since he oversees the household of God. As God's steward, he must have a firm grasp of the Word so that he can preach with sound doctrine and refute those who contradict it (1:9).

The picture that emerges from the Pastorals can be summarized as follows. The overall supervision of the church is entrusted to bishops and elders. In the case of 1 Timothy, there is a distinction between the two offices, but in the Letter to Titus the terminology of elder and bishop is used interchangeably so that it is more appropriate to speak of the presbyter-bishop. The Pastorals envision an ordination rite that consists of the laying on of hands (2 Tim. 1:6). This ordination rite presupposes that the Spirit has already designated those to be ordained (1 Tim. 1:18; 4:14). Within the narrative world of the Pastorals, Timothy and Titus function as the immediate link between Paul and the church of the Pastorals. Because his delegates have appointed bishops, deacons, and

24. The text of 1 Tim. 5:17 presupposes that the elders rule, perhaps as a council of elders, and that some but not all of these elders preach and teach.

25. Note that in the address of Phil. 1:1 Paul greets the "bishops and deacons" at Philippi. This twofold order is somewhat similar to the twofold order of bishop and deacons envisioned in 1 Timothy.

presbyters, as Paul instructed them, the church has been nourished by the sound doctrine that enables it to perform good works.

TRAINED FOR GOOD WORKS

Although Timothy and Titus have faithfully handed on what Paul entrusted to them, false teachers have arisen within the church. No longer content with the sound doctrine that has been handed on to the church, these people are engaged in religious speculation that involves myths and endless genealogies. In the view of the Pastorals, such teachers are immoral, and they are threatening the moral fabric of the church since there is an intimate connection between sound teaching and the morally good life. Those who adhere to sound teaching will live a morally good life distinguished by *eusebeia* ("devoutness," "piety," "godliness") and good works, whereas those who abandon the sound teaching handed on to the church will lead godless lives (*asebeia*) and no longer be fit for good works.

The False Teaching

Paul devotes a great deal of time within the narrative world of the Pastorals to warning Timothy and Titus about false teachers who have already infiltrated the church, and of what will happen "in the last days," presumably the time of the Pastorals. According to 1 Timothy, some people are already teaching a different doctrine, occupying themselves with myths and endless genealogies, which promote speculation rather than God's plan. Although they are ignorant of the true purpose of the law, which is intended for sinners rather than for the godly, they are foolishly presenting themselves as teachers of the law (1:3–7), presumably the Mosaic law.[26] Paul mentions two of these people, Hymenaeus and Alexander, who, he says, have ruined their faith by rejecting the guidance of conscience (1:19–20). Toward the end of his first letter to Timothy, therefore, Paul warns his delegate of what will happen in the last days. There will be people who renounce their faith, preferring "deceitful spirits and teachings of demons," and there will be liars with corrupt consciences who forbid people to marry and require them to abstain from certain foods (4:1–3). Paul characterizes their teaching as "profane myths and old wives' tales" (4:7), and he warns Timothy that those who do not agree with the sound words of Jesus Christ and the teaching that is in accord with godliness understand nothing (6:3–4).

26. The Pastorals assume that the Mosaic law is intended for sinners rather than for the saved. In this regard, there is some continuity with Paul's own teaching inasmuch as Paul says that the justified are no longer under the law. However, the Pastorals never deal with the salvation-historical role of the law, nor do they personify it in the way Paul does.

In his second letter to Timothy, Paul again warns his young delegate about "wrangling over words" (2:14), "profane chatter" (2:16), "stupid and senseless controversies" (2:23), and he points to Hymenaeus and Philetus as examples of people who have turned from the truth by saying that the resurrection of the dead has already occurred (2:17–18). As in 1 Timothy, Paul warns his assistant of what will happen in the last days. People will have the outward form of godliness, but they will deny its real power. They will infiltrate households and lead women astray. Like Jannes and Jambres, the opponents of Moses, the minds of these people are corrupt, their faith is counterfeit, and they oppose the truth (3:1–9). The time is coming, then, when people will no longer be satisfied with sound doctrine but seek teachers who suit their own needs. Instead of adhering to the truth, they will listen to myths (4:3–4).

In his letter to Titus, Paul warns Titus of rebellious people who are idle talkers and deceivers, "especially those of the circumcision," an indication, perhaps, that the false teachers are Jewish Christians, though not necessarily Judaizers.[27] They are upsetting whole households, paying attention to Jewish myths, and reverting to questions of purity and impurity, presumably the dietary prescriptions of the Mosaic law. Most importantly, they deny God by their actions, and so they are "unfit for any good work" (1:10–16). Titus is to avoid the controversies, genealogies, dissensions, and quarrels about the law that characterize this false teaching (3:9).[28]

The main outlines of the false teaching described in the narrative world of the Pastorals can be summarized as follows. Its proponents have become weary of the sound teaching Paul handed on to Timothy and Titus, therefore they are indulging in religious speculation that involves myths, genealogies, and the Jewish law. They present themselves as teachers of the law and appear to have made inroads among certain women, perhaps the younger women of the church, to whom their teaching was especially attractive. They forbid marriage, perhaps among the younger women of the church, whom they encourage to become teachers.[29] They require people to abstain from foods that they view as unclean. Some of these teachers have also claimed that the resurrection has already taken place, which suggests a misunderstanding about the

---

27. There is no indication in the Pastorals that Jewish Christians are requiring Gentiles to adopt a Jewish way of life, as was the case at Galatia. Rather, the problem seems to be that, in the view of the Pastorals, certain Jewish Christian members of the church have misused the law by trying to assert that they are teachers of the law.

28. If the teaching described in the Letter to Titus is the same as that described in 1 and 2 Timothy, there are several indications that this teaching derives from the circle of Jewish Christian believers.

29. Note the strong insistence in 1 Tim. 3:11–15 that women are to be submissive and that Paul does not allow them to teach or to have authority over a man. Women will be saved by childbearing. In 1 Tim. 5:14 Paul insists that young widows marry. Compare this with 1 Corinthians 7, where Paul exhorts widows (no age specified) to remain as they are.

general resurrection of the dead, although the Pastorals never defend the general resurrection of the dead as Paul does in 1 Corinthians 15.[30]

The Moral Life

To combat this false teaching and those who propound it, Paul presents a vision of the moral life that is related to the sound teaching he handed on to Timothy and Titus. Adherence to this teaching leads to good works and a life of piety, devotion, and godliness (*eusebeia*), whereas deviation from it results in a godless or an impious life (*asebeia*) devoid of good works. The concept of *eusebeia* ("godliness") plays a central role in 1 Timothy. For example, Paul requests prayers for kings and those who are in authority so that "we [the church] may lead a quiet and peaceable life in all godliness and dignity" (2:2). He encourages Timothy to train himself in godliness since it is valuable in every way "for both the present life and the life to come" (4:7–8). He warns Timothy that those whose words do not agree with the sound words of Jesus Christ and the teaching that is in accord with godliness understand nothing and have a morbid craving for controversy (6:3–4). Timothy, therefore, must pursue "righteousness, godliness, faith, love, endurance, [and] gentleness" (6:11).

In 1 Tim. 3:16 Paul relates this godliness to the epiphany of Christ Jesus: "Undeniably great is the mystery of devotion (*to tēs eusebeias mystērion*): Who was manifested in the flesh, vindicated in the spirit, seen by angels, proclaimed to the Gentiles, believed in throughout the world, taken up in glory" (NAB). The godliness with which the Pastorals are concerned, then, is rooted in the mystery of redemption; and apart from this mystery, which was manifested in the epiphany of Jesus Christ, godliness cannot be practiced. This mystery of godliness is the key to understanding the religious devotion (*eusebeia*) that distinguishes believers from unbelievers. Since those who diverge from this sound teaching, which communicates the mystery of the faith, will not be able to practice *eusebeia*, the Pastorals insist upon sound teaching.

In 1 Timothy Paul provides his younger delegate with a great deal of practical instruction about living a morally good life, which is pleasing to God. Timothy is to fight the good fight, having faith and a good conscience (1:18–19).[31] He is to instruct women to adorn themselves with good works, to be submissive, and to live lives of faith, love, holiness, and modesty (2:9–15). In the face of a dangerous moral asceticism, Paul reminds Timothy that "everything created by God is good, and nothing is to be rejected, provided it

---

30. Ephesians and Colossians speak of believers already having been raised up with Christ, but this does not seem to have presented a problem or resulted in a denial of the general resurrection of the dead. In the Pastorals the situation seems to be quite different.

31. The manner of life that Paul commends to Timothy is the manner of life that he himself has lived. See 2 Tim. 4:7.

is received with thanksgiving" (4:4). Believers are to provide for relatives, especially their family members (5:8), younger widows are to marry and manage their household well (5:14). Slaves are to regard their masters "as worthy of all honor, so that the name of God and the teaching may not be blasphemed" (6:1).[32] Those who are rich are "to do good, to be rich in good works, generous, and ready to share" (6:18). The picture that emerges is that of a well-ordered household in which all, especially women and slaves, know their place and perform good works that will bring credit to the faith. Family relationships, marriage, and the goodness of creation are all affirmed.

The Letter to Titus, which is similar in genre to 1 Timothy, also provides concrete moral instruction. Titus is to teach older men to be "temperate, serious, prudent, and sound in faith, in love, and in endurance" (2:2). Older women are to be "reverent in behavior" and to encourage the young women (2:3–4). Younger men are to be self-controlled (2:6). Slaves are to be "submissive to their masters" so that they may be "an ornament to the doctrine of God our Savior" (2:9–10). Titus is to be a model of good works (2:7).

In 2 Tim. 2:20–21 Paul provides a metaphor that helps to clarify this vision of the moral life. He begins by noting that in a large household there are a variety of vessels, not only precious vessels of gold and silver, but vessels of wood and clay, some intended for special use, others for general use. Next, he applies this metaphor to the church, which is the household of God, pointing out that those who cleanse themselves of what is adverse to sound teaching will become "special utensils" useful to the owner of the house, namely God, because they will be "ready for every good work." This metaphor of the household of God indicates the ecclesial way in which the Pastorals view the morally good life. All within the great household of God, no matter their social status, have the potential to be special utensils for God's use to produce good works.

Justified by Grace

The relationship that the Pastorals draw between sound teaching, godliness, and good works does not mean that they have forgotten Paul's teaching on justification by faith. The Pastorals are profoundly aware that salvation is the result of God's grace rather than human works. But since the Pastorals are no longer engaged in the same debates that Paul was when he wrote Galatians and Romans, they have reformulated his teaching on justification, as has Ephesians, in terms of being saved by grace. For example, 2 Tim. 1:9–10 affirms that God "saved us and called us with a holy calling, not according to our works but according to his own purpose and grace. This grace was given to us in Christ Jesus before the

---

32. Whereas in his letter to Philemon, Paul exhorts Philemon to receive Onesimus as a brother, the Pastorals, like Colossians and Ephesians, exhort slaves to be submissive to their masters.

ages began, but it has now been revealed through the appearing of our Savior
Christ Jesus, who abolished death and brought life and immortality to light
through the gospel." Although Paul's language of being justified by faith apart
from doing the works of the Mosaic law has been replaced by the vocabulary of
being saved by grace, the Pastorals affirm Paul's enduring theological insight that
salvation depends on God's grace rather than human effort. For the Pastorals,
this grace was revealed in the epiphany of the Savior, Jesus Christ. It was this
epiphany, not human works, that abolished death and effected life.

The same point is made in Titus 3:4–7. At one time those who now belong
to the household of God were like the rest of sinful humanity. "But when the
goodness and loving kindness of God our Savior appeared, he saved us, not
because of any works of righteousness that we had done, but according to his
mercy, through the water of rebirth and renewal by the Holy Spirit. This Spirit
he poured out on us richly through Jesus Christ our Savior, so that, having
been justified by his grace, we might become heirs according to the hope of
eternal life." The language of this text, which employs the vocabulary of righteousness and justification, is closer to that of Romans and Galatians than it is
to 2 Timothy. The references to baptism ("the water of rebirth") and the
renewal of the Holy Spirit recall the arguments of Galatians 3, that those who
have received the gift of the Spirit are justified and all who have been baptized
into Christ are Abraham's descendants. But like the text of 2 Timothy, the
emphasis has shifted from being justified by faith apart from doing the works
of the Mosaic law to being saved by God's mercy and justified by God's grace
rather than by "works of righteousness," which, in the present context, refers
to good works rather than to the works of the Mosaic law.[33]

For the Pastorals, the grace of God, which saves and justifies, made its
appearance in the epiphany of Christ. It is this grace that enables believers to
perform good deeds. "For the grace of God has appeared, bringing salvation
to all, training (*paideuousa*) us to renounce impiety (*asebeian*) and worldly passions, and in the present age to live lives that are self-controlled, upright, and
godly (*eusebōs*), while we wait for the blessed hope and the manifestation
(*epiphaneian*) of the glory of our great God and Savior, Jesus Christ. He it is
who gave himself for us that he might redeem us from all iniquity and purify
for himself a people of his own who are zealous for good deeds (*kalōn ergōn*)"
(Titus 2:11–14). The morally good life then is the outcome of salvation rather
than the means to salvation, and it is possible only because God's grace trains
people to live upright lives. Being zealous for good deeds is a matter not of
"works righteousness" but of God's work in Christ.

---

33. The Pastorals speak of faith as a virtue or as the content of what is believed rather than the
trusting faith that Paul speaks of in his letters. The two concepts are not opposed since the content
of the faith requires an act of faith on the part of the believer, but there is a shift of emphasis.

The vision of the morally good life that the Pastorals provide is deeply rooted in the salvation that made its appearance in Christ Jesus, the mystery of faith that is the content of the sound teaching Paul entrusted to Timothy and Titus, and that they must entrust to faithful witnesses. The morally good life is the outcome and goal of God's gracious epiphany in the epiphany of Jesus Christ. It is a life lived in and for the household of God, in which each person can be God's special utensil for good works. False teaching is a danger and threat to the life of the household of God because those who embrace unsound teaching are no longer useful utensils in God's household.

CONCLUSION

The Pastorals present New Testament theology with a theological paradox. On the one hand, they affirm the Pauline tradition and begin a process whereby the Pauline correspondence will eventually be viewed as Scripture. Their author (or authors) clearly revered the memory of the great apostle, and these letters present Paul's teaching as the effective antidote to the false teaching that plagued the church they address. On the other hand, their theology has important gaps and omissions when one compares the theological vision of the Pastorals with Paul's own theology. A few examples will suffice. One looks in vain in the Pastorals for Paul's profound analysis of the human condition, which portrays humanity under the powers of sin, death, and the law. Nor does one find Paul's paradoxical theology of the cross, or his apocalyptic vision of the parousia, when the general resurrection of the dead will occur and the kingdom will be handed over to God, even though the Pastorals complain that some are claiming that the resurrection of the dead has already taken place. The Pastorals refer to the Spirit, but the Spirit no longer plays the same dynamic role that it does in Paul's correspondence. Finally, the church is no longer viewed as the body of Christ or the temple of God, and there is no discussion about its relationship to Israel or to the future of Israel. When compared with Paul's own writings, the theology of the Pastorals is reserved. It is concerned to preserve the church, which is being assaulted by false teaching that threatens its structured life. Consequently, the Pastorals claim the Pauline tradition as the deposit of faith that has been handed on to them from Paul through Timothy and Titus. Although the content of this deposit is never explicitly defined, it is evident that it is intimately related to the salvation that has occurred in the epiphany of God in the epiphany of Jesus Christ. The Pastorals are aware of the major moments in the work of salvation (Christ's passion, death, resurrection, ascension, parousia), but they cast the event of salvation in the language of epiphany. God's salvation appeared in Christ, who will appear again. By this epiphany God graciously saved humanity and equipped believers for good works. In the final and last epiphany, Christ Jesus will appear as God's judge to consummate all things. In the meantime, believers must learn to live in the household of God.

This new presentation of Paul's theology does not include the whole of his theology, and some elements within this theology appear to have regressed from Paul's theology, for example, his understanding of the role of women within the church. The theology of the Pastorals, however, maintains the essential element of the Pauline deposit: the manifestation of God in Jesus Christ, salvation by grace rather than by human effort, the relationship between the indicative of salvation and the moral imperative, and the hope that there will be a future appearance of the Savior. The enduring contribution of these letters is to have solidified the Pauline inheritance. By claiming Paul as the one from whom they have ultimately received the deposit of faith, they have made the Pauline tradition an integral element of the church's faith.

PART THREE

The Johannine Tradition

The Gospel of John and the Johannine Epistles constitute the third great theological tradition of the New Testament, the Johannine tradition. Like the Synoptic Gospels, the Fourth Gospel recounts Jesus' ministry to Israel, which climaxes in his saving death and resurrection. Like the Pauline Letters, the Johannine Epistles proclaim the significance of what God has done in Christ. But there is a notable difference between the Johannine tradition on the one hand and the Synoptic and Pauline traditions on the other. Whereas the starting point of the Synoptic Gospels is Jesus' proclamation of the kingdom of God and the starting point of the Pauline tradition is the gospel of what God has effected in Christ's death and resurrection, the starting point of the Johannine tradition is the incarnation, the firm conviction that the eternal Word of God became flesh in Jesus of Nazareth. The Gospel expresses this in its programmatic statement, "And the Word became flesh and lived among us, and we have seen his glory, the glory as of a father's only son, full of grace and truth" (John 1:14). The Johannine Epistles affirm this by their insistence that *Jesus*, in all of his humanity, is the Christ (1 John 2:22), the Son of God (1 John 5:5), the one who has come *in the flesh* (1 John 4:1; 2 John 7).

This new starting point does not mean that the Johannine tradition diminishes the importance of Jesus' public ministry to Israel or the significance of his saving death and resurrection. Like the Synoptic Gospels, the Johannine Gospel presents an extended narrative of Jesus' ministry. Like the Pauline Letters, the Johannine Gospel and Epistles understand the significance of Jesus' death and resurrection. But the Johannine tradition views these events through the prism of the incarnation. For example, in the Gospel Jesus comes to Israel proclaiming what he has heard and seen in the presence of the Father rather than the kingdom of God. Consequently, his death is his glorification rather than a moment of humiliation and defeat; it is his return to the One who

259

sent him into the world. Those who believe that Jesus has come from the Father have already passed from death to life. In the Johannine Letters, the test of faith is whether one believes that Jesus—in all of his humanity—is the Christ, the Son of God, the one who has come in the flesh. Those who believe this are in communion with God and love the children of God.

Although the Fourth Gospel and the Johannine Epistles share this common starting point, as well as themes such as faith, love, light, and life, there are differences between them. The most obvious is genre. The Gospel is a narrative that recounts Jesus' life; the Epistles are letters intended to strengthen and encourage believers who have already accepted the gospel. The Gospel focuses on Jesus' relationship to the world and to his own (his disciples); the Epistles are addressed to believers who have been traumatized by the recent departure of those who no longer confess that Jesus, in all of his humanity, is the Christ, the Son of God. In the Gospel, Jesus experiences opposition from "the Jews" and from "the world." The community of believers to whom the Epistles are addressed experiences opposition from those who once belonged to their community but have now left them. Thus, whereas the world hated Jesus, now it is those who have left the community who hate the members of the community. The most significant difference, however, is the way in which the Gospel and Epistles develop the theological implications of the incarnation. Whereas the focus of the Gospel is the "revelation" that the preexistent Son brings from the Father, the focus of the Letters is the "communion" that believers enjoy with God and each other when they love each other and confess that *Jesus* is the Christ, the Son of God. For this reason, in the third part of this work I present the Gospel under the rubric of the "revelation" that the Son brings from the Father, and I present the Epistles under the rubric of the "communion" that believers enjoy with God and with one another.

9

A Theology of Revelation

The Gospel of John

Although most would agree that the incarnation is the starting point for the Johannine tradition, the beginning point for a Johannine theology is disputed.[1] Should it begin with an analysis of the human condition apart from Christ (Bultmann and Gnilka), with Christology and soteriology (Strecker and Stuhlmacher), or with the revelation that the Son brings from the Father (Hahn)? Each of these starting points makes eminent sense since the Fourth Gospel is a story of *God* who "so loved *the world* that he gave *his only Son*, so that everyone who believes in him may not perish but may have eternal life" (John 3:16). A New Testament theology, then, could begin with an analysis of the human situation before and apart from God's revelation in Christ and then consider God's salvific work in Christ. Or it could begin with the Son who reveals the Father to the world and then consider the human condition in light of this revelation. Wherever it begins, it must maintain the intimate relationship between God and Jesus that characterizes the Fourth Gospel.

Christology and theology are so intimately related in the Fourth Gospel that it is impossible to discuss the Son without speaking of the Father, just as it is impossible to discuss the Father without speaking of the Son.[2] Moreover, since the Son is the light of the world who comes to reveal what he has seen and heard in the presence of the Father, the true situation of the world can only be known in light of the revelation the Son brings from the Father. Consequently, an

---

1. See Ferdinand Hahn, *Theologie des Neuen Testaments*, 2 vols. (Tübingen: Mohr Siebeck, 2002), 1:599.

2. Rudolf Schnackenburg (*Jesus in the Gospels: A Biblical Christology* [Louisville: Westminster John Knox Press, 1995], 246) notes that theology and Christology "are so close to each other and interrelated" that it is a false alternative to have to decide "whether one is to understand the Gospel of John christologically or theologically."

analysis of Johannine theology can begin with the Son or with the Father, or even with the world, so long as it respects how all three are interrelated.

Although the expressed purpose of the Gospel ("that you may come to believe that Jesus is the Messiah, the Son of God, and that through believing you may have life in his name," 20:31) suggests a christological starting point, Jesus' statement before Pilate ("For this I was born, and for this I came into the world, to testify to the truth," 18:37) points to the theological dimension of Jesus' mission: to witness to the truth he has seen and heard in the presence of the Father. Yet it is not a matter of Christology or theology—it is both. To believe that Jesus is the Messiah, the Son of God, is to believe that he comes from God and witnesses to the truth. To belong to the truth to which Jesus witnesses is to believe that he is the Messiah, the Son of God. Perhaps, then, the most important category for understanding the theology of the Fourth Gospel is *revelation*, the Son's revelation to the world of what he has seen and heard in the Father's presence.

The category of revelation, however, presents its own problems since it is difficult to summarize the content of what Jesus reveals apart from his constant message that he comes from God and will return to the Father who sent him into the world. Bultmann states the problem in an often quoted remark, "Thus it turns out in the end that Jesus as the Revealer of God *reveals nothing but that he is the Revealer*."[3] Although there is some truth to this statement, it claims too much because it says too little. To be sure, Jesus does not reveal a series of propositional truths about God, but his words and works, especially his saving death, by which he glorifies the Father and the Father glorifies him, reveal the essence of God's love for the world, a love whereby God sends his Son not to condemn but to save the world (3:17). The Son's revelation of the Father, then, is a fruitful point of departure for Johannine theology so long as the meaning of this revelation is not reduced to new or esoteric "information" about God. Understood within the narrative world of the Fourth Gospel, the Son's revelation of the Father is the disclosure of the intimate and unheard-of relation of the Father and the Son whereby each abides in the other so that to see and hear the Son is to see and hear the Father.

Since the Son's revelation of the Father is communicated through the Gospel narrative, this chapter begins with the story the Gospel tells in order to establish a narrative framework for understanding the Gospel's theology. The chapter has five parts: (1) the story the gospel tells; (2) the sending of the Son into the world; (3) the sin of the world; (4) the community of believers: the church; and (5) the mutual glorification of the Father and the Son.

3. Rudolf Bultmann, *Theology of the New Testament*, 2 vols. (London: SCM, 1952–55), 2:66.

THE STORY THE GOSPEL TELLS

The overall structure of the Gospel is clear. It begins with a prologue (1:1–18) that provides the reader with information about God, Jesus, and the world that is crucial for understanding the narrative that follows. Next, it tells the story of the Son who comes into the world to reveal what he has seen and heard in the presence of the Father only to be rejected by the world (1:19–12:50). Having been rejected by the world, the Son turns to his own—the disciples whom the Father has given to him—and reveals the depth of God's saving love for them and the world by his saving death upon the cross, which the Gospel describes as the hour of the Son's glorification and return to the Father (13:1–20:29). The story concludes with a statement in which the narrator explains why he has written (20:30–31) and with an epilogue that appears to have been added at a later stage in the Gospel's composition and now belongs to the canonical text (21:1–25).

The Prologue

Although the Johannine prologue presents scholars with a series of questions regarding its origin and literary structure, its function within the canonical text is clear: to orient the reader or listener to the narrative that follows. Without the prologue it would be difficult to make sense of the claims that Jesus makes about himself and his relationship to God, for example, "Before Abraham was, I am" (8:58); "The Father and I are one" (10:30). Without the prologue, which reveals that Jesus is the incarnation of the preexistent Word of God, such claims appear delusional or, as Jesus' opponents maintain, blasphemous (10:33). But in light of the prologue, those who hear or read the Gospel begin to understand why Jesus can and does make such claims, even if they do not comprehend the full depth of their meaning. The prologue, then, is indispensable for reading the Gospel as its author wants it to be read.

Francis Moloney notes that the prologue manifests a three-part structure: the Word in God becomes the light of the world (vv. 1–5); the incarnation of the Word (vv. 6–14); and the revealer, the only Son, turned toward the Father (vv. 15–18).[4] The first part introduces the preexistent Word of God through whom all things were made. The Word is so intimately associated with God that the prologue can say that the Word is what God is ("and the Word was God," 1:1), a theme that will be echoed in Thomas's confession at the end of the Gospel ("My Lord and my God!" 20:28). Because everything has been created through

---

4. Francis J. Moloney, S.D.B., *The Gospel of John* (SP 4; Collegeville, MN: Liturgical Press, 1998), 34.

the agency of this preexistent Word, this life-giving preexistent Word is the light that dispels the darkness in which humanity finds itself. In addition to introducing the Word and setting the stage for what follows, the opening words of the prologue echo the first words of Genesis ("In the beginning . . ."), thereby relating the preexistent Word of the Gospel to God's creative word ("And God said . . . ," Gen. 1:3, 6, 9, 11, 14, 20, 24, 26).[5]

Whereas the first part of the prologue speaks of the relationship of the pre-existent Word to God, the second (John 1:6–14) describes the entrance of the Word into the world of human beings, culminating in the prologue's central statement, "And the Word became flesh and lived among us" (1:14). This part of the prologue makes four points. First, John came as a witness to the Word.[6] As a witness to the Word, he testified to the light that the Word brought into the world, clearly indicating that he himself was not the light but only a witness to it. John's testimony and the theme of witness will play an important role in the narrative that follows. Second, the prologue describes the entrance of the Word into the world and the world's response to the Word (vv. 10–11), even though the incarnation of the Word has not yet been described (v. 14). The world's ignorance of the Word, even though the world came into being by the Word, and the refusal of the Word's own people to accept him, presage themes that will be developed in the rest of the narrative: the hostility of "the Jews" and the hatred of "the world" for Jesus and his disciples.[7] Third, despite this rejection, some have believed in the Word, and, because they have, the Word has given them the power to become children of God (vv. 12–13). This theme will also be developed in the Gospel, especially in relation to the community of Jesus' disciples. Fourth, the preexistent Word through whom God made the world became flesh (*ho logos sarx egeneto*). This is undoubtedly the most important statement of the prologue and of the Gospel, and it is the vantage point from which the Fourth Gospel views and understands Jesus: the incarnation. Jesus of Nazareth, the one of whom Pilate says, "Here is the man!" is the Word made flesh. Consequently, to see Jesus is to see the enfleshment of the preexistent Word of God. Because the Word is God, Jesus can say to Philip, "Whoever has seen me has seen the Father" (14:8). But the very incarnation of the Word, by which the Word is revealed to the world, paradoxically conceals the

5. Although the concept of the Word is certainly influenced by the motif of God's divine wisdom, which was instrumental in the work of creation (Prov. 8:22–26; Wis. 7:22–8:1; Sir. 24:1–22), there is also a relationship with God's creative word in Genesis 1.

6. One of the significant differences between the Fourth Gospel and the Synoptic Gospels is the way in which they present John the Baptist. Whereas the Synoptics highlight John's ministry of baptism, the Fourth Gospel presents him as one who witnesses to Jesus.

7. Throughout this chapter I put the expression "the Jews" in quotation marks to indicate that it possesses a technical meaning in the Fourth Gospel, which I will discuss below. In the Fourth Gospel the expression functions as a concrete example of the refusal of "the world" to believe that Jesus comes from the Father. It tends to reflect the debate between the Johannine community and its opponents rather than the debate between Jesus and the Jewish people of his day.

Word from those who refuse to believe. The Gospel, however, will be unrelenting in its demand that one must accept the enfleshed Word in order to see the Father, and the world will be equally unrelenting in its refusal to believe that the one it knows as "Jesus" comes from and reveals the Father.

The third part of the prologue (vv. 15–18) begins with a reprise of John's testimony, but this time the testimony points to the preexistence of the Word incarnate ("He who comes after me ranks ahead of me because he was before me," v. 15). The voice of the community for whom this Gospel was originally intended also testifies that the community of believers has received "grace upon grace" (v. 16). For, whereas the law was given through Moses, grace and truth have come through Jesus Christ (v. 17, the first time that the incarnate Word is named). Moloney shrewdly notes, "This is not a negative assessment of the former gift; it is a Christian perspective that respects the gift of God given through Moses but insists that the former gift is now perfected in the gift of the truth that took place in and through the event of Jesus Christ."[8] Although there will be intense hostility between Jesus and "the Jews," the Gospel will clearly acknowledge that "salvation is from the Jews" (4:22), and Jesus will say that if "the Jews" believed in Moses, they would believe in him (5:46). Moreover, he will claim that Abraham "rejoiced that he would see my day" (8:56). Thus there is a certain salvation-historical perspective in the Fourth Gospel, albeit different from that found in Matthew, Luke, or Paul. The enfleshment of the Word in Jesus and the sending of the Son into the world are not so much the fulfillment of prophecy as they are God's way of bringing to perfection a former revelation, thus the expression "grace upon grace" (v. 16).

After verse 14 it is no longer possible to speak merely of "the Word" since the Word has become flesh in Jesus Christ. The final verse of the prologue refers to the "only Son, who is close to the Father's bosom" (v. 18).[9] This designation of God as "Father" and the incarnate Word as "the Son" will dominate the rest of the narrative in which Jesus claims that he is the Son whom the Father has sent into the world to reveal the Father to the world. The prologue now explains how Jesus can make this claim. No one but the Son has ever seen God. Although the Old Testament narrates theophanies to Moses and select prophets, from the vantage point of the Fourth Gospel no one can claim to have seen God in the way that the Son has seen and heard the Father.[10] Moses spoke with God, Isaiah was transported into the heavenly sanctuary, and

---

8. Moloney, *Gospel of John*, 40.

9. This is the alternate reading of the NRSV, which reads "heart."

10. Among the major theophanies of the Old Testament are the following: Gen. 6:5–9:17 (God appears frequently to Noah before and after the flood); Gen. 17:1–21; 18:1–15 (God appears to Abraham); Exod. 3:1–4:17 (God appears to Moses from the burning bush); Exod. 19:3–31:18; 32:31–34:28 (Moses receives the Covenant Code from God); 1 Kgs. 19:9–18 (God appears to Elijah); Job 38:1–41:26 (God answers Job's complaints); Isa. 6:1–13 (Isaiah sees God in the temple); Ezek. 1:1–28 (Ezekiel has a vision of God).

Ezekiel had a vision of God, but no figure in Israel's history ever dwelt in God's bosom. The startling claim of the Fourth Gospel, then, is that Jesus has seen and heard the Father because he is the incarnation of the preexistent Word.

The major movement and themes of the prologue can be summarized in this way. The preexistent Word, who is what God is, and through whom God created the world, entered human history by becoming flesh in Jesus of Nazareth. Because Jesus is the incarnate Word, he is the only Son, the one who has seen the Father. Accordingly, he comes into the world to reveal the Father. This revelation is life for a world that dwells in a darkness of which it is not even aware. Consequently, those who refuse to believe in the Son refuse to believe in God who sent him, whereas those who believe that God has sent the Son into the world become children of God because they are born of God.

The Son's Revelation to the World

The first part of the Johannine Gospel narrates how the Son came into the world to reveal the Father only to be rejected by the world (1:19–12:50). The narrative unfolds in the following way: the witness of John and his disciples to Jesus (1:19–51); the initial manifestation of Jesus' glory (2:1–4:54); Jesus reveals himself during the feasts of "the Jews" (5:1–10:42); the rejection of resurrection and life (11:1–12:50).

The Witness of John and His Disciples to Jesus

One of the major themes of the Fourth Gospel is the theme of witness—Jesus' witness to the Father and the Father's witness to Jesus. What Jesus does and says is what Moses and the Scriptures proclaim. Both testify that Jesus comes from God. Accordingly, it is appropriate that, in the Fourth Gospel, John should be cast in the role of a witness to Jesus rather than as the one who baptizes him, and that the first part of the Gospel should open with John's witness. John testifies to "the Jews" that he is not the Christ, Elijah, or the prophet (1:19–28), and then to his disciples that Jesus is "the Lamb of God who takes away the sin of the world" (1:29, 36), the one on whom the Spirit descended and remains, the Son of God (1:33–34). John's witness leads two of his disciples to follow Jesus. One of them, Andrew, testifies to his brother Simon that they have found the Messiah (1:41). Jesus then summons Philip to follow him. Philip in turn testifies to Nathanael, "We have found him about whom Moses in the law and also the prophets wrote, Jesus son of Joseph from Nazareth" (1:45). Although skeptical at first, Nathanael eventually confesses that Jesus is the Son of God, the King of Israel (1:49). Jesus, however, promises that Nathanael will see greater things: "heaven opened and the angels of God ascending and descending upon the Son of Man" (1:51). Thus the witness of John results in disciples for Jesus, and the witness of Jesus' own disciples leads to further witnesses, thereby indicating that those who believe in Jesus must testify to him.

All of the titles that emerge in this section are true (Jesus is the Lamb of God who takes away the sin of the world, the Son of God, the Messiah, the King of Israel), but none of them can be understood apart from the prologue and Jesus' promise to Nathanael that he will see the angels of God ascending and descending upon the Son of Man. Because Jesus is the incarnate Word of God, he is the new point of communication between God and humanity, the Son who reveals the Father to the world, the one through whom God reveals himself to the world.

The Initial Manifestation of Jesus' Glory

Having promised Nathanael that he will see greater things, Jesus begins to reveal his glory. This glory, which will play a major role throughout the Gospel, is the glory Jesus enjoyed in God's presence "before the world existed" (17:5). By revealing this glory, Jesus reveals the Father. Although the full revelation of this glory will not occur until the hour of Jesus' death, he begins to reveal his glory through a series of signs whereby his disciples believe in him. The initial manifestation of this glory occurs in 2:1–4:54, a section that begins with Jesus' first sign at Cana of Galilee, where he changes water into wine. It then concludes with a second sign in Cana, where he heals the son of a royal official. Between these signs, Jesus goes to Jerusalem during Passover and cleanses the temple, speaks with Nicodemus, and then with the Samaritan woman. At the end of his ministry in Samaria, the inhabitants of that city confess, "This is truly the Savior of the world" (4:42).

For those who believe in Jesus, his signs point to his glory and the significance of his ministry. For example, the first sign at Cana signals the new revelation that he brings, "the good wine" that God has saved for last. The second, the healing of the royal official's son, points to Jesus as the giver of life, a theme that will be developed in a more dramatic way when Jesus raises Lazarus from the dead. But it is not merely Jesus' signs that reveal his glory. Everything he does and says indicates his glory and so reveals the Father to the world. Thus the cleansing of the temple points to Jesus as the new temple of God, the place where all will worship the Father "in spirit and truth" (4:23). Since no one can see the kingdom of God "without being born from above" (3:3), however, Jesus tells Nicodemus that he must be born of "water and Spirit" (3:5), foreshadowing a major theme of the Gospel: Jesus is the one who gives the Spirit. This theme of the Spirit is developed further when Jesus tells the Samaritan woman that he is the source of "living water" (4:10), "a spring of water gushing up to eternal life" (4:14).

In the midst of this section, the Gospel provides brief summaries of its central theme to remind its audience why Jesus has come into the world (3:16–21,

31–36). "God so loved the world that he gave his only Son" (3:16). "The Father loves the Son and has placed all things in his hands" (3:35). Therefore, whoever believes in the Son already has eternal life. To summarize, the initial manifestation of Jesus' glory shows that he has come from God to reveal the Father to the world. He is the new temple where those born of water and the Spirit worship God in spirit and truth. He is the one who gives the living water that is the Spirit.

Jesus Reveals Himself during the Feasts of the Jews

The events of 5:1–10:42 take place during four Jewish feasts. On the first, an unnamed "feast of the Jews" that occurs on the Sabbath, Jesus reveals that the Father has shown the Son everything and entrusted him with the work of raising the dead and giving life, as well as with the power to exercise judgment (5:1–47). Next, on the Feast of Passover, Jesus reveals that he is the bread of life who has come down from heaven and those who eat this bread will live forever (6:1–71). During the Feast of Tabernacles (7:1–10:21), he proclaims that he is the source of living water (7:37–39), the light of the world (8:12) who has come into the world for judgment (9:39), the good shepherd who freely lays down his life for his sheep (10:11). Finally, on the Feast of Dedication (10:22–39), Jesus reveals himself as the one whom the Father has consecrated and sent into the world (10:36).

To understand this section, it is important to recall that toward the end of the prologue, the community that stands behind the Fourth Gospel confesses, "From his fullness we have all received, grace upon grace" (1:16). In this section of the narrative, which deals with the feasts of "the Jews," the Gospel explains the meaning of this confession by showing how these feasts find their perfection and deepest meaning in the one who has come from the Father. Jesus' work of healing on the Sabbath shows that he does what God continues to do even on the Sabbath: he gives life and exercises the power of judgment. Consequently, whereas "the Jews" would prohibit Jesus from working on the Sabbath because they view him only as a man rather than as the one who comes from God, Jesus' activity on the Sabbath reveals his true identity and the deepest meaning of the Sabbath. In a similar vein, the Gospel presents Jesus as the perfection of the Jewish Feast of Passover. Whereas the ancestors of "the Jews" ate manna in the wilderness and died, Jesus is the true bread of life, and whoever eats this bread will live forever (6:58). By presenting himself as the light of the world and the source of life-giving water—the Spirit—during the Feast of Tabernacles, Jesus shows how this Jewish feast, in which water and light play such a central role, finds its perfection in the revelation he brings from the Father. Finally, by declaring that he is the one whom the Father has consecrated and sent into the world, Jesus reveals that, as the revelation of the Father, he replaces the altar of the temple whose rededication the feast commemorated. From the point of view of the Fourth Gospel, Jesus perfects these feasts by bringing "grace upon grace." For those who believe that he comes from God, it is futile to celebrate these feasts apart from Jesus. The grace these feasts once brought to Israel comes to its perfection in the grace that attends the one whom the Father has consecrated and sent into the world.

"The Jews" as portrayed in the Fourth Gospel, however, refuse to believe that Jesus comes from God. In their view, he is a blasphemer because he claims a relationship with God to which no human being has a right. The basic charge "the Jews" bring against him is found in two verses that frame this section. In the first, the Johannine narrator notes, "For this reason the Jews were seeking all the more to kill him, because he was not only breaking the sabbath, but was also calling God his own Father, thereby making himself equal to God" (5:18). In the second, "the Jews" explain why they are about to stone Jesus, "It is not for a good work that we are going to stone you, but for blasphemy, because you, though only a human being, are making yourself God" (10:33). The central question, then, is who is Jesus? From where does he come? Although "the Jews" think they know his origin and identity (7:27), they do not. Jesus comes from God, and he presents a series of "witnesses" who testify on his behalf: his Father, John, the works that he does, and the Scriptures (5:31–39). Consequently, this section can be viewed as a trial that comes to its climax on the Feast of Dedication when "the Jews" gather around Jesus and ask, "How long will you keep us in suspense? If you are the Messiah, tell us plainly" (10:24). It is at this "trial" that "the Jews" pick up rocks to stone Jesus for blasphemy (10:31–33).[11]

Jesus' revelation on these four feasts of the Jews is the most sustained account of how the light came into the world to reveal the Father, only to be rejected by his own. It is here more than anywhere else that the christological question of the Gospel is raised in its most acute form: Who is Jesus, and where has he come from?

The Rejection of Resurrection and Life

Although "the Jews" try to arrest and kill Jesus during the feasts of Tabernacles and Dedication (7:30, 44; 8:59; 10:31), he escapes their schemes because his "hour" has not yet arrived (7:30; 10:39). But after the feasts of the Jews, when the Greeks ask to see him, Jesus realizes that the hour has come for the Son of Man to be glorified (12:20–23). In 11:1–12:50 the Gospel narrates the events that lead to the world's rejection of Jesus and the arrival of this hour: the raising of Lazarus from the dead, the decision of the Sanhedrin to hand

---

11. This scene on the Feast of Dedication is the Johannine counterpart to the Synoptic trial before the Sanhedrin. This explains why the Johannine passion narrative has a "hearing" before Annas (18:19–24) but not a trial scene before the Sanhedrin.

Jesus over to the Romans, the anointing at Bethany, Jesus' entrance into Jerusalem, and the desire of the Greeks to see him.[12]

Throughout the narrative thus far, Jesus has performed a number of signs that reveal his glory and show that he comes from God. In one of the Gospel's many ironies, however, the sign that most explicitly points to life—the raising of Lazarus from the dead (11:1–44)—results in the Sanhedrin's decision to put Jesus to death (11:45–53). This sign, which not even the religious authorities can deny, should indicate to the most skeptical critic that Jesus comes from God. Indeed, the chief priests and Pharisees acknowledge that Jesus is performing many signs (11:47). Nevertheless, despite his signs they refuse to believe that he comes from God. Instead, Caiaphas counsels the Sanhedrin "that it is better for you to have one man die for the people than to have the whole nation destroyed" (11:50).

From this point on, the events unfold rapidly. Mary anoints Jesus, and Jesus interprets her loving gesture as an anointing for burial (12:7). Large crowds insist upon seeing not only Jesus but Lazarus, so that when Jesus enters Jerusalem as its royal Messiah the Pharisees complain, "You see, you can do nothing. Look, the world has gone after him!" (12:19). The statement is both true and false. The crowds have come to see Jesus because he has raised Lazarus, but the sign has not led them to faith in Jesus as the resurrection and the life. When some seek to see Jesus, however, he knows that his hour has come, the hour when the Son of Man will be "lifted up" and draw everyone to himself (12:32).

The first part of the Gospel concludes with a narrative comment that summarizes the result of Jesus' ministry: "Although he had performed so many signs in their presence, they did not believe in him" (12:37). The first part also explains why Jesus came into the world: "I have come as light into the world, so that everyone who believes in me should not remain in the darkness" (12:46). But the world has not believed, and so the light of the world withdraws from the world. The first part of the Gospel (1:19–12:50), then, illustrates the words of the prologue: "He was in the world, and the world came into being through him; yet the world did not know him. He came to what was his own, and his own people did not accept him" (1:10–11).

The Revelation of the Son to the Disciples the Father Entrusted to Him

Having withdrawn from the world, Jesus turns to his disciples, whom the Father has given him, in order (1) to prepare them for his departure, (2) to assure them

---

12. The Greeks who seek to see Jesus are probably Gentiles, representatives of the scattered children of God.

that he will send another Paraclete,[13] and (3) to pray for them and those who will believe in him because of their word (13:1–17:26). Jesus then embarks upon his passion, which is the hour of his glorification (18:1–19:42), after which he appears to Mary of Magdala and his disciples (20:1–29). The Gospel concludes with a statement of its purpose (20:30–31) and an extended epilogue (21:1–25).

Although the present canonical form of the farewell discourse is the result of a long and complicated editorial process, the purpose of the discourse is clear: (1) to remind the disciples of what Jesus has said and done; (2) to assure them that he will not leave them as orphans in the world; (3) to prepare them for his imminent death by explaining that he is returning to the Father; and (4) to pray for them and those who will believe in him because of their testimony. Before the discourse begins, however, Jesus humbles himself as if he were a slave and washes his disciples' feet, thereby foreshadowing his slavelike death upon the cross whereby he will cleanse them (13:1–11). He then instructs the disciples to follow his example (13:12–15), and he gives them a new commandment: that they should love one another as he has loved them (13:34–35). Next he explains the significance of his death and why he must leave them: his death is his return to the Father from whom he came, and it is for their benefit. By returning to the Father who sent him into the world, he will be able to prepare a place for them so that they can be with him (14:2–3). By returning to the Father, he will also be able to send them another Paraclete, the Spirit of truth, who will teach and remind them of what he has told them (14:16, 26). In the time after his death, they must remain in him by keeping his words (15:1–10), which he summarizes in the commandment to love one another (15:11–17). The world will hate them just as it hated him (15:18–25), but the Paraclete will enable them to testify on Jesus' behalf (15:26–27). Throughout this discourse, the disciples struggle to understand where Jesus is going and why they cannot follow (13:36; 14:5; 16:16–18). Therefore, after speaking in "riddles," Jesus tells them plainly, "I came from the Father and have come into the world; again, I am leaving the world and am going to the Father" (16:28). Although the disciples appear to understand (16:29–30), it is apparent from Jesus' response that they do not fully comprehend what he has said (16:31–32). They will not understand until he has been raised from the dead.

The discourse concludes with a prayer (17:1–26) that opens with Jesus asking the Father to glorify him with the glory he had before the foundation of the world (17:1–5). Jesus then prays for his disciples, asking the Father to keep them in the Father's name (17:11) and to consecrate them in the truth (17:17). Finally, he prays for all who will believe through their word so that all may be one (17:20–26).

---

13. Jesus is the first Paraclete in the sense that he is the one who has been the advocate for his disciples.

The Johannine passion narrative presents Jesus' crucifixion as the death of the good shepherd who freely lays down his life for his sheep and as the completion of the work the Father has given him to accomplish. When Judas and a cohort of soldiers come to arrest Jesus, he willingly surrenders himself to them (18:5, 8). Because he is the good shepherd, no one takes his life from him; he freely surrenders it. When Pilate claims to have the power to release or crucify him, Jesus replies that Pilate would have no power if it were not given to him from above (19:10–11). The destiny of the Son of Man does not depend on Pilate's authority but on the will of the Father, who determines Jesus' work. Thus, when the Johannine Jesus dies on the cross, his final words are, "It is finished" (19:30). What is finished is the work that the Father has given the Son to accomplish, the work of revealing the Father's love for the world, a work that is completed by Jesus' death on the cross.

Although the account of Jesus' resurrection is often viewed as anticlimactic because the Gospel places such emphasis on his death as the hour of his glorification and return to the Father, the resurrection plays an indispensable role within the narrative. For it is only in light of the resurrection that the disciples finally understand that Jesus' death was his departure to the Father and the moment of his glorification. To be sure, the disciples thought they understood the significance of Jesus' death before his crucifixion (16:29–30), but the events of the passion and the disciples' inability to comprehend their significance have shown otherwise. Therefore, even though the resurrection may appear to play a less prominent role in the Fourth Gospel than it does in the Lukan or Pauline writings, it remains the key to unlocking the mystery of Jesus' person. This is why it is only after the resurrection that Thomas can echo the prologue ("And the Word was God," 1:1) with his confession, "My Lord and my God!" (20:28).

In a brief narrative comment, the Fourth Evangelist explains that the purpose of the Gospel is to enable those who hear or read it to believe that Jesus is the Messiah, the Son of God, so that through this faith they may have life.[14] Like Thomas's confession, this comment echoes the prologue, which describes the Word as the mediator of life (1:4) and says that all who accepted the incarnate Word were given the power to become children of God (1:12). The primary goal of the Gospel, then, is to sustain and bring people to life by faith in the one whom the Father has sent into the world so that they may share in the life of the Father.

---

14. There is an important textual problem in 20:31. Whereas in some manuscripts the verb "believe" is in the aorist subjunctive tense, suggesting that the Gospel is addressed to nonbelievers ("so that you may believe"), in others it is in the present subjunctive tense, suggesting that the Gospel is addressed to believers ("so that you may continue to believe"). The decision one makes here depends, in large measure, upon one's understanding of the Gospel's purpose. Overall, it seems more likely that the primary audience of the Gospel consists of those who already believe.

Chapter 21 is an extended epilogue, added at a latter stage, which recounts an appearance of the risen Lord to his disciples in Galilee. At this appearance, Peter is rehabilitated and commissioned to care for the flock of the good shepherd.

The major movement of the Fourth Gospel can be summarized in this way. The Son came into the world to reveal the Father to the world. By the signs he performs and the words he speaks, the Son reveals what he has heard and seen in the presence of the Father. But the world refuses to believe that the Son has come from the Father. Consequently, the Son turns to the disciples whom the Father has given him in order to prepare them for his departure and to send them into the world to do what he has done. Having prepared the disciples for the time when he will leave the world, the Son glorifies the Father by completing the work the Father has entrusted to him. In doing so, he manifests the Father's love for the world and provides those who believe in the Son the opportunity to share in the very life the Son enjoys with the Father.

THE SENDING OF THE SON INTO THE WORLD

The theology of the Fourth Gospel is a theology of revelation: the revelation about the Father, which the Son brings to the world for the life of the world. The starting point for a Johannine theology, then, is the sending of the Son into the world to reveal the Father to the world. Accordingly, this section will discuss: (1) the sending of the Son, (2) the relationship between the Father and the Son, (3) the identity of the Son, and (4) the revelation of the Son.

The Sending of the Son

The most fundamental claim Jesus makes in the Fourth Gospel is that he comes from God and is returning to God, who is his Father. He calls God his Father and openly refers to himself as the Son whom the Father has sent into the world to reveal what he has seen and heard in the presence of the Father. Everything within the Gospel, then, revolves around a single claim: that the Father has sent the Son into the world. Because this claim is central to Jesus' revelation, those who refuse to obey and honor the Son whom the Father has sent into the the world do not honor and obey the Father who sent him. Or put another way, those who believe in Jesus believe in the one who sent him, whereas those who refuse to believe in the one whom the Father sent into the world cannot believe in the Father whom the Son reveals. The christological claims of the Fourth Gospel, then, have been so identified with its theological claims about God that it is no longer possible to speak of Jesus apart from the God who sent him, just as it is no longer possible to speak of God apart from the Son whom the Father sent into the world. Christology has become theology, and theology has become Christology.

This implosion of Christology into theology and of theology into Christology is rooted in the fundamental claim of the prologue that the Word became flesh (1:14). Because the one whom the Father has sent into the world is the Word incarnate, the prologue can make yet another claim that is foundational for the narrative that follows: "No one has ever seen God. It is God the only Son (*monogenēs theos*), who is close to the Father's bosom, who has made him known" (1:18). Moses and the prophets may have stood in God's presence and seen his radiant glory and even heard his voice, but only the Son preexisted with God before the foundation of the world. In this sense, then, no one but the only begotten Son has seen God. The sending of the Son into the world, then, is not to be confused with a prophetic call whereby God sends a prophet to bring his word to the people. Nor is it a metaphor that identifies Jesus as one chosen and elected to bring God's word to the world. The sending of the Son points to the Gospel's central claim: that the human one whom the world knows as the son of Joseph (1:45; 6:42) is the Word incarnate. Consequently, Jesus comes with a claim that scandalizes his contemporaries: he reveals what he has seen and heard in the presence of his Father.

The Fourth Gospel uses two verbs to describe the sending of the Son into the world (*apostellō* and *pempō*). It employs *apostellō* in the aorist tense,[15] with "God," "the Father," "that one," "the living Father," or "you" as the subject, and "the Son," "whom," or "me" as the object. Thus the focus is on Jesus as the one whom God sent into the world. For example, the Gospel's programmatic statement says, "God did not send the Son into the world to condemn the world, but in order that the world might be saved through him" (3:17). Then, in a recapitulation of the prologue (3:31–36), the evangelist notes, "He whom God has sent speaks the words of God, for he gives the Spirit without measure" (3:34). In the rest of the Gospel, Jesus identifies himself as the one sent by God, the God whom Jesus calls his Father.

Jesus knows God because he is from God, and God sent him (7:29). He did not come of his own but was sent by God (8:42). Because he is the one whom the Father sanctified and sent into the world, he does not blaspheme when he says that he is God's Son (10:36). Eternal life is to know God and the one whom God has sent into the world (17:3). Therefore, the one work God requires is that people should believe in the one whom God has sent (6:29). Jesus' disciples are those who believe that God sent him into the world (17:8, 25). Therefore, after completing the work the Father entrusted to him, Jesus sends them into the world just as the Father sent him into the world (17:18; 20:21). The ultimate

15. For occurrences of *apostellō*, see 3:17, 28, 34; 5:36, 38; 6:29, 57; 7:29; 8:42; 10:36; 11:42; 17:3, 8, 18, 21, 23, 25; 20:21.

goal of Jesus' revelation, then, is that the world should believe that the Father has sent him (11:42). Only then will the world receive the life the Son brings from the Father (6:57). If the world accepts the testimony of Jesus' works, it will see that these works testify that the Father has sent him into the world (5:36).

When the Fourth Gospel employs the verb *pempō*, it is usually in a participial phrase that functions as an adjective and describes God as the one who sent the Son.[16] In most instances the Greek phrase consists of an article, the aorist participle, and an accusative pronoun that describes God as the one who sends Jesus, for example, "My food is to do the will of him who sent me and to complete his work" (4:34). Here and in other instances the verb emphasizes God as *the sending one*. Jesus' food is to do the will of the one who sent him (4:34; 6:38), and the will of the one who sent him is that he should lose nothing of all that God has given him but raise it up on the last day (6:39). Because the Son comes from God, those who do not honor the Son do not honor the Father who sent him (5:23), whereas those who believe in the one who sent him have eternal life and do not come under judgment (5:24). Jesus insists that what he teaches is not his own but the teaching of the one who sent him (7:16). If "the Jews" do not know who Jesus is, it is because they do not know the one who sent him (7:28). The one who sent Jesus testifies on his behalf (8:18). The one who sent him is true (8:26), and he is always with him since Jesus always does what is pleasing to him (8:29). To believe in Jesus is to believe in the one who sent him (12:44), to see him is to see the one who sent him (12:45), and to receive him is to receive the one who sent him (13:20). Jesus never speaks on his own because the Father who sent him has commanded him what to say (12:49; 14:24). If the world hates Jesus' disciples, it is because it does not know the one who sent him (15:21). Therefore it does not know that by his death Jesus is returning to the one who sent him into the world (7:33; 16:5).

The two verbs that the Gospel employs for "sending" are complementary in their function. *Apostellō* points to Jesus as the one whom God has sent into the world and *pempō* to God as the one who sends him into the world. The sending of the Son into the world, then, is both a christological and theological statement: christological inasmuch as it identifies Jesus as *the Son* whom the Father sent into the world, theological inasmuch as it identifies God as *the Father* who sent the Son into the world. These sending formulas are important soteriological statements because they explain why the Father sent the Son into the world: not to condemn the world but to save the world by revealing the Father to the world. If the world is to be saved, then, it must believe that Jesus—in all of his humanity—is the one whom God sent into the world. To see and hear the incarnate one is to hear and sèe the Father who sent him.

---

16. For occurrences of *pempō*, see 4:34; 5:23, 24, 30, 37; 6:38, 39, 44; 7:16, 18, 28, 33; 8:16, 18, 26, 29; 9:4; 12:44, 45, 49; 13:20; 14:24; 15:21; 16:5; 20:21.

The Relationship between the Father and the Son

The Fourth Gospel is emphatic that the one who sent Jesus into the world is the Father and that Jesus is his Son. Jesus, however, does not come into the world to reveal that God is like a Father—something already known from Israel's Scriptures—but to reveal that God is *his* Father apart from whom Jesus can do nothing.[17] Consequently, to hear and see the Son is to hear and see the Father. Within the theological world of the Johannine Gospel, there is no access to God apart from the revelation of the Son. For this reason, Jesus says to "the Jews," "It is my Father who glorifies me, he of whom you say, 'He is our God,' though you do not know him" (8:54–55). The Fourth Gospel explains the intimate relationship between the Father and the Son in a number of discourses directed to "the Jews" and to Jesus' disciples.[18]

The Father Has Shown All Things to the Son

The first of these discourses occurs in chapter 5 when Jesus explains why he works on the Sabbath ("My Father is still working, and I also am working," 5:17), leading the Johannine narrator to comment that "the Jews" were seeking all the more to kill Jesus not only because he broke the Sabbath "but was also calling God his own Father, thereby making himself equal to God" (5:18). Although Jesus is equal to God, he does nothing on his own. For just as a son can do only what he sees his father doing, Jesus does only what his Father has shown him (5:19). Thus he works on the Sabbath just as his Father continues to work on the Sabbath by giving life and rendering judgment.[19] Because the Father loves the Son, he shows him everything he does (5:20). Consequently the Father has given the Son the power to raise the dead to life and render judgment so that people may honor the Son just as they honor the Father. But if one does not honor the Son, one cannot honor the Father who sent the Son into the world. Those who hear what the Son says and believe in the Father who sent him have already passed from death to life (5:21–24).

17. The following are examples of where, in the Old Testament, the Israelites acknowledge God as "Father" and of where God refers to Israel as his son/children: Exod. 4:22; Deut. 14:1; 32:6; Ps. 68:6; Isa. 63:16; 64:8; Jer. 3:4, 19; 31:9; Hos. 11:1; Mal. 1:6; 2:10. There are also passages where God's relationship to the king is likened to that of a father to a son (2 Sam. 7:14; Pss. 2:7; 89:27–28).

18. On the concept of God in the Fourth Gospel see the important monograph of Marianne Meye Thompson, *The God of the Gospel of John* (Grand Rapids: Eerdmans, 2001); and the chapter of Francis J. Moloney, S.D.B., "Telling God's Story: The Fourth Gospel," in *The Forgotten God: Perspectives in Biblical Theology* (ed. A. Andrew Das and Frank J. Matera; Louisville: Westminster John Knox Press, 2002), 107–22.

19. On the background of the idea that God continues to give life and render judgment even on the Sabbath, see C. H. Dodd, *The Interpretation of the Fourth Gospel* (Cambridge: Cambridge University Press, 1953), 320–24.

The Father who is the source of all life has given the Son the gift to have life in himself and the authority to execute judgment (5:27). The Son, then, is the resurrection and the life (11:25–26), and the hour is coming when the dead will hear his voice and come forth in a resurrection that leads to life if they have done good, or to condemnation if they have done evil (5:28–29). The Son, then, does nothing on his own because he is so intimately united with the Father that he does only the will of the one who sent him (5:30). The Son of God is the one who does only what he has seen and heard in God's presence.

The works the Father has given Jesus to complete (to give life and exercise judgment) testify that the Father has sent him (5:36). In addition to these works, the Father testifies on Jesus' behalf, but the world does not receive this testimony because it refuses to believe in the one whom the Father has sent into the world (5:37–38), preferring the praise of the world to the glory of God (5:44). The Father-Son relationship, then, is so intimate that there is no access to the Father apart from the Son, no faith in God without believing in the one to whom the Father has given the power to give life and the authority to render judgment.

The Father Gives the Son as the True Bread from Heaven

Chapter 6 presents Jesus as the bread of life whom the Father is giving to the world. When the crowd quotes Scripture ("He gave them bread from heaven to eat," 6:31) and asks Jesus for a comparable sign, Jesus interprets the text in the following way. It was not Moses who gave them bread from heaven; rather it is his Father who is presently giving them the true bread from heaven (6:32), which Jesus identifies with himself: "I am the bread of life" (6:35). In saying this, Jesus is not claiming autonomy for himself. For he has not come down to do his own will but the will of the one who sent him (6:38): that he should lose nothing of what God has given him but raise it up on the last day (6:39). So he concludes, "This is indeed the will of my Father, that all who see the Son and believe in him may have eternal life; and I will raise them up on the last day" (6:40). The theme of the Son raising believers on the last day runs throughout this discourse (6:39, 40, 44, 54) and recalls what Jesus has already said in the Sabbath discourse in which he presented himself as the life-giver (5:21, 26, 28–29). The Son is the bread of life and the giver of life because "the living Father" through whom he lives has sent him (6:57).

The crowd, however, is scandalized by Jesus' words. How can the son of Joseph claim to be the bread of life who has come down from heaven (6:41–42)? Many of Jesus' own disciples find his teaching difficult and offensive (6:60). Aware of this, he tells the crowd that no one can come to him unless drawn to him by the Father who sent him (6:44). Those who hear and learn from the Father come to him, although he is the only one who has seen the Father (6:45–46). To those disciples who do not believe, he says, "For this reason I have told you that no one can come to me unless it is granted by the Father" (6:65). The presence of Jesus in the world and the ability to recognize him as the Son whom the Father has sent into the world, as the true bread of life, is a gift from God that must be embraced. Those who accept the gift believe in the scandal of the incarnation—that the son of Joseph is the one whom the Father has sent into the world. By embracing the gift, they reveal that the Father has drawn them to Jesus. Conversely, those who refuse the gift are scandalized by the incarnate Word, and their refusal to receive the gift reveals that they have not been drawn to Jesus by the Father.[20]

The Father and the Son Are One

During the feasts of Tabernacles and Dedication, the question of Jesus' identity comes to center stage (7:25; 8:53; 10:24). Jesus speaks not only of where he has come from but where he is going (7:33; 8:21). If "the Jews" do not know who he is, it is because they do not know where he comes from and where he is going (8:14). The question of Jesus' relationship to the Father (from whom he came and to whom he will return) is crucial, then, for understanding who Jesus is. The debates of chapters 7–10 echo themes introduced during the Sabbath discourse of chapter 5 about Jesus' relation to the Father and the work of judgment the Father has entrusted to him (8:15, 16, 26; 9:39). The one who gives life and raises the dead is the one who judges, not in the sense that he judges anyone (8:15) but in the sense that his presence brings the world to a moment of judgment when it must decide whether Jesus comes from God (9:39).

Jesus insists that his teaching is not his own but belongs to the one who sent him. However, those who resolve to obey the will of God will know if Jesus' teaching is from God or if he is merely speaking on his own (7:16–17). That some cannot discern this can only mean that they have not resolved to do God's will.

When Jesus declares that he is the light of the world (8:12), the Pharisees accuse him of testifying on his own behalf (8:13). Jesus, however, insists that his testimony is valid because, unlike them, he knows his origin and destiny (8:14). But there is another who testifies on his behalf—his Father. When they ask, "Where is your Father?" he replies that they do not know him or his Father. For if they knew him, they would know who his Father is (8:19). Once more, it is the relationship between Jesus and the Father that resolves the christological question. To know Jesus is to know the Father, and to know the Father is to know Jesus. If Jesus' opponents do not know him, it is because they

---

20. The Johannine concept of predestination or divine determinism appears to work in this way: a person's faith is evidence that the Father has drawn such a one to the Son. Conversely, a person's refusal to believe indicates that such a one has not been drawn to the Father by the Son. The Gospel, however, never says that certain people are prevented by God from believing in Jesus.

do not know his Father; and because they do not know his Father, they do not know him.[21]

The essential difference between Jesus and those who do not believe in him is that whereas they are "from below," he is "from above," and whereas they are "of this world," he is "not of this world" (8:23). Because he comes from above, he declares what he has heard from his Father just as the Father instructed him. But since those who do not believe belong to this world, they cannot understand that Jesus is speaking to them about God as his Father (8:26–29).

This question of Jesus' Father comes to a climax in an especially bitter dialogue in which the Fourth Gospel makes a sharp distinction between Jesus' Father and the father of his opponents (8:31–59). The debate begins with Jesus speaking to "the Jews" who believed in him, promising that if they continue in his word, they will know the truth and the truth will make them free (8:31–32). Unaware that they are not yet free of sin, "the Jews" assert that they are Abraham's children (8:33). But Jesus retorts that if they were truly Abraham's children, they would do what Abraham did, and if God were their Father they would love the Son because he comes from God (8:39–42). That they neither love Jesus nor do what Abraham did becomes the occasion for the Johannine Jesus to make the most frightful statement of the New Testament, "You are from your father the devil" (8:44).[22] That these words are not to be taken literally—as if the devil physically fathered the Jewish people—is evident from 8:56, where Jesus affirms that Abraham is the ancestor of the Jews. What then is the meaning of the Gospel's harsh indictment of "the Jews" in 8:44, that the devil is their father?

The Gospel's harsh and unfortunate indictment in 8:44 reflects the fierce debates between the Johannine community and the Jewish synagogue, toward the end of the first century, over the person of Jesus and his relationship to God. From the point of view of the Johannine community, one cannot honor the Father apart from honoring the Son whom the Father sent into the world. Consequently, according to the logic of the Johannine community, those who do not accept the revelation that the Son brings from the Father cannot be from God (8:47), and if they are not from God they must be from the devil. While Christianity will continue to confess that Jesus comes from the Father, it should be evident that it can no longer engage in this first-century polemic.

---

21. The argument, of course, is circular, as is so much of the argument in this Gospel for which the indispensable key is faith in the one whom God sent into the world. If one does not believe in the Son, one cannot know the Father. Conversely, ignorance of the Father means one cannot believe in the Son. If one truly understood God, then, one would believe that God sent Jesus into the world.

22. I employ the expression "Johannine Jesus" to signal that it is unlikely that these are the words of the historical Jesus.

Jesus expresses his love for those who know that he comes from the Father in his good shepherd discourse (10:1–21). Because he is the good shepherd, he knows his sheep with the same intimacy that the Father knows him and he knows the Father (10:14–15). Indeed, the reason the Father loves him is that the Son lays down his life in order to take it up again for the sake of his sheep (10:17). In doing this, he fulfills the commandment he received from the Father (10:18).

On the Feast of Dedication, when "the Jews" ask Jesus to tell them if he is the Messiah, he points to his works—all that he has said and done. His works testify that he is the Messiah, but they refuse to believe because they are not his sheep, and so they do not hear his voice (10:25–27). Then, in his most important statement thus far, Jesus plainly proclaims, "The Father and I are one" (10:30), leading "the Jews" to pick up stones to put him to death "because you, though only a human being, are making yourself God" (10:33). Once more, it is the offense of the incarnation that becomes the occasion for those who do not believe to stumble and fall. Those who do not believe that Jesus is the incarnate Word cannot understand that he is "the one whom the Father has sanctified and sent into the world" (10:36). However, it is not blasphemous for such a one to call himself the Son of God, because he does the works of his Father. If they believed in these works, they would understand that the Father is in Jesus, and Jesus is in the Father (10:38).

Jesus' revelation to the world ends with a statement that summarizes his work in light of his relation to the Father (12:44–50). Its content can be summed up in this way. To believe in Jesus is to believe in the one who sent him. To see Jesus is to see the one who sent him. Jesus has come as the light of the world, not as its judge. Those who reject him will not be judged by him but by the word he has spoken, a word that is not his own but the word of the Father who sent him. For those who believe in him, that word is eternal life. Thus he has spoken to the world, not on his own, but as the Father has instructed him.

The Son Reveals the Father to His Disciples

In his farewell discourse to his disciples (13:1–17:26), Jesus reveals that he has come from the Father and is going to the Father (16:28). Although the disciples do not comprehend the full significance of what Jesus says because he has not yet returned to the Father, when the Paraclete whom Jesus will ask the Father to give them (14:16) reminds them of all that Jesus has said (14:26), they will understand. In this discourse, Jesus speaks about his unity with the Father, developing what he said earlier, "The Father and I are one" (10:30). But now a new element is added: Jesus' disciples will also share in this intimate union with him and the Father.

The discourse begins with a narrative comment that the hour had come for Jesus to return to the Father (13:1). This theme of returning to the Father is the key to unlocking what follows, for until the disciples comprehend that

Jesus' death is a return to the Father, they cannot understand why he must leave them. When he returns to the Father, he will prepare a place for them in his Father's house so that where he is they may also be (14:1–3). The disciples, however, still do not know where Jesus is going, so he explains that he is the way, the truth, and the life, and no one comes to the Father but through him (14:6). To know Jesus is to know the Father (14:7) so that whoever has seen Jesus has seen the Father, for the Father is in Jesus and Jesus is in the Father (14:9–10). These remarkable statements indicate that for the Johannine believer there is no other way to see, hear, or know God apart from Jesus, the incarnate Word. The Fourth Gospel's understanding of the incarnation enables it to proclaim that Jesus is in the Father, and the Father is in him (14:11). Thus it is imperative for disciples to believe that Jesus' death is a return to the Father from whom he came.

Jesus' departure, however, will not leave the disciples bereft of his presence, since the Father will send them another Paraclete. Then they will know that Jesus is in the Father, and they are in him, just as he is in them (14:20). Moreover, those who love Jesus will be loved by the Father, and Jesus will love them and reveal himself to them (14:21). To love Jesus is to keep his word that he received from the Father (14:24). Jesus' return to the Father, then, has important consequences for the disciples. By it they will understand his union with the Father, and the Father will love them as he has loved Jesus.

In the metaphor of the vine (15:1–17), the union between Jesus and the Father is expanded to include the disciples. Jesus is the vine, the disciples are the branches, and the Father is the vinegrower. By remaining in the vine, they will produce the fruit of love, and as they produce this fruit, the Father will prune them so that they will produce even more fruit. Jesus has chosen the disciples and made known to them everything he has heard from the Father so that they will bear fruit—the fruit of love—that will last (15:15–16). But the world will hate them just as it hated Jesus, a hatred that is ultimately directed at God, since "whoever hates me hates my Father also" (15:23).

When Jesus tells the disciples that in a little while they will no longer see him but then in a little while they will see him again (16:16), they are puzzled because they do not understand that he is going to the Father. It is at this point that Jesus plainly reveals that he came from the Father and has come into the world, and now he is leaving the world and going to the Father (16:28). He then prays to his Father for the disciples that "they may be one, as we are one" (17:11). For just as the Father sent him into the world, he is about to send them into the world (17:18). The unity between Jesus and the Father, which has been a hallmark of the entire Gospel, is now extended to the disciples, who must do what Jesus has done.

The relationship between Jesus and the Father can be summarized in the following points: (1) The Father shows the Son everything and grants the Son the power to give life and render judgment. (2) The Father loves the Son and gives all things to the Son. (3) Through the works that the Son does, the Father testifies that he has sent the Son into the world. (4) The Son does only what the Father commands him, and he speaks only what he hears and sees in the Father's presence since he comes to do the Father's will. (5) The Father and the Son are one. Therefore, to honor the Son is to honor the Father, and to dishonor the Son is to dishonor the Father. (6) The Son's death is a return to the Father by which the Son prepares a place for his disciples. (7) The disciples will share in the intimate union of the Father and the Son and be sent into the world by the Son just as the Son was sent into the world by the Father. (8) Because the Son comes from the Father and returns to the Father, everything that he says and does reveals the Father. There is no other way to the Father but through the Son.

The Identity of the Son

The most important information about Jesus' person is found in the Gospel's prologue, which identifies him as the incarnation of the preexistent Word, and in Jesus' self-revelation about his relationship to the Father. In addition to what the prologue says and what Jesus relates about himself, the Fourth Gospel attributes a number of titles to Jesus. Some are traditional designations already found in the Synoptic tradition (Christ, Son of God, King of Israel, the King of the Jews, Prophet, and Lord) whereas others are distinctively Johannine (the Lamb of God, the Savior of the world, the only Son, and God). Moreover, as in the Synoptic tradition, Jesus often refers to himself as the "Son of Man." These titles receive their full meaning when interpreted in light of the prologue and what Jesus says about himself in the Gospel narrative.

Messiah, Son of God, King of Israel

The comment by the evangelist at the conclusion of chapter 20, which explains the purpose of the Gospel, indicates that the Gospel's most important confessional titles are "Messiah" and "Son of God": "But these are written so that you may come to believe that Jesus is the Messiah, the Son of God, and that through believing you may have life in his name" (20:31). That this statement comes at the end of the Gospel is significant since the Gospel narrative—starting with the prologue—has defined these two titles for its audience. As in the rest of the New Testament, then, it is not the categories of Messiah and Son of God that determine who Jesus is but Jesus who determines what it means to be God's Son, the Messiah.[23]

---

23. On this point see Frank J. Matera, "Transcending Messianic Expectations: Mark and John," in *Transcending Boundaries: Contemporary Readings of the New Testament: Essays in Honor of Francis J. Moloney* (ed. Rekha M. Chennattu and Mary L. Coloe; Biblioteca de Scienze Religiose 187; Rome: Libreria Ateneo Salesiano, 2005), 201–16.

Christos is already identified with Jesus in the prologue: "The law indeed was given through Moses; grace and truth came through Jesus Christ" (1:17).[24] In this verse *Christos* is employed as part of Jesus' name rather than in a titular sense. The same phenomenon occurs in Jesus' prayer to the Father: "And this is eternal life, that they may know you, the only true God, and Jesus Christ whom you have sent" (17:3). But the titular sense of *Christos* is always close at hand, and its use as part of Jesus' name in these texts indicates that messiahship has become so closely aligned with Jesus that the community of believers can call Jesus the Messiah, Jesus Christ. The text of 1:17 also indicates that, from a salvation-historical perspective, Jesus plays the primary role in God's redemptive plan inasmuch as he is the one in whom the grace, which is the truth, is revealed.

In the narrative that follows the prologue, the Gospel begins to employ *Christos* in a titular sense. John the Baptist testifies to "the Jews" that he is not the Messiah (1:20) and then to his disciples that Jesus is "the Lamb of God who takes away the sin of he world" (1:29), "the Son of God" (1:34), thereby identifying the coming Messiah as the Lamb of God and Son of God. Andrew declares to his brother Simon, "We have found the Messiah (which is translated Anointed)" (1:41),[25] and Philip tells Nathanael, "We have found him about whom Moses in the law and also the prophets wrote" (1:45). Nathanael, in turn, exclaims to Jesus, "Rabbi, you are the Son of God! You are the King of Israel!" (1:49), only to be told that he will see "the angels of God ascending and descending upon the Son of Man" (1:51). From this chain of acclamations, it is apparent that for the Fourth Gospel the Messiah is the one to whom the Scriptures testify, the royal Son of God, the King of Israel, the one who is the point of communication between heaven and earth. The rest of the narrative will show how Jesus is this Messiah.

Before John the Baptist disappears from the Gospel narrative, he again testifies that he is not the Messiah but has been sent ahead of the Messiah (3:28). The Johannine narrator then provides a narrative comment that expands upon John's final witness and identifies Jesus—the Messiah to whom John has just witnessed—as "the one who comes from above," "the one who comes from heaven," "the one who testifies to what he has seen and heard," "he whom God has sent," the Son in whose hands the Father has placed all things (3:31–36).

In the next episode, Jesus speaks to a Samaritan woman about "living water" (4:10). When the woman asks Jesus if he is "greater than our ancestor Jacob" (4:12), he replies that this living water will become "a spring of water gushing up to eternal life" (4:14). Next, he speaks of an hour when true worshipers will

24. If "grace and truth" form a hendiadys, then this grace is the truth. See Moloney (*Gospel of John*, 33), who renders the text "the gift that is the truth."

25. Andrew employs the traditional Hebrew word for the Messiah in its Greek transcription, *Messias*, which the Johannine narrator then translates as *Christos*.

worship the Father "in spirit and truth" (4:23), leading the woman to express her faith that the "Messiah is coming" (4:25).[26] At this point Jesus openly declares, "I am he" (4:26), thereby affirming that as the Messiah he is the giver of the Spirit (life-giving water), which enables people to worship God in spirit and truth. The villagers of that city add a further dimension to Jesus' messiahship when they confess, "This is truly the Savior of the world" (4:42).

Although Jesus clearly proclaims that he is the Messiah to the Samaritan woman, his messiahship is a disputed question in Jerusalem during the Feast of Tabernacles. The crowd wonders if the authorities know that he is the Messiah, since he speaks so openly and they say nothing (7:26). But the crowd is also skeptical, since it thinks that it knows where Jesus comes from, and when the Messiah comes, "no one will know where he is from" (7:27). The remark, of course, is ironic. The crowd thinks that it knows Jesus' origin and so disqualifies him from being the Messiah, but in fact it does not know his origin—he comes from God. Some in the crowd, however, believe in him as the Messiah because of the signs he has done (7:31). The crowd remains divided, however, some believing that he is the Messiah, others questioning his credentials to be the Messiah since they only know him as a Galilean, whereas the Messiah is "descended from David and comes from Bethlehem" (7:42).

The Fourth Gospel is not interested in Jesus' Davidic origin in the way that the Gospels of Matthew and Luke are. Like the Gospel of Mark, it has a kind of "messianic secret," albeit of a different sort. The Messiah is the one who comes from God; therefore his human origins are of no account. Because he comes from God, his presence is hidden and secret until people believe in him as the one whom the Father has sent into the world.

On the Feast of Dedication, "the Jews" ask Jesus, "How long will you keep us in suspense? If you are the Messiah, tell us plainly" (10:24). By calling God his Father and claiming to be the one whom God has sent into the world, Jesus has told them that he is the Messiah. But because they refuse to believe his claims, his messiahship is hidden from them. Nevertheless, he responds by telling them that the works he has done testify to him, but "the Jews" do not believe because they are not his sheep (10:25–26). When he tells them that he and the Father are one (10:30), therefore, they can only accuse him, the one whom the Father has consecrated and sent into the world, of blasphemy for claiming to be God's Son (10:33). Because the Fourth Gospel has reinterpreted messiahship in light of Jesus, rather than Jesus in terms of traditional messianic categories, no answer can satisfy Jesus' opponents so long as they refuse to believe that he comes from God.

Toward the end of Jesus' public ministry, Martha confesses that he is the Messiah, the Son of God, the one coming into the world (11:27). Although the

---

26. The narrator again employs the Greek form of the Hebrew, *Messias*.

confession is formally correct and foreshadows what the Johannine narrator will say at the end of the Gospel (20:31), within the context of the narrative not even Martha has understood Jesus. For whereas he asks her if she believes that he is the resurrection and the life (11:25–26), she ignores his question and responds with a traditional confession that Jesus is the Messiah, the Son of God who is coming into the world. As Francis Moloney has shown, she has not yet understood that as the Messiah Jesus is *already* the resurrection and the life.[27] Another inadequate expression of Jesus' messiahship occurs when he enters Jerusalem and the crowds greet him as "the King of Israel" (12:13). As in the case of Martha's confession, the acclamation is formally correct but inadequate since it presupposes that Jesus is the royal Davidic Messiah. To counter this notion of messiahship, Jesus mounts a donkey to present himself as the humble royal figure described in Zeph. 3:14–15 and Zech. 9:9, an action whose significance his own disciples comprehend only after his glorification (John 12:16).

There is no "trial" before the Sanhedrin at which the question of Jesus' messiahship is raised because "the Jews" asked the question at the Feast of Dedication (10:22–39), and after the raising of Lazarus they decide to put Jesus to death (11:45–53). Instead, there is a single sustained trial before Pilate in which the question of Jesus' kingship and origin plays a central role. At the outset of the trial, the accusation against Jesus is that he is a messianic pretender, "the King of the Jews" (18:33). When asked if he is the king of the Jews, Jesus responds that his kingdom is not of this world but that he has come into the world to testify to the truth (18:36–37). As the trial progresses the real issue emerges: Jesus has claimed to be the Son of God (19:7). This new development leads Pilate to ask the only question that can clarify who Jesus is: "Where are you from?" (19:9). But Pilate does not understand the truth (18:38), and he is not ready to accept that Jesus comes from God.

The Johannine understanding of messiahship can be summarized in this way: the Messiah is the Son of God, the one who comes from God to testify to the truth he has heard and seen in the Father's presence. He is the king of Israel not because he restores the Davidic kingdom but because he brings the Spirit and reveals the Father to the world. To know that Jesus comes from God is to know that he is the Messiah, the Son of God.

Distinctively Johannine Titles

In addition to the titles it shares with the Synoptic Gospels, the Fourth Gospel employs a number of distinctive titles, identifying Jesus as the Lamb of God, the Savior of the world, the only Son, and God. Whereas the first two titles are soteriological in nature, the last two point to Jesus' deepest identity with

27. Francis Moloney, "Can Everyone Be Wrong? A Reading of John 11.1–12.8," *NTS* 49 (2003): 505–27.

God. Since none of these titles occurs with regularity throughout the Gospel, however, it is best to view them as auxiliary titles that clarify what it means to call Jesus the Messiah, the Son of God.

John testifies that Jesus is the Lamb of God on two occasions. On the first, he declares, "Here is the Lamb of God (*ho amnos tou theou*) who takes away the sin of the world!" (1:29). He further identifies Jesus as the one who ranks ahead of him because he was before him (an allusion to the preexistence of the Word), as the one on whom the Spirit descended and remained, and as the Son of God (1:30–34). On the next day, he identifies Jesus as the Lamb of God to two of his disciples, who then follow Jesus (1:35–39). Rudolf Schnackenburg notes that there have been several suggestions about the background for this title: the servant of Isaiah 53 who, like a lamb, is led to slaughter and whose life is an offering for sin (Isa. 53:7, 10–12); the paschal lamb, who is also mentioned in 1 Cor. 5:7; the sacrificial lamb of the Jewish cult (Exod. 29:38–42); the lamb in the account of the binding of Isaac in Genesis 22; and the slaughtered lamb of the book of Revelation (Rev. 5:6–10).[28] None of these suggestions, however, completely explains the Lamb of God image in the Fourth Gospel. Schnackenburg concludes that while the servant of Isaiah and the paschal typology may be the strongest candidates, it is most likely that the Fourth Evangelist, perhaps stimulated by such texts, created this expression. Within the Gospel, the image of the lamb now points to Jesus' salvific work of taking away "the sin of the world," which, within the narrative world of the Fourth Gospel, is the refusal to believe God's revelation. The world lives in the darkness of sin and ignorance that can be removed only by the light that the Son brings: the Son's revelation of the Father. As the one whom the Father sent into the world, Jesus the Lamb of God takes away the sin of the world by revealing the Father to the world, a revelation that comes to its climax in Jesus' saving death on the cross, the moment of his glorification.

The designation of Jesus as "the Savior of the world" occurs only once in the Gospel, at the end of the encounter between Jesus and the Samaritan woman (4:42). Apart from 1 John 4:14, it appears nowhere else in the New Testament. Its use in 1 John, however, is suggestive since 1 John clearly identifies the Savior of the world as the Son whom the Father has sent: "And we have seen and do testify that the Father has sent his Son as the Savior of the world." Both expressions (the Lamb of God and the Savior of the world) highlight Jesus' salvific work. As the Lamb of God he takes away the world's sin of unbelief, and as the Savior of the world he is the Son whom the Father has sent not to condemn the world but in order that the world might be saved through faith in the only Son of God (3:17).

---

28. Schnackenburg, *Jesus in the Gospels*, 276–81. In Isaiah 53 the focus is primarily on the servant who is like a lamb. The Passover lamb was not understood as a sacrificial lamb. The lamb of the temple sacrifice was a daily offering for sins. In the binding of Isaac, a ram rather than a lamb is supplied for Isaac. The lamb of the book of Revelation is a slaughtered lamb.

Thomas's confession, "My Lord and my God!" (20:28), is a christological high point of the Gospel. Those who confess that Jesus is the Messiah, the Son of God (20:31), also know that he is their Lord and their God. The significance of Thomas's confession is that it echoes what the prologue says of the Word: "In the beginning was the Word, and the Word was with God, *and the Word was God*" (1:1). In light of the resurrection, Thomas now believes that the risen One is the Word that was with God in the beginning, the very Word that was incarnate in Jesus. The risen Lord is not a second god, nor does he displace God. The distinction between the Son and the Father remains. The Son is not the Father, but he is "God" inasmuch as he is the incarnation of the Word.

This Son is God's only begotten (*monogenēs*), a term that occurs twice in the prologue (1:14, 18) and twice in a narrative comment that functions as a reprise of the prologue (3:16, 18). In every instance *monogenēs* indicates the uniqueness of the Son, even though the word "son" does not occur in 1:14, 18, though it does in 3:16, 18. While those who are born from above can become children of God (*tekna tou theou*, 1:12), the Fourth Gospel never speaks of them becoming sons/children of God or sons/children of their heavenly Father in the way that the Gospel of Matthew does (Matt. 5:9, 45). There is only one Son, the only begotten Son of the Father, the one who was with the Father before the foundation of the world.[29]

The Son of Man

As in the Synoptic Gospels, Jesus speaks of himself as the Son of Man a number of times in the Fourth Gospel.

- The angels of God will ascend and descend upon the Son of Man (1:51).
- No one has ascended into heaven except the Son of Man, who descended from heaven (3:13).
- What will the disciples do if they see the Son of Man ascending to where he was before? (6:62).
- The Son of Man will be lifted up (3:14; 8:28; 12:34).
- The Father has given the Son authority to execute judgment because he is the Son of Man (5:27).
- The Son of Man gives the food that endures for eternal life (6:27), and unless people eat the flesh and drink the blood of the Son of Man (6:53), they will not have life in themselves.
- The hour has come for the Son of Man to be glorified by God (12:23; 13:31).
- In one instance Jesus asks, "Do you believe in the Son of Man?" (9:35).

The Johannine Gospel employs the Son of Man tradition in a new and creative manner. There are no references to a future coming of the Son of Man

---

29. First John maintains this line of thought, referring to believers as *tekna* rather than *huioi*. See 1 John 3:1, 2, 10; 5:2.

on the clouds of heaven to render judgment as there are in the Synoptic
Gospels, only a single statement about the Son of Man who already executes
judgment (5:27). Moreover, those sayings that deal with the passion of the Son
of Man speak of him being "lifted up" or "glorified." As for the rest of the Son
of Man sayings, there is little or no relationship between them and the Synoptic tradition.

As in the Synoptic Gospels, the designation "Son of Man" is not a confessional title. The Gospel has not been written "so that you may come to believe
that Jesus is the *Son of Man*" (compare 20:31). Rather, the Son of Man designation allows the Gospel to point to Jesus (1) as the incarnate one who is the
point of communication between heaven and earth, (2) the one who will be
lifted up on the cross and glorified by God, (3) the one who is the bread from
heaven and whose body and blood believers must eat and drink, and (4) the
one whose presence already effects judgment. Consequently, if people are to
have life, they must believe in the Son of Man. They must believe that Jesus
is the incarnate one who has come from God. A review of the Son of Man sayings will clarify these points.

After Nathanael enthusiastically confesses that Jesus is the Son of God, the
King of Israel, Jesus promises that he will see the heavens opened and the
angels of God ascending and descending upon the Son of Man, thereby alluding to the episode in Gen. 28:12 when, in a dream, Jacob saw a ladder between
earth and heaven upon which the angels of God were ascending and descending. For the Fourth Gospel, Jesus has become this ladder, the new point of
communication between heaven and earth, the one through whom the Father
is revealed to the world.

In the sayings that deal with his death, Jesus says that the Son of Man will be
lifted up (*hypsoō*). As nearly all commentators note, the verb has a double meaning: to lift up or to exalt. Jesus will be physically lifted up on the cross, and this
lifting up will be the moment of his exaltation, for his death will be his return
to the Father. Because Jesus' death is his return to God, other Son of Man sayings speak of the glorification of the Son of Man. The one who will be lifted up
in crucifixion is none other than the one who has descended from heaven.

In his conversation with Nicodemus, Jesus begins by saying that no one has
ever ascended into heaven except the one who descended from heaven, the Son
of Man (3:13). He then recalls the episode of Moses, who lifted up the serpent
in the wilderness to heal the Israelites (Num. 21:4–9), and says that the Son of
Man must also be lifted up (upon the cross) so that all who believe in him may
not perish (John 3:14). In this way Jesus affirms that eternal life comes from
believing that the one lifted up in crucifixion is none other than the one who
descended from and ascended to heaven. In 8:28 Jesus tells "the Jews" that
when they have "lifted up" the Son of Man (upon the cross) they will realize

that "I am he (*egō eimi*), and that I do nothing on my own, but I speak these things as the Father instructed me." That is, they will comprehend that the crucified One is the one who came from God. In 12:32 Jesus says that when he is "lifted up from the earth" he will draw all people to himself. Realizing that Jesus is referring to his death, the crowd asks, "We have heard from the law that the Messiah remains forever. How can you say that the Son of Man must be lifted up? Who is this Son of Man?" (12:34). Because he speaks of his death, the crowd disqualifies Jesus from messiahship. It cannot comprehend how the Son of Man, who must be lifted up in crucifixion, can be the Messiah, who endures forever. It does not realize that the Son of Man is the incarnate one who comes from God.

Because the Son of Man is the incarnate one, the lifting up of the Son of Man is his exaltation. Thus, when Jesus realizes that the hour for his passion has arrived, he says, "The hour has come for the Son of Man to be *glorified*" (12:23). When Judas leaves to betray him, thereby setting the events of the passion in motion, Jesus exclaims, "Now the Son of Man has been *glorified*, and God has been glorified in him" (13:31). The glorification of the Son of Man takes place when he is lifted up on the cross. Only those who believe that Jesus came from God and is returning to God, however, can understand that his death is his glorification.

Only those who believe that Jesus has come from God, then, can comprehend what Jesus means when he exhorts the crowd to strive for the food that the Son of Man will give them (6:27) and to eat the flesh of the Son of Man and drink his blood if they are to have life (6:53). When Jesus' disciples find his teaching too difficult to accept, he asks what they will do if they see the Son of Man ascending to where he was before (6:62). In other words, if they do not believe that he has come down from heaven as the bread of life, how will they believe when he ascends to his Father by being lifted up on the cross?

Finally, although the Fourth Gospel does not speak of a final apocalyptic judgment, it understands the central role the Son of Man plays in God's work of judgment. This judgment, however, is already taking place as people believe in or refuse to believe in Jesus as the one whom the Father has sent into the world. Thus when Jesus says that the Father has given the Son "authority to execute judgment, because he is the Son of Man" (5:27), he means that God has given the Son this authority because he is the one who comes from God, the human one who is the Word incarnate.

The point of the Son of Man sayings, then, is not so much to identify Jesus as the Son of Man as it is to emphasize that the human one who will be lifted up on the cross is the point of communication between heaven and earth, the bread of life, the one to whom the Father has given all judgment because this one is the incarnate Word, the one whom the Father has sent into the world.

The Revelation of the Son

In his *Theology of the New Testament*, Rudolf Bultmann makes the following observation about Jesus' words in the Fourth Gospel:

> Jesus' words never convey anything specific or concrete that he has seen with the Father. Not once does he communicate matters or events to which he had been a witness by either eye or ear. . . . His theme is always just this one thing: that the Father sent him, that he came as the light, the bread of life, witness for the truth, etc.; that he will go again, and that one must believe in him. . . . Jesus is not presented in literal seriousness as a pre-existent divine being who came in human form to earth to reveal unprecedented secrets. Rather, the mythological terminology is intended to express the absolute and decisive significance of his word—the mythological notion of pre-existence is made to serve the idea of the Revelation. His word does not arise from the sphere of human observation and thought, but comes from beyond. . . . It is an authoritative word which confronts the hearer with a life-and-death decision.[30]

Much of what Bultmann affirms in this provocative statement is correct.[31] Although the Fourth Gospel presents Jesus as the one who comes into the world to reveal the Father, Jesus never communicates "matters or events to which he had been a witness by either eye or ear," nor does he disclose "unprecedented secrets" about God. Rather, he reveals that he comes from the Father and is returning to the Father (16:28), and those who see him see the Father (14:9). The revelation of the Fourth Gospel, then, is not found in new "information" about God—and certainly not in divine or esoteric secrets—but in an encounter with Jesus that reveals the Father. This revelation can be summarized by reviewing a series of "I am" sayings in which Jesus makes a number of claims about himself. Seven of these statements occur with a predicate (I am the bread of life; I am the light of the world; I am the gate; I am the good shepherd; I am the resurrection and the life; I am the way, the truth, and the life; I am the vine), whereas others occur in an absolute form, without a predicate: "I am."

I Am the Bread of Life

In the bread of life discourse, Jesus presents himself as the bread of life (6:35, 48), the living bread that came down from heaven (6:51). In making this claim, he equates himself with the bread of God "which comes down from heaven

30. Bultmann, *Theology of the New Testament*, 2:62.

31. Bultmann's contention that the sending of the Son into the world is a mythological statement is questionable, since the Gospel is quite insistent that Jesus is God's incarnate Word (1:14), a statement that Bultmann would also classify as part of the Gospel's mythology meant to communicate the truth that Jesus' word is authoritative. The manner in which Bultmann writes here, however, can be misleading since the Gospel never claims that Jesus came to reveal "unprecedented secrets." It would be more precise to say that the Son came to reveal the Father's love for the world.

and gives life to the world" (6:33). Because he is the bread of life, those who come to him will never be hungry, and those who believe in him will never be thirsty (6:35). As the bread of life, he has not come down to do his own will but the will of the one who sent him so "that all who see the Son and believe in him may have eternal life; and I will raise them up on the last day" (6:40). Accordingly, whereas the Israelites ate manna in the wilderness and died, those who eat this bread "will live forever" (6:58).

In revealing that he is the bread of life that comes down from heaven, Jesus reveals that the Father is the giver of all life who will raise up the dead on the last day. Most importantly, there is no need to search for this life apart from the Son, who reveals the Father. To believe in Jesus is to eat this bread of life that the Father gives to the world, thereby participating in eternal life in the present, confident that even if one should die the Son will raise the believer on the last day in accordance with the Father's will.

I Am the Light of the World

During the Feast of Tabernacles, Jesus proclaims, "I am the light of the world. Whoever follows me will never walk in darkness but will have the light of life" (8:12). The light that Jesus brings is the life that comes from the Father who sent him into the world (1:4). Jesus comes into the world so that those who believe in him will not dwell in the darkness (12:46). As long as Jesus is in the world, he is the light of the world (9:5) so that those who do what is true may come to the light (3:21). It is imperative, then, that people walk while they have the light (Jesus) lest the darkness overtake them (12:35). The world, however, prefers the darkness to the light (3:19–20).

In revealing that he is the light of the world, Jesus discloses that God is light and so the source of all life and truth. Although the Fourth Gospel never explicitly identifies God as light, 1 John does: "This is the message we have heard from him and proclaim to you, that God is light and in him there is no darkness at all" (1 John 1:5). The community that stands behind this letter understands that in revealing himself as the light of the world, Jesus discloses the God in whom there is no darkness, the God who is the source of life and truth. To hear and see Jesus, then, is to live in the light of God, which is the life that comes from God.

I Am the Gate, the Good Shepherd

In his discourse on the good shepherd, Jesus proclaims that he is both the gate through which the sheep enter the sheepfold (10:7, 9) and the good shepherd (10:11, 14) who knows his sheep and lays down his life for them. Those who enter through him will be saved (10:9) because he came that they might have life in abundance (10:10). This life comes at the cost of the life of the good shepherd, who freely lays down his life for the sheep just as the Father has commanded him (10:11, 15, 17, 18). The metaphor of the shepherd is rooted in the Old Testament metaphor of God as the shepherd of the individual Israelite (Psalm 23) and of the nation (Ezek. 34:11–16). By proclaiming that he is the good shepherd, Jesus reveals that he is the one in whom God now shepherds his people. There is no other access to life apart from the Son, for he is both the gate through which people must enter into eternal life and the good shepherd who lays down his life for the life of the sheep. By identifying himself as the gate and the good shepherd, Jesus reveals how God gives life through the death of the good shepherd, making Jesus the gateway to life.

I Am the Resurrection and the Life

When Martha complains that if Jesus had been present, her brother would not have died, Jesus assures her that her brother will rise again. Martha assumes that Jesus is speaking of the final resurrection of the dead and affirms her faith in the general resurrection of the dead. Jesus, however, replies that he is the resurrection and the life so that those who believe in him, even if they die, will live, and those who live and believe in him will never die (John 11:25–26). This complex response goes far beyond Martha's belief in the general resurrection of the dead. By affirming that he is the resurrection and the life, Jesus affirms that those who believe in him already share in resurrection life. Therefore, even if they die, the resurrection life they already enjoy through faith in the Son will not be taken from them. Those who enjoy this resurrection life will never die, for they will never be eternally separated from God.

By proclaiming that he is the resurrection and the life, Jesus reveals that God is the fullness of life, which not even death can destroy. To be sure, there will be a general resurrection of the dead, but for the Johannine believer resurrection life has already begun through faith in the Son, who communicates the very life of the Father to the world. When believers are raised from the dead, then, they will continue in a resurrection life they already enjoy in the Son.

I Am the Way, the Truth, and the Life

In the farewell discourse, when Thomas says, "Lord, we do not know where you are going. How can we know the way?" (14:5), Jesus replies that he is the way, the truth, and the life, and that no one comes to the Father except through him. To know Jesus, then, is to know the Father (14:6–7). The "way" leads to the Father. The "truth" is the word that the Father has entrusted to the Son (17:17). The reason Jesus came into the world was to testify to this truth (18:37). The law came through Moses, but the grace that is the truth came through Jesus Christ (1:17). "Life," of course, refers to eternal life, which those who believe in the Son already experience (3:16), a life that will continue for believers even after death because the Son will raise them from the dead (5:28–29). The Son mediates such life because just as the Father has life in himself, so he has granted the Son to have life in himself (5:26). In proclaiming that he is the way, the truth, and the life, then, Jesus reveals that the fullness of life and truth is found only in God. Accordingly, those who believe in the Son as "the way" will come to the Father, who is the source of "truth" and "life."

I Am the Vine

In his metaphor of the vine, Jesus proclaims that his Father is the vinegrower (15:1), he is the vine, and his disciples are the branches (15:1, 5). Apart from him and the Father, they cannot bear fruit. For the branches to bear fruit they must live in the vine and be pruned by the vinegrower. By proclaiming that he is the vine, then, Jesus again reveals that he is the way to the Father, the gate through whom the sheep must enter, the one who reveals the Father as the source of life.

As one looks back, it should be apparent that all of these sayings (I am the bread of life; I am the light of the world; I am the gate; I am the good shepherd; I am the resurrection and the life; I am the way, the truth, and the life; I am the vine) reveal Jesus and the Father in relation to eternal life. There is no other way to this life but through the Son, and there is no other source of life but the Father. To believe in the Son, therefore, is to receive life from the Father, which life not even death can destroy. The Son of God does not reveal "unprecedented secrets," as Bultmann notes, but he does reveal the way to life. He reveals the one thing the world most needs: life that will not perish, eternal life, which is found in the Father and mediated through the Son.

I Am

In a number of instances, Jesus simply affirms "I am" (*egō eimi*) without adding a predicate. In some instances, this expression appears to be a formula of identification, for example, when Jesus tells the disciples on the storm-tossed sea, "It is I; do not be afraid" (6:20), or when he identifies himself to the arresting party, "I am he" (18:5, 6, 8).[32] But in other cases there is another sense. For example, Jesus tells "the Jews" they will die in their sins "unless they believe that *egō eimi*" (8:24). He says that when they have lifted up the Son of Man they "will realize that *egō eimi*, and that I do nothing on my own, but I speak these things as the Father instructed me" (8:28). He warns his disciples what is about to happen so that when it occurs they may believe that *egō eimi*. In each instance the audience will realize that Jesus is who he claims to be, namely, the one who came from the Father. Accordingly, if "the Jews" do not believe that he is who he claims to be, they will die in their sins, although they

---

32. It is possible that there is an epiphany element in these statements as well since, when Jesus appears to the disciples, he is walking on the sea (6:19), and when he identifies himself to the arresting party, those who would apprehend him step back and fall to the ground (18:6).

will realize who he is after he has been lifted up. As for the disciples, they will remember what Jesus said, and then realize that he is who he claimed to be—the one whom the Father sent into the world.[33] To summarize, the "I am sayings," those with predicates and those without predicates, reveal Jesus as the one who comes from and reveals the Father. To receive this revelation is not only to understand who Jesus is but who God is as well.

The Christology of the Fourth Gospel is a theology of God inasmuch as Jesus reveals the Father to the world. In the view of the Fourth Gospel, to know who Jesus is, is to know who God is, and to know who God is, is to know who Jesus is. This is why the Fourth Gospel makes such harsh statements about "the Jews" and "the world." Within the narrative world of this Gospel, these expressions often stand for those who do not believe that Jesus comes from the Father; and because they do not, they do not know God.

THE SIN OF THE WORLD

The Son comes into the world to reveal the Father to the world so that the world may know the truth and dwell in the light that is life. In revealing the Father to the world, the Son discloses that the world is enslaved to sin and in need of salvation. This is not a two-step process, however, as if the Son first reveals the Father to the world and then, in a second act of revelation, discloses the sinfulness of the world. Rather, it is in the very act of revealing the Father to the world that the Son reveals that the world dwells in darkness and falsehood. For just as one becomes aware of the darkness only when the light shines, so the world does not know its true condition until the Son comes as the light of the world who reveals the Father. A discussion of the sending of the Son into the world, then, necessarily leads to a consideration of the situation of the world in light of the Son's revelation.

The Salvation and Judgment of the World

The concept of "the world" (*ho kosmos*) in the Fourth Gospel is somewhat elusive since it can refer to the world of creation or, when employed as a figure of speech, to the world of human beings. For example, when the prologue says that the world came into being through the agency of the Word (1:10), or when Jesus asks the Father to glorify him with the glory he had in the Father's presence before the world existed (17:5), the created world is in view. But when Jesus teaches that the bread of God is that which comes down from heaven

---

33. In a final "I am saying" in 8:58 ("Very truly, I tell you, before Abraham was, I am") the Gospel points to Jesus' preexistence.

"and gives life to the world" (6:33), or when the Pharisees complain that the world has gone after Jesus (12:19), "the world" is a metonymy for human beings. This is especially clear when the Johannine narrator remarks that "the light has come into *the world*, and *people* loved darkness rather than light because their deeds were evil" (3:19). Inasmuch as human beings live in the created world, then, the distinction between the world of creation and the world of humanity is fluid. For example, when Jesus says, "I came into this world for judgment" (9:39), or when Martha confesses that Jesus is "the one coming into the world" (11:27), both dimensions of "the world" are in play. Jesus has come from the Father into the world of creation, and in doing so he comes into the world of human beings.

A more important distinction is that between the world as the object of God's love and "the world" as a figure of speech for unbelief. Because the world came into being through the agency of the Word (1:10), God loves the world and gave his only Son, "so that everyone who believes in him may not perish but may have eternal life" (3:16). Thus God did not send the Son into the world to condemn it but to save it through his only Son (3:17). The Son comes into the world, then, as the true light of the world (1:9), and those who follow him do not walk in darkness (8:12; 9:4–5; 11:9; 12:46). The Son is "the Savior of the world" (4:42), "the prophet who is to come into the world" (6:14). He is the "living bread" that has come down from heaven and gives his flesh "for the life of the world" (6:51). Because he comes to save the world, the Son declares to the world what he has heard in the Father's presence (8:26). The Father has sanctified and sent him into the world (10:36), and although all judgment is in his hands, the Son has come not to judge but to save the world (12:47). The Father and the Son, then, are one in their will to save the world.

There would be no need for God to send his Son into the world unless the world were in need of salvation.[34] That the Son comes as the light of the world indicates that the world dwells in darkness, and his promise of eternal life reveals that the world does not possess the fullness of life. The Fourth Gospel never explains the origin of the world's predicament in the way that Paul does (see Rom. 5:12–21), but it is quite insistent that the world finds itself in a situation characterized as darkness, sin, death, and utter denial of the truth that is God.[35] The most surprising aspect of this predicament is that the world is not

34. Paul argues in a similar way when he notes that if righteousness comes through the law, then Christ died for nothing (see Gal. 2:21). In other words, why would God have sent his Son if humanity could find righteousness through the law?

35. Georg Strecker (*Theology of the New Testament* [Louisville: Westminster John Knox Press, 2000], 489) notes: "The Fourth Evangelist does not reflect on the cause of humanity's state of unsalvation. He does not take up the Jewish tradition of the fall of Adam into sin or the corresponding idea of 'original sin.' Neither is it a matter of fate, as though humanity had been unconditionally delivered over to this destiny as in Gnosticism but it is a matter of a historical event, even if it is not presupposed that each person has made a conscious decision against the truth."

aware of it.[36] Consequently, even though the light has come into the world, the world prefers the darkness to the light because its deeds are evil (John 3:19).

The reaction of the Pharisees to the healing of the man born blind is an indication of the world's predicament. Although they cannot dispute that Jesus has given sight to a man who was blind from birth, they refuse to believe that Jesus comes from God. When he says that he has come into the world for judgment "so that those who do not see may see, and those who do see may become blind" (9:39), the Pharisees respond, "Surely we are not blind, are we?" (9:40). In response, Jesus says, "If you were blind, you would not have sin. But now that you say, 'We see,' your sin remains" (9:41). The "sin of the world" is its refusal to believe in the one who brings the light that is life; this sin is the world's denial that it dwells in sin.

Jesus comes as the Lamb of God to take away the sin of the world (1:29), but the world hates him and his disciples. The world is under the power of "the ruler of this world" (12:31; 14:30; 16:11). Because Jesus does not belong to the world and testifies that its works are evil, the world hates him (7:7). Since it hates him, it also hates his disciples, whom he has chosen out of the world and whom he will send into the world (15:18–19; 17:18). The disciples will experience persecution and sorrow in the world, and the world will rejoice because of their trials (16:20), but Jesus has cast out the ruler of this world (12:31) and overcome the world (16:33). When the Paraclete comes he will prove that the world was wrong about sin because it did not believe in the one whom the Father sent into the world, about righteousness because Jesus has returned to the Father from whom he came, and about judgment because through Jesus' revelation of the Father the ruler of this world has been cast out (16:8–11).

To summarize, the world, which is the object of God's love, finds itself in a predicament of which it is not even aware until the light comes into the world to expose the darkness in which it dwells. Because its deeds are evil and it prefers to dwell in the darkness, the world does not realize that it is under the control of "the ruler of this world." Left to itself, the world is blind to the truth of its predicament. Its fundamental sin is unbelief—a refusal to believe that the Son reveals the Father. This Johannine analysis of the human condition discloses that humanity prefers to live apart from God's revelation lest it be compelled to see itself for what it truly is. It fears God's revelation because in revealing the Father, the Son reveals humanity to itself. It proclaims that apart from God humanity cannot enjoy the light that is life. Making use of existen-

---

36. Strecker (ibid., 489–90) puts it this way: "Life in falsehood, sin, and subjection to death points to a situation that is objectively hopeless but of which the individual is not aware. . . . There is no escape hatch from one's being in this world of untruth; it is total. And this situation is all the more hopeless, since the worldly human being takes untruth for truth, darkness for light, and death for life (cf. 9:40–41)."

tial philosophy, Bultmann describes the world in this way: "Thus the world creates for itself a *security* of its own and operates within it as that which is *familiar and to be taken for granted*. It shrugs off the disturbance that is created for it by the appearing of Jesus with its incredulous question: 'How can this be?' (3:9), or with similar 'how's' (6:42; 7:15; 8:33; 12:34)."[37]

The Jews and the World

One of the most distinctive aspects of the Fourth Gospel is its frequent use of the expression "the Jews" (*hoi Ioudaioi*). Whereas the Synoptic Gospels identify Jesus' opponents as the Pharisees, the scribes, the Sadducees, and the high priests, it is the Pharisees, who are often identified as "the Jews," who remain Jesus' primary protagonists in the Johannine Gospel. The expression "the Jews" is troublesome and elusive: troublesome because it can engender hostility toward the Jewish people; elusive because it has several nuances of meaning within the Gospel narrative. This phrase, which I have placed in quotation marks throughout this chapter, is treated here because the Fourth Gospel tends to employ "the Jews" as a way of exemplifying the world's refusal to believe in Jesus as the one who comes from God.

Before analyzing this expression, I think it is important to state that the Gospel clearly affirms that Jesus is a Jew and that "salvation comes from the Jews" (4:9, 22). Although the Gospel lacks a fully developed salvation history comparable to that found in Luke–Acts, it insists that Abraham rejoiced that he saw Jesus' day (8:56), that Moses wrote about Jesus (5:46), that Isaiah saw his glory and spoke about him (12:41), and that the Scriptures are about him (1:45; 5:39). For this reason, Strecker writes, "There is a *line of salvation history* that leads from the history of Israel to Jesus."[38] But it is also evident that there is a religious separation between those who now believe in Jesus as the one who has come from the Father and "the Jews" inasmuch as the Johannine narrator frequently refers to the feasts of "the Jews" in a way that distances those who believe in Jesus from those who do not (2:13; 5:1; 6:4; 7:2; 11:55; 19:42). "The Jews" have become a cause of fear for those who would believe in Jesus (7:13; 9:22; 20:19), threatening to expel, or actually expelling, them from the synagogue (9:22; 12:42; 16:2). Consequently, those who believe in Jesus as the Messiah are not at home in the synagogues of "the Jews," and they do not celebrate the feasts of "the Jews" as they once did, since Jesus is the perfection of those feasts. Although those who have embraced the Gospel's message about Jesus are confident that he is the fulfillment of Israel's deepest longing—the perfection of the law given through Moses (1:17)—they have distanced themselves

37. Bultmann, *Theology of the New Testament*, 2:32.
38. Strecker, *Theology of the New Testament*, 492.

from "the Jews." "The Jews," as portrayed in the Fourth Gospel, have become the Gospel's primary example of the world's refusal to believe.

It should be clear at this point that "the Jews" of the Gospel narrative cannot simply be equated with the Jewish people of Jesus' ministry, as if all of Jesus' Jewish contemporaries willfully refused to believe in him. Indeed, even this Gospel is aware that some Jews believed in Jesus, though not all arrived at the fullness of faith (2:23; 8:31; 12:11). Within the Fourth Gospel "the Jews" is a literary and theological expression that points to the unbelief of the world in a concrete manner. Although the Fourth Evangelist undoubtedly views the concept as rooted in history, the contemporary reader will do best to see this expression as a figure of speech—unfortunate in its formulation since it is open to misinterpretation—that points to the world's unbelief: the refusal of every age to accept the revelation of the Son.

Who Are "the Jews"?

There are moments within the Gospel when "the Jews" refers to the Jewish crowds without any particular note of hostility. For example, many of "the Jews" come to console Martha and Mary at the death of their brother Lazarus (11:19, 31, 33, 45). To be sure, they do not fully understand what Jesus is about, but then neither do Martha and Mary. As Moloney notes, everyone is wrong, no one comprehends the significance of Jesus' claim to be the resurrection and the life.[39] But in this particular story, "the Jews" are not expressly presented as Jesus' opponents, nor do they represent the Jewish leadership. They are those who have come to console Martha and Mary.[40]

The situation, however, is quite different in the healing of the man born blind. Within this narrative the man is brought to the Pharisees (9:13, 16), who are then identified as "the Jews" (9:18). When the man's parents (who are Jewish) are asked about their son and give a vague reply, the Johannine narrator remarks, "His parents said this because they were afraid of the Jews; for the Jews had already agreed that anyone who confessed Jesus to be the Messiah would be put out of the synagogue" (9:22). Since the parents themselves are Jews, it is evident that "the Jews" are not the Jewish people but a leadership group opposed to Jesus, in this case the Pharisees whom Jesus condemns at the end of the episode (9:40–41). Other examples of this use of "the Jews" occur throughout the Gospel. "The Jews" who send priests and Levites to John (1:19) are identified as the Pharisees (1:24). When the narrator notes that it was Caiaphas who had advised "the Jews" that it was better for one person to die for the people (18:14), he recalls an earlier episode in which Caiaphas coun-

---

39. Moloney, "Can Everyone Be Wrong?"

40. In the view of the Johannine narrator, however, such consolation is misplaced since Jesus is the resurrection and the life. Therefore, death has already been overcome.

sels the chief priests and the Pharisees (11:47–50). "The Jews," then, cannot simply be equated with the crowds or the Jewish people. In many instances they are a leadership group opposed to Jesus, most notably the Pharisees.

The Hostility of the Jews

In the great middle section of the Gospel (chaps. 5–10), which narrates a series of events that occur during the Jewish feasts of Passover, Tabernacles, and Dedication, the hostility between Jesus and "the Jews" is especially acute. It is in this section more than any other that the Gospel presents "the Jews" as an example of the world's refusal to believe that Jesus comes from the Father. According to the Johannine narrator, "the Jews" began to persecute him because he violated the Sabbath (5:16). When Jesus explains that he "works" on the Sabbath because his Father is still working, "the Jews" seek to kill him because, in addition to violating the Sabbath, he was calling God his Father and making himself equal to God (5:18). In the discourse that follows, Jesus accuses "the Jews" of refusing to accept the testimony of John, the testimony of his own Father, the testimony of the Scriptures, and the testimony of Moses (5:31–47). In the view of the Johannine narrative, "the Jews" are an example of "the world" that is incapable of believing because it is more interested in receiving human praise than the glory that comes from the only true God (5:44). "The Jews," then, provide a narrative example of a world closed in upon itself, thinking that it already enjoys eternal life in its Scriptures, when instead those Scriptures point to the giver of eternal life (5:39–40). The world thinks that God's love dwells in its midst, but it does not accept the one whom the Father has sent in his name (5:42–43). In a word, the world represented by the expression "the Jews" thinks it already enjoys salvation and so refuses to accept the salvation that comes from God.

The audience for the bread of life discourse is the large crowd that Jesus fed with the five barley loaves and the two fish, the same people who proclaim that he is the prophet who is coming into the world (6:14). But as the discourse progresses and Jesus claims that *he* is the bread of life that has come down from heaven, the narrative portrays "the Jews" complaining about Jesus because he says that he is the bread that comes down from heaven (6:41). Next, when Jesus proclaims that he is the living bread and whoever eats this bread will live forever, "the Jews" dispute among themselves and ask, "How can this man give us his flesh to eat?" (6:52). Thus, at two moments when Jesus makes important claims (that he is the bread of life and those who eat this living bread will live forever), it is "the Jews" who complain and dispute among themselves. As in the previous episode, the Fourth Evangelist employs "the Jews" as an example of the world's unbelief. The world represented by "the Jews" is scandalized by the incarnation. Since the world thinks that it knows Jesus' origin, it refuses to believe that he came down from heaven (6:42). It refuses to believe that "this

man" can give his flesh to eat (6:52). The world of unbelief is constrained by
its own self-imposed limits of what it is willing to believe God can do.

At the Feast of Tabernacles "the Jews" are still mystified by Jesus. They are
astonished by the learning of someone who has not been taught according to
their system of learning (7:15). They do not understand what he means when
he says that he is going to the one who sent him, and they will not be able to
follow him (7:33–35; 8:21–22). The problem is that even though the world
symbolized by "the Jews" thinks that it knows God, it does not, for only if the
world knows Jesus can it know God (8:19). The world represented by "the
Jews," then, is not even aware that its knowledge of God is deficient.

The conflict reaches its high point when Jesus speaks to "the Jews" who had
believed in him (8:31). But as the conversation develops, it is apparent that
their faith is inadequate. "The Jews" think of themselves as free because they
are Abraham's descendants. What "the world" represented by "the Jews" does
not understand is that it is enslaved to sin, and, because it is, its father is the
devil (8:44). The situation of the world, then, is that it thinks of its enslavement to sin as freedom and does not realize that it is under the ruler of this
world. The climactic statement of this discourse, "You are from your father
the devil, and you choose to do your father's desires" (8:44), is one of the most
unfortunate statements of the New Testament, and Christians will do well to
avoid any notion that the Jewish people are demon-possessed. The statement
is best taken as a metaphor for unbelief that can be applied to all who willfully
align themselves with a world that is blind to its own enslavement to sin. The
world, as the Fourth Gospel understands it, refuses to believe because Jesus
tells it the truth (8:45): it is enslaved to sin. When the world refuses to believe
this revelation, it shows that its father is the devil.

After Jesus' discourse on the good shepherd, "the Jews" are once more
divided, some thinking that he is demon-possessed or out of his mind, others
are not so sure (10:19–21). Consequently, at the Festival of Dedication, they
demand that Jesus tell them plainly whether he is the Messiah (10:24). That
Jesus has already told them that he comes from the Father has made no impression upon them. They have even refused to believe in the works he had done.
Consequently, it will make little difference if he tells them that he is the Messiah. For the Fourth Evangelist "the Jews" characterize the unbelief of the
world, and because they do, they do not understand what Jesus means when
he says, "The Father and I are one." For them his self-revelation is blasphemous and deserves death. When the expression "the Jews" is understood as
pointing to the unbelief of the world, then it reveals the true condition of the
world—the world refuses any revelation beyond its own understanding of
God. The world refuses to accept that God reveals himself in the incarnate
one. The world refuses any revelation that it cannot explain.

The King of the Jews

Except for a reference to the debates during the Feast of Tabernacles (13:33), there is no mention of "the Jews" in Jesus' farewell discourse, which now speaks of the hostility of "the world" that the disciples must face. "The world" that will hate Jesus' disciples plays the same role that "the Jews" played during Jesus' ministry. Understood in a hostile sense, "the world" and "the Jews" refer to the same reality: the refusal of humanity to believe in the one whom God sent into the world. In the passion narrative, however, "the Jews" reappear once more as those who oppose Jesus and bring him to Pilate. The question is whether Jesus is the King of the Jews. From the point of view of "the Jews," he cannot be since he does not fit their understanding of what it means to be the Messiah. From the point of view of the narrative, however, there is an ironic sense in which the title is correct: Jesus is the King of the Jews because he testifies to the truth (18:37). But just as the world confuses darkness with light and slavery with freedom, so it confuses falsehood with truth; and because it does, it does not recognize the true King of the Jews when he appears.

The main point of this exposition can be summarized in this way. The Fourth Gospel employs the expressions "the Jews" and "the world" to highlight humanity's refusal to believe in the one whom God sent into the world. "The world" is the more abstract and universal concept, "the Jews" a more concrete manifestation of disbelief. Together, they reveal the depth of the human predicament from which humanity cannot extricate itself because it refuses to believe in anything beyond itself. The light discloses the darkness, which is sin and falsehood: the sin of refusing to believe that God has revealed himself in the human one; the falsehood of mistaking the lie for the truth. Only by embracing the Son's revelation can "the world" understand its true situation.

THE COMMUNITY OF BELIEVERS: THE CHURCH

In revealing the Father to the world, the Son discloses that the world dwells in a darkness of which it is not even aware, confusing falsehood with truth and death with life. Although the world refuses to believe this revelation of its predicament, some within the world no longer belong to the world because Jesus has chosen them out of the world to be his disciples. A discussion of the situation of the world, then, leads to a consideration of the community of those who believe in the Son's revelation, namely, Jesus' disciples. These disciples, as portrayed within the Fourth Gospel, represent more than the followers of the earthly Jesus. They point to the community of those who believe that Jesus came from God; they represent the church. A discussion of the disciples, then, entails a consideration of Johannine ecclesiology, albeit in a limited sense, since the Gospel is primarily a narrative about Jesus rather than an exposition of ecclesiology. But through the story it tells, it does disclose something of Johannine ecclesiology.[41] This section, then, deals with the following topics within the framework of Johannine ecclesiology: (1) the community of Jesus' disciples; (2) the Spirit and the community of Jesus' disciples; (3) sacraments: Baptism and Eucharist; (4) the church's experience of salvation: Johannine eschatology.

The Community of Jesus' Disciples

The disciples, as portrayed in the Johannine Gospel, are the historical link between Jesus and the church. They stand as witnesses to his ministry, death, and resurrection, and they form the nucleus of the church that believes in him. Within the Johannine Gospel, Jesus' first disciples come from the circle of John the Baptist, thereby establishing a link among John, Jesus, and the church (1:35–37). In the first part of the Gospel, the disciples are present with Jesus as he reveals himself to the world. They believe in him when he reveals his glory at Cana of Galilee (2:11). They remember what he says and does, although they do not always understand the full significance of his words and deeds at the time (2:22; 12:16). Some even find his teaching so difficult that they no longer follow him (6:66). When Jesus asks the Twelve if they also want to leave, however, Peter responds, "Lord, to whom can we go? You have the words of eternal life" (6:68). In the Fourth Gospel Jesus' disciples are those who abide in his word because they believe that he comes from the Father with the words of everlasting life.

The Fourth Gospel never names the Twelve, nor does it report their call in the way the Synoptic Gospels do. The only explicit reference to them is in 6:70, "Did I not choose you, the twelve? Yet one of you is a devil." Nevertheless, it seems to assume that these twelve are the inner circle of Jesus' disciples whom he addresses in his farewell discourse.[42] Although spoken to this inner circle, the farewell discourse is ultimately directed to the church, a community of disciples that abides in Jesus' words. Within this discourse, the disciples are portrayed (1) as chosen and elected, (2) as in the world but not of it, (3) as sharing an intimate relationship with the Father and the Son, (4) as a community that follows Jesus' commandment to love one another, and (5) as sent into the world for mission by Jesus.

---

41. See the study of the Johannine church by Raymond E. Brown, *The Community of the Beloved Disciple: The Life, Loves, and Hates of an Individual Church in New Testament Times* (New York: Paulist Press, 1979).

42. This does not mean that discipleship is limited to the Twelve. The text of 6:66 already points to a wider circle of disciples, and Jesus tells "the Jews" that if they continue in his word, they are truly his disciples (8:31).

The Father has given the disciples to Jesus, and so they ultimately belong to the Father (17:9). For this reason Jesus reveals the name of the Father to them (17:6), and while he is with them he protects them in that name (17:12). Because the Father has given the disciples to him, Jesus can say that he has chosen and elected them (6:70; 13:18; 15:16). Consequently, he loves "his own" to the very end (13:1), and he appoints them to go forth and bear fruit that will last (15:16). It is not the disciples who have chosen Jesus, but Jesus who has chosen them out of the world, and for this reason the world hates them (15:16, 19). Inasmuch as the community of Jesus' disciples belongs to the Father and has been chosen by Jesus, the church is a community of the chosen and elect that belongs to God, a theme that runs throughout the Pauline Letters. This divine election, however, is not to be interpreted as a double predestination whereby some have been called to salvation and others have not. Discipleship is available to all who believe that Jesus comes from the Father. It is by abiding in Jesus' word that disciples know they have been chosen, whereas those who refuse to abide in his word show they have not been chosen.

Although Jesus' disciples do not belong to the world, they continue to live in the world. They came "from the world," and before they embraced Jesus' word they lived in its darkness unaware of their sin. But they now believe that the Father sent Jesus into the world (17:8). Although Jesus is no longer in the world, the disciples are in the world (17:11). Being in the world, however, is not the same as belonging to the world (17:14). To be in the world is to live in the created world, whereas to belong to the world is to align oneself with the world's self-understanding, to live in the darkness that is sin. Because the disciples no longer belong to the world, just as Jesus did not belong to the world, the world hates them (15:19). Inasmuch as the community of Jesus' disciples are those who live in the world without being of the world, they form a sanctified community that has been consecrated in the truth that is God's word (17:17). The church, which is God's chosen and elect community, then, is a sanctified community that must live in the world without being of the world.

Since the community of Jesus' disciples is a sanctified community that lives in the world but not according to the world, it enjoys a new relationship with Jesus and the Father. Jesus is in the Father, the disciples are in him, and he is in them (14:20). Inasmuch as they are in Jesus who is in the Father, they are also in the Father. If they love Jesus by keeping his word, the Father will love them, and Jesus and the Father will dwell in them (14:23). In his prayer for his disciples, Jesus prays for their unity and sheds further light on this mystery of mutual indwelling. First, he prays that his own disciples may be one as he and the Father are one (17:11). Next he prays for unity between his disciples and those who will believe through their word so that all disciples, present and future, may be in the Father and the Son, just as the Father dwells in the Son and the Son in the Father (17:20–21). Thus Jesus will be in the disciples and the Father in Jesus so that the disciples may be completely one and the world may know that the Father sent the Son (17:23).

The most concrete description of this indwelling is found in the figure of the vine. Here it is necessary to recall the frequent exhortations to "abide" in Jesus and his love (15:4, 5, 6, 7, 9). If the disciples abide in him, the true vine, they will bear much fruit. As they bear fruit, the Father will prune them so that they may bear even more fruit. The fruit that the disciples bear is the fruit of loving one another as Jesus has loved them. When the disciples bear the fruit of this love, the Father will be glorified, and they will truly be Jesus' disciples (15:8). As the community of Jesus' disciples, then, the church enjoys a "mystical" union with the Son, and through the Son with the Father. This communion of the church, which Paul calls *koinōnia*, is rooted in the church's indwelling in the Son, and through the Son, in the Father.

Because the community of Jesus' disciples enjoys such an intimate union with the Father and the Son, it must reflect this unity to the world. Therefore, Jesus gives his disciples a new commandment that they love one another as he has loved them. In this way all will know that they are his disciples (13:34–35; 15:12–17). Jesus' commandment is new because his disciples must love one another in the way he has loved them by laying down his life for their sake (15:13). As the good shepherd, he has laid down his life for the sheep (10:11), and for this reason the Father loves him (10:17). In addition to loving one another, the disciples must love Jesus by keeping his commandments (14:15). If they do this, the Father will love them (14:21, 23). Therefore, just as Jesus has done what the Father commanded so that the world may know that he loves the Father (14:31), so the disciples must keep his commandments. His love for them is rooted in the Father's love for him. Just as the Father has loved him, so he has loved them, and so they must abide in his love (15:9).

Jesus' love commandment must be seen in the context of the Father's love for him and his love for the disciples. As the Father has loved the Son, the Son has loved the disciples, and as the Son has loved the disciples, the disciples must love one another so that the world will know that they are Jesus' disciples. By keeping his commandment (the whole of his revelation), the community of his disciples will express its love for him, and be loved by him and the Father. The church, as the community of Jesus' disciples, is a community rooted in love.

Although the disciples have been taken out of the world and no longer belong to the world, the community of Jesus' disciples is a missionary community. Because the disciples have believed that the Father sent Jesus into the world, Jesus sends them into the world (17:18; 20:21), where they will encounter trouble and persecution (16:1–4). The world will hate them just as it hated him (15:18), but Jesus will ask the Father to send them another Paraclete to strengthen them. Thus, although the world is the realm of unbelief, God does not abandon it. The world remains the object of God's love even after Jesus' death. For this reason, the church, as the community of Jesus' disciples, is essentially a missionary community.

The Spirit and the Community of Jesus' Disciples

Like the Synoptic Gospels, the Fourth Gospel presents Jesus as the Spirit-endowed Son of God. Although this Gospel refrains from describing his baptism (since it presents John as a witness to Jesus rather than as the one who baptizes him), John testifies that he saw the Spirit descending from heaven and remaining on Jesus. John then discloses that the one who sent him to baptize said, "He on whom you see the Spirit descend and remain is the one who baptizes with the Holy Spirit" (1:33), and he testifies, "This is the Son of God" (1:34). From the outset of the Gospel, then, it is clear that Jesus is the Spirit-endowed Son of God upon whom the Spirit descends and remains.

In the narrative that follows, Jesus speaks of the importance of this Spirit. He tells Nicodemus that "no one can enter the kingdom of God without being born of water and Spirit" (3:5), and he tells the Samaritan woman that God is Spirit and must be worshiped in spirit and truth (4:24). To those disciples who find his teaching on the bread of life difficult to receive, he says that it is the Spirit that gives life, whereas the flesh is useless. Jesus' words are spirit and life (6:63). Because no one can enter the kingdom of God or worship God apart from the Spirit, Jesus promises the Samaritan woman "living water" that will gush up to eternal life (4:10, 14), and during the Feast of Tabernacles he promises "rivers of living water" to those who come to him (7:38). This living water is the Spirit that Jesus intends to bestow upon those who believe in him, for, as the Johannine narrator notes, "as yet there was no Spirit, because Jesus was not yet glorified" (7:39). After Jesus' death, blood and water flow from his side (19:34), and when he appears to his disciples, he breathes upon them saying, "Receive the Holy Spirit" (20:22).[43] Jesus is the one who "gives the Spirit without measure" because he comes from above and speaks what he has heard (3:31–34). This is why his words are "spirit and life" (6:63), and his disciples believe that he has "the words of eternal life" (6:68).

In addition to this story of Jesus and the Spirit, which runs throughout the Gospel narrative, the Fourth Gospel refers to the "Paraclete" whom Jesus and the Father send to the disciples after Jesus returns to the Father. The precise meaning of Greek *paraklētos* is disputed.[44] Latin writers translated it as

---

43. The reference to "blood and water" flowing from Jesus' side is sometimes taken as referring to the Eucharist and baptism. See Moloney, *Gospel of John*, 505–6. This sacramental meaning, however, is not accepted by all commentators. The logic of the Gospel's narrative suggests that whereas the blood confirms the reality of Jesus' death, the water points to the Spirit he gives by his death, and which he subsequently gives to his disciples by breathing the Spirit upon them.

44. See the entry in BDAG s.v. *paraklētos*.

advocatus, giving the sense of someone called to the aid of another, whereas Greek writers understood it in a more active sense, as helper or advisor. Accordingly, it has been translated as "Comforter" (KJV), "Helper" (NASB), "Counselor" (RSV, NIV), and "Advocate" (NAB, NRSV). The precise meaning of the term and its role in the Gospel's understanding of the Spirit, however, is best determined by examining the five passages of the farewell discourse in which it appears.

The first Paraclete saying occurs in 14:15–17. If the disciples love Jesus, they will keep his commandments. He, in turn, will ask the Father to send them another Paraclete who will be with them forever. The Paraclete is identified as "the Spirit of truth," which indicates that the very essence of the Spirit is truth. The world cannot see or recognize this Spirit, but the disciples will know the Paraclete because it will abide with them and in them. By speaking of "another" Paraclete, Jesus suggests that the Paraclete will function as he did, revealing "the truth" as he did (thus the name, "the Spirit of truth"). Just as the Father gave Jesus to the world, so the Father will give the Paraclete to the disciples, and just as the world did not recognize that Jesus came from the Father, so it will not be able to recognize the Paraclete when he comes. The disciples, however, who recognize that Jesus came from the Father, will know the Paraclete, with whom they will enjoy a mutual indwelling.

In the second saying (14:25–26), the function of the Paraclete is more precisely defined: the Paraclete will teach the disciples everything and remind them of what Jesus said to them. The Paraclete is now identified as "the Holy Spirit." Whereas in the first saying Jesus said that he would ask the Father to give them another Paraclete, now he says that the Father will send the Paraclete in his (Jesus') name. The Paraclete, then, comes from the Father through the intercession of, or in the name of, Jesus. He does what Jesus did and reminds the disciples of everything he said. By doing so, he makes Jesus' teaching present to the disciples and to those who will follow them.

The third Paraclete saying (15:26–27) occurs after Jesus tells his disciples that the world will hate them. If Jesus had not spoken to the world and performed the works that he did, the world would not be guilty of sin. But now the world is without excuse; for it has hated both Jesus and his Father (15:22–25). Against this backdrop, Jesus says that he will send the Paraclete to the disciples from the Father. The Paraclete, who is again called the Spirit of truth, will testify on Jesus' behalf, and the disciples will do the same since they have been with Jesus from the beginning. The preceding verses, in which Jesus accuses the world of being without excuse, suggest that the disciples, supported by the Paraclete, will now testify against the world, which refused to believe in Jesus or his works. Unlike the first two sayings in which Jesus says that the Father will send the Paraclete, Jesus now says that he will send the Paraclete. But as in the first two sayings, it is clear that the Paraclete comes from the Father.

The fourth saying (16:7–11) occurs after Jesus speaks of the persecution and hardship the disciples will endure (16:1–4a). Jesus did not tell the disciples these things at the beginning, because he was with them (16:4b). But now that he is returning to the Father, he tells them what they must endure. Although the disciples are saddened, it is to their advantage that Jesus go, for if he does not depart, the Paraclete will not come to them. But if Jesus leaves, he will send them the Paraclete. This Paraclete will then sustain the disciples in their time of trial by proving the world wrong about sin, righteousness, and judgment. The world will be shown to be in sin because it did not believe in Jesus. It will be shown to have been wrong about righteousness because Jesus has returned to the Father. And it will be shown to have been mistaken about judgment because Jesus has cast out the ruler of this world. As in the third saying, Jesus is the one who sends the Paraclete, who will expose the sin and guilt of the world, thereby assisting the disciples in their time of trial and persecution.

In the fifth and last saying (16:12–15), Jesus promises that the Paraclete, the Spirit of truth, will guide the disciples in all truth because he will not speak on his own but only what he hears, and he will declare to them what is to come. He will glorify Jesus because he will declare to the disciples what belongs to Jesus. The work of the Paraclete and his relation to Jesus, then, is analogous to Jesus' work and his relation to the Father. Just as everything that belongs to the Father belongs to Jesus, so everything that belongs to Jesus belongs to the Father. Just as Jesus glorifies the Father by declaring what belongs to the Father, so the Paraclete will glorify Jesus by declaring what is his to the disciples. This fifth saying, then, explains what Jesus means when he says in the first saying that the Father will send the disciples "another" Paraclete. The work of the Paraclete continues the work of Jesus.

The central points of the Paraclete sayings can now be summarized. First, the Paraclete continues the work of Jesus by teaching and reminding the disciples of what Jesus did. Second, the Paraclete will sustain the disciples in the trials they will face after Jesus' departure by testifying on his behalf and proving that the world, not Jesus, was in the wrong. Third, the Paraclete will enable the disciples to testify to the world that Jesus came from the Father. Consequently, as Jesus constituted the disciples as a community during his lifetime, so the Paraclete will constitute the disciples as a community of believers—the church—after Jesus' departure. The Spirit of truth, the Paraclete, continues the work of Jesus in the church so that disciples may hear and remember the words of eternal life from generation to generation.

Sacraments: Baptism and Eucharist

The Fourth Gospel does not explicitly speak of what the later church calls "sacraments" since it is primarily a narrative about Jesus. But inasmuch as the

Gospel was composed within and for a community of believers, it reflects to some degree the Johannine community's experience of worship and sacraments. Consequently, although one should not expect to find a fully developed sacramental theology in this or any New Testament writing, it is not unreasonable to search for clues that point to the Johannine understanding of the sacraments, more specifically, baptism and the Eucharist.

Although the Fourth Gospel is more intent upon presenting John as a witness to Jesus rather than as the one who baptized him, there is no doubt that John baptized (1:25, 26, 28). The purpose of his divinely appointed task, however, was to reveal the Spirit-endowed Son of God to Israel (1:31, 33).[45] The Johannine Gospel also reports that Jesus and his disciples baptized (3:22). A few verses later, however, the Johannine narrator notes that it was not Jesus who was baptizing but his disciples (4:1–2). This clarification is necessary because Jesus comes to baptize with the Holy Spirit, not with water, as John has already testified (1:33), an event that occurs when the risen Lord breathes the Spirit upon his disciples and says, "Receive the Holy Spirit. If you forgive the sins of any, they are forgiven them; if you retain the sins of any, they are retained" (20:22–23).[46] There is an interesting line of development, then, regarding baptism in the Fourth Gospel. John baptizes in order to reveal Jesus to Israel. During the early period of Jesus' ministry his disciples, many of whom were former disciples of John, also baptize with water, although the purpose of this water baptism is never explained. Most importantly, after his resurrection Jesus baptizes his disciples with the Holy Spirit, just as John said he would.

Although there is no description within the Gospel narrative of Jesus "instituting" the sacrament of baptism, there are texts that point to the sacrament, the most important being Jesus' conversation with Nicodemus. The dialogue begins with Jesus affirming that one cannot enter the kingdom of God without being born *anōthen*, a word that can mean "from above" or "again" (3:3). When Nicodemus mistakenly thinks that he must be born a second time, Jesus replies that no one can enter the kingdom of God "without being born of water and Spirit" (3:5). Although Jesus does not explicitly speak of "baptism," the community of his disciples—the church—now understands his response to Nicodemus in terms of baptism. Those who enter the community are "born from above" through the power of the Spirit, which is given to them through water baptism in Jesus' name. Baptism, then, is a sacrament of *water and the*

45. Unlike the Synoptic Gospels, John the Baptist does not call people to repentance to prepare the way for the Lord. His role is to baptize and testify that Jesus is the Messiah.

46. On a literary level, the statement of 4:2 may refer only to the remark in 4:1 (that the Pharisees heard that Jesus was baptizing and making more disciples than John). Thus Jesus did baptize as noted in 3:22, but at this particular moment (noted in 4:1) he was not baptizing. On a historical level, it may well be that Jesus practiced water baptism for a time. But in the period after Jesus' death and resurrection, the church sees that Jesus' most important baptism is the gift of the Spirit.

Spirit, water signifying the "living water" that is the Spirit. It is not simply a rite of washing but a sign that points to the living water that is the Spirit. By the gift of this Spirit believers are born from above so that they enter the kingdom of God.

As important as this teaching is, it is only the beginning of Jesus' revelation, belonging to what the Gospel calls "earthy things" (*ta epigeia*, 3:12) in contrast to "heavenly things" (*ta epourania*, 3:12). Hebrews 6:1–2 makes a similar distinction between "basic teaching" and going on "toward perfection." This distinction is not meant to denigrate baptism but to indicate that it is a gateway to further revelation. Those who have been born from above are now in a position to hear and understand "heavenly matters."

Before beginning his farewell discourse, Jesus washes his disciples' feet (John 13:3–11). When Peter objects to this, Jesus replies that Peter will have no share with him unless he allows Jesus to wash him. Peter then asks Jesus to wash not only his feet but his hands and head as well, at which point Jesus replies, "One who has bathed does not need to wash, except for the feet, but is entirely clean" (13:10). Jesus' remark indicates that the washing of his disciples' feet points to something else. By this action, which is the work of a slave, Jesus is indicating that he will wash his disciples by his slavelike death on the cross. After Jesus' death, the Johannine community understands its baptismal practice in light of Jesus' action. Baptism recalls what Jesus did when he washed the disciples' feet; it is not a complete bath but points to the cleansing bath that comes from Jesus' death. By being baptized, believers enter into the cleansing action of Jesus' saving death on the cross.[47] It is not the rite of baptism that saves but that to which it points: the Lord's cleansing death on the cross.

By breathing the Spirit upon his disciples, the risen Lord confers the Spirit upon them as John foretold (1:33). This text also contributes to a Johannine understanding of baptism. The action of "breathing on" (*enephysēsen*, 20:22) the disciples recalls how God breathed life into the first human being (Gen. 2:7), and the gift of the Spirit brings with it the forgiveness of sins (Ezek. 36:25–27). For the Johannine community, baptism bestows new life, which results in the forgiveness of sins, and those who have been baptized are now empowered by the Lord to extend this forgiveness to others as well.

Although the Fourth Gospel does not narrate the institution of the Eucharist, it contains an extended discourse on the bread of life that has come down from heaven (John 6:25–59). The discourse is Jesus' homily on the text of Ps. 78:24: "He gave them bread from heaven to eat" (John 6:31). Jesus

---

47. On these points see Hahn, *Theologie*, 1:693; Rudolf Schnackenburg, *The Gospel according to John* (3 vols.; vol. 1, New York: Herder & Herder, 1968; vol. 2, Seabury, 1980; vol. 3, Crossroad, 1982), 3:21–22.

begins by stating the true meaning of the text: it is not Moses who gave them bread from heaven but Jesus' Father, who is presently giving them the true bread that comes down from heaven and gives life to the world (6:32–33). Jesus then identifies himself as this bread that has come down from heaven, and he promises that whoever believes in him will have eternal life (6:47). Those who "eat" this bread (a metaphor for believing in Jesus as the bread of life) will not die but live forever (6:50–51ab).

Toward the end of the discourse (6:51c–58), the verb "eating" takes on a different sense. It is no longer simply a metaphor for believing in Jesus.[48] In 6:51c Jesus identifies the bread that *he* will give for the life of the world as his flesh (*sarx*). When the Jews ask how he can give his flesh to eat (*phagein*, 6:52), he develops his thought further. Unless they eat the flesh of the Son of Man *and drink his blood*, they will not have life in themselves. Employing a graphic verb for eating (*trōgeōn*), Jesus says that on the last day, he will raise up those who "eat" his flesh and "drink" his blood because his flesh is real food and his blood real drink, therefore those who "eat" his flesh and "drink" his blood abide in him and he in them (6:53–57). The discourse concludes with the true meaning of Ps. 78:24: the Israelites ate bread in the wilderness and died, but those who eat this bread will live forever (John 6:58).

Within the context of the discourse "bread" has two meanings. First, it refers to Jesus as the bread who has come down from heaven. Those who "eat" this bread by "believing" in Jesus have eternal life. But in the final part of the discourse (6:51c–58), the change of verbs for eating, from *estheōn* to *trōgeōn*, and the introduction of "flesh" and "blood" indicate that bread has taken on a eucharistic meaning. Jesus the true bread of life is now present to the believing community in and through the Eucharist it celebrates. Rather than do away with the need to believe that Jesus has come down from heaven, the Eucharist provides each generation with a sacramental way to appropriate this truth.

The "sacramental theology" reflected in the Fourth Gospel can be summarized in this way. Baptism is a birth from above through the power of the Spirit. It enables the believer to enter into the saving mystery of Jesus' cleansing death; it leads to new life and the forgiveness of sins. The Eucharist is the way in which believers appropriate Jesus, the bread of life that has come down from heaven. When they believe in him as the bread that has come down from heaven and eat his flesh and drink his blood in the Eucharist, they have life in themselves and the promise of future resurrection life.

---

48. Many commentators, most notably Rudolf Bultmann (*The Gospel of John: A Commentary* [Philadelphia: Westminster, 1971], 234–37), view these verses as the addition of an ecclesiastical redactor who was interested in sacraments. This position is still adopted by Hahn, *Theologie*, 1:696–98. But since in this New Testament theology I am concerned with the canonical text, and since there is no textual evidence for this position, it is best to treat these verses as part of the text and not separately.

The Church's Experience of Salvation: Johannine Eschatology

The community of those who believe in Jesus as the one whom the Father has sent into the world cannot be understood apart from the Johannine concept of life or eternal life that the Son brings to those who believe in him. This concept, in turn, is integral to the Fourth Gospel's distinctive presentation of eschatology: its experience of, and its hope for, God's final redemptive work.

The Johannine Gospel is quite clear about its purpose: it has been written so that people may believe that Jesus is the Messiah, the Son of God, and through this faith "have life in his name" (20:31). It is not surprising, then, that life/ eternal life plays such a prominent role in the narrative.[49] Jesus promises the Samaritan woman "a spring of water gushing up to eternal life" (4:14). He teaches that he is the bread of God that has come down from heaven "and gives life to the world" (6:33). He comes as the good shepherd so that people "may have life, and have it abundantly" (10:10). He reveals that he is "the way, and the truth, and the life" (14:6), and in his prayer to the Father he says that eternal life is to know the only true God and the one whom God has sent, Jesus Christ (17:3). What is surprising, at least to those unfamiliar with the Gospel, is its insistence that those who believe in Jesus *already* share in this life, which is eternal life. For example, the one who believes in the Son "has eternal life" (3:36). Anyone who hears Jesus' word and believes in the one who sent him "has eternal life, and does not come under judgment, but has passed from death to life" (5:24). The believer already possesses eternal life (6:47). Consequently, the believer need not wait until the last day to attain eternal life. The life that Jesus brings *is* eternal life, and those who believe in him already share in this eschatological gift.

This distinctive Johannine understanding of life/eternal life raises the question of Johannine eschatology. How is this concept of eternal life as a reality already experienced related to a more traditional eschatology that hopes and waits for the Lord's parousia and the general resurrection of the dead? In the Synoptic Gospels and the Pauline Epistles, there is a vibrant hope that Christ will come again. But in the Johannine Gospel this hope appears to have faded. There are no sayings about the return of the Son of Man at the end of the ages as in the Synoptic Gospels. Nor is there any description of the Lord's parousia and the events that will occur at that time, as there are in Paul's Letters. Consequently, Johannine eschatology is often described as a "realized eschatology" because the future has been collapsed into the present, whereas the eschatology of the Synoptic Gospels and the nondisputed Pauline letters is called a "consistent eschatology" because it anticipates a series of final

---

49. Although the Gospel speaks of "life" and "eternal life," the two expressions refer to the same reality. Life is eternal life.

dramatic events (the return of Christ, the general resurrection of the dead, and the final judgment) whereby God will be victorious over sin and death.

The Fourth Gospel still alludes to these dramatic eschatological events. For example, in his Sabbath discourse Jesus says, "Do not be astonished at this; for the hour is coming when all who are in their graves will hear his [the Son's] voice and will come out—those who have done good, to the resurrection of life, and those who have done evil, to the resurrection of condemnation" (5:28–29). Here there is an unmistakable reference to the resurrection of the dead and the judgment that will accompany it. In the bread of life discourse, in which Jesus promises that those who eat his body and drink his blood "have eternal life" (6:54), he says that he will raise up the believer on the last day (6:39, 40, 44, 54). Another allusion to "the last day" occurs at the end of Jesus' public ministry when he warns, "The one who rejects me and does not receive my word has a judge; *on the last day* the word that I have spoken will serve as judge" (12:48). Finally, although the Gospel of John does not speak of the Lord's parousia as Paul and the Synoptic writers do, the farewell discourse includes a number of intriguing sayings about Jesus coming to the disciples "again" (14:3, 18, 28), as well as promises that they will see him "again" (16:16, 22). While the sayings of chapter 16 now refer to the resurrection, those of chapter 14 appear to allude to the Lord's return, albeit without the apocalyptic imagery found in Paul and the Synoptic writers.

Rudolf Bultmann attributed these more traditional eschatological sayings (especially 5:28–29; 6:39, 40, 44, 54; 12:48) to a later "ecclesiastical redactor."[50] In doing so, he attempted to make the Fourth Gospel more internally consistent with itself. A New Testament theology, however, does not enjoy this luxury since its primary object is the canonical text rather than a hypothetical, reconstructed text. Moreover, even if Bultmann is correct, the later redactor is not necessarily betraying the earlier layers of tradition since the tensions these texts appear to introduce may be intended to clarify the Gospel's eschatology.

A profitable starting point for approaching Johannine eschatology is the expression "the hour is coming, and is now here" (4:23; 5:25). In 4:23 "the hour" is the hour when people will worship the Father in spirit and in truth, whereas in 5:25 it is the hour when the dead will hear the voice of the Son of God and live. From the perspective of a traditional eschatology, this hour is the last or final hour. But from the viewpoint of Johannine eschatology, it is an hour that is *already* occurring in Jesus' life and ministry. Although God will be worshiped in spirit and truth and the dead will be raised on the last day, the believer *already* participates in these realities through faith in the Son of God.

---

50. Bultmann, *John*, 219–20, 261–62. Hahn (*Theologie*, 2:714–15) also attributes these sayings to a later redactor.

The same juxtaposition of present and future occurs in the bread of life discourse: "This is indeed the will of my Father, that all who see the Son and believe in him may have eternal life; and I will raise them up on the last day" (6:40). On the one hand, the believer already enjoys eternal life by believing in Jesus; on the other, the believer will be raised up on the last day. A similar juxtaposition of present eternal life and a future resurrection is found in 6:54: "Those who eat my flesh and drink my blood *have eternal life*, and *I will raise them up on the last day*."[51] This juxtaposition of present eternal life and a future resurrection suggests the continuity between present and future for the Fourth Gospel, thereby underscoring the importance of the gift already received. Resurrection life *is* a continuation of the life/eternal life that the believer has already received by believing in the one whom God sent into the world.

The conversation between Martha and Jesus is helpful for grasping Johannine eschatology. Martha begins by lamenting that if Jesus had been present, her brother would not have died (11:21). Jesus then speaks of the resurrection of the dead in traditional terms, "Your brother will rise again" (11:23), which Martha confirms, "I know that he will rise again in the resurrection on the last day" (11:24). At this point, however, Jesus reinterprets this traditional eschatology for her: "I am the resurrection and the life. Those who believe in me, even though they die, will live, and everyone who lives and believes in me will never die" (11:25–26). It is no longer sufficient to believe in the general resurrection of the dead. Those who believe *already* enjoy resurrection life because the one in whom they believe *is* the resurrection and the life. Because they *already* possess this life, they will live even if they die, and they will not suffer eternal death because the eternal life they *already* possess cannot be taken from them. Consequently, even though they must face physical death, they will not lose the eternal life they already enjoy. Their resurrected life will be the continuation of a life they already possess.

The future is not as important for the Fourth Evangelist as it is for Paul and the Synoptic writers. The more traditional temporal perspective that looks forward to an apocalyptic victory at the close of the ages has given way to a more vertical approach because the one who is from above has come into the world. Believers will suffer physical death, and so there is still need for a resurrection from the dead. But since those who have believed in the Son of God have already passed from death to life, there is no need for the kind of

---

51. The inclusive translation of the NRSV misses the point that Jesus speaks of raising the individual believer from the dead. This emphasis upon the individual is significant since Paul and Acts tend to focus on the general resurrection of the dead, whereas the Fourth Gospel has begun to emphasize the resurrection of the individual on the last day. The difference is subtle but important.

apocalyptic scenario found in other New Testament writings. Resurrection means resurrection to a life the believer already possesses.[52]

The main points of Johannine ecclesiology can now be summarized. The church has been chosen and elected by Jesus, who sends it into the world, just as the Father sent him, so that the world may believe. This community of disciples enjoys the gift of the Paraclete, the Spirit of truth, who reminds them of all that Jesus said and did, and sustains them during times of persecution. Through the Paraclete, then, Jesus is present to the church once more. This church also experiences the Spirit and the life that the Spirit gives through baptism and the Eucharist. This life is eternal life, so real and present that for this community of believers the future has invaded the present.

THE MUTUAL GLORIFICATION
OF THE FATHER AND THE SON

The sending of the Son into the world results in the mutual glorification of the Father and the Son in which the community of Jesus' disciples now participates. Because the world prefers its own glory to the glory that comes from God, it dwells in darkness. Only when it acknowledges that the Son glorifies the Father and that the Father glorifies the Son does the world pass from the darkness of death to the light of life. The Johannine concept of glorification, then, completes the Gospel's theology.

As the preexistent Word that dwelt in God's presence before the world existed, the Son already enjoyed the very glory of God (17:5). In coming into the world, the Son reveals this glory by accomplishing the work the Father gave him to do. This "work" is the entire revelation the Son brings through his words and deeds, a work that culminates in his death, whereby he glorifies the Father and the Father glorifies him. Depending upon how one evaluates Jesus' relation to God, the incarnation conceals or reveals this glory. The community that stands behind the witness of the Fourth Gospel confesses: "The Word became flesh and lived among us, and we have seen his glory" (1:14), because it believes in the Son. But the world looks upon the incarnate one and sees a human being who glorifies himself rather than God. The incarnation, then, is the scandal and paradox that underly the Gospel narrative. This paradox comes to its climax in Jesus' death, which the believer understands as the act by which the Father glorifies the Son, whereas the world views the same event as the just punishment of one who has blasphemed and led God's people astray.

In the first part of the Gospel, the Son reveals his glory and God's glory in the works he does. For example, Jesus' first sign reveals his glory, and his disciples

---

52. It is important to recall that the Fourth Gospel tends to emphasize the resurrection of the individual rather than describe an apocalyptic scene of the general resurrection of the dead.

believe in him (2:11). The raising of Lazarus leads to God's glory, and the Son is glorified through this victory of life over death (11:4, 40). The works that Jesus does throughout his ministry, then, disclose his glory because they testify that he comes from God in whose presence he enjoyed God's glory. Even Isaiah saw his glory and spoke about him (12:41). In revealing Jesus' glory, then, these works glorify God because the Son does only what the Father commands him to do.

It is Jesus' death, however, that is the culminating act whereby the Son glorifies the Father and the Father glorifies the Son, and it is this understanding of death as glorification that is the distinctive trait of Johannine theology. On several occasions the Gospel refers to Jesus' death in terms of his glorification. For example, the evangelist notes that during Jesus' ministry there was no Spirit yet "because Jesus was not yet glorified" (7:39), that is, Jesus had not yet died. The disciples understand the significance of Jesus' actions only when he is glorified (12:16), that is, after he has died. When the time approaches for his death, Jesus says, "The hour has come for the Son of Man to be glorified" (12:23), that is, to be lifted up on the cross. During the farewell discourse, the hour is so close that Jesus speaks as if it has already occurred: "Now the Son of Man has been glorified, and God has been glorified in him" (13:31). In the prayer before his death, he prays that the Father will glorify the Son so that the Son may glorify the Father (17:1). In all of these instances, Jesus is referring not to the resurrection as the moment of his glorification but to his death, whereby he will glorify God, and God will glorify him. In the Fourth Gospel, the power of the resurrection already makes itself felt in Jesus' death, even as death and resurrection remain distinct events.

Although the evangelist understands the violence and brutality of crucifixion, he chooses to present Jesus' death as a moment of glorification rather than as a moment of humiliation, a paradox that only a faith rooted in the incarnation can comprehend. Consequently, the Son does not die with a cry of dereliction but says, "It is finished" (19:30), referring to the work the Father gave him to do. The lifting up of the Son of Man on the cross becomes the moment of his exaltation, and the Son's death is the occasion for his departure and return to the Father. This remarkable understanding of death means that the resurrection does not play quite the same role in the Fourth Gospel that it does in other New Testament writings, where it functions as God's vindication of Jesus. To be sure, the evangelist narrates the account of the empty tomb and the appearances of Jesus to his disciples. But there is a sense in which the resurrection in the Fourth Gospel appears to be primarily for the benefit of Jesus' disciples, a way of confirming that his death was the moment of his glorification.[53]

---

53. This statement needs to be balanced by other data such as Jesus' words to Mary, after his resurrection, that he has not yet ascended to his Father (20:17). Thus, even though the Gospel portrays Jesus' death as a return to the Father, it also maintains the traditional view of his return to the Father as an ascension that occurs after the resurrection.

The Gospel presents Jesus' death as a moment of glorification because it understands Jesus' death in light of the incarnation. Because the Word became flesh, the death of the Son is not a moment of humiliation, no matter how the world judges it. Death has become his departure and return to the Father, the Son's moment of glorification. This distinctive understanding of the crucifixion requires believers to see God's glory where the world cannot.

CONCLUSION

Whereas the Synoptic tradition highlights Jesus' preaching of the kingdom of God, the Johannine tradition highlights Jesus' preaching about himself as the one whom the Father sent into the world. For the Synoptic tradition Jesus is the messianic Son of God, the royal descendant of David. He announces the kingdom of God and enters into its transcendent realm by his saving death and resurrection. Having been raised from the dead, he is now enthroned at God's right hand as Messiah. God is revealed in Jesus' proclamation of the kingdom, a revelation that comes to its climax in Jesus' death and resurrection.

For the Johannine tradition Jesus remains the messianic Son of God, but the emphasis is now on his origin. Jesus the Messiah is the incarnation of the pre-existent Word of God who reveals what he has seen and heard in the Father's presence. Although he does not proclaim the kingdom of God, he does reveal the life that the kingdom brings. He teaches what he has seen and heard in the Father's presence and those who believe that he comes from the Father have already passed from death to life. Because Jesus comes from God, his death is the moment of his glorification and return to the Father who sent him into the world to reveal what he has seen and heard in the Father's presence.

Whereas the Pauline tradition focuses on Christ's saving death and resurrection, the Johannine tradition focuses on Christ's incarnation. The Pauline emphasis on Christ's death and resurrection makes the cross the locus of God's salvation, the place where believers see God's redemptive work in the crucified Christ. The cross reveals God's power in weakness, God's wisdom in folly, God's victory over every cosmic power. The cross reveals that God is the one who justifies the ungodly and reconciles humanity and the cosmos to himself. The cross reveals how God vindicates the righteous Christ by raising him from the dead. Thus the cross reveals the God of hope, the God who raises the dead.

The Johannine emphasis on the incarnation makes the person of the Son the locus of salvation, the one in whom God is revealed to the world. Whereas Paul highlights the scandal of the cross, John emphasizes the scandal of the incarnation. This scandal is the Gospel's claim that the Word became flesh. It is Jesus' claim that to hear and see him is to see and hear the Father who sent him into the world. For the Johannine Gospel, the scandal of the incarnation is the locus of God's revelation. In this scandal God is revealed to the world.

Although these three great theological traditions present God's revelation in Christ from different vantage points, they agree that Jesus is the locus of God's revelation to the world. In and through him, believers encounter God. This encounter occurs in the experience of the inbreaking kingdom of God that Jesus announces, in the scandal of the cross that the Pauline Gospel proclaims, and in the scandal of the incarnation that the Johannine Jesus claims for himself. In every case, Jesus remains the locus of God's revelation.

10

A Theology of Communion with God

1 John

The relationship of the Johannine Epistles to one another and to the Fourth Gospel is complex and disputed. Although a majority of commentators maintain that the Epistles were written after the Gospel and presuppose its theology, a strong minority argues that they predate the Gospel and represent an earlier form of Johannine theology.[1] The relationship of the Epistles to one another is no less complex. On the one hand, 1 John does not identify its author, and it lacks a letter salutation and closing, raising the question of its genre.[2] On the other, 2 and 3 John are true letters, and in both the author identifies himself as "the elder." In terms of content, however, 1 and 2 John are similar insofar as they both refer to a group that no longer confesses that Jesus is the Christ, whereas 2 and 3 John deal with the issue of hospitality, albeit differently.[3]

Although there is no unanimity about the relationship of the Epistles to the Gospel or of the Epistles to one another, I assume that the Epistles were written after the Gospel by someone who was closely associated with those who

---

1. For example, Strecker (*Theology of the New Testament*, 421–22) argues that the Epistles were written before the Gospel because they exhibit an earlier form of Johannine theology. He also argues that 2 and 3 John were composed before 1 John.

2. Raymond E. Brown (*An Introduction to the New Testament* [New York: Doubleday, 1997], 392) notes that 1 John has none of the features expected of a letter and that scholars disagree about its genre. He suggests that it may be "a written exhortation interpreting the main themes of the Fourth Gospel in light of secessionist propaganda that had a certain plausibility and continued to attract followers."

3. Whereas in 2 John 10–11 the elder warns the recipients not to offer hospitality to anyone whose teaching does not correspond with his own, in 3 John 9 the elder complains that Diotrephes refuses to offer hospitality to his (the elder's) emissaries.

were responsible for the production of the Gospel.[4] I also assume that the author of 2 and 3 John was probably the author of 1 John. This author, the elder, whom I shall call John, writes to assure a community, which has recently suffered the trauma of schism, that its members are in communion with the bearers of the authentic Johannine tradition, and so in communion with God. If this reconstruction is correct, 1 John was originally a circular letter that dealt with a crisis within the community occasioned by the departure of some of its members, and 2 John was a cover letter that warned other communities not to offer hospitality to the emissaries of those who had left the community. As for 3 John, it appears to have been occasioned by the refusal of a particular church leader, Diotrephes, to offer hospitality to the emissaries of the elder.[5] According to this scenario, the canonical order of the material is the chronological order in which the letters were composed.

Overall, the Johannine Epistles presuppose a situation that can be summarized as follows. A group of believers from within the community—sometimes referred to as the secessionists—have recently left the community.[6] In the view of 1 John, they have denied that *Jesus* is the Christ, the Son of God.[7] This is not to say that they no longer believed in Christ. To the contrary, they appear to have held a high Christology that emphasized the divinity of Christ at the expense of his humanity. In light of this Christology, they affirmed that they enjoyed a profound communion with God and were without sin. This Christology, however, severed the link between Jesus (the human one in whom the

4. Raymond E. Brown (*The Epistles of John: Translated with Introduction, Notes, and Commentary* [AB 30; Garden City, NY: Doubleday, 1982] 32–35) and John Painter (*1, 2, and 3 John* [SP 19; Collegeville, MN: Liturgical Press, 2002], 58–74) offer helpful discussions regarding the relationship between the Gospel and the Epistles. Both believe that the Gospel precedes the Epistles. The history of how the Fourth Gospel came into being is complicated and disputed. Many argue that the Gospel was composed in stages, within a Johannine school or circle that treasured and handed on the witness of the Beloved Disciple. The author of 1 John appears to have been a member of this circle, or closely associated with it. On the composition of the Gospel, see Raymond E. Brown, *An Introduction to the Gospel of John*, edited, updated, introduced, and concluded by Francis J. Moloney (New York: Doubleday, 2003), 40–89.

5. Although Diotrephes was an independent-minded leader, who refused to accept the authority of the elder and offer hospitality to his emissaries, there is no indication that he belonged to or favored the secessionists; otherwise it is difficult to understand why the elder sent emissaries to him in the first place.

6. Brown (*Epistles of John*, 47–86) has reconstructed the position of the secessionists and then employed this reconstruction in his interpretation of the Epistles. Painter (*1, 2, and 3 John*, 88–93) also provides a profile of the opposition. Judith Lieu (*The Theology of the Johannine Epistles* [NTT; Cambridge: Cambridge University Press, 1992], 15) acknowledges that the Epistles were written in the context of opposition and debate over the authentic interpretation of the Fourth Gospel but argues that "however serious the schism, the polemic against the specific views and claims of opponents does not control the letter or its thought."

7. The italics are meant to emphasize that it was the human one, Jesus, whom the secessionists refused to confess as the Christ, the Son of God. Thus they denied the incarnation.

Word became flesh) and the Christ, the Son of God. Having effectively separated Jesus from the Christ, the Son of God, they were on the way to what later theology would call Docetism.[8]

The secessionists undoubtedly thought that their Christology offered a profound understanding of Christ that brought them a more perfect communion with God because they were no longer hindered by the flesh of Jesus. From the point of view of 1 John, however, this Christology not only misunderstood the nature of the incarnation, it misrepresented the authentic meaning of communion with God. For, in denying that Jesus is the Christ, the secessionists misunderstood the paradoxical way in which God (1) manifested his love to the world, (2) effected the forgiveness of sins, and (3) enabled humanity to be in communion with God. In a word, although the secessionists viewed their Christology as a teaching that brought them into closer communion with God, the Johannine Epistles argue that it is precisely this teaching that prevents authentic communion with God. In response to this crisis, the Johannine Epistles develop a theology of communion that is rooted in the incarnation.

Although the Johannine Epistles were occasioned by a particular problem within the church, there is something enduring about their theology. The theology of these writings, especially 1 John, draws an intimate relationship between faith and praxis, offering a series of ethical and christological tests whereby believers can determine if they are in communion with God. Those who do not pass these tests are not in communion with God, no matter what they claim for themselves. Focusing on the motif of communion, in this chapter I present material under the following headings: (1) communion with God; (2) ethical tests for communion with God; (3) christological tests for communion with God; (4) love and communion with God; and (5) sin, sinlessness, and communion with God.

COMMUNION WITH GOD

The trauma caused by the departure of some members of the community inevitably raised the question of which group was in communion with God: those who left the community or those who remained? Who were the authentic bearers of the tradition: the secessionists with their new understanding of Christ, or those who continued to confess that Jesus, the human one, was the

---

8. Docetism is the name for a heresy that developed in the second century. Strecker (*Theology of the New Testament*, 438) writes, "They could grasp the Christian confession of the saving significance of Jesus only to the extent that they could make a strict distinction between the heavenly Christ, whom they acknowledged, and the earthly human Jesus. It was only the latter, in their understanding, who had suffered and died on the cross, while the former only 'appeared' to be identical with Jesus."

Christ, the Son of God? Fully aware of what is at stake, the author of 1 John begins with a prologue (1:1–4) in which he associates himself with the original witnesses of the Johannine tradition ("we") who testify to what they have heard, seen, and touched with their own hands so that the recipients of the letter may have *koinōnia* ("fellowship," NRSV; "communion," author's translation) with them.

From the point of view of 1 John, there are two reasons why *koinōnia* with the bearers of the original tradition ("we") is crucial for communion with God. First, the group with which 1 John associates itself faithfully testifies to what it has seen, heard, and touched from the beginning: the message about the Word of life that was enfleshed in Jesus, the Messiah, the Son of God. John, then, insists that what he communicates to the recipients of the letters ("you") is an authentic tradition that has been faithfully handed on from the beginning. Second, those with whom John associates himself ("we") already enjoy *koinōnia* with the Father and his Son, Jesus Christ, because they know and abide in the truth of what they have heard, seen, and touched. For the recipients ("you") to have *koinōnia* with God, they must be in communion with the original witnesses of the faith, those whom John identifies as "we."[9]

Although an initial reading of the prologue could suggest that the second group is not yet in *koinōnia* with the first, it soon becomes apparent that John addresses believers who share his faith in the original tradition of the community and so are in communion with God. John affirms that their sins are forgiven, that they have known him (Jesus) from the beginning, that they have conquered the evil one, that they know the Father, that they are strong, and that the word of God abides in them (2:12–14). But apprehensive that the community may be questioning its relationship to God because of the schism that has so recently traumatized it, John assures its members of their relationship to the original bearers of the tradition, and so to God. The central theological issue of 1 John, then, is *koinōnia*, which is often translated as "fellowship" but is better rendered "communion." For whereas fellowship suggests a social relationship between two parties, the *koinōnia* of which John speaks is participation in a shared reality (the life of God) whereby believers are in communion with one another. It is communion with God and Christ, then, that grounds the *koinōnia* believers have with one another.

Communion with God can be summarized as follows. The message to which the original witnesses testify is about "the word of life" (1:1). Those who are in communion with God already participate in this life. This life is eternal life (1:2; 5:11), and it cannot be destroyed by death. Believers have passed from

---

9. John uses "we" in two ways. At times it refers to the original bearers of the tradition with whom the author of 1 John associates himself, see 1:1–4. At other times John employs "we" to associate himself with the community; see 2:1–3. Lieu (*Theology of the Johannine Letters*, 23–27) has a helpful discussion regarding the relationship of the author to the community.

death to life (3:14); and John writes in order that they may know that they have eternal life (5:13; see also John 20:31).

Intimately related to this life are the concepts of light and love. John reminds his recipients of the message that the original witnesses ("we") proclaimed to them: "that God is light and in him there is no darkness at all" (1:5). As the epistle progresses, John also defines this message in terms of love, reminding his listeners that the message they have heard from the beginning is that they should love one another (3:11). He then provides a theological reason for this love, "Whoever does not love does not know God, for God is love" (4:8). Thus John defines God in two ways: as light and as love. To be in communion with God is to walk in the light and to abide in God's love, for only those who love their fellow Christians dwell in this light (2:9–10). To be in communion with God is to participate in God's own life, which is light and love.

The concepts of truth, knowledge, and abiding are also important for understanding *koinōnia*. Those who walk in the light of life by loving God and their fellow Christians know God and abide in the truth. Knowledge of God is not a mere intellectual understanding of God. It is a deep and intimate experience of the Father and the Son, and it results in confidence and assurance that casts out all fear. Those who know God dwell and abide in the truth; they enjoy an intimate communion with God and one another. If the community continues to abide in what it has heard from the beginning, it will abide in the Son and the Father (2:24).[10]

In addition to light, love, truth, knowledge, and abiding, John employs two other concepts to explain what he means by being in communion with God. First, he affirms that the recipients of the letter have been anointed by the Holy One so that they have knowledge (2:20). This anointing abides in them and teaches them all things (2:27).[11] Second, John affirms that although their final destiny has not yet been revealed, the recipients of the letter have been begotten by God and are already called children of God (3:1). Born of God, they have conquered the world (5:4).

Communion with God, then, is participation in the life of God, which is light and love. Those who participate in this life know the truth of God, which is revealed through Jesus Christ and the Spirit; they dwell in this knowledge, which is the truth. Their participation in the life of God makes them children

10. The concept of truth plays an important role in 2 and 3 John (see 2 John 1, 2, 3, 4; 3 John 1, 3, 4, 8, 12). Strecker (*Theology of the New Testament*, 430) writes, "'The truth' means the revealed reality of God, in which one can participate because it takes hold of one (cf. 2 John 2) or one finds oneself 'in' it or 'walking' in it (cf. 2 John 4; 3 John 3–4)."

11. Although the meaning of this anointing is disputed, there are two reasons why it is likely that it refers to the Spirit that the community has received from Jesus. First, in the Gospel Jesus is called "the Holy One of God" (John 6:69). Second, in the remaining christological tests, John calls upon the community to test the spirits to determine if they are from God (4:1); and he argues that the Spirit, the water, and the blood agree in their testimony about Jesus Christ (5:6).

of God and provides them with an anointing whereby they know the truth. But how do believers know if they are truly in communion with God and one another?

ETHICAL TESTS FOR COMMUNION WITH GOD

Aware that those who have left the community also affirm that they are in communion with God, John provides a number of ethical tests to determine if one is in communion with God. Six of these tests occur within the first two chapters of 1 John, the first three beginning with the phrase, "If we say . . ." (1:6, 8, 10), and the last three with the formula "whoever says . . ." (2:4, 6, 9).

The first test (1:6–7) draws an immediate connection between *koinōnia* with God and the ethical life. One cannot claim to have communion with God and continue to walk in the darkness. Those who make such claims are liars, and they do not practice the truth; they are no longer living in accordance with the message of life they received from the beginning. Correcting this false understanding of communion, John notes that those who walk in the light, as Jesus did, enjoy *koinōnia* with one another, and the blood of Jesus cleanses them from their sins. Although one might have expected John to say that they have *koinōnia* with God, the emphasis upon *koinōnia* with one another anticipates a theme that will reoccur throughout the letter: there is no communion with God apart from communion with one's fellow Christians.

In the second test (1:8–9), John criticizes those who claim that they have no sin, arguing that such people deceive themselves and the truth is not in them. Conversely, those who confess their sins will be forgiven and cleansed from all unrighteousness. This second test suggests that those who left the community claim to have no experience of sin because they are in communion with God. From the point of view of John, this claim is false since it does not take into consideration the ongoing task of living a morally good life.

In the third test (1:10), John develops the theme of sinfulness further. Those who say that they have not sinned make "him" a liar,[12] and his word does not dwell in them. For John, Jesus Christ came as an atoning sacrifice for the sins of the whole world. Therefore, if believers sin, they have an advocate with the Father, Jesus Christ (2:1–2). Any claim not to have sinned calls into question the atoning sacrifice of the Son and his role of advocate before the Father.

Taken together, the first three tests affirm the ethical dimension of communion with God. Those who do not behave in a way that accords with the light, which is the life of God, are not in communion with God, no matter

---

12. Here "him" refers to God since this verse belongs to a larger unit (1:5–10) that deals with communion with God.

what they claim for themselves. Since all have sinned, those who wish to be in communion with God must acknowledge their sinfulness.

The ethical dimension of *koinōnia* with God comes into even sharper focus in the remaining tests. In the fourth test (2:3–5a), John assures his audience: "we may be sure that we know him, if we obey his commandments." He then proceeds to argue that the one who says, "I have come to know him," but does not obey his commandments, is a liar. Conversely, the love of God reaches perfection in those who obey God's Word. Although John does not identify these commandments, the following verses indicate that it has in view the commandment the community received from the beginning: believers should love one another (2:7–8).

The fifth test (2:5b–6) is also prefaced by a statement of assurance: "By this we can be sure that we are in him." The test that follows requires those who say, "I abide in him," to walk as Jesus walked. As the letter will make clear, Jesus walked in righteousness and love.

The sixth test (2:9–11), with its reference to light and darkness, recalls the first (1:6), and it completes the theme of keeping the commandments. Whoever says "I am in the light" and hates his fellow believer is still in the darkness, whereas the one who loves lives in the light. Dwelling in the light, then, requires one to love the other members of the community.

By these six tests, John establishes an intimate bond between communion with God and the moral life, a communion that finds its fullest expression in love for one's fellow believer. To be in communion with God is to know God and dwell in God's light, which is life. But since there is no communion with God apart from doing the commandments of God, anyone who claims to be in communion with God without living an ethically good life is a liar. The ethical tests for determining if one is in communion with God, then, affirm a central theological tenet: communion with God requires one to live a morally good life.

CHRISTOLOGICAL TESTS FOR COMMUNION WITH GOD

In addition to these ethical tests, John provides a series of christological tests to determine if one is in communion with God. That both the ethical and christological tests are necessary shows that John draws an intimate connection between faith and praxis. Those who do not confess that Jesus is the Christ cannot walk in the light, whereas those who walk in the light confess that Jesus is the Christ. In this way John makes Christology the foundation of the moral life, and the moral life the expression of authentic faith in Christ.

John presents his christological tests in three passages (2:18–27; 4:1–6; 5:4b-12). In the first, he warns his audience that it is the last hour because there are many antichrists who deny that Jesus is the Christ.[13] In the second, he exhorts the community to test the spirits, since any spirit that does not confess that Jesus Christ came in the flesh is not from God. In the third, he reminds the community that its faith in Jesus as the Son of God conquers the world. In each passage the test is similar: those who are in communion with God are those who confess that the human one, Jesus, is the Christ, the Son of God. The fundamental test, then, is faith in the incarnation.

In the first test (2:18–27), John identifies the secessionists as antichrists and liars who deny that Jesus is the Christ. Although they have left the community, their departure reveals that they never belonged to it. For, if they were God's children, they would never have left the community. Their refusal to acknowledge that Jesus is the Christ identifies them as antichrists, whose appearance signals the last hour. By denying that Jesus is the Christ, they have denied the Father and the Son, for Jesus is the Son who reveals the Father.

John is confident about the faith of those who have remained in the community, since they "have been anointed by the Holy One" (2:20). Because the community has received this anointing of the Spirit from Jesus the Christ, it has knowledge, and it knows the truth (2:20–21). As long as this anointing abides within it, the community has no need for others to teach it, for it abides in the truth that Jesus is the Christ. The first christological test, then, establishes a close relationship between faith in Jesus as the Christ and communion with God. The one who denies that Jesus is the Christ denies the Father and the Son, whereas the one who confesses the Son has the Father (2:22–23).

The second christological test (4:1–6) is similar to the first but it calls upon the community to test the spirits. For, although the community has been anointed by the Holy One, there are false prophets who do not confess Jesus. These prophets are the antichrists and liars of whom John has already spoken in the first test. They are called false prophets because they are led by a spirit of error. Thus there are two spirits: the spirit of truth and the spirit of error. The first is from God, the second from the world. But how is the community to distinguish between them? Believers can be sure that "every spirit that confesses that Jesus Christ has come in the flesh is from God" (4:2), whereas "every spirit that does not confess Jesus is not from God" (4:3). The spirit that does

---

13. The only occurrences of "antichrist/s" in the New Testament are in the Johannine Epistles (1 John 2:18, 22; 4:3; 2 John 7). This use of the term in these epistles is striking inasmuch as it refers to believers, albeit believers who have left the community. The Gospel of Mark speaks of "false messiahs" and "false prophets" (Mark 13:22) who will appear at the end time, before the parousia. In 2 Thess. 2:3 Paul refers to a lawless figure, whose coming is the work of Satan. And, of course, the book of Revelation speaks of the two "beasts" (Rev. 13:1, 11) who do the bidding of Satan. Although there is no unified teaching in the New Testament about these figures (antichrists, false messiahs, false prophets), there is a consensus that deceiving figures, who are in league with Satan, will arise in the last days to test the elect.

not confess Jesus is the spirit that refuses to acknowledge the incarnation, the coming of the Christ in the flesh of Jesus.

John is confident that the members of the community are from God and that they have conquered the false prophets because the one who is in them is greater than the one who is in the world. The one in them is the Spirit of God, the Spirit of truth, which abides in them. This is the one who is greater than the spirit of error that informs the false prophets who deny that the Christ has come in the flesh. The christological test John proposes here, then, is intimately related to the experience of the Spirit. Only those who acknowledge the identity of Jesus Christ as the one who came in the flesh possess the Spirit of God. Only they belong to God.

John begins his third christological test (5:4b–12) by stating that the victory that conquers the world is "our faith" (5:4b). Building upon this affirmation, he identifies those who conquer the world as the ones who believe that "Jesus is the Son of God" (5:5). The world is the realm of those who refuse to confess that Jesus Christ has come in the flesh. John has already instructed the members of the community not to love the world or the things of the world since the world and its desires are passing away (2:15–17). He assures them that their faith in Jesus as the Son of God has overcome the world.

Since the secessionists also believe in the Son of God, John must distinguish the faith of the community from the faith of those who have left it. Authentic faith believes in "the one who came by water and blood . . . not with the water only but with the water and the blood" (5:6). Behind this enigmatic statement lies a profound difference between the Johannine community and the secessionists. Whereas the latter affirm that the Son of God was manifested to the world when John baptized Jesus in the waters of the Jordan, the Johannine community affirms that the Son of God was also manifested in the shedding of Jesus' blood on the cross. For John, then, the affirmation that the Son of God was manifested at Jesus' baptism is true but inadequate since it does not take into account Jesus' atoning death on the cross, the moment when he handed over the Spirit.

For John there are three witnesses who testify on behalf of Jesus the Christ, the Son of God: *the waters of John's baptism*, when Jesus was identified as the Son of God (John 1:34); *the blood of Jesus shed on the cross*, whereby Jesus Christ became an atoning sacrifice for sins (1 John 2:1–2); and *the Spirit, which Jesus handed over on the cross* (John 19:30). Previous to Jesus' death, there was no Spirit because Jesus had not yet been glorified (John 7:39). But at his death Jesus handed over the Spirit (John 19:30), which he had promised during the Feast of Tabernacles (John 7:37–39). These three witnesses, whose testimony agree (1 John 5:7–8), are God's witnesses to his Son. To refuse to believe their testimony is to make God a liar. To accept their testimony is to receive eternal life, which God makes available in his Son. It is one's faith in Jesus as the Son of God, who came in water and the flesh, that discloses if one has life (5:12).

To summarize, one must confess that Jesus is the Christ, the one who came in the flesh, by water and by blood. This faith is corroborated by the anointing the community has received, the Spirit of truth. It is this confession that determines if one has the Father, if one is from God, if one has conquered the world, and if one has eternal life.

LOVE AND COMMUNION WITH GOD

In his description of Christian love, John establishes an intimate connection between faith and the moral life that can be summarized as follows: those who believe that Jesus is the Christ are born of God and their love for the one who begat them leads them to love God's children (5:1). This understanding of love, however, is restrictive since the children of God are those who confess that Jesus is the Christ. Consequently, it explicitly excludes the secessionists, and it does not include those who have not yet come to faith in Jesus Christ. But this profound love is available to all since God sent his Son into the world as an atoning sacrifice for the sins of the entire world (2:2). As the world is drawn into God's love through faith in Jesus, the Son of God, so it is drawn into the intense love that those begotten by God have for each other, a love that is the fruit of communion with God.

Before embarking upon his first description of love (3:12–24), John reminds the community of the message it has heard from the beginning: believers should love one another (3:11). Such love provides them with knowledge and assurance that they are in communion with God. By the love they have for one another, the members of the community know they have passed from death to life, whereas those who do not love abide in death (3:14). When believers love in truth and action, they know they belong to the truth (3:18–19).

Because they have the example of Jesus, who laid down his life for them, the members of the community know how to love one another. Therefore, they should lay down their lives for one another (3:16). For inasmuch as their love is rooted in God's love for them, they cannot expect God's love to abide in them if they see fellow believers in need and refuse to assist them (3:17).

John discloses his understanding of the intimate relationship between faith and praxis in the way he summarizes God's commandment: "we should believe in the name of his Son Jesus Christ and love one another, just as he has commanded us" (3:23). Here John joins the christological confession of the community with the love commandment. To abide in God's love one must believe and love; there is no separation between faith and praxis.

Whereas John's initial description of love (3:12–24) highlights the need for the community's members to love one another as Christ loved them, his second description (4:7–5:4a) draws a close relationship between love for God and love for one's fellow Christian. This relationship between love for God and love for one's fellow Christian is rooted in God's love for the believer, which God manifested by sending his only Son into the world.

Believers ought to love one another because love is from God (4:7), who has loved them (4:11). They are profoundly aware of this love because God sent his only Son into the world so that they might have life through the Son (4:9). The initiative for love, then, begins with God, who sent his only Son as an atoning sacrifice for sins (4:10). Those who do not love cannot know God because God is love (4:8, 16). Conversely, those who love are born of God; they know God, and they abide in God (4:7, 16). Because they are born of God, they love God's children (5:1).

There is an intimate connection, then, between God's own love, the believer's love for God, and the love believers should have for one another. Those who say they love God but hate their brothers and sisters are liars; for those who refuse to love their brothers and sisters, whom they can see, cannot love God, whom they have not yet seen (4:20). The commandment the community has received, then, is that those who love God must love one another.

The love for one's brothers and sisters of which John speaks is love for the other members of the community, for these are the ones who believe that Jesus is the Christ and so have been born of God (5:1). In contrast to them, the "liars" are those who have shown their hatred for their brothers and sisters by leaving the community and refusing to confess that Jesus is the Christ.

To understand why John limits the circle of love to those within the community, it is important to recall the link he establishes between God's own love and the sending of the Son into the world. Since God revealed his love by sending his only Son into the world, love begins with God. Since God manifested his love by sending his Son into the world, those who do not confess the Son cannot understand the depth of God's love. Conversely, those who confess that God has sent the Son into the world, and that Jesus is this Son, enjoy a profound communion with God and with one another, provided they love one another.

The Johannine concept of love is restrictive when compared to Jesus' commandment to love one's enemy. This restrictiveness is, in part, the result of an inner-community conflict waged within a dualistic framework of light and darkness, truth and falsehood: those who do not dwell in the light of truth do not love their brothers and sisters and so cannot love God. But there is something else at work here. Those who dwell in the light of the truth enjoy a profound communion with God and one another that others do not and cannot enjoy. To be sure, such an understanding of love runs the risk of a sectarianism that can quickly devolve into self-righteousness. But it need not. It can also become an incentive to bring the world into this circle of God's love. For God sent his Son into the world as an atoning sacrifice, "for our sins, and not only for ours but also for the sins of the whole world" (2:2).

SIN, SINLESSNESS, AND COMMUNION WITH GOD

There is a tension in what John says about sin, sinlessness, and communion with God that is difficult to resolve.[14] On the one hand, he condemns those who claim to be without sin (1:8, 10). On the other, he affirms that those who abide in Christ and are born of God do not sin (3:6, 9a; 5:18); indeed, they cannot sin (3:9b). To further complicate the matter, despite his teaching on sinlessness, John clearly acknowledges that believers sin and can be forgiven (2:1; 5:16). Thus there is a twofold tension within the epistle. On the one hand, there is a tension between the teaching of John and his opponents regarding sinlessness. On the other, there is a tension in John's own teaching, which acknowledges that believers sin even as he affirms his teaching on sinlessness.

The tension in John's teaching on sinlessness is helpful for explaining the difference between his teaching and that of the secessionists. Whereas John presents a paradoxical doctrine of sinlessness, which is tempered by the realization that believers sin, the secessionists claim that sin is no longer a reality in their lives because they have been freed and enlightened by the Son of God.[15] Thus John has the secessionists in view when he writes: "If we say that we have no sin, we deceive ourselves, and the truth is not in us" (1:8); or "If we say that we have not sinned, we make him a liar, and his word is not in us" (1:10). From the perspective of John such affirmations betray the truth because Jesus, whose death was an atoning sacrifice for the sins of the whole world, continues to act as an advocate before the Father on behalf of those who sin (2:1–2). The secessionists' understanding of sinlessness, then, does not comprehend the full significance of Jesus' atoning death or his role as an advocate before the Father. Most importantly, their departure from the community reveals the true nature of their teaching. For if they were truly without sin, they would never have left the community; they would have continued to love its members.

The tension within John's own teaching is more difficult to resolve. The most complete presentation of this teaching is in 3:4–10, a section in which John provides a way for the community to distinguish between the children of

---

14. Brown (*Epistles*, 412–15) lists seven solutions: (1) "Two different writers are involved." (2) "The author's statements are directed to two different groups of adversaries." (3) "The author is thinking of specific kinds of sin when he says that the Christian does not or cannot sin." (4) "The author is thinking only of special or elite Christians when he says that those begotten by God do not or cannot sin." (5) "The author means that Christians do not or cannot sin habitually even though there are occasional lapses." (6) "The author is thinking on two different levels" (the pastoral and the ideal). (7) "The author is speaking in two different literary contexts."

15. Brown (*Epistles*, 82) suggests that the secessionists may have derived their position from certain texts of the Gospel. For example, on the basis of John 8:31–34, they might have concluded that they were free from sin, and on the basis of 9:41, they might have claimed that they were not guilty because they are not blind. If this reconstruction is correct, there was a struggle between the secessionists and the author of 1 John over the authentic interpretation of the Johannine tradition.

God and the children of the devil. The main lines of the argument can be summarized as follows. Sin is lawlessness (*anomia*), and those who commit sin are guilty of lawlessness. Jesus, the Son of God, was revealed to take away sins, and there was no sin in him. Therefore, the one who abides in him does not sin, whereas the children of the devil commit sin. In contrast to them, those who have been born of God do not sin since God's seed dwells in them; indeed, they cannot sin.[16] The children of God and the children of the devil, then, are revealed by their deeds. Those who follow the path of lawlessness align themselves with the children of the devil, whereas those who follow the way of righteousness, which expresses itself in love for one's brothers and sisters, belong to God.

This distinction between the children of the devil and the children of God admits of no compromise. Sin, which is lawlessness, identifies one with the devil, who has sinned from the beginning, whereas righteousness, which is expressed in love, identifies one with the sinless Son of God.[17] John repeats this teaching at the end of the letter (5:18–20). But before doing so, he admonishes the members of the community to petition God on behalf of a fellow believer who sins, provided that the sin is not mortal (5:16–17).[18] Immediately after this statement, in which John acknowledges the presence of sin in the community, he reaffirms his teaching that "those who are born of God do not sin" (5:18). In effect, John reaffirms his teaching on sinlessness even as he acknowledges that believers can and do sin.

The tension in 1 John is similar to that in Paul's teaching on sin and baptism in Romans 6. On the one hand, Paul affirms that those who have died with Christ are freed from sin. Dead to sin, they are alive to God. But Paul is keenly aware that even those who have died with Christ in baptism can still sin. For although they have already been justified and reconciled to God, they will not be finally saved until the parousia and the general resurrection of the dead. Thus believers live with a tension in their lives; they live between what has already happened and what has not yet occurred.

Although John does not develop his theology of Christian existence with the clear eschatological reservation that Paul does (already justified but not yet

---

16. The inability to sin, impeccability, is a much stronger claim than sinlessness. For whereas one who is presently sinless may sin at some future time, one who is impeccable cannot sin. Rather than try to reconcile this statement of impeccability with John's acknowledgment that Christians sin, it may be best to see this statement from a paraenetic perspective, as does Strecker (*Theology of the New Testament*, 445).

17. John appears to equate righteousness and the love commandment inasmuch as righteousness involves keeping God's commandment, which for John is the love commandment (2:7–11; 3:11–17, 23–24; 4:7–8).

18. John need not explain what he means by a sin that is mortal since the members of the community understand this terminology. The context of the letter suggests that John is referring to the denial that Jesus is the Christ, the Son of God.

saved), he understands that even though believers are already God's children it has not yet been revealed what they will be (1 John 3:2). In effect, John implicitly acknowledges that believers have not attained perfect communion with God. Since they have not, the power of sin remains a danger in their lives. On the one hand, John affirms that believers are in communion with God and dwell in the light. On the other, he is aware that they can and do sin (2:1; 5:16). When they do, they show that they are no longer abiding in Christ and acting as God's children. But if their sin is not mortal, they can be restored to communion with God. In effect, John juxtaposes two important truths, which he expects his audience to hold in tension: sinlessness in Christ and sin in the Christian life.[19]

In the end, there is an unresolved tension in John's teaching on sin, sinlessness, and communion with God. The secessionists avoided this tension by refusing to take into account the reality of sin in their lives. John provides a more realistic view of the Christian life, albeit at the cost of consistency. Christians live a sinless life so long as they abide in Christ and belong to God. But experience shows that even those who have been born of God fail. At such moments they must call upon the one who is their advocate before the Father.

CONCLUSION

In this chapter I have presented the theology of 1 John under the rubric of communion with God. Those who believe that Jesus is the Christ are begotten of God and are in communion with God. Because they are begotten of God, they love those whom God has begotten. In this way 1 John establishes an intimate connection between faith and praxis.

For John there is an inherent opposition between sin and communion with God. Consequently, those who abide in Christ and belong to God ought to be sinless, and if they truly belong to God they will be. Yet John acknowledges the reality of sin within the community of those who are in communion with God. He draws a distinction between sin that is mortal and sin that is not, and he reminds his audience that those who do sin have an advocate before the Father who pleads on their behalf.

Although John speaks eloquently about the relationship between love for God and love for the other, his understanding of love is narrower in scope than

---

19. Frank Thielman (*Theology of the New Testament: A Canonical and Synthetic Approach* [Grand Rapids: Zondervan, 2005], 548) puts it well: "It seems likely that the Elder has instead expressed two sides of a single truth with a simplicity typical of his style elsewhere. Fellowship with God and the claim to be without sin are incompatible. At the same time, everyone who abides in God does not, indeed cannot, sin. The Elder apparently expects his readers to allow each statement to qualify the other."

Jesus' teaching as presented in the Synoptic Gospels. For whereas Jesus calls upon his disciples to love the neighbor and even the enemy, John calls upon his recipients to love those begotten of God, those who believe that Jesus is the Christ. In presenting his teaching on love in light of his Christology, John highlights a new dimension of love: its origin in God. But if God is love and Jesus Christ comes to reveal God's love to the world, only those who believe that Jesus is the Christ fully comprehend this love and the communion it effects.

PART FOUR

Other Voices

In addition to the Synoptic tradition, the Pauline tradition, and the Johannine tradition, there are a number of other voices in the New Testament: the Letter to the Hebrews, the Letter of James, 1 and 2 Peter, the Letter of Jude, and the book of Revelation.

The unknown author of Hebrews is one of the great theologians of the New Testament. Equal in theological stature to Paul and John, he develops a new and dynamic Christology that presents Jesus, the Son of God, as a high priest according to the order of Melchizedek. Making use of imagery from the Day of Atonement, he finds a new way to explain the meaning and significance of Jesus' death.

The letters attributed to James, Peter, and Jude (along with the Johannine Epistles) make up the Catholic or General Epistles. Although this category is a later construct, the writings of this collection play an important role in the New Testament canon, providing a counterweight to the powerful witness of the Pauline tradition.[1] For example, whereas the Pauline tradition vigorously proclaims that one is justified by God's grace on the basis of faith in Jesus Christ, the Catholic Epistles remind the justified that their new status in Christ does not exempt them from the responsibility of living a morally good life or from God's impending judgment. This is not to suggest that the Pauline tradition dispenses believers from the ethical life. Paul's teaching on justification by faith can be misunderstood, however, and there were some who did employ his law-free gospel as an excuse for a libertine way of life. Although the Catholic

---

1. On the importance of the Catholic Epistles and their role in the New Testament, see Jacques Schlosser, ed., *The Catholic Epistles and the Tradition* (BETL 176; Leuven: Leuven University Press, 2004). The essays of Jacques Schlosser ("Le corpus des Épîtres catholiques," pp. 3–41) and Robert Wall ("A Unifying Theology of the Catholic Epistles: A Canonical Approach," pp. 43–71) highlight the canonical role of the Catholic Epistles.

Epistles do not match Paul's dynamic, apocalyptic theology, they emphasize the importance of the moral life and warn believers of the impending judgment all must face.

In addition to providing a counterweight to the Pauline Epistles, the Catholic Epistles remind believers of other significant figures who play a role in the New Testament: (1) James, a brother of the Lord, the leader of the church at Jerusalem, and the premier representative of Jewish Christianity; (2) Peter and John, disciples and apostles who testify to what they have heard and seen; (3) Jude, the brother of James and Jesus, a family member of the Lord who appears to have played an important role in the period after Jesus' death and resurrection. Although the letters attributed to these persons may not have been written by them, the attribution of these writings to James, Peter, John, and Jude suggests that not only were they renown figures in the early church, they were also viewed as important witnesses to the Jesus tradition. Those who wrote in their names sought to preserve this distinctive witness, a witness that was surely treasured and preserved in the circles that honored and revered these figures.

The book of Revelation is a fitting conclusion not only to the New Testament but to the entire Bible. It presents a new and vibrant Christology of Christ as the slaughtered Lamb who has been taken up into God's presence and is worthy to reveal what is soon to take place. Revelation's vision of the new Jerusalem, which descends from heaven as the bride of the Lamb, provides yet another way to envision God's apocalyptic victory.

Although no single theme unites these diverse writings, they share several theological motifs: (1) the need for conduct that coheres with the gospel, (2) the assurance that there will be a final judgment at which the wicked will be punished and the just rewarded, (3) a conviction that suffering and affliction are part of the Christian life in the time before God's final victory, (4) warnings that false teachers will appear in the last days, and (5) exhortations for the faithful to persevere and maintain the apostolic teaching they have received. These writings remind readers that in addition to the three great theological traditions of the New Testament, there are other voices that need to be heard.

11

A Theology of Priesthood
and Sacrifice

The Letter to the Hebrews

The unknown author of the Letter to the Hebrews ranks as one of the great theologians of the New Testament, comparable to Paul and John in the depth of his theological insight.[1] This writing, which the author identifies as "my word of exhortation" (13:22), presents a profound reflection on the meaning and significance of Jesus' death in terms of the Day of Atonement, arguing that Jesus was a high priest according to the order of Melchizedek whose death inaugurated a new covenant that effected the forgiveness of sins once and for all times. This portrayal of Jesus' death, whereby he entered the heavenly sanctuary and was designated a high priest according to the order of Melchizedek, is the most innovative and remarkable aspect of the author's theology. No other New Testament writer explicitly portrays Jesus as a priest, let alone as a high priest.[2]

Despite its unique portrayal of Jesus as a high priest, Hebrews stands within the mainstream of New Testament theology. Like the vast majority of New Testament writings, it identifies Jesus as the Son of God and acknowledges the centrality of his death in God's redemptive plan. Its author is deeply aware that, apart from God's salvific work in Christ, humanity is burdened with sin and does not have full access to God. He values Israel's Scriptures as God's Word, which already speaks of Christ. He recognizes the importance of the community of the church and the need for perseverance and faith. He understands that the consummation of all things is yet to occur. To be sure, the author of

---

1. Although the church in the East tended to view Hebrews as Pauline and canonical from as early as the third century, the question of authorship has always presented a problem. Today there is general agreement that Paul was not its author.

2. Some authors see priestly motifs in John 17, which is often referred to as Jesus' high priestly prayer, but the Fourth Gospel does not explicitly portray Jesus as a priest. In Rev. 1:13 the one like a Son of Man appears to be dressed as a priest, but the priestly motif is not developed.

Hebrews presents many of these traditional ideas in his own way, but when all is said and done, he stands within the mainstream of the New Testament tradition. In a word, the author is both traditional and innovative: traditional in his understanding of Jesus as the Son of God whose death was redemptive; innovative in his presentation of Jesus as a high priest whose death fulfilled what the Day of Atonement prefigured.

A discussion of the theology of Hebrews should begin with a distinction between *what* the author seeks to accomplish and *how* he accomplishes his task. For, even though Hebrews is one of the most—perhaps the most—explicitly theological writings of the New Testament, its main purpose is to persuade a community of believers, some of whom are in danger of apostatizing, to persevere in faith so that they can enter God's Sabbath rest, the heavenly sanctuary, the city of God. To convince this community of faltering believers to remain steadfast in their faith, the author develops a theology of Jesus the Son of God, a high priest according to the order of Melchizedek, the pioneer and perfecter of faith, the one who has entered the heavenly sanctuary by his death and so effected the eternal forgiveness for sins. Consequently, doctrinal exposition is in the service of moral exhortation in Hebrews. This is not to suggest that the theology of Hebrews is unimportant. But it is a salutary reminder that the theology of Hebrews, like the theology of most other New Testament writings, is occasional in nature.[3]

The precise historical circumstances that generated this letter, like the identity of its author, are unknown.[4] Suffice it to say that the author was likely writing to believers in Italy (13:24), possibly those in Rome who had already suffered persecution (10:32–33) and were threatened with further afflictions (13:13). In the view of the author the community has grown "dull in understanding" (5:11), and he is fearful that some may apostatize. Therefore, he exhorts them to hold to their original confession of faith and to endure the trials of the present so that they can enter God's Sabbath rest (4:1–11). Why the author chose the theme of the high priesthood of Christ is shrouded in mystery. Was the community in need of further assurance that its sins were forgiven? Was the community in danger of reverting to Jewish practices? Did the author develop this theology of priesthood and sacrifice on his own? These and other questions remain unanswered.[5]

---

3. Not all would agree with this assessment. Some would argue that Hebrews' primary purpose is doctrinal exposition, e.g., Albert Vanhoye, *Structure and Message of the Epistle to the Hebrews* (SubBi 12; Rome: Pontifical Biblical Institute Press, 1989).

4. See Barnabas Lindars, *The Theology of the Letter to the Hebrews* (NTT; Cambridge: Cambridge University Press, 1991), 1–25; Craig R. Koester, *Hebrews: A New Translation with Introduction and Commentary* (AB 36; New York: Doubleday, 2001), 64–79.

5. The title, which was added later, has suggested to many that the author was writing to Jewish Christians who were in danger of reverting to Jewish practices. Lindars (*Theology of Hebrews,* 4–15) argues that the problem has to do with the consciousness of sin, a constant theme in Hebrews: the community needs assurance that its sins have been forgiven.

Hebrews is the most explicitly christological writing of the New Testament. Accordingly, in this chapter I present Hebrews' theology in light of its understanding of Christ and his sacrifice, concluding with a comparison of the theologies of Hebrews and Paul: (1) Jesus, the Son of God; (2) Jesus, a high priest; (3) Jesus, the mediator of a new covenant; (4) Jesus, the pioneer and perfecter of faith; (5) Jesus and the children God has given him; and (6) Hebrews and Paul.

JESUS, THE SON OF GOD

The author of Hebrews constructs his theology of priesthood and sacrifice on his confession that Jesus is the Son of God. Without this prior confession, the author cannot effectively argue that Jesus is a high priest according to the order of Melchizedek, nor can he persuade his audience that Jesus' death is the redemptive act by which God deals with sin once and for all. Accordingly, before he embarks upon his theology of priesthood and sacrifice, he must remind his audience of what it already knows and confesses: Jesus is the eternal Son of God.

The centrality of the title "the Son of God" is evident when he writes, "Since, then, we have a great high priest who has passed through the heavens, Jesus, the Son of God, let us hold fast to our confession" (4:14). The confession of the community is not that Jesus is a great high priest (a teaching with which it seems to be unfamiliar) but that he is the Son of God.[6] Accordingly, the author builds on the community's confession of Jesus as the Son of God in order to show that as the Son of God, Jesus is a great high priest who has passed through the heavens by his atoning death on the cross. It will, of course, be important for the author to emphasize the humanity of Jesus as well as his intimate and unique relationship to God, if he is to present Jesus as a merciful and faithful high priest, and this the author will do. But before doing so, he must establish the foundation on which he will build his theology of priesthood and sacrifice: the sonship of Jesus.

The author constructs his theological foundation in the first two chapters, where he shows that the Son of God is superior to the angels. Although this point seems obvious, his intent is to show that *Jesus*, the Son of God, is superior to the angels, even though he was, for a little while, made lower than them (2:9). In a word, before the author can consider priesthood and sacrifice, he must deal with what theology calls the incarnation. How is it that Jesus, the

---

6. Koester (*Hebrews*, 126–27) makes the point that central to the community's confession was its acknowledgment of Jesus as the Son of God. Hebrews refers to the community's confession in two other places. In 3:1 it speaks of "Jesus, the apostle and high priest of our confession," and in 10:23 it speaks of "the confession of our hope." It is clear from 4:14, however, that Jesus' status as God's Son is the foundation for confessing Jesus as apostle and high priest.

one whom the community confesses as the Son of God, is greater than the angels? Only when the author answers this question will he take up the issues of priesthood and sacrifice.

He summarizes the essential elements of his Son of God theology in the proem that prefaces the discourse that follows (1:1–4). The opening verses allude to the whole span of God's salvific plan: from the creation of the universe to the exaltation of the Son. The proem, however, does not start at the beginning but in the middle, with the Son by whom God has spoken in these last days, and whom God appointed as the heir of all things. Thus the first mention of the Son is a reference to the incarnate One who has been exalted, even though the name "Jesus" will not appear until 2:9. Previously God spoke by prophets in fragmentary ways, but in these, the last days, God has spoken "by a Son." The author is not implying that God has many sons. Rather, he is contrasting the ways in which God formerly spoke in many and various ways, through the prophets, with the way in which God has most recently spoken in a final and definitive way, through a Son.[7]

Having begun with the incarnate Son, the author moves back to a period before creation and affirms that the Son, by whom God has spoken, is the one by whom "he also created the worlds." Put in theological terms, the incarnate Son is the preexistent Son. This Son, through whom God created the universe, is "the reflection of God's glory" and "the exact imprint of God's very being." Not only is he the one through whom God created the universe, he is the one who sustains creation by his powerful word.

Having spoken of the incarnation and creation, the author turns to the present, the time of the Son's exaltation, anticipating the theme of priesthood and sacrifice he will develop. After the Son made purification for sins by his death, he sat down at the right hand of "the Majesty on high." This purification for sins refers to the Son's work as a high priest, and his session at the right hand of God presupposes his death and resurrection by which he entered into the heavenly sanctuary. Within the first three verses of the proem, then, the author moves from the role of the Son in history as the one by whom God has spoken in a final and definitive way, back to his role in creation, and forward again to his exaltation at God's right hand. Thus he speaks of the incarnation, the preexistence, and the exaltation of the Son.[8]

The result of the Son's exaltation is that he has become as much superior to the angels as the name he has inherited is "more excellent than theirs" (1:4).

---

7. In both instances, however, it is the same God who has spoken, making clear that there is a unity in God's divine plan. Hebrews does not say why God spoke only in various and fragmentary ways by the prophets.

8. For a full exposition of this, see John Meier, "Structure and Theology in Heb. 1, 1–14," *Bib* 66 (1985): 168–89; idem, "Symmetry and Theology in the Old Testament Citation of Heb 1, 5–14," *Bib* 66 (1985): 504–33.

Although some have proposed that the name the Son inherited is *kyrios*, as in the Philippians hymn, or that it is "high priest," the concept that dominates the rest of the discourse, it is more likely that the name is "Son" since, in the very next verse, the author quotes Ps. 2:7 and asks, "For to which of the angels did God ever say, '*You are my Son*; today I have begotten you'?" (Heb. 1:5). When he affirms that the Son has "become" superior to the angels and that "the Son" has inherited the name "Son," then, he is speaking of the Son who "for a little while was made lower than the angels" (2:9), when he shared in the flesh and blood of his brothers and sisters (2:14). In other words, although the author will not speak of Jesus as the incarnate Son of God until chapter 2, he is already speaking of Jesus as the exalted Son of God in chapter 1. There is a paradoxical sense, then, in which the preexistent Son inherits the name "Son" at his exaltation. The author does not speculate about the preexistent Son. Rather, he is primarily concerned with the earthly Jesus, who inherits the name "Son" by learning obedience through what he suffered and so became perfect (5:8–9), that is, he attained the goal for which God intended him.[9] Consequently, when the author affirms that the Son has become superior to the angels, he means that *Jesus*, who is now exalted as Son of God at God's right hand, is superior to the angels.

Although some have suggested that the author found it necessary to combat a false teaching about the superiority of the angels to the risen Christ, it is more likely that he introduces the theme of the Son's superiority to the angels in order to prepare for his theology of priesthood and sacrifice, since, as high priest, Jesus the Son of God must enter into the heavenly sanctuary. Moreover, by highlighting the superiority of Jesus to the angels, the author is able to emphasize the abasement of the Son who shared in the flesh and blood of his brothers and sisters in order to free them from "the one who has the power of death, that is, the devil" (2:14). Thus there is a certain similarity between the structure of the Christ hymn in Philippians and the opening chapters of Hebrews, both of which presuppose the preexistent status of the Son, his abasement, and his exaltation because of his obedience to God.

The author "proves" that the Son is superior to the angels by a catena of seven scriptural quotations through which God speaks (1:5–14). All of the quotations presuppose the exaltation and enthronement of Jesus, as the Son of God, at God's right hand. Consequently, the author is contrasting the angels not with the preexistent Son but with Jesus, the Son of God, who is now exalted at God's right hand. Writing from this perspective, he asks which of the angels did God ever call his Son (Ps. 2:7; 2 Sam. 7:14)? The implied answer is none.

---

9. The theme of perfection appears throughout Hebrews (see 2:10; 5:9; 7:19, 28; 9:9; 10:1, 14, 40; 12:23). It is best taken as a way of expressing the completion or fulfillment of a person's or object's goal. For Hebrews, one is perfected when one has finally arrived at the purpose and goal of God's plan.

Rather, when God introduced the Son into the heavenly world, at the Son's exaltation, he commanded the angels to worship him (see Deut. 32:43).[10] Whereas God made the angels his servants (Ps. 107:4), God established the throne of the Son forever (Ps. 45:6–7), for the Son will endure forever (Ps. 102:25–27). Returning to the question that opened the catena, the author asks, to which of the angels did God ever say, "sit at my right hand" (Ps. 110:1)? Daring to call upon God as his only authority, the author establishes that the exalted Son of God, whose earthly name has not yet been mentioned, is superior to the angels because God enthroned and called him his Son.

For the author of Hebrews, the destiny of humanity, as outlined in Psalm 8, has already been achieved in Jesus, the Son of God, the great high priest who has passed through the heavens. But before Jesus, the Son of God, could fulfill his destiny, it was necessary for him to be made, for a little while, lower than the angels (Heb. 2:9). The author explains this abasement of the Son as a matter of sharing in the flesh and blood of humanity so that he might be a merciful and faithful high priest and make atonement for sins (2:14–18). Thus, although he does not explicitly develop a teaching of the incarnation in the way that the Fourth Gospel does when John writes "the Word became flesh" (John 1:14), the author of Hebrews presupposes an understanding of the incarnation. The one "for whom and through whom all things exist" (Heb. 2:10) was not ashamed to call those whom he brought to salvation his brothers and sisters (2:11). Rather he shared in their humanity and became like them in every respect but sin.

The author's Son of God theology moves from the abasement to the exaltation of the Son. During the period of his earthly life, Jesus was already Son of God (5:8), but he was not yet perfected because he had not yet reached his appointed goal as high priest; he had not yet passed through the heavens into the heavenly sanctuary by the sacrifice of his own death. During the period of his earthly sojourn, then, Jesus, the Son of God, was made lower than the angels inasmuch as he had not yet been exalted at God's right hand. During this period, although he was the Son of God, he learned in an experiential way what it meant to be obedient. When finally brought to perfection by the attainment of his goal, however, Jesus was exalted at God's right hand, superior to the angels, having inherited a name ("Son") that is superior to theirs. From the vantage point of Jesus' exaltation, the author can now speak of the Son as the one through whom and for whom all things exist, the one through whom God created the universe.

Without this Son of God theology, the author would not be able to develop his theology of priesthood and sacrifice since he envisions a priesthood that goes beyond the human limitations of the Levitical priesthood. For example,

---

10. This interpretation is disputed, and some would argue that Hebrews is referring to the incarnation or the parousia rather than to the exaltation. But the scriptural texts of the catena seem to have the period of the Son's exaltation in view.

when discussing Melchizedek, he affirms that Melchizedek is like the Son of God since he has "neither beginning of days nor end of life" (7:3). When comparing the Levitical priesthood with the priesthood of Jesus, the author notes that whereas the law appoints as high priests those who are subject to weakness, God's oath appoints "a Son who has been made perfect forever" (7:28). The high priest that the author envisions must be human and divine: human so that he can be merciful and compassionate, divine so that he and his sacrifice will endure forever.

JESUS, A HIGH PRIEST

The most innovative aspect of Hebrews' theology is the argument that Jesus is a high priest according to the order of Melchizedek. With this teaching, the author introduces two theological concepts: (1) Jesus is a priest; (2) Jesus' priesthood derives from the order of Melchizedek. The author must argue vigorously for both ideas since neither has a historical foundation in the life of Jesus or in the history of Israel. Israel's priests were drawn from the tribe of Levi, and they traced their ancestry to Aaron. There was no priesthood according to the order of Melchizedek. Nor was there any tradition that, in the last days, a high priest would arise from the lineage of Melchizedek. As for Jesus, he was disqualified from the priesthood because he did not belong to the tribe of Levi (7:13–14).

The author is aware of the difficulties he faces, and he acknowledges that what he will say is "hard to explain" and goes beyond "the basic teaching about Christ" (5:11; 6:1). Whereas the basic teaching about Christ undoubtedly encompassed the story of his ministry, which culminated in his death and resurrection, the author seeks to explain the significance of that story in terms of Israel's priesthood and cult for a community of believers who no longer shared in either.[11] In one of the most theologically creative arguments of the New Testament, therefore, the author argues that the public execution of Jesus— the shameful act of his crucifixion—was nothing less than a sacrificial offering of a high priest who, by this act, entered into the heavenly sanctuary, the true holy place. To accomplish this theological task the author must show that Jesus was qualified to be a priest and that he derives his priesthood from the order of Melchizedek. After explaining the nature of Jesus' priesthood, the author will present Jesus' death as an act of atonement that inaugurated a new covenant because it effected the forgiveness of sins once and for all time.

---

11. Because the community did not have its own cult, priesthood, and sacrificial offering, it may have felt the need for these things, especially since it lived in a world where priests and temples abounded.

Qualified to Be a Priest

The first explicit statement about Jesus' priesthood in Hebrews comes at the conclusion of the discussion of Jesus' abasement whereby the Son was made lower than the angels so that he might free his brothers and sisters from the fear of death by sharing in their humanity: "Therefore he had to become like his brothers and sisters in every respect, so that he might be a merciful and faithful high priest in the service of God" (2:17). In 4:14–15 the author again emphasizes the humanity of Jesus, but this time he also points to the transcendent nature of Jesus' priesthood: "Since, then, we have a great high priest who has passed through the heavens, Jesus, the Son of God, let us hold fast to our confession. For we do not have a high priest who is unable to sympathize with our weaknesses, but we have one who in every respect has been tested as we are, yet without sin." From these initial statements about Jesus' priesthood, it is apparent that the author intends to present Jesus' priesthood from two vantage points: his humanity and his sonship.[12]

It is important for the author to present Jesus as a merciful high priest who can sympathize with the weaknesses of his brothers and sisters since he also portrays Jesus as the pioneer of salvation, the forerunner, the perfecter of faith (2:10; 6:20; 12:2), who by his death has already entered the heavenly sanctuary, into which his brothers and sisters must follow if they hope to attain God's Sabbath rest. Were Jesus merely a divine figure, it would be impossible for them to follow him into the sanctuary or for him to sympathize with their weakness. Before explaining Jesus' transcendent priesthood according to the order of Melchizedek (7:1–28), therefore, the author must describe Jesus' qualifications for priesthood (5:1–10).

The author is aware that a high priest must minister to his brothers and sisters. Therefore, he notes that every high priest is chosen from among human beings to deal with matters that pertain to God and to offer sacrifices for sins, his own sins as well as the sins of the people. Aware of his own weakness, he is able to deal with the ignorant and wayward. No one, however, can take this honor upon himself; he must be called to it (5:1–4). On the basis of this description, the author shows that Jesus is qualified to be a high priest (5:5–10). First, employing Psalms 2 and 110 in a new and creative manner, the author deduces that God called the Son (Ps. 2:7) to be a priest when he said, "You are a priest forever, according to the order of Melchizedek" (110:4). Second, describing Jesus' cries to God for deliverance from death, the author estab-

---

12. Note that Hebrews also presents Jesus' sonship from two vantage points. On the one hand, the Son is superior to the angels. On the other, he was made, for a while, lower than them.

lishes that the Son truly shared in the human situation of his brothers and sisters.[13] Therefore, he can sympathize with their weaknesses.

The comparison is not perfect, however, since in the case of the Son human weakness did not lead to sin but became a way for the Son to learn obedience through what he suffered, thereby being perfected and so the source of eternal salvation for those who follow in his path. In affirming that the Son was made perfect (*teleiōtheis*, 5:9), the author means that through his repeated obedience to God, the Son attained the goal for which God destined him. In affirming that the Son learned obedience through suffering, the author indicates that the incarnate Son learned the meaning of obedience inasmuch as God's will required him not only to endure the sufferings of the cross but to submit his will to God's will again and again.[14]

Jesus' "ordination" to priesthood is the culmination of a lifetime of obedience, which finds its climax in the cross. So the author concludes his discussion of Jesus' qualifications for priesthood by saying that after he had attained God's will by his obedience, Jesus was "designated by God a high priest according to the order of Melchizedek" (5:10).[15] In this way the author acknowledges that Jesus was not a high priest during the days of his earthly life but was designated one at the completion of his life's work.

According to the Order of Melchizedek

The author derives his notion of a priesthood according to the order of Melchizedek from Psalm 110, a psalm that the New Testament normally employs to argue for the enthronement of the risen Lord as God's Messiah: "The LORD says to my lord, 'Sit at my right hand until I make your enemies your footstool.'"[16] The author, however, goes further than other New Testament writings by introducing what the psalm says in verse 4: "The LORD has sworn and will not change his mind, 'You are a priest forever according to the order of Melchizedek.'" Presuming that the entire psalm is speaking about the Messiah, the author deduces that the one who has been enthroned at God's right hand as Messiah (Ps. 110:1) is also a priest according to the order of Melchizedek (110:4). Since the author intends to make use of the Day of Atonement to explain the significance of Jesus' death, however, he speaks of Jesus as

13. Whether this refers to Gethsemane is disputed. But the outcome of the debate does not affect the argument. The point Hebrews makes is that Jesus truly shared in human weakness.

14. Koester (*Hebrews*, 299) expresses it well, "Although Jesus was never disobedient to God, he could not demonstrate obedience until he was placed in situations where the will of God was challenged and obedience was required."

15. Note that Ps. 110:4 only speaks of a priest, whereas Hebrews calls Jesus a high priest.

16. Psalm 110 is cited in several other places in the New Testament: Mark 16:19; Rom. 8:34; 1 Cor. 15:25; Eph. 1:20; Col. 3:1.

"a *high priest* according to the order of Melchizedek" (Heb. 5:10; 6:20), whereas the psalm speaks only of "a *priest* according to the order of Melchizedek."

Although Psalm 110 may have once alluded to the double honor of kingship and priesthood conferred upon David when he captured the Jebusite city that became Jerusalem, Israel did not develop a theology of a priesthood according to the order of Melchizedek. Therefore, it is necessary for the author of Hebrews to explain how and why Jesus can be called a high priest according to the order of Melchizedek, a task that he undertakes in chapter 7. He proceeds in two steps. First, he argues that Melchizedek was superior to Abraham, and so superior to his Levitical descendants (Heb. 7:1–10). Second, he explains why it was necessary to replace the Levitical priesthood with a priesthood according to the order of Melchizedek (7:11–28). From this argument it will become apparent that just as the author recognizes that Jesus was not a priest during his lifetime but was designated one when he was made perfect, so he understands that the priesthood according to Melchizedek did not make its appearance until Jesus was perfected.

Apart from Ps. 110:4, Melchizedek appears only one other time in the Old Testament, in the account of Gen. 14:17–20, where he is identified as king of Salem (which Ps. 76:2 identifies as Jerusalem) and priest of God Most High. Melchizedek blesses Abraham, and Abraham gives him one-tenth of his possessions. The author of Hebrews seizes upon the fact that the Genesis account makes no reference to Melchizedek's genealogy and concludes from this omission that Melchizedek resembles the Son of God, having neither beginning nor end of days, therefore "he remains a priest forever" (Heb. 7:3).[17] Next, he concludes that Melchizedek is superior to Abraham since Abraham is blessed by Melchizedek (7:7). Moreover, since Abraham was the ancestor of Levi, the one to whom all Levitical priests trace their descent, the author can claim that Levi paid tithes to Melchizedek through Abraham, thereby establishing the superiority of Melchizedek to Levi and his priestly descendants. Melchizedek, then, is a type of the Son of God, and he foreshadows a priesthood that finds its completion in Christ.

Having established the superiority of Melchizedek to Abraham (7:1–10), the author explains the need for a new priesthood (7:11–28). If the Levitical priesthood could have effected "perfection" (*teleiōsis*), there would have been no need for another priesthood according to the order of Melchizedek (7:11). This change of priesthood, however, necessitates a change of law (7:12), since the law, like the Levitical priesthood, was weak and ineffectual and could make nothing "perfect" (*eteleiōsen*, 7:19). As in earlier uses of the concept of "perfection," the author has in view the completion of God's plan.

---

17. Note that Hebrews says that Melchizedek resembles the Son of God. It does not say that the Son of God resembles Melchizedek. There is no suggestion that Melchizedek is greater than the Son, even though the Son is a priest according to the order of Melchizedek.

The argument he employs here is analogous to that which Paul employs in Galatians: "for if justification comes through the law, then Christ died for nothing" (Gal. 2:21); and "if a law had been given that could make alive, then righteousness would indeed come through the law" (Gal. 3:21). For Paul the manifestation of righteousness in Christ indicates that it was never the purpose of the law to effect justification or give life. For the author of Hebrews the appearance of a new priesthood indicates that neither the Levitical priesthood nor the law could attain the ultimate purpose of God's will. Thus it is apparent to the author that God had always intended that there would be a priesthood according to the order of Melchizedek.

The author does not ask why God established the Levitical priesthood and the law if neither could bring people to perfection. The author's failure to do so is due in part to the fact that he does not analyze the human condition in the insightful way that Paul and John do. To be sure, the author is aware that humanity is under the power of the devil (2:14–15), but he never says that the devil frustrated the purposes of the priesthood and the law in the way that Paul argues that the power of sin made it impossible for those under the law to do its just requirements. For the author of Hebrews the Levitical priesthood was ineffectual and needed to be replaced by a priesthood that could attain God's purpose.

The author affirms that the uniqueness of Jesus' priesthood arises from the way it was given, "through the power of an indestructible life" (7:16) and by an oath (7:21). Because of his exaltation to God's right hand, Jesus can no longer die, and "he holds his priesthood permanently" (7:24), making intercession for his brothers and sisters (7:25). Unlike the Levitical priests who were appointed by a commandment that designated them as priests because they belonged to the tribe of Levi, Jesus was appointed as a high priest when God swore, by an oath, that Jesus is a priest forever, according to the order of Melchizedek (7:21). Anticipating an argument yet to be made, the author concludes that Jesus is "the guarantee of a better covenant" (7:22); and, unlike other priests, he has no need to offer daily sacrifices, since he did this "once for all when he offered himself" (7:27).

The contrast between Jesus' priesthood and the Levitical priesthood could not be greater. The Levitical priests were appointed by a commandment regarding physical descent and were subject to death; Jesus was appointed by God's oath and lives forever. The Levitical priests offered sacrifices for their own sins as well as those of the people; Jesus is "holy, blameless, undefiled, separated from sinners, and exalted above the heavens" (7:26). For the author Jesus must be like his brothers and sisters in every way, apart from sin, so that he can sympathize with their weakness; and he must be the Son of God so that his priesthood can endure forever. Herein lies the importance of the author's initial discussion of the Son who was made, for a little while, lower than the angels but has become as much superior to them "as the name he has inherited is more excellent than theirs" (1:4).

For the author priesthood and sonship are inextricably bound together: apart from his priesthood, Jesus has no ministry; and apart from his sonship, Jesus' priesthood is ineffective. Consequently, it is necessary for Jesus to exercise his priesthood as God's Son and to fulfill his ministry as a high priest according to the order of Melchizedek.

JESUS, THE MEDIATOR OF A NEW COVENANT

The author's purpose in identifying Jesus as the Son of God, a great high priest according to the order of Melchizedek, is ultimately soteriological; that is, he seeks to explain how God effected salvation, once and for all, through Jesus Christ. Therefore, having identified Jesus as a high priest, the author explains the nature and significance of Jesus' sacrifice. To accomplish this, he employs the promise of a new covenant and the rite of the Day of Atonement to argue that Jesus' death was a high priestly act whereby he entered the true holy of holies, the heavenly sanctuary, thereby effecting forgiveness of sins, once and for all, and so inaugurating the promised new covenant.

This comparison between Jesus' shameful death on the cross and the entrance of the high priest into the Holy of Holies on the Day of Atonement is one of the boldest statements in the New Testament. On face value, Jesus' crucifixion was the execution of a criminal. But the author makes it the completion and perfection of Israel's cult, arguing that the alleged criminal was a high priest, and that his death was the perfect sacrifice for sins. The author sees the presence of the divine in the secular.

In his earlier discussion of priesthood, the author noted that every high priest is put in charge of things pertaining to God "to offer gifts and sacrifices for sins" (5:1). But in that initial comparison (5:1–10), he did not explain what "gifts and sacrifices" Christ offered, since he was concerned to explain the nature of his priesthood. Having established that Jesus is a high priest according to the order of Melchizedek (7:1–28), he embarks upon the task of explaining the nature and significance of the sacrifice Jesus offers, since "it is necessary for this priest also to have something to offer" (8:3).

The author, however, cannot equate Jesus' sacrifice with the gifts and sacrifices offered by the ministers of the Mosaic covenant, since Jesus was not qualified to be a Levitical priest and serve in the temple. Moreover, since a change of priesthood means a change of law (7:12),[18] he concludes that Jesus'

---

18. The point of the argument is that since the Levitical priesthood was established by the Mosaic law, the end of that priesthood is the end of that law.

sacrifice belongs to a new and better covenant, making Jesus "the mediator of a better covenant" (8:6). Accordingly, the author turns to the promise of a new covenant found in Jer. 31:31–34. But instead of identifying the text as coming from the prophet Jeremiah, he writes, "God finds fault with them when he says . . ." (8:8). Just as he argued that there would have been no need for a new priesthood if perfection could have been attained through the Levitical priesthood (7:11), so he argues that there would not have been any need for a new covenant if the first covenant had been without fault (8:7). For him the first covenant and its cult did not and could not effectively deal with sin.

Whereas Paul's concern with the text of Jeremiah is the promise that God will write his law upon the hearts of the people (2 Cor. 3:2–6), the author of Hebrews is more concerned with the words, "For I will be merciful toward their iniquities, and I will remember their sins no more" (Heb. 8:12; see also 10:17). The problem, then, is what he calls the "consciousness of sin" (10:2). If the old cult, established by the first covenant, had been able to deal effectively with sin, those who belonged to the first covenant would no longer have any consciousness of sin. Their sins would have been forgiven, once and for all. The daily and annual repetition of the cultic rites of the first covenant, however, testify that this was not the case. Consciousness of sin—a realization that sin has not been effectively dealt with—remained an enduring problem.

For the author the sanctuary in which the cult was carried out under the first covenant was "a sketch and shadow of the heavenly one" (8:5).[19] It consisted of (1) the Holy Place where the priest offered daily sacrifices, and (2) the place beyond the curtain, the Holy of Holies, into which the high priest entered once a year, on the Day of Atonement, to offer sacrifices for himself and the people. It is this second sanctuary, the Holy of Holies, with which the author is most interested, since he will draw a comparison between the yearly sacrifice of the high priest on the Day of Atonement and the singular sacrifice of Christ, a high priest according to the order of Melchizedek.

The author argues that the continual repetition of the rite of atonement, whereby the high priest entered the Holy of Holies once each year, was the way in which the Holy Spirit was already indicating that the way into the heavenly sanctuary had not yet been opened (9:8). For as long as this rite continued, it was evident that sin had not been dealt with in a final and definitive manner. The gifts and sacrifices offered in the earthly sanctuary "cannot perfect the conscience of the worshiper" (9:9) because they do not and cannot assure worshipers that their sins have been forgiven. Thus the need for a new and better sacrifice.

The author sees this new sacrifice in the death of Christ. When Christ came as high priest, he did not enter the old sanctuary made by hands, but "he

---

19. Hebrews speaks of the sanctuary or tent rather than of the temple.

entered once for all into the Holy Place," with his own blood, and he obtained "eternal redemption" for those whom he sanctified (9:12).[20] In saying that Christ entered "the Holy Place," the author is no longer referring to "the Holy Place" of the first sanctuary (9:2). Rather, he has in view "heaven itself" (9:24), which Christ "entered" by his death. Having entered this holy place, Christ attained his goal; he has been perfected. Having been perfected, he is established as a high priest forever, according to the order of Melchizedek.

The nature and significance of Christ's death is of great importance in Hebrews. Playing on the word *diathēkē*, which means "will" as well as "covenant," the author argues that just as a will does not take effect until the death of the testator, so the new covenant could be effected only by the death of its testator (9:15–18). Thus it was necessary for Christ to die in order to become the mediator of a new covenant. To show the difference between the many sacrifices of the first covenant and the singular sacrifice of the new covenant, the author interprets the words of Psalm 40 as words spoken by the Son[21] upon his entrance into the world: "Sacrifices and offerings you have not desired, but a body you have prepared for me; in burnt offerings and sin offerings you have taken no pleasure. Then I said, 'See, God, I have come to do your will, O God'" (Ps. 40:6–8, as quoted in Heb. 10:5–7). The quotation highlights the distinctive nature of Christ's sacrifice: it was not the death of an unwilling animal but the sacrifice of one who freely came to do God's will. Consequently, there is no need to repeat this sacrifice. Indeed, it cannot be repeated, since Christ, having risen, can no longer die. The author emphasizes Christ's singular sacrifice, whereby he died once (*hapax*), in order to distinguish between the old and the new cult. Whereas the priests of the old covenant *stand* day after day, offering the same sacrifices that cannot effectively deal with sin, Christ *sits* enthroned at God's right hand, having offered a single sacrifice of himself, which deals with sins past, present, and to come.

The author's intricate theology of priesthood and sacrifice is based on three concepts: (1) a new priesthood according to the order of Melchizedek, (2) a new covenant, and (3) a single sacrifice that effects atonement and the forgiveness of sins once and for all. The new element in this soteriology is the manner in which he portrays the nature and significance of Christ's death. Like Paul, John, and the Synoptics, the author of Hebrews affirms the centrality of Christ's death in God's redemptive work: a death that effects the forgiveness of sins. Unlike them, he presents this death as the cultic act of a high priest, arguing that the crucifixion was nothing less than the entrance of the true high priest into the heavenly sanctuary. The resurrection does not play as central a

---

20. One would have expected Hebrews to say that Christ entered the Holy of Holies, but it does not since heaven has no need for such an inner chamber. All is holy.

21. The text does not explicitly identify the speaker as "the Son," but this is clearly implied.

role in this theology as it does in the theologies of Paul and the Synoptics since Christ's death is his entrance into the heavenly sanctuary. In this regard, Hebrews is like the Fourth Gospel, in which the resurrection—while hardly denied—is taken up into the Son's death, which the Fourth Evangelist portrays as the Son's return to the Father. The author of Hebrews is aware of the resurrection (see 13:20), but he prefers to present it in terms of the high priest's entrance into the heavenly sanctuary, thereby showing the soteriological significance of Jesus' death and resurrection.

JESUS, THE PIONEER AND PERFECTER OF FAITH

As important as the Christology of Hebrews is, it is ultimately at the service of exhortation since the purpose of Hebrews is to exhort a faltering community to hold to its confession of faith in Jesus, the Son of God, whose destiny embodies their hope (4:14; 10:22).[22] Consequently, there is a studied juxtaposition of doctrinal exposition and moral exhortation in Hebrews that comes to its climax in 12:1–2, when, after recounting past examples of faith (11:4–40), the author focuses the attention of the audience on Jesus, "the pioneer and perfecter of our faith" (12:2). In making this statement, the author affirms that Jesus is both "the originator *and* the consummator of faith."[23] Jesus' faith—which is best understood as faithful obedience—is the prototype of faith, "but not one to be transcended by later improvements, for he is also faith's paragon."[24] In calling Jesus the pioneer of faith, the author is hardly implying that Jesus was the first to believe, as is evident from the long list of those who believed before him. Rather, he is insisting that "Jesus *originates* faith in the sense that 'he is the first person to have obtained faith's ultimate goal, the inheritance of the divine promise, which the ancients only saw from afar.'"[25]

His portrayal of Jesus as the pioneer and perfecter of faith is intimately related to his eschatology. For if Jesus is the one who has already attained the goal that God has set for humanity, then believers know what their eschatological salvation will be and how to attain it—by firmly fixing their gaze on Jesus and following his example.

In several ways the author presents Jesus as the one who has already attained the goal, thereby becoming perfected. In 2:5–9 he employs Psalm 8 to argue that

22. See Frank J. Matera, "Moral Exhortation: The Relationship between Moral Exhortation and Doctrinal Exposition in the Letter to the Hebrews," *TJT* 10 (1994): 164–84.

23. N. Clayton Croy, *Endurance in Suffering: Hebrews 12.1–13 in Its Rhetorical, Religious, and Philosophical Context* (SNTSMS 98; Cambridge: Cambridge University Press, 1998), 176.

24. Ibid.

25. Ibid. The quotation is from Attridge, *The Epistle to the Hebrews: A Commentary on the Epistle to the Hebrews* (Hermeneia; Philadelphia: Fortress, 1989), 356.

humanity's destiny has found its initial realization in Jesus. For although everything is not yet subjected to humanity as the psalm promises, believers can already
"see Jesus, who for a little while was made lower than the angels, now crowned
with glory and honor" (Heb. 2:9). In other words, Jesus is already exalted at God's
right hand, and his enemies are being subjected to him, thereby fulfilling humanity's destiny in his person. Although he does not employ Paul's concept of the new
or eschatological Adam, the author's use of Psalm 8 here makes a similar point:
Christ is the new human being, the pattern of what is to be.

Jesus has attained this goal by passing through the heavens as a great high
priest (4:14), by entering into the inner shrine (6:19–20), where he is seated at
the right hand of the Majesty in heaven and ministers in the true sanctuary
(8:1–2). He is the one who blazed the trail for others to follow, and so he is "the
pioneer of their salvation" (2:10), the "forerunner" on their behalf (6:20), "the
pioneer and perfecter" of their faith (12:2). This is not to imply that those who
follow Jesus will also be priests who enter into the heavenly sanctuary by the
sacrifice of their death. For the author there is only one priest whose death deals
with sin once and for all. But by entering the heavenly sanctuary, Jesus provides
those who will follow him with an example of faithfulness and obedience that
they can comprehend because he was tested as they are (4:15), and he learned
obedience through what he suffered (5:8). Thus the perfected Jesus, having
completed his goal, is the source of eternal salvation for all who obey him (5:9).

The author is aware of the traditional notion of the parousia, the return of
the Lord at the end of the ages. He notes that having offered his sacrifice for
sins, Christ "will appear a second time, not to deal with sin [for he has already
done that], but to save those who are eagerly waiting for him" (9:28). The author
even betrays traces of an imminent parousia: "as you see the Day approaching"
(10:25; also see 10:37). But rather than develop its eschatology in terms of the
imminent return of the Lord, Hebrews focuses on the need for believers to be
faithful and obedient and endure the sufferings of the present so that they can
attain the salvation that Jesus, their great high priest, has obtained for them.

In his exposition of Psalm 95 (Heb. 3:7–4:10), the author explains that
whereas the wilderness generation was unable to enter God's Sabbath rest
because of its unbelief and disobedience (3:19; 4:6), there is still a Sabbath rest
for God's people (4:9). But to enter that rest one must be faithful and obedient. The Sabbath rest that the author has in view is access to God by entrance
into the heavenly sanctuary. Consequently he speaks of "better things" in
regard to salvation (6:9), a "better hope" through which believers approach
God (7:19), "a better covenant" (7:22; 8:6), "better sacrifices" (9:23), "a better
resurrection" (11:35), a "better word" (12:24). In a word, believers know that
they possess "something better and more lasting" (10:34).

In his encomium of faith, the author speaks of these better things in terms
of a city "whose architect and builder is God" (11:10), for people of faith have

always known that "they are seeking a homeland" (11:14). Therefore, they desire "a better country, that is, a heavenly one" (11:16). But they did not receive what was promised because, although they believed, their faith could not attain its goal until the pioneer and perfecter of faith completed his course by entering into the heavenly sanctuary.

Aware that salvation has *already* made its appearance in Christ but is *not yet* complete, the author notes that believers have come "to Mount Zion and to the city of the living God, the heavenly Jerusalem" (12:22). Here they have "no lasting city," but "are looking for the city that is to come" (13:14). The city that is yet to come is the heavenly sanctuary into which Jesus has already entered as high priest. But rather than explicitly speak of the heavenly sanctuary, the author refers to a heavenly city, thereby making clear that believers do not enter the sanctuary as priests in the way Jesus did. Rather, they will form a new community in the heavenly city, where they will enjoy God's Sabbath rest.

To summarize, the author's eschatology is intimately related to his presentation of Jesus as the pioneer and perfecter of faith. As the one who has finished the course, Jesus has brought faith to its completion in a way that no one before him did. The Christian life, then, is a matter of following in Jesus' path of obedience and faithfulness, a way made possible because Jesus has blazed a trail for others to follow. Those who endure, despite suffering and affliction, will attain to the heavenly city, the place of God's Sabbath rest, the heavenly sanctuary. The author does not explain the relationship between the parousia and this final salvation in the way that Paul does in 1 Corinthians 15, but he does remind his readers that there is a goal to God's plan that will not be attained until the end, when Christ will appear a second time.

JESUS AND THE CHILDREN GOD HAS GIVEN HIM

Although its doctrinal sections deal primarily with issues of Christology and soteriology, the purpose of Hebrews is to exhort its audience to maintain its original confession. Consequently, even though *ekklēsia* occurs only twice in this writing (2:12; 12:23), the author is vitally interested in the ecclesial life of the community he addresses.

The community meets on a regular basis (10:25), has "leaders" (13:7, 17, 24), and its members have undergone basic teaching about Christ (6:1). The author speaks of baptism as enlightenment (6:2–4; 10:32), and his cryptic remark about "an altar from which those who officiate in the tent have no right to eat" (13:10) may be a reference to the Eucharist.[26] The community has

---

26. So Ferdinand Hahn, *Theologie des Neuen Testaments*, 2 vols. (Tübingen: Mohr Siebeck, 2002), 1:438.

already endured "a hard struggle with sufferings," and some of its members have been exposed to abuse and persecution (10:32–34). The author, however, is fearful that some may apostatize. His purpose then is to exhort and encourage the community by reminding it that the apostle and high priest of its confession (3:1) has dealt with sin once and for all.

To reinforce its message, the author introduces three harsh warnings that there will be no second repentance for those who apostatize. First, it is impossible to restore to repentance those who willfully apostatize after having been enlightened since "they are crucifying again the Son of God and are holding him up to contempt" (6:4–8). Second, there is no longer a sacrifice for sins for those who willfully persist in sin but a fearful punishment for those who spurn the Son of God (10:26–31). Third, those who, like Esau, despise their birthright will find no second chance to repent (12:16–17). It is not that God cannot restore them, but that, as Craig Koester notes, God would be offering apostates what they have already rejected. Therefore, "God permits their decision to stand; he allows them to terminate the relationship."[27] Such apostasy has not yet occurred, and the author expresses his confidence that it will not (6:9). His harsh warnings, however, emphasize the importance of Christ's singular sacrifice for sins and the need for the members of the community to persevere in faithful obedience until they attain their goal.

For the author, the church can be viewed from two perspectives. From the perspective of its present situation, one can understand it as "the wandering people of God."[28] The church is like Israel in the wilderness, journeying in search of the promised land of God's Sabbath rest. This image, which plays an important role in the author's interpretation of Psalm 95, finds its counterpart in the account of the cloud of witnesses who lived by faith as they searched for the city whose architect and builder is God (Heb. 11:10), and for the better country that is heaven (11:16). From the perspective of what it will be, however, the church is "the assembly (*ekklēsia*) of the firstborn who are enrolled in heaven" (12:23).

Less concerned than Paul about the continuity of the church with Israel, the author of Hebrews employs these two images (the wandering people of God and the assembly of the firstborn) to draw a contrast between the church of its day and Israel of old. Israel failed to enter God's rest because of its disobedience (4:6), but there remains a Sabbath rest for the people of God (4:9), which the author identifies as the church, seemingly to the exclusion of Israel. Whereas Israel of old came to Mount Sinai, which could not be touched under the threat of death (12:18, 20), the church has come to Mount Zion, the city

---

27. Koester, *Hebrews*, 322.

28. This is the title of Ernst Käsemann's celebrated monograph, *The Wandering People of God: An Investigation of the Letter to the Hebrews* (Minneapolis: Augsburg, 1984).

of the living God, the heavenly Jerusalem (12:22). For the author of Hebrews the church is the beneficiary of a new covenant, which has made the first covenant obsolete (8:13). In a word, the author is no longer interested in the fate of Israel in the way that Paul is in Romans 9–11. Whereas Paul anguishes over the failure of Israel to believe (Rom. 9:1–5) and proclaims that in God's plan "all Israel will be saved" (11:26), the author of Hebrews associates Israel with the wilderness generation, which has been replaced by the church.

For the author the church is God's house, over which Christ faithfully rules as a son (Heb. 3:6) because, through his suffering and death, he brought its members to God. To show this, the author places the words of Psalm 22 in the mouth of the exalted Christ, who says to God, "I will proclaim your name to my brothers and sisters, in the midst of the congregation (*ekklēsia*) I will praise you" (Heb. 2:12). The "congregation" is the heavenly assembly (12:23) brought into existence by Christ. Again, speaking the words of Scripture, this time from Isaiah, the exalted one proclaims, "Here am I and the children whom God has given me" (2:13, quoting Isa. 8:17). The "children" (*ta paidia*) are the members of the church, whom Christ received on the occasion of his exaltation. For the author of Hebrews, then, the members of the church can be viewed as Christ's children, as well as his brothers and sisters: his children because God has given them to him; his brothers and sisters because he shared in their flesh and blood.

The ecclesiology of Hebrews, incipient though it be, is clearly related to its Christology and soteriology. By his incarnation and death, Christ has brought the church into being and sanctified its members (Heb. 2:11). By the example of his faithful obedience he has shown God's people how to live so that they can join "the assembly of the firstborn who are enrolled in heaven" (12:23).

HEBREWS AND PAUL

Although the church in the West did not judge Hebrews to be Pauline until the fourth century, it was regarded as Pauline and canonical in the Greek and Syrian churches as early as the third century. Accordingly, in most manuscripts Hebrews occurs between the last Pauline letter addressed to the churches (2 Thessalonians) and the first letter addressed to individuals (1 Timothy), an exception being Papyrus 46, which places it between Romans and 1 Corinthians.[29] Contemporary scholarship is unanimous in its judgment that Paul was not the author of Hebrews, but there is a continuing debate about its relation to the Pauline tradition. L. D. Hurst notes: "The introduction last century of

---

29. Werner Georg Kümmel, *Introduction to the New Testament* (Nashville: Abingdon, 1975), 392–93.

the 'Alexandrian' interpretation of Hebrews soon made it fashionable to see little if any connection between Hebrews and Paul."[30] But his own examination of the data leads Hurst to conclude that, although the differences between Hebrews and Paul rule out viewing Hebrews as deuteropauline "in the sense of literary borrowing by a Pauline disciple," the similarities rule out the view that the author *could not* have been, at some time, a Pauline disciple. He suggests: "If it is recognized that there is a sense in which the apostolic tradition grew in a way in which Paul and his associates may have had a significant part, there may be a basis for claiming Pauline influence in the epistle without recourse to the literary solution."[31]

Although some will disagree with Hurst's highly qualified sense of viewing Hebrews as deuteropauline, his suggestion is helpful since a New Testament theologian should be interested in the theological relationships among the writings of the New Testament. This issue is especially acute in the case of Hebrews and Paul since there is a long tradition—not to mention the present order of the canon—that relates Hebrews to the Pauline writings. More importantly, since Paul and the author of Hebrews are among the most creative "theologians" of the New Testament, it is important to know the extent to which their unique theological perspectives diverge and converge.

Hurst summarizes fifteen points of convergence originally noted by Hans Windisch, and he adds eleven more: (1) a similar view of the incarnation, (2) Christ's humiliation, (3) his obedience, (4) his offering for us, (5) the presentation of Christ as an *apolytrōsis* ("redemption") for sin, (6) Christ's intercession for us, (7) the superiority of the new covenant, (8) the inheritance of an exalted name, (9) a reference to signs and wonders, (10) the depiction of Christ as humanity's brother, (11) the example of Abraham's faith, (12) the negative example of the wilderness generation, (13) the portrayal of the Christian life as a race, (14) conversion as enlightenment, (15) the use of similar Old Testament passages, (16) Christ's death as the defeat of evil powers, (17) Christ's death as expiation, (18) waiting for Christ's return, (19) a Pauline-like ending, (20) righteousness by faith, (21) the description of Christians as descendants of Abraham, (22) Paul's assertion that the gospel was preached in advance to Abraham and Hebrews' insistence that Abraham saw and greeted the promise from afar, (23) the rebuke that the readers are fit for milk (elementary teaching) but not meat (advanced teaching), (24) the use of *teleios* in regard to maturity, (25) Christian teaching as a *themelios* ("foundation"), and (26) the nature of stewards as faithful.[32]

---

30. See the helpful summary of the debate in L. D. Hurst, *The Epistle to the Hebrews: Its Background of Thought* (SNTSMS 65; Cambridge: Cambridge University Press, 1990), 107.

31. Ibid. 124.

32. Ibid., 108. Hurst's list contains the appropriate scriptural citations. Koester (*Hebrews*, 54–55) also provides a list.

To be sure, many of these items are used in different ways and contexts, and the particular point of comparison is not always as important for one author as it is for the other. For example, righteousness by faith (number 20) does occur in Heb. 11:7, but it hardly plays the central role in Hebrews that it does in Paul's theology. Nevertheless, it is apparent that the theologies of Hebrews and Paul enjoy some points of convergence, especially in their Christologies and soteriologies.

In addition to these points of convergence, however, there are undeniable divergences. Kümmel summarizes the most important: (1) Whereas Paul consistently refers to Christ's resurrection, Hebrews speaks of Christ's exaltation or entrance into the heavenly sanctuary. (2) Whereas Paul's soteriology focuses on justification and reconciliation, Hebrews prefers the notions of cleansing, sanctification, and perfection. (3) The dominant idea of Hebrews, the high priesthood of Christ, does not occur in Paul's writings. (4) The "new covenant" plays a more central role in Hebrews' theology and is clearly related to Christ's priesthood. (5) Hebrews has nothing to say about justification by faith apart from the works of the law or the opposition between the Spirit and the flesh, or being "with" Christ. (6) Paul calls for faith in Christ, Hebrews for faithfulness and obedience patterned after the faithfulness of Christ. (7) The concepts of Gentile and Jew do not play a role in Hebrews, nor is Hebrews concerned about the destiny of Israel in the way that Paul is. (8) Hebrews views the law in terms of Israel's cult, whereas Paul views it in terms of the moral life and its salvation-historical role. (9) Paul never speaks of the impossibility of a second repentance. (10) The parousia and the general resurrection of the dead play central roles in Paul's apocalyptic theology, whereas Hebrews is more concerned with entrance into God's Sabbath rest, the heavenly sanctuary, the city of God.[33]

Overall these points of divergence are more persuasive than the points of convergence since they highlight structural differences between the theologies. Put another way, whereas the points of convergence indicate that the author of Hebrews and Paul made use of common Christian tradition, the points of divergence show how each refashioned that tradition in new and creative ways. For example, Paul views Jesus' death and resurrection as the event whereby God justified the ungodly, reconciled the world to himself, and released the power of the Spirit, thereby transferring humanity from the realm of sin to the realm of God's grace. Accordingly, believers are no longer under the law, for they are led and guided by the Spirit. The response to this act of grace is trusting faith in Christ, reliance on what God has done rather than doing the works of the law. Believers have already been justified and reconciled, but they will not be finally saved until the parousia, when the dead will be raised incorruptible.

---

33. Kümmel, *Introduction to the New Testament*, 395. I have slightly modified and expanded upon his list.

The author of Hebrews takes the same redemptive event but interprets it differently. He presents the death of Jesus as a cultic act whereby a great high priest according to the order of Melchizedek entered into the heavenly sanctuary, leading the way for others to follow. By Christ's death, which inaugurates a new covenant, sin has been dealt with once and for all time. There will be no further sacrifice for sin. Rather than present the response to this redemptive event as faith in Christ, apart from doing the works of the law, the author of Hebrews calls upon his audience to be faithful and obedient in the way Jesus, the pioneer and perfecter of faith, was. The eschatological goal is no longer expressed in terms of resurrection from the dead but in the language of entrance into God's Sabbath rest, the heavenly sanctuary, the city of God.

The ways in which Hebrews and Paul express God's redemptive event differ. Some might even argue they are irreconcilable. Both, however, speak of God's redemptive work in Christ. Both view this death as the eschatological event by which God deals with sin in a final and definitive way. Both agree that Jesus is the Son of God, the one through whom God offers salvation to the world. The difference is the way in which each presents this event, which, when all is said and done, cannot be explained by merely recounting the historical circumstances of the crucifixion. Both affirm that what appears to have been the execution of a criminal was indeed the locus of God's redemptive work. Paul chose to express this reality in the language of justification and reconciliation, the author of Hebrews in the cultic language of priesthood and sacrifice. Both, however, came to a similar conclusion regarding the significance of this death: it is God's final and definitive word.

12

A Theology of Wisdom and Perfection

The Letter of James

Insofar as it appears to contradict Paul's teaching on justification by faith, the Letter of James has always presented a challenge—perhaps the most formidable challenge—to the unity of the theology in the New Testament. It is not surprising then that some theologies of the New Testament focus their attention on those verses in James that deal with faith and works (2:14–26) in order to determine if there is a way to reconcile the teaching of James and Paul. The result of this approach is a somewhat truncated presentation of the letter's theology. In recent years, however, there has been a renewed and vibrant interest in the study of the person of James and the letter attributed to him.[1] This renewal has allowed scholars to read James on its own terms rather than as a foil for Paul's teaching on justification by faith, and it presents New Testament theology with an opportunity to mine a rich theological vein that has often been overlooked.

The author of the letter identifies himself as "James, a servant of God and of the Lord Jesus Christ," and his intended audience as "the twelve tribes in the Dispersion" (1:1). Questions about the letter's authorship, audience, and date, however, have spawned an intense debate, which is chronicled in most introductions to the New Testament.[2] On the one hand a number of scholars argue, on the basis of material that seems to reflect the earliest traditions about Jesus, that the author of the letter is James the brother of the Lord. On the other hand others contend, on the basis of style, rhetoric, and the letter's seemingly anti-Pauline polemic, that James is best attributed to an unknown Hellenistic writer of a later period. Still others urge a mediating position by maintaining that

---

1. The essay of Bruce Chilton, "James, Jesus' Brother," in *The Face of New Testament Studies: A Survey of Recent Research* (ed. Scot McKnight and Grant R. Osborne; Grand Rapids: Baker, 2004), 251–62, provides a helpful summary of recent research on the person of James.

2. See Kümmel, *Introduction to the New Testament*, 403–16; Udo Schnelle, *The History and Theology of The New Testament Writings* (Minneapolis: Fortress, 1998), 383–98.

the letter was written in behalf of James, either during his lifetime or shortly thereafter.[3]

As is the case with so many debates regarding dating and authorship, there is insufficient evidence to arrive at a solution to which all will ascribe. Contemporary scholarship, however, has convinced many that even if the letter is pseudonymous, it reflects traditions that have their origin in circles that revered the memory and teaching of James. Moreover, literary and rhetorical approaches to James have effectively argued that James is more than a collection of unrelated moral maxims. When examined in light of its rhetoric, it discloses a literary and rhetorical unity that has implications for its theological stance.[4] Finally, canonical approaches have emphasized that inasmuch as the letter purports to have been written by James, this is how it functions in the church's Scripture.[5] All of these insights are helpful for a New Testament theologian who is interested in the theology of the text as well as the history behind it. Accordingly, in this chapter I begin with a presentation of the literary and rhetorical unity of James before proceeding to a discussion of the theological vision that informs this letter. After listening to the voice of James on its own terms, I conclude with a brief comparison between the theology of James and that of Paul.

THE LITERARY AND RHETORICAL UNITY OF JAMES

Although the classic commentary of Martin Dibelius was instrumental in removing the Letter of James from under the shadow of Paul's theology of jus-

---

3. Kümmel (*Introduction to the New Testament*, 412–13) presents two arguments for the authorship of James: (1) the simple self-designation that opens the letter, and (2) the letter's contact with the Gospel tradition. He then lists five arguments against the authorship of James: (1) the cultured language of the text; (2) the lack of any references to the cultic aspects of the law; (3) the omission of any mention of the author's relationship to Jesus; (4) the nature of the discussion of faith and works in chapter 2, which suggests that James was written sometime after Paul's debate on justification; (5) the rather late addition of James to the canon. Peter H. Davids (*The Epistle of James: A Commentary on the Greek Text* [NIGTC; Grand Rapids: Eerdmans, 1982], 2–22) and Patrick J. Hartin (*James* [SP 14; Collegeville, MN: Liturgical Press, 2003], 16–25) propose a mediating position. Davids concludes that "it is likely that either James received assistance in the editing of the work, or that his teaching was edited at a later date (perhaps after his death), as the church spread beyond Jerusalem and began to use Greek more exclusively" (p. 22). Hartin favors a solution that views "the composition of the letter as having taken place shortly after the death of James at Jerusalem. A close associate of James with an excellent ability in Greek writes in his name to those Christian-Jewish communities in the Diaspora who recognized James's leadership and authority" (p. 25).

4. This approach can be seen in the commentaries of Davids and Hartin mentioned above.

5. Brevard S. Childs (*The New Testament as Canon: An Introduction* [Philadelphia: Fortress, 1984], 431–45, here 444–45) is a representative of this approach. He concludes, "The historical stages through which the epistle of James developed are unknown, and the several reconstructions remain speculative. The danger of first deciding on a hypothesis regarding authorship and date of composition lies in twisting the subsequent reading of the canonical text in order to support the theory." Robert W. Wall ("James, Letter of," *DLNT*, 545–61) discusses a canonical approach to James.

tification by faith, it tended to view the letter as a collection of unrelated moral exhortations.[6] A closer examination, however, suggests that James introduces his major topics in the opening chapter and develops them in the rest of the letter. If this is correct, there is a literary unity to James that can be viewed as the outward expression of its inner theological vision.

Announcing the Topics

After the initial salutation, the first chapter of James can be divided into two parts (vv. 2–11 and 12–25) that culminate in a description of what James understands by religion that is "pure and undefiled" (vv. 26–27).[7] The first two parts are similar, each beginning with the topic of testing or temptation, then moving to the topic of wisdom or gifts from above before concluding with a statement about rich and poor or hearing and doing the word. In these subunits, the attentive reader finds vocabulary and themes that will be repeated as the letter progresses.

A. Testing (vv. 2–4)   A′. Temptation (vv. 12–16)
B. Wisdom (vv. 5–8)   B′. Every perfect gift from above (vv. 17–18)
C. Poor and rich (vv. 9–11)   C′. Listeners and doers of the word (vv. 19–25)
           D. Pure and undefiled religion (vv. 26–27)

The first unit (vv. 2–4) begins with a theme that serves as a leitmotif for the rest of the letter: testing, which requires endurance, brings faith to perfection so that believers may be "mature and complete" in their faith. As the letter progresses, James will relate testing to the end time, perfection to the law, and explain his understanding of faith.

In the second unit (vv. 5–8), James introduces the theme of wisdom, which he relates to faith and prayer. James assumes that he is addressing those who are (or should be) wise because they observe the perfect law of liberty. But since he is aware that there may be some within the community who lack this gift, he encourages them to petition God for wisdom, the supreme gift that enables believers to live wisely in this life. Repeating the theme of faith introduced earlier, James encourages his audience to ask for wisdom in faith, drawing a contrast between faith and doubt. Introducing yet another theme that will appear again, James compares the doubter to one who is double-minded (*dipsychos*). Such double-mindedness is the opposite of the perfection to which James

6. Martin Dibelius, *James: A Commentary on the Epistle of James* (Hermeneia; Philadelphia: Fortress, 1976), 3.

7. The use of "James" can be confusing since "James" can refer to the real or implied author of the letter or to the letter itself. In this chapter most instances of "James" refer to the author of James rather than the letter, thus the frequent uses of the pronouns "he" and "his" when referring to "James." Uses that refer to the letter should be self-evident.

summons his readers, and it is incompatible with the ideal of friendship with God that James will propose in chapter 4.

In the third unit (1:9–11), James introduces the theme of poor and rich, noting the great reversal of fortunes God has already effected for the community of the wise. The lowly members of the community should boast that God has raised them up, and the rich should boast that God has brought them low. James notes that life in this world is transitory, and, even though there are social and economic differences in the present life, the rich will fade away like the grass of the field.

The fourth unit (vv. 12–16) begins by returning to the major theme of the first unit: the need for endurance in testing. Instead of simply restating what has already been said, however, James introduces new themes that he will develop further. For example, the one who endures the test of temptation will receive the eschatological gift of "the crown of life." James also begins to flesh out his understanding of God and the human condition. Countering a view of God as the one who causes temptation, James maintains that God can neither be tempted nor does God tempt anyone with evil. The source of temptation is desire, which gives birth to sin, which in turn gives birth to death. It is important, then, for the community not to be deceived. The origin of its trials and temptations is not in a malevolent deity but in the human condition that needs gifts from on high if it is to be healed.

In the fifth unit (vv. 17–18), James speaks of these gifts and of the graciousness of God, "the Father of lights," in whom there is no change. Every perfect gift is from God and, as James has already suggested, the most important of these gifts is wisdom from above. The community of the wise, then, can be utterly confident since "the Father of lights" has already given it a new life "by the word of truth," which is the gospel. This community is "a kind of first fruits of his creatures." Its members are what others are destined to be.

Having reminded the community that they have received the gospel that has given them life, in the sixth unit (vv. 19–25) James exhorts those who have embraced "the word of truth" to "be quick to listen" and to "be doers of the word." If believers are quick to listen, they will welcome "the implanted word" that has the power to save their souls. This "implanted word" is the gospel they received at baptism, "the word of truth" that has made them the firstfruits of the redeemed.

Listening to the implanted word finds its completion in doing the word. Accordingly, James urges the community of the wise to be doers of the word and not merely hearers of it. James now begins to relate the word to "the perfect law, the law of liberty." This perfect law is the Mosaic law, which the community of the wise observes in light of the implanted word of the gospel, the word of truth. For James, there is no opposition between law and gospel, as there is in Romans and Galatians. The law, as lived by and interpreted by Jesus, remains in force. It is a perfect law because it is the expression of God's will. It is the law of liberty because perfect observance leads to freedom from desire and sin.

Having announced its major topics of testing, wisdom from above, rich and poor, listening to and doing the word, James concludes (vv. 26–27) with a definition of true religion that focuses on the social responsibility of the community of the wise. Those who are wise will care for orphans and widows and keep themselves "unstained by the world." Here it is interesting to note that although James speaks only of the moral dimensions of the law, he continues to employ the language of the ritual law to express the goals and demands of the religious life. Religion is to be "pure and undefiled." Believers are to be "unstained" by the world.

James qualifies the truly religious person in yet another way. Those who are religious must be able to "bridle their tongues." This theme recalls what James has already said about those who are "double-minded," and he will develop it further in chapter 3.

To summarize, this rich introduction places the entire letter under a number of themes that function as keys to unlocking the literary unity of James. Those who have received the implanted word are truly wise, for they have access to wisdom from above. Because they are wise, they know that the testing of their faith leads to perfection and that such faith expresses itself in doing the perfect law of liberty. Faith in action as well as in word is pure and undefiled religion.

Developing the Topics

Having announced his major topics in the opening chapter, James explores and expands upon these themes in what follows. In chapter 2 he deals with faith, the law, and the need for faith to express itself in works. In chapter 3 he examines the importance of controlling the tongue and distinguishing between two kinds of wisdom. In chapter 4 he explores the human condition. And in chapter 5 he develops the topics of the rich, the eschatological hope of believers, the importance of truthful speech, and the power of prayer. In every instance the topics of these chapters echo and expand upon what James has already said in chapter 1.

Faith

Faith is central to James's understanding of the Christian life, as the remarks about the testing of faith (1:3) and the need to ask for wisdom in faith (1:5) indicate. In chapter 2 James develops his understanding of faith in three steps. First he argues that those who show favoritism toward the rich at the expense of the poor are betraying their faith in their glorious Lord Jesus Christ

(2:1–7).[8] Returning to the theme of the lowly and the rich announced in 1:9–11, James reminds his listeners that God chose the poor to be rich in faith and to be heirs of the kingdom he promised. Anticipating a theme he will develop in chapter 5, James reminds his recipients that it is the rich who oppress them and blaspheme the excellent name of Christ that was invoked over them at their baptism. True faith, then, must not discriminate on the basis of social differences if it is to be perfect and complete.

Second, James emphasizes the importance of keeping the whole law (2:8–13), thereby highlighting the unity of faith and law in his theological vision. For James the Mosaic law is "the royal law" (2:8) because it was given by God, who is the King of the universe, the one whose kingdom Jesus proclaimed (Mark 1:15). It is "the law of liberty" (Jas. 2:12; see also 1:25) because its observance leads to the freedom to do God's will. Although James recognizes the importance of the love commandment as stated in Lev. 19:18 (a commandment that plays a central role in the teaching of Jesus and Paul), he does not summarize the law in this commandment. Rather, he insists that one must observe all of the commandments.[9] To violate one commandment is to violate the entire law, for God's will is one.

Third, James argues that faith without works is dead (2:14–26), and on three occasions he notes that a person is "justified by works" (2:21, 24, 25). This section is the most controversial aspect of James's teaching. But instead of reading it in light of Paul's teaching on justification by faith apart from doing the works of the Mosaic law, it is important that we listen to James's voice. Whereas the issue for Paul was how a person is transferred from the realm of sin and death to the realm of grace and life, the issue for James is the nature of faith. Is it possible to have faith apart from works? Can such faith save a person? For James an abstract notion of faith has no power to save, and it will not stand the test of God's judgment. Faith, without works of loving-kindness, is dead. In affirming that Abraham and Rahab were justified by works, James is not so much setting faith and works in opposition to each other as he is arguing against a concept of faith that he views as barren because it expresses itself in words but not in deeds. Because this kind of faith cannot save or justify, James affirms that a person is justified by works that manifest faith.

By the end of chapter 2, James has made his position clear. Faith comes to perfection through testing and steadfast endurance; it never doubts. It shows

---

8. James 2:1 presents several exegetical problems, not the least of which is whether the genitive is objective, "believe in our glorious Lord Jesus Christ," or subjective, "hold the faith of our glorious Lord Jesus Christ." Hartin (*James*, 116–17, 128–31) presents a number of interesting arguments in favor of the subjective genitive.

9. Although James insists that one must do all of the commandments of the law, he never refers to the cultic or dietary prescriptions of the law, a puzzling fact since Acts and Galatians portray James as a law-observant Jew.

no partiality to the rich; it does not stand in opposition to the law; it is manifested and active through good works that assist those in need.

Perfection in Speech and Wisdom from Above

In the opening chapter, James spoke of the wisdom that comes from God (1:5), and he warned that the religion of those who do not bridle their tongue is worthless (1:26). In chapter 3 James takes up these topics in reverse order: the importance of taming the tongue (3:1–12), two kinds of wisdom (3:13–18).

James compares the tongue to a bit in the mouth of a horse and to the rudder of a great ship. Like these small instruments, the tongue is meant to control the body. However, whereas the bit and the rudder carry out the purpose for which they were intended, the tongue does not. Here James is utterly pessimistic. He affirms that if someone is perfect in speech, such a person is perfect and capable of keeping the whole body in check. But the reality is that no one has been able to tame the tongue. Pointing to the contradictions in human life, James notes that people bless and curse with the same tongue, thereby showing that their devotion to God is not whole and entire.

What James says about the tongue reveals a great deal about his understanding of the human condition. He describes the tongue as "a world of iniquity," affirming that "it stains the whole body" (3:6). Like Paul and John, James assumes that a human being cannot attain perfection apart from God's grace. If perfection is to be attained, there is need for the implanted word of the gospel, the word of truth, wisdom that comes from above.

James indicates that there are two kinds of wisdom (3:13–18). On the one hand, some mistakenly assume that worldly behavior characterized by envy, ambition, and boasting is wisdom. But James assures his audience that this wisdom "does not come down from above" (3:15). True wisdom is pure, peaceable, gentle, willing to yield, full of mercy, without any trace of partiality or hypocrisy (3:17). As is evident from the qualities that characterize the wisdom from above, those who are endowed with it will control the tongue. The solution to the human predicament, then, is the gift of wisdom, which, when fully embraced, allows those who receive it to be perfect in speech. This wisdom enables believers to do the perfect law of liberty in light of the implanted word of the gospel.

The Human Condition

Chapter 4 is the fullest expression of James's anthropology. Developing themes announced in chapter 1 and pursuing themes found in chapter 3, James explains the reason for conflicts and disputes within the communities he addresses.

In 1:14–15 James explained temptation in terms of desire (*epithymia*), which leads to sin and death. In 3:14–16 he argued that envy and selfish ambition are the result of a wisdom that is "earthly, unspiritual, devilish." Building upon this earlier analysis of the human condition, James identifies human craving (*hēdonē*) as the origin of conflicts and disputes (4:1). What humans do not have, they want. What they cannot obtain, they covet. What they ask for, they ask for in the wrong way because they want it for their own pleasure (*hēdonē*). In effect, human beings are divided; for by seeking what they crave, they find themselves in friendship with the world rather than in friendship with God. What they must do is resist the devil, humble themselves, and draw near to God. Otherwise they will remain double-minded (*dipsychoi*, 4:8; see also 1:8).

Returning to the theme of speech (4:11–12), James asks why believers continue to speak against one another. James warns that if they speak evil of one another and judge fellow believers, they will be judging the law. Recalling his earlier injunction that believers must be doers of the word (1:22), James explains that those who judge the law, by speaking ill of others, make themselves judges of the law rather than doers of it. For those who judge others assume the prerogative of God, the sole lawgiver and judge.

James sees the arrogance of the human person in the attitude of those who plan business ventures without any thought of their mortality (4:13–17). Such people forget the utter frailty of humanity, which is like "a mist that appears for a little while and then vanishes." The section concludes with James's description of sin as the deliberate failure to do what a person knows is right.

James does not distinguish between the human condition before and after Christ. What is found in chapter 4 can be applied to the believer as well as to the unbeliever. For James the human condition is conflicted and double-minded even among believers, since not all have appropriated the wisdom from above. Because they are driven by desire, humans seek to be friends with God and friends with the world. What the implanted word requires, and what James urges, is a life of perfection characterized by full and complete devotion to God.

Riches, Endurance, Truthfulness, and the Prayer of Faith

In chapter 1 James encouraged his readers to endure their trials (1:2–4) and to pray for wisdom in faith without wavering (1:5–8). He exhorted the rich to boast in their lowliness because their possessions are fleeting (1:9–11), and he warned that the religion of those who do not bridle their tongue is worthless (1:26). In chapter 5 James develops a series of variations on these topics.

The chapter begins with a harsh condemnation of the rich (5:1–6).[10] Like those who boast about their future business enterprises without considering their mortality (4:13–17), the rich have not understood the fleeting nature of the human condition. In an ironic statement, James notes they have "laid up

---

10. Here James is not speaking about the rich in the community, as is the case in 1:9–11, but about the rich in general, especially those whose hoarding of wealth results in the oppression of those within the community.

treasure for the last days" (5:3), but now that "the last days" have arrived their riches are rotting and the cries of those whom they defrauded are a witness against them, reaching "the ears of the Lord of hosts."

Because "the last days" have arrived, James encourages his audience to be patient until the coming of the Lord, recalling the patience of the prophets and the endurance of Job (5:7–11). This unit is a strong testimony to James's eschatological hope and his firm conviction that the parousia is near. It is also remarkable for its fourfold use of "Lord," which in the first two instances refers to Christ (5:7, 8) and in the last two instances to God, the Lord of hosts (5:10, 11). The ease with which James identifies Christ and God as Lord suggests that James has a more exalted Christology than is often thought.

In a brief statement that at first appears out of place, James exhorts his listeners not to employ oaths but to speak plainly and truthfully (5:12), a statement reminiscent of Jesus' teaching in the Sermon on the Mount (Matt. 5:33–37). This saying, however, is not so much an injunction against taking oaths as it is a variation of James's constant exhortation to bridle and tame the tongue. Those who are perfect need not take oaths because when they say yes they mean what they say, and when they say no they mean what they say.

Having exhorted the community to pray for wisdom with faith without doubting, James encourages the suffering to pray and the sick to summon the elders of the church to pray over them and to anoint them in the name of "the Lord," which here refers to Christ (5:13–18). James affirms that this prayer made in faith will save the sick, the Lord (Christ) will raise them up, and their sins will be forgiven. The members of the church, then, are to confess their sins to one another and pray for one another so that they may be healed. Pointing to the example of Elijah, James is unwavering in his faith that the prayer of the righteous "is powerful and effective" (5:16).

The letter concludes abruptly, without the final greeting or blessing characteristic of Paul's letters, reminding the audience that, in addition to saving the sinner, those who bring back believers who have wandered "from the truth" will "cover a multitude of sins" (5:19–20). So this letter, which focuses on issues of "social justice," concludes with an admonition to care for those who have strayed from the truth, which in this instance refers to the gospel, "the word of truth" mentioned in 1:18.

The literary and rhetorical unity of James is found in the way the author develops the several topics he announces in his opening chapter: the need for perseverance in faith, which leads to perfection; the need to ask for wisdom with faith, without doubting, lest one be viewed as double-minded; the great reversal that God has effected for the lowly and the rich; the fleeting nature of life; the eschatological crown that awaits those who endure temptation; the human condition, which is characterized by desire; the generosity of God, who grants every good gift; the need to be doers as well as hearers of the word; the need to bridle the tongue; and the nature of true religion. James achieves unity by recycling these themes in a variety of ways rather than by presenting them in a systematic fashion.

James attains his rhetorical goal by contrasting (a) faith without works and faith that is active along with works, (b) the wisdom of this world and the wisdom from above, (c) partial and perfect observance of the law, (d) boasting in oneself and boasting in God, (e) prayer that doubts and prayer made in faith, (f) being double-minded and being perfect, (g) partiality and impartiality, (h) being controlled by the tongue and taming the tongue, and (i) the fleetingness of life and the enduring judgment of God. The Christian life is a choice between the demands of the world and the requirements of God, between compromise and total allegiance to God. Those who choose the first path are perfect, whereas those who choose the second are double-minded.

THE THEOLOGICAL VISION OF JAMES

The literary and rhetorical unity of James suggests that this letter possesses a unified theological vision of the Christian life. To affirm this is to challenge a widespread assumption that even though James contains a great deal of practical and helpful moral exhortation, it has little to say about the Christian life. To be sure, James does not present an imposing Christology and soteriology such as is found in the Fourth Gospel, the Pauline Letters, or the Epistle to the Hebrews. But just as recent studies have shown that there is a literary and rhetorical unity to the letter, so they have argued that the theological vision of the letter is richer than has usually been supposed.[11] In the case of James, there are at least three important theological assumptions: the enduring importance of the law for the Christian life; the significance of the implanted word of the gospel that calls upon believers to observe the law perfectly; and the gift of wisdom from above.

The Law

For James the Mosaic law is and remains "the perfect law, the law of liberty" (1:25; see 2:12), "the royal law" (2:8) of the great king, which must be observed in all of its commandments if one is to be perfect. There is no conflict between this law and the gospel, which James identifies as "the implanted word" (1:21),

<hr>

11. For helpful surveys of James's theology, see Andrew Chester and Ralph P. Martin, *The Theology of the Letters of James, Peter, and Jude* (NTT; Cambridge: Cambridge University Press, 1994), 6–62; Hahn, *Theologie des Neuen Testaments*, 1:395–407; Adolf Schlatter, *The Theology of the Apostles: The Development of New Testament Theology* (Grand Rapids: Baker, 1998), 82–103; Georg Strecker, *Theology of the New Testament* (Louisville: Westminster John Knox Press, 2000), 654–82.

"the word of truth" (1:18). James never explains the precise relationship between the law and the gospel, but one suspects that his understanding of their relationship is similar to what is found in the Gospel of Matthew: Jesus' interpretation of the law and the manner in which he observed the law in his life shows believers how to observe the law perfectly, thereby making it a law of liberty for them. The manner in which James appears to allude to Jesus' teaching, especially as found in the Sermon on the Mount, suggests that James's understanding of the law is deeply informed by a stream of tradition that he shares with the Synoptic Gospels. For example, when James calls upon his audience not to swear by heaven or by earth or by any other oath (5:12), he appears to be echoing Jesus' own teaching as remembered in the Sermon on the Mount (Matt. 5:33–37).[12]

Like the Sermon on the Mount, the Letter of James views the goal of the Christian life as perfection: complete and undivided loyalty to God (Jas. 1:4; 3:2; Matt. 5:48). Faith must be expressed without doubting; there must be no partiality; and speech must be gracious and truthful at all times. In a word, one cannot simultaneously be in friendship with God and in friendship with the world. Although he assumes that the faith of those who endure testing and temptation will be brought to perfection, James is keenly aware that human beings—even those who have embraced the word of truth—are imperfect. This imperfection can be seen in the way people abuse speech by both blessing and cursing "those who are made in the likeness of God" (Jas. 3:9). Rather than control their tongue, such people are controlled by it. Within the letter, then, the tongue becomes a metaphor for a power and force beyond human control. Nevertheless, James seems to envision the possibility of controlling the tongue when he affirms, "Anyone who makes no mistakes in speaking is perfect" (3:2). James's understanding of the human condition, then, can be summarized as follows. The life of human beings is fleeting, for they are like the flower of the field that quickly fades (1:10), a mere mist that quickly passes away (4:14). What most characterizes them is the divided self that expresses itself in "double-mindedness" (1:8; 4:8) and is driven by desire (1:14; 4:1–2). The fearsome prospect that human beings face, whether they realize it or not, is that they must stand in judgment before God and give an account of themselves (5:9).

Unlike Paul, John, and the Synoptic writers, James does not focus on the redemptive event that has the power to overcome the human predicament. He does not speak of the death of Christ and its power to overcome sin and reconcile humanity to God. Nor does he refer to the transforming power of the resurrection or the general resurrection of the dead. James does not even employ the word "gospel." Instead, his focus is on the enduring value of the

---

12. Davids (*James*, 47–48) provides a list of possible relations between James and the Synoptic tradition.

law, presumably as interpreted and lived by Jesus. This is not to say that James is unaware of Christ's saving death and resurrection. The use of "Lord" in conjunction with the name Jesus Christ (1:1; 2:1), or as a way to refer to the exalted Christ (5:7–8, 14–15), implies the event of Christ's death and resurrection, and it indicates that James confesses Jesus as the one whom God has exalted at his right hand.[13]

The Implanted Word

James understands the transforming power of what has been effected through Jesus Christ, for he states that God has given believers a "birth by the word of truth, so that we should become a kind of first fruits of his creatures" (1:18). James notes that the implanted word "has the power to save your souls" (1:21). These expressions refer to the gospel and point to the redemptive significance of its message. On the one hand, the gospel is a salvific message that brings about a new birth so that those who embrace it are the firstfruits of God's creatures. On the other hand, this word is an implanted word, a gift from above, and it touches the deepest self of those who embrace it. It has the power to save because it is God's gift, which pierces the inner self.

The theological problem of James is not his teaching on faith and works, as is often supposed, but his understanding of the relationship between the law and the implanted word. Although it would be theologically satisfying to say that the implanted word enables believers to carry out the law, James never explicitly affirms this. However, it is apparent that James views those who have embraced the word as a people who are the firstfruits of a harvest yet to come. They are living in the last days, for the Judge is at the door, and the Lord is near.

The way in which the letter begins is revealing. James addresses "the twelve tribes in the Dispersion" (1:1). If one thinks that the letter is addressed to Jewish Christians, one will suppose that its author is identifying them as the eschatological people of God. But if one holds that the letter is addressed to Gentile Christians, one will argue that it is identifying them as the Israel of God, much as Paul does in Gal. 6:16. In either case, the theological point is similar: the implied audience is the eschatological people of God, which has received the implanted word, the word of truth, the gospel. This people, which has been

---

13. There are instances when it is not clear whether James is referring to Jesus or to God as Lord, for example, 4:10, 15. J. Ramsey Michaels ("Catholic Christologies in the Catholic Epistles," in *Contours of Christology in the New Testament* [ed. Richard N. Longenecker; Grand Rapids: Eerdmans, 2005], 268–91, here 273) writes, "James does not intend that we sort out his uses of 'Lord'—assigning some to God and others to Jesus. To James, 'the Lord' of the Hebrew Bible and 'the Lord Jesus Christ' are one and the same. He has no interest in distinguishing between them as 'Father' and 'Son,' only in recognizing and honoring one 'Lord' and 'God.'"

born anew by that word, is expected to observe the law perfectly. This is not to say that perfect observance of the law is the means to salvation. But it does suggest that even though James is aware that believers have not yet attained this goal, the word of truth urges them to observe the law perfectly.

Wisdom

In addition to the law and the implanted word, wisdom plays an important role in James's theology. Wisdom comes from God, who gives "generously and ungrudgingly" (1:5), and it is one of the perfect gifts that comes down "from the Father of lights" (1:17). The good works that James requires of believers are "born of wisdom" (3:13). But James is aware that there is another kind of wisdom that gives rise to "envy and selfish ambition," a wisdom James identifies as "earthly, unspiritual, devilish" (3:15). Therefore, it is important for believers to distinguish between the two if they are to be in friendship with God rather than in friendship with the world. Although James does not explain the relationship of the law, the implanted word, and wisdom from above, there may be such a relationship since Israel viewed its law as an expression of God's wisdom (see Sirach 24, especially v. 23), and the Gospel of Matthew portrays Jesus in the guise of divine wisdom (see Matt. 11:25–30 and note the similarity to Sir. 24:19–22).

Wisdom from above allows believers to practice a religion that is "pure and undefiled before God" (Jas. 1:27), and it leads to friendship with God. Such religion expresses itself in deeds of loving-kindness toward the lowly and oppressed. These deeds are not a means of obtaining salvation but a concrete expression of faith. For this reason James insists that, apart from works, faith is dead.

The contours of the theology embedded in the Letter of James can be summarized as follows. The word of truth about Jesus Christ, which is the implanted word of the gospel, has made those who embrace it members of the eschatological people of Israel, the twelve tribes of Israel that have been restored by the gospel.[14] The goal of this eschatological people is perfection, which comes from faithful endurance and perfect observance of the law of liberty. Such people live as a community of the wise because they have received the gift of wisdom from the Father of lights. They express their religion in deeds that accompany and testify to their faith in Jesus Christ. They are aware that the Lord is near and

---

14. Hartin (*James*, 53–55) has an interesting excursus on the theological significance of James's address to the twelve tribes of the Dispersion. He argues that "this expression should be read against the background of Israel's hope in a restored twelve-tribe kingdom" (p. 53), and he notes the theological implication of this vision is that "God is at work bringing this restoration to birth (1:18)" (p. 55). The vision of James "still lies at the heart of the world of Israel and sees no incompatibility between being a follower of Jesus and an adherent of Israel's traditions" (p. 55).

that the Judge is at the door. When God's judgment takes place, there will be a further reversal of fortunes in favor of the poor and oppressed.

PAUL AND JAMES

Comparing James and Paul is a bit unfair and, perhaps, unwise. Paul and his interpreters, after all, have elaborated a rather extensive theology that focuses on the death and resurrection of Christ, whereas James is a single letter that never explicitly refers to Christ's death and resurrection. The Spirit plays a central role in Paul's vision of the Christian life, but it is never mentioned in James.[15] Paul is concerned about the place of Gentiles in the people of God; James never speaks of them. Paul develops an elaborate theology of the resurrection of the dead in conjunction with his understanding of the parousia, whereas James simply notes that the Lord is near and the Judge is at the door. And, as has often been noted, Paul insists that the believer is justified by God's grace on the basis of faith, apart from doing the works of the Mosaic law (Rom. 3:20, 28; Gal. 2:16), whereas James affirms that one is justified by works that manifest one's faith, not by faith alone (Jas. 2:21, 24, 25). The differences between the two are such that any comparison is akin to the proverbial comparison of apples and oranges. James and Paul configure their understanding of the Christian life differently.

Paul configures his theology in light of the apocalyptic event of Christ's death and resurrection. This event establishes a new creation, so that the power of sin is overcome and Gentile and Jew become one in Christ. James configures his theology around wisdom from above and the perfect law of liberty. Those who observe the law and live according to the wisdom that comes from God will attain the wholeness and perfection for which they were intended. Within the canon, James and Paul temper each other, the Pauline Letters reminding believers that trusting faith in Christ is the only way into God's new creation, and James reminding believers that those who have entered this new creation cannot use their faith as an excuse for not doing good works. In the words of Brevard Childs, "The letter bears witness that, correctly interpreted, the Old Testament continues to function as a norm for Christian living even after the resurrection."[16] Left to itself, the Letter of James is an insufficient exposition of the Christian life since it does not present or deal with the salvific death and life-giving resurrection of Christ. But it does offer

---

15. Davids (*James*, 56) suggests that "James has a wisdom pneumatology, for wisdom in James functions as the Spirit does in Paul." This is an interesting suggestion, but one should not overlook that James never explicitly speaks of the Spirit.

16. *New Testament as Canon*, 438.

a reliable presentation of the responsibilities entailed in the Christian life. Paul's Letters, by contrast, present an insightful exposition of the Christ event, and they highlight the centrality of the moral life. Left to themselves, however, they can and have been misunderstood. So it is necessary to read the Pauline corpus with James readily at hand, just as it is important to read James in light of the Pauline corpus.

13

A Theology for a Time of Affliction and Disorder

1 and 2 Peter and Jude

The letters of Peter and Jude present New Testament theology with a problem. On the one hand, contemporary scholarship tends to view these letters as pseudepigraphical: letters written in the name of Peter and of Jude. On the other, these letters purport to be the writings of significant figures of the early church: Peter, a disciple and apostle of the Lord; Jude, a brother of James and Jesus. Moreover, although 2 Peter presents itself as Peter's second letter, it is usually treated with Jude rather than with 1 Peter. To be sure, 2 Peter and Jude are closely related to each other inasmuch as both oppose false teachers who have called into question the reality of judgment and the Lord's parousia. But despite this kinship between them, there is little doubt that 2 Peter presents itself as part of the Petrine tradition and that it wants to be read as such. What, then, is the relationship between these three letters, and how should New Testament theology approach them?

A fruitful line of inquiry is to view these letters as instruction for Christians whose faith is being threatened by a world hostile to the faith of the community and by false teachers within the community. In the case of 1 Peter, the focus is on how Christians ought to live in a hostile world. It affirms that since Christians are aliens and exiles in this world, they must follow in the footsteps of Christ, who suffered for them. They are not to flee from the world but to live as Christians in the world so that, by the example of their lives, they can convince others of the genuineness of their faith.

If the concern of 1 Peter is Christian existence in a hostile world, the concern of 2 Peter and Jude is the threat of false teaching to the life of the church. In both letters the focus is on a danger that comes from within the community itself rather than from the world outside of the community. Viewed in this way, both letters complement 1 Peter, which is primarily concerned with external threats to the life of the community. Second Peter provides a defense for the church's hope in the Lord's parousia in the face of false teachers, and Jude advances the argument by offering a scriptural analysis of false teachers. Both 2 Peter and Jude urge their audiences not to be led astray by false teachers who dismiss the Lord's parousia and the judgment that will attend it, because there will be no escape from God's judgment. All three letters remind their audiences that believers are related to the apostolic generation that assures the continuity of their faith with the faith of those who preceded them. All three affirm that the moment of judgment will not be delayed. Viewed together, they present the church with instructions in a time of affliction and disorder: afflictions from outside the church and disorders from within the church. First Peter presents a theology of Christian existence in a hostile world. Second Peter complements this theology with a theology of Christian hope in the face of false teachers. Jude deepens this theology with a theological analysis of false teaching.

FIRST PETER: A THEOLOGY OF CHRISTIAN EXISTENCE

Originally written for believers in Asia Minor who were being abused and reviled because of their Christian faith, 1 Peter reminds its recipients of their new identity as the people of God, provides them with instructions for living in the world as Christians, and offers a rationale for the suffering they are presently experiencing. Read in light of these themes, the letter can be viewed as a theology of Christian existence, a profound reflection on what it means to live as a Christian in the world.[1]

As is the case with the Letter of James, the question of authorship has played a significant role in the discussion of 1 Peter, with some scholars defending its Petrine authorship and others maintaining that the letter is pseudonymous. In recent years, however, the emerging consensus is that the letter had its origin in a Petrine circle that revered the teaching and memory of Peter.[2] Accordingly, whereas an earlier generation tended to view 1 Peter as part of, or closely related to, the Pauline school, recent scholarship is more inclined to understand it as

---

1. The word "Christian" (*christianos*) occurs only three times in the New Testament (Acts 11:26; 26:28; 1 Pet. 4:16). First Peter, however, is the only New Testament writing that explicitly calls its recipients Christians, thus the rather frequent use of the term in this chapter as compared to previous chapters.

2. Martin (in Chester and Martin, *Theology of James, Peter, and Jude*, 90–94, here 92) writes, "Yet the insight that a document like 1 Peter may well be the final product of a group associated with Peter in his lifetime and intent on publishing his teaching after his demise is gaining ground, and holds out the most promise for future understanding." For a summary of recent scholarship, see Robert L. Webb, "The Petrine Epistles: Recent Developments and Trends," in *Face of New Testament Studies*, 373–90.

the representative of a distinctive theology associated with a circle of believers who revered the memory of Peter.

The debate about the letter's authorship, however, has not affected its interpretation as much as one might expect.[3] For whether the letter was written by Peter or by another in his name, its purpose remains the same: to strengthen believers who are being abused and ridiculed for their faith by providing them with a theological rationale for their suffering. By invoking Petrine authorship, the letter associates itself with one of the most revered figures of the early church. Appointed by Jesus to tend his sheep (John 21:15–19), Peter followed his Lord as a disciple and, according to *1 Clement*, eventually suffered for him.[4] Inasmuch as Peter's own life was marked by suffering and revilement for the sake of Christ, he is the ideal apostle to encourage others in their suffering for the gospel.

Although 1 Peter contains numerous baptismal allusions, recent scholarship is no longer inclined to view it as a baptismal homily or as the remnants of a baptismal liturgy.[5] Moreover, rhetorical studies have strengthened the case for its literary unity and called into question partition theories.[6] First Peter, then, is best viewed as a circular letter sent to Gentile churches in Asia Minor from a Petrine circle located in Rome. Written in a Greek style that can be characterized as literary Koine, it celebrates the new identity of its recipients, seeks to persuade them that their suffering as Christians is integral to this identity, and provides them with an ethic for living in an environment hostile to their faith. The theological logic of the letter can be summarized as follows: Christian identity undergirds Christian behavior and provides believers with a rationale to suffer for their faith. This discussion is organized under the following categories: (1) a theology of Christian identity, (2) a theology for living in the world, (3) a theology of suffering for Christ, and (4) First Peter in theological perspective.

A Theology of Christian Identity

The author of 1 Peter develops the theme of Christian identity in two ways. On the one hand, he describes the present situation of believers in language

---

3. Childs (*New Testament as Canon*, 456) makes this point: "the historical critical decisions regarding the book's authorship and dating have not affected the book's interpretation as much as one might expect."

4. See *1 Clement* 5, especially 5.4, "Peter, who because of unrighteous jealousy suffered not one or two but many trials, and having thus given his testimony went to the glorious place which was his due."

5. The most explicit reference to baptism is 3:20–21, which interprets the account of Noah's rescue from the destructive waters of the flood as a figure pointing to baptism. There appear to be implicit references to baptism in 1:3 and 2:2, which speak of "a new birth," "newborn infants," and "spiritual milk."

6. See Barth L. Campbell, *Honor, Shame, and the Rhetoric of 1 Peter* (SBLDS 160; Atlanta: Scholars Press, 1998); and Steven Richard Bechtler, *Following in His Steps: Suffering, Community, and Christology in 1 Peter* (SBLDS 162; Atlanta: Scholars Press, 1998).

reminiscent of Israel's exile and dispersion. On the other, he celebrates the new status of Christians in terms of the salvation and inheritance that is already theirs as the people of God. These two descriptions reveal the inherent tension and paradox of the Christian life: Christians have attained a new status as the people of God, and yet they live as aliens and exiles in this world since their new faith has alienated them from the world in which they live.

Aliens and Exiles

The author highlights the present trying circumstances of the letter's recipients in his greeting, where he identifies them as "the exiles of the Dispersion in Pontus, Galatia, Cappadocia, Asia, and Bithynia" (1:1). Their status as "aliens and exiles" (2:11) is to be taken metaphorically rather than as an indication of their social position within society.[7] Understood metaphorically, this expression indicates that even though the recipients are living in the land of their birth, their Christian faith has made them like strangers and aliens to their compatriots, who are abusing and ridiculing them. Thus, while they are the recipients of an inheritance that is being kept for them in heaven (1:4), they are also aliens and exiles, living far from their true homeland. Their situation, then, is analogous to that of Israel during the period of the Babylonian captivity, as well as to the situation of those Israelites who live in the Dispersion far from the land of Israel. Inasmuch as the present is the time of their exile (1:17), believers should not be surprised at "the fiery ordeal" that is taking place among them (4:12).

Because they have become "aliens and exiles" in the world, it is all the more urgent that believers "abstain from the desires of the flesh that wage war against the soul" (2:11), lest they become conformed to the world once more. Accordingly, they must conduct themselves honorably among the Gentiles, even though their moral life may cause their Gentile compatriots to speak ill of them. Although the original recipients of the letter were Gentile, the author distinguishes them from "the Gentiles." As aliens and exiles, they are the people of God whose homeland is in heaven.

The People of God

The author calls the audience aliens and exiles in this world because he views them as the people of God. Echoing words that Hosea originally applied to Israel, he affirms that at one time the recipients of this letter were not a people, but now they have become God's people (2:10; see Hos. 1:9; 2:23). Consequently, even when he identifies them as "exiles of the Dispersion," the

---

7. John H. Elliott (*A Home for the Homeless: A Social-Scientific Criticism of 1 Peter, Its Situation and Strategy* [Minneapolis: Fortress, 1990], 37–49) interprets the expression in terms of the recipients' social status rather than metaphorically.

author reminds his audience that they were "chosen," "destined," and "sanctified by the Spirit" for the purpose of being "obedient to Jesus Christ and to be sprinkled with his blood" (1 Pet. 1:2). The final phrase alludes to the covenant ceremony described in Exod. 24:3–8, when Moses sprinkled the people of Israel with blood in order to seal their promise of obedience to the covenant. By applying the same phrase to his audience, the author affirms that "Christians have become elect sojourners in accordance with God's plan empowered by the sanctifying action of the Spirit to the end that they be the people of a new covenant, which like the covenant with Israel entails obedience and sacrifice, in this case the sacrifice of Christ."[8]

The author reminds his audience that they have been ransomed from their former way of life by "the precious blood of Christ," whom he compares to "a lamb without defect or blemish" (1 Pet. 1:19). The image of the lamb recalls the Passover lamb whose blood protected Israel at the time of its deliverance from Egypt (Exodus 12). According to 1 Peter, God destined Christ for this redemptive work "before the foundation of the world," but it is only now, "at the end of the ages," that Christ has been revealed for their sake (1 Pet. 1:20). In a remarkable statement that highlights God's redemptive plan on behalf of the recipients, the author affirms that this plan was revealed to the prophets—who had already "testified in advance to the sufferings destined for Christ and the subsequent glory"—that they were serving not themselves but the recipients of the letter (1:10–12).

Redeemed by the precious blood of Christ, believers have been given "a new birth" in virtue of Christ's resurrection from the dead (1:3). This new birth makes them the beneficiaries of an inheritance in heaven, which the author describes as "imperishable, undefiled, and unfading" (1:4). Their salvation, then, has already been secured for them, and it will be revealed in the last time. But at the present time, inasmuch as they are still in exile from their heavenly home where their inheritance is kept for them, they will suffer trials so that the genuineness of their faith will praise God when Christ is revealed. The proof of their faith is that even though they have not seen the Lord, they love and believe in him (1:8–9).

First Peter's most important statement about the identity of its recipients occurs in 2:4–10, where the author reminds them that they are a spiritual house, God's own people. Employing a series of scriptural texts (Isa. 28:16; Ps. 118:22; Isa. 8:14) that make use of the word "stone," the author identifies believers as a spiritual house constructed of "living stones," the cornerstone being Christ, the stone that the builders rejected. By coming to Christ, who is "a living stone," believers, who themselves are "living stones," are being built

8. Paul J. Achtemeier, *1 Peter: A Commentary on 1 Peter* (Hermeneia; Minneapolis: Fortress, 1996), 89.

into "a spiritual house" in which they are a holy priesthood, which offers spiritual sacrifices acceptable to God (1 Pet. 2:4–5).

This description of the community, rich in theological imagery, associates believers with Christ, the stone who was rejected by the builders but chosen by God, and it identifies them as a spiritual house, which is a living temple. Unlike the old temple, however, which was serviced by the Levitical priests, those who believe in Christ are themselves the priests of this temple, and through Christ they offer themselves as a spiritual sacrifice to God.[9]

Making use of imagery originally applied to Israel, the author identifies the letter's recipients as "a chosen race" (see Isa. 43:20), "a royal priesthood" (see Exod. 19:6), "a holy nation" (see Exod. 19:6), "God's own people" (see Exod. 19:5; Isa. 43:21). As God's people, their task is to glorify the mighty acts God has worked on their behalf, when he called them "out of darkness into his marvelous light" (1 Pet. 2:9). Although the author of 1 Peter identifies its recipients with titles and prerogatives originally reserved for Israel, he never takes up the question of Israel and the Gentiles in the way that Paul does. He does not argue that the recipients of the letter have replaced Israel, nor does he call them a new Israel or the Israel of God. He is more intent upon affirming that those who are being built into the spiritual house, whose cornerstone is Christ, enjoy the full prerogatives of the people of God.

The manner in which 1 Peter identifies its recipients can be summarized as follows. Those who are Christians have been chosen to be God's priestly and royal people who are being formed into a spiritual house of worship in which they offer themselves in sacrifice to God. Their election is the result of God's eternal plan whereby Christ ransomed them from their former way of life. Inasmuch as their inheritance is in heaven, they live as exiles and sojourners in this world.

A Theology for Living in the World

Although Christians live as aliens and exiles in a world that is hostile to them, the author of 1 Peter does not encourage them to withdraw from the world but to live in the world in a manner worthy of their new status as God's people. By doing so, they will silence those who revile them for their faith and will lead such people to praise God. The author develops this teaching in 2:11–3:12, a section that provides believers with practical guidance and instruction for living in the world as Christians.

---

9. Donald P. Senior (in Donald P. Senior, C.P., and Daniel J. Harrington, S.J., *1 Peter, Jude and 2 Peter* [SP 15; Collegeville, MN: Liturgical Press, 2003], 53) writes: "This section binds together the destiny of the Christians with their crucified and risen Master. The Christians, too, are 'living stones.' . . . The Christians form a 'spiritual *house*,' fitting the author's view of the community as the new temple, a notion reinforced in the subsequent references to priesthood and offering of sacrifices."

The author addresses his initial admonition to all believers (2:11–12). Inasmuch as they are aliens and exiles in the world, they must abstain from the desires of the flesh and conduct themselves honorably among the Gentiles. In urging believers to live honorably among those who shame them, the author introduces a theme he will develop throughout this section: good conduct can bring others to glorify God. For 1 Peter, then, there is a missionary dimension to living in the world.

In 2:13–17 the author urges the recipients of the letter to accept the authority of every human institution, be it the authority of the emperor or of his delegates. This injunction recalls Paul's instruction in Rom. 13:1–7. But unlike the text of Romans, which grounds its argument in the authority God has given to the governing authorities, the author of 1 Peter argues that it is God's will that Christians silence the ignorant and foolish by doing what is right. Once more, the behavior of Christians in the world is missionary in nature; its purpose is to silence critics and bring them to God.

In 2:18–25 the author turns his attention to Christian slaves, urging them to accept the authority of their masters, the authority not only of those who are kind and gentle but even of those who are harsh.[10] The author is aware that such obedience will entail suffering for Christian slaves, but he argues that if they endure, their conduct will be a credit to them in God's sight.[11] Drawing a distinction that he will make again, the author notes that although there is no credit in suffering for what is wrong, there is for enduring suffering in behalf of doing what is right (2:20; also see 3:17). This admonition to Christian slaves concludes with a rationale for suffering, relating the suffering of the Christian to the suffering of Christ (2:21–25).[12]

In 3:1–6 the author urges Christian wives to accept the authority of their husbands, especially if their husbands are not believers. Reminding wives that even Sarah obeyed Abraham and called him her lord, he identifies them as daughters of Abraham. Once more, the motivation for this conduct is missionary in nature. The author is hopeful that husbands who are disobedient to the word (the gospel) will be won over, without a word, by the pure and reverent conduct of their wives. Conduct in accord with one's Christian identity, then, is a proclamation of the gospel.

10. In this section 1 Peter is addressing *Christian* slaves rather than slaves in general. The author's goal is to provide them with a rationale for the suffering they are enduring, not to support the institution of slavery.

11. The Greek word translated "credit" is *charis*. The sense of the phrase is that Christian slaves will find "favor" in God's sight by suffering justly.

12. Although the author employs the christological passage of 2:22–25 to encourage Christian slaves to endure their suffering in the way the innocent Christ did, it is apparent from 2:21 and 3:9 (both of which speak of the Christian vocation) that the example of Christ's innocent suffering, described in this passage, is intended for the entire Christian community. For just as 2:21 says that Christian slaves were *called* to suffer without retaliating, so 3:9 notes that all the members of the Christian community were *called* not to repay evil with evil.

The author's instruction to Christian husbands is brief (3:7). He affirms that even though wives belong to "the weaker sex," their husbands must honor them because they too are "heirs of the gracious gift of life." Although this statement sounds demeaning to contemporary ears, it is important to read it in the context of a society that did not accord women the same social status it accorded men. Read against this background, the affirmation that Christian wives are *coheirs* with their husband is significant because it highlights the equality of man and woman in light of the inheritance that is being kept for them in heaven (1:4).

The author's instruction, which began with an exhortation to the entire community of believers (2:11–12), concludes with an admonition for all to seek unity and mutual love (3:8–12). Urging believers not to retaliate when they are abused, he reminds them that their election as God's people calls them to repay evil and abuse with blessing. He provides an extended quotation from Psalm 34 to support an argument he has been making throughout this section: those who seek eternal life must turn away from evil and do good. There is no place, then, for retaliation in the Christian life, even when Christians are abused; for when they repay evil with evil, Christians betray their vocation as God's people who have been redeemed by the suffering of the innocent Christ.

Inasmuch as the author exhorts slaves to be obedient to their masters and wives to their husbands, his theology is problematic. Read in isolation, apart from the social and historical circumstances that gave rise to it, this theology can mistakenly suggest that the author approves of slavery and the subjugation of women. The purpose of his instruction, however, is not so much to validate the culture of his day as it is to encourage believers to live in the world in a manner that reflects their Christian identity so that they can proclaim the gospel by the conduct of their lives. The culturally determined aspects of the text need not serve as a guide for contemporary Christian behavior, whereas the admonition to live in the world in a manner that reflects one's Christian identity remains an enduring value.[13]

A Theology of Suffering for Christ

The author is keenly aware that the recipients of the letter are already enduring suffering for the sake of their faith in Christ, and his purpose is to support

---

13. There is an important hermeneutical issue here, namely, how does one decide what is culturally determined and what is of enduring doctrinal or spiritual value? There is no simple response to this question, and even professional exegetes will disagree with one another on this point. But unless one is wedded to an unbending theory of verbal inerrancy, one must acknowledge that the Word of God is communicated in and through human words that are historically and culturally bound. Consequently, the exegete and the theologian must continually search for the enduring Word of God in these human words.

them in this suffering lest they falter. Accordingly, he encourages them not to be surprised "at the fiery ordeal" that has already begun among them (4:12), and he reminds them that other Christians throughout the world are also suffering (5:9).[14] To strengthen them during this period of their suffering, he relates their suffering to the suffering of Christ and argues that, whereas it is shameful to suffer for doing what is wrong, there is great honor in suffering as a Christian (4:13–16).

This relationship between Christian identity and suffering is a central element in the theology of 1 Peter. For unless believers understand why they are suffering, it is unlikely they will persevere as Christians when they encounter suffering. Consequently, in addition to urging believers to live in the world in a way that is worthy of their dignity as Christians, the author provides them with a rationale for the suffering they are presently experiencing, arguing that this suffering is a participation in the sufferings of Christ.

The author refers to the "sufferings of Christ" (*pathēmata Christou*) on three occasions. First, he notes that the Spirit of Christ, which inspired the prophets, "testified in advance to the sufferings destined for Christ and the subsequent glory" (1:11). Second, he encourages the recipients to rejoice insofar as they "are sharing Christ's sufferings" (4:13). Finally, he reminds them that Peter himself is an elder and "a witness of the sufferings of Christ" (5:1). The present suffering that the recipients endure, then, is not a cause for shame, even though it dishonors them in the estimation of their contemporaries. Rather, they are participating in the sufferings of Christ, foretold by the Spirit of Christ; they are enduring sufferings to which Peter himself testifies by his own participation in the sufferings of Christ.

On several occasions, the author argues that there is no shame in suffering for doing what is right. When encouraging Christian slaves to accept the authority of their masters, he notes that if they do what is right and suffer for it but endure, they will enjoy God's approval (2:20). Addressing the whole community of believers, he asks who will harm them if they are eager to do what is good, noting that they will be blessed if they suffer for what is right (3:13–14). For it is better to suffer for doing good than to suffer for doing evil (3:17); and it is better to suffer as a Christian than as an evildoer (4:14–16).

To support his argument that it is better to suffer for doing good than for doing evil, the author employs two hymnlike passages in which the suffering of Christ plays a central role. In the first (2:22–25), he supports his exhortation to Christian slaves to endure their suffering by noting that although the

14. Recent scholarship suggests that the Christians who are being addressed by 1 Peter are facing revilement and ridicule from their contemporaries rather than systematic persecution from local governing authorities.

innocent Christ was abused, he did not retaliate in kind. When he suffered, he did not threaten but entrusted himself to God. In this way Christ bore the sins of humanity in his body, on the cross. In the second passage (3:18–22), the author supports his contention that it is better to suffer for doing good than for doing evil by noting that Christ also suffered, the righteous one for the unrighteous, in order to bring people to God. The passage goes on to describe Christ's ascent into heaven, his proclamation to the spirits in prison, and his enthronement at God's right hand.

In the passages noted above, the author employs the example of Christ to encourage Christians in their suffering: they should be prepared to suffer as did the innocent Christ, who suffered and did not retaliate. But in addition to providing believers with the example of Christ, these passages suggest that there is a purpose in the sufferings Christians endure. For inasmuch as Christ's sufferings were redemptive, participation in his sufferings is redemptive as well.[15] If God vindicated the suffering Christ, believers can be confident that God will vindicate them as well, transforming their shame into honor.

By grounding suffering in the believer's new identity as a Christian and by relating the sufferings of the Christian to the suffering of Christ, the author provides the most comprehensive theology of suffering in the New Testament. This does not mean that Christians should actively seek suffering or that all suffering is in accordance with God's will. Although the author notes that it is better to suffer for doing good than for doing evil, he qualifies his statement by saying, "if suffering should be God's will" (3:17). When he exhorts believers who are suffering to entrust themselves to a faithful Creator, he speaks of "those suffering in accordance with God's will" (4:19), thereby suggesting that not all suffering is in accordance with God's will. The suffering the author has in view is that which results from conduct in accord with Christian identity. Suffering that is in accordance with God's will is the result of conduct worthy of one's identity as a Christian. Understood in this way, 1 Peter's theology of suffering is similar to Jesus' beatitude in the Sermon on the Mount: "Blessed are those who are persecuted for righteousness' sake, for theirs is the kingdom of heaven" (Matt. 5:10).

First Peter's theology of Christian existence can be summarized as follows. Because of their new identity, Christians are to conduct themselves in the world as God's own people. If they live in this way, they can be confident that the suffering that results from their conduct will be a participation in the sufferings of Christ and in accord with God's will.

---

15. To say that Christian suffering is redemptive is not to suggest that Christ's suffering was inadequate for salvation. Rather, this statement affirms that when Christians suffer with and for Christ, their suffering acquires a new meaning because of their association with Christ.

First Peter in Theological Perspective

In this section I have viewed the theological logic of 1 Peter through the prism of Christian existence in the world. The author, however, develops a number of subsidiary topics to support his theological vision. Among the most important are those relating to Christology, ecclesiology, and eschatology.[16]

The author does not so much develop a Christology as presuppose a Christology. For example, he presupposes an understanding of the preexistence of Christ when he speaks of the "Spirit of Christ" at work in the prophets (1:11), and he exhibits a rather elaborate understanding of the postexistence of Christ when he speaks of Christ's proclamation to the spirits in prison (3:19), his resurrection, his enthronement at God's right hand, and the subjugation of angels, authorities, and powers to him (3:21–22).

The enigmatic comment in 3:19–20 about Christ's proclamation to the imprisoned spirits has proven difficult to interpret ("in which also he went and made a proclamation to the spirits in prison, who in former times did not obey, when God waited patiently in the days of Noah").[17] Some read it in light of the equally enigmatic passage in 4:6 about the gospel being proclaimed to the dead ("For this is the reason the gospel was proclaimed even to the dead"), and they conclude that both texts refer to Christ's preaching to the lost souls of the generation of the flood. Others argue that 3:19–20 refers to the judgment Christ pronounced upon the fallen angels *as he ascended* to heaven.[18] On balance, the second view is more convincing since there is no mention in 3:19–20 of Christ descending to the imprisoned spirits. Rather, he makes his proclamation to these spirits as he ascends to heaven, thereby sealing their fate and assuring Christians that these cosmic forces no longer have any power over them.

The most important christological contribution of 1 Peter is found in three hymnlike passages (1:18–21; 2:22–25; 3:18–22) that highlight Christ's suffering and redemptive death.[19] Drawing upon the motif of the Suffering Servant found in Isaiah 53, the first focuses on the redemptive death of Christ. The second, which also makes use of the Suffering Servant motif, presents Christ as a model of innocent suffering, by whose wounds sinners have been healed. The third begins with the suffering of Christ and describes his victorious

---

16. The purpose of this chapter has not been to catalogue every theological topic in 1 Peter but to identify the "theological logic" of the letter, which develops a theology of Christian existence.

17. See William Joseph Dalton, *Christ's Proclamation to the Spirits: A Study of 1 Peter 3:18–4:6* (AnBib 23; Rome: Pontifical Biblical Institute Press, 1965).

18. According to this interpretation, the proclamation of the gospel to the dead (4:7) would refer to the proclamation of the gospel to those who were alive but have since died.

19. On these passages see Frank J. Matera, *New Testament Christology* (Louisville: Westminster John Knox Press, 1999), 174–84.

ascent into heaven, where he is presently enthroned over the cosmic powers. The result is a presentation of Christ that has his preexistence and post-existence in view but finds its center of gravity in Christ's sufferings.

Although the author never employs the word *ekklēsia*, he has a great deal to say about the church. The church is a community of people who are being built into a "spiritual house" (2:4), whose cornerstone is Christ and whose members are the "living stones" of this building, God's own people. The community is both charismatic and structured. On the one hand its members have been given gifts for the benefit of the whole community (4:10–11), on the other there are elders who are responsible for the life of the community, which is "the flock of God" (5:1–3). The "chief shepherd," however, remains Christ (5:4).

Although the author identifies the church by titles that were once reserved for the people of Israel ("chosen race," "royal priesthood," "holy nation"), he never takes up the question of Israel and the Gentiles, nor does he address the role of the law in the Christian life. For this author Christians have become the people of God. However, he never explains how he understands the relationship of this people to historical Israel.

The eschatology of 1 Peter is, in some ways, akin to Paul's eschatology. The author insists that salvation is about to be revealed "in the last time" (1:5). He exhorts his readers to endure their sufferings so that their faith will be fire-tested and result in praise and glory "when Jesus Christ is revealed" (1:7). He is confident that there will be a day of judgment (2:12); he warns that the end is near (4:7) and the time of judgment is at hand (4:17); and he anticipates the "glory to be revealed" when the "chief shepherd appears" (5:1, 4). But unlike Paul, the author does not develop an apocalyptic scheme in which death is destroyed, the dead are raised incorruptible, and the Son hands over the kingdom to God (1 Cor. 15:24–28). He affirms that believers have an inheritance, which is being kept for them in heaven (1:4). But since he does not adopt Paul's apocalyptic scheme, he does not explain how believers will enter into this inheritance.

In the end, the most important theological contribution of 1 Peter is its description of Christian existence in the world. All other themes, important though they be, are in the service of this theological vision.

SECOND PETER: A THEOLOGY OF CHRISTIAN HOPE

Second Peter is one of the most problematic writings of the New Testament. Although it purports to be Peter's farewell testament (1:12–15) and explicitly notes that this is the second letter the apostle has written (3:1), it is usually studied in conjunction with the Letter of Jude rather than with 1 Peter, which, from a canonical perspective, it complements.[20] This pairing of 2 Peter with Jude reflects the judgment of most contemporary scholars that 2 Peter is pseudonymous and makes use of material found in Jude.

In an influential and often quoted essay, Ernst Käsemann highlighted the problematic character of this letter in yet another way.[21] Arguing that it was directed at gnostics, who had attacked the church's eschatology, he criticized its defense of primitive Christian eschatology as lacking "any vestige of Christological orientation."[22] More importantly, he viewed 2 Peter as the onset of early Catholicism, claiming that in 2 Peter, "The messenger of the Gospel has become the guarantor of the tradition, the witness of the resurrection has become the witness of the *historia sacra*, the bearer of the eschatological action of God has become a pillar of the institution which dispenses salvation, the man who is subject to the eschatological temptation has become the man who brings *securitas*."[23]

Denigrated as an example of early Catholicism, 2 Peter was relegated to the periphery of New Testament studies. In recent years, however, there has been a renewed interest in this writing.[24] Rather than criticize 2 Peter as an example of early Catholicism, contemporary scholars have paid closer attention to the rhetorical and theological argument it seeks to make in light of the genre it employs: a farewell discourse within the context of a letter.

Just as 2 Timothy employs the form of a letter to convey Paul's final testament before he departs from this life, so 2 Peter employs the letter form to transmit Peter's testament to the church before he dies. Aware that his death will come soon (1:14) and that false teachers will appear after he has departed (2:1), Peter writes so that, after his death, the recipients of the letter will be able to recall his teaching (1:15). Thus the letter functions as a testament of Peter's apostolic teaching so that, when false teachers arrive, the church will remember what Peter taught.

In 2 Peter the great apostle warns that in the last days false teachers will infiltrate the church and scoff at the promise of the parousia. Accordingly, Peter

20. Childs (*New Testament as Canon*, 476) writes: "From a canonical perspective it is significant to note that whereas an explicit connection is made between I and II Peter, no such linkage is made between Jude and II Peter."

21. Ernst Käsemann, "An Apologia for Primitive Christian Eschatology," *Essays on New Testament Themes* (SBT 1/41; London: SCM, 1964), 169–95.

22. Ibid., 178.

23. Ibid., 177.

24. Webb ("Petrine Epistles," in *Face of New Testament Studies*, 387–88) summarizes the new situation in this way: "First, rather than being characterized as 'early catholic' and theologically suspect, 2 Peter may now be considered theologically astute and quite sophisticated. Second, the opponents are not gnostic, but rather are to be found represented in various forms of Hellenistic thought. Third, Jude and 2 Peter are recognized as different, not only in identity of opponents and sociocultural context, but also in terms of theology and argumentation. Now the way is paved for further developments."

mounts a spirited defense of the parousia. Käsemann was correct, then, when he argued that 2 Peter is an apologia of primitive Christian eschatology, and contemporary scholarship is correct when it views 2 Peter as a pseudonymous letter written after Peter's death in response to an issue affecting the church at the end of the apostolic age. Second Peter, however, is not merely a naive defense of the parousia nor does it isolate the parousia from the rest of the Christian message. For 2 Peter the denial of the parousia has ramifications for the entire Christian message. For if the false teachers are correct, then one cannot trust the apostolic witnesses who handed on the gospel. Thus 2 Peter deals with a question that continually confronts Christian theology: the relationship between the faith of the apostolic generation and every generation that follows.

Second Peter is a testament to Peter's apostolic witness, which seeks to remind and assure the church that its faith in its Lord and Savior[25] and its hope in the parousia are grounded in the promises of the prophets and the witness of the apostles. In this discussion of 2 Peter I consider the following topics: (1) the testament of Peter; (2) Peter's defense of the parousia; (3) Peter's testament and the false teachers; and (4) Second Peter and the parousia.

The Testament of Peter

In the greeting, "Simeon Peter"[26] identifies the recipients of this letter as having received "a faith as precious as ours through the righteousness of our God and Savior" (1:1), thereby establishing an important relationship between Peter's faith and the faith of those to whom he writes. Their faith is as "precious" (*isotimon*) as the faith of the apostolic generation because it comes through the righteousness of Jesus Christ, whom Peter boldly identifies as "our God and Savior."[27] This righteousness of Jesus Christ, which brings the faith of believers into existence, points to "the fairness and lack of favoritism which gives equal privilege to all Christians."[28] At the outset of the letter, then, Simeon Peter, "a servant and apostle of Jesus Christ," establishes an important link between himself and those to whom he writes; he and they share a common faith.

Aware that his death is imminent (1:14) and eager to preserve this precious faith, Peter provides his audience with a final testament of his teaching (1:3–11). The initial verses of this testament (1:3–4) summarize the essential content of the gospel Peter has handed down to them. Christ's divine power

25. "Lord and Savior" is the distinctive way in which 2 Peter refers to Christ. See 2:20; 3:2, 18. Jesus is also called "Savior" in 1:1 and 1:11.

26. The use of "Simeon Peter" here is striking, and it recalls Acts 15:14, where Peter is also called "Simeon." Compare 1 Pet. 1:1, which simply speaks of "Peter."

27. This is one of the few instances in the New Testament where Jesus is called God. Other instances are John 1:1; 20:28; Rom. 9:5; Titus 2:13; Heb. 1:8–9.

28. Richard J. Bauckham, *Jude, 2 Peter* (WBC 50; Waco: Word, 1983), 168.

has already given them everything they need for life and godliness in the present world, and in the world to come. They have received this gift through the knowledge of Christ, who called them by his own glory and goodness, when they first embraced the gospel.[29] Because of this gospel, they have been set free from the corruption of this world to "become participants of the divine nature" (*theias koinōnoi physeōs*). The testament of Peter's preaching, then, is about the power of the gospel, which enables believers to escape from the corruption of this life so that they can participate in God's life.

In 2 Peter, however, the author is aware that believers must repeatedly confirm their election by their good conduct if they are to enter into the eternal kingdom of their Lord and Savior. Consequently, he provides them with a catalogue of virtues, each virtue building upon the one that precedes it, and all climaxing in love: faith is to be supported by goodness, goodness by knowledge, knowledge by self-control, self-control by endurance, endurance by godliness, godliness by mutual affection, and mutual affection by love (1:5–7). Those who lack these virtues will be like people who are nearsighted and blind. Worse still, they will forget that their past sins have been cleansed. For this reason, believers must confirm their call and election by living a virtuous life grounded in the salvation they have received.

Peter's testament summarizes the Christian message in a way that is understandable to his Hellenistic audience. He speaks of escape from the corruption in this world and participation in the divine nature, and he refers to a number of familiar virtues, such as godliness and self-control. But as the election theology of this passage indicates, and as will become more apparent as the letter progresses, the theology of 2 Peter is deeply rooted in traditional biblical categories as well. Thus Peter's testament provides an interesting blend of Hellenistic and Jewish Christian categories.

In 1:12–15 Peter explains why he is writing. He is aware that his death is at hand. Because of this, he intends to keep on "reminding" the recipients of this letter of what he has told them, even though they know and are established in the truth they have received. In this way, when he is no longer present to them, they will be able "at any time to recall these things" (1:15). Thus 2 Peter functions as a permanent testament to his teaching so that, when he is no longer present, his teaching will be present to the church.[30]

29. It is not clear who the subject is in 1:3–4. It could refer to God or to Christ. On the one hand, the closest referent is Jesus in 1:1, on the other it is normally God who calls believers (1:3). Bauckham (*Jude, 2 Peter*, 177) interprets the subject as Christ, though most commentators construe it as referring to God.

30. Remembering is an important theme in 2 Peter. Believers must recall and remember what they have learned and been taught, especially from Peter. See the references to reminding, remembering, recalling, being attentive in 1:12, 13, 15, 19; 3:1, 2. The opposite of such behavior is to be forgetful (1:9) or to ignore something (3:5).

In 3:1–4 Peter explains why the church must remember and recall what he has said and taught. In the last days people will question the promise of Christ's coming, insisting that nothing has changed and that everything has remained the same since the beginning of creation. When this happens, it will be important for believers to "remember the words spoken in the past by the holy prophets, and the commandments of the Lord and Savior spoken through your apostles" (3:2). Peter writes, then, to arouse and remind believers of the apostolic message.

Read as a pseudonymous letter written at the end of the first century or at the beginning of the second century, 2 Peter provides a window into the situation of the church at that time. Read within its canonical context, it functions as a letter that every generation of believers can read in order to recall and remember the apostolic message, especially in times of crisis.

Peter's Defense of the Parousia

As is evident from the remarks of 3:1–4, the central issue in 2 Peter concerns the apparent delay of the parousia. Everything has remained the same; nothing has changed. Christ has not come; the parousia has not taken place. Why, then, should the church continue to hope that the parousia, and the judgment that attends it, will occur? Is it not apparent that the prophecies that foretold the parousia, and the witness of the apostolic generation that testified to the parousia, were mistaken? Aware of these objections, Peter undertakes a vigorous defense of the parousia. In doing so, he provides an apologia not only for the parousia but for the whole fabric of the Christian message. For if the prophets and the apostolic witnesses were mistaken when they testified to the parousia, then the entire gospel can be called into question.

In 1:16–21 Peter replies to two objections: (1) the apostles employed "cleverly devised myths" when they proclaimed the power and coming (*parousia*) of the Lord Jesus Christ; (2) the prophetic word was merely a human word rather than God's word.[31] In response to the first, Peter affirms that he was an eyewitness to the transfiguration, on the holy mount, when God revealed Jesus as his Son (1:16–18). For Peter the transfiguration was the fulfillment of Psalm 2, the moment when God installed Jesus as his messianic Son on "the holy mountain," thereby appointing him to the task that he would exercise at the parousia.[32] As an eyewitness to the transfiguration, Peter rebukes those who contend that the hope for the parousia was a "cleverly devised myth." Having been present when God appointed Jesus to the task he will carry out

---

31. Bauckham (*Jude, 2 Peter*) identifies 1:16–18; 1:20–21; 2:3b–10a; 3:5–7; and 3:8–10 as sections in which 2 Peter replies to the objections of those who deny the parousia.

32. This point is made by Bauckham (*Jude, 2 Peter*, 221–22).

at the parousia, Peter can assure his audience that their hope for the parousia is grounded in a reliable apostolic witness.

In response to the second objection, Peter reminds his audience that in addition to his eyewitness testimony, they also possess the prophetic message that points to the parousia. Comparing the prophetic message to a lamp shining in the dark and the parousia to the dawning day with its morning star, Peter suggests that even though the prophetic message is not fully intelligible at the present time, it will become so when the parousia occurs.

Affirming the power and truth of prophecy, Peter insists that "no prophecy of scripture is a matter of one's own interpretation" because prophecy is not the result of human beings willing prophecy into existence but of human beings being moved by the Holy Spirit, and so speaking God's word (1:20–21). Thus, whereas those who deny the ancient prophecies of the parousia say that the prophets were speaking their own words rather than God's, Peter contends that the power of those prophecies did not derive from those who spoke them but from the power of the Spirit that impelled them to speak.[33] The ancient prophecies, then, confirm the parousia, even though they only point to the parousia like a dim lantern shining in the dark.

Having defended the apostolic witness and the prophecies that point to the parousia, in 2:4–10a Peter provides four arguments to assure his audience that there will be a day of judgment. In the first three, he recalls three examples of past judgment. First, God did not spare the angels who sinned (see Gen. 6:1–4). Second, God did not spare the ancient world at the time of the flood. Third, God destroyed Sodom and Gomorrah. Each of these examples contributes to Peter's defense of the parousia and the day of judgment. First, the imprisoned angels witness to the parousia because they are being guarded in the netherworld (Tartaros) "until the judgment" (2 Pet. 2:4). Second, the destruction of the world at the time of Noah witnesses to the parousia because just as the ancient world was destroyed, so the present world will be destroyed. Third, the destruction of Sodom and Gomorrah witnesses to the parousia because just as those cities were annihilated by fire, so the elements that compose the universe will be destroyed by fire (see 3:10). In his fourth argument, Peter reminds his audience how God rescued the righteous Lot from the lawless people of his day, and he concludes that God knows how to rescue "the godly from trial" and "keep the unrighteous under punishment until the day of judgment" (2:9).

---

33. The text can be construed in two ways, depending upon how one understands the phrase "one's own interpretation." If the phrase refers to the reader of Scripture, it means that one cannot interpret Scripture as one wishes because the Spirit has already given the text its meaning. If it refers to the prophet, it means that it is not the prophet who gives the text its prophetic meaning but the Spirit at work within the prophet. Bauckham defends this second interpretation (*Jude, 2 Peter*, 229–31). This text has often been a point of contention between Protestants and Catholics over the interpretation of Scripture.

This skillful use of scriptural arguments demonstrates that even though in 2 Peter the author has begun the process of interpreting the Christian faith in Hellenistic categories, he is firmly rooted in the world of Israel's Scriptures. It also suggests that these examples from the Old Testament may be the kind of texts that Peter has in view when he speaks of "the prophetic message" (1:19) that points to the parousia, even though these texts do not come from the Prophets.

Peter's most explicit argument on behalf of the parousia occurs in 3:5–10, where he responds to those who scoff, "Where is the promise of his coming? For ever since our ancestors died, all things continue as they were from the beginning of creation!" (3:4). In response to their criticism, Peter provides two arguments. First, he asserts that those who scoff at the parousia "deliberately ignore" (3:5) the power of God's Word. By that Word, God created the world from the watery chaos that preceded it, and by water the world was once destroyed. If the Word of God created the world, then it can also destroy the world, and indeed it will, this time by fire. Second, the recipients of the letter must "not ignore this one fact" (3:8): that God does not reckon time as humans do. One day in God's sight is like a thousand years, and a thousand years are like a single day. The apparent delay of the parousia and its attendant judgment is not a delay on God's part but a manifestation of God's mercy and an invitation to repent.

The argument of 2 Peter contrasts the behavior of the false teachers who deliberately *ignore* the power of God's Word with the behavior of believers who must not *ignore* God's mercy, thereby establishing a fault line between the two groups. Those who deliberately ignore what God has done in the past will be destroyed, whereas those who remember will be saved. It is all the more important then for believers to read and remember Peter's testament again and again.

Peter's defense of the parousia can be summarized as follows. The hope of the parousia is founded on (1) the apostolic eyewitness to the transfiguration, (2) prophetic testimony, (3) God's past judgment of sinners, (4) the power of God's Word to destroy as well as to create, and (5) the realization that God does not act as humans do.

Peter's Testament and the False Teachers

Peter writes a farewell testament because he knows that, after his departure, there will be false teachers among the elect just as there were false prophets among the people of Israel (2:1). Although these teachers have not yet appeared (since, from the point of view of the letter, Peter is still alive), Peter gives a detailed description of them in chapter 2. Contemporary exegesis explains this description in two ways. First, it is based upon the description of the false teacher in the Letter of Jude, which the author of 2 Peter edits for his own purposes. Second, it reflects the description of the false teachers that the pseudonymous author of 2 Peter opposes. Although both explanations are helpful for understanding the historical situation that occasioned 2 Peter and the manner in which the letter was composed, neither explains the theological nexus the letter draws between Peter's testament and the false teachers.

Whereas the purpose of Peter's testament is to remind believers of the salvation that has allowed them to "escape from the corruption that is in the world" and "become participants of the divine nature" (1:4), Peter's description of the teachers is unrelenting. Their ways are licentious, and they are greedy; they are bold and willful; they are like irrational animals. They slander what they do not understand, and their eyes are full of adultery. They promise freedom but are slaves of corruption. Thus they are like "waterless springs" and "mists driven by a storm" (2:17) since their teaching cannot provide what it promises. It would have been better for them not to have known "the way of righteousness" than to turn away from it (2:21).

This description of the false teachers stands in sharp contrast to Peter's final exhortation, when he asks the recipients of the letter what sort of persons they should be if all things are to be dissolved at the parousia (3:11). Peter's response is they should lead "lives of holiness and godliness, waiting for and hastening the coming day of God" (3:11–12). Waiting and hoping for the parousia, then, should be an impetus to live "without spot or blemish" (3:14).

The contrast Peter establishes between the behavior of the false teachers who deny the parousia and lead others astray, on the one hand, and those who follow Peter's testament and patiently wait for the parousia, on the other, clarifies the theological purpose of chapter 2. False teaching has profound implications for the soundness of the Christian life.[34] Peter's harsh description of the false teachers in chapter 2 reminds believers that if they abandon his testament for the promises of the false teachers, they will deviate from the way of righteousness. The denial of the parousia by the false teachers is not a minor issue that one can choose to ignore. It is the denial of the faith handed on by the apostles and confirmed by Israel's Scriptures. As the praxis of the false teachers shows, those who deny that there will be a day of judgment will inevitably fall from the way of righteousness and will no longer participate in the divine nature. Unable to participate in the divine nature, they will no longer share in salvation.

Second Peter and the Parousia

Second Peter deals with a crucial issue of New Testament theology: the meaning and significance of the parousia. What is the parousia? When will it occur? What will happen when it does?

---

34. There is an interesting relationship between 2 Peter and the Pastorals, both of which argue that good conduct flows from good teaching and bad conduct from false teaching.

For the Synoptic tradition, the return of the Son of Man at the end of the ages will be the occasion for the glorious Son of Man to gather the elect into the kingdom of God, which will have come in power. The Pauline tradition is similar to this line of thought, although it no longer refers to Jesus as the Son of Man. At the parousia, the risen Lord—the firstfruits of the general resurrection of the dead—will return. The dead will be raised incorruptible, and the Son will hand over the kingdom to his Father.

Both traditions, however, are aware of the problem posed by the parousia and its apparent delay. The Synoptic tradition insists that no one knows the day or hour of the parousia, not even the Son; therefore disciples must work as industrious servants until their Lord appears. The Pauline tradition is also aware that no one knows the time or the season of the parousia, and it must deal with those who deny the resurrection of the dead and act as if the end time has already arrived. In the deuteropauline letters, although hope for the future has not been set aside, Paul's apocalyptic vision begins to give way to a scenario that speaks of the believer's inheritance in heaven rather than the general resurrection of the dead.

The most radical transformation of the parousia, however, occurs in the Johannine tradition. To be sure, this tradition still speaks of the future resurrection of believers, but it no longer refers to the parousia. Whereas the Synoptic Gospels point to the glorious coming of the Son of Man, the Johannine Jesus promises the coming of the Paraclete, who will remind the church of all that Jesus said and did. Hope for the future is not set aside, but the experience of future salvation and the present experience of salvation have begun to merge.

For 2 Peter the reality of the parousia is nonnegotiable. The parousia will be the definitive moment of God's judgment, and it will effect a transformation of the world as it is presently known. In describing the parousia, however, Peter does not speak of the return of the glorious Son of Man, as does the Synoptic tradition, or of the general resurrection, as does Paul. The focus is on God rather than on Christ, with the emphasis on divine judgment. The "day of the Lord" (3:10), which is also called "the day of God" (3:12), will come suddenly like a thief, the heavens will pass away, the elements[35] will be dissolved, "and the earth and everything that is done on it will be disclosed" (3:10).[36] When the

---

35. The "elements" (3:10, 12) could refer to (1) the four elements that were thought to be the building blocks of the world (earth, air, fire, water), (2) angelic beings, (3) the heavenly bodies (planets, stars). Here they appear to refer to the heavenly bodies, all of which will be dissolved by fire and so exposed to God's judgment.

36. The Greek behind "will be disclosed" is *eurethēsetai* ("it will be found"). This enigmatic reading has occasioned a host of variant readings, all discussed by Bauckham (*Jude, 2 Peter*, 317–21). The sense of this difficult reading seems to be that when the heavenly bodies (the elements) are dissolved by fire, then the works of humans "will be found," that is, they will be revealed or disclosed for what they are, and so subject to God's judgment.

heavenly bodies have been dissolved by fire, then the earth and everything that humans have done will be apparent and exposed to God's judgment.

Even though the heavens will be set ablaze and the elements melt with fire (3:12), the parousia will not be the end of the world but the occasion for its transformation. This moment of apocalyptic destruction will bring about "new heavens and a new earth, where righteousness is at home" (3:13). This hope is firmly grounded in the vision of the book of Isaiah (see Isa. 65:17 and 66:22),[37] and it echoes other references to righteousness in 2 Peter (1:1; 2:5, 21). The parousia then is crucial to the fabric of the Christian message for 2 Peter. If there is no parousia, there is no judgment. If there is no judgment, there is no righteousness. If there is no righteousness, the world will not be transformed.

The enduring theological contribution of 2 Peter is not so much in the arguments it makes in behalf of the parousia as in its recognition that hope for the parousia is an indispensable element of Christian faith. That hope, which Peter eloquently describes in terms of new heavens and a new earth filled with God's righteousness, affirms that God will have the last word. The descriptions of the parousia in Paul, the Synoptics, and 2 Peter may differ, but the central affirmation they make does not: there will be a final redemptive act of God that will set all things aright.

JUDE: A THEOLOGY OF HERESY

The authorship, date, and destination of the Letter of Jude are disputed. While a number of scholars argue that the author was Jude, one of the brothers of the Lord, the majority tends to view Jude as a pseudonymous letter composed at the end of the first or at the beginning of the second century.[38] Nearly all agree, however, that even though Jude is classified as one of the Catholic Epistles, supposedly intended for a general audience, it was written for a specific occasion: to warn its recipients of false teachers who had infiltrated their midst. Although there is considerable disagreement about the identity of these intruders and the nature of their teaching, there is a growing consensus that they were antinomians, similar in their approach to the faith as were the Spirit-filled believers

---

37. Bauckham (*Jude, 2 Peter,* 326) notes that this promise is found throughout Jewish apocalyptic literature. He points to *Jub.* 1:29; *1 Enoch* 45:4–5; 72:1; 91:16; *Sib. Or.* 5:212; *2 Apoc. Bar.* 32:6; 44:12; 57:2; *4 Ezra* 7:75; *Bib. Ant.* 3:10.

38. Whereas Bauckham (*Jude, 2 Peter,* 14–16) argues that the letter was written by Jude the brother of Jesus, Harrington (*1 Peter, Jude and 2 Peter,* 183) proceeds on the assumption that the letter is pseudepigraphical, though it "may well have had historical connections to Jude, James, and the family of Jesus."

at Corinth.[39] Like those Spirit-filled Corinthians, the intruders seem to have emphasized their present experience of salvation to the detriment of a future judgment and the coming parousia.[40] Thus there is a similarity between 2 Peter and Jude inasmuch as both affirm the certainty of divine punishment for those who lead others astray and deviate from the way of righteousness.

Although Jude and 2 Peter share a great deal of material in common, especially their descriptions of the false teachers, they construct their theologies differently. Whereas 2 Peter argues that hope for the parousia is a constitutive element of Christian faith, the Letter of Jude is concerned with the phenomenon of error within the Christian community. Employing examples from Israel's past and pointing to the prophetic words of Enoch and the predictions of the apostles, Jude develops something akin to a theology of heresy, showing that the Scriptures provide a storehouse of types and examples for judging and understanding false teachers and their errors. Furthermore, he maintains that the apostles predicted the appearance of false teachers, and Enoch foretold their destruction. Read in light of the historical situation that occasioned it, the Letter of Jude provides its recipients with a way to understand what is occurring: the intruders and their errors were foreshadowed in the types and examples found in Scripture, and their coming and judgment were prophesied. From a canonical and theological perspective, the letter functions in an analogous way. In addition to warning the Christian community of those who can destroy the faith that has been handed on to it, the letter provides a way for the community of every age to understand the phenomenon of heresy. Those who deviate from the faith do not possess superior moral and theological insight; they are merely repeating a destructive pattern of behavior of which there are innumerable types and examples in Scripture.[41] These examples and

39. Martin (*Theology of James, Peter, and Jude*, 68–75, here 69) provides a description of the false teachers. He notes that there is "a point of contact with 1 Corinthians in which Paul's controversy with Corinthian enthusiasts conceivably turned on the nature of Christian existence and their attitude to 'the flesh,' i.e. human nature. For the Corinthians, who imagined that they had already become like the angels and so were free from all earthly constraints following their baptismal resurrection (1 Cor. 4.8), the claims of morality were treated with an attitude that Paul cannot condone, especially when it led to pride (1 Cor. 5.2, 6) and sexual/bodily indulgence (1 Cor. 6.12–20)."

40. Martin (ibid., 72) writes, "Evidently the teaching opposed here has to do with the denial of apocalyptic elements in the Christian message either by way of a spiritualizing device that in turn arose of the teachers' belief that the fullness of salvation was achieved here and now, or a general scepticism, mirrored in, but not identical with 2 Peter 3.3, that cast doubt on the hope of a future parousia of the Lord."

41. The point made here is indebted to the observation of Childs (*New Testament as Canon*, 492). He notes that the concern of 2 Peter "is to address the question of how the fixed apostolic traditions represented by the figure of Peter function as written scripture for later generations of Christians." In contrast to 2 Peter, the Letter of Jude "addresses the phenomenon of heresy and not any one specific form of error. Indeed, what characterizes the approach is that heresy is now dealt with as a theological referent, and not simply as an historical danger confronting a particular congregation."

types are intended to remind believers that even they can fall from the faith that was handed on to them. Jude then invites believers to reread the stories of former rebellions so that the faithful will be able to recognize perversion of the truth when it appears again, as indeed it will.[42]

If 2 Peter is a farewell testament in the form of a letter, Jude is a homily in the form of a letter.[43] In the homiletic portion of the letter (vv. 5–23), Jude brings forth a series of examples and types from the Old Testament (vv. 5–13), as well as prophecies from Enoch and the apostles (vv. 14–19) to explain what is presently happening. Having shown how these types and examples apply to the present situation of his audience, Jude appeals to its audience to persevere in the faith and to assist those who are in danger of falling from it (vv. 20–23). Surrounding this "homily" is a greeting (vv. 1–2), an explanation of why Jude writes (vv. 3–4), and a doxology (vv. 24–25). The letter can be outlined as follows.

vv. 1–2	Letter greeting
vv. 3–4	Occasion for writing
vv. 5–23	A "homily" that actualizes Scripture
vv. 5–13	Examples from Scripture and their application
vv. 14–19	Predictions from Enoch and the apostles and their application
vv. 20–23	Appeal to persevere and save faltering believers
vv. 24–25	Doxology

Greeting and Occasion

Jude identifies himself in two ways. He is a servant of Jesus Christ and a brother of James (v. 1). By calling himself a servant of Jesus Christ rather than a brother of Jesus, Jude acknowledges his new relationship to Jesus, whom he now confesses as the risen Lord. This new relationship makes his former familial relationship to Jesus insignificant.[44] He does, however, acknowledge his familial

---

42. This point is suggested by Lewis R. Donelson, *From Hebrews to Revelation: A Theological Introduction* (Louisville: Westminster John Knox Press, 2001), here 93: "We cannot learn all Jude wants us to learn simply by reading Jude. We need also to read the stories of Cain, Sodom, Balaam, and Korah. We need to read those stories while thinking about ourselves. Jude is not simply citing in order to reinforce a theological point. Jude is inviting a reading not just of itself but of other texts. Jude is creating a permanent connection between past and present."

43. Harrington (*1 Peter, Jude and 2 Peter*, 161) makes this point when he writes that he regards Jude "as a homily in the form of a letter and 2 Peter as a testament in the form of a letter."

44. In Mark 6:3 the brothers of Jesus are identified as "James and Joses, and Judas and Simon." In Matt. 13:55 they are identified as "James and Joseph and Simon and Judas." The author of Jude is, or is identifying himself with, the brother called Judas/Jude, since he calls James his brother. The precise relationship of Jude and Jesus has been debated from earliest times. Is he the brother of Jesus, a son of Joseph and Mary? Is he a son of Joseph by a previous marriage but not a child of Mary? Or is "brother" being used in the sense of cousin? The question raised here and the solutions proposed to answer it reflect dogmatic concerns about the perpetual virginity of Mary.

relationship to his brother James, who identifies himself as "a servant of God and of the Lord Jesus Christ" (Jas. 1:1) rather than as a brother of Jesus. The recipients of the letter are identified as "called" and "beloved in God" (Jude 2), two appellations that highlight their election and mark them as belonging to the people of God. They are being kept safe for Jesus Christ; that is, they are being protected from defilement for the parousia. Other allusions to the parousia will occur in verses 14, 21, and 24.

In verses 3–4 Jude explains that he originally intended to write about the salvation that he and they share in common, suggesting a more irenic letter that would have dealt with the nature of the faith entrusted to them. The unexpected arrival of intruders, however, has forced him to alter his plans. Consequently, he now writes to urge them "to contend for the faith that was once for all entrusted to the saints." Although this phrase is often interpreted negatively, as an example of "early Catholicism," because it concerns the faith that is to be believed rather than the act of believing, references to the content of the faith are not unusual in the New Testament. Paul, the great champion of the act of faith, employs brief formulas to summarize the content of the gospel he preaches (1 Cor. 15:3–5), and there are occasions when he refers to the faith as the content of what is to be believed (2 Cor. 1:24). Jude's purpose in speaking of the faith "that was once for all entrusted to the saints" is to emphasize the continuity between the faith of the recipients of this letter and the faith entrusted to all believers, the saints. This is the faith for which they should contend and from which they must not deviate.

Certain intruders, however, have deviated from this faith, and Jude now identifies them, noting that they were designated long ago for the condemnation they will receive. In affirming this, Jude highlights a point he will develop: there is nothing new about what is happening. Scripture foreshadowed the false teachers and their errors long ago.

The false teachers who intruded into the community were themselves Christians, at least in name. But they perverted "the grace of our God into licentiousness," thereby denying the Lord and Master, Jesus Christ. This charge suggests that the intruders may have been teachers who embraced a radical form of Paul's gospel of freedom and grace, by which they justified living in a libertine manner. A similar problem occurred among those Corinthians who boasted, "All things are lawful for me" (1 Cor. 6:12).

Examples from Scripture and Their Application

Having alerted his recipients about the intruders, Jude interprets the dangers that threaten the community in light of scriptural types from Israel's past (vv. 5–13). He begins with three examples of disbelief, rebellion, and sexual immorality (vv. 5–7), which he portrays as types of the error the intruders have introduced (v. 8). Next (v. 9), he recalls an event from the *Assumption of Moses*, a lost work known from patristic citations, which he also applies to the intruders (v. 10). Finally, Jude recalls three more Old Testament examples (v. 11), which he applies to the intruders (vv. 12–13).[45]

The first three examples (vv. 5–7) recall (1) the failure of the wilderness generation to enter the promised land because of its disbelief; (2) the rebellion of the angels who, in their lust for human women, left their heavenly abode; and (3) the immorality of the inhabitants of Sodom and Gomorrah who sought to have sexual intercourse with the angels who visited Lot.[46] Jude actualizes these stories and presents them as types from the past that foreshadow what is presently occurring. Accordingly, in verse 8 he describes the intruders as "these dreamers" who "defile the flesh, reject authority, and slander the glorious ones" (v. 8).[47] The implication is that by defiling their flesh through their immoral behavior, the intruders are mimicking the lust of the fallen angels and the inhabitants of Sodom and Gomorrah. By rejecting authority, they are manifesting the disbelief of the wilderness generation and the rebellion of the angels who left their heavenly domain. The charge of slandering the glorious ones is then contrasted with the behavior of the archangel Michael, which Jude describes in the next verse (v. 9).

According to the *Assumption of Moses*, Michael and the devil contended for the body of Moses, the devil laying claim to the body because it belonged to the realm of matter and because Moses murdered the Egyptian.[48] Although an archangel, Michael refused to insult the devil, a fallen angel, commending him to God for punishment instead. In contrast to Michael's respectful behavior, the intruders have slandered angels, whom Jude calls "the glorious ones." The accusation of slandering angels accords with Jude's portrayal of the intruders. Their focus on the present experience of salvation and ecstatic experiences has mistakenly convinced them that there will be no judgments for them and that they themselves will judge angels.[49] In verse 10 Jude comments on and actu-

---

45. The beginning of each application section is clearly indicated by the word *houtoi*: "these dreamers," v. 8; "these people," v. 10; "These are . . . ," v. 6; "These are . . . ," v. 19.

46. For Israel's disbelief in the wilderness, see Numbers 13–14. For the story of the angels, see Gen. 6:1–4 and its development in *1 Enoch* 6–16. For the story of Sodom and Gomorrah, see Genesis 19.

47. This is the first of five instances where Jude employs the pronoun *houtoi* ("these") when speaking of the intruders. In every instance, *houtoi* marks the beginning of a section in which Jude applies an example from the past to the present. See vv. 10, 12, 16, 19 for the other four occurrences of *houtoi*.

48. Bauckham (*Jude, 2 Peter*, 73–74) has gathered the patristic texts that refer to the *Assumption of Moses* and this dispute between Michael and the devil.

49. See Paul's remark in 1 Cor. 6:3, "Do you not know that we are to judge angels—to say nothing of ordinary matters?" Here Paul is referring to the role that believers will play at the eschaton. He is fully aware, however, that believers will also stand in judgment before the judgment seat of God/Christ (Rom. 14:10; 2 Cor. 5:10). The intruders, however, appear to have denied that they would face such a judgment.

alizes the story of Michael and the devil. Whereas Michael was respectful of even the devil, "these people slander whatever they do not understand." For Jude, those who deviate from the faith that was entrusted to them do not understand what they are saying, since the very essence of false teaching is to deny the truth.

In verse 11 Jude brings forth three more Old Testament types: Cain, Balaam, and Korah. The first was a murderer, the second led Israel astray, and the third rebelled against Moses.[50] Actualizing these examples, Jude warns his recipients that "these" men are blemishes on their love feasts (perhaps their eucharistic banquets). He then applies four metaphors to them: they are water-less clouds; they are trees without fruit; they are wild waves; they are wander-ing stars. Just as the actions of Cain, Balaam, and Korah were destructive to others, so the actions of the intruders are destructive for the life of the com-munity. Because they are waterless clouds and dead trees, their teaching does not refresh or bear fruit. Like Cain's offering, their actions are not pleasing to God. Because they are wild waves and wandering stars, they lead people astray as did Balaam and Korah.

Predictions of Enoch and the Apostles and Their Application

Having actualized six examples of error and rebellion from the past, in verses 14–19 Jude recalls and actualizes two prophecies from the past. The first (vv. 14–15) comes from *1 Enoch*. Although *1 Enoch* is not part of the Old Testament canon, Jude views it as a prophetic work since its purported author, Enoch, had been taken up to heaven, where he heard and saw heavenly mysteries.[51] According to Jude, Enoch prophesied long ago about the coming of the Lord and the destruction of the intruders. Therefore, Jude actualizes the prophecy and applies it to the intruders, whom he calls, "These . . . grumblers and mal-contents" (v. 16). By indulging their own lusts and by their bombastic speech, they reveal that they are the ones of whom Enoch prophesied, for they are peo-ple whose deeds are ungodly; they are people who have spoken against the Lord. The prophecy of Enoch is not about wicked people in general; it is about these people.

In verses 17–19 Jude reminds his audience of "the predictions of the apos-tles of our Lord Jesus Christ," who already foretold that, in the last time,

---

50. For the story of Cain, see Gen. 4:8. For the story of Balaam, see Numbers 22–24 and 31:16, which blame Balaam for the episode of 15:1–5, which recounts how the men of Israel engaged in sexual intercourse with the Moabite women. For the story of Korah, see Numbers 16.

51. On the basis of Gen. 5:24 ("Enoch walked with God; then he was no more, because God took him"), it was assumed that Enoch was taken to heaven, where he heard and saw heavenly mysteries. The literature written in Enoch's name (*1, 2, 3 Enoch*) deals with the mysteries Enoch saw and heard in heaven.

scoffers would appear who would indulge their own ungodly lusts. Jude actualizes this prediction as well by identifying the intruders as the scoffers of whom the apostles spoke. He calls them "these worldly people" (*houtoi . . . psychikoi*), devoid of the Spirit, who are causing divisions" (v. 19). His description of them as *psychikoi* recalls Paul's distinction between those who are *psychikoi* ("unspiritual," 1 Cor. 2:14) and those who are *pneumatikoi* ("spiritual," 1 Cor. 2:15). The intruders think they possess the Spirit, but they do not. Their dreams and bombastic speech show they are merely *psychikoi*. Their appearance is a clear sign that the last days, predicted by the apostles, have arrived.

Appeal and Doxology

Jude's "homily" concludes with an appeal to his audience (vv. 20–23). Whereas the teaching and behavior of the intruders are devoid of the Spirit, which they claim to possess, and destructive of the community, which they would teach, the recipients of the letter are to build themselves upon their most holy faith. They are to pray to the Holy Spirit, and keep themselves in the love of God as they wait for the mercy of the Lord Jesus Christ, which he will manifest at his parousia.[52] In addition to caring for themselves, they must care for others, especially those in danger of being led astray by the intruders. Employing a three-part formula, Jude encourages them to have mercy on those who are wavering, to save others, and to have mercy on still others, being careful not to be defiled by them.[53]

The letter concludes with an elaborate doxology (vv. 24–25) that praises the "only God our Savior" who has the power to prevent believers from falling from the faith and who can enable them to "stand without blemish in the presence of his glory." This last phrase is Jude's fourth and final allusion to the parousia (see vv. 1, 14, 21), a further indication of how central the theme of judgment is to this letter.

Conclusion

The main point of Jude can be summarized as follows. False teachers can never bring a new perspective to the gospel, for they merely repeat past errors whose type can be found in Scripture. Their appearance is the fulfillment of prophecy and a sign that the last days have arrived. Since the arrival of false teachers ironically witnesses to the Lord's parousia and judgment, believers must be

---

52. Note the Trinitarian structure of this exhortation.

53. The text of Jude 23 presents one of the most difficult textual problems in the New Testament. Whereas witnesses such as Sinaiticus and Alexandrinus list three groups, as is also reflected in the NRSV, others such as Vaticanus list only two: "have pity on those who doubt snatching them from the fire, but have pity on others in fear."

strengthened in the faith that has been entrusted to them and care for those whose faith is being threatened.

Although the appearance of the false teachers did not herald the last days or immediate judgment as Jude thought it would, his letter is an invitation to learn from the past. Jude affirms that teaching that perverts the gospel repeats errors that have occurred often in the history of God's people. His letter invites believers to become familiar with the errors of the past in order not to repeat them in the future.

14

A Theology of God's Final Victory over Evil

The Book of Revelation

Inasmuch as it witnesses to God's final victory over evil, the book of Revelation—also called the Apocalypse of John—provides a fitting conclusion to the New Testament and to the entire Christian Bible. As a conclusion to the New Testament, Revelation assures its audience that God has already won the victory through the death of Christ, the slaughtered Lamb. In the time before the final appearance of God and his Christ, however, those who follow the Lamb must witness to the victory that God has already obtained in Christ. As a conclusion to the entire Christian Bible, Revelation provides its audience with a vision of a new heaven and a new earth, where God will dwell with his people in a new Jerusalem, the city of God. Through the use of imagery, symbolism, and hundreds of allusions to the Old Testament, the book of Revelation weaves the central themes of the Old and New Testaments into an apocalyptic vision of God's triumph over evil.[1]

Written toward the end of the first century for Christians living in Asia Minor under the powerful and all-pervasive rule of the Roman Empire, the book of Revelation warned its original listeners not to compromise their faith by submitting to and participating in the cult of the emperor.[2] Put simply, they

1. The New Testament theologies of Ferdinand Hahn, I. Howard Marshall, Georg Strecker, and Frank Thielman provide helpful summaries of the theology in the book of Revelation. The most helpful summary of Revelation's theology, however, is the monograph of Richard Bauckham, *The Theology of the Book of Revelation* (NTT; Cambridge: Cambridge University Press, 1993).

2. David E. Aune ("Revelation to John," *The Westminster Dictionary of New Testament and Early Christian Literature and Rhetoric* [Louisville: Westminster John Knox Press, 2003], 399) notes that whereas the prevailing view in the nineteenth century was that the book of Revelation was written shortly after the death of Nero (A.D. 68), most contemporary authors date the book to the latter part of the reign of Domitian (ca. A.D. 95), with some proposing a later date, during the reign of Trajan (A.D. 98–117).

were to worship God alone and not the beast—the might and force of the Roman Empire. Viewed in terms of its original setting, then, Revelation addressed a specific historical situation: the relationship of the church to the Roman Empire of the first century. Any interpretation of this writing, therefore, must begin with an appreciation and understanding of how it functioned for its original audience.

For New Testament theology, however, the theological significance of the Book of Revelation is not limited to the historical circumstances that originally occasioned its writing. This is not to claim that Revelation is an encoded document that predicts future historical events. To be sure, it does say something about the future: about God's victory over Satan and the beasts; the fall of Babylon (Rome) and the appearance of a new Jerusalem. But it is not a book of predictions secretly encoded in the seven seals, the seven trumpets, the seven bowls, and so on. Every attempt to decode these symbols and apply them to future historical events inevitably misunderstands the nature and purpose of this writing.

The book of Revelation is as concerned with the past and the present as it is with the future. Its purpose is not so much to predict the future as it is to remind listeners that God has already won the decisive victory over evil. Consequently, those who compromise with evil and worship its representatives find themselves in opposition to God. The future that God has prepared—the only future that really matters—belongs to those who witness to Jesus and worship God, no matter how powerful the forces of evil may be.

For the original audience of Revelation, the power of this evil was embodied in the oppressive rule of the Roman Empire, which required them to worship the emperor rather than God and the Lamb. For contemporary readers, this evil is embodied in any "beast" that requires them to worship it rather than God and the Lamb. The theological significance of the book of Revelation, then, is its prophetic call to worship God and bear witness to Jesus. Revelation views the present and future in light of what God has already done, and it understands and witnesses to the future from God's point of view.[3]

The book of Revelation communicates its theology through the story it tells. Therefore, I begin this chapter with a discussion of the narrative of Revelation and its theological significance. I then consider four aspects of the narrative's theology. This chapter consists of five parts: (1) the narrative of the book of Revelation; (2) God and his victory; (3) Christ and his victory; (4) God's people and their victory; and (5) God's enemies and their defeat.

---

3. Bauckham (*Theology of Revelation*, 7) writes, "The effect of John's visions, one might say, is to expand his readers' world, both spatially (into heaven) and temporally (into the eschatological future), or, to put it another way, to open their world to divine transcendence."

THE NARRATIVE OF THE BOOK OF REVELATION

Written to be read aloud and heard (1:3), the book of Revelation is a dramatic presentation of what must soon take place. To its first audience, who lived in an oral culture, the public reading of this prophecy must have been a dramatic and moving experience that provided them with a view of their present circumstances *as seen from heaven*. The proclamation of this prophecy would have assured the church that, despite its present afflictions, its future was linked to the victory of God and the Lamb. Before we turn to specific aspects of Revelation's theology, then, it will be helpful to recount the main movements of its story.

The framework of Revelation (1:1–8; 22:6–21) indicates that it is an apocalypse, a prophecy, and a letter. As an apocalypse, it *reveals* what "must soon take place" (1:1). As a prophecy, it *testifies* to the Word of God and Jesus Christ (1:2). As a letter, it *addresses* seven churches in the Roman province of Asia (1:4). Thus Revelation can be described as an apocalyptic prophecy communicated in the form of a letter, intended to be read aloud in the assemblies of the churches of Asia Minor.

The author, who identifies himself as John (1:1, 4, 9), was a prophet who belonged to a prophetic guild (22:9). According to his own account, he received this prophecy on the island of Patmos, where he was exiled because of his faithful witness to the Word of God and Jesus (1:9). Having received this revelation of Jesus Christ through an angel (1:1; 22:6), he communicates it in the form of a letter to the churches of Asia. The content of the book of Revelation, then, is the revelation given to Jesus Christ by God, made known to John by an interpreting angel, and communicated to the churches in the form of a letter.[4]

The Message of the Risen Lord to the Seven Churches
(1:9–3:22)

John's prophecy begins with a vision of the risen Christ (1:9–20), whom he describes in language that alludes to "the one like a son of man" mentioned in Dan. 7:13. The risen Christ identifies himself as "the first and the last," "the living one" who was dead but now lives forever and holds "the keys of Death and of Hades" (Rev. 1:17–18). Standing in the midst of seven golden lampstands, which represent the seven churches, and holding seven stars, which represent the angels of the churches, the risen Christ commands John to write

---

4. Although John says that he received this revelation from Jesus Christ, this does not exclude John's personal involvement in the composition of Revelation. For even after he had received the revelation, it would have been necessary for him to communicate in writing the vision he had experienced, a process that might have taken several years.

what he sees and send it to the churches of Ephesus, Smyrna, Pergamum, Thyatira, Sardis, Philadelphia, and Laodicea.[5]

The messages of the risen Lord to the seven churches (2:1–3:22) function as imperial edicts to warn and assure the churches. Each message has four parts: a description of the risen Lord, an evaluation of the spiritual status of the particular church, admonitions or encouragements, and a promise to those who heed what the Spirit says to the churches.[6]

In the first part of each message, the risen Lord identifies himself in a way that echoes some aspect of John's inaugural vision: "These are the words of him who holds the seven stars in his right hand, who walks among the seven golden lampstands" (2:1); "the first and the last, who was dead and came to life" (2:8); "who has the sharp two-edged sword" (2:12); "the Son of God, who has eyes like a flame of fire, and whose feet are like burnished bronze" (2:18); "who has the seven spirits of God and the seven stars" (3:1); "the holy one, the true one, who has the key of David, who opens and no one will shut, who shuts and no one opens" (3:7); "the Amen, the faithful and true witness, the origin of God's creation" (3:14). These introductory statements remind the churches that their Lord, who has been victorious over death, is all-knowing.

In the second part of the message, the risen Lord reveals that he knows the character and worth of each of the churches (2:2, 9, 13, 19; 3:1, 8, 15). He finds nothing to criticize in the churches of Smyrna and Philadelphia, but he admonishes the church of Ephesus for abandoning its first love, the church of Pergamum for holding to the teaching of Balaam and the Nicolaitans, the church of Thyatira for tolerating the prophet Jezebel, the church of Sardis for not being vigilant, and the church of Laodicea for being lukewarm.[7] These statements inform the churches that the risen Lord knows their sufferings, their endurance, and their failures.

Having revealed the status of the churches, in the third part of the message the risen Christ encourages and admonishes the churches. The church at Ephesus must repent and do the works it first did (2:5). The church at Smyrna must

5. Since the prophecy of the book was sent to these seven churches, the book of Revelation can be viewed as a circular letter sent to and read by all of these churches, perhaps in the order in which they are listed. Only later would it have been copied and preserved by these churches.

6. Raymond E. Brown (*An Introduction to the New Testament* [New York: Doubleday, 1997], 784–85) outlines each of the letters in this way. For a historical-critical analysis of each letter, see Colin J. Hemer, *The Letters to the Seven Churches of Asia in Their Local Setting* (Biblical Resource Series; Grand Rapids: Eerdmans, 2001).

7. Hemer (ibid., 94) concludes that "Nicolaitanism was an antinomian movement whose antecedents can be traced in the misrepresentation of Pauline liberty, and whose incidence may be connected with the special pressures of emperor worship and pagan society." The position of those who espoused the teaching of Balaam (whose name is used as a simile) probably indicates a similar error. Although the identity of Jezebel is unknown, Hemer (ibid., 128) suggests that she may have taught Christians to accommodate themselves to certain idolatrous and immoral practices of the trade guilds for the sake of their livelihood.

not fear what it is about to suffer (2:10). The church at Pergamum is to repent (2:16). The church at Thyatira is warned about what will happen to those who consort with the prophet Jezebel and her followers (2:20–23). The church at Sardis must repent and awaken from its spiritual slumber (3:3). The church at Philadelphia is assured that the Lord will protect it from the hour of trial (3:10). The church of Laodicea is advised to be earnest and repent, for the Lord is standing at the door (3:19–20). Although each church receives a slightly different encouragement or admonition, there is a consistent message to all of the churches: the Lord will sustain those who endure and punish those who do not.

The final part of each message is a promise to those who conquer by refusing to submit to the evil that threatens the churches. Those who are victorious in the present struggle will eat from the tree of life (2:7); they will not be harmed by the second death (2:11); they will be given the hidden manna and a new name written on a white stone (2:17); they will exercise authority over the nations and the morning star (2:26–28); they will be clothed in white robes (3:5); they will be made a pillar in the temple of God (3:12); and they will have a place on the throne with the risen Lord (3:21). Although the precise meaning of these images is elusive, their overall meaning is not. Those who conquer with Christ will live in the new Jerusalem described at the end of this revelation (21:1–22:5).

The purpose of John's inaugural vision can be summarized as follows. The risen Lord, who has already conquered the power of death, is fully aware of the situation in which the churches find themselves. If they hope to participate in his victory over death, they must conquer by witnessing to him and refusing to compromise their faith. For although the present circumstances of the churches are dire and oppressive, the risen Lord has already conquered and is fully aware of their trials.

John's Vision of God and the Lamb (4:1–5:14)

The promise of the risen Lord at the end of chapter 3, "To the one who conquers I will give a place with me on my throne, just as I myself conquered and sat down with my Father on his throne" (3:21), provides a transition to the throne room scene that follows in chapters 4–5.

Suddenly, John sees an open door in heaven, and the voice that spoke to him earlier (1:10) instructs him to come up. Upon entering heaven, he finds himself in the throne room of God, where God is seated on the throne surrounded by twenty-four elders, the seven spirits of God, and four living creatures who cry out without ceasing, "Holy, holy, holy, the Lord God the Almighty, who was and is and is to come" (4:8). In response to the cry of the four living creatures, the twenty-four elders sing, "You are worthy, our Lord and God, to receive glory and honor and power, for you created all things, and by your will they existed and were created" (4:11).

John sees a scroll with seven seals in the right hand of God, which no one in heaven or on earth can open. But then one of the elders tells him that the Lion of the tribe of Judah, the Root of David, has conquered and will open the scroll. These metaphors suggest a powerful Davidic Messiah. But instead of a lion, John sees a Lamb with seven horns, seven eyes, and the seven spirits of God. The Lamb, who appears to have been slaughtered, is the Messiah who has conquered by his death. When the Lamb takes the scroll from the right hand of God, the twenty-four elders sing a new song in which they proclaim that the Lamb is worthy to open the scroll, "for you were slaughtered and by your blood you ransomed for God saints from every tribe and language and people and nation" (5:9). This song is followed by another, sung by thousands of angels who acclaim the Lamb as worthy to receive power, and wealth, and wisdom and might (5:12). Finally, every creature sings, "To the one seated on the throne and to the Lamb be blessing and honor and glory and might forever and ever!" (5:13), and the four living creatures respond, "Amen!" In this scene Revelation portrays the Lamb as being in the very sphere of God, worthy to receive the same honor and glory as the one seated on the throne.

The throne room scene opens a new phase in the book of Revelation; for whereas previously John was on earth, now he has been taken into heaven, where he will see what is happening and what is about to happen from an entirely new perspective. The Lamb will open the scroll, and the opened scroll will reveal the seven trumpets and the seven bowls of God's wrath, as well as numerous other visions. John will see the suffering that the church must still endure if it is to conquer, the punishments that God will inflict upon those who refuse to repent, and the final victory that God will bring about for those who conquer with the Lamb.

The vision of God as the one seated on the throne reminds the church to worship God alone, and the metaphor of the slaughtered Lamb shows that if believers are to conquer the world, they must follow in the footsteps of the slaughtered Lamb. Conquering the world is not a matter of exercising power and might, however, but of worshiping the one who sits on the throne, testifying to the Lamb, and resisting evil to the point of shedding one's blood, if necessary.

Seven Seals, Trumpets, and Bowls, and Three Interludes
(6:1–16:21)

The events that occur from this point on are complicated by three interludes that interrupt the opening of the seven seals, the blowing of the seven trumpets, and the pouring out of the seven bowls of God's wrath. Thus there is an interlude between the sixth and seventh seal (the sealing of the 144,000 and

the vision of a vast multitude that no one could count; 7:1–17), a second interlude between the sixth and the seventh trumpet (the little scroll and the two
witnesses; 10:1–11:14), and a third between the seventh trumpet and the seven
bowls of God's wrath (the woman and the dragon, the two beasts, and three
visions of hope; 12:1–14:20). The material is structured as follows.

> The first six seals
> *First interlude*: The sealing of the 144,000; the vast multitude
> The seventh seal and the first six trumpets
> *Second interlude*: The vision of the little scroll; the two witnesses
> The seventh trumpet
> *Third interlude*: The woman and the dragon; two beasts; three visions
> of hope
> The seven bowls

Although they complicate the structure of this section, the purpose of these
interludes is to assure the faithful that their witness to Jesus is not in vain since
God has been and will be victorious. Consequently, although John will recount
the fall of Babylon and the appearance of a new Jerusalem in chapters 17–22,
these interludes provide the faithful with preliminary visions of God's victory.
In effect, Revelation tells its story of punishment, suffering, judgment, and victory several times in chapters 6–16 before recounting the judgment and fall of
Babylon and the appearance of the new Jerusalem in chapters 17–22. This
story can be summarized as follows.

The First Six Seals (6:1–17)

Having received the scroll from the right hand of the one seated on the throne
(5:7), the Lamb begins to open the seals. The opening of the first four seals
releases four horses, each with its rider: one who conquers; a second who takes
peace from the earth; a third who brings famine; and a fourth rider named
Death, who has authority over a fourth of the earth "to kill with sword, famine,
and pestilence" (6:8). With the opening of the fifth seal, John sees the souls of
those who have been slaughtered on behalf of the Word of God, under the altar
of God. He hears them cry out and ask how much longer before God judges
and avenges their blood. They are told to rest yet a little longer until their number is complete. When the Lamb opens the sixth seal, there is a great earthquake
and cosmic signs in the heavens. These cause the rulers of the earth to hide, for
they are aware that the great day of the wrath of God and of the Lamb is at hand.

The First Interlude (7:1–17)

Before the Lamb opens the seventh seal, there is an interlude. John sees four
angels standing at the four corners of the earth, and another with the seal of
the living God. This angel tells the four angels not to damage the earth or sea

until he has marked the foreheads of the servants of God with this seal. The angel then marks 144,000, twelve thousand from each of the twelve tribes of Israel. Following this, John sees a great multitude beyond counting, standing before the throne of the Lamb, crying out, "Salvation belongs to our God who is seated on the throne, and to the Lamb!" (7:10). The vision of the 144,000 assures the faithful, who must still suffer and witness on behalf of God and the Lamb, that God has sealed and protected them, whereas the vision of the great multitude provides the faithful with a vision of the final victory they will gain by their witness to God and the Lamb.[8] Thus, even though the seventh seal has not been opened, the victory of God has already been announced.

The Seventh Seal and the First Six Trumpets (8:1–9:21)

When the Lamb opens the seventh seal there is silence in heaven for a half hour in anticipation of what will be revealed (8:1). The opening of the seal reveals seven angels, standing before God, with the seven trumpets, which God has given to them. The opening of the seventh seal, then, begins a new cycle of suffering, punishment, judgment, and victory. John recounts the blowing of the first four trumpets (8:7–12) in the succinct way that he described the opening of the first four seals, describing the blowing of the fifth and sixth trumpets in greater detail (9:21). The blowing of the first four trumpets results in a series of cosmic disturbances that destroy a third of everything they afflict. The fifth trumpet, also called the first woe, brings a vast horde of locusts, which are allowed to torture those who do not have the seal of God on their foreheads (9:4). The sixth trumpet, also called the second woe, unleashes a cavalry of two hundred million. Although a third of humanity is destroyed, the rest of humanity refuses to repent (9:21).

The Second Interlude (10:1–11:14)

Before the blowing of the seventh trumpet, John introduces a second interlude in which he recounts two more visions: the little scroll and the two witnesses. In the first vision, a mighty angel gives John an open scroll, which John must eat so that he can prophesy "about many peoples and nations and languages and kings" (10:11). The content of the scroll is God's assurance that there will be no more delay; for when the seventh angel blows his trumpet "the mystery of God will be fulfilled, as he announced to his servants the prophets" (10:7). The vision of two prophets (11:1–14), who are described in language

---

8. Reviewing the function of these two visions, G. R. Beasley-Murray (*Revelation* [New Century Bible; Grand Rapids: Eerdmans, 1974], 168) writes: "The pause was made up of two visions, the first anticipating the trials as though they were future (although the story had almost reached its end), the second looking back on them as concluded. The second advanced on the first, not only from the temporal viewpoint, but in hinting that the preservation of the Church, of which the first vision spoke, did not mean the immunity of the Church from suffering."

reminiscent of Moses and Elijah, is a parable for the church, which must witness to Jesus during its time of suffering and affliction. The church will be afflicted by the beast that comes up from the bottomless pit, and many of its members will be put to death (11:7). But just as the breath of life entered anew into the two prophets who were slain, so it will enter into God's faithful when God raises them from the dead (11:11–12). Like the first interlude, this interlude assures the church that despite its present afflictions it will be victorious through its witness to God and the Lamb.

The Seventh Trumpet (11:15–19)

After the second interlude, the seventh angel blows his trumpet. The blowing of the seventh trumpet, which is the third woe, consummates God's victory. The kingdom of this world becomes the kingdom of God and his Messiah (11:15), and God's wrath comes upon the nations that raged against his prophets and saints (11:18). Like the first interlude, the second concludes with a vision of God's eschatological victory, assuring the church that God will be victorious.

The Third Interlude (12:1–14:20)

Before describing his vision of the seven bowls, John introduces a third interlude, longer than the first two, in which he recounts his vision of a woman and a dragon, a vision of two beasts, and three visions of hope. In the first vision (12:1–18), the pregnant woman symbolizes Israel, which gives birth to the Messiah, despite fierce opposition from Satan, the dragon. The woman's child is then "snatched away and taken to God and to his throne," a reference to Christ's death and resurrection. In heaven Michael is victorious over the dragon and casts him and his angels out of heaven. Thrown down to earth, the dragon pursues the women and the rest of her children. This woman, who gave birth to the Messiah, is the people of God whom Satan is presently afflicting. The purpose of the vision can be summarized as follows. God's victory over Satan has already been won in heaven by the birth, death, and resurrection of the slaughtered Lamb, the Messiah. But Satan continues to afflict the church on earth. Those who are privy to John's vision, however, understand that Satan will not be victorious because he has already been defeated in heaven.

Although defeated in heaven, Satan is still capable of leading the elect astray. To accomplish this, he employs the two beasts. The first, which rises from the sea (13:1), represents the Roman Empire and its rulers. The second, which rises from the earth (13:11), represents the imperial cult, which requires the inhabitants of the earth to worship the image of the first beast, to whom the dragon (Satan) has given its power, throne, and authority (13:2). To participate in this cult is to worship Satan.

After these two visions of the trials and tribulations that the faithful must endure, John concludes this interlude with three visions of hope that point to God's eschatological victory. In the first, he sees another vision of the 144,000. But now they have conquered and are standing with the Lamb on Mount Zion singing a new song before the throne of God that no one else could learn (14:1–5). Next he sees a vision of three angels (14:6–13). The first announces that the hour of judgment has come; the second proclaims the fall of Babylon/ Rome; and the third warns that those who worship the beast and receive its mark will drink the wine of God's wrath. Finally, John sees a vision of the one like the Son of Man, with a sharp sickle in his hand, ready to gather his elect (14:14–16). This is complemented by the vision of an angel, with a sickle in his hand, who is ready to reap the earth for the winepress of God's wrath. For a third time Revelation concludes its interludes with a vision of God's eschatological victory on behalf of the elect.

The Seven Bowls (15:1–16:21)

Before the seven angels pour out the seven bowls of God's wrath, John sees a vision of a new exodus. Those who have conquered the beast are now standing beside a sea of glass, singing the song of Moses and the song of the Lamb (15:2–4). Each of the seven angels is given a golden bowl filled with the wrath of God. The bowls of God's wrath punish those who opposed God and worshiped the image of the beast with plagues similar to those that afflicted Egypt at the time of the exodus. But this time there is no interlude between the sixth and seventh bowl, as there was between the sixth and the seventh seal and between the sixth and the seventh trumpet. God's judgment is immediate and complete. When the seventh angel pours out his bowl, a voice from the throne says, "It is done!" (16:17). The great city (Babylon) is split into three parts, the cities of the nations fall, and Babylon is given the cup of God's wrath to drink.

Although the structure of this section is intricate, its message is clear. At the present time, the church must struggle by witnessing to God and the Lamb against the dragon and the beasts that represent it. Although this witness leads to suffering and death, God's victory on behalf of the elect has already been won in heaven. Therefore, no matter how difficult the tribulations the elect must endure, God's holy ones will not be defeated so long as they remain faithful to God and the Lamb.

The Fall of Babylon (17:1–19:10)

This section is best viewed as a further description of the seventh bowl, which announced the destruction of Babylon: "God remembered great Babylon and gave her the wine-cup of the fury of his wrath" (16:19). It is not a description of new events that take place after the seven bowls but an explanation of how God pours out his wrath against Babylon.[9]

One of the seven angels who poured out the wrath of God invites John to view the judgment of Babylon, "the great whore who is seated on many waters" (17:1). Carried away in the spirit, John sees a woman seated on a scarlet beast that has seven heads and ten horns, clothed with purple and scarlet. On her forehead is the name "Babylon the great, mother of whores and of earth's abominations" (17:5). The woman on the beast, who is drunk with "the blood of the saints and the blood of the witnesses to Jesus" (17:6), is Rome. She stands in sharp contrast to the woman described in chapter 12, who represents Israel and the church.

The angel explains "the mystery" of the woman and the beast to John in coded language that suggests that the seven-headed beast represents one of the Roman emperors, most likely Nero (17:7–18). The ten horns symbolize ten kings who will join the beast and make war on the Lamb, only to be conquered by the Lamb. The Lamb is the Lord of lords and the King of kings (17:14), titles that will be applied to the victorious Christ in 19:11–16.

Another angel comes down from heaven and proclaims a dirge over Babylon (18:2–3), and a voice calls upon the elect to leave the great city because plagues will come upon her in a single day, and she will be burned with fire (18:4–8). Next, the kings of the earth (18:9–10), its merchants (18:11–17a), and its seafarers (18:17b–19) sing their dirges over the city, each lamenting how judgment has come upon the city in a single hour. The chapter concludes with rejoicing in heaven (18:20), and with an angel throwing a great millstone into the sea and proclaiming that the great city will be thrown down with just such violence (18:21–24).

John now hears the voice of a great multitude proclaiming God's victory over the great whore and announcing, for the first time, the marriage of the Lamb (19:1–8), which will be described in chapter 21. In anticipation of these nuptials, the angel tells John to write, "Blessed are those who are invited to the marriage supper of the Lamb" (19:9). In response, John tries to worship the angel, but the angel replies that he must not do so, for only God is worthy to be worshiped (19:10).

This description of the fall of Babylon is enigmatic inasmuch as chapter 18 presents it as both past and future. On the one hand, an angel cries out, "Fallen, fallen is Babylon the great!" (18:2). But on the other, the mighty angel who throws the millstone into the sea says, "With such violence Babylon the great city *will be* thrown down, and *will be* found no more" (18:21). This tension indi-

---

9. This point is made by Beasley-Murray (*Revelation*, 248): "This section, which flows without a break into a description of the parousia of Christ (19:11ff.), is a unity. It expands and explains the judgment of the seventh bowl, which was briefly described in 16:17–21."

cates that Revelation is portraying the fall of Babylon from two perspectives. From the vantage point of those who are still suffering, the fall of the great city is a future event. But from the perspective of heaven, it has already occurred in the victory of the Lamb.

The Victory of Christ and the New Jerusalem (19:11–22:5)

Having announced the destruction of the great city, the book of Revelation recounts Christ's victory over the dragon and the beasts and then describes the appearance of a new city, the heavenly Jerusalem, the bride of the Lamb.

Heaven is opened, and John sees a white horse, whose rider is called "Faithful and True" (19:11). The rider, who is Christ, leads the armies of heaven against the beasts and the kings of the earth (19:19).[10] The ensuing battle is brief, and the beast and the false prophet (the beast from the earth) are quickly captured and thrown into the lake of fire, and the rest of their armies are killed by the sword.[11] Following this, an angel seizes the dragon (Satan, the devil) and throws him into a pit, where he is bound for a thousand years (20:1–3). Those who did not worship the beast come to life and reign with Christ for a thousand years. This is the first resurrection (20:5). After a thousand years, Satan is released to attack the saints of God once more. But his assault upon them and the beloved city is futile, and Satan is thrown into the lake of fire with the beast and the false prophet (20:7–10). The final judgment and the second resurrection occur, and Death and Hades are cast into the lake of fire (20:14). God's victory is complete. All of God's enemies have been defeated, and it is time for the new Jerusalem, the city of God, the bride of the Lamb, to appear.

The events described above, especially the millennium, are among the most enigmatic in the book of Revelation. But they need not be, if one interprets them theologically rather than chronologically. The description of the rider on the white horse and the battle that ensues (19:11–21) is the way in which Revelation presents the parousia. The millennium, which is identified as the first resurrection (20:1–6), is the way in which Revelation affirms that Christ will vindicate the martyrs. Having been put to death because of their witness to the Lamb, they now reign with Christ for a thousand years. The eschatological battle that follows the millennium (20:7–10) indicates that Satan's final assault upon the followers of the Lamb will be utterly futile. Satan is cast into the lake of fire and the final judgment ensues, when even Death and Hades are

---

10. This battle is foreshadowed in 17:12–14, which explains that the ten horns of the beast are ten kings who, together with the beast, will make war upon the Lamb. That war is finally described in chap. 19.

11. Note how this accords with the dirges of chap. 18, which express amazement that Babylon's fall is "in one hour" (18:10, 17, 19).

thrown into the lake of fire (20:11–15).[12] This is the second death, from which
there is no resurrection. Construed chronologically, these images make little
sense, but interpreted theologically they point to God's victory at Christ's
parousia, when the martyrs will be vindicated, Satan will be defeated, and all
will face the judgment of God.[13]

The book of Revelation concludes with a description of the new heaven and
the new earth that God's victory has won (21:1–22:5). The bride of the Lamb,
first announced in 19:7, is identified as the Holy City, the new Jerusalem,
where God dwells with mortals. The city has no temple, for its temple is God
and the Lamb; and it has no need of sun or moon, for God is its light, and its
lamp is the Lamb. The throne of God and the Lamb is in the city, and there
God's servants will worship him. They will see God face-to-face, and God's
name will be on their foreheads. Thus the new Jerusalem, the bride of the
Lamb, stands in utter contrast to the great city of Babylon.

This prophecy provides those who hear or read it with privileged information about the fundamental conflict that underlies and determines human reality: the struggle between all that is good and all that is evil. Those who hear
or read this prophecy understand that even though this conflict is still being
waged against God's people on earth, God has already won the victory through
the death of his Messiah, the slaughtered Lamb. Consequently, although the
dragon and the beast continue to assault God's people on earth, those privy to
this prophecy know the outcome of the conflict: God will be victorious on
earth as he is in heaven.

GOD AND HIS VICTORY

The book of Revelation is about God. It identifies God as the Alpha and the
Omega, the beginning and the end (1:8; 21:6); the one who is, who was, and
who is to come (1:4, 8; 4:8; see also 11:17; 16:5); the Lord God, the Almighty
(1:8; 4:8; 11:17; 15:3; 16:7; 19:6; 21:22); the one seated on the throne (4:2, 3,
7; 5:1, 7, 13; 6:16; 7:10, 15; 19:4; 21:5).[14] God is the one who gives this revelation to Jesus Christ (1:1); and God is the one from whom the Lamb receives
the seven-sealed scroll (5:7).

12. First Corinthians 15 provides a similar vision of the end, when it speaks of death, the last
enemy, being defeated at the parousia and the general resurrection of the dead. See 1 Cor.
15:23–26.

13. On the millennium see Bauckham, *Theology of Revelation*, 106–8, especially 107: "This
shows that the theological point of the millennium is solely to demonstrate the triumph of the
martyrs: that those whom the beast put to death are those who will truly live—eschatologically,
and that those who contested his right to rule and suffered for it are those who will in the end rule
as universally as he—and for much longer: a thousand years!"

14. Bauckham (ibid., 25–35) provides an extended discussion of these four titles.

By portraying God as the one seated on the throne, the book of Revelation affirms that God alone is worthy of worship. So on two occasions, when John is about to worship the angel who guides him, the angel replies, "You must not do that! I am a fellow servant with you and your comrades. . . . Worship God!" (19:10; 22:9). Likewise the angel who proclaims "an eternal gospel" says, "Fear God and give him glory . . . and worship him who made heaven and earth, the sea and the springs of water" (14:7). This command to worship God highlights the central conflict within the narrative world of the book of Revelation: the conflict between those who worship God and those who worship the beast. Whereas those who follow the Lamb worship God, those who bear the mark of the beast worship the one whom the beast represents: Satan, the great dragon. It is not surprising, then, that Revelation develops its theology of God within the context of worship and liturgy. This prophecy enables those who hear and read it to enter the very throne room of God, where they witness the worship of the heavenly court. Through this description of the heavenly liturgy and its summons to worship God, Revelation develops its theology of God.

The most important description of this heavenly liturgy occurs in the throne vision of chapters 4–5, in which John sees "a throne, with one seated on the throne" (4:2). John portrays the one seated on the throne as having the appearance of "jasper and carnelian" (4:3). The rest of his description concerns those who surround the throne (the twenty-four elders, the seven spirits of God, and the four living creatures) and the worship they offer to the one seated upon it.[15] The four living creatures unceasingly cry out, "Holy, holy, holy, the Lord God the Almighty, who was and is and is to come" (4:8). In response to their cry, the twenty-four elders sing, "You are worthy, our Lord and God, to receive glory and honor and power, for you created all things, and by your will they existed and were created" (4:11). After this description of the heavenly liturgy, John notes that the one seated on the throne holds a seven-sealed scroll in his right hand, which he gives to the Lamb (5:1, 7). Three more hymns follow, two in honor of the Lamb, and a third that praises both the Lamb and the one seated on the throne: "To the one seated on the throne *and to the Lamb* be blessing and honor and glory and might forever and ever!" (5:13).

This privileged view of the heavenly liturgy identifies God in several ways: (1) as the one seated on the throne; (2) as the one whose holiness renders him totally other; (3) as the one who has always been and who will come; and (4) as the Creator who alone is worthy to receive glory, honor, and power. The only appropriate response to the one seated on the throne is the kind of worship that

---

15. Beasley-Murray (*Revelation*, 114) notes that the twenty-four elders have "quasi-priestly functions." It is doubtful, therefore, that they should be seen as representatives of the old and new Israel. The second group of angels, the four "living creatures," who are closer to the throne, are described in imagery reminiscent of Ezekiel 1 and Isaiah 6. The seven spirits of God are the plentitude of God's own Spirit. On the seven spirits, see Bauckham, *Theology of Revelation*, 110–15.

the heavenly court renders to him. Apart from the Lamb, there is no one else worthy of worship. Revelation, then, discloses its understanding of God in terms of worship and praise. Although God cannot be described or circumscribed, God can and must be worshiped; for it is by worshiping the one seated on the throne that creation acknowledges the majesty and otherness of God.

As the Lamb opens the seven-sealed scroll, which reveals the vision of the seven trumpets and the seven bowls, Revelation develops its theme of worship through a series of hymns. In the interlude between the sixth and the seventh seal, the great multitude standing before the throne and the Lamb cries out that salvation belongs to God, who is seated on the throne, and to the Lamb (7:10), and the angels of the heavenly court attribute to God, "Blessing and glory and wisdom and thanksgiving and honor and power and might" (7:12). Next, one of the elders identifies this multitude as those who "have washed their robes and made them white in the blood of the Lamb" (7:14). Having testified to Jesus by the sacrifice of their lives, they stand before the throne and worship God, and the one seated on the throne shelters them and wipes away every tear (7:15–17). The interlude between the sixth and seventh seal suggests that worship is the expression and experience of God's victory.

After the seventh angel blows the seventh trumpet, a loud voice in heaven proclaims, "The kingdom of the world has become the kingdom of our Lord and of his Messiah, and he will reign forever and ever" (11:15). The twenty-four elders then worship God by giving thanks for the victory he has won (11:17–18). But whereas earlier God was acclaimed as the one who is and who was and who is to come (1:4, 8; 4:8), now God is referred to as the one who is and who was (11:17), without any reference to a future coming, for God's victory is complete. After Michael and his angels expel the great dragon from heaven, John again hears a loud voice proclaiming this victory, "Now have come the salvation and the power and the kingdom of our God and the authority of his Messiah" (12:10). This victory is the expulsion of Satan, and it is the heavenly counterpart of the victory of the Lamb, Christ's death upon the cross. For Revelation, God is the one who is victorious, and to worship God is to celebrate God's victory.

Before the seven angels pour out the seven plagues, John has a vision of those who have conquered the beast, and he hears them sing the song of Moses and of the Lamb. This hymn praises the Lord God Almighty, whose ways are just and who alone is holy, concluding, "All nations will come and worship before you, for your judgments have been revealed" (15:4). When the third angel pours out his bowl, this angel also proclaims the justice of God, the Holy One, who is and who was (16:5). As in 11:17, there is no need to speak of God as the one who will come because God's victory is complete. The hymns of chapter 19 celebrate this victory and ascribe salvation, glory, and power to God who has judged the great whore (19:2). A voice from the throne says, "Praise our God, all you his servants, and all who fear him, small and great" (19:5); and the voice of a great multitude cries out that the Lord God Almighty reigns (19:6). Thus the central motif of all the hymns is constant: God is worthy of praise because God has been victorious and reigns forever and ever.

The book of Revelation expresses its understanding of God in terms of worship and praise. God is the one seated on the throne, who is worthy of worship and praise because he has won the victory over the beast through the blood of the Lamb. To worship God is to affirm and participate in this victory.

CHRIST AND HIS VICTORY

The book of Revelation establishes an intimate relationship between God and Christ. At the beginning of this prophecy, God identifies himself as "the Alpha and the Omega" (1:8), and at the end he says, "I am the Alpha and the Omega, the beginning and the end" (21:6). At the beginning of this prophecy, the one like the Son of Man says, "I am the first and the last" (1:17), and at the end, "I am the Alpha and the Omega, the first and the last, the beginning and the end" (22:13). In effect, Revelation applies to Christ what it applies to God. As God is the Alpha and Omega, the beginning and the end (1:8; 21:6), so Christ is the first and the last, the Alpha and the Omega (1:17; 22:13). For the book of Revelation, Christ has always belonged to the reality of God.[16]

The throne vision in chapters 4–5 portrays this intimate relationship between God and Christ in yet another way. In this scene there are five hymns, two to the one seated on the throne (4:8, 11), two to the Lamb (5:9–10, 12), and one to God and the Lamb (5:13). Whereas the first two hymns praise God as creator, the second and third praise the slaughtered Lamb as redeemer. The fifth hymn ascribes blessing, honor, glory, and might to God and the Lamb, allowing the Lamb to share in what properly belongs to God. Thus the book of Revelation relates Christ to God in virtue of Christ's preexistence and his saving death on the cross.

This intimate relationship between God and Christ is also apparent in the nexus that Revelation establishes between the victory of God and the victory of Christ. Christ's victory on the cross is God's victory, and God's victory is Christ's victory. Thus the 144,000 cry out, "Salvation belongs to our God who is seated on the throne, *and to the Lamb!*" (7:10). When the seventh angel blows his trumpet, he says, "The kingdom of the world has become the kingdom of our Lord *and of his Messiah*" (11:15). After Michael expels the dragon from

---

16. See the discussion by Bauckham (ibid., 54–58) on the first and the last. On p. 57, he notes that in calling Christ the first and the last, the beginning and the end, Revelation unambiguously states that Jesus Christ belongs to "the fullness of the eternal being of God."

heaven, a voice proclaims, "Now have come the salvation and the power and the kingdom of our God *and the authority of his Messiah*" (12:10). This victory inaugurates the marriage of the Lamb (19:7), whose bride is the Holy City of the heavenly Jerusalem (21:9–10). That city needs no temple because God and the Lamb are its temple (21:22), and it requires no sun or moon because God is its light, and the Lamb is its lamp (21:23).

Revelation expresses Christ's victory in several ways. The greeting of the letter to the seven churches describes Jesus as "the faithful witness, the first-born of the dead, and the ruler of the kings of the earth," who "freed us from our sins by his blood, and made us to be a kingdom, priests serving his God and Father" (1:5–6). John then sees a vision of Jesus as one like the Son of Man standing in the midst of seven golden lampstands (the seven churches), holding seven stars (the angels of the churches), with a sharp two-edged sword (the Word of God) coming from his mouth. Once dead, he is alive forever, and now he possesses the keys of Death and Hades (1:12–18). When the risen Christ addresses each of the seven churches, he identifies himself in language that recalls this vision and the victory he has won through his death and resurrection (2:1, 8, 12, 18; 3:1, 7, 14). The first three chapters of Revelation, then, present Christ as one who has been victorious over death. Having conquered death, he promises a share in his victory to those who are faithful.

Whereas the vision of the one like a Son of Man portrays the victory of the resurrected Christ, the metaphor of the slaughtered Lamb expresses the victory of the crucified Christ. By this metaphor, Revelation forestalls any notion that Jesus is a national messiah who wins the victory through the exercise of power and might.[17] To be sure, Revelation affirms that Jesus is the Messiah, "the Lion of the tribe of Judah, the Root of David" (5:5). But it then proceeds to identify the Lion of the tribe of Judah as the slaughtered Lamb, an understanding of messiahship comparable to Paul's theology of the crucified Messiah. By employing the metaphor of the slaughtered Lamb, Revelation portrays Christ as the Messiah who conquers by his death. Having ransomed a people for God by shedding its blood (5:9–10), the slaughtered Lamb is worthy to open the seven-sealed scroll, which reveals the whole plan of God. The victory of the slaughtered Lamb is the victory of the cross. To use Pauline language, it is a victory won through the weakness and folly of the cross.

The book of Revelation knows yet another aspect of the victory of Christ—the victory that Christ will win at the parousia. It describes this victory twice. First, at the end of the long interlude between the seven trumpets and the seven

---

17. Revelation does employ military imagery in its description of the parousia, when it portrays Christ returning on a white horse with the armies of heaven (19:11–21). This description of the parousia in military terms, however, is to be taken as a metaphor for the consummation of God's victory, which Christ wins at the parousia.

bowls, John sees a vision of one like the Son of Man, seated on a cloud, with a golden crown and a sharp sickle, who reaps the harvest of the earth (14:14–16). Then, after the destruction of Babylon, the one who is called "Faithful and True," "the Word of God," "King of kings and Lord of lords" goes forth with the armies of heaven and conquers the beast and the kings of the earth (19:11–21). Thus the victory of Christ has three dimensions: the victory of the cross, the victory of the resurrection, and the victory of the parousia.

Although the book of Revelation identifies Christ in several ways, its most distinctive contribution to New Testament theology is its presentation of him as the slaughtered Lamb.[18] This metaphor defines messiahship in light of Christ's victory on the cross and summons believers to follow the Lamb by being faithful to God, even unto death. In addition to this distinctive contribution, Revelation contributes to a growing understanding within the New Testament of Christ's relationship to God by affirming that Christ is the beginning and the end of all things, the Alpha and the Omega. Revelation does not present an explicit statement of preexistence, such as is found in the Fourth Gospel, because it does not develop a theology of the incarnation. But it does understand and present Christ as one who, in some way, already existed with God.

GOD'S PEOPLE AND THEIR VICTORY

The book of Revelation presents its theology of the church—the people of God—in two ways. First, John communicates the words of the risen Lord to the seven churches of Asia Minor. In this initial vision, the risen Lord encourages and admonishes his churches, promising an eschatological reward to those who are victorious. Second, John is taken up into heaven, where he sees visions of the church's apocalyptic struggle with, and ultimate victory over, Satan and the beast. In the initial vision of chapters 1–3, the focus is on the local community, the *ekklēsia*, and it is not yet apparent that the churches will be victorious. But in the visions of chapters 4–22, the outcome of the struggle

18. Charles H. Talbert ("The Christology of the Apocalypse," in *Who Do You Say That I Am? Essays on Christology in Honor of Jack Dean Kingsbury* [ed. Mark Allan Powell and David R. Bauer; Louisville: Westminster John Knox Press, 1999], 166–84) provides a complete list of titles applied to Christ in Revelation: Lord; Christ/Messiah; the Son of God; the faithful witness/martyr; the firstborn of the dead; the first and the last; the living one; the holy one; the true one; the one who has the key of David; the Amen; the origin of God's creation; the beginning and the end; the Alpha and the Omega; the Lion of the tribe of Judah; the Root of David; the Lamb; the Word of God; the bright morning star; the one who has the sharp two-edged sword. Jan A. du Rand ("Soteriology in the Apocalypse of John," in *The Soteriology of the New Testament* [ed. Jan G. van der Watt; Leiden: Brill, 2005], 465–504) provides an analysis of the soteriology in Revelation, especially in reference to the Lamb.

is never in doubt: the people of God will be victorious because the Lamb has already been victorious. Thus, whereas the opening chapters of Revelation describe the church as a local congregation that must win the victory, the remaining chapters portray the church as the eschatological people of God who have been victorious.[19] This prophecy enables the church on earth to see itself from the vantage point of God and the Lamb and so to understand its present struggle in an entirely new way.

At the outset of this prophecy, John reminds the churches that Jesus Christ loves them, has freed them from their sins by his blood, has made them a kingdom of priests to serve God, and is coming soon (1:5–7). The one like the Son of Man walks amid the churches, the seven golden lampstands, which are meant to enlighten the world by their witness to Jesus. Although the churches may not experience the full presence of their Lord, there is nothing he does not know about their circumstances. He is aware of their strengths and weaknesses, their perseverance and their failures. He knows that while some of them do not tolerate evildoers and have suffered great afflictions, others have been corrupted by those who urge them to compromise their faith by participating in the cult of the emperor. Among the corrupting elements of the church are the Nicolaitans (2:15), the prophet Jezebel (2:20), and those who hold to the teaching of Balaam (2:14). It is imperative, therefore, for the churches to repent because the exalted Son of Man is coming soon (2:5, 16; 3:3, 11, 20). The primary purpose of the seven letters, then, is to encourage and admonish the churches during this time of trial and tribulation.

The visions that follow the seven letters encourage the churches to persevere in their struggle by showing them the victory that those who follow the Lamb will win. For example, when the Lamb opens the fifth seal, John sees that the souls of those who have already been martyred are under the altar of God (6:9–11). Although they ask God to avenge their blood, they are told that their number is not yet complete, signaling that others must endure their fate before the victory can be won. Between the opening of the sixth and the seventh seals, John recounts how the 144,000 servants of God (12,000 from every tribe of Israel) are marked with the seal of God on their forehead so that they can endure the eschatological woes that are about to come (7:1–9).[20] Following this, he sees "a great multitude that no one could count, from every nation," standing before the throne of the Lamb, robed in white (7:9), whom one of the twenty-four elders identifies as those who "have come

---

19. Although there are several references to the church (*ekklēsia*) in chaps. 1–3, there is only one reference to the church in the remaining chapters (22:16), since chaps. 4–5 present the church as the people of God. Jan Lambrecht ("The People of God in the Book of Revelation," *Collected Studies on Pauline Literature and on the Book of Revelation* [AnBib 147; Rome: Pontifical Biblical Institute Press, 2001], 379–94) shows the relationship between these two ecclesiologies.

20. Bauckham (*Theology of Revelation*, 76–80) describes the 144,000 as an army of martyrs.

out of the great ordeal" by washing their robes and making them white in the blood of the Lamb (7:14). The appearance of this multitude suggests that the first group has passed through the great eschatological struggle that the church must face and has now become an international multitude beyond counting, the eschatological people of God who have conquered by their witness to the Lamb.[21]

The parable of the two witnesses (11:1–14) and the tale of the woman and the dragon (12:1–17) provide the church with further assurance that its testimony and struggle will not be in vain. For just as God vindicated these two witnesses by raising them from the dead, so God will vindicate the church's witness. Just as the dragon was not able to conquer the woman, so Satan will not be able to conquer the people of God.

John has yet another vision of the 144,000, but this time they are standing with the Lamb on Mount Zion, singing a song that only they could learn (14:1–5). They are the redeemed, the firstfruits for God and the Lamb, the ones who follow the Lamb wherever he goes. John then sees those who have conquered the beast and its image, standing beside a sea of glass, singing the song of Moses and the Lamb (15:2–3). This new vision does not necessarily point to a different group of people. Whether it be the 144,000, the great multitude, the two witnesses, or the woman who is pursued by the dragon, these images and metaphors point to the people of God, who have conquered by their testimony to the Lamb.

Revelation recounts the final victory of God's people in its description of the new heaven and the new earth, and the Holy City, the new Jerusalem (21:1–27). This new city is the place where God dwells with his people (21:3). It is "the bride, the wife of the Lamb" (21:9). Although the book of Revelation never explicitly identifies the church with the new Jerusalem, there is an intimate relationship between them insofar as the Holy City is the dwelling place of the eschatological people of God. The description of this new city as the bride of the Lamb suggests that the new Jerusalem, the city in which the redeemed live with God, is the way in which the book of Revelation presents its eschatological vision of the church.

To summarize, the book of Revelation portrays the church as both a local community and as the eschatological people of God. Its victory, which is the victory of the Lamb, can be won only by testifying to Jesus, at the cost of blood if necessary. There can be no compromise between the church and the world, only witness to God and the Lamb. It is by such testimony that the people of God win their victory.

---

21. The relationship between these two groups is problematic and disputed. The juxtaposition of the two groups suggests that the witness of the 144,000 has led others to follow the Lamb. Thus the 144,000 from every tribe of Israel have become an international multitude.

GOD'S ENEMIES AND THEIR DEFEAT

In chapters 12–13 the book of Revelation introduces the great red dragon (12:3), the beast from the sea (13:1), and the beast from the earth (13:11)—a satanic trinity that stands in opposition to God, the Lamb, and the people of God.[22] The dragon is Satan; the beast from the sea is the imperial power of Rome; and the beast from the earth represents the imperial cult. The dragon has already persecuted the woman (Israel) pregnant with child (the Messiah), but it has failed to prevent the birth of the Messiah (the slaughtered Lamb), who has been taken up to God and his throne. Michael and his angels have already cast the dragon out of heaven and thrown him down to the earth, where he wages war against the woman and the rest of her children, the eschatological people of God, "who keep the commandments of God and hold the testimony of Jesus" (12:17). In order to conquer the people of God, the dragon gives "his power and his throne and great authority" (13:2) to the beast that rises out of the sea, the imperial power of Rome. This beast is allowed to make war on the saints and conquer them, and is "given authority over every tribe and people and language and nation" (13:7). Thus it stands in sharp contrast to the slaughtered Lamb, who ransomed "saints from every tribe and language and people and nation" by his blood (5:9). The second beast, which enforces the imperial cult, exercises the authority of the first and requires everyone to be marked on their right hand or forehead with the name of the beast, thereby establishing a contrast with the 144,000 who bear the name of the Lamb and his Father on their foreheads (14:1).

Chapters 19–20 describe the defeat of this satanic trinity in three stages: the parousia, the millennium, and the final battle at Gog and Magog. At the parousia Christ, who is "Faithful and True," comes forth with the armies of heaven and defeats the beast and the kings of earth. As a result of this battle, the beast and the false prophet (the second beast) are cast into the lake of fire (19:11–21). Next, the dragon is bound and cast into a pit for a thousand years, while those who did not worship the beast or its image, or receive its mark on their foreheads or hands, reign with Christ for a thousand years (20:1–6). Finally, when the dragon is released, there is a climactic battle at Gog and Magog, after which Satan is cast into the lake of fire, with the beast and the false prophet, forever (20:7–10).

In the period between the victory that the Lamb has already won and the final defeat of the dragon and the beasts, the eschatological people of God play their own role in conquering and defeating this satanic trinity. The risen Lord

---

22. This term is used by Bauckham (*Theology of Revelation*, 88–89). Although Revelation does speak of "the beast that comes up from the bottomless pit" in 11:7, this satanic trinity is not introduced until chaps. 12–13.

summons the churches to participate in this eschatological struggle when he promises that those who conquer will eat from the tree of life (2:7), will not be harmed by the second death (2:11), will be given the hidden manna and a white stone with a new name (2:17) and authority over the nations and the morning star (2:27–28), be clothed in white robes (3:5), be made a pillar in the temple of God (3:12), and be given a place on his throne (3:21). But it is only in chapters 12–13 that Revelation explains what and how the churches must conquer to be victorious: they must conquer the dragon and the beasts by witnessing to God and the Lamb. Accordingly, the church must also play a role in the defeat of God's enemies by actively resisting the imperial rule of Rome, which arrogates to itself the worship that belongs to God. Richard Bauckham puts it well: "John's message is not, 'Do not resist!' It is, 'Resist!—but by witness and martyrdom, not by violence."[23]

In chapters 17–18 the book of Revelation portrays the defeat of God's enemies in another way, the fall of Babylon (Rome). The pouring out of the seventh bowl (16:17–21) announces the fall of great Babylon, which stands in sharp contrast with the new Jerusalem. Chapter 17 then portrays the city as a great whore sitting on a scarlet beast, "drunk with the blood of the saints and the blood of the witnesses to Jesus" (17:6). Bauckham notes that the saints are not called to conquer Babylon in the way that they are summoned to conquer the dragon and the beast but to come out of her and not take part in her sins, lest they share in her plagues (18:4).[24] Another city awaits the followers of the Lamb, the new Jerusalem, where "nothing unclean will enter . . . nor anyone who practices abomination or falsehood" (21:27). Whereas fallen Babylon becomes "a dwelling place of demons" (18:2), the new Jerusalem is God's dwelling place among mortals (21:3).

The defeat of God's enemies is God's victory over the dragon and the beasts, which results in the fall of Babylon and the appearance of a new Jerusalem. Although the victory is ultimately the work of God and the Lamb, the eschatological people of God share in this victory by actively resisting Satan and his deputies.

CONCLUSION

Although the imagery of the book of Revelation is complex and at times confusing, its theology is remarkably clear and traditional. Christ's death upon the cross was God's decisive victory over Satan. By shedding his blood, the slaughtered Lamb gained an international people for God from every race, tongue,

23. Ibid., 92.
24. Ibid., 89.

and nation. This people is in continuity with historical Israel, which gave birth
to the Davidic Messiah, the Lion of the tribe of Judah. Although the decisive
victory has already been won, its final consummation has not yet occurred. In
this regard, the eschatology of Revelation is similar to Paul's eschatology:
believers are already justified but not yet saved. The martyrs already rest under
the altar of God, but their final salvation will not be complete until the eschatological people of God enter the city of God. Revelation's understanding of
salvation is also reminiscent of Hebrews' theology, which portrays salvation in
terms of entering into God's Sabbath rest, approaching Mount Zion, the city
of the living God, the heavenly Jerusalem, as well as entry into the heavenly
sanctuary.

The theology of Revelation was forged in the fires of persecution and
oppression, and it stands as a powerful reminder that there can be no compromise between good and evil. One cannot worship God and the beast, or, as
Paul writes, one cannot drink from the cup of the Lord and the cup of demons
(1 Cor. 10:21). But whereas Paul affirms the goodness of God's creation and
provides believers with a way to engage the world in a positive manner, the
book of Revelation does not. Its understanding of reality, reminiscent of the
dualism of the Fourth Gospel, does not allow it to develop a theology of positive engagement with the world. Therefore, although the eschatological
vision of Revelation makes it a fitting conclusion to the New Testament and
to the entire Bible, its theology must be supplemented by those writings that
provide a fuller understanding of the Christian life in this world (such as is
found in the Synoptic Gospels, Ephesians, Colossians, and the Pastoral Epistles) without setting aside the eschatological dimension of the Christian life.

Conclusion

The Diverse Unity of New Testament Theology

Having investigated the diverse theologies in the New Testament, we can now broach the question of the unity of New Testament theology. Can one speak of *the theology* of the New Testament as well as of the *theologies* in the New Testament, or is the New Testament merely a collection of diverse writings, some theologically related to one another, others not?

Inasmuch as the New Testament is a collection of writings, most of which were composed independently of one another, it might seem that there is little purpose in trying to establish *the* theology of the New Testament. After all, the book that is now called the New Testament is the result of a long and intricate process whereby the church determined which writings were normative and authoritative for faith and worship. Moreover, the authors of the New Testament wrote for diverse communities of believers, from Jerusalem to Rome, in order to exhort, admonish, and instruct believers in their new faith. They were not writing theological essays for a volume that would one day be called the New Testament.

However, inasmuch as the church identified these particular writings as Scriptures that witness to God's self-revelation in Jesus Christ, the unity of the New Testament is a presupposition of faith. That is, faith presupposes that these writings, as diverse as they may be, are related to one another because they witness to God's self-revelation in Christ. Viewed from the perspective of faith, then, the search for the unity of the New Testament is an example of faith seeking to understand what it believes: that there is unity in the diverse theologies of the New Testament because each writing witnesses to God's self-revelation in Jesus Christ.

Historians, of course, will and should approach the task differently. The unity of New Testament theology is not a presupposition of faith for the historian but a hypothesis to be tested. Although these two approaches to the unity of New Testament theology differ, they are not diametrically opposed to each other. For even though believers presuppose the unity of the New Testament, they must investigate and establish the inner connections among its writings, relationships that are not always immediately apparent. In doing so, they must resist the temptation to mute the diverse voices of the New Testament.

Several recent works have dealt with the unity of New Testament theology. For example, François Vouga offers a theological and hermeneutical interpretation that focuses on the human subject in light of God's revelation in Christ.[1] Juxtaposing diverse writings and blocks of material, he shows "how, at the interior of the New Testament, the dialogue and controversy over the great themes of Christian theology (what is the gospel, the kingdom, salvation, life, faith, hope, love?) renders an account of the event of the revelation of God, who, in the history of the hellenized and Jewish West, *disrupts the perception that the human subject has of itself.*"[2] Vouga's themes come from the central message of the New Testament writings, which has its origin in a common experience: an encounter with the uniqueness of a word outside the ordinary and beyond all the probabilities of common human reason.[3] The New Testament writings identify this experience in a variety of ways, for example, the presence of the kingdom, the coming of Emmanuel, the Savior of Israel and Lord of the nations, the incarnation of the Word of God, the resurrection of a crucified Messiah.[4] The event of this word results in the appearance of a subject ("Le surgissement du sujet") that structures its new life according to the theological virtues of faith, hope, and love.[5] This new existence of the subject is rooted in the resurrection of Christ, which leads to a new understanding of human existence.[6] In the present this new existence is lived within the social sphere of the church,[7] where believers hope for a future in which God's word will be the last word.[8] Vouga's understanding of the unity of the New Testament can be summarized in this way: the diversity of the New Testament writings is a paradoxical witness to the unity of the New Testament that testifies to the singular event of the gospel in a multiplicity of ways.

After studying the individual writings of the New Testament, Peter Stuhlmacher summarizes the central message of the New Testament in six statements.

---

1. *Une théologie du Nouveau Testament* (MdB 43: Geneva: Labor et Fides, 2001). Vouga's interest in the human subject and the implications of the New Testament for the subject's understanding of existence recalls Rudolf Bultmann's program of existential interpretation. Vouga's method, however, is not wedded to a particular existential philosophy as was the case with Bultmann.

2. Ibid., 21.
3. Ibid., 31.
4. Ibid.
5. Ibid., 113.
6. Ibid., 221.
7. Ibid., 315.
8. Ibid., 391.

1. "The chief witnesses of the New Testament *join in confessing the one God, who has definitively revealed himself in his one Son, consubstantial with him, and who has brought about the salvation of the world in him.*"
2. "According to the New Testament the common confession of the one God, who has definitively revealed himself in and through Christ, is connected to the *proclamation of the one apostolic gospel of God about Jesus Christ.*"
3. "*The (major) New Testament witnesses teach in common that the crucifixion of Jesus is to be understood as an atoning death performed for 'the many' in God's commission.*"
4. "*The New Testament writers are in agreement in seeing in Jesus' resurrection the creative act (which affects all human beings) of the one God, who brings the dead to life, and they are in agreement in teaching the expectation of the parousia and the last judgment.*"
5. "*The individual witnesses of the New Testament join in calling those who believe in Jesus Christ to an exemplary praxis of love of God and neighbor.*"
6. "*According to the unanimous witness of the New Testament, the Holy Spirit who proceeds from the one God and his Christ bears and determines the witness, the knowledge of the faith, and the sanctification of the community of Jesus Christ.*"[9]

The recent work of Ferdinand Hahn is the most ambitious example of a New Testament theology to date. Comprehensive in scope, it consists of two volumes.[10] Hahn begins his second volume by noting that a treatment of the theologies of the various New Testament writings is not a theology of the New Testament if the focus is merely on what is distinctive. One can speak of a New Testament theology only if there is an effort to correlate the different elements and explain Christian faith.[11] Accordingly Hahn views the work of New Testament theology as akin to that of fundamental theology. It should integrate what has been learned about the earthly Jesus and develop a unified conception of the New Testament.[12] Hahn undertakes this synthetic task by employing, as his guiding principle, the revelation of the one God who created all things and made himself known to humanity and to the world.[13] With this guiding theme in view, he divides his second volume into five parts.

In the first, he insists that the Old Testament is the presupposition for all parts of the early Christian tradition, for it was the normative Scripture for the early church. As the church's Scripture, the Old Testament witnesses to God's action in creation and history as well as to God's future salvific activity. Adopting the

9. Peter Stuhlmacher, *Biblische Theologie des Neuen Testaments*, 2 vols. (Göttingen: Vandenhoeck & Ruprecht, 1992, 1999), 2:309–11.
10. Ferdinand Hahn, *Theologie des Neuen Testaments*, 2 vols. (Tübingen: Mohr Siebeck, 2002).
11. Ibid., 2:1. "Von einer Theologie im strengen und eigentlichen Sinn kann doch nur dort gesprochen werden, wo es um einen Gesamtzusammenhang geht, bei dem in einer durchreflektierten Weise zum Ausdruck gebracht wird, was christlicher Glaube ist und beinhaltet." (One can only speak of theology, in a strict and proper sense, where there is an overall framework that expresses what Christian faith is, and consists of, in a manner that is thoroughly thought out.)
12. Ibid., 2:33.
13. Ibid., 2:26–27.

Old Testament as its Bible, the early church read Israel's Scriptures in light of God's action in Christ.

Since an analysis of early Christian texts shows that the concept of revelation was of prime importance for the early Christian message, in part two Hahn takes up the theme of "The Revelatory Act of God in Jesus Christ." This revelation occurs with the inbreaking rule of God that Jesus proclaimed and realized through his ministry, which then became the basis for the church's Christology. Hahn notes that inasmuch as the Spirit was at work in Jesus' ministry and proclamation, there is an implicit Trinitarian structure in the witness of the New Testament.

In the third part ("The Soteriological Dimension of God's Revelatory Act") Hahn considers the human condition, the problem posed by the law, the redemption of humanity, and the gospel as the proclamation and realization of salvation. Then, since the redemption of humanity leads to new life, Hahn takes up the topic of "The Ecclesial Dimension of God's Revelatory Act" in part four. This allows him to discuss a number of themes such as discipleship and faith, the nature of the church, baptism, Eucharist, prayer, creeds, worship, the gifts of the Spirit, mission, and the ethical life. This discussion of the present aspect of the Christian life leads to the final part in which Hahn considers the future hope of the Christian life ("The Eschatological Dimensions of God's Revelatory Act").

Hahn is aware that the New Testament writings express these themes differently and that there are tensions among them, for example, their understanding of the law, the relationship between works and faith, and most importantly the tension between present and future eschatology. Nevertheless, there is a remarkable agreement and convergence among the New Testament writings in regard to God's revelatory activity in Christ.[14] The unity of the New Testament does not consist in uniformity ("Gleichförmigkeit") but in a multifaceted development of the early Christian message.[15] The decisive characteristic of the early Christian message is its faith in the God of the Old Testament and his promises, which, for the early church, found their culmination in the person and history of Jesus Christ.[16]

Hahn argues forcefully for the inner unity of the New Testament. His proposal, like Stuhlmacher's, is similar to the church's rule of faith, a narrative account of God's revelatory activity that began at creation, continued with the election of Israel, and culminated in Jesus Christ. However, whereas Stuhl-

---

14. Ibid., 2:803–5.

15. Ibid., 2:805. "Die Einheit des Neuen Testaments besteht nicht in Gleichförmigkeit, sondern in einer vielgestaltigen Entfaltung der urchristlichen Botschaft." (The unity of the New Testament does not consist in uniformity but in a multifaceted unfolding of the early Christian message.)

16. Ibid., 2:805–6.

macher focuses more intently on God's work of reconciliation in Christ, Hahn employs the more embracing theme of revelation to disclose the inner unity of the theology in the New Testament.

Finally, the recent works of I. Howard Marshall and Frank Thielman, both of which deal with the theologies in the New Testament, conclude with chapters on the theological unity of the New Testament.[17] After his survey of the theologies in the New Testament, Marshall concludes that the New Testament presents a religion of redemption in which there are four stages common to all writers: (1) a situation of human need, sin, that places people under divine judgment; (2) a saving act of God accomplished in Jesus Christ; (3) a new life for those who believe, mediated by the Holy Spirit, a life that people experience individually and communally; (4) hope for the consummation of all things.[18] Although more detailed, Thielman's analysis is similar. He maintains that the writings of the New Testament converge on five issues: (1) the human problem and God's answer to it in Jesus; (2) faith as God's gracious initiative; (3) the Spirit as the eschatological presence of God; (4) the church as the people of God; and (5) the consummation of all things.[19]

Although these five authors structure their proposals differently, each of them deals with similar themes: humanity's need for salvation; God's response to humanity's plight; the person of Christ; the individual believer and the community of the church; the power of the Spirit and the life of the faithful; the consummation of all things at the parousia, the general resurrection of the dead, and the final judgment. Moreover, the manner in which they develop their proposals suggests that there is an underlying narrative that guides the diverse writings of the New Testament. This is not to say that all of the New Testament writings exhibit this narrative in detail. They do not. The appearance of certain themes again and again, however, indicates that the authors of the New Testament were aware that they and those for whom they wrote were part of a history in which God has acted on their behalf. The recurrent themes of their writings and the events of this history provide the foundation for what can be called "the master story" of the New Testament.

The unity of New Testament theology is grounded in the implied master story to which these writings witness. This story can be summarized in this way: Humanity finds itself in a predicament of its own making from which it cannot extricate itself. This predicament, which is experienced as a profound alienation

17. I. Howard Marshall, *New Testament Theology: Many Witnesses, One Gospel* (Downers Grove, IL: InterVarsity Press, 2004); Frank Thielman, *Theology of the New Testament: A Canonical and Synthetic Approach* (Grand Rapids: Zondervan, 2005).

18. Marshall, *New Testament Theology*, 717–18. There are also four chapters (7, 19, 24, 30) in which Marshall shows the relationships among the various writings of the New Testament.

19. These are the sectional headings that Thielman employs to structure his material (*Theology of the New Testament*, 681–724).

from God, is the result of humanity's rebellion against God. It affects Jew and Gentile alike. Because humanity cannot reconcile itself to God or free itself from this predicament, God has graciously sent his own Son into the world to redeem the world. Those who believe and accept this gracious offer of salvation, Jew and Gentile alike, are incorporated into a community of believers that God has redeemed and sanctified through Christ. Redeemed and sanctified, this new community lives by the power of God's Spirit as it waits for the consummation of all things. Although this consummation is expressed in different ways (the parousia, the general resurrection of the dead, the final judgment), the New Testament writings agree that God will be victorious and Christ will be the agent of God's victory. How the writings of the New Testament contribute to and verify this narrative I will summarize under the following headings: (1) humanity in need of salvation; (2) the bringer of salvation; (3) the community of the sanctified; (4) the moral life of the sanctified; and (5) the hope of the sanctified.

HUMANITY IN NEED OF SALVATION

There is an intimate relationship between the salvation the gospel brings and the human condition. On the one hand, people embrace the gospel because it responds to a profound need in their lives. It promises healing, forgiveness, deliverance from evil, reconciliation with God, and salvation from death itself. On the other hand, those who experience this salvation begin to comprehend the predicament in which they find themselves apart from the gospel. They are conscious of the power of sin and their former alienation from God. They understand that what they once thought was true was a lie. Now that they dwell in the light, they realize that they had been living in darkness. Whether proclaimed by Jesus or by the early church, the gospel unmasks the human condition. To speak of soteriology, then, is to talk about Christian anthropology, and to talk about Christian anthropology is to speak of soteriology.[20]

The Synoptic Tradition

The gospel begins with Jesus' proclamation that the kingdom of God is making its appearance in his ministry. The good news that Jesus brings is God's own good news—God's gospel—that the kingdom of God is at hand. This kingdom is a dynamic reality. It is the power of God, the sphere in which those who embrace the kingdom acknowledge God's rule over history and creation. In and

---

20. For an overview of the soteriology in the New Testament, see Arland J. Hultgren, *Christ and His Benefits: Christology and Redemption in the New Testament* (Philadelphia: Fortress, 1987); Jan G. van der Watt, ed., *Salvation in the New Testament: Perspectives on Soteriology* (NovTSup 121; Leiden: Brill, 2005).

through Jesus' ministry, God's kingdom invades the human sphere. People experience the salvation the kingdom brings through the forgiveness of sins and the healing God offers through Jesus' ministry. Those who believe see the hidden presence of God's rule and understand that the kingdom of God is in their midst.

The manner in which Jesus casts out demons and frees his contemporaries from the power of Satan is a powerful indication that the kingdom of God has come upon them (Luke 11:20). These exorcisms reveal humanity's profound need to enter into the kingdom of God, the sphere where God rules over history and creation. To be sure, God always rules over history and creation. The powerful presence of Satan, however, shows that humanity has not submitted to God's rule. Having refused to dwell in the sphere of God's rule, humanity finds itself in bondage to Satan's rule.

Israel's initial response to Jesus' proclamation of the kingdom indicates that the gospel responds to a profound need for healing and forgiveness. The Synoptic Gospels recount numerous stories of people who believe that Jesus has the power to save them. When people approach Jesus with faith in his power to save them, this is precisely what he does (Mark 2:5; 5:34).

Jesus' gospel of the kingdom effects salvation and reveals the human condition. On the one hand, he offers people a concrete experience of what it is like to live in the sphere of God's rule where people are reconciled to God and to one another because they acknowledge God's rule over their lives. When Jesus heals the physical ills of his contemporaries, frees them from Satan's bondage, forgives their sins, and raises the dead, they experience the kingdom of God. On the other hand, the salvation the kingdom brings exposes the true state of the human condition. Apart from the kingdom, people find themselves alienated from God and in profound need of forgiveness. Having rebelled against God's rule, they have allowed Satan to rule over their lives. Israel, then, needs to be reformed and restored if it is to enter into the sphere of God's rule, and the Gentiles must turn from idols to the living and true God.

The kingdom of God enters a new phase through Jesus' death and life-giving resurrection. Jesus gives his life as a ransom for many (Mark 10:45) and pours out his blood for the forgiveness of sins (Matt. 26:28). After Jesus' resurrection, God bestows upon him all authority in heaven and on earth (Matt. 28:18), and Jesus enjoys the glory that befits God's Messiah (Luke 24:26). As the risen One, Jesus enters into the sphere of God's rule in a decisive way that cannot be reversed because he has entered into resurrection life. Those who follow him by surrendering their lives will also enter into the transcendent realm of the kingdom when they receive eternal life at the resurrection of the dead.

In the Acts of the Apostles, the early church witnesses to Jesus' resurrection and proclaims the forgiveness of sins in his name. Those who repent and are baptized experience the forgiveness of their sins, receive the gift of the Holy Spirit, and are incorporated into a community of believers destined to be saved

(Acts 2:38, 47). The risen Lord is the focal point of salvation, for there is no other name by which people can be saved (4:12). This salvation, which is already experienced in the forgiveness of sins, the gift of the Holy Spirit, and the communal life of church, reveals the human predicament. The present generation is a "corrupt generation" (2:40) that was complicit in the death of God's Messiah, although it did not fully comprehend what it was doing (3:17). Furthermore, the forgiveness of sins in Jesus' name suggests that the Mosaic law could not adequately deal with the problem of sin (13:39). Thus the church proclaims that Gentiles and Jews alike "will be saved through the grace of the Lord Jesus" (15:11).

In addition to the present dimension of salvation the church already enjoys, Acts points to the salvation believers will experience at the end of the ages. Peter looks forward to the return of the Messiah, "the time of universal restoration that God announced long ago through his holy prophets" (3:21). Because the Messiah has been raised from the dead, Paul anticipates the general resurrection of the dead, which is Israel's hope and the fulfillment of God's promise (26:6–7).

In Acts the proclamation of what God has done in Jesus includes the forgiveness of sins, the gift of the Spirit, and resurrection from the dead. This salvation proclaims that humanity is in profound need of forgiveness, without which it cannot enter into the new life the resurrection brings, the transcendent realm of the kingdom where Jesus is enthroned as Lord and Messiah.

To summarize, whereas the subject of Jesus' gospel is the kingdom of God, the subject of the church's proclamation is the gospel of what God had accomplished in Jesus Christ. This is not to suggest that the early church abandoned Jesus' proclamation of the kingdom of God. It did not. The early church preached the kingdom of God by its proclamation of the death and resurrection of Jesus, who entered into the kingdom of God as Lord and Messiah. By entering into the transcendent sphere of the kingdom of God, the risen Lord became the subject of the gospel the early church proclaimed. The church's proclamation of God's good news, then, is in continuity with Jesus' proclamation of the kingdom. For in preaching the gospel of what God had done in Christ, the early church proclaimed the fulfillment of the kingdom of God in the one who had already entered its transcendent realm. This gospel promises that just as Jesus entered into God's kingdom by his death and resurrection, those who believe in him will enter into the transcendent sphere of the kingdom at the general resurrection of the dead.

The Pauline Tradition

The gospel is the content of Paul's preaching. By "the gospel" Paul means the good news of what God has done in the saving event of Christ's death and resurrection. Paul also speaks of "the gospel of God," by which he means God's own good news; "the gospel of Jesus Christ," by which he means the good news about Jesus Christ; and "my gospel," by which he means the gospel of God that he (Paul) proclaims. Because this gospel focuses on the death and resurrection of Christ, Paul refers to the gospel he preaches as "the message about the cross" (1 Cor. 1:18) and the "mystery of God" (1 Cor. 2:1). Thus whereas Jesus' gospel announced the inbreaking power of God's kingdom, Paul's gospel proclaimed the way in which God's power manifested itself in Christ's death and resurrection, thereby making the kingdom of God available to all who believe in Christ.

A former Pharisee, Paul understood the importance of the law and the covenant God had made with Israel, and he hoped for the resurrection of the dead. But when God revealed that the one whom Paul judged to be a law-breaker was none other than God's Son, the former Pharisee reassessed his understanding of the Mosaic law, the nature of the righteousness he had attained under that law, and the power of sin. This reassessment occurred throughout Paul's ministry as he faced challenges from those who opposed his gospel and as crises arose in the congregations he had established, especially at Galatia and Corinth. The essential content of the gospel, however, was communicated to Paul when God revealed his Son to him (Gal. 1:16). In light of that revelation, Paul understood that Christ would occupy the central place in his life that the law formerly had.

Paul's understanding of the human condition, in light of Christ, can be summarized in this way. Previous to the appearance of Christ, humanity was under the power of sin, which frustrated humanity's efforts to do God's will as expressed in the law. Sin entered the world through Adam's transgression of God's commandment, and with sin came death. The power of sin was especially apparent in the Gentile world, which worshiped the creature rather than the Creator. As a result of its idolatry, the Gentile world found itself in a sinful predicament from which it could not extricate itself (Rom. 1:18–32). Although the Jewish people had the advantage of knowing God's will because God had graciously given them the gift of Torah, they also transgressed God's commandments (2:1–29). In Paul's view, all are under the power of sin (3:9).

Previous to his call and conversion, Paul was confident that he was blameless "as to righteousness under the law" (Phil. 3:7). But inasmuch as his legal observance drove him to persecute those who confessed Jesus as the Son of God, Paul considered his former gains under the law as a loss (Phil. 3:8). In light of the righteousness he received through his faith in Christ, he saw the human condition in a new way. Apart from Christ, humanity does not understand its own actions. Even though unredeemed humanity may know what is good, it does not do the good it knows because it is under the power of sin (Rom. 7:14–20).

Human beings cannot attain righteous before God on the basis of legal observance because they are under the power of sin that Adam's transgression introduced into the world. Reasoning from the salvation that God effected in Christ to the human situation, Paul asks why Christ died if righteousness could have come through the law (Gal. 2:21). If the law had the power to give people life, then righteousness would have come through the law (3:21). The law then must have played a different role in God's redemptive plan. Its salvation-historical purpose was not to effect righteousness but to act as Israel's disciplinarian until Christ came (3:24). With the appearance of Christ, the law's salvation-historical role ended, for "Christ is the end of the law" (Rom. 10:4).

Paul's analysis of the human condition reveals that humanity is in a predicament from which it cannot free itself. Enslaved to the power of sin, humanity is under God's judgment, threatened with death, which brings eternal separation from God. Humanity is in dire need of salvation.

For Paul this salvation comes in and through the gospel he proclaims. Although the word of the cross about Christ crucified is "a stumbling block to Jews and foolishness to Gentiles" (1 Cor. 1:23), Paul is not ashamed of the gospel because it is the power of God that effects salvation for Jew and Greek alike. The proclamation of the gospel reveals God's righteousness: God's uprightness and covenant faithfulness (Rom. 1:16–17). God revealed this righteousness through the foolishness and weakness of the cross. The cross then was the place of atonement (Rom. 3:25) where God justified, redeemed, and reconciled humanity to himself. On the cross, Christ redeemed humanity "from the curse of the law" (Gal. 3:13). On the cross, Christ died for all (2 Cor. 5:14–15). By means of Christ's death, God reconciled humanity to himself, allowing his Son to stand as humanity's representative before God so that humanity could stand in the righteousness of Christ before God (2 Cor. 5:19, 21).

The death of Christ is a salvific event for Paul, a death whereby Christ "gave himself for our sins to set us free from the present evil age" (Gal. 1:4), a death whereby Paul experienced Christ's personal love (Gal. 2:20). At the heart of Paul's theology is the conviction that "Christ died for our sins in accordance with the scriptures" (1 Cor. 15:3).

Whereas the death of Christ highlights Christ's redemptive work on behalf of humanity, Christ's resurrection foreshadows the final salvation humanity will experience at the parousia and the general resurrection of the dead. Humanity has already been justified and reconciled to God though Christ's death (Rom. 5:9–10), but it will not be saved until the last enemy—death—is destroyed. Thus the general resurrection of the dead plays a central role in Paul's soteriology. He is confident that this general resurrection of the dead has already begun in Christ, "the first fruits of those who have died" (1 Cor. 15:20). He believes that the new age, characterized by life in the Spirit, has already made its appearance in Christ. Because the general resurrection has already begun in Christ, the parousia, which heralds the general resurrection of the dead, is imminent. When Christ returns, the dead will be raised incorruptible, and death will have been destroyed (1 Cor. 15:26). Transformed by the power of the resurrection, those who have believed in Christ will inherit the kingdom of God (1 Cor. 15:50). Thus God's work of salvation in Christ will be complete, and God will be all in all. Justified, reconciled, redeemed, and sanctified by God's work in Christ, humanity will be changed and transformed at the general resurrection so that it can enter the imperishable kingdom of God.

In the period between what God has already done in Christ and the general resurrection of the dead, humanity lives in the new creation God has effected in Christ (2 Cor. 5:17; Gal. 6:15). Living in this new creation, it experiences the power of the resurrection through life in the Spirit (Romans 8; Galatians 5). This Spirit, which empowers believers to fulfill the law (Gal. 5:13–26), is the "first installment" (2 Cor. 1:22) of the resurrection life believers will enjoy at the general resurrection of the dead.

Although Paul provides a more detailed and insightful analysis of salvation and the human condition than the Synoptic writers do, there is a convergence in the anthropology and soteriology of the Synoptic and Pauline traditions. Both affirm that human beings have a profound need for peace and reconciliation with God because they have sinned. God provides the means for this reconciliation in and through Christ. The final act in the drama of salvation, however, will not occur until the parousia, when those who belong to Christ will enter into the kingdom of God by the resurrection of the dead.

Those who wrote in Paul's name built upon and developed his anthropological and soteriological insights. This is especially true for Colossians and Ephesians, which present Paul's soteriology in cosmic terms. For Colossians, Christ is the head of the body, which is the church, and through him "God was pleased to reconcile to himself all things, whether on earth or in heaven, making peace through the blood of the cross" (Col. 1:20). Through the cross, Christ triumphed over the cosmic powers (2:15) so that there is no further need for "self-abasement and worship of angels" (2:18). Inasmuch as the church is the body of the risen Christ, Colossians can also say that believers have been raised up with Christ (3:1), even though the general resurrection of the dead has not yet occurred. For Colossians the gospel is the revelation of God's mystery, which is Christ (2:2), a mystery that reveals how all things in heaven and on earth have been reconciled to God.

Ephesians also identifies Christ as the head of the church, which is his body (1:22). Through the blood of Christ, believers have found redemption, in the forgiveness of their trespasses (1:7). Formerly they were "dead" because of their trespasses and sins (2:1), but now they have been made "alive together with Christ" (2:5). They have been saved by God's grace rather than by their works (2:8–9). Because Christ, the head of the church, has been raised up and seated at God's right hand (1:20), they have been raised up and seated with him "in the heavenly places" (2:6). For Ephesians, Christ is the sphere in which a new humanity is being created, the place where the ancient hostilities between Gentile and Jew are being abolished (2:11–22). In Ephesians the gospel reveals the mystery of Christ, "that the Gentiles are coheirs, members of the same body, and copartners in the promise in Christ Jesus through the gospel" (3:6).

The Pastorals affirm that "Christ Jesus came into the world to save sinners" (1 Tim. 1:15). Therefore, he gave himself as a ransom for all (1 Tim. 2:6), and he gave himself "for us that he might redeem us from all iniquity and purify for himself a people of his own who are zealous for good deeds" (Titus 2:14). Those who desire to be saved must come to the knowledge of the truth, which is the "glorious gospel" God entrusted to Paul (1 Tim. 1:11). This gospel is the content of the "sound teaching" Paul entrusts to Timothy and Titus (2 Tim. 1:13; Titus 2:1).

This gospel promises God's gracious gift of salvation in and through Jesus Christ. God desires that everyone be saved and come to the knowledge of the truth (1 Tim. 2:4). He is "the Savior of all people, especially of those who believe" (1 Tim. 4:10). In language reminiscent of Paul's teaching on justification, 2 Timothy notes that God saved and called people, not according to their works, but according to his own purpose and grace, which was given to them in Jesus Christ before time began (2 Tim. 1:9). This grace was manifested through the appearing of the Savior, Christ Jesus, who abolished death and brought life and immortality through the gospel. It is this gospel for which Paul has been appointed apostle and teacher (2 Tim. 1:9–11).

The Letter to Titus also draws upon Paul's teaching on justification. Those who have accepted the faith were "once foolish, disobedient, led astray, slaves to various passions and pleasures" (3:3). But when the goodness and kindness of God appeared, they were saved, not because of any works of righteousness they had done "but according to his mercy, through the water of rebirth and renewal by the Holy Spirit" (3:5). The Savior God poured out this Spirit through the Savior, Jesus Christ, so that having been justified by his grace they might become heirs to the hope of eternal life (3:6). Those who embrace the salvation the gospel brings have rejected "impiety and worldly passions," as they wait for the manifestation of their great God and Savior, Jesus Christ (2:12–13).

Although the Pastorals do not provide the same insightful analysis of the human condition that the nondisputed Pauline writings do, salvation plays a central role in these letters. The initial epiphany of Jesus Christ "abolished death and brought life and immortality" (2 Tim. 1:10). At his final epiphany, the Savior will judge the living and the dead (1 Tim. 4:1).

The Johannine Tradition

The Johannine tradition provides a keen analysis of the human condition and of the salvation God offers in Jesus Christ. But whereas the starting point of the Synoptic tradition is the gospel of the kingdom, the Johannine tradition begins with the revelation the Son brings from the Father.

Sent into the world to reveal what he has seen and heard in God's presence, the Son discloses the human condition. This is not a two-step process, however, whereby the Son first reveals what he has heard and seen in God's presence and then reveals the human condition. Rather, the revelation the Son brings is a disclosure of the human condition. For in revealing the light in which God dwells, the Son discloses the darkness in which the world lives. In revealing the eternal life that God gives, the Son discloses the death for which the world is destined—eternal separation from God. And in revealing the truth that is God, the Son exposes the sin of the world, which prefers to live in the darkness rather than in the light of God. The revelation the Son brings to the world, then, exposes the predicament in which humanity finds itself: a profound alienation from God. Unaware of its blindness (John 9:40–41), humanity desperately needs the salvation the Son brings from the Father.

Jesus' claim that he reveals what he has seen and heard in the presence of the Father derives from the Gospel's central affirmation: "the Word became flesh and lived among us" (John 1:14). As the enfleshment of God's Word, Jesus is the Lamb of God who takes away the sin of the world (1:29). He is the Savior of the world (4:42; 1 John 4:14), the only Son of God, whom God sent into the world "so that everyone who believes in him may not perish but may have eternal life" (John 3:16). Jesus freely lays down his life for the sheep (10:11, 15, 17, 18), and he dies "for the nation" (11:51). In the words of 1 John, his death was "an atoning sacrifice for sins" (1 John 2:2; 4:10).

Those who believe in the Son have eternal life (John 3:36), whereas those who refuse to believe are already condemned (3:18). When the Son raises the dead on the last day (6:39, 40, 44, 54), the eternal life believers experience will be brought to completion. The relationship between the Johannine and the Synoptic traditions can be expressed in this way. Whereas the preferred soteriological category of the Synoptic tradition is the kingdom of God, the central soteriological category of the Johannine tradition is the life that the Son of God grants to those who believe that he comes from the Father. Whereas the imagery of the kingdom implies life with God, the Johannine category of eternal life enables the Johannine tradition to express the salvific reality of the kingdom in a way that responds to the deepest longing of the human spirit.

Other Voices

In addition to the three great traditions of the New Testament (the Synoptic, Pauline, and Johannine traditions), the Epistle to the Hebrews, the Letter of James, the Petrine Letters, and the book of Revelation also speak of salvation and the human condition, albeit in different ways. With its theology of sacrifice and priesthood, Hebrews makes the most significant contribution. Arguing that perfection could not be attained through the Levitical priesthood (Heb. 7:11) and that the animal sacrifices of the Levitical cult could not adequately deal with sin (10:1–4), Hebrews maintains that Jesus was a high priest according to the order of Melchizedek. As a high priest, he entered into the heavenly sanctuary by his death in order to deal with sin once and for all. Hebrews views the human predicament as a "consciousness of sin" (10:2) from which only the Son of God could free humanity by the sacrifice of his own blood.

The book of Revelation also focuses on the redemptive death of Christ, whom it presents as the slaughtered Lamb. By his blood, the Lamb has ransomed for God saints from every tribe and language and people and nation (Rev. 5:9), making them a "kingdom, priests serving his God and Father" (1:6). By the victory of his death, the slaughtered lamb has won a new people for God. The manner in which Revelation portrays the conflict between those who worship God and those who worship the beast indicates that those who do not follow the Lamb belong to Satan and the beast. Apart from the victory of the Lamb, humanity is under Satan's power.

Like Hebrews and Revelation, 1 Peter is conscious of the redemptive value of Christ's blood. Believers have been "sprinkled" with the blood of Christ (1 Pet. 1:2). They were "ransomed" from the futile ways they inherited from their ancestors by "the precious blood of Christ," whom 1 Peter compares to a lamb "without defect or blemish" (1:18–19). Because of what God has done in Christ, believers have been born anew "through the living and enduring word of God" (1:23). Once they were not a people, now they are God's people. Once they did not experience God's mercy, now they have experienced God's mercy (2:10). Because of what God has done in Christ, they have become "a chosen race, a royal priesthood, a holy nation, God's own people" (2:9).

Second Peter expresses the salvation believers have received and the situation from which they have been rescued when it affirms that they have escaped "from the corruption that is in the world" and become "participants of the divine nature" (2 Pet. 1:4). For James, salvation is related to the wisdom that comes from above (Jas. 1:5; 3:13, 15, 17), which enables people to live a life of perfection in accordance with the royal law, the law of liberty (2:8, 12). Apart from such wisdom, people are driven by the "cravings" that are at war within them (4:1). They are in friendship with the world rather than in friendship with God (4:4).

Although the writings of the New Testament express it in different ways, the salvation that the gospel brings reveals that humanity is in a predicament from which it cannot extricate itself. The gospel is God's response to this profound need for salvation that is fulfilled in Jesus Christ. But who is the bringer of this salvation to whom the New Testament testifies?

THE BRINGER OF SALVATION

Just as there is an intimate relationship between the salvation that the gospel brings (soteriology) and the gospel's revelation of the human condition (Christian anthropology), so there is a necessary relationship between the salvation that the gospel brings (soteriology) and the bringer of salvation (Christology).[21] The gospel effects the salvation it promises because the one who brings this salvation—Jesus—is the eschatological agent of God's salvific work. Were he not appointed by God to bring salvation, Jesus would not be the Savior. It is not surprising, then, that the person and identity of Jesus is of central concern to the writers of the New Testament. Although the various writers of the New Testament express their understanding of Jesus in different ways, all affirm Jesus' unique relationship to God and his indispensable role in the salvation God offers to remedy the human predicament. Jesus is the bringer of salvation because he is the one whom God has chosen, designated, and sent into the world. He is the savior because in and through him God provides the definitive remedy for the plight that affects the human condition.

The many ways in which the New Testament identifies Jesus correspond to the different ways in which it describes the salvation God effects in Jesus Christ. For example, whereas the Synoptic Gospels identify Jesus as the messianic Son of God who inaugurates God's kingdom, Paul identifies Jesus as the eschatological Adam who counters the history of sin that Adam introduced into the world. Whereas John identifies Jesus as the Son who comes from God to reveal the Father to the world, Hebrews identifies Jesus as a high priest according to the order of Melchizedek who deals with sin once and for all. Understanding the ways in which the New Testament identifies Jesus, then, provides an insight into the salvation God effects in and through him.

21. On the Christology of the New Testament, see Oscar Cullmann, *The Christology of the New Testament* (London: SCM, 1959); Marinus de Jonge, *Christology in Context: The Earliest Christian Response to Jesus* (Philadelphia: Westminster, 1988); James D. G. Dunn, *Christology in the Making: A New Testament Inquiry into the Origin of the Doctrine of the Incarnation* (2nd ed.; Grand Rapids: Eerdmans, 1989); Frank J. Matera, *New Testament Christology* (Louisville: Westminster John Knox Press, 1999); Ben Witherington III, *The Many Faces of the Christ: The Christologies of the New Testament and Beyond* (Companions to the New Testament; New York: Crossroad, 1998).

The Synoptic Tradition

For the Synoptic tradition, Jesus is preeminently the herald of the kingdom of God. He preaches and teaches about the kingdom, and through his healings and exorcisms he manifests the inbreaking power of God's rule. By his death and resurrection, he enters into the transcendent realm of the kingdom that he heralds.

Because Jesus announced and effected the kingdom of God through his ministry, death, and resurrection, the Synoptic tradition identifies him as God's anointed one (the Christ), Israel's promised Messiah. The application of this title to Jesus, however, required the Synoptic writers to explain what they meant when they identified Jesus as the Messiah since he had suffered such a shameful death. If he was the Davidic Messiah, why did he not restore the Davidic monarchy? If he was the Messiah, why did he not restore the kingdom to Israel? Instead of measuring Jesus against traditional messianic expectations, however, the early church defined its understanding of messiahship in terms of Jesus. To be sure, the church continued to search Israel's Scriptures for proofs and prophecies that Jesus was Israel's expected Messiah. But it now read Israel's Scriptures in light of Jesus' death and resurrection. Consequently, the early church defined its understanding of the Messiah in light of what God had accomplished in Jesus Christ. The crucified and risen Jesus now defined what it meant to be God's anointed one. This understanding of the Messiah became the church's hermeneutic for reading Israel's Scriptures, especially the Psalms and the Prophets. For the early church now saw the pattern of Jesus' death and resurrection in texts from the Psalms and Prophets that described the vindication of the righteous sufferer.

Within the Synoptic tradition, the designations "Son of God" and "Son of Man" play a crucial role in identifying Jesus as the Messiah. The first, "Son of God," identifies Jesus' relationship to God. The second, "Son of Man," clarifies his destiny.

Jesus enjoys a unique relationship to God because he is the Son of God. To be sure, there were other sons of God, most notably the angels of God's court (Job 1:6), the people of Israel (Exod. 4:22), the Israelite king (Ps. 2:7), and the righteous sufferer (Wis. 2:18). But in the view of the Synoptic Gospels, Jesus enjoyed a unique relationship to God that became fully apparent at his death and resurrection. The Synoptic writers refer to this relationship in several texts. In their accounts of Jesus' baptism and transfiguration, they narrate how God identifies Jesus as his beloved Son (Matt. 3:17; 17:5; Mark 1:11; 9:7; Luke 3:22; 9:35). In other instances, they narrate that Jesus speaks of himself as God's Son and/or refers to God as his Father. For example, in a saying shared by Matthew and Luke, Jesus reveals the intimate relationship he enjoys with the Father (Matt. 11:27; Luke 10:22). At the conclusion of his temple discourse

Jesus explicitly refers to himself as "the Son" and to God as "the Father" (Mark 13:32). In the Garden of Gethsemane, he prays to God as his Father (Matt. 26:39, 42; Luke 22:42), employing an intimate form of address according to the Markan Gospel ("Abba," Mark 14:36). Jesus' sonship also plays a central role in the passion narratives. The religious leaders ask Jesus if he is the Messiah, the Son of God (Matt. 26:63; Mark 14:61; Luke 22:67), and according to the Matthean Gospel they mock him for having claimed to be God's Son (Matt. 27:42–43). In doing so, they employ the language Satan used when he tested Jesus in the wilderness (Matt. 4:3, 6; see also Luke 4:3, 9).

Each of the Synoptic Gospels presents Jesus as the Son of God in a slightly different manner. In the Markan Gospel, the Roman centurion is the only human character within the narrative to confess that Jesus was truly God's Son (Mark 15:39), an indication that only those who acknowledge Jesus as the crucified Messiah can understand the nature of his unique relationship to God. In the Matthean Gospel, Jesus is conceived through the power of the Holy Spirit, apart from the agency of a human father (Matt. 1:18, 20). Even during Jesus' lifetime his disciples confess that he is the Son of God (Matt. 14:33; 16:16), although they will not fully comprehend the significance of their confession until his resurrection from the dead. The Lukan Gospel also insists that Jesus was conceived by the power of God's Spirit, rather than through the agency of a human father, and identifies Mary's child as the Son of God (Luke 1:35). For Luke "Messiah" and "Son of God" have become interchangeable terms, as is evident from Luke 4:41.[22]

If "Son of God" is the way in which the Synoptics identify who the Messiah is, "Son of Man" explains Jesus' destiny as the Messiah. That destiny can be seen in the destiny of the one like a son of man described in Daniel 7. Just as God vindicated the one like a son of man, so God will vindicate his Messiah, who must suffer and die before rising from the dead. In all of the Synoptic Gospels, then, Jesus' passion predictions are intimately related to Peter's messianic confession. The one whom Peter confesses as the Messiah is the one who must follow the path of the Son of Man who will be rejected, suffer, and die before entering into his glory (Matt. 16:21; Mark 8:31; Luke 9:22). The Synoptic Gospels agree that Jesus the Messiah is the Son of God who must endure the fate of the suffering Son of Man. After this period of suffering and rejection, however, God will vindicate the Messiah just as he vindicated the one like a son of man described in Daniel 7. Vindicated by God, the Messiah will return on the clouds of heaven as the glorious Son of Man to gather the elect and judge those who judged him.

---

22. The demons shout that Jesus is "the Son of God," and Jesus rebukes them because they know that he is "the Messiah." This exchange shows that the two titles are interchangeable for Luke.

In the Acts of the Apostles, "Son of God" and "Son of Man" recede into the background[23] as the church proclaims that the risen Jesus is "Lord" and "Messiah" (Acts 2:32). "Lord" is the way in which the church addresses, speaks about, and prays to Jesus because he has been exalted at God's right hand, whereas "Messiah" is the content of the church's proclamation. This Christology, which focuses on the ascension and exaltation of Jesus, resolves the problem raised by the unfulfilled promise that the angel made to Mary: that her son would sit upon the throne of David and rule over the house of Jacob forever (Luke 1:32). The prophet Anna had spoken of the child Jesus to all who were "looking for the redemption of Israel" (Luke 2:34), and the two disciples on the road to Emmaus were clearly disappointed that Jesus had not redeemed Israel in the way they expected (Luke 24:21). But with Jesus' resurrection, ascension, and exaltation, the Acts of the Apostles reveals that the risen and exalted Lord is the enthroned Messiah (Acts 2:36) who will restore all things (3:21).

The Gospels and Acts employ other titles to explain who Jesus is and what he has done. They identify him as the holy one of God (Mark 1:24) and, in a qualified sense, as the son of David (Matt. 1:1). They present him as a prophet (Luke 7:16), and call him "Emmanuel" (Matt. 1:23), "the holy and righteous one," "the author of life" (Acts 3:14–15). Of course, his name "Jesus" signifies that he will save his people from their sins (Matt. 1:21). The primary contribution of the Synoptic writers, however, is to *redefine* the notion of messiah in light of Jesus. The Messiah is the one who suffered, died, rose from the dead, the one who will return at the end of the ages as God's eschatological agent. The Messiah is God's Son, whose destiny is the fate of the Son of Man.

The Pauline Tradition

Whereas the Christology of the Synoptic tradition embraces Jesus' life and ministry as well as his death and resurrection, the Christology of the Pauline tradition focuses on the salvific event of Christ's death and resurrection, which anticipates his parousia and the general resurrection of the dead. In addition to the parousia, the Pauline tradition speaks of Christ's preexistence. Consequently, the earliest Christology of the New Testament, which is represented by the nondisputed Pauline letters, is one of the most sophisticated Christologies in the New Testament. It is also an intensely personal Christology insofar as it is rooted in Paul's experience of the risen Lord.

Paul's Christology begins with his call and conversion, when God revealed "his Son to me" (Gal. 1:16). From that moment on, Paul understood the cru-

---

23. "Son of Man" occurs only in Stephen's speech (Acts 7:56). "Son of God" occurs only in Acts 9:20, in reference to Paul's preaching. But as was the case in Luke 4:41, it is clear from Acts 9:20 and 9:22 that "Messiah" and "Son of God" are interchangeable titles for Luke.

cified Jesus as the risen Lord, the Son of God, the eschatological Adam, the one who has already entered into God's new creation, where he shares in the very glory of God so that he is the image of God (2 Cor. 4:4; see also Col. 1:15). Paul also understood that Jesus was the Messiah, the descendant of David (Rom. 1:2; 9:5).

Although Acts reports that Paul regularly proclaimed that Jesus was the Messiah (Acts 9:22; 17:3; 18:5; 18:28), in his own letters Paul does not discuss Jesus' messiahship or try to prove that he was the Messiah. In his letters, *Christos* is no longer a messianic title but a way in which Paul identifies Jesus. This is not to say that Jesus' messiahship is unimportant to Paul. For even though *Christos* becomes associated with Jesus' name, Paul is undoubtedly aware of the messianic connotation of this name when he writes "Christ," "Jesus Christ," "Christ Jesus." For example, Paul's discussion in 1 Cor. 1:18–25 of "Christ crucified" as "the power of God and the wisdom of God" indicates that Paul, like Mark, views Jesus as the crucified Messiah.

Paul regularly refers to Jesus as "Lord," and to a lesser extent as "Son" or "Son of God." "Son" or "Son of God" identifies who Jesus is in relationship to God, whereas "Lord" highlights Jesus' exalted status in light of the resurrection. In relationship to God, Jesus is the Son of God. In relationship to believers, he is their Lord, the one whom God has exalted by virtue of the resurrection, and they are his servants.

Paul's gospel is about God's Son (Rom. 1:3, 9), who, through his own death, reconciled humanity to God (Rom. 5:10). In the fullness of time God sent his Son, born of a woman, born under the law, into the world to redeem those who were under the law (Gal. 4:4–5). For Paul the experience of Christ's love is so personal that he can say the Son of God "loved *me* and gave himself for *me*" (Gal. 2:20). Believers have been called into communion (*koinōnia*) with God's Son, whom Paul identifies as Jesus Christ, their Lord (1 Cor. 1:9). By virtue of his resurrection from the dead, the Son is the firstborn of a large family (Rom. 8:29), and believers have been "predestined" to be conformed to the image of God's Son (Rom. 8:29).

Jesus is Lord because he has been raised from the dead. Those who confess that he is Lord and believe that God raised him from the dead will be saved (Rom. 10:13). Because Jesus has been raised from the dead, Paul identifies him as "the Lord of glory" (1 Cor. 2:8), the one bathed in God's own glory. Bathed in the glory of God, Christ is the "image of God" (2 Cor. 4:4), the eschatological Adam. The acknowledgment of his lordship is a confession of faith empowered by the Spirit. Therefore, no one can say that "Jesus is Lord except by the Holy Spirit" (1 Cor. 12:3). For believers there is only one God, who is the Father, and one Lord, who is Jesus Christ, "through whom are all things and through whom we exist" (1 Cor. 8:6). In calling Jesus "Lord," Paul acknowledges that God has exalted Jesus, and that Jesus has entered into the realm where God dwells. Because the risen Lord has entered into the sphere of God, Paul begins his letters with greetings that boldly associate Jesus with God, for example, "Grace to you and peace from God our Father *and* the Lord Jesus Christ" (1 Cor. 1:3).

Paul's Christology is not exhausted by the names and titles he applies to Jesus. For example, his soteriology reveals that Jesus is the justifier, the reconciler, the redeemer, the sanctifier, the liberator, even though Paul never explicitly employs these titles. Moreover, the frequent use Paul makes of expressions such as "in Christ" and "in the Lord" suggests that he views the risen Lord as having transcended the limits of time and space so that believers are already united with him through faith and sacrament. Because believers have been baptized into Christ (Rom. 6:3; Gal. 3:27), they are "the body of Christ" (1 Cor. 12:27).

The manner in which Paul views Christ as a corporate personality is especially evident in his understanding of Christ as the eschatological Adam (Rom. 5:12–21; 1 Cor. 15:21–22, 45–49). The first human being, Adam, introduced sin and death into the world by his disobedience to God. By his obedience to God, the new Adam, Christ, introduced resurrection life into the world. Humanity now stands in solidarity with either Adam or Christ. Those who remain "in Adam" are under the power of sin, which leads to death. Those who have been baptized "into Christ" have been transferred to the realm of God's grace, which leads to life. Christ is the eschatological Adam because he is the new human being, the one in whom humanity sees its destiny because Christ is the firstfruits of the general resurrection from the dead.

Although Paul's Christology is primarily concerned with the salvific event of Christ's death and resurrection, he also speaks of Christ's preexistence. For example, when he says that the spiritual rock that followed Israel in the wilderness was Christ, he intimates that Christ already existed at the time of Israel's wanderings in the wilderness (1 Cor. 10:4). When he says that God in the fullness of time sent his Son, he hints at the incarnation (Gal. 4:4). Paul's most explicit affirmation of preexistence, however, is in the Philippian's hymn (2:6–11), where he affirms that the one who was in the form of God emptied himself and took the form of a slave so that he was found to be in human form. To be sure, Paul's purpose in this hymn is paraenetic rather than speculative. He is more interested in summoning the Philippians to imitate the example of Christ than he is in speculating about Christ's preexistence. But that he speaks about Christ's preexistence is an indication that he views Christ as more than a human being who has been exalted to God's right hand. The Christ of Paul's Christology is God's Son in a unique manner. Paul can go so far as to say that Jesus is God (Rom. 9:5).

The Christ hymn of Col. 1:15–20 dominates and defines the Christology of Colossians. Echoing 2 Cor. 4:4, it affirms that Christ is "the image of the invisible God." Developing Paul's theology of the body of Christ (1 Cor. 12:27), it calls Christ "the head of the body," which is the church. Recalling Paul's metaphor of the risen Christ as the "first fruits of those who have died" (1 Cor. 15:20), it names Christ "the firstborn from the dead." Building upon Paul's understanding of Jesus as the Lord "from whom are all things and for whom we exist" (1 Cor. 8:6), it presents Christ as the one in, through, and for whom all things were created, whether on earth or in heaven. In light of Paul's theology of reconciliation (2 Cor. 5:18–20), it presents Christ as the one in whom the fullness of God dwelt so that through him God was pleased to reconcile all things to himself, whether on earth or in heaven.

As the creative and redemptive agent of God, Christ and his victory are cosmic in scope. He now sits enthroned at "the right hand of God" (Col. 3:1), superior to the cosmic powers (2:10) whom God defeated through Christ's death on the cross (2:15). Consequently, those whom God has rescued from the power of darkness have been transferred "into the kingdom of his beloved Son," in whom they have "redemption and the forgiveness of sin" (1:14). In language that approaches the Johannine doctrine of the incarnation, Colossians writes that "in him [Christ] the whole fullness of deity dwells bodily" (1:19). For Colossians, Christ is the revelation of the mystery of God (1:26; 2:2; 4:3).

Ephesians develops the cosmic Christology of Colossians in relationship to the church, whose head and savior is Christ (Eph. 5:23). God manifested his great power when he raised Christ from the dead "and seated him at his right hand in the heavenly places" (1:20), above every cosmic power. Having put all things under Christ's feet, God has made him "the head over all things for the church" (1:22). In virtue of his resurrection and session at God's right hand, Christ has become the focal point of God's redemptive plan. The elect were chosen "in Christ before the foundation of the world to be holy and blameless" (1:4). Through Christ they were destined for adoption as God's children (1:5), and in him they have "redemption through his blood" (1:7). God's salvific plan, then, is "to gather up all things" in Christ, "in heaven and things on earth" (1:10). In effect, Ephesians develops Paul's Adam theology in a new direction by portraying Christ as the one who "abolished the law with its commandments and ordinances" in order to "create in himself one new humanity" in which Jew and Gentile are at peace with God (2:15). The body of Christ, which is the church, is the place where this new humanity and reconciliation are taking form. Thus the Christology of Ephesians is intimately related to its ecclesiology.

The Pastorals know that Jesus Christ was a descendant of David, that he stood before Pontius Pilate, and that he was raised from the dead (1 Tim. 6:13; 2 Tim. 2:8). They affirm that Christ came into the world to save sinners (1 Tim. 1:15) and that he gave himself as a ransom for all (2:6). Manifested in the flesh, he was vindicated in the Spirit and taken up into glory (3:16). In noting that

Christ is the one mediator between God and humanity, 1 Timothy strongly affirms Christ's humanity (2:5–6).

The most distinctive aspect of the Pastorals' Christology, however, is the manner in which they predicate the title "savior" to God and Christ. First Timothy reserves the title for God (1 Tim. 1:1; 2:3; 4:10), but 2 Timothy and Titus apply it to God (Titus 1:3; 2:10; 3:4) and to Christ (2 Tim. 1:10; Titus 1:4; 3:6). Moreover, the text of Titus 2:13 appears to identify Jesus Christ as "our great God and Savior."[24] The Pastorals predicate "Savior" to both God and Christ because they view the epiphany of Christ as the manifestation of God's grace. The goodness and loving-kindness of the Savior God appeared (Titus 3:4) in the epiphany or manifestation of the Savior Christ Jesus (2 Tim. 1:10). Having been manifested in the flesh at his initial appearing, vindicated in the Spirit by his resurrection, and taken up into glory (1 Tim. 3:16), Christ will appear at the end of the ages to judge the living and the dead (1 Tim. 6:14; 2 Tim. 4:1, 8; Titus 2:13).

Whereas the Christology of the Synoptic tradition begins with Jesus' proclamation of the kingdom of God and seeks to explain how the crucified Jesus can be the Messiah, the Christology of the Pauline tradition focuses on Christ's death and resurrection in order to explain the saving significance of that event. Colossians and Ephesians present this event as cosmic in scope, and the Pastorals view the appearance of Christ, the Savior, in the flesh as the epiphany of God's salvation. Although these two traditions present the person of Jesus from different perspectives, they testify to his unique relationship with God that makes him the bringer of salvation.

The Johannine Tradition

Johannine Christology is traditional and innovative. On the one hand, like the Synoptic tradition it affirms that "Jesus is the Messiah, the Son of God" (John 20:31), and it makes frequent use of the designation "Son of Man." And like the Synoptic tradition it develops its Christology through the story it tells. On the other hand, the Johannine Gospel tells the story of Jesus in a new way, and it understands the confessional titles "Messiah" and "Son of God," as well as Jesus' self-designation as the "Son of Man," from a new perspective, the perspective of the incarnation. Consequently, whereas the Synoptic tradition begins with Jesus' proclamation of the kingdom, and whereas the Pauline tradition focuses on the saving event of Jesus' death and resurrection, the starting point of the Johannine tradition is the incarnation. Jesus the Christ, the Son of God, is the enfleshment of God's eternal word. Everything the Gospel says about Jesus and

---

24. The text, however, could be translated "of the great God, and our savior," in which case "God" is not predicated of Jesus.

everything that he claims for himself is rooted in the climax of the prologue: "And the Word became flesh and lived among us, and we have seen his glory, the glory as of a father's only son, full of grace and truth" (John 1:14).

The Johannine tradition (the Gospel and the Epistles) develops its Christology from the perspective of the incarnation, and it is only in light of the incarnation that one can understand what this tradition means when it identifies Jesus as the Messiah, the Son of God. Jesus' own claims can be summarized in this way. He is the Son whom the Father sent into the world to reveal what he has seen and heard in the Father's presence. Because he is the Son, the Father loves him and "shows him all that he himself is doing" (John 5:20), giving him the power to give life "to whomever he wishes" and giving "all judgment to the Son" (5:21–22). Consequently, Jesus makes numerous claims about himself. He is the bread of life (6:35), the light of the world (8:35), the gate (10:35), the good shepherd (10:11), the resurrection and the life (11:25), the way, and the truth, and the life (14:6), the true vine (15:1). Whereas the Synoptic Jesus proclaims the kingdom of God, the Johannine Jesus proclaims that he is the Son who comes from the Father, the one whom the Father has sent into the world. To believe in the Son of Man is to believe that Jesus is the one whom God sent into the world for the salvation of the world.

As in the Synoptic Gospels, "Messiah" and "Son of God" are the central confessional titles of the Johannine Gospel. But whereas the Synoptic and Pauline traditions disclose the significance of Jesus' messiahship and sonship through Jesus' death and resurrection, in the Johannine tradition it is the incarnation that explains why and how Jesus is the Messiah, the Son of God. The crucial question for the Fourth Gospel concerns Jesus' origin. Where does he come from? The world, which is from below, thinks that it knows Jesus' origin, so it judges that he cannot be the Messiah because he comes from Galilee rather than from Bethlehem (John 7:40–44; see also 7:25–31). What the world does not know and refuses to believe is that Jesus comes from above. He is the Messiah because he is the Son whom the Father sent into the world to reveal what he has seen and heard in the Father's presence. Thus when "the Jews" ask Jesus to tell them if he is the Messiah, he refuses to answer because he knows they will not believe. But he does affirm that he and the Father are one (10:22–30). As the Son of God, the Messiah is the one "whom the Father has sanctified and sent into the world" (10:36).

This new perspective extends to Jesus' use of "Son of Man." For whereas in the Synoptic Gospels Jesus refers to himself as the Son of Man to highlight (1) his present earthly circumstances and authority, (2) his suffering and rejection, and (3) his future vindication, the Johannine Jesus employs this designation to highlight that he is the earthly one who comes from God. In referring to himself as the Son of Man, then, Jesus highlights that he, in all of his humanity, is the point of communication between heaven and earth (1:51). He, in all of his humanity, will ascend to heaven because he comes from heaven (3:13; 6:62). He, in all of his humanity, has been given God's authority to judge (5:27). When he is lifted on the cross, therefore, he will be glorified because his death will be his return to the Father from whom he came (8:28; 12:23; 13:31).

Like the Gospel, the Johannine Epistles develop their Christology from the perspective of the incarnation. But whereas the Gospel communicates its Christology through the story it tells, the letters were written in response to a crisis occasioned by those who denied or misunderstood the significance of the incarnation. Confessing their faith in the Christ, the Son of God, those who had left the community no longer acknowledge that *Jesus*, in all of his humanity, was the Christ, the Son of God. Having developed a Christology that was docetic in nature, they misunderstood the full implications of the Gospel's claim that "the Word became flesh" (John 1:14). In response to this Christology, the Johannine Letters affirm that the one who denies that *Jesus*, in all of his humanity, is the Christ is the antichrist (1 John 2:22; 2 John 7). And they proclaim that the one who confesses that "Jesus Christ has come in the flesh is from God" (1 John 4:2). To confess the Christ, the Son of God, is to confess that the Son was revealed in the death of Jesus on the cross as well as in the waters of Jesus' baptism (5:6). Placing more emphasis on the redemptive nature of Jesus' death than does the Gospel, 1 John affirms that Jesus is an "atoning sacrifice" (*hilasmos*) for sins (2:2; 4:10), a term that recalls Paul's use of *hilastērion* ("a sacrifice of atonement") in Rom. 3:25.

Other Voices

Apart from the three great traditions discussed above, Hebrews makes the most significant contribution to the Christology of the New Testament. Like the great traditions, its most important christological category for identifying Jesus is "Son of God." Thus, even when the author speaks of Jesus as a high priest, he identifies him as "the Son" or "the Son of God" (Heb. 4:14; 5:5; 7:28). Like the Synoptic tradition, the author of Hebrews is aware of Jesus' sufferings during the period of his earthly life (5:7). Like the Pauline tradition, he sees the destiny of humanity already accomplished in Jesus (2:9). Like Colossians, he emphasizes the Son's role in creation (1:2). Like the Johannine tradition, he has intimations of the incarnation (2:14). But unlike any other tradition, he explicitly presents Jesus as a high priest according to the order of Melchizedek who entered into the heavenly sanctuary by his death on the cross in order to deal with sin once and for all. The most significant contribution of this Christology, then, is its soteriological dimension. The death of Jesus upon the cross was a cultic act that dealt with the problem of sin in a way that the sacrifices of the Levitical priesthood could not.

Like the Christology of Hebrews, the Christology of the book of Revelation is both traditional and innovative. It is traditional inasmuch as John the Elder presents Jesus as the Messiah (Rev. 5:5; 11:15; 12:10), the risen Lord, "the first born of the dead" (1:5), the one like the Son of Man (1:13; 14:14). It is innovative, however, in the way he portrays Jesus as the slaughtered lamb (5:6), a striking metaphor that suggests weakness and defeat. In Revelation John employs this expression to emphasize that God's victory occurred on the cross through the death of Jesus. Thus, just as Paul proclaims the wisdom and power of God in the weakness and folly of the cross, so John announces the victory of God in the apparent weakness and defeat of the slaughtered Lamb. By portraying Christ as the slaughtered Lamb, John shows that Jesus is God's powerful Messiah in virtue of his faithful witness unto death. In portraying him as the risen Son of Man, John shows that Jesus is triumphant over death. Having been slaughtered like a lamb, Jesus has been vindicated by God and is "worthy to take the scroll and to open its seals" (5:9). Vindicated by God because of his faithful witness, he is intimately associated with the one who sits on the throne (5:13; 7:10). Like God, he is the Alpha and the Omega (1:8; 22:13), the beginning and the end.

First Peter portrays Christ as the righteous One who suffered for sins once and for all (*hapax*). As the righteous One, he suffered for the sake of the unrighteous in order to bring them to God. Having been put to death in the flesh, he has been brought to life in the spirit by virtue of the resurrection (1 Pet. 3:18). An unblemished lamb, he ransomed others by his precious blood (1:18–19). Although he suffered insult from others, he did not retaliate but bore the sins of others in his body on the cross to free people to live for righteousness (2:23–24). Thus he is the shepherd and guardian of souls (2:25), the chief shepherd of the flock who will appear at the end of the ages (5:4). His sufferings, however, were not unexpected; for the Spirit of Christ had already revealed them to the prophets (1:10–11), suggesting that Christ enjoyed some sort of preexistence with God.

The remaining writings of the New Testament do not develop significant christologies. In its defense of the parousia, however, 2 Peter does provide an interesting witness to Jesus' transfiguration, when God identified Jesus as his beloved Son (2 Pet. 1:16–21). By their references to the "Lord Jesus Christ" James and Jude disclose their understanding of Jesus as the risen Lord (Jas. 1:1; 2:1; 5:7; Jude 17, 25).

The diverse ways in which the writings of the New Testament present Jesus are due, in large measure, to their starting points. Whereas the Synoptic tradition begins with Jesus' ministry of preaching the kingdom, the Pauline tradition focuses on the event of Christ's death and resurrection, and the Johannine tradition begins with the incarnation. Hebrews begins with Christ's sacrifice, Revelation with the victory Christ has won on the cross, and 1 Peter with

Christ's sufferings. Although these diverse starting points lead the New Testament writers to frame their Christologies differently, there is an emerging consensus that the bringer of salvation was God's Messiah, the Son of God. But how does the New Testament portray the community of the sanctified that confesses and worships the bringer of salvation?

THE COMMUNITY OF THE SANCTIFIED

Just as there is an intimate relationship between soteriology and Christology, so there is a nexus between soteriology and ecclesiology.[25] The salvation Christ brings gathers people into a community of believers who have been sanctified and set aside for service to God. But since the writings of the New Testament present their understanding of Christ and the salvation he brings from different starting points, they portray this sanctified community in a variety of ways. For example, the Synoptic tradition presents the church as a community of disciples because it begins with Jesus' proclamation of the kingdom of God. The Pauline tradition portrays the church as a sanctified community, the body of Christ, and the temple of God because it begins with Christ's redemptive death and resurrection. The Johannine tradition portrays the church as a community of disciples who enjoy the communion of the Father and the Son because it begins with the incarnation. For all of these traditions the church is the outcome of God's salvific work in Christ. Those who have been redeemed live in a sanctified community as they wait for the coming of their Lord.

The Synoptic Tradition

Because the kingdom of God is making its appearance in his ministry, Jesus gathers a community of disciples to be with him and to learn from him so that they can proclaim the kingdom of God. The immediate circle of Jesus' disciples consists of "the Twelve," whom Jesus appoints and names as apostles (Mark 3:14). Throughout his ministry, Jesus teaches and instructs them about the kingdom of God and how they are to live as a community in the new age. By appointing the Twelve to be with him and proclaim the kingdom, Jesus indicates that his disciples are the nucleus of a restored Israel that will live in

---

25. On the ecclesiology of the New Testament, see Raymond F. Collins, *The Many Faces of the Church: A Study in New Testament Ecclesiology* (New York: Crossroad, 2003); Mark Bockmuehl and Michael B. Thomason, eds., *A Vision for the Church: Studies in Early Christian Ecclesiology* (Edinburgh: T. & T. Clark, 1997); Howard Clark Kee, *Who Are the People of God? Early Christian Models of Community* (New Haven: Yale University Press, 1995); Paul S. Minear, *Images of the Church in the New Testament* (1960; repr. NTL; Louisville: Westminster John Knox Press, 2004); Rudolf Schnackenburg, *The Church in the New Testament* (New York: Herder & Herder, 1956).

righteousness because God rules over their lives. Because they are the nucleus of this restored Israel, they will judge the tribes of Israel in the eschatological age (Matt. 19:28; Luke 22:30).

Jesus' proclamation of the kingdom of God, however, brings him into conflict with Israel, especially with its leaders who refuse to accept his authority (Matt. 21:23; Mark 11:28; Luke 20:2). Because they reject his ministry, Jesus warns Israel's leaders that the kingdom of God will be taken from them "and given to a people that produces the fruits of the kingdom" (Matt. 21:43). The people to whom Jesus refers are the members of his congregation, his church, which he establishes after Peter confesses that Jesus is the Messiah, the Son of the living God (Matt. 16:16–19).

In the Acts of the Apostles, that portion of Israel that repents and believes that Jesus is the Messiah is the reestablished Israel, over which the twelve apostles rule. Born of the Spirit on Pentecost, this church devotes itself to the teaching of the apostles, holds all things in common, and meets in the temple area (Acts 2:42–47). But just as the religious leaders opposed Jesus, so they oppose those who preach and act in his name. Consequently, Israel is divided over its Messiah. Those who repent and believe in Jesus as the Messiah are the restored and renewed Israel. Those who refuse to repent find themselves, in the words of Gamaliel, "fighting against God" (5:39).

At its inception the Jerusalem church is composed of Jewish believers: Jesus' own disciples and those from Israel who have repented and believed in the gospel. But with the conversion of the household of Cornelius (Acts 10), the beginning of the Pauline mission (Acts 13–14), and the decision of the Jerusalem church not to impose circumcision and the full burden of the Mosaic law upon Gentile converts (15:1–29), the church rapidly expands into Asia Minor, Greece, and even to Rome. Jesus' "little flock" (Luke 12:32) rapidly becomes a community of Gentiles and Jews who call upon the name of the Lord. The Jerusalem church remains a stronghold for thousands of Jewish Christians who are "zealous for the law" (Acts 21:20), but by the end of Acts it appears that the future of the church will be among the Gentiles (see 28:28).

According to the Synoptic Gospels, the church grows out of the community of disciples that Jesus established when he preached the kingdom of God. As the nucleus of a restored Israel, its purpose is to proclaim and witness to the inbreaking rule of God. In the Markan Gospel, this community is Jesus' new family, composed of those who do God's will (Mark 3:33–35). It is to this community that Jesus reveals the mystery of the kingdom (4:11). For the Markan Gospel, with its strong critique of the temple, the church is the new temple of God, "not made with hands" (14:58), that comes into existence with Jesus' death on the cross, when the curtain of the old temple is "torn in two, from top to bottom" (15:38).

In the Matthean Gospel, Jesus' conflict with Israel results in the establishment of a new congregation, the church. Jesus' missionary discourse in chapter 10 provides instruction for the church's missionaries, and his discourse on community life in chapter 18 provides guidance for forgiveness and discipline within the church. In his Great Commission at the close of the Gospel, Jesus commands the eleven disciples to preach the gospel to all the nations (Matt. 28:16–20). Although it does not use the term, the Matthean Gospel appears to conceive of the church as "a new Israel" that replaces historical Israel.

Luke–Acts offers the most complete ecclesiology of the Synoptic tradition. It chronicles the growth of the church from the community of Jesus' disciples to its birth at Pentecost, then narrates how the church's witness to Jesus' resurrection progressed from Jerusalem to Judea, to Samaria, to the ends of the earth, embracing Gentiles as well as Jews. For Acts the church is the restored and reestablished Israel, God's own congregation, which "he obtained with the blood of his own Son" (Acts 20:28). The appearance of the church is the outcome—not the betrayal—of Jesus' preaching of the kingdom. The church is not the kingdom of God but that sphere in which believers already acknowledge God's rule over their lives.

The Pauline Tradition

Paul's understanding of the church grows out of the gospel he preaches about Jesus Christ. The church is the community of those who have been sanctified in Christ and called to be saints (1 Cor. 1:1). Its members have been washed, sanctified, and justified in the name of the Lord Jesus Christ and in the Spirit of God (6:11). They were bought at a price (6:20), through the death of their Lord, who redeemed and freed them from sin. Although *ekklēsia* is the manner in which Paul most frequently identifies the church,[26] the Pauline tradition employs other metaphors as well: the body of Christ, the temple of God, the household of God.

Paul employs *ekklēsia* in a variety of ways. In most instances it refers to a local assembly of believers in a particular city or province, for example, "the church at Cenchreae" (Rom. 16:1), "the churches of Galatia" (Gal. 1:2; 1 Cor. 16:1), "the churches of Asia" (1 Cor. 16:19), or "the churches of Macedonia" (2 Cor. 8:1). But Paul can also speak of "all the churches of the Gentiles" (Rom. 16:4), "all the churches of Christ" (Rom. 16:16), "all the churches of the saints" (1 Cor. 14:33), or simply "all the churches" (2 Cor. 8:18; 11:28). In all of these instances, he has local communities in view. At other times he refers to the

---

26. Rom. 16:1, 4, 5, 16, 23; 1 Cor. 1:2; 4:17; 6:4; 7:17; 10:32; 11:16, 18, 22; 12:28; 14:4, 5, 12, 19, 23, 28, 33, 34, 35; 15:9; 16:1, 19 (twice); 2 Cor. 1:1; 8:1, 18, 19, 23, 24; 11:8, 28; 12:13; Gal. 1:2, 13, 22; Eph. 1:22; 3:10, 21; 5:23, 24, 25, 27, 29, 32; Phil. 3:6; 4:15; Col. 1:18, 24; 4:15, 16; 1 Thess. 1:1; 2:14; 2 Thess. 1:1, 4; 1 Tim. 3:5, 15; 5:16; Phlm. 2.

church in a particular house. For example, there is a church in the house of Prisca and Aquila (Rom. 16:1–5; 1 Cor. 16:19), as there is in the house of Gaius, "who is host to me and to the whole church" (Rom. 16:23).

For Paul the church is an assembly of believers. When discussing abuses at the celebration of the Eucharist, he writes, "when you come together as a church" (1 Cor. 11:18). When addressing the question of spiritual gifts, he notes, "If, therefore, the whole church comes together and all speak in tongues . . ." (1 Cor. 14:23). In these texts, *ekklēsia* refers to a gathering or assembly of God's holy ones rather than to a place or institution. The *ekklēsia* is the local assembly in which the Spirit is active, dispensing gifts for building up the church (1 Cor. 14:4, 5, 12). Without this Spirit, there would be no church.

On several occasions Paul refers to "the church of God," "the churches of God," or simply "the church," but he still has the local congregation in view. In 1 Cor. 15:9 and Gal. 1:13, for example, he describes himself as someone who persecuted "the church of God," undoubtedly referring to the Jerusalem congregation. In 1 Cor. 1:1 and 2 Cor. 1:2, he addresses his letters to "the church of God that is in Corinth," thereby bestowing upon his Gentile congregation a title originally reserved for the Jerusalem church.

In 1 Cor. 10:32 and 11:22, "the church of God," probably still refers to the local community at Corinth, but one starts to detect the beginnings of a different usage wherein "the church of God" has a more general sense.[27] The authors of Colossians and Ephesians may have sensed this, for when they describe the church as the body of Christ, they portray the church as universal in scope.[28]

The body of Christ metaphor, which plays a prominent role in Colossians and Ephesians, appears in only two other Pauline writings, 1 Corinthians and Romans. But since Colossians and Ephesians may have been written by others in Paul's name, they probably develop the concept of the church as the body of Christ on the basis of what they found in 1 Corinthians and Romans.

The "body of Christ" can refer to the crucified body of Christ (Rom. 7:4) or to the eucharistic body of Christ (1 Cor. 10:16). But in 1 Cor. 12:27 Paul relates it to the Corinthian church ("Now you are the body of Christ and individually members of it"), as is apparent from the next verse: "And God has appointed *in the church* first apostles, second prophets, third teachers" (12:28).[29]

Paul does not develop an abstract theology of the church as the body of Christ. Rather, he employs the concept in response to problems plaguing the

---

27. This is the suggestion of Joseph A. Fitzmyer, *Paul and His Theology: A Brief Sketch* (2nd ed.; Englewood Cliffs, NJ: Prentice-Hall, 1989), 96.

28. In Ephesians and Colossians, *ekklēsia* has all but lost its local sense. See Eph. 1:22; 3:10, 21; 5:23, 24, 25, 27, 29, 32; Col. 1:18, 24. However, Col. 4:15 and 16 refer to a local congregation.

29. The Greek text of 1 Cor. 12:27 does not have a definite article (*hymeis de este sōma Christou*) and could be translated, "you are a body belonging to Christ."

Corinthian community. For example, in 1 Cor. 10:14–22 he warns that participation in the table of the Lord (the Eucharist) and the table of demons (idol worship) is mutually exclusive. In making his argument, he reminds the Corinthians that the Eucharist is a sharing in the "body of Christ," and then he notes, "Because there is one bread, we who are many are one body" (10:17). In 12:12–26 Paul employs an extended metaphor of the body to remind the Corinthians that just as there are many members in a human body, each with its own role, so the church has many members, each with spiritual gifts: "For just as the body is one and has many members, and all the members of the body, though many, are one body, so it is with Christ. For in the one Spirit we were all baptized into one body—Jews or Greeks, slaves or free—and we were all made to drink of one Spirit" (12:13). After explaining the need for diversity in the human body (12:14–26), Paul tells the Corinthians that they are the body of Christ (12:27). Then employing *ekklēsia* for the first time with this image, he lists the different ministries and gifts God has appointed for the church (12:27–31).

In 1 Cor. 12:12–31 and Rom. 12:3–8, Paul has the local community in view when he speaks of the body of Christ, and he uses the metaphor to highlight the different gifts and functions within the local congregation. But the church is not merely like a body. It *is* one body in Christ because its members participate in the eucharistic body of Christ (1 Cor. 10:16–17). The local *ekklēsia* participates in, and belongs to, the body of Christ because its members have been baptized into Christ's body (12:13) and share his eucharistic body (10:16). As members of Christ's body, each has a different function for the common good. Therefore, when Paul asks the factious Corinthian community, "Has Christ been divided?" (1:13), he is referring to the church at Corinth. When he tries to dissuade the Corinthians from immorality by reminding them that their bodies are members of Christ (6:15), he is speaking to them as members of the church whose bodies are members of Christ.

Colossians and Ephesians develop Paul's metaphor of the body in a new way. First, whereas Paul speaks of the body of Christ, the authors of these letters speak of Christ as the "head" (*kephalē*) of the body, which is the church (Col. 1:18; 2:19; Eph. 1:22–23; 4:15–16; 5:23). This new image allows the authors to explain the relationship between Christ and his church more clearly than Paul did in Romans 12 and 1 Corinthians 12. For example, the author of Colossians notes that the church is nourished by the head, who is Christ, and grows with a growth that comes from God (Col. 2:19). In a similar way, the author of Ephesians exhorts his audience to grow into Christ who is the head, from whom the whole body grows (Eph. 4:15–16). The author also combines the head and body metaphor with the metaphor of marriage (5:22–33). Comparing the relationship of Christ and his church to the relationship of husband and wife, he describes Christ as the head of the church, his body, of which he is the Savior. Because he loved the church and handed himself over for it to make it holy, the church should be subject to Christ, who nourishes and cares for the church, which is his body.

Second, when the authors of Colossians and Ephesians identify the church as the body of Christ, they understand *ekklēsia* in a more universal sense than Paul did. Here *ekklēsia* refers to the whole church as a single entity. Accordingly, God has subjected all things to Christ and made him head over all things for the sake of the church, which is Christ's body (Eph. 1:22–23). Christ, in turn, has created a new humanity in himself so that he might reconcile Gentile and Jew in one body through the cross (2:15–16). Accordingly, the church is the showpiece of Christ's work of reconciliation. It is filled with the "fullness" of Christ who is filling all things with the fullness of God (1:23).[30] In the church, God reveals the mystery, hidden for ages but now revealed to the holy apostles and prophets, that "the Gentiles have become fellow heirs, members of the same body, and sharers in the promise in Christ Jesus through the gospel" (3:6).

The temple of God is akin to the body of Christ metaphor. Aware that those who are in Christ have been called, elected, sanctified, and set apart for worship in the Spirit, Paul views the church as the temple of God. He reminds the Corinthian community that they are God's holy temple because God's Spirit dwells in them (1 Cor. 3:16–17). As the temple of the living God, believers are as different from unbelievers as is light from darkness (2 Cor. 6:16). Employing similar imagery, the author of Ephesians reminds his Gentile audience that they are now "citizens with the saints and also members of the household of God" (Eph. 2:19). Built on the foundation of the apostles and prophets, with Christ as the cornerstone, they are growing into a holy temple in the Lord (Eph. 2:21).

The metaphor of the household of God, first mentioned in Eph. 2:19, plays an important role in the Pastoral Epistles, which view the church as a vast household, governed by God's stewards and servants. The imagery allows the author of the Pastorals to present the church as an ordered community in which all the members know their role and place, but this metaphor lacks the vibrancy of Paul's understanding of the church as a Spirit-filled community or the mystical quality of the church in the body of Christ metaphor as developed in Colossians and Ephesians. Nevertheless, the author is aware that the church is more than an organization; it is a people for whom Jesus Christ gave himself so that he might "purify for himself a people of his own who are zealous for good deeds" (Titus 2:14).

The church plays a central role in Pauline theology because it is the community of the redeemed, the place where God's redemptive work can be seen. It is a community of those who have been chosen and consecrated for service

---

30. Here "fullness" (*plērōma*) refers to the very being of God.

to God. Whereas the nondisputed Pauline writings focus on the church as a local Spirit-filled community, the other letters begin to view the church as a cosmic reality or as the household of God that preserves the rich deposit of faith. All of the letters, however, emphasize that the church is the place where God's redemptive work in Christ can be experienced. The manner in which the Pauline tradition relates Israel and the church is more complex. Although Paul insists that God has not rejected his people (Rom. 11:1), he writes, "not all Israelites truly belong to Israel" (Rom. 9:6). For Paul the church is "the Israel of God" (Gal. 6:16), the community of those who have been justified on the basis of faith in Christ. For Ephesians the church is the place where a new humanity is taking form, the body of Christ, in which Jew and Gentile are reconciled to each other (Eph. 2:11–18).

The Johannine Tradition

Because the Johannine tradition begins with the incarnation, its understanding of the church focuses on the intimate relationship between Jesus and his disciples.[31] Unlike the world, which refuses to believe that Jesus comes from the Father, Jesus' disciples believe that he is the one whom the Father has sent into the world. Unlike those who abandon Jesus, they confess that he has "the words of eternal life" (John 6:68). Consequently, Jesus calls the disciples his "friends" to whom he has revealed everything he has heard from his Father (15:15). It was not the disciples who chose him; it was Jesus who chose them and appointed them to go and bear fruit that will last (15:16).

The Johannine Gospel explains the intimate relationship that exists between Jesus and his disciples through the metaphor of the vine (15:1–10). Jesus is the vine; his Father is the vinegrower; and the disciples are the branches. The disciples abide in Jesus, and he abides in them (15:4). Jesus loves the disciples just as the Father has loved him. If they keep his commandments, they will abide in his love just as he has kept the Father's commandments and abides in God's love (15:9–10). Thus the church abides in Jesus, who abides in the Father. Jesus prays that his Father will sanctify the disciples in truth, which is the word he has revealed to them from the Father (17:17). He also prays that future generations of disciples will be one so that as the Father dwells in Jesus, and Jesus dwells in the Father, the disciples may dwell in Jesus and the Father. By this example of love, the world will come to believe that the Father sent Jesus into the world (17:20–21).

The Johannine tradition is aware of the role that the salvific event of Jesus' death and resurrection played in the creation of the church. When alluding to his crucifixion, Jesus says "And I, when I am lifted up from the earth, will draw

---

31. The word "church" appears only three times in the Johannine tradition (3 John 6, 9, 10).

all people to myself" (12:32). In his discourse on the good shepherd, he identifies himself as the good shepherd who lays down his life for the sheep (10:11, 15). The church is the community of those drawn to Jesus by his death on the cross. Its members are the sheep for whom he lays down his life. Although the disciples are saddened by the prospect of his departure, Jesus assures them that his return to the Father—his death—is advantageous for them. For when he returns to the Father, he will send them the Advocate, the Holy Spirit, who will teach them everything and remind them of all that he has said (14:26).

In chapter 21, which is often viewed as an epilogue or appendix to the Gospel, the risen Lord reconstitutes his scattered sheep and designates Simon Peter to feed his lambs and sheep (21:15–19). This scene has a number of interesting connections with other Gospel texts. On the one hand, it describes how the risen Lord reconstitutes his scattered flock, an encounter the Markan Gospel suggests but never describes (Mark 14:28; 16:7). On the other, it highlights the ministry Peter exercises in the reconstituted flock, a ministry reminiscent of the ministry Jesus promises Peter, after Peter's confession at Caesarea Philippi (Matt. 16:17–20). It also recalls Jesus' word to Peter at the Last Supper: "Simon, Simon, listen! Satan has demanded to sift all of you like wheat, but I have prayed for you that your own faith may not fail; and you, when once you have turned back, strengthen your brothers" (Luke 22:31–32).

Viewed from the vantage point of the Gospel, the Johannine church is a chosen community of disciples who believe that Jesus has come from the Father. Its members enjoy an intimate relationship with Jesus and the Father. Guided by the Advocate, this community stands in stark contrast to the world that hates it just as it hated Jesus.

The incarnation is the starting point for the ecclesiology of the Johannine Epistles as is apparent from the manner in which these letters identify those who belong to the community and those who do not. Those who do not confess that Jesus Christ has come in the flesh are deceivers and antichrists, who have gone into the world (2 John 7). In contrast to them stands the authentic community of those who believe Jesus is the Christ, the Son of God. Those who hold to this faith have fellowship/communion (*koinōnia*) with the original witnesses of the Gospel tradition who testify to "what was from the beginning, what we have heard, what we have seen with our eyes, what we have looked at and touched with our hands, concerning the word of life" (1 John 1:1). Those who are in fellowship with the original witnesses are in communion with "the Father and with his Son Jesus Christ" (1:3). The members of this community acknowledge their sins because they know that Jesus is the atoning sacrifice for their sins and for the sins of the whole world (2:2). They dwell in the light because they love the members of the church. Although what they will be has not yet been revealed, they know that they are already God's children (3:2). They belong to God, whereas the "whole world lies under the power of the evil one" (5:19).

Because of its new starting point, Johannine ecclesiology stands somewhere between the ecclesiology of the Synoptic tradition and that of the Pauline tradition. Like the Synoptic tradition, it views the church as a community of disciples. Although it does not develop the theme, it is aware that Jesus has chosen "the twelve" (John 6:71). But whereas the Synoptic tradition views the church in light of the inbreaking kingdom of God, the Johannine tradition develops its understanding of the church in light of the revelation that the incarnate One brings from the Father. Because of this revelation, the Johannine community is in intimate communion with the Son and with the Father. Like the Pauline tradition, then, the Johannine tradition emphasizes the intimate, almost mystical, relationship that believers enjoy with their Lord. But whereas the Pauline tradition does this through the metaphor of the body of Christ, the Johannine tradition accomplishes this through the metaphor of the vine and the branches. For the Pauline tradition believers are in Christ because they have been baptized into his death and resurrection; for the Johannine tradition they are in communion with Christ because they have believed in the revelation he brings from the Father.

Although the Johannine Gospel (but not the Epistles) makes frequent references to "the Jews," it does not struggle with the question of Israel and the church in the way that the Gospel of Matthew, Luke–Acts, and Romans 9–11 do. The Gospel affirms that "salvation is from the Jews" (John 4:22) and says that if people believed in Moses they would believe in Jesus (5:46), but it does not present the community of Jesus' disciples as a new or restored Israel. Nor is it as explicitly interested in the Gentile question as the Synoptic Gospels are.[32] For the Fourth Gospel, Jesus has become the new temple (2:19–22), the place where people will worship God in Spirit and truth (4:23). Jesus is the one who replaces Israel's feasts. The community of Jesus' disciples is not so much a new Israel or the restored people of God as it is a new entity born of the Son's revelation from the Father. Those who do not belong to this new community belong to the world, the sphere of darkness that refuses to embrace God's truth.

Other Voices

Apart from its use in the book of Revelation, *ekklēsia* occurs only three times in the remaining writings of the New Testament (Heb. 2:12; 12:23; Jas. 5:14).[33]

---

32. It does manifest an interest in the Gentiles in John 12:20–23. When the Greeks express their desire to Philip to see Jesus, Jesus realizes that the hour has come for the Son of Man to be glorified.

33. In the book of Revelation it occurs in 1:4, 11, 20; 2:1, 7, 8, 11, 12, 17, 18, 23, 29; 3:1, 6, 7, 13, 14, 22; 22:16. The term *syneklektē* (literally, "chosen together") in 1 Pet. 5:13 may also refer to the church, thus the translation of the NRSV, "sister church."

But inasmuch as Hebrews, James, 1 and 2 Peter, Jude, and the book of Revelation address particular churches that are experiencing problems from within and outside the church, they contribute to the New Testament's understanding of the church.

First Peter offers the most significant ecclesiology of these writings. Its author addresses the recipients as "exiles of the Dispersion . . . who have been chosen and destined by God the Father and sanctified by the Spirit to be obedient to Jesus Christ and to be sprinkled with his blood" (1 Pet. 1:1–2). For 1 Peter the church is (1) a sanctified community, (2) in exile from its true homeland, (3) brought into existence by Christ's death. The members of this sanctified community are "living stones," and they are being built into a "spiritual house" whose cornerstone is Christ (1 Peter 4–5). The people of this spiritual house are "a holy priesthood" that offers spiritual sacrifices to God through the mediation of Jesus Christ (2:5). They are "a chosen race, a royal priesthood, a holy nation, God's own people" (2:9). The book of Revelation makes a similar point when John says that Jesus Christ "made us to be a kingdom, priests serving his God and Father" (Rev. 1:6; see also 5:10; 20:6). There are "elders" (*presbyteroi*) in the church that 1 Peter addresses (1 Pet. 5:1), as there are in the congregation that the Letter of James addresses (Jas. 5:14). The "chief shepherd" (*archipoimenos*) of the flock, however, is Christ (1 Pet. 5:4).

The book of Revelation offers two perspectives on the church. The letters to the seven churches in Asia Minor portray the church in the midst of its earthly struggle (Revelation 2–3). If the church on earth is to conquer, it must witness to God and the Lamb and resist every temptation to compromise with Satan and the beast. The remaining visions of the book of Revelation present the struggles the church is presently enduring from the point of view of God. Having been taken into the heavenly court, John is shown the victorious church: an army of martyrs, the 144,000 (7:1–8; 14:1–5) who shed their blood for the Lamb, and he sees the Holy City, the new Jerusalem, where those who have conquered will dwell (21:9–14). In addition to the vision of the 144,000, John sees a great multitude "from every nation, from all tribes and peoples and languages" (7:9), an indication that the victorious church will be composed of Gentiles as well as of Jews. The church is both new and in continuity with Israel.

The Letter of James emphasizes continuity with Israel when James addresses the recipients as "the twelve tribes in the Dispersion" (Jas. 1:1), encouraging them to be doers of the word by persevering in "the perfect law, the law of liberty" (1:25). The church is a community guided by wisdom from above (3:15, 17). In it the elect live in friendship with God rather than in friendship with the world (4:4).

The author of Hebrews employs numerous examples from Israel's Scriptures, and he exhorts the recipients to persevere so that they can enter into God's Sabbath rest (Heb. 3:7–4:11). Like Israel's ancestors, the church is still in search of a heavenly homeland (11:16), though it has approached "the city of the living God, the heavenly Jerusalem . . . the assembly of the firstborn who are enrolled in heaven" (12:22–23). Despite the use of imagery from Israel's Scriptures, the author sees little continuity between historical Israel and the church. A "new covenant" has appeared, making the first one obsolete (8:13), suggesting that the church has replaced Israel.

Second Peter and Jude do not develop significant images or metaphors for the church, in part because they must warn the church of false teachers who threaten the life of the community (2 Pet. 2:1–3; Jude 3–4). Their admonitions remind the church that evil can come from within as well as from outside the church.

The ecclesiology of the New Testament is complex, making use of a variety of images and metaphors. The church is a community of disciples, a sanctified community, the temple of God, a spiritual building, the body of Christ, the twelve tribes of the Dispersion, the wandering people of God, the flock of the good shepherd, the true vine, to mention only a few images and metaphors. Although the New Testament writers have different starting points for their ecclesiology, they agree on one point: the church has come into existence through Christ's death and resurrection. But how is this new community to live in the period between its Lord's resurrection and parousia?

THE MORAL LIFE OF THE SANCTIFIED

Just as the experience of salvation determines the way in which the New Testament writers understand the person of Jesus and the community of the sanctified that believes in him, so this experience of salvation determines the way in which the writers of the New Testament exhort believers to live within this sanctified community.[34] Put another way, "the indicative of salvation" (what God has done in Christ) grounds "the moral imperative" (how believers ought to live in Christ). The community of those who have been sanctified in and through Christ ought to live in a way that corresponds to the gift they have received.

The writers of the New Testament, however, structure the moral life of the sanctified community differently because they have diverse starting points. For example, the Synoptic Gospels begin with Jesus' preaching of the kingdom of God, thereby making the kingdom the moral horizon for Jesus' moral teach-

---

34. On the moral teaching of the New Testament, see Richard B. Hays, *The Moral Vision of the New Testament: A Contemporary Introduction to New Testament Ethics* (New York: HarperCollins, 1996); Frank J. Matera, *New Testament Ethics: The Legacies of Jesus and Paul* (Louisville: Westminster John Knox Press, 1996); Wolfgang Schrage, *The Ethics of the New Testament* (Philadelphia: Fortress, 1988); Rudolf Schnackenburg, *Die sittliche Botschaft des Neuen Testaments*, 2 vols. (HTKNT Sup 1–2; Freiburg: Herder, 1986–88).

ing, whereas the Johannine tradition begins with the incarnation, making faith in Jesus, the one who comes from the Father, the moral horizon of these writings. In the Pauline tradition and most other New Testament writings, God's redemptive work in Christ's death and resurrection is the moral horizon of the ethical demands these writings make.

The different ways in which the New Testament writers understand and express their soteriology, then, influences how they present the moral imperatives of the gospel. All of these writers, however, agree that the moral life should be lived within a sanctified community of like-minded believers.

The Synoptic Tradition

Jesus does not so much develop a new set of ethical requirements as he refocuses Israel's moral demands in light of the inbreaking kingdom of God. Because the kingdom of God is making its appearance in his ministry, he summons Israel to repent and believe that the kingdom is at hand (Matt. 4:17; Mark 1:14–15; Luke 4:43; 5:32). Repentance entails turning from sin in order to do God's will in light of the inbreaking kingdom. For example, in the Markan Gospel Jesus identifies those who do the will of God as the members of his new family, which is being established by the appearance of the kingdom (Mark 3:34–35). In his dispute with Israel's religious leaders, he accuses them of abandoning God's commandment in favor of their religious traditions (7:8), and he teaches that moral impurity comes from within rather than from outside a person (7:17–23). In his teaching on divorce, Jesus returns to God's will as originally expressed in the book of Genesis (Mark 10:6–9), and when asked what is the first commandment, he responds that the two most important commandments are to love God and to love one's neighbor as oneself (12:28–31). Although the Markan evangelist notes that Jesus declared all foods clean (7:19), he does not portray Jesus as challenging or abolishing the law. When a rich man asks Jesus what he must do to inherit eternal life, Jesus quotes from the Decalogue (10:19). When the man responds that he has kept the commandments from his youth, Jesus summons him to do more than the law requires: to sell his possessions and give the money to the poor and to follow him (10:21).

The Gospels of Matthew and Luke summarize Jesus' moral teaching in their distinctive accounts of his great sermon: the Sermon on the Mount (Matthew 5–7) and the Sermon on the Plain (Luke 6:17–49). The Matthean Gospel insists that Jesus has come not to destroy the law and the prophets but to fulfill them. Therefore, Jesus challenges his disciples to practice a righteousness that exceeds the righteousness of the scribes and the Pharisees (Matt. 5:17–20). In providing his own commentary on certain aspects of Israel's law, Jesus intensifies the demands of the law by requiring his disciples to do more than the law requires (5:21–48). He summarizes the law and the prophets by saying, "In everything do to others as you would have them do to you" (7:12). When identifying love of God and love of neighbor as the two great commandments, the Matthean Jesus adds, "On these two commandments hang all the law and the prophets" (22:40), thereby revealing that these two commandments function as Jesus' hermeneutical principle for interpreting the law and the prophets.

The ethical demands of Jesus' Sermon on the Plain in Luke's Gospel do not make any reference to the Mosaic law or to the prophets. Composed with a Gentile audience in view, this version of Jesus' great sermon requires disciples to love their enemies and not to judge each other. Revoking the law of reciprocity, Jesus asks his disciples what credit there is in loving those who love them since even sinners do the same (Luke 6:32). Then, invoking the law of reciprocity, he promises that if they are merciful and do not judge others, God will not judge them (6:37). As in the Gospels of Mark and Matthew, the commandment to love God and one's neighbor plays a central role in the moral teaching of the Lukan Jesus. But in the Lukan Gospel, Jesus defines what he means by the neighbor through the parable of the Good Samaritan (10:30–37).

The Gospels of Matthew and Luke enhance Jesus' moral teaching in two ways. First, the Matthean Gospel emphasizes the importance of doing what Jesus commands and warns its audience that there is an impending judgment that no one can escape. Second, the Lukan Gospel warns disciples about the danger of riches and the misuse of possessions. This is not to suggest that these themes are exclusive to these Gospels. The Markan and Lukan Gospels know that there will be a final judgment, and the Matthean and Markan Gospels are aware of the dangers that riches and possessions pose. But the theme of judgment plays a more central role in the Matthean Gospel (Matt. 13:36–43; 25:31–46), just as the theme of possessions plays a more important role in the Lukan Gospel (Luke 12:13–21; 16:1–13). Because the kingdom of God is making its appearance in his ministry, Jesus warns his disciples that they must "do" what he commands them (Matt. 7:13–27; Luke 6:43–49). Because the kingdom is at hand, his disciples must be prepared to leave *all* of their possessions in order to follow him (Mark 10:28; Matt. 19:27; Luke 14:33).

The Acts of the Apostles provides an interesting example of how the early church adapted the moral demands of its Lord. Whereas Jesus' original followers embraced an itinerant ministry that required them to leave family and home (Luke 9:57–62), the early church lived as a community of believers whose members shared their possessions in common (Acts 2:42–47; 4:32–35). The kingdom of God continues to be an integral part of the church's teaching, but, as the final words of Acts indicate, Jesus has now become an integral part of the church's message: "He [Paul] lived there two whole years at his own expense and welcomed all who came to him, *proclaiming the kingdom of God and teaching about the Lord Jesus Christ* with all boldness and without hindrance" (Acts 28:30–31).

Since the Lukan Gospel has already presented the moral teaching of Jesus, there is no need for Acts to repeat this instruction. The readers of Acts can assume that the apostles' teaching about Jesus includes Jesus' teaching about the moral life. In Acts the fundamental moral imperative is that people should repent and be baptized in the name of Jesus Christ for the forgiveness of their sins (Acts 2:38). Apart from this imperative, Acts communicates its ethical teaching through the stories it tells. The manner in which the central characters of Acts live out their lives provides future generations with examples for living their Christian lives.

The Pauline Tradition

Whereas the moral horizon of the Synoptic tradition is the inbreaking kingdom of God, the moral horizon of the Pauline tradition is the saving event of Christ's death and resurrection.[35] Paul and those who wrote in his name call upon their converts to live in a particular way because of the new life they have received in and through God's work in Christ. This relationship between the indicative of salvation and the moral imperative is apparent in the structure of several Pauline letters. For example, in Romans, after presenting his teaching on justification by faith, Paul begins his moral exhortation, "I appeal to you therefore, brothers and sisters, by the mercies of God, to present your bodies as a living sacrifice, holy and acceptable to God, which is your spiritual worship. Do not be conformed to this world, but be transformed by the renewing of your minds, so that you may discern what is the will of God—what is good and acceptable and perfect" (Rom. 12:1–2). In the exhortation that follows (12:1–15:13), Paul draws out the moral implications of the gospel he has developed in the first eleven chapters of the letter. Believers must offer themselves to God. Why? Because God has been merciful to them. Believers must no longer conform themselves to this age but be transformed by the renewal of their minds. Why? Because they have been incorporated into the new Adam, the realm of God's Spirit, where it is possible to discern God's will. The moral instruction of Romans 12–15:13, then, is intimately related to Paul's teaching about the righteousness of God and the justification of the believer. Indeed, if Paul could not produce such a moral exhortation, his gospel of justification by faith would be in vain.

The same pattern occurs in Galatians. After defending his gospel of justification by faith in Gal. 1:1–5:12, Paul begins his moral exhortation in this way: "For you were called for freedom, brothers and sisters; only do not use your freedom as an opportunity for self-indulgence, but through love become slaves

---

35. On Paul's ethic see James D. G. Dunn, *The Theology of Paul the Apostle* (Grand Rapids: Eerdmans, 1998), 625–69, to which many of the ideas in this section are indebted.

to one another" (5:13). Paul then develops an extended moral exhortation that shows how the moral life of the justified is related to his teaching on justification by faith (5:13–6:10). Although the justified are no longer under the law since they have been incorporated into Christ, the Spirit leads and guides them, producing the fruit of the moral life within them.

The pattern also occurs in Colossians and Ephesians. In the first two chapters of Colossians, Paul presents Christ as the one in, through, and for whom the world was created and reconciled to God. Then, on the basis of this cosmic Christology, he exhorts his converts to live a moral life: "So if then you have been raised with Christ, seek the things that are above, where Christ is, seated at the right hand of God" (Col. 3:1). The ethical teaching that follows in chapters 3–4 is the working out of the gospel Paul presents in the first two chapters of the letter. In Ephesians, after an extended teaching on reconciliation in chapters 1–3, Paul begins his moral exhortation in this way, "I therefore, the prisoner in the Lord, beg you to lead a life worthy of the calling to which you have been called" (Eph. 4:1). The moral exhortation that follows in chapters 4–6 instructs believers how to live as a community that has been reconciled in and through Christ.

Although the Pastorals do not present the same kind of structure, the moral imperative of these letters remains grounded in the indicative of salvation inasmuch as the author argues that the ability to perform good works depends upon sound teaching. The grace of God, which has made its appearance in Christ Jesus, trains believers "to renounce impiety and worldly passions, and in the present age to live lives that are self-controlled, upright, and godly" (Titus 2:12). Those who reject sound teaching will be incapable of doing good works. The sound teaching of the gospel, then, summons and equips believers to live a morally good life.

This relationship between the indicative of salvation and the moral imperative is also evident in a number of statements in which Paul exhorts his converts to live a morally good life. For example, in Gal. 5:25 he writes, "If we live by the Spirit, let us also be guided by the Spirit." In 1 Corinthians Paul warns his converts not to engage in prostitution, since their bodies are members of Christ and temples of the Holy Spirit. Indeed, they have been purchased at the price of Christ's death (1 Cor. 6:15–20). Consequently, it is incongruous for them to engage in immorality. In Rom. 6:1 Paul asks, "What then are we to say? Should we continue in sin in order that grace may abound?" He then explains why believers should not persist in sin: "we have been buried with him by baptism into death, so that, just as Christ was raised from the dead by the glory of the Father, so we too might walk in newness of life" (Rom. 6:4). The manner in which Paul concludes this comparison ("so we too might walk in newness of life") is surprising, since one might have expected him to write, "just as Christ was raised from the dead by the glory of the Father, *so we will be raised from the dead.*" But instead of completing the analogy in this way, he employs the believer's baptismal union with Christ to motivate his converts to live a morally good life. Having been united with Christ through baptism, believers have died to an old way of life so that they "might walk in newness of life."

Paul (and those who wrote in his name) does not provide his converts with an entirely new ethic. Like Jesus, he presupposes the moral heritage of Israel, even when he tells his converts that they are no longer under the law. He never makes an explicit distinction between the moral and cultic aspects of the law, although he assumes that those who are in Christ are no longer bound by the law's ritual prescriptions. Believers are no longer under the regime of the law, but their behavior should not violate its moral prescriptions.

It should not be surprising, then, that the Pauline Letters contain extensive lists of virtues to strive for and vices to avoid. In Romans he writes, "let us live honorably as in the day, not in reveling and drunkenness, not in debauchery and licentiousness, not in quarreling and jealousy" (Rom. 13:13). In Philippians he exhorts the community, "whatever is true, whatever is honorable, whatever is just, whatever is pure, whatever is pleasing, whatever is commendable, if there is any excellence and if there is anything worthy of praise, think about these things" (Phil. 4:8–9). In the Pastorals, Paul tells Timothy to pursue "righteousness, godliness, faith, love, endurance, gentleness" (1 Tim. 6:11). Similar exhortations are found in Col. 3:5–17 and Eph. 4:25–32.

Because most of his converts came from and lived in a Gentile world, which was often marked by sexual excess and idolatrous worship, Paul cautions them to avoid immorality of every kind. He expects his converts to avoid the kind of immorality already condemned in Israel's Scriptures and to practice the kind of behavior that many Hellenistic moral philosophers extolled. So he reminds the Thessalonians that they should abstain from fornication because God's will for them is their sanctification (1 Thess. 4:3).

The distinctive aspect of the Pauline moral tradition is not to be sought in a new moral code, as if Paul and his followers developed an ethic entirely different from that in Israel's Scriptures or in the writings of the Hellenistic moral philosophers. Rather, it is present in the way the Pauline tradition relates the moral life of believers to the person of Christ. In some instances, Christ provides a model for the moral life of the believer. For example, in Romans Paul writes, "We who are strong ought to put up with the failings of the weak, and not to please ourselves. Each of us must please our neighbor for the good purpose of building up the neighbor. For Christ did not please himself" (Rom. 15:1–3). In Philippians he employs the example of Christ to present the Philippians with a pattern for their own behavior. Just as Christ humbled himself, so they should "do nothing from selfish ambition or conceit, but in humility regard others as better than yourselves. Let each of you look not to your own interests, but to the interests of others" (Phil. 2:3–4). In other instances, it is the believer's intimate association with Christ's death and resurrection that provides the motivation for the moral life of the believer. Believers have been baptized into Christ's death (Rom. 6:3), they have been raised up with him (Col. 3:1). They are even seated with him in the heavenly places (Eph. 2:6) inasmuch as they belong to his body, the church. Because they are so intimately related to Christ through the mystery of his death, resurrection, and exaltation, they are to live lives worthy of their calling.

The Pauline tradition grounds the moral imperative in the indicative of salvation. Believers ought to act in a morally good way because they have been called, justified, reconciled, sanctified, and saved in and through Christ. They can act in this new way because the power of the Spirit is at work in them, leading and guiding them. They have been raised up with Christ, and they are the beneficiaries of sound teaching that trains them to do good works.

The Johannine Tradition

Whereas the starting point for the moral teaching of the Synoptic tradition is Jesus' gospel about the kingdom and the starting point for the Pauline tradition is the gospel about Jesus Christ, the starting point for the moral teaching of the Johannine tradition is the incarnation. As the incarnation of the eternal Word of God, Jesus is the Son whom the Father sent into the world to reveal the Father to the world in order to save the world from the darkness of sin. The fundamental moral demand of the Fourth Gospel, then, is to believe in Jesus as the one whom the Father sent into the world. Consequently, when the crowds ask Jesus what they must do to perform *the works of God*, he responds, "This is *the work of God*, that you believe in him whom he has sent" (6:29). God does not require a multiplicity of works but a singular work: faith in the one whom God sent into the world.

The Son's proclamation that the Father sent him into the world to reveal the Father to the world is the Johannine equivalent of Jesus' proclamation of the kingdom of God in the Synoptic Gospels. Just as the inbreaking of God's rule summons people to live a new life, so the revelation the Son brings from the Father calls people to live in a new way. By disclosing what he has heard and seen in the presence of the Father, the Son reveals the Father's love for the world and the sin of the world. By embracing this revelation, those who believe that Jesus comes from the Father see themselves and the world in an entirely new way. For the first time, they perceive that what the world calls truth is a lie, what the world calls light is darkness, and what the world calls life is death. In the light of the Son's revelation, they comprehend that they have been living in the darkness of sin that leads to eternal separation from God. The revelation that the Son brings from the Father, then, is salvific because it enables believers to see themselves and the world as they truly are before God, who is light. In light of this revelation that comes from the Father, they understand that they can and must live in a new way.

In the Fourth Gospel, the Johannine Jesus describes this new life as abiding in love. Before returning to the Father who sent him into the world, Jesus gives his disciples a new commandment: they should love one another as he loved them (John 13:34; see also 15:11–17). In giving this commandment to his disciples, Jesus does not quote from Deut. 6:4–5 and Lev. 19:18, as he does in the Synoptic Gospels. The object of this new commandment is not one's neighbor, much less one's enemies, but one's fellow disciple. The Johannine love commandment is a *new* commandment because Jesus "gives" it to his disciples as his parting gift before he returns to the Father. The primary content of this new commandment is the love that his disciples should have for one another because of the intimate relation they enjoy with him. By keeping his commandments they abide in his love, just as he has kept his Father's commandments and abides in the Father's love (John 15:10).

The Johannine love commandment is exclusive, not because Jesus and his disciples hate the world but because only those in communion with Jesus and the Father can extend this kind of love to one another. As others come to believe that Jesus comes from the Father, they will be included in this communion of love.

The Johannine Epistles develop their teaching about the moral life in response to those who have left the community and no longer confess "that Jesus Christ has come in the flesh" (2 John 7). From the point of view of the epistles, the secessionists have betrayed Jesus' commandment that his disciples should love one another. By leaving the community and denying that *Jesus* is the Christ, the secessionists no longer love the members of the community; they no longer love God's children. In the face of this crisis, 1 John reminds those who continue to believe that Jesus is the Christ that to be in communion with God they must walk in the light and acknowledge their sins (1 John 1:5–10). Referring to Jesus' new commandment as "an old commandment," which the community has known from the beginning, 1 John warns believers that those who claim to be in the light but hate the members of the community are in the darkness. Walking in the light means loving those who believe that Jesus is the Christ (2:7–11). The primary ethical requirement for the community of believers, according to 1 John, is to love those who belong to the community. The motivation for this love is God's own love. Because God has loved them and sent his Son as an atoning sacrifice for their sins, believers ought to love one another (4:10–11).

Faith and love, then, are the fundamental ethical demands of the Johannine Epistles. One must believe that Jesus is the Christ. Those who believe that he has come in the flesh are born of God. Because they are God's children, they will love those begotten of God (5:1).

Other Voices

Of the remaining New Testament writings, the Letter of James offers the most significant ethical contribution. Like the Gospel of Matthew, James puts a premium on doing what the law requires. He describes the law as "the perfect law, the law of liberty" (Jas. 1:25; see also 2:12). Because the law is the perfect law of liberty, which brings freedom to those who observe it, James requires perfect observance, noting that "whoever keeps the whole law but fails in one point has become accountable for all of it" (2:10). However, even though he singles out the love commandment ("You shall love your neighbor as yourself") as "the royal law according to the scripture" (2:8), James does not say that love fulfills the law (see Rom. 13:10; Gal. 5:14) or that the Law and the Prophets "hang" on the love commandment (see Matt. 22:40). James requires people to do the law in its entirety, although it is not clear if his understanding of the law includes the ritual prescriptions of the law.

Because believers must be doers of the law, James argues that "faith apart from works" is barren (Jas. 2:20). Faith without works cannot save a person because faith without works is dead (2:14, 26). In a statement that stands in tension with Paul's teaching on justification by faith, James proclaims that "a person is justified by works and not by faith alone" (2:24). James and Paul, however, view faith and works differently. Whereas Paul understands faith as trust in and submission to God, James presents faith as an intellectual assent to the truth. Whereas Paul understands works as the moral and ritual prescriptions of the Mosaic law, James understands works as good deeds. For James good deeds are an indication of faith; for Paul faith is the disposition out of which those who entrust themselves to God do good deeds.

James's understanding of wisdom also informs his vision of the moral life. A morally good life is born from wisdom from above (3:13–18). Those who lack wisdom, therefore, should ask God for this gift, and it will be given to them "generously and ungrudgingly" (1:5). God, "the Father of lights," bestows every perfect gift upon believers and gives them a "birth by the word of truth," so that they "would become a kind of first fruits of his creatures" (1:18). James too draws a relationship between the moral imperative and the indicative of salvation. Those who have been born by "the word of truth" are the "first fruits" of a people who are doers of the word because wisdom from above rules their lives.

The Epistle to the Hebrews, 1 Peter, and the book of Revelation ground their moral exhortation in the salvation Christ has won through his suffering and death on the cross. These writings employ moral exhortation to encourage those who are enduring persecution and affliction to persevere in their faith. For example, the author of Hebrews uses the soteriology and Christology of Christ's high priesthood to encourage a community that appears to have lost its original fervor. To encourage this faltering community, the author juxtaposes doctrinal expositions with moral exhortations. Since God has spoken through a Son (Heb. 1:5–14), the recipients of the Son's revelation must pay greater attention to what they have heard (2:1–4). Since Christ is a high priest who has offered himself as a perfect sacrifice for their sins (7:1–10:18), believers should hold fast to their confession without wavering; there will be no further sacrifice for sins (10:19–39). The author employs the example of Israel's failure in the wilderness to provide his audience with an example of unfaithfulness (3:7–4:11). He also employs examples of faith from the past (chap. 11), which culminate in the faithfulness of Jesus (12:2), to encourage believers to persevere in their faith, for they have not yet resisted to the point of shedding their blood (12:4).

Whereas the starting point of Hebrews is the salvation Christ has won as a high priest, the point of departure for 1 Peter is the salvation the community has experienced in virtue of Christ's sufferings. By his sufferings, Christ bore their sins so that they might live for the sake of righteousness (1 Pet. 2:24). Consequently, Peter reminds his audience that Christ suffered for them, leaving them an example so that they might follow in his footsteps (2:21). Since Christ suffered on their behalf, believers should adopt his attitude and live "no longer by human desires but by the will of God" (4:2). The moral life according to 1 Peter, then, involves imitating and learning from the sufferings of Christ. Although there is shame in suffering for having done evil, there is no shame in suffering as a Christian (4:15–16).

The soteriological starting point of the book of Revelation is the victory God has won through the death of his slaughtered Lamb, the Christ. Although believers may not comprehend the full implications of the struggle they are enduring during the period of their earthly sojourn, the author of the book of Revelation assures them that the death of Christ has already determined the outcome of the conflict in which they are engaged. Therefore, they will be victorious if they are faithful. Because this conflict is so fundamental, there is no room for compromise or accommodation. Accordingly, in Revelation John requires his audience to choose between worshiping God and worshiping the beast. Those who witness to the Lamb by worshiping God will enter the Holy City, the new Jerusalem, whereas those who serve the beast, and so worship Satan, will be cast into the fiery lake and suffer the second death.

Second Peter and Jude warn their readers of false teachers (2 Peter 2; Jude 5–6). In this regard they are like the Pastorals, which argue that sound teaching leads to a godly life and false teaching leads to an immoral life. By warning the church about these false teachers, 2 Peter and Jude affirm the connection between the gospel and a sound moral life.

The writings of the New Testament present their vision of the moral life of the sanctified community in diverse ways because they adopt different starting points: the demands of the inbreaking kingdom of God; the implications of Christ's saving death and resurrection; the significance of the revelation the Son brings from the Father. Despite these different starting points, these writings ground their vision of the moral life in an experience of salvation. Believers can and should live a morally good life because of the salvation they have received in Christ.

The issue of the Mosaic law is the main point of tension among the writings of the New Testament. Whereas the Gospel of Matthew and the Letter of James highlight the importance of doing all that the law commands, the Pauline tradition speaks of Christ as the end of the law (Rom. 10:4). Yet Paul does not advocate an antinomian way of life any more than Matthew and James make Christ subservient to the law. For all three writers, Christ is the source of salvation and so the source of the moral life. But these writers do approach the moral life differently. Matthew and James suggest that Christ taught people to live in accordance with the law. In contrast to them, Paul views Christ as the goal and terminus of the law and speaks of "fulfilling" the law through the love commandment. Although each of these writers approaches the moral life differently, all agree that those who belong to the sanctified community of the church must live in a way that is pleasing to God because God's final victory is at hand. What, then, does the community of the sanctified hope for?

THE HOPE OF THE SANCTIFIED

Just as the soteriology of the New Testament grounds and determines the way in which its writers present their Christology, ecclesiology, and ethical teaching, so it grounds their eschatology, their vision of God's final victory in Christ.[36] To be sure, the sanctified community already experiences something of this victory. The Synoptic Gospels insist that the kingdom of God has made its appearance in the life and ministry of Jesus. Acts and the Pauline tradition claim that believers already experience the gift of the Spirit. The Johannine tradition affirms that believers have already passed from death to life. The Epistle to the Hebrews maintains that Christ has effectively dealt with sins. And the book of Revelation reminds believers of the victory that the slaughtered Lamb has already won. But all of the New Testament writings, even the writings of the Johannine tradition, maintain that there will be a consummation of all things in the future. The kingdom of God will come in power. The dead will be raised incorruptible. God's enemies will be defeated in a final and definitive manner. As was the case with their Christology, ecclesiology, and

36. For the eschatology of the New Testament, see G. B. Caird, *New Testament Theology*, completed and edited by L. D. Hurst (Oxford: Clarendon, 1994), 238–78; Hahn, *Theologie des Neuen Testaments*, 2:738–98; Donald Guthrie, *New Testament Theology* (Downers Grove, IL: InterVarsity Press, 1981), 790–892; Vouga, *Théologie du Nouveau Testament*, 391–437.

ethics, the New Testament writers present their eschatology in diverse ways because of their different starting points: Jesus' preaching about the kingdom of God, the gospel of Jesus' death and resurrection, and the revelation that the Son brings from the Father.

The Synoptic Tradition

The eschatology of the Synoptic tradition begins with Jesus' preaching about the kingdom of God. Jesus proclaims, "The time is fulfilled, and the kingdom of God has come near" (*ēngiken hē basileia tou theou*, Mark 1:15; see also Matt. 4:17), and when he sends his disciples on mission, he instructs them to make the same announcement (Matt. 10:7; Luke 10:9). When the Pharisees ask him when the kingdom of God will come, he responds, "The kingdom of God is not coming with things that can be observed; nor will they say, 'Look, here it is!' or 'There it is!' For, in fact, the kingdom of God is among you (*hē basileia tou theou entos hymōn estin*)" (Luke 17:20–21). When people accuse Jesus of casting out demons by the power of Beelzebul, he responds, "But if it is by the finger of God that I cast out the demons, then the kingdom of God has come to you (*ephthasen eph' hymas hē basileia tou theou*)" (Luke 11:20). Inasmuch as the kingdom of God has made its appearance in Jesus' ministry, the eschaton (the new age) has broken into and made its appearance in the present age (the old age).

Despite Jesus' proclamation of the kingdom, most of his contemporaries do not perceive the kingdom's presence in his ministry. Consequently, Jesus reveals the mystery of the kingdom to his disciples (Matt. 13:11; Mark 4:11; Luke 8:10). At the present time, the kingdom is hidden in Jesus' ministry so that only those who believe can see it. But when it is revealed in all of its power, no one will be able to deny its presence. Thus the kingdom is *already* present in Jesus' ministry, perceptible to those who believe, but it has *not yet* been manifested in power.

From the perspective of the Synoptic Jesus, the coming of the kingdom in power is imminent. Before his transfiguration, he tells his disciples, "there are some standing here who will not taste death until they see that the kingdom of God has come with power" (Mark 9:1; Matt. 16:28; Luke 9:27). At the Last Supper, when he explains the significance of his death to his disciples, Jesus takes a vow of abstinence not to drink the fruit of the vine until that day he drinks it in the kingdom of God (Matt. 26:26–29; Mark 14:22–25; Luke 22:15–20). Thus, despite his impending death, Jesus anticipates entering into the realm of God's kingdom in a new and definitive way.

Because death cannot prevent Jesus from entering into the transcendent realm of God's kingdom, he will return at the end of the ages as the glorious Son of Man who will gather the elect and judge the nations (Mark 13:27; Matt. 25:31–46). Although Jesus describes the events that will precede his return, he insists that the Son of Man will return suddenly and unexpectedly. Therefore, not even the Son knows the day or the hour of this event, only the Father (Matt. 24:36; Mark 13:32). Because the Son of Man's parousia will be sudden and unexpected, it is imperative for the disciples to be vigilant (Matt. 24:44; Mark 13:35–37; Luke 12:40).

Except for the saying in Luke 21:31 ("when you see these things taking place, you know that the kingdom of God is near"), Jesus does not make an explicit connection between his parousia and the coming of the kingdom. The Synoptic tradition seems to suppose that Jesus has already entered into the transcendent realm of the kingdom through his death and resurrection. Having entered into the kingdom, he will return in his capacity as the glorious Son of Man at the end of the ages to gather the elect into the transcendent realm of God's kingdom. The hope of the sanctified, then, can be expressed in this way: those who belong to the community of the sanctified hope for the return of the Son of Man and their own entry into the kingdom the Father has prepared for them from the foundation of the world (Matt. 25:34).

The Acts of the Apostles provides a transition from the Synoptic Gospels to the rest of the literature in the New Testament, especially the Pauline Letters. The hope of the early church, as described in Acts, remains focused on Jesus' return and the kingdom of God. In the forty days between his resurrection and ascension, the risen Lord continues to speak to his apostles about the kingdom (1:3). Philip proclaims the good news about the kingdom of God and the name of Jesus Christ to the Samaritans (8:12). In the synagogue at Ephesus, Paul speaks boldly and persuasively about the kingdom of God for three months (19:8). In summing up his ministry, he reminds the Ephesian elders how he proclaimed the kingdom of God among them (20:25). Acts then ends with Paul preaching the kingdom of God in Rome (28:31).

Although there is no mention of the "Son of Man" in Acts apart from Stephen's final words (7:56), the early church continues to wait for the return of its Lord. After Jesus' ascension, the angels tell the Eleven, "This Jesus, who has been taken up from you into heaven, will come in the same way as you saw him go into heaven" (1:11). Peter encourages the people of Israel to repent so that God will send them the Messiah at the time designated for the "universal restoration that God announced long ago through his holy prophets" (3:21). Paul warns the Athenians that God "has fixed a day on which he will have the world judged in righteousness by a man whom he has appointed, and of this he has given assurance to all by raising him from the dead" (17:31).

Because God has raised his Messiah from the dead, the early church hopes for the general resurrection of the dead. In his defense speeches, for example, Paul insists that he is on trial for the resurrection of the dead, what he identifies as "the promise made by God to our ancestors" (26:6). At the end of Acts, he tells the Jewish community at Rome that he is a prisoner for the sake of "the hope of Israel" (28:20), by which he means the general resurrection of the dead that the Messiah's resurrection initiated. The early church's hope in the resurrection of the dead, as portrayed in Acts, provides an important link between the preaching of Jesus about the kingdom and the early church's preaching about Jesus. Jesus proclaimed the kingdom of God and entered into its transcendent realm by his death and resurrection. Those who believe in him hope to enter into that same kingdom when the Son of Man gathers the elect. The general resurrection of the dead, then, is an essential component of the church's hope for the kingdom and the return of its Lord.

The Pauline Tradition

God's redemptive work in Christ stands at the core of Pauline theology. But as important as this redemptive work is, it is not finished. Consequently, believers live in hope as they wait for the final act of God's redemptive work, which will attain its goal at the parousia, when the dead will be raised incorruptible. This hope for Christ's parousia is present in nearly all of the Pauline writings, although it plays a greater role in some letters than in others.[37]

Paul's vibrant hope for the parousia is intimately related to his belief in the general resurrection of the dead that Christ's resurrection initiated. For inasmuch as the general resurrection of the dead has already begun in one man, then the parousia (the moment when Christ will return as God's eschatological judge and the dead will be raised) is forever imminent no matter how long it may be delayed.[38] The redeemed, then, are already living in the new age, which is marked by the outpouring of God's Spirit. But inasmuch as the general resurrection of the dead has not yet occurred, and will not take place until Christ returns, they are also living in the old age as well. Those who are in

---

37. The Pauline writings employ a variety of terms when they refer to the return of Christ at the end of the ages. (1) *Parousia* occurs in 1 Cor. 15:23; 1 Thess. 2:19; 3:13; 4:15; 5:23; 2 Thess. 2:1, 8. The basic meaning of the term is "presence," but in these texts it takes on a technical meaning since it refers to the presence of the Lord at the end of the ages. (2) *Apokalypsis* occurs in 1 Cor. 1:7; 2 Thess. 1:7. In these texts it refers to the "revelation" or "unveiling" of Christ that will occur at the end of the ages. (3) *Hē hēmera, hē hēmera tou theou, hē hēmera tou Christou;* "the day," "the day of the Lord," "the day of Christ" (1 Cor. 1:8; 2 Cor. 1:14; Phil. 1:6, 10; 2:16). In these cases the Old Testament notion of "the day of the YHWH" is applied to the return of Christ as God's eschatological judge. (4) *Epiphaneia* (1 Tim. 6:14; 2 Tim. 4:1, 8; Titus 2:13). This term, which is distinctive of the Pastorals, refers to the manifestation of Christ at the end of the ages. There is a certain similarity between it and the notion of the "revelation" or "disclosure" of the Lord at the end of the ages.

38. In 1 Thess. 4:17 Paul seems to believe that he will be alive at the parousia, and in 1 Corinthians 7 his instructions concerning marriage seem to presuppose that the end is near. In other texts he reckons with the possibility that he may die before the parousia (Phil. 1:23; 2 Cor. 5:1–5). Although Paul may have been mistaken about "when" the parousia will occur, his basic theological insight remains intact: the parousia can occur at any moment because the general resurrection of the dead has already happened in Christ.

Christ, then, live between what has already happened and what has not yet occurred, the general resurrection of the dead.

Paul's own understanding of the parousia emerges piecemeal since his correspondence is occasional in nature. In 1 Thessalonians his discussion focuses on the fate of those who have already died, and he presents the parousia as an imperial visitation. Christ will descend from heaven, and those who have died in him will be raised. Then the living will be taken up with them in the clouds to meet the Lord (1 Thess. 4:13–18). In 1 Corinthians 15 Paul presents the parousia within the context of the general resurrection of the dead. At the end of the ages, when everything has been subjected to Christ, Christ will return and the dead will be raised incorruptible. When the last enemy, death, has been destroyed, the Son will hand over the kingdom to his Father, and God will be all in all (1 Cor. 15:20–28). At the parousia all will be transformed, the living as well as the dead, and they will bear the image of the eschatological Adam, the risen Christ (1 Cor. 15:42–57).[39] In 2 Corinthians the resurrection continues to play a central role. Paul writes that "the one who raised the Lord Jesus will raise us also with Jesus, and will bring us with you into his presence" (2 Cor. 4:14). Paul affirms his faith that if his body is destroyed by death, he will be clothed with a heavenly dwelling (2 Cor. 5:1–5). Although the imagery has changed, and there is no explicit reference to the parousia or the general resurrection of the dead, Paul is still speaking of the resurrection body he hopes to receive after death. In 2 Thessalonians the discussion focuses on the retribution the returning Lord will inflict on those who are presently afflicting those who believe in the gospel (2 Thess. 1:5–10) and on the events that must take place before the Lord's return (2 Thess. 2:1–12). The entire discussion occurs without any reference to Christ's resurrection or the general resurrection of the dead. In 2 Thessalonians Paul continues to present the parousia as an imperial visitation, but instead of highlighting the gathering of the elect, he emphasizes the punishment the returning Lord will inflict upon those who oppose the gospel.

The parousia does not play as central a role in Paul's other letters, although it continues to inform his theology. In Philippians he writes, "The Lord is near" (Phil. 4:5), and he reminds his converts that their citizenship is in heaven. When the Savior comes from heaven, he will transform their earthly bodies and conform them to his own glorious body (Phil. 3:2–21). What Paul writes here clearly reflects his theology of the parousia and the general resurrection of the dead, as outlined in 1 Corinthians 15. In Romans he exhorts his audience to be vigilant since their salvation is closer than when they first became

---

39. Although Acts 24:15 speaks of "a resurrection of both the righteous and the unrighteous," when Paul writes about the resurrection from the dead, he speaks only of believers, since it is those who believe in Christ and presently enjoy the gift of the Spirit who will enjoy resurrected life.

believers (Rom. 13:11–12). Although he does not take up the topic of the parousia, his hope for the transformation that will occur at the resurrection of the dead plays an important role in his theology, especially in Romans 8. Believers already enjoy the gift of the Spirit, and they can be confident that if the Spirit of God, who raised Jesus from the dead, dwells in them, then God, who raised Jesus from the dead, will raise their mortal bodies through the Spirit that dwells in them (8:11). The sufferings of the present time then cannot be compared to the glory that is to be revealed when not only believers but the whole of creation will be set free from its bondage to decay "and obtain the freedom of the glory of the children of God" (8:21). Believers, then, are waiting for the redemption of their bodies (8:23) that will occur at the parousia, when the resurrection of the dead takes place.

Paul maintains the tension between what has "already" occurred in Christ and what has "not yet" happened. Believers have already been justified and reconciled to God, but they have not yet been saved because the general resurrection of the dead has not yet occurred. When Paul does speak of believers as saved, he is careful to note that they have been saved "in hope" (Rom. 8:24); they hope and trust that they will be saved because they have already been justified and reconciled (5:9–10). They will not be finally saved, however, until the last enemy, death, has been destroyed at the general resurrection of the dead. The parousia, which ushers in the general resurrection of the dead, then, is the final act of God's redemptive work in Christ. This is not to say that what God did in Christ was insufficient. But it does affirm that as long as believers are subject to death and decay, God's redemptive work is not complete.

The parousia does not play as prominent a role in the deuteropauline letters as it does in the nondisputed Pauline correspondence. Discussion of the general resurrection of the dead tends to recede, and there is a tendency to speak of believers as saved and raised up. This is not to say that these letters no longer hope for a final manifestation of God's redemptive work in Christ. They do, but there is a shift in emphasis from the future to the present, as will become even more apparent in the Gospel of John. This is evident in Colossians and Ephesians, which employ the spatial imagery of the hope that is stored up in heaven for believers. For example, the author of Colossians speaks to the hope that is laid up for the believer in heaven (Col. 1:5), and he encourages the recipients to set their minds "on things that are above" (3:2). Believers already share in "the inheritance of the saints in light," and they have been transferred from the power of darkness to the kingdom of God's beloved Son (1:12–13). The author of Ephesians says that they have been saved by grace and even speaks of them as raised up with Christ and seated with him in the heavenly places (Eph. 2:5–6).

Although the overall tendency of Colossians and Ephesians is to underline what has already happened, the authors are still aware that God's work of salvation is not yet finished. For example, even though the author of Colossians says that believers have been raised up with Christ, he affirms that Christ will appear again (Col. 3:1, 4). The author of Ephesians does not allude to the parousia or to the appearance of Christ, but does refer to God's plan to gather up all things in Christ, in heaven and on earth, in the fullness of time (Eph. 1:10). Moreover, inasmuch as both letters speak of believers as already raised up with Christ, they show that they have not forgotten Paul's teaching about the general resurrection of the dead. To be sure, the emphasis is on the present aspect of resurrection life: believers already enjoy something of Christ's resurrection because they have been raised up with him in baptism. But what they enjoy is hidden or stored up for them in heaven. It is only when Christ is revealed that they will be revealed with him in glory (Col. 3:4).

The authors of Colossians and Ephesians emphasize the present aspect of the resurrection because of their ecclesiology, which views the church as the body of the cosmic Christ. Inasmuch as believers belong to the body, which is growing into Christ, they are raised up with him. Both authors understand that the final goal has not yet been attained, however, for the church is still struggling to attain "the measure of the full stature of Christ" (Eph. 4:13).

The author of the Pastoral Epistles develops an epiphany theology that is similar in some respects to Paul's theology of the parousia. God will bring about the epiphany or manifestation of Jesus Christ at the right time (1 Tim. 6:14). This manifestation will be the moment when Christ Jesus will judge the living and the dead (2 Tim. 4:1) and reward with righteousness those who have longed for his coming (2 Tim. 4:8). On that day Christ will be manifested as the great God and Savior of those who believe (Titus 2:13). The author, however, never presents this epiphany as the moment when the general resurrection of the dead will occur. For him the final epiphany or manifestation of Christ is the completion of his first epiphany. At his first epiphany Christ appeared in the flesh to bring salvation; at his last epiphany he will appear as the judge of the living and the dead.

The Pauline teaching about what believers hope for is expressed in a variety of ways, not all of which are fully compatible with one another. In Paul's own letters, hope focuses on the general resurrection of the dead, which will occur at the parousia. Believers are already justified and reconciled to God, but they are not yet saved because death has not yet been destroyed. What believers hope for, then, is resurrection from the dead. In Colossians and Ephesians, hope is something that is stored up in heaven, where believers have already been raised up with Christ through their baptismal union with him. The fulfillment of the believer's hope will occur after death. Neither the author of Ephesians nor the author of Colossians, however, develops the apocalyptic aspect of Paul's thought, so that one begins to wonder how central the parousia is to their theological thought. In the Pastorals, the parousia does play a role, but it becomes Christ's second epiphany at which he will judge the living and the dead. There is no mention of the resurrection of the dead. To summarize, the Pauline Letters affirm that the present life of the believer has not yet attained its final goal. But whereas the general resurrection of the dead plays a prominent role in Paul's own thought, it tends to recede in the letters of his followers.

The Johannine Tradition

While hope for a final act of salvation plays a central role in the Synoptic and Pauline traditions, the present experience of salvation plays a more prominent role in the Johannine tradition. For example, Jesus says that anyone who believes his word and believes in the one who sent him "has eternal life, and does not come under judgment, but has passed from death to life" (John 5:24). He affirms that those who do not believe in him are already condemned "because they have not believed in the name of the only Son of God" (John 3:18). Thus when Martha confesses that her brother will rise in the resurrection on the last day, Jesus responds that he *is* the resurrection and the life so that those who believe in him will live, even if they die, and everyone who lives and believes in him will never die (11:24–26). In a word, resurrection life is already present and available to those who believe in Jesus.

For the Johannine tradition the essence of salvation is life, which in Johannine parlance is the eternal life believers *already* experience because they believe Jesus is the incarnate one who has come to reveal the Father to the world. In revealing the Father to the world, Jesus communicates the light of God, which is life, to those who believe his word. This is why Jesus says that he is the way, the truth, and the life (John 14:6). It is not surprising, then, that scholars frequently point to the Johannine tradition as an example of "realized eschatology," by which they mean an eschatology that maximizes the present dimension of salvation. The consequence of such an eschatology is that believers are more fully aware of the salvation they already experience.

Because the Johannine tradition emphasizes the present aspect of salvation, it does not say as much about the future dimension of salvation as does the Synoptic tradition. For example, although the Johannine Jesus frequently refers to himself as the Son of Man, he never speaks of the imminent return of the Son of Man. Instead of giving a farewell discourse about the destruction of Jerusalem and the return of the Son of Man, the Johannine Jesus delivers an extended farewell discourse in which he speaks of his return to his Father. After returning to the Father, Jesus will send his disciples another Advocate, the Holy Spirit, who will remind them of all that Jesus said and did. Thus the Johannine tradition does not describe or promise an imminent apocalyptic event comparable to the return of the Son of Man and the final manifestation

of the kingdom (the Synoptic tradition) or the parousia and the general resurrection of the dead (the Pauline tradition). There is no need for such an
apocalyptic event because, through the incarnation of God's eternal Word,
believers already experience eternal life, a life that will continue despite death.
The eschatological hour is now.

Although the Johannine tradition emphasizes the present aspect of salvation to a greater extent than the Synoptic and Pauline traditions, it has not
done away the future dimension of salvation. For example, in his bread of life
discourse, Jesus says that he will raise up those who believe in him on "the last
day" (John 6:39, 40, 44, 54). At the end of his public ministry, he warns that
on "the last day" the word he has spoken will judge those who have rejected
him and not received his word (12:48). Although he does not speak about the
return of the Son of Man, he does promise his disciples that, when he returns
to his Father, he will prepare a place for them, and he will "come again" to take
them to himself that where he is, they may be (14:3). The Johannine tradition
is aware of the general resurrection, of the final judgment, and of the Lord's
return. But it does not present these events in the apocalyptic manner that the
Synoptic and Pauline traditions do.

It is no longer necessary for the Johannine tradition to present the future
hope of believers in such an apocalyptic manner because it places a premium
on the eternal life believers already possess. The life believers presently enjoy
is eternal life. Consequently, their resurrection from the dead will be a continuation of the eternal life that the Son has already given them. This is why
it is not incongruous for the Johannine tradition to juxtapose two of Jesus' sayings, one that emphasizes the eternal life believers already enjoy, the other that
promises resurrection of the dead. "Very truly, I tell you, anyone who hears
my word and believes him who sent me *has eternal life*, and does not come
under judgment, but has passed from death to life. Very truly, I tell you, *the
hour is coming, and is now here*, when the dead will hear the voice of the Son of
God, and those who hear will live. For just as the Father has life in himself, so
he has granted the Son also to have life in himself" (John 5:24–26). Although
believers already enjoy eternal life, they will die. But they will also rise in virtue
of the eternal life they already enjoy. There is no need for the Fourth Gospel
to dwell on apocalyptic events when there is such continuity between the life
believers already have and the life they will enjoy.

Like the Gospel, 1 John affirms that believers already enjoy eternal life
(1 John 5:11, 13). Here John also affirms that they have passed from death to life,
although he attributes the reason for this passage to their love for one another
(3:14). Believers who stand in continuity with the original witnesses of the
Johannine community and walk in the light are in communion with the Father
and his Son, Jesus Christ (1:3, 6–7). But as in the Gospel, in 1 John the author
is aware that there is a future dimension to salvation, although he never refers

to the resurrection of the believer or to the last day. Rather he speaks of Christ's revelation and parousia. Believers are to abide in Christ so that when he is revealed they will not be put to shame at his coming (*parousia*, 2:28). They already are God's children, but what they will be has not yet been revealed. When Christ is revealed, however, they will be like him and see him as he is (3:2). Although the language is more restrained than that found in the apocalyptic scenarios of the Synoptic and Pauline traditions, there is a vibrant hope for what will happen in the future. Somewhat curiously, then, whereas Colossians and Ephesians tend to tone down Paul's apocalyptic scenario, the Johannine Letters appear to have heightened the Fourth Gospel's eschatological hope.

Other Voices

Of the remaining New Testament writings, 2 Peter and the book of Revelation deal most explicitly with the theme of eschatology. Second Peter offers a theological defense for the apparent delay of the parousia. What appears to be a delay in the coming of the Lord is a sign of the Lord's patience. It is intended as a time for repentance (2 Pet. 3:1–10). Hope for the parousia does not rest on "cleverly devised myths" but on the testimony of those who were eyewitnesses of the Lord's majesty at the time of his transfiguration (1:16). The Lord's coming will be sudden and unexpected. The heavens will pass away, and the elements will be dissolved with fire. Accordingly, believers are waiting for "new heavens and a new earth, where righteousness is at home" (3:10, 13).

The eschatological hope of the book of Revelation is more detailed. Like 2 Peter, John the Elder speaks of "a new heaven and a new earth" (Rev. 21:1), but he also describes the "holy city, the new Jerusalem," where believers will live with God and the Lamb (21:9–27). Entry into this city requires an intense struggle. Believers must contend with the beast and witness to the Lamb if they hope to dwell in God's city. Through his account of the seven seals, the seven trumpets, and the seven bowls, John describes the judgment of God in gruesome detail, culminating in the fall and destruction of Babylon. The Son of Man is still associated with the parousia (14:14–16), but John is not limited to the Son of Man imagery when describing the parousia, as 19:11–16 shows. Moreover, only he speaks of a thousand-year reign of the saints (20:1–20) and of the first resurrection (20:5–6). Although his imagery is unlike that of any other New Testament writing, his eschatological hope coheres with other New Testament writings: God will be victorious over evil. Christ will be the agent of God's victory, and the saints will enjoy life with God.

The author of Hebrews develops a unique eschatology that is closely related to its Christology and soteriology. He argues that inasmuch as Jesus has entered into the heavenly sanctuary to offer a perfect sacrifice for sins, Jesus has become the "pioneer" (*archēgos*, Heb. 2:10) of faith, the one who blazed the trail that leads to salvation for those who follow in his footsteps. Having entered into God's Sabbath rest by his high priestly work, he shows others the way to that rest. This is why the author says that there still remains a Sabbath rest for God's people (4:9).

Drawing upon examples from Israel's past, the author describes the hope that lies before believers as "the city that has foundations, whose architect and builder is God," "a better country, that is, a heavenly one" (11:10, 16). Because of what lies before them, the author exhorts his readers to fix their eyes on Jesus, the pioneer and perfecter of their faith (12:1–2), reminding them that they "have come to Mount Zion and to the city of the living God, the heavenly Jerusalem" (12:22). In his only explicit reference to the second coming, he notes that "Christ, having been offered once to bear the sins of many, will appear a second time, not to deal with sin, but to save those who are eagerly waiting for him" (9:28).

For 1 Peter, believers have "an inheritance that is imperishable, undefiled, and unfading" (1 Pet. 1:4), kept for them in heaven. This inheritance comes from their new birth through the resurrection of Jesus Christ. Their salvation will be revealed "in the last time," when "Jesus Christ is revealed (*apokalyphthēnai*)" (1:5, 7), when the chief shepherd "appears" (*phanerōthentos*, 5:4).

Because the Letter of James focuses on the moral life, the coming of the Lord plays an important role in this letter as well. Believers must be patient until the "coming of the Lord" (*parousia tou kyriou*, Jas. 5:7). The Judge is standing at the doors (5:9), and when he comes, those who have oppressed the poor will be punished (5:1–6).

The hope of the sanctified is expressed in diverse ways in the New Testament because its writers have different starting points: the kingdom of God, the death and resurrection of Christ, the incarnation. But amid this diversity, there is a constant theme: God's work of salvation will be brought to completion when the Son of Man returns, the dead are raised, the final judgment takes place, and believers enter into their Sabbath rest, the Holy City, the new Jerusalem, where there will be a new heaven and a new earth. No single metaphor expresses the whole reality. But taken together, these metaphors point to God's transcendent victory in Christ.

A FINAL WORD

Three elements account for the diverse unity of New Testament theology: (1) an experience of salvation in Jesus Christ, (2) an underlying narrative that recounts the story of salvation, and (3) the diverse starting points that the New Testament writers employ to express the salvation God has effected in Christ. The first two elements account for the unity of New Testament theology, the last for the diverse ways in which the New Testament writers communicate their understanding of what God has accomplished in Christ.

New Testament theology begins with soteriology. Apart from soteriology, there would be no need for Christology, ecclesiology, Christian ethics, or eschatology. The experience of the salvation God has accomplished in and through Christ determines how the New Testament writers understand Christ, the church, the moral life, and the hope of the sanctified. Although this experience of salvation can and does differ from person to person, and so from writing to writing, there is an overall consensus in the writings of the New Testament that God has rescued believers from the powers of sin and death that threaten their relationship to God. The early Christians believed that their sins had been forgiven in a new and definitive way through God's work in Christ, and because God had forgiven their sins in and through Christ, they now stood in a new relationship to the Creator. The kingdom had dawned, the resurrection of the dead had begun in Christ, and they were justified, reconciled, redeemed, and sanctified. This experience of forgiveness assured them that death no longer had the same power over their lives that it had when they were alienated from God. In addition to this experience of forgiveness, the first Christians enjoyed an experience of God's own Spirit within their lives, which convinced them that their new life would continue beyond death. This experience of salvation in all of its manifestations (healing from sickness, freedom from Satan, the forgiveness of sins, the gift of the Spirit) helps to explain the unity in the theology of the New Testament.

A second element that accounts for the unity of New Testament theology is the narrative about salvation that the New Testament writings exhibit, sometimes explicitly, other times implicitly. A composite of this narrative can be summarized in five points. (1) Humanity finds itself in a predicament from which it cannot extract itself. It is under the powers of sickness, demons, sin, and death. But most importantly, humanity is alienated from God, and it cannot reconcile itself to God. It cannot usher in the kingdom of God; it cannot control the power of sin; it cannot grant itself eternal life. It does not even understand the full depth of its sinful condition. (2) Consequently, God has sent his own Son into the world to redeem the world. The appearance of the Son marks the inbreaking of the kingdom of God, and the Son reveals the Father to the world. His death and resurrection effect reconciliation with God and anticipate God's final victory over death at the general resurrection of the dead. (3) This act of salvation brings into existence a community of believers who have been redeemed and sanctified by God's work in Christ. This community—the church—consists of Gentiles and Jews. Although there has been a rupture with historical Israel, this new community sees itself as being in continuity with God's salvation-historical plan for Israel. (4) Because it is a sanctified community, it lives in the light of the inbreaking kingdom of God. It is led by the Spirit, illumined by the revelation it has received from the Son, and it lives in accordance with the pattern of Christ's saving death and resurrection. (5) Finally, in light of the salvation it has already received, the community looks forward to God's final act of salvation in Christ. It anticipates God's final coming in Christ and the eternal life that will attend it: resurrection from the dead, entrance into the heavenly sanctuary, the new Jerusalem.

This composite summary draws upon several New Testament traditions, and the narrative it recounts does not occur, in its entirety, in every single New Testament writing. But the underlying drama of the narrative—the need for salvation, redemption in Christ, the appearance of a new community, a new way of life, and a new hope for the future—is present in all three great traditions and in other voices of the New Testament.

The third element—the different starting points of the three great New Testament traditions—accounts for the diverse ways that the writings of the New Testament present their experience of salvation and their understanding of this narrative. Because the Synoptic tradition begins with Jesus' proclamation of the kingdom of God, it views the narrative and the experience of salvation in light of God's inbreaking kingdom. Because the Johannine tradition begins with the incarnation, it views the narrative in terms of the sending of the Son into the world and the experience of salvation in light of the revelation the Son brings from the Father. And because the Pauline tradition and most of the remaining writings of the New Testament begin with the gospel of Jesus' death and resurrection, they view the narrative from the perspective of the cross, and salvation in terms of the forgiveness of sins and God's victory over death. This is not meant to imply that John and the Synoptics ignore Christ's death and resurrection, or that Paul is ignorant of the kingdom of God and the revelation the Son brings. Rather, it is intended to highlight that the New Testament writings have different starting points for recounting the narrative of what God has done in Christ and expressing the salvation that God's work in Christ has effected.

The unity of New Testament theology is a diverse unity: a unity that expresses itself in a multiplicity of ways because no one way can fully capture the mystery that is God in Christ. To insist upon only one way is to deny the mystery. To insist upon only one way is to foolishly imagine that human beings can comprehend the mystery that is God. The diverse unity of the New Testament is the only unity of the New Testament. It is the only unity that stands in awe before the mystery.

Bibliography

Adam, A. K. M. *Making Sense of New Testament Theology: "Modern" Problems and Prospects*. StABH 11. Macon, GA: Mercer University Press, 1995.

Alexander, T. Desmond, Brian S. Rosner, D. A. Carson, and Graeme Goldsworthy, eds. *New Dictionary of Biblical Theology: Exploring the Unity and Diversity of Scripture*. Downers Grove, IL: InterVarsity Press, 2000.

Balla, Peter. *Challenges to New Testament Theology: An Attempt to Justify the Enterprise*. Peabody, MA: Hendrickson, 1997.

Barr, James. *The Concept of Biblical Theology*. Minneapolis: Fortress, 1999.

Barth, Gerhard. "Über Probleme und Trends bei neutestamentlichen Theologien." *KD* 48 (2002): 261–75.

Bauckham, Richard. *The Theology of the Book of Revelation*. NTT. Cambridge: Cambridge University Press, 1993.

Baur, Ferdinand Christian. *Vorlesungen über neutestamentliche Theologie*. Ed. F. F. Baur. 1864. Repr. Darmstadt: Wissenschaftliche Buchgesellschaft, 1973.

Beyschlag, Willibard. *New Testament Theology or Historical Account of the Teaching of Jesus and of Primitive Christianity according to the New Testament Sources*. 2 vols. Edinburgh: T. & T. Clark, 1895. (German original, 1891–92.)

Boers, Hendrikus. *What Is New Testament Theology? The Rise of Criticism and the Problem of a Theology of the New Testament*. GBS. Philadelphia: Fortress, 1979.

Bonsirven, Joseph. *Theology of the New Testament*. Westminster, MD: Newman Press, 1963. (French original, 1951.)

Braun, Herbert. "The Problem of a Theology of the New Testament." *JTC* 1 (1965): 169–83.

Bultmann, Rudolf. *Theology of the New Testament*. 2 vols. London: SCM, 1952–55. (German original, 1948–53.)

Caird, G. B. *New Testament Theology*. Completed and edited by L. D. Hurst. Oxford: Clarendon, 1994.

Carson, D. A. "Current Issues in Biblical Theology." *BBR* 5 (1995): 17–41.

———. "New Testament Theology." Pages 796–814 in *Dictionary of the Later New Testament and Its Developments*. Ed. Ralph P. Martin and Peter H. Davids. Downers Grove, IL: InterVarsity Press, 1997.

Chester, Andrew, and Ralph P. Martin. *The Theology of the Letters of James, Peter, and Jude*. NTT. Cambridge: Cambridge University Press, 1994.

Childs, Brevard S. *Biblical Theology of the Old and New Testaments: Theological Reflection on the Christian Bible*. Minneapolis: Fortress, 1992.

Conzelmann, Hans. *An Outline of the Theology of the New Testament*. New York: Harper & Row, 1969. (German original, 1967.)

Cullmann, Oscar. *Christ and Time*. London: SCM, 1962. (German original, 1946.)

———. *Salvation in History*. NTL. London: SCM, 1967. (German original, 1965.)

Descamps, A. "Réflexions sur la méthode en théologie biblique." In *Sacra Pagina: Miscellanea biblica Congressus Internationalis Catholici de Re Biblica*. Ed. J. Coppens, A. Descamps, and E. Massaux. 2 vols. BETL 12–13. Paris: Gabalda, 1959. 1:132–57.

Dodd, C. H. *The Apostolic Preaching and Its Developments*. London: Hodder & Stoughton, 1936.

———. *According to the Scriptures: The Sub-Structure of New Testament Theology*. New York: Scribner, 1953.

Donahue, John R. "The Changing Shape of New Testament Theology." *TS* (1989): 314–35.

———. "The Literary Turn and New Testament Theology: Detour or New Direction?" *JR* 76 (1996): 250–75.

Donfried, Karl L., and I. Howard Marshall. *The Theology of the Shorter Pauline Letters*. NTT. Cambridge: Cambridge University Press, 1993.

Dunn, James D. G. *Unity and Diversity in the New Testament: An Inquiry into the Character of Earliest Christianity*. 2nd ed. Valley Forge, PA: Trinity International Press, 1990.

———. *The Theology of Paul's Letter to the Galatians*. NTT. Cambridge: Cambridge University Press, 1993.

Ebeling, Gerhard. "The Meaning of Biblical Theology." *JTS* 6 (1955): 210–25.

Esler, Philip F. *New Testament Theology: Communion and Community*. Minneapolis: Fortress, 2005.

Feine, Paul. *Theologie des Neuen Testaments*. 8th ed. Berlin: Evangelische Verlagsanstalt, 1953. (First published 1910.)

Fuller, Reginald H. "New Testament Theology." Pages 565–84 in *The New Testament and Its Modern Interpreters*. Ed. Eldon Jay Epp and George W. MacRae. Philadelphia: Fortress, 1989.

Furnish, Victor Paul. *The Theology of the First Letter to the Corinthians*. NTT. Cambridge: Cambridge University Press, 1999.

Gnilka, Joachim. *Theologie des Neuen Testaments*. HTKNT Sup 5. Freiburg: Herder, 1994.

Goppelt, Leonhard. *Theology of the New Testament*. 2 vols. Grand Rapids: Eerdmans, 1981–82. (German original, 1975–76.)

Grant, Frederick C. *An Introduction to New Testament Thought*. Nashville: Abingdon, 1950.

Green, Joel B. *The Theology of the Gospel of Luke*. NTT. Cambridge: Cambridge University Press, 1995.

Guthrie, Donald. *New Testament Theology*. Downers Grove, IL: InterVarsity Press, 1981.

Haacker, Klaus. *The Theology of Paul's Letter to the Romans*. NTT. Cambridge: Cambridge University Press, 2003.

Hafemann, Scott J., ed. *Biblical Theology: Retrospect and Prospect*. Downers Grove, IL: InterVarsity Press, 2002.

Hahn, Ferdinand. *Theologie des Neuen Testaments*. 2 vols. Tübingen: Mohr Siebeck, 2002.

Hanson, Paul D. "The Future of Biblical Theology." *HBT* 6 (1984): 13–24.

Harrington, Wilfrid J., O.P. *The Path of Biblical Theology*. Dublin: Gill & Macmillan, 1973.

Hasel, Gerhard. *New Testament Theology: Basic Issues in the Current Debate*. Grand Rapids: Eerdmans, 1978.

———. "The Nature of Biblical Theology: Recent Trends and Issues." *AUSS* 32 (1994): 203–15.

———. "Recent Models of Biblical Theology: Three Major Perspectives." *AUSS* 33 (1995): 55–75.

———. "Proposals for a Canonical Biblical Theology." *AUSS* 34 (1996): 23–33.

Holtzmann, Heinrich Julius. *Lehrbuch der neutestamentlichen Theologie*. 2 vols. Freiburg: Mohr (Siebeck), 1897.

Hübner, Hans. *Biblische Theologie des Neuen Testaments*. 3 vols. Göttingen: Vandenhoeck & Ruprecht, 1990, 1993, 1995.

Jeremias, Joachim. *New Testament Theology: The Proclamation of Jesus*. New York: Scribner, 1971. (German original, 1971.)

———. *Jesus and the Message of the New Testament*. Repr. ed. K. C. Hanson. Fortress Classics in Biblical Studies. Minneapolis: Fortress, 2002.

Jervell, Jacob. *The Theology of the Acts of the Apostles*. NTT. Cambridge: Cambridge University Press, 1996.

Käsemann, Ernst. "The Canon of the New Testament and the Unity of the Church." Pages 95–107 in *Essays on New Testament Themes*. SBT 1/41. London: SCM, 1964. (German original, 1951–52.)

———. "The Problem of a New Testament Theology." *NTS* 19 (1973): 235–45.

Keck, Leander E. "Problems of New Testament Theology. A Critique of Alan Richardson's *An Introduction to New Testament Theology*." *NovT* 7 (1964): 217–41.

Kraftchick, Steven J., Charles D. Myers Jr., and Ben C. Ollenburger, eds. *Biblical Theology: Problems and Perspectives: In Honor of J. Christiaan Beker*. Nashville: Abingdon, 1995.

Kraus, Hans-Joachim. *Die biblische Theologie: Ihre Geschichte und Problematik*. Neukirchen-Vluyn: Neukirchener Verlag, 1970.

Kümmel, Werner Georg. *The Theology of the New Testament according to Its Major Witnesses: Jesus—Paul—John*. Nashville: Abingdon, 1973. (German original, 1969.)

Küss, O. *Die Theologie des Neuen Testaments: Eine Einführung*. Regensburg: Pustet,.1937.

Ladd, George Eldon. *A Theology of the New Testament*. Ed. Donald A. Hagner. 2nd ed. Grand Rapids: Eerdmans, 1993.

Lemcio, Eugene E. "The Unifying Kerygma of the New Testament." *JSNT* 33 (1988): 3–17.

Lemonnyer, Antoine. *Théologie du Nouveau Testament*. Paris: Bloud & Gay, 1928. Rev. and ed. Lucian Cerfaux, 1963.

Lieu, Judith. *The Theology of the Johannine Epistles*. NTT. Cambridge: Cambridge University Press, 1991.

Lincoln, Andrew T., and A. J. M. Wedderburn. *The Theology of the Later Pauline Letters*. NTT. Cambridge: Cambridge University Press, 1993.

Lindars, Barnabas. *The Theology of the Letter to the Hebrews*. NTT. Cambridge: Cambridge University Press, 1991.

Lohse, Eduard. *Grundriss der neutestamentlichen Theologie*. Stuttgart: Kohlhammer, 1974.

Luz, Ulrich. *The Theology of the Gospel of Matthew*. NTT. Cambridge: Cambridge University Press, 1995. (German original, 1993.)

Marshall, I. Howard. *New Testament Theology: Many Witnesses, One Gospel*. Downers Grove, IL: InterVarsity Press, 2004.

Martin, Ralph. "New Testament Theology: Impasse and Exit." *ExpTim* 91 (1980): 264–69.

Matera, Frank J. "New Testament Theology: History, Method, and Identity." *CBQ* 67 (2005): 1–21.

———. "Christ in the Theologies of Paul and John: A Study in the Diverse Unity of New Testament Theology." *TS* 67 (2006): 237–56.

Meinertz, Max. *Theologie des Neuen Testaments.* 2 vols. Bonn: Peter Hanstein, 1950.

———. "Sinn und Bedeutung der neutestamentlichen Theologie." *MTZ* 5 (1954): 159–70.

Morgan, Robert. *The Nature of New Testament Theology.* SBT, 2/25. Naperville: Allenson, 1973.

Morgan, Robert, and John Barton. *Biblical Interpretation.* Oxford: Oxford University Press, 1988.

Morris, Leon. *New Testament Theology.* Grand Rapids: Zondervan, 1986.

Müller, Mogens. "Neutestamentliche Theologie als Biblische Theologie: Einige grundsätzliche Überlegungen." *NTS* 43 (1997): 475–90.

Murphy-O'Connor, Jerome. *The Theology of the Second Letter to the Corinthians.* NTT. Cambridge: Cambridge University Press, 1991.

Neill, Stephen. *Jesus through Many Eyes: Introduction to the Theology of the New Testament.* Philadelphia: Fortress, 1976.

Perrin, Norman. "Jesus and the Theology of the New Testament." *JR* 64 (1984): 413–31.

Räisänen, Heikki. *Beyond New Testament Theology: A Story and a Program.* 2nd ed.; Philadelphia: Trinity Press International, 2000.

Reumann, John, ed. *The Promise and Practice of Biblical Theology.* Minneapolis: Fortress, 1991.

———. *Variety and Unity in New Testament Thought.* Oxford Bible Series. Oxford: Oxford University Press, 1991.

Richardson, Alan. *An Introduction to the Theology of the New Testament.* New York: Harper & Brothers, 1958.

Robinson, James M. "The Future of New Testament Theology." *DrewG* 45 (1974–75): 175–87.

Rowe, C. Kavin. "New Testament Theology: The Revival of a Discipline: A Review of Recent Contributions to the Field." *JBL* 125 (2006): 393–419.

Sandys-Wunsch, John, and Laurence Eldredge. "J. P. Gabler and the Distinction between Biblical and Dogmatic Theology: Translation, Commentary, and Discussion of His Originality." *SJT* 33 (1980): 133–58.

Schelkle, Karl Hermann. *Theology of the New Testament.* 4 vols. Collegeville, MN: Liturgical Press, 1971. (German original, 1968–76.)

Schlatter, Adolf. *The History of the Christ: The Foundation for New Testament Theology.* Grand Rapids: Baker, 1997. (German original, 1909.)

———. *The Theology of the Apostles: The Development of New Testament Theology.* Grand Rapids: Baker, 1998. (German original, 1910.)

Schlier, Heinrich. "The Meaning and Function of a Theology of the New Testament," and "Biblical and Dogmatic Theology." Pages 1–19, 26–37 in *The Relevance of the New Testament.* New York: Herder & Herder, 1968. (German originals, 1957, 1963.)

Schmithals, Walter. *The Theology of the First Christians.* Louisville: Westminster John Knox Press, 1997. (German orginal, 1994.)

Schnackenburg, Rudolf. *New Testament Theology Today.* New York: Herder & Herder, 1963.

Scott, Ernest F. *The Varieties of New Testament Religion.* New York: Scribner, 1944.

Scroggs, Robin. "Can New Testament Theology Be Saved? The Threat of Contextualisms." *USQR* 42 (1988): 17–31.

Smith, D. Moody. *The Theology of the Gospel of John.* NTT. Cambridge: Cambridge University Press, 1995.

Spicq, C. "Nouvelles réflexions sur la théologie biblique." *RSPT* 42 (1985): 202–19.

Stauffer, Ethelbert. *New Testament Theology.* London: SCM, 1955. (German original, 1941.)

Stevens, George B. *The Theology of the New Testament.* 2nd rev. ed. International Theological Library. Edinburgh: T. & T. Clark, 1918. (First published 1899.)

Strecker, Georg. "Das Problem der Theologie des Neuen Testaments." Pp. 1–31 in *Das Problem der Theologie des Neuen Testaments.* Ed. Georg Strecker. Wege der Forschung 367. Darmstadt: Wissenschaftliche Buchgesellschaft, 1975.

———. *Theology of the New Testament.* Louisville: Westminster John Knox Press, 2000. (German original, 1996.)

Stuhlmacher, Peter. *How to Do Biblical Theology.* PTMS 38. Allison Park, PA: Pickwick, 1995.

———. *Biblische Theologie des Neuen Testaments.* 2 vols. Göttingen: Vandenhoeck & Ruprecht, 1992, 1999.

Telford, W. R. *The Theology of the Gospel of Mark.* NTT. Cambridge: Cambridge University Press, 1999.

Theissen, Gerd. *The Religion of the Earliest Churches: Creating a Symbolic World.* Minneapolis: Fortress, 1999. (German original, 1999.)

Thielman, Frank. *Theology of the New Testament: A Canonical and Synthetic Approach.* Grand Rapids: Zondervan, 2005.

Via, Dan O. *What Is New Testament Theology?* GBS. Minneapolis: Fortress, 2002.

Vouga, François. *Une théologie du Nouveau Testament.* MdB 43. Geneva: Labor et Fides, 2001.

Watson, Francis. *Text and Truth: Redefining Biblical Theology.* Grand Rapids: Eerdmans, 1997.

Weinel, H. *Biblische Theologie des Neuen Testaments: Die Religion Jesu und des Urchristentums.* 4th rev. ed. Tübingen: Mohr, 1928. (First published 1911.)

Weiss, Bernard. *Biblical Theology of the New Testament.* 2 vols. Edinburgh: T. & T. Clark, 1882. (German original, 1868.)

Wilckens, Ulrich. *Theologie des Neuen Testaments.* Vol. 1, parts 1–4. Neukirchen-Vluyn: Neukirchener Verlag, 2002, 2003, 2005.

Yarbrough, Robert W. "Modern Reception of Schlatter's New Testament Theology." Pages 417–31 in Adolf Schlatter, *The Theology of the Apostles: The Development of New Testament Theology.* Grand Rapids: Baker, 1998.

Young, Frances. *The Theology of the Pastoral Letters.* NTT. Cambridge: Cambridge University Press, 1994.